The Media Guide 1996

Paul Fisher, Steve Peak and Emma Johnson

Fourth Estate • London

Published in Great Britain by:
Fourth Estate Ltd, 6 Salem Road, London W2 4BU
The fourth annual edition

A catalogue record for this book is available from the British Library
ISBN 1-85702-372-2

Acknowledgements: Rachel Cave, Dr Judy Clark, Andrew Culf, Charles Grant,
Roger Harrison, Gerald Knight, Gary Phillips, Cedric Pulford, Owen Wintersgill

Picture research: Donna Halfpenny-Peters

Picture credits: page 10, Garry Weaser; page 12, The Guardian; page 14, Martin Argles; page 16 and page 17, Graham Turner;
page 26 E Hamilton West; page 27,Martin Argles; page 92, Thomas Nam Nguyen; page 124, Frank Martin; page 126, Sean Smith;
page 127, E Hamilton West; page 129, David Sillitoe; page 132, The Guardian; page 135, David Sillitoe; page 137, The Guardian; page
141, Kenneth Saunders; page 143, E Hamilton West; page 148, The Guardian; page 150 and page 155, Graham Turner; page 161, Peter
Johns; page 167, David Sillitoe; page 251, Frank Martin; page 253, Graham Turner; page 255 The Guardian; page 257, The Guardian

Set in News Gothic
Printed in Great Britian by Bath Press

The international media group

Pearson's mission is to be a major international provider of media
content, renowned for distinctive products that deliver
information, education and entertainment in ways that people want.

Pearson plc, 3 Burlington Gardens, London W1X 1LE.

PRINT

BROADCASTING

INSIDE CONTACTS

OUTSIDE CONTACTS

THE STATE

DISASTERS AND EMERGENCIES

BUSINESS

PRESSURE AND ADVICE GROUPS   328

INTRODUCTION

The media is becoming increasingly important, certainly to itself and quite possibly to the public as well. Every week in newspaper, TV and radio bulletins there is news about the news. When the leader of the opposition has pow-wows with the big chief media owner, that's news. When government ministers pick fights with newspapers and television interviewers, that's news too.

Among the studious young, there is a fascination about the media as shown by the record numbers who are applying for media studies courses. As a route into a journalistic career the value of these courses is unproven, but as an academic area its interest is undeniable. The feeling is that to understand the media is to understand the world we live in.

It is a truism that the media changes the world we see, as well as merely reflecting it. In the midst of disasters people smile to camera becasue they know they'll soon be on TV or in the papers. Those who produce television programmes and newspaper articles are drilled into delivering the quick hit and, as a result, public debate must be conducted in soundbites and attitudes crisp enough to impress those with the shortest of attention spans.

The media which shapes our reality is also reshaping itself. The scale and the speed of change, both in organisational and technological terms, have been dramatic. Consider the past decade. In 1985 satellite TV had not been launched, Rupert Murdoch was yet to move his newspapers to Wapping, independent TV producers only worked for Channel 4, ITV franchises were yet to be auctioned off, the BBC dominated the radio scene, the print and broadcast unions were still powers to be reckoned with and nearly every journalist still had to use a typewriter. In 1985 headline writers struggled to find puns for the chip which did not involve fish, or old blocks or shoulders.

Today, everything has changed. Now journalists, and many others too, have to be familiar with on-screen make up computers, video journalism, satellite TV and the whole hype around the information superhighway. The arrival of Internet has been one of the stories of the mid-1990s. The fascination is that here is a media channel with none of the conventional controls. Anyone with a computer and phone can communicate directly with large numbers of other people without having to go through any kind of intermediary. The promise is of a new species of mass media without the restrictive paraphenalia of editors, house styles or owners with their own political/commercial agendas.

Meanwhile the media owners are doing very nicely. In commercial broadcasting alone, mid-1995 was a landmark time. By then independent radio's share of the listening audience had exceeded that of the BBC's for the first time, BSkyB had captured 4 per cent of the national television audience, the number of satellite dish owners had crept above three million and the cable companies had signed up their millionth subscriber.

Despite the erosion of its old position the BBC has had its charter renewed and is reasserting itself in general esteem. It can still lay claim to being the voice of the nation and at the same time is presenting a leaner, fitter, more commercial face to the licence-paying public and to its political masters. The 1995 BBC annual report had the appearance of any other big company's accounts and contained the upbeat financial background to match.

Across all media sectors - newspapers, TV, radio, - the urge to diversify into other areas has been added to the old jostle of buying out the competition. Determined media owners have lobbied successfully to relax legislation about who can own what. Concentrations of ownership are necessary for corporate survival, both in global markets and for increasing the scope of media operations. But who will benefit? Does more media mean better coverage and greater understanding or merely a greater quantity of infotainment?

There are other questions equally important to those working in the media business. Viewed from within, the permutations of fresh ownership are infinitely fascinating. The only certainty is that next year will bring more change.

GUIDE TO THE GUIDE

This book is designed for those who want to know about the media. It is a practical guide for those working in the media, who want to work in it or who work regularly with journalists and programme makers. If it's in the media, it's in the Media Guide. We hope.

The book has two aims. The first is to list the British media organisations and companies that play a role in shaping any and every aspect of newspapers, magazines, television and radio. Beyond the business of listing and fitting things into categories are descriptions and explanations of a complex industry. The print and broadcast chronicles have been given extra space because they have proved useful for all kinds of people. The second aim is to provide a handbook of the world outside the media, particularly for journalists creating stories.

As the media expands, so does the need for up-to-date information to assist people round it. And this book expands along with its subject area. The redesigned and reorganised fourth edition of the Media Guide is the biggest yet and has more contacts squeezed onto more pages. To reflect the interest that many young people have in various kinds of media studies, the guide's coverage of training and education has been expanded into separate sections on Training for the Press, Broadcast Training and Media Studies. There are also new sets of pages covering the ethnic press, cross media ownership, awards and prizes, think tanks, how to make complaints and the Internet.

Those of us who compile guides need guidance. That's why we ask people who use this book to complete the questionnaire on page 225. We want to know which bit of the media you work in and what would make the book more useful. So, if it's not in the media guide (and you think it should be), tell us.

The guide splits into four parts:

PRINT starts with a chronicle of key events across the sector. Then it looks at national and regional newspapers and their owners. The leading magazine publishers and their main titles are listed, along with a directory of magazine phone numbers. Then comes agencies, support organisations, press mags and yearbooks.

BROADCASTING begins with an even longer chronicle of events. There are separate entries on BBC television, commercial television in its many forms, radio and then the various broadcasting back-up organisations.

INSIDE CONTACTS mops up the media related things that wouldn't slot easily into the first two categories: lobbyists; think tanks; books; libraries; and 1996 anniversaries.

OUTSIDE CONTACTS moves outside the industry to provide a contacts' directory of information and phone numbers in the areas most often consulted by journalists.

There is a full index at the back which covers the first three specifically media sections of the book. The final Outside Contacts part is not indexed, although it is easy enough to find what's there by turning back a page to the second contents spread. Otherwise all entries in the rest of the book with an address are indexed. The few sections comprising phone numbers only are not indexed. These are:

Magazines	82
Independent TV producers	180
Book publishers	249
Advice groups	328

Alan Rusbridger, who became Guardian editor in January 1995, faces the Sky News cameras

PRINT CHRONICLE

Key events between August 1994 and July 1995

* Many newspapers keep cutting their prices; but the cost of newsprint goes up and up for all
* The birth of the broadloid as the broadsheets use tabloid tricks in their struggle for circulation
* Trinity International Holdings becomes the biggest fish in the regional pond
* Blair meets Murdoch: Labour's old media enemy becomes its lover - or is it just good friends?

Harmsworth Magazines closes
Early August: Harmsworth Magazines, the Daily Mail and General Trust's main consumer magazines subsidiary, is effectively closed. Its five key titles - including Shooting Times and The Field - are sold to IPC. Other publications are moved elsewhere in DMGT. The subsidiary stays in existence, but not as an operator. The deal brings to end Harmsworth's five-year struggle to become a major competitor in consumer publishing. IPC's overall position is strengthened, making it the predominant in the country interests market.

Murdoch snuggles up to Labour
8 August: Rupert Murdoch frightens the Tory Party by saying "I could even imagine myself supporting the British Labour leader, Tony Blair." This may be a signal that the long-running political battle between Mr Murdoch's newspapers and Labour could be coming to an end. His remarks appear in Der Spiegel, the German magazine. Today is already supporting Labour openly. News International papers have waged a sporadic campaign against Tory leader John Major for over a year. His predecessor, Margaret Thatcher, was strongly backed by Mr Murdoch. In early September Mr Blair appoints Today's political columnist Alastair Campbell as his personal press secretary. Also in September Messrs Murdoch and Blair meet for dinner, with their wives. "Absolutely nothing of exclusive interest to News International was discussed," reports a company spokeswoman. Mr Murdoch had organised the unusual event. [>7 February]

Yachting World libel case
8 August: Almost 100 magazine editors and publishers attend a meeting about the recent £1.45 million High Court libel award against Yachting World following a performance report on a revolutionary yacht design. Legal experts say the nub of the case involves a discrepancy between the claims of the manufacturer and the findings of the reviewing journalist. This has implications for all journalists and media involved in product testing. Many of those at the meeting, called by the Periodical Publishers Association, feel the case could seriously curtail product testing in all media, which would be against the interests of consumers.

Newspaper price cuts
15 August: Ian Hargreaves, the new editor of the Independent starts work, launching a fresh era for the paper under its changed ownership. The price war amongst the national papers is seen as his top priority. Rupert Murdoch started the struggle in July 1993 by cutting the price of the Sun to 20p, followed the next month by the Times to 30p. On 23 June 1994 the Daily Telegraph dropped from 48p to 30p and the next day the Times was slashed to 20p. The Independent had tried to stay out of the struggle, but its price of 50p now seemed too high, so on 1 August it was cut to 30p. The price war hits the newspaper profits hard. Murdoch's News Corporation lost £45 million of profits in the year to June 1994, despite large increases in circulations. Telegraph profits fell by 12 per cent in the first half of 1994, before the full financial impact of cutting its price had been felt. "Severe effects" are expected says its chairman Conrad Black. On 22 August the Sun has to put up its price to 22p because of the rise in the cost of newsprint. But three days later its advertising rate, and those of the Times and News of the World, are increased 15 per cent, showing that the News International is likely to continue the price cutting campaign for some time. The company will keep its prices down, and circulations therefore up, thus providing the commercial justification for the higher advertising rates. In July the Times circulation increases to almost 599,000 (524,000 in June), the Sun to 4.17 million (4.16 million) and the Telegraph to 1.07 million (1.01 million). [>21 October]

Reed Elsevier chairman resigns

15 August: The man who oversaw the creation of the giant magazine company Reed Elsevier will receive one of the largest executive pay-offs in Britain in recent years. Peter Davis, co-chairman until his resignation in June 1994 after a management argument, will be given a compensation package of £2.02 million. [>15 March]

Press Complaints Commission row

22 August: The future of Press Complaints Commission chairman Lord McGregor is thrown into doubt when he becomes embroiled in a controversy over nuisance phone calls made to a friend of the Princess of Wales. The News of the World had alleged on 21 August that Princess Diana had been making "cranky" calls to the art dealer Oliver Hoare. This was followed up in much of the media. Lord McGregor tells Radio Four today that articles about the Princess did not breach the commission's code. However, he also admitted that he had not read the original story in the News of the World. This prompts criticisms that his intervention has been a public relations disaster, and that he has unnecessarily brought the Press Complaints Commission into the case. A leading firm of headhunters has already been appointed to seek a replacement for the 72-year old peer, whose term of office is not due to expire until the end of 1995. [>21 November]

Sunday Express editor resigns

25 August: Eve Pollard resigns as editor of the Sunday Express after a failure to reverse years of circulation decline. She was appointed in May 1991, moving from the editorship of the Sunday Mirror. Ms Pollard converted the Sunday Express to tabloid format in 1992, but circulation still declined. Her husband Sir Nicholas Lloyd is editor of the Daily Express. She is replaced by Brian Hitchens, aged 58, former editor of the Daily Star who had recently been censured by the Press Complaints Commission for labelling homosexuals as "poofters" and "pansies". Insiders expect he will try to revive the Express by making it more right-wing, and more macho. Mr Hitchens shakes the paper by bringing five Daily Star senior executives with him. His former deputy, Philip Walker, succeeds him on The Star. [>12 February]

Mellor attacks News International

29 August: David Mellor criticises Baroness Thatcher for allowing Rupert Murdoch to secure a dominant position in the British newspaper and TV market. The former National Heritage

David Mellor

secretary says News International's effective control of satellite TV alongside its ownership of 35 per cent of the national press was "an unfortunate development for the future of this country. No-one in their right mind would want any more organs of opinion owned by News International," he tells an audience at the Edinburgh International Television Festival. "One of the great self-inflicted wounds of Britain in the 1980s has been to allow so many national newspapers to fall into the hands of foreign companies who sometimes delight in demonstrating that they have no long-term interest in Britain and its well-being." [>19 September]

Privacy ruling

30 August: A rape victim wins £10,000 damages from a newspaper which published the name of her street, in what is believed to be the first case of its kind. The Sexual Offenses (Amendment) Act 1992 bans the media from publishing a rape complainant's name, address or picture, if likely to lead to her identification. The Herald and Post, a Thomson Group local paper in Bedfordshire and Hertfordshire, published the street name and other material that identified her.

Mirror investigation unit closes

Late August: The Daily Mirror's investigations unit fades away when its last chief, Peter Hounam, leaves the paper. The unit had been run for 13 years by Paul Foot until he quit, in March 1993. His campaigning stories gave the Mirror a unique popular position in the national press in the 1980s.

Women in journalism

Late August: The first steps are taken in setting up the Women in Journalism group to help promote better conditions for females. This is the result of the strong feeling across the media that women are kept in lower ranks, despite playing key roles and having large staff numbers. A survey finds that the 15 ITV companies have 106 people in executive directorships · 102 of them men. On the broadsheet newspapers, the survey reveals that only two of the 63 top editorial jobs are held by women. [>15 June]

Local paper feeds cable

5 September: The first live news service from a provincial British newspaper to a cable television channel starts today when the Bristol Evening Post begins a nightly service to United Artists. It represents a victory for the provinces because the local paper has beaten the Mirror Group Newspaper's proposed Live TV onto the screen. [>15 September]

Cable infotainment from MGN

15 September: Mirror Group Newspapers announces plans to launch a national cable TV channel, called Live TV. This will be a joint scheme with five of the biggest telephone and cable TV companies, providing 24-hour "infotainment" to subscribers. A local version of Live TV will be developed with Midland Independent Newspapers. On 18 September MGN carries out a dawn raid on Scottish Television, buying 14.9 per cent of its shares for £37.4 million (the holding later goes up to 20 per cent, the maximum permitted legally). The two surprise initiatives by MGN show the group is now strongly diversifying into broadcast media because of the possible long-term decline of the print sector. Until today MGN has expressed little interest in broadcasting. Now the group is joining the cross-media expansion of other big print companies, including Pearson, Associated Newspapers and the Guardian Media Group. On 19 October former Sun editor Kelvin MacKenzie becomes MGN's executive director in charge of all the group's television interests. Until he quit the Sun on 21 January 1994 he had been a prominent rival of MGN chief executive David Montgomery. MacKenzie became managing director of BSkyB, but resigned on 2 August after clashing with chief executive Sam Chisholm. [>20 April]

Cross media ownership

19 September: There should be tighter controls on cross-media ownership to defend democracy, says Lord Hollick, managing director of MAI, which owns Meridian and Anglia TV. "The case for the deregulation of broadcasting chimes with the free market approach of many governments and provides a convenient alibi for their failure to tackle the monopolistic and anti-democratic nature of some major media groups which, as it happens, also provide them with important political support. The rise of major world media corporations and their enormous potential to influence political events is now ringing alarm bells in many countries." Lord Hollick is writing in Index on Censorship. On 31 October the pressure groups Liberty and the Campaign for Press and Broadcasting Freedom publish a report saying media ownership in Britain reduces the range of editorial views and has implications for the quality of democracy. Censored: Freedom of Expression and Human Rights calls for a new licensing body, with powers to prevent excessive concentration of media ownership. The report, going to the United Nations Human Rights Committee, says that four companies control 85 per cent of all national newspapers. Over 80 per cent of the local press is controlled by 15 corporate owners. [>28 October]

Big Issue

20 September: Social security officials visit the headquarters of Big Issue, the weekly magazine sold on the streets by homeless people. In a crackdown on social security fraud the Department of Employment is seeking the names of the 700 sellers. They cannot sign on for benefits and earn more than £5 a week. The magazine sells about 250,000 copies a week, and is sold by many impoverished vendors.

Graduates favour privacy laws

29 September: Britain's newest graduates believe media intrusion into people's private lives should be curbed. A Guardian survey of this summer's graduates found four out of ten strongly supporting control over media intrusion into privacy.

Wholesalers' code

5 October: All 76 national newspaper wholesalers have signed up to a new code of practice which attempts to remove unfair restrictions on the supply of papers to retail outlets, it is announced. The agreement has been operating unofficially since July 1994, seven months after the Monopolies and Mergers Commission found certain restrictions imposed by wholesalers to be against the public interest. The new code attempts to stop wholesalers arbitrarily refusing to supply retail outlets.

MPs want tougher media law

5 October: The gulf of mistrust between politicians and the media has widened and MPs would back tougher controls on journalists, according to a survey by the Association of British Editors. Backbench MPs from both parties are united in their hostility towards the Press Complaints Commission, national newspapers and the BBC board of governors. The majority (55 per cent) of the 216 MPs who returned questionnaires support some form of statutory controls over the media, while 68 per cent back an ombudsman with statutory controls. On 7 October National Heritage secretary Peter Dorrell says publication of the government's long-awaited white paper on privacy and the press has been delayed again. Nothing is expected until 1995 at the earliest. He also says a decision on cross-media ownership is "not imminent".
[>17 February]

Sleaze

20 October: The Guardian begins exposing sleaze about Tory MPs taking cash hand-outs from lobbyists in return for asking parliamentary questions. Then the row shifts to the Treasury's chief secretary Jonathan Aitken, about who funded his weekend stay at the Paris Ritz hotel in 1993. Guardian editor Peter Preston says his reporters had sent a "cod fax" to the Ritz seeking financial information, using a mock-up of House of Commons notepaper to protect the source. On 31 October Mr Preston is summoned to explain to parliament's Serjeant at Arms about the cod fax. Lord Tebbit in the House of Lords accuses Mr Preston of behaving in a "scurrilous, scandalous, dishonest and wicked manner". On 1 November Mr Preston resigns from the Press Complaints Commission because he is worried that "too much collateral damage" from the fax row would affect the work of the commission. That evening the Commons committee of privileges unsuccessfully tries to start an investigation into the fax, but is halted by member Tony Benn threatening to publish his own account of the committee's hearings if they are held in private. The annual general meeting of the Association of British Editors on 4 November unanimously passes a resolution deploring "the threats and increasingly intemperate attacks on the press, as personified by the treatment of Peter Preston of the Guardian by members of the government and parliament". As a result of recent sleaze scandals, John Major sets up the Committee on Standards in Public Life, chaired by Lord Nolan. It will investigate the ethical behaviour of MPs and lobbyists. Its public hearings start on 17 January 1995. [>17 January]

Price wars are fair

21 October: The Office of Fair Trading decides to take no action over the newspaper price war, ruling that consumers had benefited from the commercial turmoil. The price reductions by the Times and Daily Telegraph did not amount to predatory pricing, says the OFT director-general Sir Bryan Carsberg after a three-month inquiry. "The cover price reductions ... appear not to be targeted upon any particular title". The Independent believes it is specifically under attack. The Telegraph and Times are estimated to have lost between £40 and £50 million a year in revenue. In circulation, the Times has done best, with 607,000 sold daily.

Chas biog

21 October: Jonathan Dimbleby, the junior member of the Dimbleby journalistic dynasty gets a High Court ban on the 23 October News of the World printing extracts from his new book The Prince of Wales: A Biography. The book reveals that the Prince has a strategy of using television journalists to combat the adverse coverage of the tabloid press.

Dimbleby J, a poacher turned gamekeeper

Future purchase

24 October: Pearson plc pays £52.5 million for Future Publishing. The company, founded in 1985 by Chris Anderson, produces 30 magazines, many covering computers. Mr Anderson receives over £30 million from the deal. It comes just four days after Pearson announces plans to spend £16 million buying the advertising monitoring operation Register Group, and underlines the company's determination to expand. The Financial Times says the purchase of Future "is the latest example of Pearson's strategic decision to turn itself from a conglomerate into a media, information and entertainment company".

Ziff-Davis purchase

27 October: The American multimedia company Ziff-Davis Publisher is taken over by New York investment firm Forstmann Little for £857 million. Ziff-Davis is a producer of computer magazines, trade newspapers and books. Its British subsidiary is Ziff-Davis UK. It had been 90 per cent owned by the three Ziff brothers.

Euro censure

28 October: MEPs serve notice that they can no longer tolerate the European Commission turning a blind eye to the growing concentration of media power in the hands of Rupert Murdoch, Silvio Berlusconi and a few other magnates. By an overwhelming majority the European parliament demands a precise timetable for the introduction of EU-wide legislation to ensure that genuine freedom of expression for the press and broadcasters is not submerged by the battle for monopoly control of the so-called "information superhighway". But the European Publishers' Council said on 26 October that outdated laws to prevent monopoly control of Britain's press and terrestrial television were preventing British firms competing on equal terms with the new media players in Europe, the US and Japan. [>7 November]

Mail buys T Bailey Forman

31 October: Plans by the Daily Mail and General Trust to take over one of Britain's largest family-owned regional newspaper groups are opposed by the Monopolies and Mergers Commission. The MMC says the trust's £92 million bid for Nottingham-based T Bailey Forman Ltd would be against the public interest, giving DMGT too high a concentration of papers in the north and east Midlands. Forman owns the Nottingham Evening Post and five sister titles. DMGT's subsidiary Northcliffe Newspapers already owns dailies in Derby, Leicester, Lincoln, Hull, Grimsby, Stoke and Scunthorpe, giving it the largest area of the country covered by one group. The Department of Trade and Industry then allows DMGT to have until 5 December to produce a compromise proposal. On that day the DTI gives the go-ahead because DMGT has agreed some minor changes, including setting up an independent editorial board for the Nottingham Evening Post. The government's decision is described by the Independent as "a big snub to the MMC". Northcliffe becomes Britain's largest regional group of papers.

Local decline

Late October: Circulations of most regional daily papers have gone down in the first half of 1994, ABC figures show. The improved editorial and design quality of many papers has been unable to halt the long-term gradual decline. Only the regional Sundays are going against this trend.

Mellor outburst

7 November: Former government National Heritage secretary David Mellor MP accuses the tabloid press of tactics worthy of the former East German security police. He is launching a day-long media blitz to counter charges that he had conducted a second extra-marital affair careless of the consequences for his family or his party, the Tories. Mr Mellor, clearly furious at morning headlines implying that he did not regard it as "a big deal" to desert his wife, said he had been set up by journalists intent on character assassination and motivated by "bloodlust" to hurt people as much as possible.

Court demands demo footage

10 November: Leading television and newspaper companies are ordered to supply the police with TV footage and photos of the October demo in London against the Criminal Justice Bill. Southwark Crown Court rejects arguments that the decision would place journalists covering such events at risk of attack by demonstrators.

Maxwell a trial

10 November: Robert Maxwell, owner of the Mirror newspapers was insane, says his widow Betty. She believes he suffered from megalomania in his last years and should have died in 1988, at the peak of his success, rather than 1991. His sons Ian and Kevin face fraud charges, with a complex and expensive trial being organised. By mid-February 1995 their legal aid cost to taxpayers has already topped £4 million, and the Serious Fraud Office has run up an investigation bill of £8.9 million. The final costs are expected to be much higher. The trial should be the most expensive this century. It starts on 31 May, after much delay.[>31 May]

News International job changes

14 November: Sunday Times editor Andrew Neil announces his formal separation from Rupert Murdoch's News Corporation. He will receive a £1 million pay-off after Mr Murdoch's scrapping of plans for Full Disclosure, a weekly prime-time current affairs programme on US television. Mr Neil, who went to the US on secondment for Mr Murdoch in early June, says: "It is not divorce, it is an amicable separation." His departure comes soon after Kelvin MacKenzie, former Sun editor turned managing director of BSkyB, quit News Corporation, on 2 August. Mr Neil will be succeeded at the Sunday Times by acting editor John Witherow.

Price war - latest

17 November: Conrad Black, the Daily Telegraph owner, says it is up to his rival Rupert Murdoch to stop cutting prices. "He started the war - he can finish it," says Mr Black. "The Times is paying a tremendous price for the honour of a marginal reduction in our profitability." The Telegraph group today unveils

a drop in profit for the opening nine months of 1994, from £45.2 million to £33.9 million. The price war could also be ended by a 30 per cent increase in the cost of newsprint (paper). The newsprint manufacturers have been giving publishers a discount, which has fuelled the war. But an increased worldwide demand for paper means the discounts can be ended, at least temporarily. The price battle has mainly been between Murdoch, Black and the Independent. [<21 October, >31 January]

Wakeham for PCC

21 November: Lord Wakeham (above) the former Conservative cabinet minister, is confirmed as the new chairman of the Press Complaints Commission. He takes over on 1 January 1995 from the first chairman Lord McGregor, aged 73, who is retiring 12 months early following some conflict over recent intervention in disputed cases. Lord Wakeham, aged 62, was Baroness Thatcher's chief whip for five years and was at one time leader of the House of Lords. His past roles are seen as being possible aides to the industry in fending off tighter statutory control of the press. He says the Press Complaints Commission's task is now to strengthen self-regulation of the press "beyond the bounds of reasonable political debate. That is vital, not just for the sake of the press, but for the health of our democracy". [<22 August, >25 January]

Indie is hacked off ...

24 November: The Independent runs the main headline "Revealed: How Hacker Penetrated the Heart of British Intelligence", claiming the "most serious breach of national security in recent years". A journalist says the security is at risk after a "mystery hacker" penetrated BT's computer and obtained the phone numbers of MI5, MI6, Buckingham Palace and the Prime Minister. But two days later the journalist admits he stole the information while working as a BT employee.

... and moves off to Canary Wharf

4 December: The Independent on Sunday is published for the first time from the newspaper's new offices on London's Isle of Dogs. The first Independent produced there is the 12 December issue. After five years at 40 City Road, opposite Companies House, the duo is joining the Mirror and Telegraph groups in 1 Canada Square, on Canary Wharf. This 50-storey tower block in the former West India Docks is Britain's tallest building. It has replaced Fleet Street as the nearest thing to a UK newspaper publishing hub. The three companies are packed on to just 11 floors. The Telegraphs are on floors 11-16 (there is no floor 13), the Independents are on 18 and 19, and the Mirror group (Daily Mirror, Sunday Mirror, Sunday People, Sporting LIfe) on 20-23. The tower and surrounding area are disliked by both staff and visiting members of the public. An Independent on Sunday editorial describes the 18th floor's eastern view, across the whole of East London to the mouth of the Thames: "To look out on all this is to feel the extremes of optimism and pessimism that characterise contemporary Britain. It is in that way a useful prospect for journalists and journalism. Undue despair can be corrected by the sunrise, straight downstream. Undue hope can be cancelled by what the sun mainly illuminates." [>7 July]

Prejudicial publicity

6 December: Two sisters, whose murder convictions were quashed by the Court of Appeal because of prejudicial media coverage, win the right to a review of the Attorney General's decision not to bring contempt proceedings against the newspapers concerned. Lawyers say the High Court decision could have a bearing on future media coverage of trials. Michelle and Lisa Taylor were convicted of the murder of Alison Shaughnessy in July 1992 and jailed for life. Their convictions were quashed in June 1993 partly on the grounds that press publicity had prejudiced their chances of a fair trial. Despite criticism of press behaviour by the Appeal Court, the Solicitor General decided no prosecution was necessary. Today the sisters successfully seek to have that decision reviewed. Their QC, Geoffrey Robertson, says: "This is the first occasion in British history when a court has actually held that defendants were denied the right to a fair trial by reason of prejudicial press publicity."

Spy allegations

8 December: Richard Gott (above), the literary editor of the Guardian, resigns following allegations that he had been used as a Soviet spy by the KGB. An article in the Spectator claimed that he had been recruited by the KGB in the late 1970s and reactivated in 1984. Mr Gott, aged 56, admits he had many informal meetings with members of the former Soviet Embassy, but denies being an agent or receiving payment. However, he did take expenses-paid trips abroad, and he describes this acceptance of "red gold" as "culpable stupidity". He resigns because he now believes he should have told editor Peter Preston about his Soviet contacts at the time. Mr Gott's name was leaked to the Spectator from a list of 24 prominent people which the double agent Oleg Gordievsky gave his MI5 handlers after his defection to the West in 1985. The Observer says on 11 December that "highly placed sources" had told it that they believe there was a plot to harm the newspaper as revenge for the Guardian's revelations in late October about Treasury minister Jonathan Aitken's controversial stay at the Paris Ritz. Sir Peregrine Worsthorne says in the Sunday Telegraph that he and many other people had supported the USA in a similar way to Mr Gott with the Soviet Union. "As a journalist he was no better or worse than many others on the other side".

Emap buys media titles

13 December: Emap ... Britain's second largest magazine proprietor ... buys the prominent media news magazine UK Press Gazette. After a battle with other companies, Emap pays £60 million for Maclean Hunter European Publishing, part of Rogers Communications of Canada. MHEP publishes 22 directories and 34 business magazines, and also provides seven electronic information services. The media directories include BRAD (British Rate and Data) and Media Daten in Germany. The deal greatly boosts Emap's expansion into Europe, a move initiated by the company's purchase of major French magazines in June 1994. In Britain, Emap now owns three key trade publications in the media business: UK Press Gazette, Broadcast and Media Week.

Tabloids twitch Howard

20 December: The Home Secretary, Michael Howard, is accused of making policy decisions on the whim of the tabloid press after he ordered a blanket ban on rehabilitation "holidays" for detained mental patients. The ban was issued four days after the Sun protested that a patient, convicted on four counts of manslaughter, had been sent on an escorted visit to an adventure centre after spending 18 years in secure hospitals.

Killed in action

31 December: At least 115 journalists were killed in 1994 while covering world events, says the International Federation of Journalists. Another 15 reporters disappeared in mysterious circumstances. The year has been a grim one, as the number of casualties is almost double 1993.

Regionals: don't go into morning

9 January: Regional evening papers could be making a mistake by also producing early morning editions, says Geoff Elliott, editor of the News in Portsmouth. His paper tried it three years ago but abandoned the scheme because it added few sales and many readers felt cheated. "They said that if we could produce two issues separated only by the hours of darkness, it proved how old most of our news really was."

New Guardian and Observer editors

12 January: Peter Preston, editor of the Guardian, is appointed editor-in-chief of both the Guardian and Observer. The Scott Trust and Guardian Media Group say the appointment reflects a desire to "maximise the use of the editorial talents and resources available to the two newspapers while retaining their separate and different editorial identities." Jonathan Fenby, editor of the Observer since it was bought by the Guardian 19 months ago, "has resigned by mutual agreement", the company announces. Mr Preston, aged 56, is the longest-serving national newspaper editor. He took charge of the Guardian in 1975, in succession to Alastair Hetherington. By coincidence, he is

today voted Britain's most impressive editor by a MORI poll of 34 editors. The Trust begins the selection of its new editors by setting up two advisory committees, both including journalists as members. This process is unique in the British newspaper industry. On 24 January, Alan Rusbridger, 41-year old deputy editor of the Guardian, succeeds Mr Preston. Andrew Jaspan, aged 42, editor of the Scotsman, is appointed editor of the Observer on 7 February. Mr Preston now focuses on the Observer, the circulation of which has fallen from 520,000 to 485,000 since its purchase by the Guardian in June 1993. In May, Mr Fenby moves to Hong Kong to become editor of the South China Morning Post, the leading English-language paper. [>29 January]

NUJ revival
Mid-January: The National Union of Journalists is undergoing a strong revival, reveals a survey of its members. "Our members are younger and more dynamic than we thought," says the NUJ's general secretary John Foster. Five thousand people returned an NUJ questionnaire, with 32 per cent of them aged 25-34 and 68 per cent under 45. And 60 per cent are in staff jobs, despite the casualistion of the industry. Three-quarters of them earn £15,000 or more.

Emap's car magazine crashes
16 January: Emap is forced to close Carweek, the weekly motoring magazine which was launched just 18 months ago. Carweek - which cost the group about £8 million to start, run and shut - is selling only 50,000 at the time it closes. At first it sold 90,000 copies, but it went rapidly into reverse. The reasons include an overcrowded market, rising paper costs, falling sales of new cars and the large (A3) size of the magazine, which meant newsagents often stored it out of sight on their bottom shelves.[> 5June]

Nolan begins public hearings
17 January: The parliamentary Committee on Standards in Public Life, chaired by Lord Nolan, starts its public hearings into the 1994 "sleaze" scandals, following the exposure on 20 October. Its report is published on 11 May. At the same time, two other Commons committee are conducting inquiries. The Select Committee on Members' Interests is investigating whether Neil Hamilton MP should have declared a six-day stay at the Ritz Hotel in Paris, part of Lord Nolan's scandals (in June the Tory-run committee says he should have done so, but lets him off any punishment). The Privileges Committee is cross-examining two Tory MPs, David

Tredinnick and Graham Riddick, who are accused of taking £1,000 for tabling parliamentary questions. They were exposed by the Sunday Times in a major investigation in July 1994, and their case was part of the government's reason for starting the Nolan committee. The committee issues its verdict on 4 April. [<20 October, >4 April]

Wapping anniversary
21 January: Trade unionists mark the ninth anniversary of News International's overnight move in 1986 from Fleet Street to Wapping in east London. They march from Tower Hill to Wapping, highlighting the fact that unions have no effective rights inside the company's headquarters.

Tory chief loses libel suit
24 January: Paul Judge, director general of the Conservative Party, fails in his High Court libel action against the Guardian over a 1993 story suggesting his party's Central Office used "old tricks" to obstruct an inquiry into donations made to party funds by the fugitive tycoon Asil Nadir. Mr Judge will have to pay both sides' legal costs, estimated at over £300,000.

Murder of newspaper editor
24 January: The editor and owner of the prominent Indian Sikl newspaper Des Pardes is shot dead outside its Southall offices. There are fears that Tarsam Singh Purewal aged 60, has been killed by people with a rival Sikh view. Several of them are arrested in the West Midlands at the end of Mach. One is Raghbir Singh, editor of a Sikh community newspaper. No charges are brought, but the Home Office says he will be deported for "reasons of national security". He appeals against the decision, backed by the NUJ and over 100 MPs.

Row over PCC chairman
25 January: Lord Wakeham, the former government energy secretary and new Press Complaints Commission chairman, is to take up a £20,000-plus directorship with merchant bank NM Rothschild which advised on the electricity privatisation five years ago. The Labour Party protests to the Lord Nolan committee on Standards in Public Life. Lord Wakeham receives £75,000 a year for three days a week at the PCC. Then in early March he is voted on to the British Horseracing Board's industry committee. Lord Wakeham also causes controversy by suggesting Lady Thatcher's press secretary Sir Bernard Ingham as a lay member of the PCC, but it turns out that he is ineligible under the commission's rules. [<21 November, >17 February]

Bid for Observer "absurd"

29 January: The Sunday Times reports that former Observer owner Tiny Rowland is trying to buy it back from the Guardian Media Group, which will soon consider his bid. GMG confirms Mr Rowland has made an offer, but dismisses any question of a sale to him or anyone else. Mr Rowland, aged 77, said he was prepared to buy the Observer back using his personal fortune. "In two years' time there is going to be an election and I'd like, at my age, to have a bit of fun." [<12 January]

Magazine advertising campaign

30 January: A three month, £1 million campaign is launched by the Periodical Publishers Association to emphasise to advertisers and agencies the power of business and professional magazines and their influence in the market they serve.

Paper shortage heralds price war truce

31 January: Rupert Murdoch signals a possible ending of the newspaper price war he started in July 1993. He indicates that the soaring cost of newsprint could lead to price increases. The Sun dropped from 25p to 20p, the Times from 45p to 20p, forcing other papers to make similar cuts. Mr Murdoch says: "We haven't made any decision, but the price of paper has gone up by 30 or 40 per cent in the last three months. That changes the economics." His hint that his prices may rise again is greeted with relief by his opponents. They hope the war is over - but it may only be a temporary truce. A brief snipers' skirmish takes place on 25 March when the Sun and Mirror cut their prices to 10p. But this is just for the one day, because the ammunition (newsprint) shortage has escalated since the start of the year, and its cost is now rising steadily. It went up 15 per cent generally in January. Some newsprint supplies in Britain are unofficially rationed. All newspaper and magazine publishers are feeling the effects. Many newspapers are having to consider reducing their number of pages in order to remain economically viable. The global crisis is caused by a shortage of both the raw material and processing plant able to meet the steadily increasing paper demand. This increase was unexpected, suddenly replacing the oversupply since the 1980s. New plant now being planned will take two years to construct. [<17 November, >18 March]

News Corp's profits up

6 February: The profits of News Corp, Rupert Murdoch's international media group, have been boosted by its American TV interests and BSkyB. In the six months ending 31 December 1994 BSkyB made operating profits of £5 million per week. News Corp as a whole had an 8 per cent rise in after-tax profits, to £325 million. UK newspaper profits went up 13 per cent. There was also the benefit of a 15 per cent rise in newspaper advertising rates, which is cushioning the company against the rising price of newsprint.

Pearson gives Labour £25,000

7 February: Pearson, publisher of the Financial Times, donates £25,000 to Labour funds. "The Labour Party has moved much more towards the centre and are the leading opposition party, so it is logical to help them," says Pearson's chairman Lord Blakenham. The party sees the gift as the first sign that British firms now believe its claim to be more efficient at running capitalism than the Tories. [<8 August, >mid-March]

Scallywag magazine sues Tory official

14 February: The publishers of the satirical magazine Scallywag issue writs for malicious falsehood against Julian Lewis, deputy director of research at Conservative Central Office. The magazine, which stopped publication in early February, is claiming damages from Mr Lewis, who in late January contacted distributors warning them not to handle any issues containing allegedly defamatory articles about him. In November 1994 Scallywag claimed Central Office proposed an alleged dirty tricks campaign against Labour leader Tony Blair. The distributors hold on to £16,000 from Scallywag sales, forcing it to close down. On 15 February Mr Lewis serves libel writs on nine distribution companies, rather than the magazine, which has no money. The next day, Scallywag delivers a writ claiming malicious falsehood to Tory prime minister John Major. On 21 April the magazine returns, after being printed abroad, but with the legal struggle still unresolved.

Alleged office bugging at the Express

12 February: The Mail on Sunday attacks its rivals at Express Newspapers with the following five page report: "The managing director of one of Britain's leading newspaper groups agreed to the bugging of a fellow director's office in an extraordinary dispute over allegations of financial impropriety, the Mail on Sunday can reveal today ... and it took place in spite of the fact that the Daily Express has voiced concern at such practices in companies." Express Newspapers takes out legal injunctions to stop the Mail on Sunday publishing its "three-month investigation", but the High Court overturns the restrictions. "Has Dog started to eat Dog?" asks the UK Press Gazette. [<25 August, >27 March]

PCC delay

17 February: National Heritage secretary Stephen Dorrell hints that Whitehall prefers self-regulation to privacy legislation and statutory controls. A white paper has been awaited almost two years and Mr Dorrell hopes that early successes of the Press Complaints Commission will provide a self-regulatory framework on which to build. In mid-March National Heritage staff unofficially give details of a draft white paper. It proposes setting up a PCC-run compensation fund which will provide pay-outs of up to £5,000 for victims of newspaper intrusion. Other proposals include a "hotline" system, with the PCC intervening before publication when a serious complaint is received; creating criminal offenses of electronic eavesdropping and telephoto lens photography; and making appointments to the commission more independently. Officially, there is no publication date yet for the white paper; unofficially, it is indicated it will appear in April - but it does not. On 5 April, PCC chairman Lord Wakeham appeals to the newspaper industry to co-operate in cleaning up its act. He tells a press lunch at Westminster: "It is by no means certain we are going to win. We are going to have a good try to produce a system of self-regulation" rather than statutory controls. [<5 October, >late March]

Murdoch sued in libel case

19 February: A Sunday Times lead news item accuses the former Labour leader Michael Foot of being a KGB "agent of influence" at the height of the Cold War. The allegation draws condemnation and ridicule from across the political spectrum and denials from former KGB agents. The Sunday Times editor John Witherow virtually to disowns the thrust of his paper's supposed scoop. Mr Foot, aged 82, says the story is "disgraceful", adding: "As far as I know, I have never met or seen a KGB agent in my life". The allegation is derived from a book by the former KGB double-agent Oleg Gordievsky. Mr Witherow admits the claim "may be utter rubbish". Mr Foot is so angry about the accusations that on 25 February he decides to sue not only the Sunday Times for libel, but also its owner, Rupert Murdoch. This is believed to be the first time this century that a newspaper proprietor, as an individual, has been named in a libel action. In coming weeks, Mr Murdoch's solicitor denies he has a case to answer because of his distance from the editorial content of his papers. On 26 February the Sunday Times does not apologise and refuses to publish in full a 2,000 word article by Mr Foot where he calls for an "absolute withdrawal" of the accusations. The same day's News of the World prints an apology. [> 7 July]

Telegraph shares

22 February: Conrad Black announces that his Canadian-based master company Hollinger intends to buy out the minority shareholders in The Telegraph plc, of which he currently owns 58.5 per cent. A USA-quoted Hollinger subsidiary, American Publishing Company, will buy Hollinger's holding in The Telegraph and make offers for the minority shares.

In late April Mr Black says he may not be able to reach an agreed price with share sellers, as his offer will be "nowhere near" the 500p a share some are seeking. Then on 17 May he abandons his buying out plan after the independent directors of his British company fail to agree a price. The Telegraph was floated in September 1992 at 325p. In May 1994, a month before Rupert Murdoch started the current round of price cuts, the shares peaked at 620p.

United Newspapers' mag shake-up

Early March: United Newspapers stages a shake-up of its magazine sector. Morgan Grampian, its subsidiary specialising in business titles, from 1 June is being renamed Miller Freeman plc. This is to give it a public identity in line with United's American business publishing division of the same name. Morgan Grampian subsidiaries will lose their individual names, such as Benn Publications and Farming Press. The United upheaval also includes the sudden departure of four directors. A month later, United sells its consumer and leisure specialist Link House, publisher of 26 titles, to a venture capital company for £9.15 million.

Independent it isn't ...

7 March: The Independent, which for eight years has run campaigns boasting of its editorial independence, is told by the Advertising Standards Authority to withdraw the claim. As far as the authority is concerned, the paper is no different from newspapers run by the media barons. The authority says the Independent's 1994 campaign implied incorrectly that shareholders could not affect editorial policy. Its launch slogan was: "It is. Are you?". On 10 June the paper changes its title from "The Independent" to just "Independent". [>mid-March]

The Scotswoman

8 March, International Women's Day: The Scotsman becomes the Scotswoman just for today, with the women on the paper taking over management. Every decision about the content is taken by a woman, and then executed by both men and women.

Reed Elsevier success

15 March: The two year old Anglo-Dutch publisher Reed Elsevier announces a profitrise of 17 per cent to over £600 million in 1994. This surprises many City analysts, who had been expecting a poorer result following internal problems in its early days. But now Reed Elsevier looks a blueprint for international mergers and cross-border strategy. IPC Magazines profits are up 23 per cent, Reed Business Publishing 60 per cent and scientific and medical titles 16 per cent. IPC chairman John Mellon says: "The recession is over as far as Reed is concerned." [<15 August]

Readers on the right turn left

Mid-March: Readers of Conservative-supporting newspapers are switching over to Labour, according to research by MORI. Since the 1992 general election, there has been a 23 per cent swing of Daily Telegraph readers to Labour. The Telegraph is the Tories' key daily vehicle for contacting the most influential party supporters. For other papers the swing is: Today 27 per cent, Daily Mail and Times 24 per cent, Sun 23 per cent, Daily Express 18 per cent. In early May further MORI figures are analyzed. They show that in the first quarter of 1995, 45 per cent of regular readers of the Times say they support Labour, compared with 15 per cent in 1992. Figures for other papers are: the Telegraph 30 per cent, against 11 per cent in 1992; Today 19 per cent, against 43 per cent. [<7 February]

Independent survival strategy

Mid-March: A refinancing package is agreed for Newspaper Publishing, the company owning the Independent and Independent on Sunday, to raise another £20 million. With circulations still low and losses high (£25 million in the last 12 months), the Mirror Group and Tony O'Reilly's Irish media company Independent Newspapers will provide the finance by increasing their share holdings to about 43 per cent each. They will have equal numbers of directors. The Spanish group Prisa will cut its shares to roughly 12 per cent and the Italian La Repubblica group will pull out. Mr O'Reilly will be a powerful figure in the background. But day-to-day management will remain with the Mirror Group, whose chief executive, David Montgomery, will have an even stronger position. He will be trying to cut the annual combined editorial budget of both papers from £27 million to £22 million. The budget for the two Telegraphs is £42 million. Andreas Whittam Smith will stand down as chairman. On 25 May Newspaper Publishing announces it has completed the rearrangements. The two main shareholders have 43.3 per cent each, having bought La Repubblica' shares, and Prisa has 12.6 per cent. The new chairman is Liam Healy, chief executive of Independent Newspapers. New directors are appointed, including Ben Bradlee, editor of the Washington Post from 1968 until 1991. [<7 March, >25 March]

NUJ loses test case

16 March: A National Union of Journalists' major test case on union rights falls in the House of Lords. The Law Lords decide it is not unlawful to withhold pay rises from employees who refuse to sign personal contracts giving up their NUJ bargaining rights. The Lords allow the appeal of the Mail group against the victory won by NUJ FoC Dave Wilson in the Court of Appeal in 1993. This is the last British stage in his five-year fight after he was deprived of a pay rise for sticking to his union. The NUJ says the judgement legitimises employers penalising workers who refuse to give up representation by their unions and sign individual contracts. There are 145 other cases awaiting this outcome. NUJ general secretary John Foster says: "The judgement is grossly unfair, and it is incredible for the Lords to say that collective bargaining is not an important union function." The NUJ considers appealing to the European Court.

Media versus the people

18 March: The Campaign for Press and Broadcasting Freedom holds a conference at the TUC headquarters to examine the media. "There is much talk of a brave new multi-media world. But the powerful voices most often heard are those of industrial players calling for deregulation of controls on media ownership and programme obligations. This conference is about discussing the concerns of other voices - those working in the media and those concerned about the democratic and cultural importance of the media in our society."

Newsprint crisis escalates

18 March: The Department of Trade and Industry holds a meeting with representatives of the newspaper and magazine industry to discuss the security of future newsprint supplies. A worldwide shortage of paper is forecast for the next two years. Early in April it is predicted that a price rise of 15 per cent expected in July, following the 15 per cent boost in January, could in fact be 25 per cent. On 26 April the European Commission reveals an investigation into alleged price fixing by 40 newsprint producers in seven countries, including Britain. Four officers raid the London HQ of Canadian firm Abitibi-Price, the world's largest supplier of newsprint. [<31January, >3 July]

NUJ versus MGN

22 March: The NUJ's struggle to gain rights for journalists to organise independently at Mirror Group Newspapers goes public with a campaign of advertisements. These say that the Labour Party and TUC are running their own joint campaigns with the Mirror, while the company's staff have few union rights.

Police seize right-wing journal

23 March: Police in Sussex and Norfolk arrest two men and seize printing equipment connected with Tomorrow's Job, a far-right, racist journal aimed at the police.

Independent on Sunday editor quits

25 March: Ian Jack, the editor of the Independent on Sunday since 1991, resigns. The next day Mr Jack, aged 50, tells his staff he is leaving, with regret, to edit the literary magazine Granta. He breaks the news at a hastily convened meeting outside his office on the 18th floor of Canary Wharf. Mr Jack says one of the reasons for going is not wanting to be part of the way the Mirror Group runs the paper. His departure arouses more fears about the two Independents. There are rumours that Independent editor Ian Hargreaves, appointed seven months ago, will soon be replaced. On 30 April, Ian Jack says in his last Independent on Sunday: "The Independent titles have sometimes been accused of sanctimony, and sometimes with some justice, but at their heart lies a serious, liberal idea that badly needs nurturing - that good newspapers have a social as well as a commercial worth." Mr Jack is succeeded by his deputy editor Peter Wilby, aged 50. He is described by Stephen Glover, one of the Independent's founders, as "rather small and quite inconspicuous. If you were casting the part of Macbeth, you would not ring Mr Wilby." [<mid-March, >5 May]

Press privacy code revised

Late March: The newspaper code on privacy intrusion is revised following complaints about photographers using step ladders, climbing trees or cutting holes in hedges to take pictures of people in their gardens. The newspaper industry's Editor's Code Committee says these photos can only be taken without using methods like that. The "unaided view of passers-by" is the approved method. [<17 Feb > 21 April]

New Morning Star editor

1 April: John Haylet, deputy editor of the Communist national newspaper Morning Star since 1988, takes over as editor following the retirement of Dr Tony Chater, who has been in the post since 1974.

Investigative reporting investigated

3 April: A survey of 35 regional newspapers finds "only a handful were truly performing" investigative reporting. Journalism student Andrew Head found in his research, published in UK Press Gazette, that many of the so-called investigative pieces sent in by journalists "were just straightforward news reports or feature articles. And most of the reporters nominated by news desks rarely used unconventional sources or methods of research ... The two restraints cited by reporters are Britain's libel laws and a shortage of time. While the first may be beyond the industry's control, and understanding, the second is not." Only 12 of the 35 papers employed investigative reporters.

Sunday Times wins awards

4 April: Following its exposure in July 1994 of cash-for-questions corruption at Westminster, the Insight team of the Sunday Times wins two awards. The journalists have already been given the What the Papers Say panel's Investigation of the Year honour and the London Press Club's Scoop of the Year award. Today the judges in the British Press Awards bestow the Exclusive of the Year and Team Journalism prizes. By coincidence, the parliamentary Privileges Committee today suspends the two Conservative MPs at the centre of the Sunday Times investigations. Graham Riddick and David Tredinnick are debarred from the Commons for 10 and 20 days respectively. Insight had revealed that the two MPs had agreed to accept £1,000 to ask parliamentary questions. But the committee also condemns the newspaper for entrapping and deceiving MPs in order to show that they would take cash for asking the questions. The paper fell "substantially below" the standards expected of legitimate investigative journalism. The Sunday Times, however, believes its four top awards prove it was acting fully and justifiably in public interest. Its exposure had helped force the government to set up the Nolan committee after the 20 October stories in the Guardian. On 2 June the PCC decides to reopen its investigation into the complaint about the Sunday Times by Mr Riddick when the Privileges Committee indicates a discrepancy about the reasons for the start of the newspaper's probe. [<17 January, >11 May]

Another MP resigns in scandal

9 April: Richard Spring, Conservative MP for Bury St Edmunds, becomes the fifth parliamentary private secretary to quit a ministerial job following investigations by Sunday newspapers. He resigns hours after today's News of the World alleges he had three-in-a-bed sex after dinner at home last Sunday.

FT closes London printing plant

19 April: Financial Times owner Pearson announces it is to close its East India Dock printing plant in London, which was completed just seven years ago at a cost of £44 million. For the first time in its 107-year history the FT will not have its own printing plant. The building, close to the Blackwall Tunnel entrance, has won several design awards. The main reason is that a northern plant is needed to enhance circulation. East India Dock also suffers from over-capacity. A contract has been signed with West Ferry Printers, jointly owned by the Telegraph and Express groups. The FT says it foresees further consolidation in the newspaper printing industry as technological change continues to weaken the links that have bound publishers and printers.

Mirror boosts profits

20 April: The Mirror Group reports a rise in its underlying profits of 44 per cent to £189.3 million in 1994, despite static circulations and little improvement in advertising revenues. New technology and the move to Docklands have helped keep the group's costs under control, along with the 22 per cent cut in staff in the past couple of years. The burden of Robert Maxwell has now largely been shaken off. Today the Mirror Group also announces it is launching Live TV, a 24-hour cable television channel on 12 June (see Broadcast Chronicle).

New PCC members

21 April: The Press Complaints Commission appoints four new lay members, all titled. One is Baroness Smith, widow of John Smith, the former Labour leader. The commission now has a non-industry majority among its 16 members. The appointments are announced by chairman Lord Wakeham at the annual Scottish Press Fund lunch. He says: "The PCC's independence from the press must be unyielding ... The new commission members will both reinforce the message that our independence bites and enhance the substance of our decision-making process." Lord Wakeham also warns he would be stinging in his criticism of editors who use spurious public interest arguments to justify flouting the code of practice.
[<late March, >23 May]

Journalist tests law on sources

24 April: A test case which could force the government to change the law to give greater protection to journalists' sources goes to the European Court of Human Rights in Strasbourg. Geoffrey Robertson QC argues that English law breaches the European convention on Human Rights by threatening journalists with up to two years imprisonment and unlimited fines for keeping sources' identities secret. He represents William Goodwin, aged 28, who was found guilty of contempt of court five years ago for disobeying a court order to reveal a source. Mr Goodwin, then a trainee reporter on the Engineer, a trade paper, had been leaked information about the financial difficulties of a private company, Tetra Ltd. The company asked the court to compel him to identify the informant so it could sue for breach of confidence. When he refused he was fined £5,000 for contempt. He is backed by the NUJ and other organisations. Last year the European Commission of Human Rights decided the order against Mr Goodwin violated the human rights convention. In a surprise move, the Strasbourg court refers the case to a full hearing of the European Court of Human Rights.

Magazines and the future

2 May: Magazines will continue to grow in importance and influence into the next millennium, despite the anticipated growth of electronic information services. This is the prediction of a Henley Centre report prepared for the Periodical Publishers Association annual conference. The PPA says the report comes at a time when more people are both reading and buying magazines. The Henley Centre believes the growth in the number and diversity of magazine titles will continue because of several key factors. There will be a consistent fragmentation of social identities, plus continued expansion of leisure interests. The development of the "small office home office" (SOHO) polarisation between income groups and the consequent increase in the diversity of lifestyles, needs and aspirations will drive magazine development. So will young people's needs to assert their individuality and to differentiate themselves from preceding generations.

O'Reilly goes global

5 May: Tony O'Reilly, joint controller of the Independent and Independent on Sunday, buys a stake in New Zealand's largest newspaper group, Wilson and Horton. He purchases 28.3 per cent of the shares, and effectively takes over management. This is part of an international expansion programme by Mr O'Reilly's Irish-based company Independent Newspapers. In September 1994 it invested £50 million in Australian radio. In February 1995 £50 million was spent on taking control of South Africa's Argus Newspapers. The next month the 29.9 per cent ownership of the UK's Independent papers rose to 43 per cent, at a reported cost of £35 million.
[<25 March, late June]

Nolan acts to stamp out sleaze

11 May: Following media exposures, the government's Committee on Standards in Public Life lays down "seven principles of public life". These will guard against what it says have been "slackness in the observation and enforcement of high standards" in a fast-changing social climate. John Major's cabinet accepts the broad thrust of the report from the committee, chaired by Lord Nolan. The report is said to be the toughest judgement of its kind this century. If implemented fully, it will have a dramatic effect on the working lives of MPs. It says MPs should undertake no paid parliamentary services for lobbyists. The committee was set up following investigative journalism by the Guardian and the Sunday Times.

Murdoch criticises NoW editor

11 May: Rupert Murdoch delivers a public rebuke to his News of the World editor following one of the Press Complaints Commission's toughest adjudications so far. He says Piers Morgan is a "young man" who has gone "over the top" in his coverage of a story on 2 April about psychological problems being suffered by Countess Spencer, sister-in-law of the Princess of Wales. The paper splashed with the headline "Di's Sister-in-law in Booze and Bulimia Clinic" and went on to describe how she had decided to seek treatment in a last ditch attempt to save her marriage. Husband Earl Spencer, brother of the princess, complains bitterly to the PCC, saying: "If ever proof was needed that sections of the tabloid newspaper business in this country are riddled with hypocrisy and evil then it was provided today ... To use someone's medical illness to fill your newspaper has to be the ultimate proof that sick minds dominate this part of the British media." The PCC upholds the complaint and claims the various breaches of the newspapers' Code of Practice were so grave that its chairman Lord Wakeham had written to Mr Murdoch personally. It is the first time the PCC has written to a newspaper publisher. Mr Murdoch says he had "no hesitation" in making public his remonstration with Mr Morgan, who issues a "sincere apology" to Countess Spencer. The earl and the NoW have not enjoyed good relations since his former mistress gave the paper details of their affair.

Complaints against the PCC

23 May: The Press Complaints Commission is strongly condemned at a conference on media ethics and responsibility. Leading civil liberties lawyer Geoffrey Robertson QC describes the commission as a "fraud and confidence trick" and a "secret and highly political quango". He urges the creation of a new privacy law to control the media, rather than continue to allow the PCC to rap owners across the knuckles. Graham Allen, Labour's media spokesman, calls the commission a "toothless watchdog".

BBC's domination of magazine markets

24 May: The Consumers' Association accuses the BBC of having "unfair domination" of particular magazine and book markets. The association says the BBC uses its name and airtime to promote its own publications, which often have little connection with programmes. There are examples of magazines "with little direct reference to any broadcast output. Products are sold using the BBC logo, sometimes with a trail on television (even though the BBC is barred from carrying advertising)". This means the BBC is "competing on unfair terms and failing to serve the public interest". The BBC rejects the criticism.

Maxwell's sons go on trial

31 May: The long-awaited trial of Robert Maxwell's sons Kevin and Ian begins. With two other men the pair are charged with conspiracy to defraud the trustees and beneficiaries of their company's pension schemes. Robert Maxwell ran two big publicly-quoted companies, Maxwell Communications Corporation (MCC) and Mirror Group Newspapers (MGN), until he died at sea on 5 November 1991. Kevin Maxwell, aged 36, was chief executive of MCC, while his brother Ian, 38, was chairman of MGN. Robert Maxwell was the "driving force" behind a scheme that "dishonestly put at risk" £100 million of pension fund assets, the court is told. After their father's death, it is alleged.that his sons Ian and Kevin misused £22 million of shares belonging to pensioners to try to save the companies from collapse. The trial is expected to last to Christmas. and costs up to £25 million. [<10 November]

Pepper sneezes

Early June: Denise Searle, the editor of Red Pepper magazine, resigns, in a row over cutting editorial budgets. Ms Searle believes this means tightly-written investigations will have to make way for discursive, academic articles. She said that other left-oriented magazines to adopt similar policies faded through lack of interest.

Mail journalist sacked

4 June: A long-serving journalist, whose test case over the Daily Mail's alleged victimisation of trade union members reached the House of Lords, is sacked by the newspaper. Dave Wilson was with the paper for 8 years. He fought a legal campaign against Associated Newspapers from

its announcement in 1989 that it would no longer recognise trade union agreements. Personal contracts were inroduced for all but 13 members of staff who refused to sign them. They were denied pay rises. Mr Wilson claimed this was discrimination against union members. His legal challenge under the 1978 Employment Act won the case in the Court of Apeal in 1993. But the House of Lords reversed the ruling in March 1995. The NUJ says it will take the case to the European Court of Human Rights because major issues affecting the whole trade union movement are involved.

Future of Emap

5 June: The profits of Emap rose 40 per cent to £64 million in the year to 1 Aptil 1995. Anouncing its annual returns, Emap says it plans to expand further into commercial radio. It is already the second biggest owner of these radio stations, after Capital. Radio is the fastest-growing section of Emap, which began life as a newspaper publisher. Total turnover rose 51%, from £362 million to £547 million. (<16 January)

Women's weeklies in battle

7 June: The lucrative market for women's weekly magazines starts a new battle with the launch of That's Life! by publishers Bauer. The company already takes in big profits from Take a Break (1.5 million a week) and Bella (980,000), the two top-sellers in Britain. Next are Woman, Woman's Weekly and Woman's Own, all owned by IPC, which fears that may not be enough market for another competitor.

Women weak in battle

15 June: Around 200 women set up an organisation to combat the "clubby male culture" that dominates much of journalism. The first survey of the new Women in Journalism group has found that the 20 national newspapers have only two women editors (Sunday Mirror and Sunday People) and five deputy editors. Of th 219 people attending news conferences, just 46 (21 per cent) are women, with none at the Mail on Sunday. At least 12 of the nationals have no women leader writers. One of the group's founders, former Express editor Eve Pollard, says: "Despite huge numbers of women in journalism few are influencing the future of our industry, either in the process of deciding what is printed or in senior management levels. Women want better links with other women. They want the confidence and stength in numbers to stand up to the male culture that holds so firm in many areas." (<Late August)

Hoaxer in jail - then out

20 June: Newspaper hoaxer Barry Gray receives a two year prison senence for a series of financial swindles. For many years he has sold the national press numerous fantasy tales. Operating under the name of Joe Flynn, he has persuaded almost every paper to buy stories with little connection to reality. The press is delighted with the conviction. But within hours Mr Gray is mistakenly released because of what is claimed to be a misunderstanding about how much time he has already spent in a French prison.

Green magazine attacked

Late June: Police have raided bookshops and arrested several anarchist journalists in recent months in what is being seen as an attempt to shut down Green Anarchist, the most radical underground news magazine on the animal rights and road protests fringe. The most recent raid was on a Manchester bookshop. The magazine is produced four times a year by the Green Anarchist Network, "fighting for a free society in harmony with nature".

Communicopia

Late June: The worldwide newspaper business must diversify into other media sectors in order to survive, says stockbroking firm Goldman Sachs. It concludes in a wide-ranging report that although newspapers will remain substantial business, steady decline will continue. A survey of 36 countries finds a 12 per cent fall in aggregate circulations between 1989 and 1993. The cause of the shrinkage is the rise of alternative, mainly electronic media, especially satellite and cable television combined with other services. Advertisers see this as having marketing potential around the globe, while newspapers are mainly single-nation. Many newspaper publishers are now "horizontally diversifying into other media", a process named by Goldman as "communicopia". the report says the situation in the UK "is made considerably worse by the price wars instigated by News International", which will probably cause a structural decline in profit margins. The survey shows the four biggest selling daily newspapers around the world are all Japanese, with number one selling 14.47 million in 1993. The Sun is eighth in the world.

Jobs go down...

Late June; Westminster Press and the Independent both make big cuts in jobs, partly because of the price of newsprint. The two Independents declare 43 editorial staff redundant, including some of the best-known journalists. Sales of the daily Independent are

The ace snapper snapped: Bert Hardy, photographed in 1987 with one of his most famous shots

still 50,000 (14 per cent) down on the January-June figure of 347,000. In Westminster Press, new chief executive Stephen Hill announces a series of major cuts during June, with 520 of the 3,5000 staff being axed. Parent company Pearson wants to increase operating profits by reshaping Westminster and reducing costs. The rising price of newsprint is only one factor. Closing down will be the Yorkshire on Sunday and Wetminster's training school for journalists in Hastings. This is seen not only as a major blow to Westminster Press staff, but also a fore-taste of what could happen to other publishers joining the increasing diversification into other sectors of the media. {>9 July]

...prices go up
3 July: The Times puts its price up from 20p to 25p on weekdays, and 35p on Saturdays. This follows the Sun's increase on 12 June to 25p, from its February figure of 23p. These rises are the result of the escalating cost of newsprint. They open the floodgates for other papers, with the Telegraph going up on 3 July from 30p to 35p, and many other dailies and Sundays doing the same in the following week. The Sunday Mirror goes up for the first time since 1992. All blame a 50 per cent increase in the newsprint price in the first half of 1995, with another big rise expected later in the year. The industry had been expecting lower figures, but the problem is becming even more srious. None of the benefit of the increase is being passed to the newsag-nts, however.They used to receive a percentage of sales prices, but now they will receive the same payment as before this boost. This is another blow to the many small newsagents who have been stuggling to survive. Meanwhile, the price war will continue. The increases are not a change in strategy, rather a reaction to the newsprint price rises that all papers are having to endure. The Times remains the cheapest, and is still runnng at a loss, forcing its direct competitors to do the same. The losses have brought a large increase in readership with sales of the Times going up by 82 per cent, from 366,000 during January to June 1993, when it was 45p, to 465,000 this May.

Pioneer news photographer dies

3 July: Bert Hardy, who was a role model for a generation of photographers and pioneered the use of 35mm photojournalism, dies of a heart attack, aged 82. He was best known for working with Picture Post from 1941 until it folde in 1957. He travelled the world, witnessing many wars and reporting them with a style and that appealed directly to the general public.

New National Heritage secretary

5 July: Virginia Bottomley swaps jobs with National Heritage secretary Stephen Dorrell who now becomes Health secretary. This is part of the Cabinet reshuffle following the 4 July re-election of John Major as leader of the Conservative Party, and therefore as prime minister. Virginia Bottomley becomes the fourth National Heritage secretary. First was David Mellor, followed by Peter Brooke, with Stephen Dorrell taking over in July 1994. Mrs Bottomley is expected to follow Mr Dorrell's moderate policies. Her husband, Peter, a former Northern Ireland minister, is a member of the All-Party Media Group. Jonathan Aitken resigns as Treasury Chief Secretary, saying that in the coming months he expects to be "heavily engaged in preparing for legal battles with my adversaries in the media" (the Guardian and World in Action).

Wisden apologises

7 July: The editor of Wisden Cricket monthly admits an "error of judgement" allowed the publication of an article questioning the commitment of foreign born players in the English team. The article claimed such players were less committed to the team's success. David Frith initially defended the piece, although he conceded the use of the word "negro" was not acceptable. But after West Indian born English players expressed outrage and threatened legal action, he offers his "unreserved apologies". England cricket captain Michael Atherton resigns from the editorial board.

Newspaper mountain climbed

7 July: A French climber scales Canary Wharf tower, Britian's tallest building and the 1990's version of Fleet Street. Reporters on seven national papers have the closest possible views of any story as Alain Robert, age 33, scales the 800 feet high tower. While passing c Live TV on the 24th floor Mr Robert asks the staff to give him a drink, but they cannot open the windows. Meanwhile, Canary Wharf and its surrounding new buildings have revived economically. In 1992 it went into administration and seemed to be permanently invalid. Over over the past year it has revived, with 75 per cent letting.

Sunday Times apology to Michael Foot

7 July: The former Labour leader Michael Foot (above) receives an apology and damages from the Sunday Times for its 19 February lead story alleging he was a KGB agent. Rupert Murdoch was initially included in the case on the grounds he is the hands-on proprietor who must have sanctioned the articles. Murdoch's solicitor claims his client could not be included because this was "bad law". An apology is given in the Royal Courts of Justice. On 9 July the paper prints a small, page two apology saying "it was not our intention" to make any "serious allegations ... We regret if any reader misunderstood our intention". The Sunday Times has agreed to pay Mr Foot "substantial damages" but the amount is not revealed. He says he will be giving some of it to the weekly political newspaper Tribune. [<19 February]

China opens up to Murdoch

Early July: The world's largest untapped media market opens its door to Rupert Murdoch. On 13 June News Corporation announces a technology deal in China with the People's Daily, the powerful newspaper of the ruling Communist Party. Mr Murdoch's 23-year old son Lachlan is one of the directors of the joint venture, a modest but highly significant breakthrough into China. The surprise deal suggests that Beijing has finally forgiven Mr Murdoch for claiming that his Hong Kong-based satellite TV station Star posed "an unambiguous threat to totalitarian regimes everywhere". The Chinese government's extreme hostility to Mr Murdoch forced him to drop the BBC World Service from Star to mend bridges. With a planned investment of £3.6 million, the new venture aims to "explore and develop a range of opportunities in China's rapidly developing information technology sector", the two companies say. Included are "electronic publishing, on-line information databases, data transmission networks and digital mapping". Mr Murdoch has clearly set his sights on opening up all aspects of the hitherto closed Chinese market. [<11 May, >16 July]

Black journalists' campaign

Early July: A conference of the NUJ Black Members Council launches a campaign to ensure more black journalists are recruited by the national press. The council's annual report has noted that out of 5,000 staff or contract journalists on major newspapers fewer than 30 are black. A researcher says that black journalists are too frightened to speak on the record about the "sea of white faces that still characterises national newsrooms".

Thomson to sell all newspapers

9 July: Thomson Corporation is putting its Scottish newspapers on the market and selling all its other British titles to Trinity International Holdings for £327.5 million. The Canadian-owned Thomson, former owner of the Times and Sunday Times, is withdrawing from local newspaper publishing after 35 years. Chester-based Trinity, which in the 1980s grew out of the Liverpool Post group, will more than double its size, moving from sixth to first place in the regional newspaper table. It will be buying 51 local papers in five towns and cities: Belfast, Cardiff, Chester, Middlesbrough and Newcastle. Titles include the Belfast Telegraph, Newcastle Journal and Western Mail. The purchase is referred to the Monopolies and Mergers Commission, with a report expected by 19 October. The company Scotsman Publications could fetch £150 million. Papers include the leading Scotsman, Scotland on Sunday, Edinburgh Evening News and, in Aberdeen, the Press & Journal and Evening Express. Bidding should start in August. A group of Scottish business leaders say they want to take over the newspapers and make them pro-Conservative. The Scotsman's editor says he will resign if this happens. Circulations of Scotland's national papers have been declining because the English nationals are producing successful Scottish versions. [<18 July]

Gay Gazette opens Capital Gay closes

Mid-July: Gay Gazette is launched, at the same time as Capital Gay closes down. The 14-year old campaigner is victim to the increased commercial competition in the gay market. Gay Gazette is published by Chronos, already producing Pink Paper and Boyz and two others. Publishing firm Millivres has five gay titles. The 32-page, 16,000 print-run Gay Gazette is seen as a temporary Chronos weapon to stop Capital Gay reviving.

Blair meets Murdoch

16 July: Labour leader Tony Blair is the guest speaker at a News International conference in Australia. Mr Blair flies free of charge to address 200 top-level Murdoch staff on the Hayman Islands, off the coast of Queensland. Blair talks in the broadest terms, saying how his aim is to create as much choice and diversity as possible. Blair's speech is seen as far less significant than his presence, symbolising the duo's new alignment that could change Britain's political future. They have met several times in the last year. The Mail and Express say Blair is "wooing" Murdoch. The Sun describes Blair as "a man with vision". Murdoch introduces Blair's speech, saying: "If the British press is to be believed, today is all part of a Blair-Murdoch flirtation. If that flirtation is ever consummated, Tony, I suspect we will end up making love like two porcupines - very carefully." [<13 June]

Government retreat on press privacy

17 July: The government retreats from legislation to curb intrusive behaviour by newspapers. But Virginia Bottomley, the new National Heritage secretary, urges the press to set up a compensation fund and says self-regulation will have to be toughened to prevent abuses of privacy. The heavily watered down white paper, two years in gestation, is greeted in parliament with jeers from backbench Tories. Labour expresses severe disappointment. The Press Complaints Commission and Newspaper Society welcome the self-regulation. The main proposals are: The PCC should pay compensation from an industry fund to victims of privacy intrusion; a "hot-line" between the

PCC chairman and editors should be established to head off breaches of the code of practice; the code should be tightened, and include a clearer definition of privacy; and non-industry members should sit on the PCC's code committee. Missing are tough laws to curb the press. The white paper marks the end of a six-year battle between politicians and the press. This began in July 1989 when Sir David Calcutt was appointed to chair a review into giving "further protection to individual privacy from the activities of the press". [<23 May]

Reed Elsevier sells papers and mags

18 July: The Anglo-Dutch publisher Reed Elsevier announces it is going to sell Reed Regional Newspapers, the UK's largest free newspaper publisher. RRN has a turnover of £131 million in 1994, with 2,800 employees producing 4.4 million copies each week, 80 per cent of which are free. There are four evening and 90 weekly titles. One of these is claimed to be the world's oldest newspaper, the Worcester Journal, born 1680. Also on the market will be two Dutch national daily papers and Reed's consumer publishing business: two overseas magazine groups (but not IPC Magazines) and Reed Consumer Books (including Hamlyn, Heinemann and Mitchell Beazley). The estimated £700+ million proceeds from this comparatively small part of Reed Elsevier will be used to concentrate on more profitable specialist publishing services. The sales could take a year to complete. Reed Elsevier's sale announcement comes just nine days after Thomson's, amidst rumours that Pearson would ideally like to sell its recently-axed Westminster Press.[<9 July]

Express job cuts

18 July: Express Newspapers announces 220 redundancies it claims will secure the future of its three national titles. The job losses represent nearly 15 per cent of the Daily Express, Sunday Express and Daily Star staff, and will cost £7.7 million. Managing director Andrew Cameron says the cuts are in response to a 50 per cent rise in newsprint prices this year and technological change. He denies widespread media speculation that the papers will be for sale. The Express announcement comes as the latest ABC circulation figures show all three papers are down in the first half of 1995 compared with 1994. The steadily-declining Daily Express has fallen 6.5 per cent, to the lowest point since the 1920s, and the Sunday Express 10.2 per cent. It later emerges the Express has had discussions with the Mirror Group and News International about possible integration between the companies, cutting costs by sharing most non-editorial work.

Newsprint crisis

19 July: Only a quarter of old newspapers are recycled, says a report by University College, London. Britain consumes 2.3 million tonnes of newsprint a year, but most is buried in landfill sites and 10 per cent is burned in incinerators. Incineration is steadily becoming more popular with local authorities, but the report says recycling is a better option. [<3 July]

Old law halts libel case

21 July: The libel action brought against the Guardian by the former minister Neil Hamilton and parliamentary lobbyist Ian Greer over the "cash for questions" affair is halted in the High Court. Mr Justice May stays the action after ruling that the 1689 Bill of Rights, which bans the courts from looking into parliamentary proceedings, would prevent the Guardian from getting a fair trial. If the ruling over Article 9 of the Bill were upheld in a higher court appeal, then MPs would be barred from suing over allegations, however false, about their parliamentary activities. The judge admits he is "acutely conscious" that the effect of the stay could be seen as a denial of justice to the MPs, a denial of a forum to the Guardian and even as a licence to publish untrue parliamentary material. [<20 October]

Tonight - tomorrow?

21 July: The Evening Standard's rival Tonight celebrates its first birthday. Today's special issue is the 172nd, with 32 pages. Calling itself "the only free newspaper for the whole of London", Tonight is aimed at commuters, and handed out at stations. It started as a daily, but is currently published weekly, on Fridays.

Sisters lose "trial by media" action

31 July: Two sisters convicted of murder and later freed lose their battle to force the Attorney-General to prosecute newspapers which subjected them to "trial by media". Lisa and Michelle Taylor fail to have contempt of court proceedings brought against several national papers for the reporting of their murder trial in 1992. Their convictions were quashed by the Court of Appeal in 1994, partly because of prejudicial newspaper publicity. But today two High Court judges rule that even though the reporting gave "no credit to the tabloid press", there can be no legal challenge against the Solicitor General's decision that proceedings were "not appropriate". The sisters will take the case to the House of Lords.

NATIONAL NEWSPAPERS

When Ian Jack resigned as Independent on Sunday editor in March 1995 he wrote of "the serious liberal idea that badly needs nurturing … good newspapers have a social as well as a commercial worth." A judgement of social worth depends on who is doing the defining. Commercial worth is a less slippery idea, although the extent to which a paper is in business to turn a profit depends on the proprietor. The Guardian, which is owned by a trust whose main purpose is the continuation of the paper, is at the non-profit making end of this spectrum. At the other end is Rupert Murdoch, though he presents the biggest conundrum of all because it's impossible to judge whether he is driven by desires for profit or influence. He probably wouldn't even make a distinction between the two.

What is indisputable is that every last newspaper owner is in business to wield influence as well as make a profit. It is also true that newspapers wane in importance. An Independent Television Commission survey into public attitudes revealed that the number of people who claim television is their principal source of world news is five time as great as the number who say newspapers are their main source. That alone explains why newspaper owners are diversifying into television.

Meanwhile the newspapers' struggles for circulation and influence are testing the "serious liberal idea" almost to destruction. Since mid-1993 News International, The Telegraph and, to a lesser extent, the Mirror Group have been running a price cutting campaign. Circulations of the cheapest papers increased. Equally predictable is the major hike in the the prices of newsprint. This is a cyclical problem with big buyers of paper squeezing suppliers in times of glut and being repaid in kind during shortages. It takes 18 months to bring new capacity in newsprint and the tight market will last way into 1996.

The result of intensified competition is that

National newspaper circulations

DAILIES	1965	1975	1985	1990	1995	change*
1 Sun	1,361,000	3,477,000	4,065,000	3,936,000	4,080,000	0.21%
2 Daily Mirror	4,957,000	3,943,000	3,253,000	3,907,000	2,603,000	0.99%
3 Daily Mail	2,425,000	1,725,000	1,828,000	1,669,000	1,788,000	-0.35%
4 Daily Express	3,981,000	2,798,000	1,875,000	1,560,000	1,279,000	-6.45%
5 Telegraph	1,351,000	1,323,000	1,221,000	1,086,000	1,066,000	0.82%
6 Daily Star			1,434,000	919,000	738,000	-1.19%
7 Times	258,000	315,000	480,000	432,000	647,000	33.41%
8 Today				581,000	566,000	-3.56%
9 Guardian	276,000	315,000	487,000	431,000	400,000	-0.76%
10 Financial Times	152,000	180,000	229,000	288,000	294,000	-1.09%
11 Independent				414,000	294,000	4.81%
SUNDAYS						
1 NoW	6,175,000	5,646,000	4,787,000	5,038,000	4,744,000	-0.63%
2 Sunday Mirror	5,022,000	4,284,000	3,211,000	2,911,000	2,560,000	-0.28%
3 People	5,509,000	4,218,000	3,090,000	2,589,000	2,066,000	2.69%
4 Mail on Sunday			1,605,000	1,890,000	1,959,000	-1.29%
5 Sunday Express	4,187,000	3,786,000	2,405,000	1,729,000	1,403,000	-10.24%
6 Sunday Times	1,275,000	1,396,000	1,258,000	1,187,000	1,253,000	2.65%
7 Sunday Tel.	662,000	757,000	690,000	592,000	692,000	10.82%
8 Observer	829,000	761,000	746,000	568,000	464,000	-7.44%
9 Ind. on Sunday				363,000	327,000	-2.38%

* percentage change in circulation since January-June 1994

ABC: January-June 1965-1995

the tabloids have become tackier and the broadsheets have become more like tabloids. Alan Rusbridger, the Guardian's new editor, coined the word of the year, and maybe a mention for himself in the Oxford English Dictionary, when he talked of the "broadloid". By this he means the traditional broadsheet newspapers that now run standard showbiz and royal gossip alongside their old-fashioned staples of politics and economics. With the exception of the FT, every broadsheet is at it and evidence is the space given over to the discovery of the film star Hugh Grant's session with a prostitute. Judged in terms of column inches this early July story got the following broadloid coverage (and broadloid rating):

The Independent 536 column inches
The Guardian 505
Daily Telegraph 482
Sunday Times 247
The Times 229
Sunday Telegraph 180
The Observer 42
Independent on Sunday 37
Financial Times 1 (one) inch.

Nobody could argue that such saturation coverage has anything to do with any social worth other than keeping papers in business.

National newspaper owners: the Big Seven

Seven companies account for most national paper sales. In circulation percentages, they are:

News International - 37 per cent
Dominated by Rupert Murdoch, News Innterational owns the Sun, The Times, Today, News of the World and Sunday Times. Also owned is the book publisher HarperCollins and 40 per cent of the satellite company BSkyB. Murdoch is the big baron in the new global village and his UK interests are a mere fiefdom.
America: Twentieth Century Fox, including Fox TV, The New York Post, TV Guide.
Germany: 49.9 per cent share of Vox satellite and terrestrial TV channel.
Asia: 99 per cent of Star TV covering India, China, Japan, the Phillippines, Thailand and Hong Kong.
Australia: Numerous print groups and newspapers and 15 per cent of Channel 7

Mirror Group - 26 per cent
Owns the Daily Mirror, Sunday Mirror, Daily Record and The People. The group has a 43 per cent stake in Newspaper Pulblishing, the company which runs The Independent and The Independent on Sunday. It also has a 40 per cent share in Scottish Television and owns Live TV and Wire TV.

United News and Media - 13 per cent
United Newspapers until 1 June 1995, it owns the Daily Express and Sunday Express,and also publishes over 80 local newspapers. Its magazine division, Miller Freeman, was formerly called Morgan-Grampian.

Daily Mail and General Trust - 12 per cent
It owns the Daily Mail and Mail on Sunday. The trust is the second largest regional paper owner via the Northcliffe Newspapers Group and has shareholdings in Teletext, local radio (especially the GWR Group), Reuters 20 per cent of West Country TV and 100 per cent of Channel One.

The Telegraph - 7 per cent
Owns the Daily Telegraph and Sunday Telegraph. Controlled by Conrad Black, via the Canadian company Hollinger.

Guardian Media Group - 3 per cent
Publishers of the Guardian and Observer,the Group also publishes some 50 local papers and several magazines, and owns 15 per cent of GMTV. The parent of the group is the Scott Trust, whose main object is the continuation of the Guardian.

Pearson - 1 per cent
Owners of the Financial Times, Pearson is a diverse company which spreads into most parts of the media. It owns the local newspaper group Westminster Press and the Longman Group of book publishers and in 1994 bought the magazine publisher Future Publishing. It holds a 14 per cent stake in BSkyB at least 8 per cent of which was put up for sale in July 1995,.
For more detail, see Cross Media Ownership on page 226.

NATIONAL DAILIES

Daily Express
245 Blackfriars Road, London SE1 9UX
Fax 0171-633 0244   Tel 0171-928 8000
News: Fax 0171-620 1654   Tel 0171-922 7070
Editor: Sir Nicholas Lloyd, since 1986.
Deputy editor: Craig MacKenzie
News editor: Ian Walker
Features editor: Niki Chesworth
City editor: Tom McGhie
Diary: Ross Benson
Executive editor (sport): David Emery
Picture editor: Chris Djukanovic
Managing editor: John Honeywell
Managing director: Andrew Cameron
Marketing director: Don Gray
Finance director: Paul Sergeant
Founded: 1900.
Owner: United News and Media

Daily Mail
2 Derry Street, Kensington, London W8 5TT
Fax 0171-937 3251   Tel 0171-938 6000
News: Fax 0171-937 4463   Tel 0171-938 6372
Editor: Paul Dacre, since 1992.
Deputy editor: Christena Appleyard
News editor: Ian Monk
Features editor: Richard Addis
Foreign editor: Leaf Kalfayan
Picture editor: Andy Kyle
City editor: Andrew Alexander
Diary editor: Nigel Dempster
Advertising director: Mike Ironside
Managing director: Guy Zitter
Financial director: Guy Morgan
Founded: 1896.
Owner: Daily Mail & General Trust

Daily Mirror
1 Canada Square, Canary Wharf, London E14 5AP
Fax 0171-293 3405   Tel 0171-510 3000
News Fax 0171-293 3409   Tel 0171-293 3831
Editor: Colin Myler, since April 1994.
Deputy editor: Brendan Parsons
Assistant editor/Columnist: Marjorie Proops
News editor: Eugene Duffy
Features editor: Mark Dowdney
Picture editor: Roy Morgans
Advedrtisement director: Mark Pritchett
Founded: 1903.
Owner: Mirror Group

Daily Record
Anderston Quay, Glasgow, Strathclyde G3 8DA
Fax 0141-242 3340   Tel 0141-248 7000
Editor: Terry Quinn
Deputy editor: Charles McGhee
News editor: Murray Morse
Features editor: John McGourty
Arts editor: Lucy Allsopp
Picture editor: Andy Allan
Sports editor: Bill Leckie
Advertising director: Steve Auty
Managing director: Kevin Beatty
Financial director: George Middlemiss
Founded: 1847.
Owner: Mirror Group

Daily Star
245 Blackfriars Road, London SE1 9UX
Fax 0171-633 0244   Tel 0171-928 8000
News: Fax 0171-922 7960   Tel 0171-922 7360
Editor: Phil Walker
Deputy editor: Peter Hill
Executive editor: Kay Goddard
News editor: Hugh Whittow
Features editor: Brian Dunlea
Picture editor: Mark Moylan
Sports editor: Phil Rostron
Managing editor: John Honeywell
Managing director: Andrew Cameron
Marketing director: Don Gray
Founded: 1978.
Owner: United News and Media

Daily Telegraph
1 Canada Square, Canary Wharf, London E14 5DT
Fax 0171-538 6242   Tel 0171-538 5000
News Fax 0171-513 2506   Tel 0171-538 6355
Editor: Max Hastings, since 1986.
Deputy editors: Simon Heffer & Veronica Wadley
Home editor: Sue Ryan
Features editor: Corinna Honan
Arts editor: Sarah Crompton
Foreign editor: Nigel Wade
Business editor: Roland Gribben
City editor: Neil Collins
Education editor: John Clare
Picture editor: Bob Bodman
Advertising director: Len Sanderson
Editorial director: Jeremy Deedes
Managing director: Stephen Grabiner
Financial director: Tony Hughes
Marketing director: David Pugh
Founded: 1855.
Owner: The Telegraph

Financial Times
1 Southwark Bridge, London SE1 9HL
Fax 0171-873 3076   Tel 0171-873 3000
News: Fax 0171-407 5700   Tel 0171-873 3616
Editor: Richard Lambert, since 1991
Deputy editor: Andrew Gowers
News editor: Julia Cuthbertson
Features editor: John Willman
Weekend FT editor: Max Wilkinson
Foreign editor: Quentin Peel
Picture editor: Glyn Genin
Finance director: Alan Miller
Founded: 1888.
Owner: Pearson

Guardian
119 Farringdon Road, London EC1R 3ER
Fax 0171-837 2114   Tel 0171-278 2332
Editor: Alan Rusbridger, since 1995
Deputy editor: Georgina Henry
Editor-in-Chief: Peter Preston
Home news editor: Paul Webster
Features editor: Roger Alton
Political editor: Michael White
Economics editor: Larry Elliot
Arts editor: Claire Armitstead
Media editor: John Mulholland
Foreign editor: Simon Tisdall
Technology editor: Nick Bannister
Picture editor: Eamon McCabe
Sports editor: Michael Averis
Managing director: Caroline Marland (from 1 January, 1994)
Marketing director: David Brook
Finance director: Paul Naismith
Advertisement director: Carolyn McCall
Founded: 1821
Owner: Guardian Media Group

Independent
1 Canada Square, Canary Wharf, London E14 5DL
Tel 0171-293 2000
Editor: Ian Hargreaves, since August 1994.
Deputy editor: Martin Jacques
Assistant editor: Simon Kelner
Managing editor: Colin Hughes
Associate editors: Andrew Marr, Polly Toynbee, Hamish McRae, Tom Sutcliffe
News editor: Michael Williams
Home editor: David Felton
Arts editor: Tristan Davies
Foreign editor: John Lichfield
Picture editor: Rod Sibbald
Sports editor: Paul Newman
Advertising director: Jeremy Reed
Founded: 1986.
Owner: Newspaper Publishing (see Mirror Group)

Sun
1 Virginia Street, Wapping, London E1 9XP
Fax 0171-782 5605   Tel 0171-782 4000
Editor: Stuart Higgins, since 1994.
Deputy editor: Neil Wallis
News editor: Robin Bowman
City editor: Isabelle Murray
Political correspondent: Trevor Kavanagh
Sports editor: Paul Ridley
Picture editor: Paul Buttle
Commercial director: Camilla Rhodes
Managing director: Doug Flynn
Founded: 1912 as Daily Herald; Sun in present form since 1969.
Owner: News International

Times
1 Pennington Street, Wapping, London E1 9XN
Fax 0171-782 5046   Tel 0171-782 5000
Editor: Peter Stothard, since 1992.
Deputy editor: John Bryant
News editor: James MacManus
Features editor: Graham Paterson
Arts editor: Richard Morrison
Foreign editor: Richard Owen
Business editor: Lindsay Cox
Technology editor: Nick Nuttall
Picture editor: Andrew Moger
Sports editor: David Chappell
Advertising manager: Rachel Pilgrim
Managing director: Douglas Flynn
Chief finance officer: Richard Linford
Founded: 1785.
Owner: News International

Today
1 Virginia Street, Wapping, London E1 9BS
Fax 0171-782 4823   Tel 0171-782 4600
Editor: Richard Stott
Deputy editor: Mary Riddell
News editor: Geoff Sutton
Features editor: Tina Weaver
City editor: Geoge Campbell
Political editor: Paul Wilenius
Sport editor: Mike Crouch
Founded: 1986.
Owner: News International

NATIONAL SUNDAYS

Independent on Sunday
1 Canada Square, Canary Wharf, London E14 5DL
Fax 0171-293 2045   Tel 0171-293 2000
News: Fax 0171-293 2051   Tel 0171-293 2480
Editor: Peter Wilby since May 1995
Deputy editor: Brian Cathcart
News editor: Michael McCarthy
Head of Sunday reviews: Richard Askwith
Commissioning editor (features): Sue Matthias
Political editor: Stephen Castle
Arts editor: Laurence Earle
Reviews editor: Richard Askwith
Foreign editor: Peter Walker
Picture editor: Victoria Lumens
Sports editor: Neil Morton
Ad manager: Guy Griffiths
Managing director: Charles Wilson
Founded: 1990.
Owner: Newspaper Publishing (See Mirror Group)

Mail on Sunday
2 Derry Street, London W8 5TT
Fax 0171-937 3745   Tel 0171-938 6000
Tape Room Fax 0171-937 7896/3829
Editor: Jonathon Holborow, since 1992.
Deputy editor: Rod Gilchrist
Executive editor: Peter Dobbie
Assistant editor: John Ryan
News editor: Thomas Hendry
Features editor: Andy Bull
Arts editor: John Butterworth
Business editor: Timon Day
City editor: William Kay
Picture editor: Gary Woodhouse
Sports editor: Roger Kelly
Advertising director: Simon Barnes
Financial director: Leif Mahon-Daly
Founded: 1982.
Owner: Daily Mail & General Trust

News of the World
1 Virginia Street, Wapping, London E1 9XR
Fax 0171-782 4463   Tel 0171-782 4000
Editor: Piers Morgan, since June 1994.
Deputy editor: Phil Hall
News editor: Alex Marunchak
Political editor: Chris Anderson
Features editor: Rebekah Wade
Art director: Danny Fox
Picture editor: Ian Bradley
Sports editor: Mike Dunn
Production editor: Bill Anslow
Advertising director: Camilla Rhodes
Managing editor: Stuart Kuttner

Associate editor: Robert Waren
Chairman: KR Murdoch
Managing director: Doug Flynn
Finance director: Richard Lindford
Founded: 1843.
Owner: News International

Observer
119 Farringdon Road, London EC1R 3ER
Fax 0171-837 2114   Tel 0171-278 2332
Editor: Andrew Jaspan, since 1995.
Deputy editor: John Price
Home news editor: Paul Dunn
Assistant editor (news): Mark Rosselli
Political editor: Anthony Bevins
Arts editor: Jane Ferguson
Foreign editor: Ann Treneman
Economics editor: William Keegan
Science editor: Robin McKie
Sport: Alan Hubbard
Picture editor: Greg Whitmore
Managing director: Caroline Marland (from 1 January, 1994)
Marketing director: David Brook
Finance director: Paul Naismith
Advertisement director: Carolyn McCall
Founded: 1791.
Owner: Guardian Media Group

People
1 Canada Square, Canary Wharf, London E14 5AP.
Fax 0171-293 3405   Tel 0171-293 3000
News: Fax 0171-293 3810   Tel 0171-293 3201
Editor: Bridget Rowe, since 1992.
Deputy editor: Len Gould
News editor: Tom Petrie
Features editor: Ceri Hosier
Political editor: Nigel Nelson
Arts editor: Danny Buckland
Foreign editor: Tom Petrie
Technology editor: Tom Petrie
Sports editor: Ed Barry
Business editor: Cathy Gunn
Picture editor: Paul Bennett
Finance director: John Allwood
Managing director: Charles Wilson
Head of marketing: Amanda Platell
Advertising manager: Mark Pritchett
Founded: 1881.
Owner: Mirror Group

Sunday Express
245 Blackfriars Road, London SE1 9UX
Fax 0171-620 1656   Tel 0171-928 8000
News: Fax 0171-922 7964   Tel 0171-922 7294
Editor: Brian Hitchen
Deputy editor: Henry Macrory
News editor: Shan Lancaster
City editor: John Murray
Political editor: Charles Lewington
Features editor: Peter Birkett
Picture editor: Les Wilson
Assistant editor (sports): Peter Watson
Managing editor: John Honeywell
Managing director: Andrew Cameron
Marketing director: Don Gray
Finance director: Paul Sergeant
Founded: 1918.
Owner: United News and Media

Sunday Mirror
1 Canada Square, Canary Whart, London E14 5AP
Fax 0171-293 3405   Tel 0171-293 3000
News: Fax 0171-293 3939   Tel 0171-293 3601
Editor: Tessa Hilton, since July 1994.
Executive editor: Paul Connew
News editor: Chris Boffey
Asistant editor (features): Linda McKay
Associate editor: Ric Papineau
Magazine editor: Katy Bravery
Fashion editor: Julia Robson
Picture editor: Russell Cox
Sports editor: Keith Fisher
Advertising director: Mark Pritchett
Managing director: Charles Wilson
Financial director: John Allwood
Marketing manager: Amanda Platell
Founded: 1915 as Sunday Pictorial.
Owner: Mirror Group

Sunday Sport
Great Ancoats Street, Manchester M60 4BT
Fax 0161-236 2427   Tel 0161-236 4466
Editor: Tony Lipsey, since 1994.
Deputy editor: John Wise
News editor: Nick Cracknell
Features editor: Nick Cracknell
Arts editor: John Duckworth
Picture editor: Peter Powell
Advertising manager: Alan Pollock
Managing director: John Gibbons
Financial director: Andy McIntyre
Founded: 1986.
Owner: Sport Newspapers (David Sullivan).

Sunday Telegraph
1 Canada Square, Canary Wharf, London E14 5AR
Fax 0171-538 6242   Tel 0171-538 5000
News: Fax 0171-513 2504   Tel 0171-538 7350

Editor: Charles Moore, since 1992.
Editor-in-chief: Max Hastings
Deputy editors: Frank Johnson & Kim Fletcher
News editor: Mark Palmer
Features editor: Lisa Freedman
Arts editor: John Preston
Literary editor: Miriam Gross
City editor: Neil Bennett
Foreign editor: Ivo Dawnay
Political editor: David Wastell
Picture editor: Nigel Skelsey
Advertising director: Len Sanderson
Chairman: Conrad Black
Managing director: Stephen Grabiner
Finance director: Tony Hughes
Marketing director: David Pugh
Founded: 1961.
Owner: The Telegraph

Sunday Times
1 Pennington Street, London E1 9XW
Fax 0171-782 5658   Tel 0171-782 5000
Editor: John Witherow since 1994
News editor: Mark Skipworth
Political editor: Michael Jones
Insight editor: Frank Kane
Managing editor business news and city editor: John Jay
Managing editor news review: Ian Birrell
Picture editor: Ray Wells
Sports editor: Nick Pitt
Design editor: Gordon Beckett
Style editor: Jeremy Langmead
Arts editor: David Mills
Music critic: Hugh Canning
Travel editor: Christine Walker
Advertisement manager: Marie Foulkes
Chairman: Rupert Murdoch
Founded: 1822.
Owner: News International

The European
200 Grays Inn Road, London WC1X 8NE
Fax 0171-713 1840   Tel 0171-418 7777
Editor: Charles Garside, since April 1994.
Deputy editor: Peter Taylor
News editor: David Meilton
Features editor: Julian Coman
Arts editor: Sebastian O'Kelly
Technology editor: Andrew Harvey
Picture editor: Jeanette Downing
Sport: Andrew Warshaw
Advertising manager: Michael Moore
Chief executive: Bert Hardy
Head of finance: Sarah Wilkinson
Head of marketing: Manfred Mareck
Founded: 1990.
Owner: The European (Barclay brothers).
The European is published on Thursdays, but is included here because it is a weekly.

LOCAL PAPER OWNERS

Local newspapers are local in name only. Over four fifths of this sector of the press is dominated by a handful owners, the Top Ten of whom control over 60 per cent of the market. Identifying ultimate ownership is confusing and the companies listed here are sometimes the regional subdivisions of larger organisations.

Over the past few years the tendency has been for the media combines to buy enough local titles to create regional monopolies. Emap, for example, has made itself strong in East Anglia, Essex and Cambridgeshire and Northcliffe Newspapers (which is ultimately owned by the Daily Mail and General Trust plc) dominates local newspapers in the West Country.

The process of consolidation accelerated when Trinity International paid £327.5 million for most of Thomson Regional Newspapers. The deal, which was struck in July 1995 and is likely to be approved by the Monopolies and Merger Commission by Christmas, gives Trinity 13 per cent of the market. As of writing in August 1995 the five titles in the Scotsman group still remained with Thomson.

The companies in this spread are the top local newspaper proprietors, as identified by the Newspaper Society in its PressAd database. The companies are ranked by the number of issues produced per week.

The top local paper owners

1 **Trinity International Holdings**
2 **Northcliffe Newspapers Group**
3 **United Provincial Newspapers**
4 **Reed Regional Newspapers**
5 **Westminster Press**
6 **Midland Independent Newspapers**
7 **Guardian Media Group**
8 **Midland News Association**
9 **Eastern Counties Newspapers Group**
10 **Emap**
11 **Portsmouth & Sunderland Newspapers**
12 **Southern Newspapers**
13 **Johnston Press**
14 **Caledonian Newspaper Publishing**
15 **Bristol United Press**
16 **Tindle Newspapers**
17 **DC Thomson & Co**
18 **Adscene Publishing**
19 **Southnews**

Adscene Publishing
Newspaper House, Wincheap, Canterbury, Kent CT1 3YR
Fax 01227-456444   Tel 01227-767321
23 titles. 881,000 weekly circulation.
The group publishes titles in Kent, Greater London, Lincs, Notts, Leics, South Yorks and Hereford.

Bristol United Press
Temple Way, Bristol, Avon BS99 7HD
Fax 0117-927 9568   Tel 0117-926 0080
8 titles. 1,383,000 weekly circulation.
A subsidary of the Bristol Evening Post.

Caledonian Newspaper Publishing
195 Albion Street, Glasgow G1 1QP
Fax 0141-553 1355   Tel 0141-552 6255
2 titles. 1,570,000 weekly circulation.
A company formed in 1992 by the management buyout of The Herald and The Evening Times from Lonrho and George Outram and Co.

DC Thomson & Co
80 Kingsway East, Dundee, Tayside DD4 8SL
Fax 01382-454590   Tel 01382-23131
3 titles. 920,000 weekly circulation.
A family owned company which also publishes the Beano and the Dandy.

Eastern Counties Newspapers Group
Prospect House, Rouen Road, Norwich, Norfolk NR1 1RE
Fax 01603-612930   Tel 01603-628311
40 titles. 2,529,000 weekly circulation.
ECN's primary business is local papers, mainly in East Anglia.

Emap
1 Lincoln Court, Lincoln Road, Peterborough, Cambs PE1 2RF
Fax 01733-349290   Tel 01733-68900
72 titles. 2,431,000 weekly circulation.
Emap is a magazine and local paper company. It has 14 regional newspaper centres in East Sussex, West Sussex, Kent, Beds, Bucks, Cambs, Herts, Leics, Lincs, Norfolk, Northants, Oxon, Suffolk, Warwicks, North Yorks and Humberside.

Guardian Media Group
164 Deansgate, Manchester M60 2RD
Fax 0161-832 5351   Tel 0161-832 7200
48 titles. 3,423,000 weekly circulation.
The Guardian Media Group's national titles are The Guardian and The Observer. Its local papers are publihsed by the Greater

Manchester Division, G&N Scott, Berks Press, Surrey Division and Lancs and Cheshire County Newspapers. All ordinary shares of the Guardian Media Group are owned by the Scott Trust and any dividends "shall be devoted towards building up the reserves of the company and expanding, improving and increasing the circulation of its newspapers.".

Johnston Press
53 Manor Place, Edinburgh EH3 7EG
Fax 0131-225 4580   Tel 0131-225 3361
73 titles. 1,946,000 weekly circulation.
A family dominated company with local titles mainly in Scotland and the north of England.

Midland Independent Newspapers
28 Colmore Circus, Birmingham B4 6AX
Fax 0121-233 0173   Tel 0121-236 3366
31 titles. 3,689,000 weekly circulation.
Midland Independent was formed in 1991 and concentrates activites on local papers in the West and East Midlands.

Midland News Association
51-53 Queen Street, Wolverhampton, West Midlands WV1 3BU
Fax 01902-772415   Tel 01902-313131
23 titles. 2,566,000 weekly circulation.The other big Midlands local paper company.

Northcliffe Newspapers Group
31-31 John Street, London WC1N 2QB
Fax 0171-405 1469   Tel 0171-242 7070
60 titles. 7,617,000 weekly circulation.
Northcliffe Newspapers is part of the Daily Mail and General Trust of which Associated Newspapers is the overall management company. The group publishes the Daily Mail and Mail on Sunday. Northcliffe is the second largest regional newspaper publisher and operates from 23 centres.

Portsmouth & Sunderland Newspapers
37 Abingdon Road, London W8 6AH
Fax 0171-937 1479   Tel 0171-937 9741
25 titles. 2,123,000 weekly circulation.
An old family firm founded in 1873 by the great-grandfather of the present chairman. The groups main activities are in central southern, north east England and Greater London.

Reed Regional Newspapers
Newspaper House, 34-44 London Road, Morden, Surrey SM4 5BR
Fax 0181-687 4309   Tel 0181-640 8989
82 titles. 4,993,000 weekly circulation.
Reed Regional Newspapers is a subsidiary of Reed Elsevier. One of the world's leading info-businesses, its local paper publishing is handled by Reed Northern Newspaper, Reed Midland Newspapers and Reed Southern Newspapers. RRN was put up for sale in July 1995.

Southnews
326 Station Road, Harrow, Middlesex HA1 2DR
Fax 0181-424 0601   Tel 0181-863 3933
21 titles. 873,000 weekly circulation.
A company formed in 1986 by a management team which had previosuly worked for Westminster Press or Reed Regional Newspapers.

Southern Newspapers
45 Above Bar, Southampton, Hampshire SO9 7BA
Fax 01703-630289   Tel 01703-634134
43 titles. 2,069,000 weekly circulation.
A privately owned company with other interests in property.

Tindle Newspapers
114 West Street, Farnham, Surrey GU9 7HL
Fax 01252-725007   Tel 01252-735667
42 titles. 1,321,000 weekly circulation.
Publishes through the South West and in and around London.

Trinity International Holdings
6 Heritage Court, Lower Bridge Street, Chester, Cheshire CH1 1RD
Fax 01244-341677   Tel 01244-350555
1300 titles. 12,000,000 weekly circulation.
The Liverpool Daily Post and Echo until 1985, Trinity expanded well beyond its original Merseyside territory to Argus Newspapers in London and the home counties plus titles in Wales and Scotland. It became the largest regional paper publisher in Britain with the £327.5 million purchase, in July 1995, of Thomson Corporation. Until then the Canadian owned publishing-to-holidays group had been the UK local paper market leader.

United Provincial Newspapers
PO Box 168, Wellington Street, Leeds, West Yorks LS1 1RF
Fax 01532-443430   Tel 01532-432701
81 titles. 6,020,000 weekly circulation.
United Provincial Newspapers is United Newspapers' regional newspaper publishing division. The group publishes three national papers - the Daily Express, The Sunday Express and Daily Star. Regionally it works from centres in Yorkshire and Humberside, the North West, South Wales and the South East.

Westminster Press
Newspaper House, 8-16 Great New Street, London EC4P 4ER
Fax 0171-353 7526   Tel 0171-353 1030
67 titles. 4,914,000 weekly circulation.
Westminster Press is a subsidiary of Pearson, the publisher of the Financial Times and the Economist. Westminster comprises nine regional divisions in Bradford, High Wycombe, Basildon, Darlington, Oxford, Brighton, Bath, Westmoreland and York.

LOCAL DAILIES

The papers marked with **(M)** are morning titles; the remainder are evening titles. Circulations are Mondays to Fridays, July to December 1994 and the percentage figures show circulation shifts from the corresponding period in 1993.

England

(Barrow) North West Evening Mail
Abbey Road, Barrow, Cumbria LA14 5QS
Fax 01229-832141/840164   Tel 01229-821835
Editor: Donald Martin
Owner: CN Group
Circulation: 19,266 (-4 per cent)

(Basildon) Evening Echo
Chester Hall Lane, Basildon, Essex SS14 3BL
Fax 01268-532060   Tel 01268-522792
Editor: Bob Dimond
Owner: Westminster Press
Circulation: 56,498 (+2.4 per cent)

Bath Chronicle
33 Westgate Street, Bath, Avon BA1 1EW
Fax 01225-445969   Tel 01225-444044
Editor: David Gledhill
Owner: Westminster Press
Circulation: 19,286 (-8.2 per cent)

Birmingham Evening Mail
28 Colmore Circus, Birmingham B4 6AX
Fax 0121-233 0271   Tel 0121-236 3366
Editor: Ian Dowell
Owner: Midland Independent Newspapers
Circulation: 201,007 (+0.3 per cent)

Birmingham Post (M)
28 Colmore Circus, Birmingham B4 6AX
Fax 0121-233 0271   Tel 0121-236 3366
Editor: Nigel Hastilow
Owner: Midland Independent Newspapers
Circulation: 26,071 (+0.9)

(Blackpool) Evening Gazette
Preston New Road, Blackpool, Lancs FY4 4AU
Fax 01253-766799   Tel 01253-839999
Editor: Robin Fletcher
Owner: United Provincial Newspapers
Circulation: 47,059 (-2.6)

Bolton Evening News
Churchgate, Bolton, Lancs BL1 1DE
Fax 01204-365068   Tel 01204-22345
Editor: Andrew Smith
Owner: Reed Regional Newspapers
Circulation: 44,451 (-3.9 per cent)

(Bournemouth) Evening Echo
Richmond Hill, Bournemouth, Dorset BH2 6HH.
Fax 01202-292115   Tel 01202-554601
Editor: Gareth Weekes
Owner: Southern Newspapers
Circulation: 49,979 (-0.4 per cent)

(Bradford) Telegraph and Argus
Hall Ings, Bradford, West Yorks BD1 1JR
Fax 01274-723634   Tel 01274-729511
Editor: Perry Austin-Clark
Owner: Westminster Press
Circulation: 60,090 (-4.9 per cent)

(Brighton) Evening Argus
Hollingbury Industrial Estate, Crowhurst Road,
Brighton, East Sussex BN1 8AR
Fax 01273-505703   Tel 01273-544544
Editor: Chris Fowler
Owner: Westminster Press
Circulation: 64,264 (-5.3 per cent)

Bristol Evening Post
Temple Way, Bristol BS99 7HD
Fax 0117-927 9568   Tel 0117-926 0080
Editor: Adrian Faber
Owner: Bristol United Press
Circulation: 89,219 (-3.8 per cent)

(Bristol) Western Daily Press (M)
Temple Way, Bristol BS99 7HD
Fax 0117-927 9568   Tel 0117-926 0080
Editor: Ian Beales
Owner: Bristol United Press
Circulation: 63,293 (-3 per cent)

Burton Mail
65-68 High Street, Burton-upon-Trent, DE141LE
Fax 01283-510075   Tel 01283-512345
Editor: Brian Vertigen
Owner: Yattendon Investment Trust
Circulation: 20,352 (-2.2 per cent)

Cambridge Evening News
51 Newmarket Road, Cambridge CB5 8EJ
Fax 01223-460846   Tel 01223-358877
Editor: Robert Satchwell
Owner: Yattendon Investment Trust
Circulation: 41,770 (-2.6 per cent)

(Carlisle) Evening News and Star
Dalston Road, Carlisle, Cumbria CA2 5UA
Fax 01228-512828   Tel 01228-23488
Editor: Keith Sutton
Owner: CN Group   Circulation: 27,549 (-1.6 per cent)

(Colchester) Evening Gazette
43 North Hill, Colchester, Essex CO1
1TZ
Fax 01206-769523   Tel 01206-761212
Editor: Martin McNeill
Owner: Reed Regional Newspapers
Circulation: 28,676 (-0.4 per cent)

Coventry Evening Telegraph
Corporation Street, Coventry, West Midlands
CV1 1FP
Fax 01203-550869   Tel 01203-633633
Editor: Dan Mason
Owner: Midland Independent Newspapers
Circulation: 83,087 (-2.2 per cent)

(Darlington) Northern Echo (M)
Priestgate, Darlington, County Durham DL1
1NF
Fax 01325-380539   Tel 01325-381313
Editor: David Flintham
Owner: Westminster Press
Circulation: 77,750 (-3.4 per cent)

Derby Evening Telegraph
Northcliffe House, Meadow Road, Derby DE1
2DW
Fax 01332-253027   Tel 01332-291111
Editor: Mike Lowe.
Owner: Northcliffe Newspapers
Circulation: 65,163 (-3.4 per cent)

Dorset Evening Echo
57 St Thomas Street, Weymouth, Dorset DT4
8EU
Fax 01305-760387   Tel 01305-784804
Editor: Michael Woods.
Owner: Southern Newspapers

(Exeter) Express and Echo
Heron Road, Exeter, Devon EX2 7NF
Fax 01392-442294   Tel 01392-442211
Editor: Rachael Campey
Owner: Northcliffe Newspapers
Circulation: 30,833 (-2.8 per cent)

Gloucestershire Citizen
St Johns Lane, Gloucester GL1 2AY
Fax 01452-307238   Tel 01452-424442
Assistant Editor: Bev Ward
Owner: Northcliffe Newspapers
Circulation: 37,556 (-3 per cent)

Gloucestershire Echo
1 Clarence Parade, Cheltenham, Glos GL50
3NZ
Fax 01242-578395   Tel 01242-526261
Editor: Anita Syvret
Owner: Northcliffe Newspapers Group
Circulation: 27,056 (-2.4 per cent)

Grimsby Evening Telegraph
80 Cleethorpe Road, Grimsby, Lincs DN31 3EH
Fax 01472-358859   Tel 01472-359232
Editor: Peter Moore
Owner: Northcliffe Newspapers Group
Circulation: 47,521 (-2.5 per cent)

Guernsey Evening Press
Braye Road, Vale, Guernsey, Channel Islands
Fax 01481-48972   Tel 01481-45866
Editor: Graham Ingrouille
Owner: Guernsey Press Co
Circulation: 15,764 (-0.8 per cent)

Halifax Evening Courier
King Cross Street, Halifax, West Yorks HX1 2SF
Fax 01422-330021   Tel 01422-365711
Editor: Edward Riley
Owner: Johnston Press
Circulation: 32,051 (-2.6 per cent)

Hartlepool Mail
Clarence Road, Hartlepool, Cleveland TS24
8BU
Fax 01429-869024   Tel 01429-274441
Editor: Chris Cox
Owner: Portsmouth & Sunderland Newspapers
Circulation: 26,730 (-1.6 per cent)

Huddersfield Daily Examiner
Queen Street South, Huddersfield, West Yorks
HD1 2TD
Fax 01484-423722   Tel 01484-430000
Editor: Richard Mallinson
Owner: Trinity International Holdings
Circulation: 38,480 (-1.9 per cent)

Hull Daily Mail
Blundells Corner, Beverley Road, Hull HU3
1XS
Fax 01482-584353   Tel 01482-327111
Editor: Mike Wood
Owner: Northcliffe Newspapers Group
Circulation: 92,263 (-1.9 per cent)

(Ipswich) East Anglian Daily Times (M)
30 Lower Brook Street, Ipswich, Suffolk IP4
1AN
Fax 01473-225296   Tel 01473-230023
Editor: Malcolm Pheby
Owner: Eastern Counties Newspapers
Circulation: 48,354 (-2.3 per cent)

(Ipswich) Evening Star
30 Lower Brook Street, Ipswich, Suffolk IP4
1AN
Fax 01473-225296   Tel 01473-230023
Editor: Terry Hunt
Owner: Eastern Counties Newspapers
Circulation: 30,628 (+1.6 per cent)

Jersey Evening Post
PO Box 582, Jersey, Channel Islands JE4 8XQ
Fax 01534-611622   Tel 01534-611611
Editor: Chris Bright
Owner: Jersey Evening Post
Circulation: 23,861 (-0.8 per cent)

Kent Today
Messenger House, New Hythe Lane, Larkfield,
Kent ME20 6SG
Fax 01622-719637   Tel 01622-717880
Editor: Chas Stewart
Owner: Kent Messenger Group
Circulation: 26,542 (-10.2 per cent)

Lancs Evening Post
Eastway, Preston, Lancs PR2 4ZA
Fax 01772-880173   Tel 01772-254841
Editor: Philip Welsh
Owner: United Provincial Newspapers
Circulation: 67,195 (-1.7 per cent)

Lancashire Evening Telegraph
High Street, Blackburn, Lancs BB1 1HT
Fax 01254-680429   Tel 01254-678678
Editor: Peter Butterfield
Owner: Reed Regional Newspapers
Circulation: 47,059 (-2.7 per cent)

Leicester Mercury
St George Street, Leicester LE1 9FQ
Fax 0116-262 4687   Tel 0116-251 2512
Editor: Nick Carter
Owner: Northcliffe Newspapers Group
Circulation: 117,488 (-3.7 per cent)

Lincolnshire Echo
Brayford Wharf East, Lincoln LN5 7AT
Fax 01522-545759   Tel 01522-525252
Editor: Cliff Smith
Owner: Northcliffe Newspapers Group
Circulation: 30,662 (-3.4 per cent)

Liverpool Daily Post (M)
Old Hall Street, Liverpool L69 3EB
Fax 0151-236 4682   Tel 0151-227 2000
Editor: Keith Ely
Owner: Trinity International Holdings
Circulation: 73,691 (-1.6 per cent)

Liverpool Echo
Old Hall Street, Liverpool L69 3EB
Fax 0151-236 4682   Tel 0151-227 2000
Editor: John Griffith
Owner: Trinity International Holdings
Circulation: 167,459 (-3.2 per cent)

(London) Evening Standard
2 Derry Street, London W8 5EE
Fax 0171-937 3193   Tel 0171-938 6000

Editor: Stewart Steven
Owner: Northcliffe Newspapers
Circulation: 452,140 (-3.15 per cent)

Manchester Evening News
164 Deansgate, Manchester M60 2RD
Fax 0161-832 5351   Tel 0161-832 7200
Editor: Michael Unger
Owner: Guardian Media Group
Circulation: 193,952 (-9.4 per cent)

(Middlesbrough) Evening Gazette
Borough Road, Middlesbrough, Cleveland
TS1 3AZ
Fax 01642-232014   Tel 01642-245401
Editor: Ranald Allan
Owner: Trinity international (formerly Thomson Corporation)

(Newcastle) Evening Chronicle
Groat Market, Newcastle-upon-Tyne NE1 1ED
Fax 0191-232 2256   Tel 0191-232 7500
Editor: Neil Benson
Owner: Trinity International (formerly Thomson Corporation)
Circulation: 117,492 (-2.9 per cent)

(Newcastle) Journal (M)
Groat Market, Newcastle-upon-Tyne NE1 1ED
Fax 0191-261-8869   Tel 0191-232 7500
Editor: Bill Bradshaw
Owner: Trinity International (formerly Thomson Corporation)
Circulation: 56,032 (-2.9 per cent)

(Northampton) Chronicle and Echo
Upper Mounts, Northampton NN1 3HR
Fax 01604-233000   Tel 01604-231122
Editor: David Rowell
Owner: Emap
Circulation: 30,267 (-1.4 per cent)

Northamptonshire Evening Telegraph
Northfield Avenue, Kettering, Northants
NN16 9TT
Fax 01536-85983   Tel 01536-81111
Editor: Colin Grant
Owner: Emap
Circulation: 35,980 (-3.8 per cent)

(Norwich) Eastern Daily Press (M)
Rouen Road, Norwich, Norfolk NR1 1RE
Fax 01603-612930   Tel 01603-628311
Editor: Peter Franzen
Owner: Eastern Counties Newspapers
Circulation: 79,192 (-1.3 per cent)

(Norwich) Evening News
Rouen Road, Norwich, Norfolk NR1 1RE
Fax 01603-612930   Tel 01603-628311
Editor: Claire Gillingwater
Owner: Eastern Counties Newspaper Group
Circulation: 41,563 (-2.2 per cent)

Nottingham Evening Post
PO Box 99 Forman Street, Nottingham NG1 4AB
Fax 0115-948 4116   Tel 0115-948 2000
Editor: Graham Glen
Owner: Northcliffe Newspapers Group
Circulation: Not ABC audited.

Oldham Evening Chronicle
Union Street, Oldham, Lancs OL1 1EQ
Fax 0161-627 0905   Tel 0161-633 2121
Editor: Philip Hirst
Owner: Hirst, Kidd & Rennie
Circulation: 36,009 (-3.3 per cent)

Oxford Mail
Newspaper House, Osney Mead, Oxford OX2 0EJ
Fax 01865-243382   Tel 01865-244988
Editor: Tim Blott
Owner: Westminster Press
Circulation: 34,383 (-8.4 per cent)

Peterborough Evening Telegraph
57 Priestgate, Peterborough PE1 1JW
Fax 01733-555188   Tel 01733-555111
Editor: Bob Crawley
Owner: Emap
Circulation: 28,354 (-2.4 per cent)

(Plymouth) Evening Herald
17 Brest Road, Derriford Business Park, Plymouth, Devon PL6 5AA
Fax 01752-765527   Tel 01752-765500
Editor: Alan Cooper
Owner: Northcliffe Newspapers Group
Circulation: 56,147 (-3.6 per cent)

(Plymouth) Western Morning News (M)
17 Brest Road, Derriford Business Park, Plymouth, Devon PL6 5AA
Fax 01752-765535   Tel 01752-765500
Editor: Barrie Williams
Owner: Northcliffe Newspapers Group
Circulation: 53,767 (-2.5 per cent)

(Portsmouth) News
News Centre, Hilsea, Portsmouth, Hants PO2 9SX
Fax 01705-673363   Tel 01705-664488
Editor: Geoff Elliott
Owner: Portsmouth & Sunderland Newspapers
Circulation: 78,633 (-3.3 per cent)

(Reading) Evening Post
8 Tessa Road, Reading, Berks RG1 8NS
Fax 01734-599363   Tel 01734-575833
Editor: Kim Chapman
Owner: Guardian Media Group
Circulation: 23,257 (-6.8 per cent)

Scarborough Evening News
17 Aberdeen Walk, Scarborough, Yorks YO11 1BB
Fax 01723-354092   Tel 01723-363636
Editor: David Penman
Owner: Emap
Circulation: 17,320 (+0.2 per cent)

Scunthorpe Evening Telegraph
Telegraph House, Doncaster Road, Scunthorpe, North Lincs DN15 7RE
Fax 01724-853495   Tel 01724-843421
Editor: Peter Moore
Owner: Northcliffe Newspapers Group
Circulation: 25,182 (+0.3 per cent)

(Sheffield) Star
York Street, Sheffield, South Yorks S1 1PU
Fax 0114-272 5978   Tel 0114-276 7676
Editor: Peter Charlton
Owner: United Provincial Newspapers
Circulation: 100,370 (-4.1 per cent)

Shields Gazette
PO Box 4, Chapter Row, South Shields, Tyne and Wear NE33 1BL
Fax 0191-456 8270   Tel 0191-455 4661
Editor: Ian Holland
Owner: North East Press
Circulation: 24,780 (-3.8 per cent)

Shropshire Star
Ketley, Telford, Shropshire TF1 4HU
Fax 01952-25460501   Tel 01952-242424
Editor: Andy Wright
Owner: Claverley Co
Circulation: 95,047 (-2.1 per cent)

(Southampton) Southern Daily Echo
45 Above Bar, Southampton SO14 7AA
Fax 01703-630289   Tel 01703-634134
Editor: Patrick Fleming
Owner: Southern Newspapers
Circulation: 62,535 (-1.8 per cent)

Stoke Evening Sentinel
Sentinel House, Etruria, Stoke-on-Trent, Staffs ST1 5SS
Fax 01782-280781   Tel 01782-289800
Editor: Sean Dooley
Owner: Northcliffe Newspapers Group
Circulation: 96,589 (-2.7 per cent)

Sunderland Echo
Echo House, Pennywell Industrial Estate, Sunderland, Tyne and Wear SR4 9ER
Fax 0191-534 3807   Tel 0191-534 3011
Editor: Andrew Hughes
Owner: Portsmouth & Sunderland Newspapers
Circulation: 59,930 (-2.9 per cent)

(Swindon) Evening Advertiser
100 Victoria Road, Swindon, Wilts SN1 3BE
Fax 01793-542434   Tel 01793-528144
Editor: Geoff Teather
Owner: Westminster Press
Circulation: 27,831 (-5.6 per cent)

(Torquay) Herald Express
Barton Hill Road, Torquay, Devon TQ2 8JN
Fax 01803-313093   Tel 01803-213213
Editor: J Mitchell
Owner: Northcliffe Newspapers Group
Circulation: 30,531 (-0.4 per cent)

Wolverhampton Express and Star
51-53 Queen Street, Wolverhampton, West
Midlands WV1 3BU
Fax 01902-21467   Tel 01902-313131
Editor: Warren Wilson
Owner: Claverley Co
Circulation: 209,819 (-3.5 per cent)

Worcester Evening News
Hylton Road, Worcester WR2 5JX
Fax 01905-429605   Tel 01905-748200
Editor: Malcolm Ward
Owner: Reed Regional Newspapers
Circulation: 23,886 (-2.1 per cent)

Yorkshire Evening Post
Wellington Street, Leeds, West Yorks LS1 1RF
Fax 0113-238 8536   Tel 0113-243 2701
Editor: Chris Bye
Owner: United Provincial Newspapers
Circulation: 108,587 (-4.6 per cent)

Yorkshire Evening Press
76 Walmgate, York YO1 1YN
Fax 01904-612853   Tel 01904-653051
Editor: David Nicholson
Owner: Westminster Press
Circulation: 48,629 (-3 per cent)

Yorkshire Post (M)
Wellington Street, Leeds, West Yorks LS1
1RF
Fax 0113-238 8537   Tel 0113-243 2701
Editor: Tony Watson
Owner: United Provincial Newspapers
Circulation: 79,803

Wales

(Cardiff) Western Mail (M)
Havelock Street, Cardiff CF1 1WR
Fax 01222-583652   Tel 01222-223333
Editor: Neil Fowler
Owner: Trinity International (formerly Thomson Corporation)
Circulation: 64,570 (-5.9 per cent)

South Wales Argus
Cardiff Road, Newport, Gwent NP9 1QW
Fax 01633-462202   Tel 01633-810000
Editor: Gerry Keighley
Owner: United Provincial Newspapers
Circulation: 36,744 (-3.7 per cent)

South Wales Echo
Thomson House, Havelock St, Cardiff CF1 1WR
Fax 01222-583624   Tel 01222-223333
Editor: Keith Perch
Owner: Trinity International (formerly Thomson Corporation)
Circulation: 79,844 (-2.8 per cent)

South Wales Evening Post
Adelaide Street, Swansea, Glamorgan SA1
1QT
Fax 01792-655386   Tel 01792-650841
Editor: Hugh Berlyn
Owner: Northcliffe Newspapers Group
Circulation: 69,700

Evening Leader & Chester Evening Leader
Wrexham Road, Mold, Clwyd CH7 1XY
Fax 01352-752180   Tel 01352-700022
Editor: Reg Herbert
Owner: North Wales Newspapers
Circulation: 32,178 (-1.1 per cent)

Scotland

(Aberdeen) Evening Express
Lang Stracht, Mastrick, Aberdeen AB9 8AF
Fax 01224-699575   Tel 01224-690222
Editor: Dick Williamson
Owner: Trinity International (formerly Thomson Corporation)
Circulation: 69,562 (-0.5 per cent)

(Aberdeen) Press and Journal (M)
Lang Stracht, Mastrick, Aberdeen AB9
8AF
Fax 01224-663575   Tel 01224-690222
Editor: Derek Tucker
Owner: Thomson Corporation
Circulation: 107,965 (+0.9 per cent)

(Dundee) Courier (M)
80 Kingsway East, Dundee DD4 8SL
Fax 01382-454590   Tel 01382-223131
Editor: Adrian Arthur
Owner: DC Thomson & Co
Circulation: 105,957 (-2.1 per cent)

(Dundee) Evening Telegraph
80 Kingsway East, Dundee DD4 8SL
Fax 01382-454590   Tel 01382-223131
Editor: Harold Pirie
Owner: DC Thomson & Co
Circulation: 37,170 (-3.6 per cent)

(Edinburgh) Evening News
20 North Bridge, Edinburgh EH1 1YT
Fax 0131-225 7302   Tel 0131-225 2468
Editor: Harry Roulston
Owner: Thomson Corporation
Circulation: 88,780 (-3.4 per cent)

(Glasgow) Evening Times
195 Albion Street, Glasgow G1 1QP
Fax 0141-553 1355   Tel 0141-552 6255
Editor: John Scott
Owner: Caledonian Publishing
Circulation: 139,463 (-6 per cent)

(Glasgow) Herald (M)
195 Albion Street, Glasgow G1 1QP
Fax 0141-552 2288   Tel 0141-552 6255
Editor: George McKechnie
Owner: Caledonian Publishing
Circulation: 107.618

Greenock Telegraph
2 Crawford Street, Greenock, PA15 1LH
Fax 01475-783734   Tel 01475-726511
Editor: Ian Wilson
Owner: Clyde & Forth Press
Circulation: 20,450 (-2.1 per cent)

Paisley Daily Express (M)
14 New Street, Paisley PA1 1YA
Fax 0141-887 6254   Tel 0141-887 7911
Editor: Norman McDonald

Owner: Trinity International Holdings
Circulation: 9,500

Scotsman (M)
20 North Bridge, Edinburgh EH1 1YT
Fax 0131-226 7420   Tel 0131-225 2468
Editor: James Seaton
Owner: Thomson Corporation
Circulation: 80,603 (-3.5 per cent)

Northern Ireland

(Belfast) News Letter (M)
46-56 Boucher Crescent, Belfast BT12 6QY
Fax 01232-664412   Tel 01232-680000
Editor: Geoff Martin
Owner: Tindle Newspapers

Belfast Telegraph
124-144 Royal Avenue, Belfast BT1 1EB
Fax 01232-554506   Tel 01232-264000
Editor: Edmund Curran
Owner: Thomson Corporation
Circulation: 133,436 (-2.4 per cent)

Irish News (M)
113-117 Donegall Street, Belfast BT1 2GE
Fax 01232-337505   Tel 01232-322226
Editor: Tom Collins.
Owner: Irish News
Circulation: 44,126 (+0.1 per cent)

LOCAL SUNDAYS

(Belfast) Sunday Life
124-144 Royal Avenue, Belfast BT1 1EB
Fax 01232-554507   Tel 01232-264300
Editor: Martin Lindsay
Owner: Trinity International (formerly Thomson Corporation)
Circulation: 94,415 (-3.9 per cent)

(Birmingham) Sunday Mercury
28 Colmore Circus, Birmingham B4 6AZ
Fax 0121-233 0271   Tel 0121-236 3366
Editor: Peter Whitehouse
Owner: Midland Independent Newspapers

(Dundee) Sunday Post
2 Albert Square, Dundee DD1 9QJ
Fax 01382-22214   Tel 1382-223131
Editor: Russell Reid
Owner: DC Thomson & Co
Circulation: 965,171 (-3.1 per cent)

(Glasgow) Sunday Mail
Anderston Quay, Glasgow G3 8DA

Fax 0141-242 3587   Tel 0141-248 7000
Editor: James Cassidy
Owner: Mirror Group   Circulation: 880,470 (+3.2 per cent)

(Manchester) News & Echo
George Leigh Street, Manchester M60 0DB
Fax 0161-237 3050   Tel 0161-237 9461
Editor: Tony Livesey   Owner: David Sullivan

(Newcastle) Sunday Sun
Groat Market, Newcastle-upon-Tyne NE1 1ED
Fax 0191-230 0238   Tel 0191-201 6330
Editor: Chris Rushton
Owner: Trinity International (formerly Thomson Corporation)
Circulation: 127,702 (+4.9 %)

(Plymouth) Sunday Independent
Burrington Way, Plymouth, Devon PL5 3LN
Fax 01752-780680   Tel 01752-777151
Editor: John Noble
Owner: Yattendon Investment Trust
Circulation: 41,195 (-1.2 per cent)

Scotland on Sunday
20 North Bridge, Edinburgh EH1 1YT
Fax 0131-220 2443   Tel 0131-225 2468
Editor: Brian Groom
Owner: Thomson Corporation
Circulation: 87,936 (-2 per cent)

Sunday Mercury
28 Colmore Circus, Queensway, Birmingham,
B4 6AX
Fax 0121-233 0271   Tel 0121 236 3366
Editor: Peter Whitehouse
Owner: Midland Independent Newspapers
Circulation: 146,565 (+1 per cent)

Wales on Sunday
Havelock Street, Cardiff CF1 1XR
Fax 01222-583725   Tel 01222-583720
Editor: Peter Hollinson
Owner: Thomson Corporation
Circulation: 60,923 (-7.1 per cent)

Yorkshire on Sunday
PO Box 470, Hall Ings, Bradford, West Yorks
BD1 1JR
Fax 01274-726633   Tel 01274-732244
Editor: Mike Glover
Owner: Westminster Press
Circulation: 53,832 (-10.7 per cent)

LOCAL WEEKLIES

Avon

Bristol United Press
Temple Way, Bristol, Avon BS99 7HD
Fax 0117-9279568   Tel 0117-926 0080
Bristol Observer; Keynsham Observer; Kingswood Observer;
Northavon Observer 0117-926 0080
South Avon Mercury 01275-874224
Owner: Bristol Evening Post

Community Media
15 Argyle Street, Bath, Avon BA2 4BQ
Fax 01225-460944   Tel 01225-460556
Bath & Keynsham Advertiser 01225-446800
Bristol Journal; North Avon Journal 0117-923 1061
Owner: Eastern Counties Newspapers Group

Wessex Newspapers
33 Westgate Street, Bath, Avon BA1 1EW
Fax 01225-445969   Tel 01225-444044
Bath Star; Norton Radstock Star; Somerset & Avon Guardian
Owner: Westminster Press

Weston Mercury
32 Waterloo Street, Weston super Mare, Avon
BS23 1LW
Fax 01934-612038   Tel 01934-614466
Weston Mercury; Somerset & Avon Herald
Owner: Comunity Media

Bedfordshire

Bedfordshire Times & Citizen
66 High Street, Bedford MK40 1NT
Fax 01234-351627   Tel 01234-363101
Ampthill Times 01234-363101.
Biggleswade Chronicle 01767-313479
Owner: Emap

Herald Newspapers
Unit 1, Sandridge Park, Porters Wood Road, St
Albans, Herts AL3 6PQ
Fax 01727-861199   Tel 01727 846866
Bedford/Biggleswade Herald; Mid-Beds Herald 01234-364221
Owner: Barwell Corporation

Herald & Post Group
60 Church Street, Luton, Beds LU1 3JQ
Fax 01582-24340   Tel 01582-401234
Berkhamsted Herald & Post; Hemel Hempstead Herald & Post;
Luton Herald & Post
Owner:Trinity International (formerly Thomson Corporation)

Home Counties Newspapers Holdings
63 Campfield Road, St Albans, Herts AL1 5HX
Fax 01727-851238   Tel 01727-866166
Dunstable Gazette/Leader 01582-60881
Leighton Buzzard Observer 01525-372051
Luton News 01582-21222
Owner: Home Counties Newspaper Holdings

Berkshire

Aldershot News
Penmark House, Albert Road, Aldershot, Hants
GU11 1NU
Fax: 01252-341033   Tel 01252-28221
Crowthorne Mail/News; Sandhurst Mail/News
Owner: Guardian Media Group

Berkshire Press
8 Tessa Road, Reading, Berks RG1 8NS
Fax 01734-599363   Tel 01734-575833
Reading Standard 01734-575833.
Bracknell & Ascot Times; Bracknell & Wokingham Standard;
Crowthorne Times; Wokingham Times 01734-782000
Owner: Guardian Media Group

Berks & Bucks Observer
Upton Court, Slough, Berks SL3 7NR
Fax 01753-693895   Tel 01753-523355

Maidenhead Advertiser
48 Bell Street, Maidenhead, Berks SL6 1HX
Fax 01628 770944   Tel 01628-771100
Owner: Baylis & Co

Newbury Weekly News
Faraday Road, Newbury, Berks RG14 2DW
Fax 01635-522922   Tel 01635-47000
Owner: Newbury Weekly News

Reading Newspaper Co
50 Portman Road, Reading, Berks RG3 1BA
Fax 01734-391619   Tel 01734-503030
Reading Chronicle; Woodley Chronicle; Tadley Chronicle; South
Oxon Chronicle; Reading Chronicle Midweek 01734-503030.
Ascot News; Bracknell News; Crowthorne Newsweek;
Wokingham News; Bracknell & Wokingham News Extra 01344-
56615.
Newbury Journal 01635-32771.
Owner: Trinity International Holdings .

Windsor Newspaper Co
256 Ipswich Road, Slough, Berks SL1 4EP
Fax 01753-692254   Tel 01753-825111
Ascot/Slough/South Bucks/Windsor Express
Owner: Southnews

Buckinghamshire

Buckinghamshire Advertiser
The Vale, Chalfont St Peter, Bucks SL9 9ST
Fax 01753 889060   Tel 01753-888333
Beaconsfield Advertiser; Amersham Advertiser
Owner: Southnews

Bucks Examiner
16-18 Germain Street, Chesham, Bucks HP5
1LH
Fax 01494-792333   Tel 01494-792626
Owner: Middlesex County Press

Bucks Free Press Group
Gomm Road, High Wycombe, Bucks HP13 7DW
Fax 01494-441977   Tel 01494-521212
Bucks Free Press; Midweek Free Press; South Bucks Star
Owner: Westminster Press

Central Counties Newspapers
2-4 Exchange Street, Aylesbury, Bucks HP20
1UJ
Fax 01296-393451   Tel 01296-24444
Buckingham Advertiser; Bucks Advertiser; Bucks Herald;
Thame Gazette; Buckingham & Winslow Advertiser; Brackley &
Towcester Advertiser; Bicester Review; Rugby Advertiser;
Rugby Review; Daventry Express; Hemel Hempstead Gazette;

Hemel HempsteadExpress; Banbury Guardian; Banbury Citizen;
Leamington Courier; Warwick Courier; Kenilworth Weekly
News, Leamington Review.
Owner: Emap

Herald & Post Newspapers
60 Church Street, Luton, Beds LU1 3JQ
Fax 01582-24340   Tel 01582-401234
Amersham Herald & Post
Owner: Thomson Group

High Wycombe Leader
51 Castle Street, High Wycombe, Bucks HP13
6RN
Fax 01474-473502   Tel 01474-438090
Owner: Southnews

Premier Newspapers
Napier House, Auckland Park, Bond Avenue,
Bletchley, Milton Keynes, Bucks MK1 1BU
Fax 01908-371112   Tel 01908-372279
Bletchley Citizen; Milton Keynes Citizen; Newport Pagnell
Citizen; Stony Stratford Citizen; Woburn Sands Citizen
Owner: Emap

Cambridgeshire

Cambridge Newspapers
51 Newmarket Road, Cambridge CB5 8EJ
Fax 01223-61744   Tel 01223-358877
Cambridge/Ely/Huntingdon St Ives/St Neots Weekly News
Owner: Yattendon Investment Trust

Cambridgeshire Times
51 High Street, March, Cambs PE15 9JJ
Fax 01354-52751   Tel 01354-52621
Cambridgeshire Times; Chatteris Advertiser
Owner: Eastern Counties Newspapers Group

Eastern Counties Newspapers Group
Prospect House, Rouen Road, Norwich, Norfolk
NR1 1RE
Fax 01603-612930   Tel 01603-628311
Ely Standard; Soham Advertiser; Littleport Gazette 01353-667831
Cambridgeshire Times; Chatteris Advertiser 01354-52621
Hunts Post; Ramsay Post 01480-411481
Wisbech Standard 01945-584447

Fenland Citizen
11 Union Street, Wisbech, Cambs PE13 1DN
Fax 01945-65912   Tel 01945-584372
Owner: Emap

Peterborough Evening Telegraph Co
57 Priestgate, Peterborough, Cambs PE1 1JW
Fax 01733-313147   Tel 01733-555111
Peterborough Citizen 01733-555111.
Hunts Citizen 01480-407555
Owner: Emap

Peterborough Herald & Post
Cross Street Court, 11-13 Cross Street,
Peterborough PE1 1AS
                                Tel 01733-318600
Owner: Midland Independent Newspapers

Town Crier
Unit 1, Cambridge Technopark, 645 Newmarket
Road, Cambridge CB5 8PB
Fax 01223-293913   Tel 01223-69966
Cambridge Town Crier/Ely Town Crier 01223-69966
St Ives Town Crier/Huntingdon Town Crier/St Neots Citizen
  01480-407555
Owner: Emap

Channel Islands

Guernsey Weekly Press
PO Box 57, Braye Road, Vale, Guernsey,
Channel Islands G41 3BW
Fax 01481-49250   Tel 01481-45866

Jersey Weekly Post
PO Box 582, Five Oaks, St Saviour, Jersey,
Channel Islands JE4 8XQ
Fax 01534-611622   Tel 01534-611611
Owner: Jersey Evening Post

Cheshire

Ashton Weekly Newspapers
Park House, Acres Lane, Stalybridge, Cheshire
SK15 2JR
Fax 0161-303 1922   Tel 0161-303 1910
High Peak Reporter 01457-852669.
North Cheshire Herald 0161-368 3595
Stalybridge 0161-303 1910
Owner: United Provincial Newspapers

Chester Standard
96 Watergate Street, Chester, Cheshire CH1 2LF
Fax 01244-351536   Tel 01244-351234
Owner: Chester Standard

Chronicle Newspapers
Chronicle House, Commonhall Street, Chester,
Cheshire CH1 2BJ
Fax 01244-340165   Tel 01244-340151
Chester Chronicle/Herald & Post; Crewe Chronicle; Ellesmere
  Port Pioneer; Middlewich Chronicle; Nantwich Chronicle;
  Northwich Chronicle/Herald & Post; Runcorn Weekly News;
  Runcorn-Widnes Herald & Post; South Cheshire Herald & Post;
  South Wirral Herald & Post; Whitchurch Herald; Widnes Weekly
  News; Winsford Chronicle
Owner: Trinity International (formerly Thomson Corporation)

Congleton/Sandbach/Biddulph Chronicles
11 High Street, Congleton, Cheshire CW12 1BW

Fax 01260-280687   Tel 01260-273737
Owner: Congleton/Sandbach Chronicles

Lancashire & Cheshire County Newspapers
Wood Street, Hollywood, Stockport, Greater
Manchester SK3 0AB
Fax 0161-480 4847   Tel 0161 480 4491
Knutsford Express Advertiser; Wilmslow Express Advertiser
  01625-529333.
Macclesfield Times/Express Advertiser 01625-424445.
Sale Express Advertiser 0161-928 3424
Owner: Guardian Media Group

Reed Northern Newspapers
The Academy, Bridge Street, Warrington,
Cheshire WA1 2RU
Fax 01925-414427   Tel 01925-633033
Newton & Golborne Guardian; Warrington Guardian
Altrincham Messenger; Sale Messenger 0161-477 4600.
Congleton Guardian 01260-280686.
Crewe Guardian 01270-258858.
Frodsham World; Runcorn World; Widnes World; 01928-568448.
Knutsford Guardian 01565-634114.
Macclesfield Messenger 01625-511241.
Middlewich/Northwich Guardians 01606-43333.
Wilmslow Messenger 01625-527695.
Winsford Guardian 01606-862086
Owner: Reed Elsevier

Cleveland

North Eastern Evening Gazette
105 Borough Road, Middlesbrough, Cleveland
TS1 3AZ
Fax 01642-232014   Tel 01642-245401
East Cleveland Herald & Post; Hartlepool & Billingham Herald &
  Post; Middlesbrough Herald & Post; Stockton Herald & Post
  01642-242222.
Teesside Times 01642-231889
Owner: Trinity International (formerly Thomson Corporation)

Hartlepool Star
Coniston House, Washington, Tyne & Wear
NE38 7SH
Fax 0191-417 3291   Tel 0191-417 0050
Owner: North East Press

County Durham

North of England Newspapers
PO Box 14, Priestgate, Darlington, Co Durham
DL1 1NF
Fax 01325-380539   Tel 01325-381313
Aycliffe Advertiser; Chester le Street Advertiser; Consett
  Advertiser; Darlington Advertiser; Darlington & Stockton
  Times; Durham Advertiser; Teesdale Advertiser; Wear Valley
  Advertiser
Owner: Westminster Press

Peterlee Star
Coniston House, Washington, Tyne & Wear
NE38 7SH
Fax 0191-417 3791   Tel 0191-417 0050
Owner: Sunderland & Portsmouth Publishing

Teesdale Mercury
24 Market Place, Barnard Castle, Co Durham
DL12 8NB
Fax 01833-638633   Tel 01833-637140

South Durham Times
31 Duke Street, Darlington Co. Durham DL3
7RX
Fax 01325-380348   Tel 01325-482286
Owner: NE Evening Gazette

Sunderland Echo
Echo House, Pennywell Estate, Sunderland,
Tyne & Wear SR4 9ER
Fax 0191-5343807   Tel 0191 5343011
Owner: Sunderland and Portsmouth Publishing

Cornwall

Cornish and Devon Post
Western Buildings, Launceston, Cornwall PL15
7AL
Fax 01566-776976   Tel 01566-772424
Bude and Stratton Post; Cornish & Devon Post; Camelford and
Delabole Post; Launceston and Bude Journal Gazette
Owner: Tindle Newspapers

Cornish Weekly Newspapers
Harmsworth House, Lemon Quay, Truro,
Cornwall TR1 2LP
Fax 01872-222145   Tel 01872-71451
Camborne & Redruth Leader; Falmouth & Penryn Leader;
Helston & Lizard Leader; Truro Leader; West Briton 01872-
71451.
Cornish Guardian 01208-78133.
The Cornishman; Penzance & St Ives Leader 01736-62247
Owner: Northcliffe Newspapers Group

Helston Printers
14c Wendron Street, Helston, Cornwall TR13
8PS
Fax 01326-574745   Tel 01326-574522
Helston Free Gazette; Penwith Pirate; Redruth & Camborne
Tinner
Owner: Southern Newspapers

Packet Newspapers (Cornwall)
Packet Works, Ponsharden, Falmouth, Cornwall
TR10 8AP
Fax 01326-373887   Tel 01326-373791
Camborne Redruth Packet; Falmouth Packet; Helston Packet;
The Packet; St Austell & Bodmin Packet; Truro Packet
Owner: Southern Newspapers

Putnam Newspapers
Great Place, Liskeard, Cornwall PL14 4BQ
Fax 01579-345071   Tel 01579-342174
Cornish Times 01579-342174.
Liskeard & Looe Gazette 01579-347444
Owner: Tindle Newspapers

St Ives Times and Echo
High Street, St Ives, Cornwall TR26 1RS
Fax 01736-795020   Tel 01736-795813
Owner: St Ives Times and Echo

Cumbria

Cumberland & Westmorland Herald
14 King Street, Penrith, Cumbria CA11 7AH
Fax 01768-890363   Tel 01768-862313

Cumbrian Newspapers
Dalston Road, Carlisle, Cumbria CA2 5UA
Fax 01228-512828   Tel 01228-23488
Cumberland News 01228-23488.
Cumbrian Gazette 01228-41151.
West Cumberland Times 01900-601234.
Whitehaven News 01946-691234
Owner: CN Group

Westmorland Gazette
22 Stricklandgate, Kendal, Cumbria LA9 4NE
Fax 01539-723618   Tel 01539-720555
Owner: Westminster Press

Derbyshire

Ashbourne News Telegraph
6 Market Place, Ashbourne, Derbyshire DE6
1GL
Fax 01335-300124   Tel 01335-342847
Owner: Burton Daily Mail

Ashton Weekly Newspapers
Acres Lane, Stalybridge, Cheshire SK15 2JR
Fax 0161-303 1922   Tel 0161-303 1910
Titles: Glossop Chronicle/High Peak Reporter 01457-852669.
Owner: United Provincial Newspapers

Burton Mail
65-68 High Street, Burton on Trent, Staffs DE14
1LE
Fax 01283-515351   Tel 01283-512345
Owner: Yattendon Group

Derby Daily Telegraph
Northcliffe House, Meadow Road, Derby
DE1 2DW
Fax 01332-253011   Tel 01332-291111
Belper/Derby/Heanor/Ilkeston/Ripley Express 01332-292222
Owner: Northcliffe Newspapers Group

Derbyshire Times Newspaper Group
37 Station Road, Chesterfield, Derbyshire S41 7XD
Fax 01246-230150   Tel 01246-200144
Chesterfield Gazette; Derbyshire Times 01246-200144.
Alfreton Echo 01773-834731.
Bakewell Times; Hope Valley Times 01629-582937.
Buxton Advertiser; Buxton Times 01298-22118.
High Peak Courier 01457-853003
Owner: Johnston Press

GC Brittain and Sons
Church Street, Ripley, Derbyshire DE5 3BX
Fax 01773-570109   Tel 01773-742133
Ripley & Heanor News; Ashbourne News 01773-742133.
Belper News 01773-820939.
Ilkeston Advertiser 0115-932 4285.
Matlock Mercury 01629-582432
Owner: Johnston Press

Ilkeston Advertiser
8 Heanor Road, Ilkeston, Derbyshire DE7 8ER
Fax 0115-9444990   Tel 0115-932 4285
Owner: GC Brittain and Sons

Local Network Publications
81 Saltergate, Chesterfield, Derbyshire S40 1JS
Fax 01246-234991   Tel 01246-202291
Chesterfield Advertiser; Dronfield Advertiser
Owner: Johnston Press

Trader Group Newspapers
Abbots Hall Chambers, Gower Street, Derbyshire DE1 1SB
Fax 01332-253915   Tel 01332-253999
Derby Trader; Ilkeston & Ripley Trader
Owner: Midland Independent Newspapers

Devon

Community Media
Fairoaks Close, Exeter Airport Business Park, Clyst Honiton, Exeter, Devon EX5 2UL
Fax 01392-445350   Tel 01392-447766
East Devon News; Exmouth Herald/Journal; Midweek Herald; North Devon Gazette; Sidmouth Herald
Owner: Eastern Counties Newspapers Group

Dawlish Newspapers
39 Teign Street, Teignmouth Devon TQ14 8EA
Fax 01626-888518   Tel 01626-864161
Dawish Gazette; Teignmouth News 01626 -779494

Devon and Cornwall Newspapers
63 Wolborough Street, Newton Abbot, Devon TQ12 1NE
Fax 01626-333589   Tel 01626-55577
Dawlish Post; Mid-Devon Advertiser; Teignmouth Post 01626-53555.

South Devon Times; Totnes Times Gazette 01803-864212
Owner: Tindle Newspapers

Express & Echo Publications
Heron Road, Sowton, Exeter, Devon EX2 7NF
Fax 01392-442294   Tel 01392-442211
Exeter Leader; Exmouth Leader
Owner: Northcliffe Newspapers Group

North Devon Journal-Herald
96 High Street, Barnstaple, Devon EX31 1HT
Fax 01271-221155   Tel 01271-43064
North Devon Journal 01271-43064.
Mid-Devon Gazette 01884-252725
Owner: Northcliffe Newspapers Group

South Hams Newspapers
101 Fore Street, Kingsbridge, Devon TQ7 1AF
Fax 01548-856499   Tel 01548-853101
Kingsbridge Gazette; Plympton News; Totnes News 01548-853101.
Dartmouth Chronicle 01803-832724.
Ivybridge Gazette 01752-893255
Owner: Tindle Newspapers

Tavistock Newspapers
42 Brook Street, Tavistock, Devon PL19 0HE
Fax 01822-613666   Tel 01822-613666
Okehampton Times; Tavistock Times Gazette
Owner: Tindle Newspapers

Torquay Herald & Express
Harmsworth House, Barton Hill Road, Torquay, Devon TQ2 8JN
Fax 01803-313093   Tel 01803-213213
Owner: Northcliffe

Dorset

Dorset Advertiser Series
71 High Street, Poole, Dorset BH15 1BB
Fax 01202-665717   Tel 01202-666633
Bournemouth/Christchurch/Poole Advertiser 01202-666633
Swanage Advertiser 01929-427428
Weymouth & Dorchester Advertiser 01305-776226
Owner: Southern Newspapers

Southern Newspapers
67 East Street, Bridport, Dorset DT6 3LB
Fax 01308-458080   Tel 01308-422388
Bridport & Lyme Regis News 01308-422388
West Dorset Express & Star 01308-424387
North Dorset Journal 01722-412525

Stour Valley News
Thomas Hardy House, Tenny Street, Blandford, Dorset DT11 7DR
Fax 01258-455391   Tel 01258-456067
Owner: Southern Newspapers

Western Gazette/Pulmans Weekly News
Sherborne Road, Yeovil, Somerset BA21 4YA
Fax 01935-32266   Tel 01935-74551
Owner: Western Gazette, Somerset

Essex

Echo Newspapers
Chester Hall Lane, Basildon, Essex SS14 3BL
Fax 01268-532060   Tel 01268-522792
Basildon/Rayleigh/Southend/Wickford Standard Recorder
 01268-522792.
Thurrock Gazette 01375-372293
Owner: Westminster Press

Essex Chronicle Series
Westway, Chelmsford, Essex CM1 3BE
Fax 01245-490500   Tel 01245-262421
Essex Chronicle 01245-262421.
Billericay Gazette; Brentwood Gazette 01277-219222.
Owner: Northcliffe Newspapers Group

Essex County Newspapers
43 North Hill, Colchester, Essex CO1 1TZ
Fax 01206-769523   Tel 01206-761212
Colchester Express; Essex County Standard 01206-761212.
Braintree & Witham Times; Halstead Gazette; Mid-Essex Express
 01376-551551.
Brentwood Weekly News; Chelmsford Weekly News; South
 Woodham Weekly News 01245-493444.
Clacton & Walton Gazette; Harwich Standard 01255-221221.
Maldon & Burnham Standard 01621-852233
Owner: Reed Elsevier

London & Essex Guardian Newspapers
News Centre, Fulborne Road, London E17 4EW
Fax 0181-527 3696   Tel 0181-531 4141
Epping Forest Independent; Epping Gazette; Loughton Gazette;
 Waltham Abbey Gazette 0181-531 4141.
Harlow Citizen 01992-572285
Owner: Reed Elsevier

Harlow & Epping Herald
60-62 High Street, Hoddesdon, Herts EN11 8TE
Fax 01727-86199   Tel 01992-448844
Owner: Herald Group Newspapers

Herts and Essex Newspapers
1 Fore Street, Hertford, Herts SG14 1DB
Fax 01992-589570   Tel 01992-586401
Dunmow Observer 01279-757721.
Harlow & Epping Star 01279-420333
Owner: Yattendon Investment Trust

Leigh/Rayleigh Times
34 The Broadway, Leigh on Sea, Essex SS9 1AJ
Fax 01702-78710   Tel 01702-77666
Rayleigh/Basildon/Island/Southend/Leigh and Westcliffe
Times

Saffron Walden Weekly News
51 Newmarket Road, Cambridge CB5 8EJ
Fax 01223-460846   Tel 01799-522218
Owner: Cambridge Newspapers

South Essex Recorders
539 High Road, Ilford, Essex IG1 1UD
Fax 0181-478 6606   Tel 0181-478 4444
Epping Forest Recorder 0181-478 4444.
Brentwood Recorder 01708-766044
Thurrock Recorder 01375-391144
Owner: Home Counties Newspaper Holdings

Yellow Advertiser
Acorn House, Great Oaks, Basildon, Essex SS14
1AH
Fax 01268-288640   Tel 01268-522722
Yellow Advertiser
Owner: United Provincial Newspapers

Gloucestershire

Bailey Newspaper Group
Reliance House, Long Street, Dursley, Glos
GL11 4LS
Fax 01453-544577   Tel 01453-544000
Gloucestershire County Gazette 01453-544000
Independent series 01242-519550
Stroud News & Journal 01453-762412
Wilts & Glos Standard, Cirencester 01285-642642
Wilts & Glos Standard, Stow-on-the-Wold 01451-831510

Cheltenham Newspaper Co
1 Clarence Parade, Cheltenham, Glos GL50 3NZ
Fax 01242-578395   Tel 01242-526261
Cheltenham News 01242-582363
Owner: Northcliffe Newspapers

Forest of Dean Newspapers
Woodside Street, Cinderford, Glos GL14 2NN
Fax 01594-826213   Tel 01594-822126
The Forester

Gloucestershire Newspapers
St Johns Lane, Gloucester GL1 2AY
Fax 01452-307238   Tel 01452-424442
Gloucester News
Owner: Northcliffe Newspapers Group

Hampshire

Aldershot News
Albert Road, Aldershot, Hants GU11 1NU
Fax 01252-341033   Tel 01252-28221
Aldershot Mail/News; Farnborough Mail/News; Fleet
Mail/News; Yateley Mail/News; Courier; Camberley
News/Courier; Farnham Mail; Ash Mail
Owner: Guardian Media Group

Farnham Castle Newspapers
114 West Street, Farnham, Surrey GU9 7HL
Fax 01252-724951   Tel 01252-725224
Alton Herald/Times 01420-82819
Bordon Herald/Times 01420-477272
Liphook Times; Surrey & Hants News 01252-716444
Petersfield Herald/Times 01730-263585
Owner: Tindle Newspapers

Jacob & Johnston
57 High Street, Winchester, Hants SO23 9BY
Fax 01962-842313   Tel 01962-841772
Hampshire Chronicle 01962-841772
Alton Gazette 01420-84446
Eastleigh Weekly News 01703-613000
Romsey Advertiser 01794-513396

Portsmouth Publishing & Printing
News Centre, Hilsea, Portsmouth, Hants
PO2 9SX
Fax 01705-673363   Tel 01705-664488
Bordon Post; Fareham & Gosport Journal; Hayling Islander;
 Havant Journal; Observer series; Petersfield Post; Portsmouth
 Journal; West Sussex Gazette; Journal and Guardian series.
Owner: Portsmouth and Sunderland Newspapers

Southern Newspapers
45 Above Bar, Southampton, Hants SO14 7AA
Fax 01703-630289   Tel 01703-634134
Bournemouth Evening Echo 01202-554601
Andover Advertiser 01264-323456;
Basingstoke Gazette 01256-461131
New Forest Post 01590-671122
Southampton Advertiser 01703-634134
New Forest Journal 01722-412525

New Milton Advertiser/Lymington Times
62 Old Milton Road, New Milton, Hants BH25
6EH
Fax 01425-638635   Tel 01425-613384

Hereford & Worcester

Reed Midland Newspapers
Hylton Road, Worcester WR2 5JX
Fax 01905-429605   Tel 01905-748200
Worcester Journal 01905-610171
Bromsgrove Advertiser; Droitwich Advertiser 01527-37000
Cotswold Journal Series 01386-765678
Hereford Times 01432-274413
Kidderminster Shuttle/Times; Stourport News 01562-744740
Ledbury Reporter; Malvern Gazette 01684-892200
Leominster Advertiser; Tenbury Wells Advertiser 01584-872183
Redditch Advertiser 01527-63611
Owner: Reed Elsevier

Shropshire Newspapers
Ketley, Telford, Shropshire TF1 3HU
Fax 01743-232305   Tel 01432-355353

Hereford Journal; Leominster Journal
Owner: Express and Star

Ross Gazette
35 High Street, Ross on Wye, Herefordshire HR9
5HE
Fax 01989-768023   Tel 01989-562007

Hertfordshire

Central Counties Newspapers
2 Exchange Street, Aylesbury, Bucks HP20 1UJ
Fax 01296-393451   Tel 01296-24444
Berkhamstead/Hemel Hempstead/Kings Langley/Tring Gazette
 and Express series 01442-62311
Owner: Emap

Herald Newspapers
Unit 1, Sandridge Park, Porters Wood Road, St
Albans, Herts AL3 6PH
Fax 01727-861199   Tel 01727-846866
St Albans; Stevenage; Welwyn 01727-846866
Bishops Stortford; Hoddesdon; Harlow 01992-448844
Milton Keynes; Leighton Buzzard 01908-233226
Bedford; Ampthill; Biggleswade 01234-364221
Owner:Barwell Corporation

Herald & Post Group
58 Church Street, Luton, Beds LU1 3JQ
Fax 01582-425273   Tel 01582-410234
Berkhamstead/Hemel Hempstead/Tring; Herald & Post series
 01582-401234

Herts & Essex Newspapers
1 Fore Street, Hertford, Herts SG14 1DB
Fax 01992-552766   Tel 01992-586401
Herts Mercury; Herts Star; Royston/Buntingford Mercury; Lea
 Valley Star; 01992-586401
Bishops Stortford Observer; Herts & Essex/Sawbridgeworth
 Observer 01279-757721
Cheshunt Mercury; Hoddesdon/Broxbourne Mercury 01992-
 444455
Owner: Yattendon Investment Trust

Home Counties Newspapers
63 Campfield Road, St Albans, Herts AL1 5HX
Fax 01727-851238   Tel 01727-866166
Borehamwood Advertiser; Harpenden Advertiser; Herts
 Advertiser 01727-866166
Biggleswade Comet; Hitchin Comet/Gazette; Letchworth
 Comet/Gazette; Stevenage Comet/Gazette 01462-422280
Welwyn & Hatfield Times 01707-327551

North London & Herts Newspapers
10 Silver Street, Enfield EN1 3EQ
Fax 0181-366 4013   Tel 0181-367 2345
Barnet & Finchley Press/Potters Bar Press 0181-441 3003
Cheshunt Telegraph/Enfield Gazette 0181-367 2345
Owner: East Middlesex County Press

Review Free Newspapers
The Lawns, Mt Pleasant, St Albans, Herts
AL3 4TJ
Fax 01727-852770   Tel 01727-834411
St Albans & Harpenden Review; Welwyn & Hatfield Review;
  Watford & West Herts Review 01727-834411

Royston Weekly News
3 Melbourne Street, Royston SG8 5BN
Fax 01763-244502   Tel 01763-249146
Owner: Cambridge Newspapers

Times & Observer Newspapers
124 Rickmansworth Road, Watford, Herts
WD1 7JW
Fax 01923-243738   Tel 01923-242211
Barnet Borough Times; Potters Bar Times 0181-441 7400
Borehamwood Times 0181-953 3391
St Albans Observer 01727-841133
Watford Observer 01923-242211
Owner: Westminster Press

Humberside

Driffield Post
47a Market Place, Driffield YO25 7AN
Fax 01377-241396   Tel 01377-241414

Goole Courier
8 Pasture Road, Goole, North Humberside
DN14
Fax 01405-720888   Tel 01405-763073
Owner: Reed Northern Newspapers

Goole Times & Chronicle
102 Boothferry Road, Goole, North Humberside
DN14 6AE
Fax 01405-720003   Tel 01405-720110

Grimsby & Scunthorpe Newspapers
80 Cleethorpe Road, Grimsby, South
Humberside DN31 3EH
Fax 01472-241444   Tel 01472-353184
Grimsby Target; Louth Target; Scunthorpe Target
Owner: Northcliffe Newspapers Group

Holderness/Hornsea Gazettes
1 Seaside Road, Withernsea, North Humberside
HU19 2DL
Fax 01964-615303   Tel 01964-614325

Hull Daily Mail Publications
Blundells Corner, Beverley Road, Hull, North
Humberside HU3 1XS
Fax 01482-584353   Tel 01482-327111
Now Then series; Haltemprice Advertiser; Holderness Advertiser
01482-27111.
Beverley Advertiser 01482-861447
Owner: Northcliffe Newspapers Group

Yorkshire Regional Newspapers
17-23 Aberdeen Walk, Scarborough, North
Yorks YO11 1BB
Fax 01723-354092   Tel 01723-363636
Driffield Times 01377-253213
Bridlington Free Press 01262-606606
Owner: Emap

Isle of Man

Isle of Man Newspapers
Peel Road, Douglas, Isle of Man.
Fax 01624-661041   Tel 01624-623451
Isle of Man Courier/Examiner; Manx Independent 01624-623451
Owner: Johnston Press

Isle of Wight

Isle of Wight County Press
Brannon House, 123 Pyle Street, Newport, Isle
of Wight PO30 1ST
Fax 01983-527204   Tel 01983-526741
Owner: Isle of Wight County Press

Kent

Associated Kent Newspapers
Westcliffe House, West Cliff Gardens,
Folkestone, Kent CT20 1SZ
Fax 01303-850618   Tel 01303-850999
Dover Express; Folkestone Herald; Hythe Herald; Romney Marsh
Herald 01303-850999
Chatham News/Standard 01634-841741
East Kent Gazette series; Sheppey Gazette 01795-475411
Herne Bay Times; Whitstable Times 01227-771515
Isle of Thanet Gazette; Thanet Times 01843-221313
Owner: Emap

Biggin Hill News
High Street, Westerham, Kent TN16 1AJ
Fax 01959-562760   Tel 01959-564766
Biggin Hill/County Border News
Owner: Tindle Newspapers

Courier Group of Newspapers
Longfield Road, Tunbridge Wells, Kent TN2 3HL
Fax 01892-543181   Tel 01892-526262
Kent & Sussex Courier; Tonbridge/Tunbridge Wells News in
Focus 01892-526262
Sevenoaks Chronicle 01732-452303
Owner: Northcliffe Newspapers Group

Dartford Informer
60 Lowfield Street, Dartford, Kent DA1 1HJ
Fax 01322-228207   Tel 01322-220791
Dartford/Swanley Informers
Owner: Local Publications

Kentish Times Newspapers
44 Harmer Street, Gravesend, Kent DA12 2AY
Fax 01474-320316   Tel 01474-363363
Dartford Times/Leader; Gravesend Reporter/Leader; Swanley
 Times; Sevenoks and Tonbridge Leader 01474-363363
Owner: Fletcher Newspaper Group

Kent Messenger
Messenger House, New Hythe Lane, Larkfield,
Maidstone, Kent ME20 6SG
Fax 01622-719637   Tel 01622-717880
Ashford KM Extra; Kentish Express (Ashford) 01233-623232
Canterbury KM Extra; Kentish Gazette (Canterbury) 01227-
 768181
East Kent Mercury 01304-373242
Folkestone KM Extra 01303-850676
Gravesend KM Extra 01474-333381
Kent Messenger (Maidstone); Maidstone KM Extra 01622-695666
Medway KM Extra 01634-830999
Sheerness Times Guardian; Sittingbourne KM Extra 01795-58030
Thanet KM Extra 01843-593009
Tonbridge & Tunbridge Wells KM Extra 01892-544747

Maidstone Star
Maidstone Press Centre, Bank Street,
Maidstone, Kent ME14 1PZ
Fax 01622-675071   Tel 01622-678556

Lancashire

Ashton Weekly Newspapers
Park House, Acres Lane, Stalybridge, Cheshire
SK15 2JR
Fax 0161-303 1922   Tel 0161-303 1910
Denton Reporter/Ashton under Lyme Reporter/East Manchester
 Reporter/Mossely-Saddleworth Reporter/Droylsden Reporter
Owner: United Provincial Newspapers

Fleetwood Weekly News
186 Lord Street, Fleetwood, Lancs FY7 6SW.
Fax 01253-770518   Tel 01253-772950
Fleetwood Weekly News; Thornton Cleveleys Weekly News

G & AN Scott
Drake Street, Rochdale, Lancs OL16 1PH
Fax 01706-341595   Tel 01706-354321
Rochdale Observer; Rochdale/Heywood Express 01706-354321
Accrington Observer; Hyndburn Express 01254-871444
Middleton Guardian 0161-643 3615
Moston/Middleton Express 0161-205 8031
Heywood Advertiser 01706-360626
Rossendale Express/Free Press 01706-213311
Owner: Guardian Media Group

Lancaster & District Star
Newspaper House, Abbey Road, Barrow in
Furness, Cumbria LA14 1QE
Fax 01229-832141   Tel 01524-66902
Owner: Furness Newspapers

Reed Northern Newspapers
Newspaper House, High Street, Blackburn,
Lancs BB1 1HT.
Fax 01254-682034   Tel 01254-671241
Blackburn Citizen; Darwen Citizen; Hyndburn Citizen 01254-
 671241
Blackpool Citizen; Lytham & St Annes Citizen; Thornton Citizen
 01253-729081
Burnley Citizen 01282-452139
Chorley Citizen 01257-269313
Lancaster Citizen; Morecambe Citizen 01524-382121
Leyland Citizen; Preston Citizen 01772-885711
Owner: Reed Elsevier

United Provincial Newspapers
Wellington Street, Leeds, West Yorks LS1 1RF
Fax 0113-244 3430   Tel 0113-243 2701
Blackpool Extra; Lytham St Annes Express 01253-839999
Burnley Express; Clitheroe Advertiser; Nelson Leader series
 01282-426161
Chorley Guardian 01257-264911
Garstang Courier; Longridge News 01995-602494
Lakeland Echo 01539-730509
Lancaster Guardian 01524-32525
The Visitor (Morecambe) 01524-833111
Ormskirk Advertiser 01695-572501
Preston Weekly Mail 01772-201234
Owner: United Provincial Newspapers

Leicestershire

Hinckley Times
Brunel Road, Hinckley, Leics LE10 0AB
Fax 01455-632774   Tel 01455-238383

Leicester Mercury Group
St George Street, Leicester LE1 9FQ
Fax 0116-2530645   Tel 0116-251 2512
Ashby & Coalville Mail; Leicester Mail 0116-251 2512
Loughborough Mail 01509-214661
Oadby & Wigston Mail 0116-288 9361
Owner: Northcliffe Newspapers Group

Midland Newspapers
28 Colmore Circus, Birmingham B4 6AX
Fax 0121-233 0271   Tel 0121-236 3366
Hinckley Journal; Hinckley Herald & Post 01455-891981
Leicester Herald & Post; Loughborough Herald & Post 0116-247
 1000

Rutland Times
Mill Street, Oakham, Leics LE15 6EA
Fax 0172-755599   Tel 01572-757722

Trident Midland Newspapers Ltd
Bridge Road, Coalville, Leics LE6 3QP
Fax 01530-811361   Tel 01530-813101
Ashby Times; Coalville Times; Free Leader; Swadlincote Times
 01530-813101

Welland Valley Newspapers
49 Nottingham Street, Melton Mowbray, Leics
LE13 1NT
Fax 01664-410042   Tel 01664-66666
Melton Citizen/Times; Rutland Mercury 01664-66666.
Harborough Mail 01858-462626
Owner: Emap

Lincolnshire

Gainsborough Trader News
5-7 Church Street, Gainsborough, Lincs DN21
2JJ
Fax 01427-616912   Tel 01909-483333
Owner: Four Counties Newspapers

Grantham & Melton Trader
62 Welby Street, Grantham, Lincs NG31
6GA
Fax 01476-66704   Tel 01476-74433
Owner: Four Counties Newspapers

Lincolnshire Publishing Co
Brayford Wharf East, Lincoln LN5 7AT
Fax 01522-545759   Tel 01522-525252
Boston Target; Skegness Target 01205-356262
Gainsborough Target 01427-612159
Lincoln Target 01522-545059
Retford & Gainsborough Times 01777-702275
Sleaford Target 01529-413416
Owner: Northcliffe Newspapers Group

Lincolnshire Standard Newspapers
345 High Street, Lincoln LN5 7DQ
Fax 01522-530324   Tel 01522-513030
Lincoln Standard 01522-513030
Alford & Coast Standard; Skegness Standard; Spilsby Standard
01754-610362
Boston Standard 01205-359818
Gainsborough Standard 01427-615323.
Horncastle Standard; Louth Standard 01507-604921
Sleaford Standard 01529-413646
Owner: Adscene Group

Mortons of Horncastle
Newspaper House, Morton Way, Horncastle,
Lincs LN9 6JR
Fax 01507-527840   Tel 01507-523456
Horncastle News 01507-526868
Louth Leader 01507-606656
Mablethorpe News 01507-472555
Market Rasen Mail 01673-844644
Skegness News 01754-768000

Stamford Herald & Post
Cross Street Court, 11-13 Cross Street,
Peterborough PE1 1AS
Fax 01733-318650   Tel:01733-318600
Owner: Midland Independent Newspapers

Welland Valley Newspapers
Mercury House, Sheepmarket, Stamford, Lincs
PE9 2QZ.
Fax 01780-51371   Tel 01780-65626
Grantham Citizen/Journal 01476-62291
Lincs Free Press Spalding Guardian 01775-725021
Stamford Citizen/ Mercury 01780-62255
Owner: Emap

London (North of Thames)

Advertiser North London Group
281 Ballards Lane, Finchley, London N12
8NR
Fax 0181-445 1893   Tel 0181-449 5577
Barnet/Edgware/Enfield/Finchley/Haringey Advertisers 0181-
449 5577
Owner: United Provincial Newspapers

Camden New Journal
40 Camden Road, London NW1 9DR
Fax 0171-485 3519   Tel 0171-485 8207
Owner: Camden Journal

Capital Newspapers
250-256 Kingsland Road, London E8 4DJ
Fax: 0171 241 01652   Tel 0171-254 6311
Hackney Echo; Hackney Gazette/North London Advertiser 0171-
254 6311
Camden/St Pancras Chronicle 0181-450 5272
Haringey Weekly Herald; Hornsey Journal; Islington Chronicle/
Gazette; Tottenham Weekly Herald/Journal 0181-340 6868
Kilburn Times/Advertiser; Paddington Times; Wembley & Brent
Times; Willesden & Brent Chronicle/Weekly Advertiser 0181-
450 5272

Dimbleby & Sons
14 King Street, Richmond, Surrey TW9 1NF
Fax 0181-668 9988   Tel 0181-668 4111
Brentford & Chiswick Times; Hounslow & Feltham Times;
Teddington & Hampton Times 0181-940 6030

Independent Newspapers UK
2 Whalebone Lane South, Dagenham, Essex
RM8 1HB
Fax 0181-592 7407   Tel 0181-517 5577
Barking & Dagenham Express/Post; Docklands Express; Ilford &
Redbridge Post; Romford & Havering Post; Stratford & Newham
Express; Waltham Forest Express 0181-517 5577
East London Advertiser 0171-790 8822
Owner: Independent Newspapers, Dublin

Informer Publications
11 High Street, Egham, Surrey TW20 9HZ
Fax 01784-470655   Tel 01784-433773
Ealing Informer; Harrow & Northwood Informer; Uxbridge
Informer 01895-621960.
Hounslow & Chiswick Informer 0181-943 5171
Owner: United Provincial Newspapers

London & Essex Guardian Newspapers, & Independent Group
News Centre, Fulborne Road, London E17 4EW
Fax 0181-527 3696   Tel 0181-531 4141
Chingford Guardian; Enfield Independent; Haringey Independent; Leyton & Leytonstone Guardian; Waltham Forest Guardian/Independent; Walthamstow Guardian 0181-531 4141
Owner: Reed Elsevier

London Newspaper Group
Newspaper House, Winslow Road, Hammersmith, London W6 9SF
Fax 0181-741 1973   Tel 0181-741 1622
Chelsea News; City of London Post; City of Westminster Post; Fulham Chronicle/Post; Hammersmith Chronicle/Post; Kensington News/Post; Marylebone Mercury; Paddington Mercury; Westminster & Pimlico News 0181-741 1622
Owner: Adscene Group

London Recorder Newspapers
4 High Street, Brentford, Middlesex TW8 0DX
Fax 0181-568 3446   Tel 0181-568 1313
Brent Recorder; Chiswick & Shepherds Bush Guardian; Ealing Recorder; Hammersmith & Fulham Guardian; Harrow Recorder; Hounslow Recorder; Ruislip & Northwood Recorder; Uxbridge Recorder; Wembley & Kenton Recorder
Owner: Tindle Newspapers

Middlesex County Press
326 Station Road, Harrow, Middlesex HA1 2DR
Fax 0181-863 0932   Tel 0181-427 4404
Greenford & Northolt Gazette; Hammersmith & Fulham Times; Hammersmith & Shepherds Bush Gazette; Southall & Hounslow Gazette 0181-579 3131
Barnet & Finchley Press 0181-367 2345
Ealing Gazette/Leader; London Times series; Shepherds Bush Gazette; Westminster Times 0181-579 3131
Enfield Express/Gazette 0181-367 2345
Harefield Gazette; Hayes & Harlington Gazette; Ruislip & Northwood Gazette; Uxbridge Express/Gazette/Leader 01895-627000
Brent Leader; Harrow Leader/Observer/Independent; Pinner Observer; Stanmore & Harrow Observer; Wembley Leader/Observer 0181-427 4404
Middlesex Chronicle 0181-754 8388
Owner: Southnews

South Essex Recorders
539 High Road, Ilford, Essex IG1 1UD
Fax 0181-478 6606   Tel 0181-478 4444
Iford Recorder; Leader series 0181-478 4444.
City of London Recorder; Docklands Recorder; Newham Recorder 0181-472 1421.
Dagenham & Barking Recorder Romford Recorder 01708-766044
Also published by Home Counties:
Hampstead & Highgate Express 0171-433 0000
Owner: Home Counties Newspaper Holdings

Times & Observer Newspapers
71 Church Road, Hendon, London NW4 4DN.
Fax 0181-203 9106   Tel 0181-203 0411
Hendon & Finchley Times 0181-203 0411
Barnet Times 0181-441 7400
Edgware & Mill Hill Times 0181-951 5000
Owner: Westminster Press

Yellow Advertiser
Acorn House, Great Oaks, Basildon, Essex SS14 1AH
Fax 01268-288640   Tel 01268-522722
Barking & Dagenham Yellow Advertiser; Havering & Romford Yellow Advertiser; Newham Yellow Advertiser; Redbridge Yellow Advertiser; Waltham Forest Yellow Advertiser
Owner: United Provinicial Newspapers

London (South of Thames)

Croydon Advertiser Group
Advertiser House, Brighton Road, South Croydon, Surrey CR2 6UB
Fax 0181-668 9988   Tel 0181-668 4111
Croydon Post/Advertiser; Coulsdon & Purley Advertiser 0181-668 4111
Owner: Portsmouth & Sunderland Newspapers

Dimbleby & Sons
14 King Street, Richmond, Surrey TW9 1NF
Fax 0181-948 3547   Tel 0181-940 6030
Barnes & Mortlake Times; Kingston, Surbiton & New Malden Times; Putney & Wimbledon Times; Richmond & Twickenham Times 0181-940 6030.
Wandsworth Borough News 0181-874 4226

Informer Publications
168 High Street, Egham, Surrey TW20 9HZ
Fax 01784-432771   Tel 01784-433773
Kingston Informer; Richmond & Twickenham Informer; Wimbledon Informer 0181-943 5171

Kentish Times Newspapers
38-46 Harmer Street, Gravesend, Kent DA12 2AY
Fax 01474-320316   Tel 01474-363363
Bexleyheath and Welling Times/Leader; Bromley and Beckenham Times/Leader; Chislehurst Times/Leader; Eltham and Greenwich Times; Orpington and Petts Wood Times/Leader; Sidcup & Blackfen Times 01474-363363
Erith and Crayford Times 01322-335741

Reed Regional Newspapers
26 York Street, Twickenham, Middlesex TW1 3 LJ
Fax 0181-744 3909   Tel 0181-744 9966
Esher & Elmbridge Guardian; Kingston Borough Guardian; Richmond & Twickenham Guardian 0181-744 9966
Surrey Comet 0181-744 9977
Owner: Reed Elsevier

South East London & Kentish Mercury Group
116 Deptford High Street, London SE8 4NX
Fax 0181-692 3225   Tel 0181-692 1122
Bexleyheath & Welling Mercury; Deptford & Peckham Mercury;
Greenwich & Eltham Mercury; Lewisham & Catford Mercury;
Sidcup & Bexley Mercury; Woolwich & Charlton Mercury 0181-692 1122
Owner: Westminster Press

South London Guardian
34 London Road, Morden, Surrey SM4 5BR
Fax 0181-687 4459   Tel 0181-646 6336
Balham & Tooting Guardian; Battersea Guardian; Mitcham &
Morden Guardian; Putney News; Wandsworth Guardian;
Wimbledon News 0181-646 6336.
Croydon Guardian; Dulwich Guardian; Streatham & Clapham
Guardian; Sutton Guardian 0181-644 4300.
Kingston Guardian; Richmond Guardian 0181-774 9742
Owner: Reed Elsevier

Trinity Newspapers Southern
20-22 Mid-day Court, Brighton Road, Sutton,
Surrey SM2 5BN
Fax 0181-642 4780   Tel 0181-642 7777
Epsom & Ewell Herald; Banstead Herald; Epsom & Banstead
Extra; Sutton Borough News; Sutton Herald; Streatham News
0181-769 4444.
Owner: Trinity International Holdings

Trinity Newspapers Southern
51 London Road, Reigate, Surrey RH2 9PR
                           Tel 01737-732000
East Grinstead Observer; Crawley News; Dorking Advertiser;
Leatherhead Advertiser; Surrey Mirror
Owner: Trinity International Holdings

Greater Manchester

The Advertiser
35 Booth Street, Ashton-under-Lyne, Gtr
Manchester OL6 7LB
Fax 0161-343 2997   Tel 0161-339 7611
Tameside Advertiser; High Peak Echo; Tameside Echo ; Oldham
Advertiser 0161-626 3663.
West Manchester Advertiser; Prestwich, Whitefield & Radcliffe
Advertiser; Salford City Reporter; West Manchester Echo 0161-789 5015
Owner: Guardian Media Group

Bury Times Newspaper Group
Market Street, Bury, Gtr Manchester BL9 0PF
Fax 0161-763 1315   Tel 0161-764 9421
Bury Times; The Messenger; Mid-Week Times; Prestwich Guide;
Radcliffe Times 0161-764 9421
Owner: Johnston Press

Lancashire & Cheshire County Newspapers
Wood Street, Hollywood, Stockport Gtr
Manchester SK3 0AB

Fax 0161-480 4837   Tel 0161-480 4491
Express Advertiser series; Stockport Times East/West;
Macclesfield Times; Poynton Times; Northenden News 0161-480 4491
Owner: Guardian Media Group

Leigh Reporter & Golborne Star
101 Railway Road, Leigh, Lancs WN7 4AD
Fax 01942-262209   Tel 01942-603334

Manchester Metro News
2 Blantyre Street, Gtr Manchester M15 4LF
Fax 0161-834 0556   Tel 0161-834 9677
Manchester Metro News 0161-834 9677
Bolton Metro News 01204-388001.
Heywood Advertiser/Express 01706-354321
Owner: Guardian Media Group

Reed Northern Newspapers
Churchgate, Bolton, Gtr Manchester BL1 1DE
Fax 01204-385103   Tel 01204 522345
Bolton Journal; Bury Journal; Leigh Journal 01204-22345.
Owner: Reed Elsevier

United Provincial Newspapers
PO Box 168, Wellington Street, Leeds, West
Yorks LS1 1RF
Fax 0113-242 1814   Tel 0113-243 2701
Ashton-under-Lyne Reporter; Denton Reporter; Droylsden
Reporter; East Manchester Reporter; Mossley Reporter;
Stalybridge Reporter 0161-303 1910.
Wigan Observer/Reporter 01942-228000.
Wigan Leader 01772-254841
Owner: United Provincial Newspapers

Merseyside

Reed Northern Newspapers
YMCA Buildings, Duke Street, St Helens,
Merseyside WA10 2HZ
Fax 01744-733934   Tel 01744-611861
Prescot Star; St Helens Star 01744-611861.
Newton & Golborne Guardian 01925-651131
Owner: Reed Elsevier

Trinity Weekly Newspapers
26 Tulketh Street, Southport, Merseyside PR8 1BT.
Fax 01704-539417   Tel 01704-536655
Southport Visitor 01704-536655.
Anfield & Walton Star Huyton Star; Maghull & Aintree Star;
Merseymart series 0151-236 4422.
Bebington News; Birkenhead News 0151-647 7111.
Bootle Times; Crosby Herald 0151-932 1000.
Formby Times 01704-872237.
Heswall News; Hoylake & West Kirkby News; Neston News;
Wallasey News 0151-630 2000
Owner: Trinity International Holdings

United Provincial Newspapers
PO Box 168, Wellington Street, Leeds, West
Yorks LS1 1RF
Fax 0113-242 1814   Tel 0113-243 2701
St Helens Reporter 01942-228000
Prescot Reporter 01744-22285
Owner: United Provincial Newspapers

Wirral Globe
Globe House, Catherine Street, Birkenhead,
Merseyside L41 6HW
Fax 0151-666 2200   Tel 0151-666 2222
Owner: Reed Elsevier

Norfolk

Emap Anglia Newspapers
Limes House, Purfleet Street, Kings Lynn,
Norfolk PE30 1HL
Fax 01553-767627   Tel 01553-761188
Lynn News 01553-761188
Norfolk Citizen 01553-692006
Owner: Emap

Emap Anglia Newspapers
Mere Street, Diss, Norfolk IP22 3AE
Fax 01379-650110   Tel 01379-643232
Diss Express; Harleston & Waveney Express
Owner: Emap

Eastern Counties Newspapers Group
Prospect House, Rouen Road, Norwich, Norfolk
NR1 1RE
Fax 01603-612930   Tel 01603-628311
Norwich Mercury 01603-628311
Beccles & Bungay Journal 01502-712623
Dereham & Fakenham Times 01362-692151
Diss Mercury 01379-644517
Great Yarmouth Mercury 01493-844201.
West Norfolk Mercury 01553-773401
Lowestoft Journal 01502-565141
North Norfolk News 01263-513232
Thetford & Watton Times 01842-765851
Wymondham & Attlborough Mercury 01953-601616

Northamptonshire

Herald & Post
Derngate, Northampton NN1 1NN
Fax 01604-614649   Tel 01604-614600
Brackley & Towcester Herald & Post; Corby Herald & Post;
 Kettering Herald & Post; Market Harborough Post; Northampton
 Herald & Post; Wellingborough Herald & Post
Owner: Midland Independent Newspapers

Northampton Mercury Co
Upper Mounts, Northampton NN1 3HR
Fax 01604-233000   Tel 01604-231122

Northampton Mercury
Owner: Emap

Northamptonshire Newspapers
Northfield Avenue, Kettering, Northants NN16
9TT
Fax 01536-410101   Tel 01536-81111
Northants Citizen series 01536-412412
Other Emap papers: Daventry Weekly Express 01327-703383
Owner: Emap

Northumberland

Hexham Courant
Beaumont Street, Hexham, Northumberland
NE46 3NA
Fax 01434-607872   Tel 01434-602351

Northeast Press
Chapter Row, South Shields, Tyne & Wear NE33
1BL
Fax 0191-456 8270   Tel 0191-455 4661
Berwick & Borders Gazette 01289-308775.
News Post Leader/Northumberland Gazette (Alnwick) 01665-
 602234
Owner: Portsmouth & Sunderland Newspapers

Northumberland Herald & Post
36 Bridge Street, Morpeth, Northumberland
NE61 1NL
Fax 01670 518379   Tel 01670-517362
Owner: Thomson Regional Newspapers

Tweeddale Press Group
90 Marygate, Berwick-upon-Tweed,
Northumberland TD15 1BW
Fax 01289-307377   Tel 01289-306677
Berwick Advertiser; Berwickshire News

Nottinghamshire

Eastwood & Kimberley Advertiser
23 Nottingham Road, Eastwood, Nottingham
NG16 3AH
Fax 01773-760444   Tel 01773-760444.
Owner: GC Brittain, Derbyshire

Hucknell & Bulwell Dispatch
Yorke Street, Hucknall, Nottingham NG15
7BT
Fax 0115-963 6149   Tel 0115-963 2128.
Owner: Derbyshire Times

Mansfield Chronicle Advertiser
121 Newgate Lane, Mansfield, Notts NG18
2PA
Fax 01623-654764   Tel 01623-26262
Ashfield/Alfreton Chronicle Advertiser

Mansfield Observer
Briarwood House, St John Street, Mansfield,
Notts NG18 1QH
Fax 01623-20760   Tel 01623-655655.

Newark Advertiser Co Ltd
Appletongate, Newark, Notts NG24 1JX
Fax 01636-643454   Tel 01636-643456
Dukeries Advertiser; Newark Advertiser; South Notts Advertiser;
Herald & Express

Nottingham Group
PO Box 99, Forman Street, Nottingham NG1
4AB
Fax 0115-948 4116   Tel 0115-948 2000
Long Eaton Advertiser 0115-946 1666.
Mansfield Free Press; Mansfield Recorder 01623-420000.
Nottingham Recorder; Stapleford News 0115-948 2000
Owner: Northcliffe Newspapers Group

Retford Times
57 Chancery Lane, Melford, Notts DN22 6HE
Fax 01777-708791   Tel 01777-702275

Trader Group Newspapers
52 Babington Lane, Derby DE1 1GZ
Fax 01332-253939   Tel 01332- 253999
Nottingham Herald & Post; Long Eaton Herald & Post 0115-934
2555
Owner: Midland Independent Newspapers

Worksop Newspapers
30 Watson Road, Worksop, Notts S80 2BE
Fax 01909-474849   Tel 01909-500500
Midweek Guardian; Worksop Guardian 01909 500500
Retford & Bawtry Guardian 01777 704242
Owner: W & J Linney

Oxfordshire

Central Counties Newspapers
2 Exchange Street, Aylesbury, Bucks HP20 1UJ
Fax 01296-393451   Tel 01296-24444
Banbury Citizen/Guardian 01295-264321.
Bicester Review 01280-813434.
Thame Gazette 01844-213266
Owner: Emap

Courier Newspapers (Oxford)
2 Ock Street, Abingdon, Oxon OX14 5AH
Fax 01235-554465   Tel 01235-553444
Oxford Courier; South Oxfordshire Courier

Goodhead Publishing
33 Witney Road, Eynsham, Oxon OX8 1PJ
Fax 01865-882007   Tel 01865-882424
Oxford Journal 01865-882424.
Banbury Cake 01295-256111
Owner: Goodhead Group

Henley Standard
Caxton House, Station Road, Henley-on-Thames,
Oxon RG9 1AD
Fax 01491-573571   Tel 01491-572178
Owner: Higgs and Co

Oxford & County Newspapers
Osney Mead, Oxford OX2 0EJ
Fax 01865-243382   Tel 01865-244988
Abingdon Herald; Didcot Herald; Oxford Star/Times; Wallingford
Herald; Wantage & Grove Herald
Witney Gazette 01993-704265
Bicester Advertiser 01869-241436
Owner: Westminster Press

Shropshire

Ludlow Advertiser
Advertiser Buildings, Upper Galdeford, Ludlow,
Shropshire SY8 1QE
Fax 01584-878442   Tel 01584-872183.
Owner: Reed Regional Newspapers

Oswestry Advertiser
6 Church Street, Oswestry, Shropshire SY11
2SP
Fax 01691-652530   Tel 01691-655321
Owner: North Wales Newspapers

Shropshire Newspapers
Ketley, Telford, Shropshire TF1 4HU
Fax 01952-254605   Tel 01952-242424
Bridgnorth Journal 01746-761411
Ludlow Journal South; Shropshire Journal 01584-876311
Market Drayton Advertiser; Newport Advertiser 01952-811500
North Shropshire Chronicle; Shrewsbury Chronicle 01743-363222
Owner: Claverley Co

Somerset

Mid Somerset Newspapers
Southover, Wells, Somerset BA5 2AB
Fax 01749-678067   Tel 01749-672430
Bridgwater Scan; Burnham Scan; Central Somerset Gazette;
Cheddar Valley Gazette; Mid-Somerset Scan; Shepton Mallet
Journal; Wells Journal
Owner: Westminster Press

South West Counties Newspapers
St James Street, Taunton, Somerset TA1 1JR
Fax 01823-257617   Tel 01823-335361
Burnham & Highbridge Weekly News; Midweek Gazette;
Somerset County Gazette; Taunton Express & Star 01823-
335361.
Bridgwater Mercury 01278-428112.
Chard & Ilminster News 01460-63442.
Messenger series; Yeovil Express & Star 01935-706300
Owner: Southern Newspapers

Wellington Weekly News
29 Bampton Street, Tiverton, Devon EX16 6AG
Fax 01823-665793   Tel 01271-43064
Owner: Northcliffe Newspapers Group

West Somerset Free Press
5 Long Street, Williton, Somerset TA4 4QN
Fax 01984-633099   Tel 01984-632731
News Trader; West Somerset Free Press
Owner: Tindle Newspapers

Western Gazette Co
Sherborne Road, Yeovil, Somerset BA21 4YA
Fax 01935-26963   Tel 01935-74551
Somerset Weekly News; Pulmans Weekly News; Western Gazette
series
Owner: Bristol United Press

Wessex Newspapers
33 Westgate Street, Bath, Avon BA1 1EW
Fax 01225-445969   Tel 01225-444044
Somerset & Avon Guardian 01225-444044
Somerset Standard (Frome) 01373-462379
Owner: Westminster Press

Staffordshire

Biddulph Chronicle
11 High Street, Congleton, Cheshire CW12 1BW
Fax 01260-280687   Tel 01260-273737

Burton Advertiser
65-68 High Street, Burton-on-Trent, Staffs DE14
1LE
Fax 01283-51007   Tel 01283-512345
Owner: Burton Daily Mail

Burton Daily Mail
The Publishing Centre, Derby Street, Stafford
ST16 2DT
Fax 01785-53287   Tel 01785-57700
Staffs Newsletter series; The Other One
Owner: Burton Daily Mail

Burton & Lichfield Journal
Curzon Street, Derby DE1 1LL
Fax 01332-883699   Tel 01332-369162
Derby/Nottingham/Coventry Journal; Rugby/Stratford Gazette;
Sutton Coldfield Times; Solihull/Redditch/Bromsgrove
Journal; Midland Business Today; Corporate Times; Business
Brief

Central Independent Newspapers
8 Aldergate, Tamworth, Staffs B79 7DP
Fax 01827-64246   Tel 01827-64222
Tamworth Herald 01827-64222
Burntwood Mercury; Lichfield Mercury 01543-414414
Cannock Mercury 01543-467500
Rugeley Mercury 01889-583401

Walsall Advertiser 01922-721234
Sutton Coldfield Observer; Great Bear Observer 0121-355 6161

Cheadle & Tean Times
18 Tape Street, Cheadle, Staffs ST10 1BD
Fax 01538-754465   Tel 01538-752214
Blythe & Forsbrook Echo; Cheadle & Tean Times 01538-752214
Uttoxeter Echo 01889-562479

Express & Star
51 Queen Street, Wolverhampton, West
Midlands WV1 3BU
Fax 01902-21467   Tel 01902-313131
Cannock Chronicle; Lichfield Chronicle/Express 01543-572834
Stafford Chronicle 01785-47290
Owner: Claverley Co.

Hill Bros (Leek)
Newspaper House, Brook Street, Leek, Staffs
ST13 5JL
Fax 01538-386975   Tel 01538-399599
Leek Post & Times 01538-399599
Cheadle Post & Times 01538-750011
Uttoxeter Post & Times 01889-568999

North Staffs Advertiser
Sentinel House, Etruria, Stoke-on-Trent, Staffs
ST1 5SS
Fax 01782-21447   Tel 01782-71100
Owner: Northcliffe Newspapers Group

Stafford/Chase Posts
Hickman Avenue, Wolverhampton, West
Midlands WV1 2BX
Fax 01902-456776   Tel 01902-870447
Owner: Reed Regional Newspapers

Trader Group Newspapers
Abbots Hall Chambers, Gower Street,
Derbyshire DE1 1SB
Fax 01332-253915   Tel 01332-253999
Burton Trader 01283-512000
Ilkeston & Ripley Trader 01332-253989
Owner: Midland Independent Newspapers

Stafford/Chase Posts
Hickman Avenue, Wolverhampton, West
Midlands WV1 2BX
Fax 01902-456776   Tel 01902-870447
Owner: Reed Midland

Uttoxeter Advertiser
Market Place, Uttoxeter, Staffs ST14 8HP
Fax 01889-563061   Tel 01889-562050
Burton Mail; Burton Advertiser; Staffs Newsletter 01283-512345
Owner: Burton Mail Group

Suffolk

Anglia Advertiser
8 Bevan Street, Lowestoft, Suffolk NR32
2AA
Fax 01493-652082   Tel 01502-582318
Waveney Advertiser 01502-582318
Gt Yarmouth Advertiser 01493-601206
Ipswich Advertiser 01473-611363
Norwich Advertiser 01603-740222
Suffolk Advertiser 01728-831128

Beccles & Bungay Journal
20 Blyburgate, Beccles, Sufflk NR34 9TB
Fax 01502-711329   Tel 01502-712623
Owner: Eastern Counties Newspaper Group

Cambridge Newspapers
51 Newmarket Road, Cambridge CB5 8EJ
Fax 01223-61744   Tel 01223-358877
Haverhill Weekly News 01440-703891
Newmarket Weekly News 01638-662581
Owner: Yattendon Investment Trust

East Anglian Daily Times Co
30 Lower Brook Street, Ipswich, Suffolk IP4
1AN
Fax 01473-225296   Tel 01473-230023
Ipswich Mercury 01473-230023
Bury St Edmunds Mercury; West Suffolk Mercury 01284-702588
Felixstowe Mercury 01394-284109
North Suffolk Mercury 01986-872202
Sudbury Mercury 01787-371297
Woodbridge Mercury 01394-385353
Lowestoft Journal 01502-565141
Owner: Eastern Counties Newspapers Group

Emap Anglia Newspapers
Mere Street, Diss, Norfolk IP22 3AE
Fax 01379-650110   Tel 01379-643232
Bury Citizen/Free Press 01284-768911
Fenland Citizen 01945-584372
Haverhill Echo 01440-703456
Lynn News & Norfolk Citizen 0153-761188
Newmarket Journal 01638-668441
Norfolk & Suffolk Express (Diss) 01379-643232
Suffolk Free Press 01787-375271
Owner: Emap

Surrey

Croydon Advertiser Group
Advertiser House, Brighton Road, South
Croydon, Surrey CR2 6UB
Fax 0181-668 9988   Tel 0181-668 4111
Caterham Advertiser; New Addington Advertiser 0181-668 4111
Reigate & Banstead Independent 01737-249372
Owner: Portsmouth & Sunderland Newspapers

Farnham Castle Newspapers Group
114 West Street, Farnham, Surrey GU9 7HL
Fax 01252-724951   Tel 01252-725224
Farnham Herald 01252-725224
Haslemere Herald 01428-651271
Surrey & Hants News series 01252-716444
Owner: Tindle Newspapers

Informer Publications
168 High Street, Egham, Surrey TW20 9HZ
Fax 01784-432771   Tel 01784-433773
Richmond & Twickenham Informer; Kingston Informer;
Wimbledon Informer 01784-433773
Woking Informer; Staines Informer 01784-433773
Epsom & Leatherhead Informer; Walton & Weybridge Informer
0181-943 5171
Owner: United Provincial Newspapers

The Messenger
2 Kings Road, Haslemere, Surrey GU27
2QA
Fax 01428-661658   Tel 01428-653999

Middlesex County Press
326 Station Road, Harrow, Middlesex HA1
2DR
Fax 0181-863 0932   Tel 0181-424 0044
Staines Leader; Surrey Herald & News; Walton & Weybridge
Leader 01932-561111
Owner: Southnews

South London Guardian
34 London Road, Morden, Surrey SM4
5BR
Fax 0181-687 4459   Tel 0181-646 6336
Epsom & Banstead Guardian; Esher & Elmbridge Guardian;
Leatherhead Guardian 0181-644 4300
Owner: Reed Regional Newspapers

Surrey Advertiser Newspaper Holdings
Martyr Road, Guildford, Surrey GU1 4LQ
Fax 01483-301271   Tel 01483-571234
Surrey Advertiser series 01483-571234
Esher News & Mail series 01372-463553
Surrey Times series 01483-579244
Woking News & Mail series 01483-755755
Woking Review series 01483-769991
Camberley Mail/News (from Hants group) 01252-28221
Surrey Hants Star 01252-316311
Owner: Guardian Media Group

Trinity Newspapers Southern
Trinity House, 51 London Road, Reigate, Surrey
RH2 9PR
Fax 01737-732267   Tel 0181-661 2221
Banstead Herald; Epsom & Ewell Herald/News; Leatherhead
Advertiser/News 0181-642 7777
Caterham Mirror; Dorking Advertiser; Horley Mirror; Oxted
Mirror; Surrey Mirror 01737-732000
Owner: Trinity International Holdings

Sussex

Beckett Newspapers
1 Commercial Road, Eastbourne, East Sussex
BN21 3XQ
Fax 01323-722091   Tel 01323-722091
Eastbourne Advertiser/Echo/Gazette/Herald; Hailsham Gazette;
Seaford Gazette 01323-722091
Lancing Herald; Littlehampton Gazette; Shoreham Herald;
Steyning Herald; Worthing Advertiser/Herald 01903-230051
Owner: Johnston Press

Courier Group of Newspapers
Longfield Road, Tunbridge Wells, Kent TN2
3HL
Fax 01892-543181   Tel 01892-526262
East Grinstead Courier 01342-323652
Kent & Sussex Courier 01892-526262
Owner: Northcliffe Newspapers Group

Crawley News
31-33 High Street, Crawley, West Sussex RH10
1BQ
Fax 01293-545930   Tel 01293-526474
Crawley News Extra
Owner: Trinity International Holdings

Portsmouth Publishing & Printing
News Centre, Hilsea, Portsmouth, Hants PO2
9SX
Fax 01705-673363   Tel 01705-664488
Bognor Regis Journal 01243-533660
Bognor Regis Observer 01243-827111
Chichester Observer 01243-539389
Midhurst & Petworth Observer 01703-813301
Peterfield Post 01730-268021
West Sussex Gazette (Arundel) 01903-882201
Owner: Portsmouth and Sunderland Newspapers

Southern Publishing Co
Hollingbury Industrial Estate, Crowhurst Road,
Brighton, East Sussex BN1 8AR
Fax 01273-505703   Tel 01273-544544
Brighton & Hove Leader; Newhaven & Denton Leader;
Peacehaven & Telscombe Leader; Seaford Leader
01273-544544
Burgess Hill Leader; Haywards Heath Leader 01444-245611
Owner: Westminster Press

Sussex County Press
56a Chapel Road, Worthing, West Sussex
BN11 1DQ
Fax 01903-201481   Tel 01903-209025
Littlehampton & Rustington Guardian; Shoreham , Lancing &
Steyning Guardian; Worthing Guardian
Owner: Johnston Press

Sussex Newspapers
19 Boltro Road, Haywards Heath, West Sussex
RH16 1BT

Fax 01444-416241   Tel 01444-452201
Mid-Sussex Citizen/Times 01444-452201
Crawley Observer 01293-562929
Owner: Emap

1066 Newspapers
Woods House, Telford Road, St Leonards-on-
Sea, East Sussex TN38 9LZ
Fax 01424-854284   Tel 01424-854242
Hastings Observer; Rye & Battle Observer; Adnews 01424-854242
Bexhill Observer 01424-730555
Sussex Express 01273-480601
Owner: Emap

Trinity Newspapers Southern
Trinity House, 51 London Road, Reigate, Surrey
RH2 9PR
Fax 01737-732267   Tel 01737-732000
Crawley News 01293-523282
East Grinstead Observer 01342-324333
Owner: Trinity International Holdings

West Sussex County Times
14 Market Square, Horsham, West Sussex
RH12 1HD
Fax 01403-268293   Tel 01403-253371
Horsham & District Advertiser; West Sussex County Times
01403-253371
Worthing Guardian Series 01903-209025
Owner: Johnston Press

Tyne & Wear

Newcastle Chronicle & Journal
Groat Market, Newcastle-upon-Tyne, Tyne &
Wear NE1 1ED
Fax 0191-232 2256   Tel 0191-232 7500
Gateshead Post; Newcastle Herald & Post; North Tyneside
Herald & Post; South Tyneside Herald & Post 0191-477 3245
Owner: Trinity International (formerly Thomson Corporation)

Northeast Press
Chapter Row, South Shields, Tyne & Wear NE33
1BL.
Fax 0191-456 8270   Tel 0191-455 4661
News Guardian series; Shields Gazette 0191-455 4661
South Tyneside Star; Sunderland Star; Washington Star 0191-
417 0050
Owner: Portsmouth & Sunderland Newspapers

Warwickshire

Atherstone Herald
10 Aldergate, Tamworth, Staffs B79 7DP
Fax 01827-60630   Tel 01827-60741
Coleshill Herald; Tamworth Herald; Atherstone
Herald/Tamworth Herald Extra.
Owner: Tamworth Herald Co

Central Counties Newspapers
32 Hamilton Terr, Leamington Spa, Warwicks
CV32 4LY
Fax 01926-451690   Tel 01926-888222
Kenilworth Weekly News; Leamington Spa Courier/Review;
 Warwickshire Courier. 01926-888222
Rugby Advertiser/Review 01788-535363
Owner: Emap

Coventry Newspapers
Corporation Street, Coventry, West Midlands
CV1 1FP
Fax 01203-550869   Tel 01203-633633
Leamington & Nuneaton/Rugby Telegraph 01203-633633
Bedworth Echo 01203-312785
Nuneaton Tribune 01203-351111
Owner: Midland Independent Newspapers

Leamington Spa Observer
45 The Parade, Leamington Spa, Warwicks
CV32 4BL
Fax 01926-451754   Tel 01926-451771
Stratford/Kennilworth/Rugby/Redditch & Bromsgrove
 Observer; County Standard

Stratford-upon-Avon Herald
17 Rother Street, Stratford upon Avon,
Warwicks CV37 6NB
Fax 01789-269519   Tel 01789-266261
Midweek News

Stratford-upon-Avon Observer
8 Shrieves Walk, Sheep Street, Stratford upon
Avon, Warwicks CV37 6GJ
Fax 01789 295605   Tel 01789-415717
County Standard

West Midlands

Coventry Newspapers
Corporation Street, Coventry, West Midlands
CV1 1FP
Fax 01203-550869   Tel 01203-633633
Birmingham Post & Mail 0121-236 3366
Coventry Citizen 01203-633633
Hinckley Journal 01455-611350
Hinckley Herald 01455-891981
Leicester Herald & Post 01162-471000
Venture Magazine 01203-525552
Weekley Tribune 01203-351111
Owner: Midland Independent Newspapers

Express & Star
51 Queen Street, Wolverhampton, West
Midlands WV1 3BU
Fax 01902-21467   Tel 01902-313131
Wolverhampton Chronicle 01902-313131
Cannock Chase/Lichfield/Stafford Chronicles 01543-506311
Dudley/Halesowen/Kidderminster/Stourbridge Chronicles

01345-211511
Edgbaston/Erdington/Great Barr/Sandwell Chronicles 0121-553
7171
Sporting Star 01902-313131
Walsall/Willenhall Chronicles 01922-723344
Owner: Claverley Co

Midland Newspapers
28 Colmore Circus, Birmingham B4 6AX
Fax 0121-233 0271   Tel 0121-236 3366
Weekly Observer 0121-626 6634
Solihull News 0121-705 8211
Sutton News 0121-354 7676
Walsall Observer 01922-27504
Owner: Midland Independent Newspapers

Reed Regional Newspapers (Midland)
78 Francis Road, Edgbaston, Birmingham, West
Midlands B16 8SP
Fax 0121-455 9458   Tel 0121-455 7877
Birmingham Metro News 0121-455 7877
Bromsgrove Advertiser 01527-837000
Dudley News 01384-459019
Halesowen News 0121-503 0999
Redditch Advertiser 01527-63611
Solihull Times 0121-711 4777
Stourbridge News/County Express 01384-374321
Wolverhampton AdNews series 01902-870447
Owner: Reed Elsevier

Sutton Coldfield Publishing
14b Birmingham Road, Sutton Coldfield, West
Midlands B72 1DG
Fax 0121-355 0082   Tel 0121-355 6901
Great Barr Observer; Sutton Coldfield Observer 0121-355 6061
Walsall Advertiser 01922-721234

Wiltshire

Avon Advertiser
39 Brown Street, Salisbury, Wilts SP1 2AS
Fax 01722-338506   Tel 01722-337466
Salisbury Journal 01722-412525
Owner: Southern Newspapers Group

Bailey Newspaper Group
Reliance House, Long Street, Dursley, Glos
GL11 4LS
Fax 01453-544577   Tel 01453-544000
Marlborough Times 01672-512488
Wilts & Glos Standard 01285-642642

Media in Wessex
100 Victoria Road, Swindon, Wilts SN1 3BE
Fax 01793-542434   Tel 01793-528144
Swindon Star 01793-528144
West & North Wilts Star; Wiltshire Times series 01225-777292
Wiltshire Gazette & Herald series 01380-723501
Owner: Westminster Press

Melksham/White Horse Independent News
31 Market Place, Melksham Wilts SN12 6EU
Fax 01225 908081   Tel 01225-704761

Salisbury Journal & Times
8 Rollestone Street, Salisbury, Wilts SP1 1DY
Fax 01722-333354   Tel 01722-412525
A1 Advertiser 01722-337466
Amesbury Journal; Salisbury Journal/Times 01722-412525
Other Southern papers: Devizes News 01380-729001
Owner: Southern Newspapers

Swindon Messenger
32 Morley Street, Swindon, Wilts SN1 1SG
Fax 01793-529143   Tel 01793-511011
Owner: Tinity International Holdings

Warminster Journal
36 Market Place, Warminster, Wilts BA12 9AN
Fax 01985 217680   Tel 01985-213030

Yorkshire

Ackrill Newspapers
1 Cardale Park, Harrogate, North Yorks HG3 1RZ
Fax 01423-524249   Tel 01423-564321
Pateley Bridge Herald; Harrogate Advertiser/Herald 01423 564321
Knaresborough Post 01423-869272
North Yorkshire News; Northallerton Times 01609-774592
Pudsey Times; Wharfe Valley Times 01943-850273
Ripon Gazette 01765-601248
Wetherby News 01937-582663
Owner: United Provincial Newspapers

Barnsley Chronicle
47 Church Street, Barnsley, South Yorks S70 2AS
Fax 01226-734455   Tel 01226-734734
Barnsley Chronicle; Barnsley Independent

Bradford & District Newspapers
Hall Ings, Bradford, West Yorks BD1 1JR
Fax 01274-723634   Tel 01274-729511
Aire Valley Target; Bradford Star 01274-729511
Craven Herald/Star 01756-792577
Ilkley Gazette/Star 01943-608602
Keighley News/Target 01535-606611
Wharfedale Observer/Star 01943-465555
Owner: Westminster Press

Garnett Dickinson Group
Eastwood Works, Fitzwilliam Road, Rotherham, South Yorks S65 1JU
Fax 01709-838489   Tel 01709-364721
Dearne Valley Weekender; Rotherham Record; Rotherham & South Yorks Advertiser; Sheffield Job News

Goodhead Publishing
49 West Street, Sheffield, South Yorks S1 4EQ
Fax 0114-276 1936   Tel 0114-275 3377
Sheffield Journal
Owner: Goodhead Group

Halifax Courier
Courier Buildings, King Cross Street, Halifax, West Yorks HX1 2SF.
Fax 01422-330021   Tel 01422-365711
Calderdale News; Evening Courier 01422-365711
Brighouse Echo 01484-714617
Hebden Bridge Times 01422-842106
Todmorden News 01706-815731
Owner: Johnston Press

John H Hirst & Co
Northgate, Cleckheaton, West Yorks BD19 3JA.
Fax 01274-851304   Tel 01274-874635
Brighouse Spen & Mirfield Advertiser; Heckmondwike Herald; Spenborough Guardian

Huddersfield Newspapers
PO Box A26, Queen Street South, Huddersfield, West Yorks HD1 2TD
Fax 01484-423722   Tel 01484-430000
Huddersfield Weekly News 01484-430000
Colne Valley Chronicle; Holme Valley Express; Huddersfield District Chronicle 01484-684011
Owner: Trinity International Holdings

Reed Northern Newspapers
Sunnybar, Doncaster, South Yorks DN1 1NB
Fax 01302-768095   Tel 01302-322144
Doncaster Courier/Free Press; Goole Courier
Owner: Reed Regional Newspapers

The Reporter
Wellington Road, Dewsbury, West Yorks WF13 1HQ
Fax 01924-457652   Tel 01924468282
Dewsbury Reporter; Mirfield Reporter; Spen & Calder Weekly News 01924-468282.
Batley News; Birstall News 01924-472121
Morley Observer & News 0113-252 3456
Spen Valley News 01924-422800
Owner: United Provincial Newspapers

Sheffield Newspapers
York Street, Sheffield, South Yorks S1 1PU
Fax 0114-272 5978   Tel 0114-276 7676
Sheffield Telegraph; Sheffield Weekly Gazette.
Owner: United Provincial Newspapers

G H Smith
Market Place, Easingwold, York, North Yorks YO6 3AB
Fax 01347-822576   Tel 01347-821329
Easingwold Advertiser & Weekly News

Worksop Newspapers
30 Watson Road, Worksop, Notts S80 2BE
Fax 01909-474849   Tel 01909-500500
Dinnington & Maltby Guardian 01909-550500
Eckington Leader 01246-434343
Retford & Bawtry Guardian 01777-704242
Owner: AW & J Linney

York & County Press
76 Walmgate, York, North Yorks YO1 1YN
Fax 01904-612853   Tel 01904-653051
East Yorkshire Star; Gazette & Herald; Selby Star; Thirsk &
Easingwold Star; York Star.
Owner: Westminster Press

Yorkshire Post Newspapers
Wellington Street, Leeds, West Yorks LS1 1RF
Fax 0113-244 3430   Tel 0113-243 2701
Leeds Weekly News.
Owner: United Provincial Newspapers

Yorkshire Regional Newspapers
17 Aberdeen Walk, Scarborough, North Yorks
YO11 1BB
Fax 01723-354092   Tel 01723-363636
Bridlington Free Press 01262-606606
Driffield Times 01377-253213
Scarborough Mercury series; Yorkshire Coast Leader 01723-
363636
Whitby Gazette 01947-602836
Owner: Emap

Yorkshire Weekly Newspaper Group
Express House, Southgate, Wakefield, West
Yorks WF1 1TE
Fax 01924-290451   Tel 01924-375111
Ossett & Horury Observer; Wakefield Express 01924-375111
Hemsworth Express 01977-640107
Pontefract & Castleford Express; Weekend Times 01977-702151
Selby Chronicle/Times 01757-702802
South Yorkshire Times 01709-584684
Morley Advertiser 0113-252 4020
Leeds Skyrack Express 0113-264 4278
Other Johnston papers: Doncaster Advertiser 01302-366843
Owner: Johnston Press

North Wales:
Clwyd/Gwynedd

Cambrian News
28 High Street, Lampeter, Dyfed SA48 7BB
Fax 01570 423575   Tel 01570-422602

Chronicle & Associated Newspapers
Chronicle House, Commonhall Street, Chester,
Cheshire CH1 2BJ
Fax 01244-340165   Tel 01244-340151

Deeside Chronicle 01244-821911
Clwyd Herald & Post 01244-340151
Mold & Buckley Chronicle; Flint & Holywell Chronicle 0352-
755455
Owner: Trinity International (formerly Thomson Corporation)

County Press
County Press Buildings, Bala, Gwynedd
LL23 7PG
Fax 01678-521262   Tel 01678-520262
Corwen Times; Y Cyfnod; Merioneth Express.

Dydd A'r Corwen Chronicle
Smithfield Lane, Dolgellau, Gwynned LL40 1DA
Fax 01341-422547   Tel 01341-422547

North Wales Newspapers
Mold Business Park, Wrexham Road, Mold,
Clwyd CH7 1XY
Fax 01352-700048   Tel 01352-700022
Mold & Deeside Leader 01352-700022
Bangor Chronicle; Caernarfon Chronicle; Y Cymru; Holyhead
Chronicle 01248-352051
County Times 01938-553354
Denbighshire Free Press 01745-813535
North Wales Pioneer 01492-531188
Rhyl & Prestatyn Journal 01745-343515
Wrexham Leader 01978-355151

North Wales Weekly News
Vale Road, Llandudno Junction, Gwynedd
LL31 9SL
Fax 01492-593664   Tel 01492-584321
Llandudno Advertiser; North Wales Weekly News 01492-584321
Abergele Visitor; Rhyl & Prestatyn Visitor 01745-344444
Bangor & Anglesey Mail 01248-362747
Caernarfon & Denbigh Herald; Y Herald (Caernarfon) 01286-
671111
Holyhead Mail 01407-762405
Vale Advertiser (Denbigh) 01745-815454
Wrexham & Mold Mail 01978-290400
Owner: Trinity International Holdings

Central Wales:
Dyfed/Powys

Brecon & Radnor Express/Powys County Times
Express Buildings, Brecon, Powys LD3 7AE
Fax 01874-624097   Tel 01874-622932

Cambrian News (Aberystwyth)
18 Queen Street, Aberystwyth, Dyfed SY23 1PX
Fax 01970-615497   Tel 01970-615000
Cambrian News & Welsh Gazette:
  Aberystwyth; Montgomeryshire 01970-615000
  Dwyfor 01766-513809
  South edition 01570-423567

Carmarthen Journal
18 King Street, Carmarthen, Dyfed SA31 1BN
Fax 01267-227229   Tel 01267-221234
Owner: Northcliffe Newspapers Group

County Echo & St Davids City Chronicle
6 Brodog Court, Brodog Terrace, Fishguard,
Dyfed SA65 9NF
Fax 01348-873651   Tel 01348-872179
Owner: Tindle Newspapers

County Times & Express
20 High Street, Welshpool, Powys SY21 7JR
Fax 01352-700048   Tel 01938-553354
Owner: North Wales Newspapers, Welshpool

Llanelli Star
10 Station Road, Llanelli, Dyfed SA15 1BJ
Fax 01554 775456   Tel 01554-774809
Burry Port/Gwendraeth/Lougher Stars
Owner: Northcliffe Newspapers Group

Mid-Wales Journal
17 The Bull Ring, Ludlow, Shropshire SY8 1AD
Fax 01584-876134   Tel 01584-876311
Owner: Shropshire Newspapers,Telford

South & West Wales Newspapers
Press Buildings, Hakin Road, Merlins Bridge,
Haverfordwest, Dyfed SA61 1XF
Fax 01437-760482   Tel 01437-763133
Pembroke County & West Wales Guardian; Western Telegraph &
Cymric Times 01437-763133
Cardigan Advertiser 01239-612513
South Wales Guardian 01269-592074
Owner: United Provincial Newspapers

Tenby Observer
Newspaper House, Warren Street, Tenby, Dyfed
SA70 7JY
Fax 01834-844774   Tel 01834-843262
Owner: Tindle Newspapers

South Wales:
Glamorgan/Gwent

Abergavenny Chronicle
45 Cross Street, Abergavenny, Gwent NP7 5ER
Fax 01873-77677   Tel 01873-852187
Monmouthshire Beacon 01600-712142
Owner: Tindle Newspapers

Bailey Newspaper Group
Unit 3, Pavilion Industrial Estate,
Pontnewynydd, Pontypool, Gwent NP4 6NF
Fax 01495-762302   Tel 01495-751133
The Press, Chepstow; The Press, Cwmbran; The Press, Newport;
The Press, Pontypool 01495-751133

Barry & District News 01446-733456
Penarth Times 01222-707234

Barry News
156 Holton Road, Barry, South Glamorgan CF63
4TY
Fax 01446-732719   Tel 01446-733456
Penarth Times 01222-707234
Owner: Bailey Newspaper Group

Cardiff Independent
Meridian Court, North Road, Cardiff, South
Glamorgan CF4 3BL
Fax 01222-618575   Tel 01222-615515
Owner: United Provincial Newspapers

Celtic Newspapers
Thomson House, Havelock Street, Cardiff CF1
1XR
Fax 01222-583609   Tel 01222-223333
Cynon Valley Leader 01685-873136
Blackwood Chronicle; Caerphilly Chronicle 01222-881715
Bridgend & Ogwr Post; Glamorgan Gazette 01656-652422
Gwent Gazette 01495-304589
Merthyr Express/Herald & Post 01685-385818
Neath Guardian; Port Talbot Guardian 01639-646401
Pontypridd & Llantrisant Observer; Rhondda Leader 01443-493426
Owner: Trinity International (formerly Thomson Corporation)

Glamorgan Gem
Craig House, 53 Eastgate, Cowbridge, South
Glamorgan CF7 7EL
Fax 01446-774108   Tel 01446-774484
Barry Gem; Cowbridge Gem; Llantwit Major Gem
Owner: Yattendon Investment Trust

South Wales Argus
Cardiff Road, Maesglas, Newport, Gwent NP9
1QW
Fax 01633-464202   Tel 01633-810000
Blackwood News; Chepstow News; Cwmbran & Pontypool News;
Llanelli News; Monmouth News; Newport News
Owner: United Provincial Newspapers

Swansea Press
Adelaide Street, Swansea, West Glamorgan
SA1 1QT
Fax 01792-472208   Tel 01792-468833
Swansea Herald of Wales; Neath Herald of Wales; Neath & Port
Talbot Shopper
Owner: Northcliffe Newspapers Group

Western Mail & Echo
Havelock Street, Cardiff, South Glamorgan
CF1 1WR
Fax 01222-583624   Tel 01222-223333
Cardiff Post; Vale Post; South Wales Echo; Bridgend Post;
Pontypridd Observer 01222-223333
Owner: Trinity International (formerly Thomson Corporation)

Scotland:
Borders/Dumfries & Galloway

Border Weeklies
113 High Street, Galashiels, Selkirk TD1 1SB
Fax 01896-759395   Tel 01896-758395
Border Telegraph 01896-758395
Peeblesshire News 01721-720884

Dumfriesshire Newspapers Group
96 High Street, Annan, Dumfries DG12 6DW
Fax 01461-205659   Tel 01461-202417
Annandale Herald/Observer (Lockerbie); Dumfries Courier;
Moffat News
Owner: Annandale Observer

Eskdale & Liddesdale Advertiser (Langholm)
Commercial House, High Street, Langholm,
Dumfriesshire DG13 0JH
Fax 013873 80345   Tel 01387-380012

Galloway Gazette
Victoria Lane, Newton Stewart, Dumfries DG8
6PS
Fax 01671-403391   Tel 01671-402503
Carrick Gazette; Galloway Gazette

Hawick News & Scottish Border Chronicle
24 High Street, Hawick, Roxburghshire TD9
9EH
Fax 01450-370706   Tel 01450-72204

Peebles Times
Sherwood Industrial Estate, Bonnyrigg,
Midlothian EH19 3LW
Fax 0131-663 6863   Tel 0131-663 2404
Lothian Times; Midlothian Advertiser; East Lothia News;
  Musselburgh News
Owner: Scottish County Press, Lothian

Tweeddale Press Group
90 Marygate, Berwick-upon-Tweed TD15 1BW
Fax 01289-307377   Tel 01289-306677
Berwickshire News & East Lothian Herald 01289-306677
Southern Reporter (Selkirk) 01750-21581

Wigtown Free Press (Stranraer)
Saint Andrew Street, Stranraer, Wigtownshire
DG9 7EB
Fax 01776 706695   Tel 01776-702551

Grampian/Highland

Aberdeen Journals
Lang Stracht, Mastrick, Aberdeen AB9 8AF
Fax 01224-663575   Tel 01224-690222
Aberdeen Herald & Post 01224-212622
Owner: Trinity International (formerly Thomson Corporation)

Fraserburgh Herald
12 Frithside Street, Fraserburgh, Aberdeenshire
AB43 5AR
Fax 01346-517378   Tel 01346-513900
Buchan Observer 01779-472184
Ellon Times 01358-723777

Fort William Extra
The Oban Times, PO Box 1, Oban Argyll PA34
5PY
Fax 01397-702495   Tel 01397-703003
Owner: Oban Times

Highland News Group
Henderson Road, Longman Industrial Estate,
Inverness, Highland IV1 1SP
Fax 01463-221251   Tel 01463-713700
Inverness Herald; Inverness & Highland News; Lochaber News;
  Nairnshire Herald; North Star (Dingwall) Ross-shire Herald
01463-713700
Caithness Courier (Wick); John O'Groats Journal (Wick) 01955-
  602424
Ross-shire Herald 01349-863436

Inverness Courier
PO Box 13, Bank Lane, Inverness-shire IV1
1QW
Fax 01463-243439   Tel 01463-233059

Inverurie Herald
21a Market Place, Inverurrie AB51 3PN
Fax 01467-622251   Tel 01467-625150
Deeside Piper 01330-824955
Owner: Angus County Press

J & M Publishing
13 West Church Street, Buckie, Grampian
AB56 1BN
Fax: 01542-834316   Tel 01542-832265
Banffshire Advertiser 01542-832265
Banffshire Herald 01542-886262
Huntly Express 01466-793622

Montrose Review Press
59 John Street, Montrose, Tayside DD10
8QU
Fax 01674-676232   Tel 01674-672605
Kincardineshire Observer (Laurencekirk) 01561-377283
Leader (Stonehaven) 01569-762139

Moray & Nairn Newspaper Co
175-177 High Street, Elgin, Grampian IV30
1DP
Fax 01343-545629   Tel 01343-548777
Northern Scot; Northern Scot Midweek Extra
  01343-548777
Banffshire Journal (Banff) 01261-8122551
Forres & Nairn Gazette 01309-672615
Strathspey & Badenoch Herald 01479-872102
Owner: Scottish Provincial Press

Nairnshire Telegraph
12 Leopold Street, Nairn, Nairnshire IV12 4BG
Fax 01667-455277   Tel 01667-453258

Northern Times
Sutherland Press House, Golspie, Sutherland
KW10 6RA
Fax 01408-633028   Tel 01408-633993
Owner: Scottish Provincial Press

The Orcadian
PO Box 18, Kirkwall, Orkney Isles KW15 1DW
Fax 01856- 878001   Tel 01856-878000

W Peters & Son
16 High Street, Turriff, Grampian AB53 7DT
Fax 01888-563936   Tel 01888-563589
Ellon Advertiser 01358-723899
Inverurie Advertiser 01467-62122
Turriff Advertiser 01888 563589

Shetland Times
Prince Alfred Street, Lerwick, Shetland ZE1 0EP
Fax 01595-694637   Tel 01595-693622

Stornoway Gazette
10 Francis Street, Stornoway, Isle of Lewis PA87
2XE
Fax 01851-706424   Tel 01851-702687
Owner: Galloway Group

West Highland Free Press
Unit One, Industrial Estate, Broadford, Isle of
Skye IV49 9AP
Fax 01471-822694   Tel 01471-822464

Central/Fife/Tayside

Angus County Press
Craig O'Loch Road, Forfar, Tayside DD8 1BU
Fax 01307-466923   Tel 01307-464901
Forfar Dispatch; Kirriemuir Herald; Tayside Farmer 01307-
464901
Brechin Advertiser 01356-622767
Deeside Piper (Banchory); Donside Piper 01330-824955
Inverurie Herald 01467-625150

Brechin Advertiser
13 Swan Street, Brechin, Tayside DD9 6EE
Fax 01356-625507   Tel 01356-622767
Forfar Dispatch; Kirriemuir Herald

Dunfermline Herald & Post
19-23 High Street, Dunfermline, Fife KY12 7DL
Fax 01383-621211   Tel 01383-621818
Owner: Scotsman Communications

Dunfermline Press
Guildhall Street, Dunfermline, Fife, KY12 7NS

Fax 01383-737040   Tel 01383-728201
Central Fife Times & Advertiser; Dunfermline Press; Fife &
Kinross Extra; Midweek Advertiser; Alloa & Hellfoots
Advertiser; Stirling News
Owner: A Romanes & Son

Herald Press
Burnside Drive, Arbroath, Angus, Tayside
DD11 1NS
Fax 01241-878789   Tel 01241-872274
Abroath Herald; Broughton Ferry/Carnoustie Gazette

Johnston (Falkirk)
Newmarket Street, Falkirk, Central FK1 1JZ
Fax 01324-629792   Tel 01324-624959
Falkirk Herald; Falkirk & Grangemouth Advertiser 01324 624959
Bo'ness Journal 0506-822637
Carluce Gazette 01555-771633
Lanark Gazette 01555-663937
Linlithgow Gazette 0506-844592
Owner: Johnston Press

Montrose Review Press
59 John Street, Montrose, Tayside DD10
8QU
Fax 01674-76232   Tel 01674-672605
Brechin Review; Montrose Review

Scottish & Universal Newspapers
Press Buildings, Campbell Street, Hamilton,
Strathclyde ML3 6AX
Fax 01698-425706   Tel 01698-283200
Blairgowrie Advertiser; Perthshire Advertiser; Perth Shopper
01738-626211
Stirling/Alloa Shopper; Stirling Observer 01786-451110
Strathearn Herald (Crieff) 01764-656500
Owner: Trinity International

Stirling News
65 Enterprise Park, Stirling, Stirlingshire FK7
7RP
Fax 0186-451330   Tel 01786-451175
Owner: Dunfermline Press

Strachan & Livingston
23 Kirk Wynd, Kirkaldy, Fife KY1 1EP
Fax 01592-204180   Tel 01592-261451
Fife Free Press/Leader 01592-261451
Fife Herald 01334-654638
The Advertiser; East Fife Mail 01334-423201
Glenrothes Gazette; Markinch News 01592-752289
St Andrews Citizen 01334-475855
Owner: Johnston Press

West Independent Newspapers
Herald Street, Ardossan, Strathclyde KA22 8BX
Fax 01294-466590   Tel 01294-464321
Alloa Advertiser; Stirling News 01259-215111
Kilsyth Chronicle 0236-822116
Owner: Clyde and Forth Weekly Press

Lothian/Strathclyde

Arran Banner (Isle of Arran)
Brodick, Isle of Arran KA27 8AJ
                  Tel 01770-302142

Bearsden, Milngavie & West Glasgow Courier
Academy Business Park, Unit 500, Gower Street, Glasgow, Lanarkshire G51 1PT
Fax 0141-427 0519   Tel 0141-427 7848

The Buteman
10 Castle Street, Rothesay, Bute PA20 9HB
Fax 01700-505159   Tel 01700-502503

Clyde & Forth Press
15 Colquhoun Square, Helensburgh, Dunbartonshire G84 8SE
Fax 01436-671241   Tel 01436-673434
Barrhead News; Clydebank Post; Dumbarton Reporter; Helensburgh Advertiser; Johnstone & Linwood Gazette; Paisley & Renfrewshire Gazette; Paisley People 01436-673434
Clyde Post (Greenock) 01475-726511

Clyde Weekly Press
Herald Street, Ardrossan, Strathclyde KA22 8BX
Fax 01294-466590   Tel 01294-464321
Ardrossan & Saltcoats Herald 01294-464321
Ayr Advertiser; Carrick Herald; Troon Times 01292-267631
Cumnock Chronicle 01290-426133
Irvine Times 01294-273421
Largs Weekly News 01475-689009

Community Media
11 Merry Street, Motherwell, Strathclyde ML1 1JJ
Fax 01698-269399   Tel 01698-275222
Hamilton People; Motherwell People 01698-275222
Ayr & District Leader; Irvine Leader; Kilmarnock & District Leader 01292-611666
Owner: Eastern Counties Newspapers Group

Dunoon Observer & Argyllshire Standard
219 Argyll Street, Dunoon, Argyll PA23 7QT
Fax 01369-703458   Tel 01369-703218

East Lothian Courier
18 Market Street, Haddington, East Lothian EH41 3JL
Fax 0162082-6143   Tel 0162082-2451
Owner: Border Weeklies

Johnston (Falkirk)
Newmarket Street, Falkirk, Central FK1 1JZ
Fax 01324-629792   Tel 01324-624959
Boness Journal 01506-822637
Carluke Gazette 01555-772226

Cumbernauld Advertiser/News 01236-725578
Lanark Gazette 01555-663937
Linlithgow Gazette 01506-844592
Owner: Johnston Press

D Macleod
Luggiebank House, Redbrae Road, Kirkintilloch, Strathclyde G66 2DD
Fax 0141-776 2218   Tel 0141-775 0040
Kirkintilloch Herald; Strathkelvin Advertiser 0141-775 0040
Bellshill Speaker 01698-748126
Bearsden & Milngavie Herald 0141-956 2314
Cumbernauld & Kilsyth News 01236 25578
Motherwell Times 01698-264611
Owner: Johnston Press

Oban Times
PO Box 1, Oban, Strathclyde PA34 5PY
Fax 01631-565470   Tel 01631-563058
Argyllshire Advertiser/Campbeltown Courier; Oban & West Highland Times; Oban Extra; Fort William Extra

Scotsman Communications
20 North Bridge, Edinburgh, Lothian EH1 1YT
Fax 0131-220 2443   Tel 0131-225 2468
Edinburgh Herald & Post 0131-225 2468
West Lothian Herald & Post 01506-634400
Owner: Trinity International

Scottish County Press
Sherwood Industrial Estate, Bonnyrigg, Lothian EH19 3LW
Fax 0131-663 6863   Tel 0131-663 2404
Dalkeith Advertiser; East Lothian News; Musselburgh News; Lothian Times; Peebles Times

Scottish Daily Record & Sunday Mail
40 Anderston Quay, Glasgow, Strathclyde G3 8DA
Fax 0141-242 3145   Tel 0141-248 7000
The Glaswegian
Owner: Mirror Group

Scottish & Universal Newspapers
Press Buildings, Campbell Street, Hamilton, Lanarkshire ML3 6AX
Fax 01698-425706   Tel 01698-283200
Hamilton Advertiser/World; Lanarkshire World 01698-283200
Airdrie Advertiser/World 01236-748048
Ayrshire Post/World 01292-261111
East Kilbride News/World 01355-266000
Irvine Herald 01294-222288
Kilmarnock Standard 01563-25115
Lennox Herald 01389-67711
Livingston Courier; Lothian Courier/World 01506-633544
Renfrewshire World 0141-887 7911
Rutherglen Reformer 0141-647 2271
Wishaw Press/World 01698-373111
Owner: Trinity International

Northern Ireland

Century Newspapers
46-56 Boucher Crescent, Belfast BT12 6QY
Fax 01232-664412   Tel 01232-680000
East Belfast News; North Down News

Andersonstown News
122 Anderstown Road, Belfast, County Antrim
BT11 9BX
Fax 01232-620602   Tel 01232-619000

Banbridge Chronicle
14 Bridge Street, Banbridge, County Down T32
3JS
Fax 018206-24397   Tel 018206-62322
Newry Reporter 01693-67633

Derry Journal
Buncrana Road, Derry, County Derry BT48
8AA
Fax 01504-373298   Tel 01504-265442
Donegal Democrat 00353-7251201
Donegal People's Press 00353-7421842

Impartial Reporter
8-10 East Bridge Street, Enniskillen, County
Fermanagh BT74 7BT
Fax 01365-325047   Tel 01365-324422
Lakeland Extra

Mid-Ulster Mail
52 Oldtown Street, Cookstown, County Tyrone
BT80 8BB
Fax 016487-64295   Tel 016487-62288

Morton Newspapers
Windsor Ave, Lurgan, County Armagh BT67 9BQ
Fax 01762-343618   Tel 01762-326161
Antrim Times 01849-428034
Ballymena Times 01266-653300
Ballymoney Observer/Times 012656-66216
Banbridge Leader 01820-662745
Carrick Times 01960-351992
Castlereagh Star; Ulster Star 01846-679111
Coleraine Times 01265-55260
Craigavon Echo 01762-350041
Dromore Leader/Star 01846-692076
East Antrim Advertiser 01574-272303
Larne Times 01574-272303
Lisburn Echo/Leader 01846-601114
Londonderry Sentinel 01504-48889
Lurgan Mail 01762-327777
Mid-Ulster Mail 01648-762288
Mid-Ulster Echo 01648-31780
North West Echo 01504-268459
Newtownabbey Times 01232-843621
Portadown Times 01762-336111
Roe Valley Sentinel 01504-764090
Tyrone Times 01868-752801

Mourne Observer
The Roundabout, Castlewellan Road, Newcastle,
County Down BT33 0JX
Fax 013967-24566   Tel 013967-22666

Newry Reporter
4 Margaret Street, Newry, County Down BT34
1DH
Fax 01693-63157   Tel 01693-67633

Northern Newspapers
20 Railway Road, Coleraine, County Derry BT52
1PD
Fax 01265-43606   Tel 01265-43344
Coleraine Chronicle; The Leader; Northern Constitution 01265-
43344
Antrim Guardian; Newtownabbey Guardian 01849-462624
Ballymena Guardian 01266-41221

North West of Ireland Printing County
John Street, Omagh, County Tyrone BT78
1DT
Fax 01662-242206   Tel 01662-243444
Derry People & Donegal News; Strabane Chronicle; Ulster Herald
01662-243444
Fermanagh Herald 01365-322066

Observer Newspapers (NI)
Ann Street, Dungannon, County Tyrone BT70
1ET
Fax 01868-727334   Tel 01868-722557
Ballymena Chronicle; The Democrat; Dungannon Observer;
Fermanagh News 01868-722557
Armagh Down Observer 01868-722557
Armagh Observer; Lurgan & Portadown Examiner 01861-522793
Mid-Ulster Observer 01648-762396

The Outlook
Castle Street, Rathfriland, County Down BT34
5QR
Fax 018206-31022   Tel 018206-30202
Owner: Outlook Press

Spectator Newspapers
109 Main Street, Bangor, County Down BT20
4AF
Fax 01247-271544   Tel 01247-270270
County Down Spectator; Newtownards Spectator; Newtownards
Chronicle

Strabane Weekly News
25-27 High Street, Omagh, County Tyrone BT78
1BD
Fax 01662-243549   Tel 01662-242721
Tyrone Constitution

Ulster Gazette & Armagh Standard
56 Scotch Street, Armagh, County Armagh
BT61 7DQ
Fax 01861-527029   Tel 01861-522639

OTHER DAILY PAPERS

Daily Sport
Great Ancoats Street, Manchester M60 4BT
Fax 0161-236 4535   Tel 0161-236 4466
Tabloid paper, stablemate of the Sunday Sport.(See page 35)

Evening Standard
2 Derry Street, London W8 5EE
Fax 0171-937 3193   Tel 0171-938 6000
London's evening daily.

International Herald Tribune
63 Long Acre, London WC2E 9JH
Fax 0171-240 2254   Tel 0171-836 4802
Paris-based international daily.

Jewish Chronicle
25 Furnival Street, London EC4A 1JT
Fax 0171-405 9040   Tel 0171-831 1100

Lloyds List International
1 Singer Street, London EC2A 4LQ
Fax 0171-250 0744   Tel 0171-250 1500
News on the business side of shipping, insurance and transport.

London Gazette
Room 418, HMSO Publications Centre, 51 Nine
Elms Lane, London SW8 5DR
Fax 0171-873 8219   Tel 0171-873 8300
The daily noticeboard for official and legal announcements,
published by the government.

Morning Star
1 Ardleigh Road, London N1 4HS
Fax 0171-254 5950   Tel 0171-254 0033
The socialist newspaper, once a powerful force in the labour
movement. Tony Chater, the long serving editor, left in April and
was replaced by his deputy John Haylet.

News Line
BCM Box 747, London WC1N 3XX
Fax 0171-620 1221   Tel 0171-928 3218
Left-wing tabloid newspaper, focussing on trade union and
political issues. Published by the Workers Revolutionary
Party.

Racing Post
112 Coombe Lane, London SW20 0BA
Fax 0181-947 2652   Tel 0181-879 3377
News of the racing and betting industry.

Sporting Life
1 Canada Square, Canary Wharf, London E14
5AP
Fax 0171-293 3758   Tel 0171-570 3000
The old-established racing newspaper which first appeared in
1859.

USA Today International
10 Wardour Street, London W1V 3HG
Fax 0171-734 6066   Tel 0171-734 3003
London-printed international edition of the prominent American
daily paper.

ETHNIC PRESS

Thank you to the Comission for Racial Equality
(0171-828 7022) for providing this list.

Ahmadiyya Gazette
8 Haugh Road, Glasgow G3 8TR
                              Tel 0141-334 7931
English/Urdu. Editors: S A Khalid/N Munawar

Al-Aalam
Banner House, 55-57 Banner Street, London
EC1Y 8PX
Fax 0171-608 3581   Tel 0171-608 3454
Arabic weekly. Editor: Sead Mahamed Shehabi

Al Ahram International
107-111 Fleet Street, London EC4A
2AB
Fax 0171-583 0744   Tel 0171-583 0692
Arabic daily. Editor: Atef El-Ghamry

Al Arab
159 Acre Lane, London SW2 5UA
Fax 0171-326 1783   Tel 0171-326 9381
Arabic daily. Editor: A S El Houni

Al Hayat
66 Hammersmith Road, London W14 8YT
Fax 0171-602 4963   Tel 0171-602 9988
Arabic daily. Editor Jihad El Khazen

Al Muhajir
Buspace Studios, Conlan St, London W10 5AP
Fax 0181-964 5940   Tel 0181-968 5217
Arabic weekly. Editor: Mr Assou

Amar Deep Hindi
2 Chepstow Road, London W7
Fax 0181-579 3180   Tel 0181-840 3534
Weekly. Editor: J M Kaushal

Ananda Bazar Patrika and Sunday
4 Carmelite Street, London EC4Y 0BN
Fax 0171-583 5385   Tel 0171-353 1821
Bengali/English weekly. Editor: A Sarkar

Asharq Al Awsat
184 High Holborn, London WC1V 7AP
Fax 0171-831 2310   Tel 0171-831 8181
Arabic daily. Editor: Othman Al-Omeir

The Asian
19 Parkleigh Road, London SW19 3BS
Fax 0181-543 4356   Tel 0181-543 4356
Fortnightly. Editor: Adnan Khan

The Asian Age
Suite 4, 55 Park Lane, London W1Y 3DB
Fax 0171-304 4029   Tel 0171-304 4028
Daily. Editor: M Hebbar

The Asian Express
211 Piccadilly, London W1V 9LD
Fax 0171-537 2141   Tel 0171-439 8985
Fortnightly. Editor: Vallabh Kaviraj

Asian Herald
20 Orchard Avenue, London N14 4ND
                          Tel 0181-991 9735
Quarterly. Editor: S Mazumdar

Asian Times
141-149 Fonthill Road, London N4 3HF
Fax 0171-263 9656   Tel 0171-281 1191
Weekly. Editor: Arif Ali

Asian Trader
1 Silex Street, London SE1 0DW
Fax 0171-261 0055   Tel 0171-928 1234
English/Gujarati/Urdu fortnightly. Editor: R C Solanki

Awaze Quam
Gate 2, Unit 5B, Booth Street, Smethwick,
Birmingham B66 2PF
Fax 0121-555 5874   Tel 0121-555 5921
Weekly. Editor: Narinder Singh

Black Perspective
PO Box 246, London SE13 7DL
Fax 0181-671 9267   Tel 0181-692 6986
Bimonthly.

Caribbean Times
141-149 Fonthill Road, London N4 3HF
Fax 0171-263 9656   Tel 0171-281 1191
Weekly. Editor: Arif Ali

Daily Dawn
62 Melbourne Avenue, London N13 4SX
Fax 0181-888 7553   Tel 0181-889 3408
British correspondent: Athar Ali

The Daily Jang
1 Sanctuary Street, London SE1 1ED
Fax 0171-378 1653   Tel 0171-403 5833
Urdu daily. Editor: Zahoor Niazi

Daily Millat
2 Baynes Close, Enfield, Middlesex EN1 4BN
Fax 0181-367 6941   Tel 0181-366 5082
Press correspondent: S Mustafa

Desbarata
170 Brick Lane, London E1 6RU
Fax 0171-377 1582   Tel 0171-377 1584
Bengali fortnightly. Editor: G H Khan

Diaspora
7 Thorpe Close, London W10 5XL
Fax 0181-521 6139   Tel 0181-521 6139
Quarterly. Contact: Tahira Khan

Eastern Eye
148 Cambridge Heath Road, London E1 5QJ
Fax 0171-702 7937   Tel 0171-702 8012
Weekly news for the Asian community. Editor: Sarwar Ahmed

The Filipino
28 Brookside Road, Golders Green, London
NW11 9NE
Fax: 0181-731 7195   Tel 0181-731 7195
Bimonthly.

Garavi Gujarat
1-2 Silex Street, London SE1 0DW
Fax 0171-261 0055   Tel 0171-261 1527
English/Gujarati weekly. Editor: R C Solanki

The Gleaner
176-188 Acre Lane, London SW2 5UL
Fax 0171-326 0794   Tel 0171-733 7014
Weekly Jamaican and Caribbean news. Editor: George Ruddock

Gujarat Samachar/Asian Voice/Asian Business
8-16 Coronet Street, London N1 6HD
Fax 0171-739 0358   Tel 0171-729 5453
Gujarati/English weekly.

Hind Samachar
478 Lady Margaret Road, Middlesex UB1 2NW
                          Tel 0181-575 8694
Weekly. Editor: E S Bedi

Hinduism Today
1B Claverton Street, London SW1V 3AY
Fax 0171-630 8688   Tel 0171-630 8688
Monthly. Correspondent: Rakesh K Mathur

Hurriyet
35 D'Arblay Street, London W1V 3FE
Fax 0171-255 1106   Tel 0171-734 1211
Turkish daily. Editor: Faruk Zabci

Impact International
233 Seven Sisters Road, London N4 2BL
Fax 0171-272 8934   Tel 0171-263 1417
Monthly Muslim news. Editor: Ahmad Irfan

India-Home and Abroad
1 Park Close, London NW2 6RQ
                          Tel 0181-452 4182
Quarterly. Editor: K K Singh

India Link International
42 Farm Avnue, North Harrow, Middx HA2 7LR
Fax 0181-728 5250   Tel 0181-866 8421
Monthly. Editor: Krishan Ralleigh

India Mail
150A Ealing Road, Wembley, Middx HA0 4PY
Fax 0181-903 2156   Tel 0181-900 1757
Weekly. Editor: Shiv Sharma

India Weekly
8 Charterhouse Buildings, Goswell Road,
London EC1M 7AH
Fax 0171-251 3289   Tel 0171-251 3290
Weekly. Editor: Iqbal Singh

Irish Post
464 Uxbridge Road, Hayes, Middx UB4 0SP
Fax 0181-561 3047   Tel 0181-561 0059
Weekly. Editor: Donal Mooney

Irish World
307A High Road, London NW10 2JY
Fax 0181-459 1802   Tel 0181-451 6606
Weekly. Editor: Damien Gaffney

Janomot
Unit 2, 20B Spelman Street, London E1 5LQ
Fax 0171-247 0141   Tel 0171-377 6032
Bengali weekly. Editor: Syed Samadul Haque

The Leader
2 Baynes Close, Enfield, Middlesex EN1 4BN
Fax 0181-367 6941   Tel 0181-366 5082
Editor: Syed Mustafa

London Dayori
14 Market Place, Bedale, North Yorks DL8 1EQ
Fax 01677-422375   Tel 1677-426300
Monthly. Features editor: Catherine Pollitt

Mauritian International
PO Box 4100, London SW20 0XN
Fax 0181-947 1912   Tel 0181-947 1912
Quarterly. Editor: Jacques K Lee

Mauritius News
583 Wandsworth Road, London SW8 8JD
Fax 0171-498 3066   Tel 0171-498 3066
Monthly. Editor: Peter Chellen

Milap Weekly
59-61 Broughton Road, London SW6 2LA
                          Tel 0171-385 8966
Urdu weekly. Editor: R Soni

The Muslim News
PO Box 380, Harrow, Middlesex HA2 6LL
Fax 0171-831 0830   Tel 0171-831 0428
Monthly. Editor: Ahmad J Versi

Navin Weekly
59-61 Broughton Road, London SW6 2LA
                          Tel: 0171-385 8966
Editor: Ramesh Kumar

Naya Padkar
Popin Building, South Way, Middlesex HA9 0HB
Fax 0181-795 0967   Tel 0181-795 0050
Editor: Indra Patel

New Horizon
144-146 King's Cross House, London WC1X
9DH
Fax 0171-278 4797   Tel 0171-833 8275
Monthly Arab and Muslim news. Editor: Ghazanfar Ali

New Impact
Anser House, Marlow, Bucks SL7 3HD
Fax 01628-481581   Tel 01628-481581
Bimonthly. Managing director: Elaine Sihera

New World
234 Holloway Road, London N7 6NA
Fax 0171-607 6706   Tel 0171-700 2673
Weekly news on international affairs. Editor: Dhiren Basu

Newsasia
270 Romford Road, London E7 9HZ
Fax 0181-519 3977   Tel 0181-519 3000
English/Urdu weekly. Editor: Shaheen Sultana

Nigerian News
23 Aberdeen Court, London W9 1AF
Fax 0171-266 4057   Tel 0171-266 4564
Fortnightly. Editor: Olubiyi Ayodeji

Pahayagan
49 Connaught Street, London W2BB
                          Tel 0171-402 6917
Filipino bimonthly. Editor: C Pedrosa

Parikiaki
534A Holloway Road, London N7 6JP
Fax 0171-281 0127   Tel 0171-272 6777
Weekly. Editor: Kyriacos Tsioupras

Pazar
97 Kingsland High Street, London E8 2PB
Fax 0171-275 7200   Tel 0171-275 7400
Turkish weekly.

Perdesan Monthly
478 Lady Margaret Road, Middlesex UB1 2PT
Fax 0181-575 8659   Tel 0181-575 8694
Monthly. Editor: G K Bedi

Pride Magazine
370 Coldharbour Lane, London SW9 8PL
Fax 0171-274 8994   Tel 0171-737 5559
Bimonthly. Editor: Deidre Forbes

Probashi Samachar
20 Orchard Avenue, London N14 4ND
                          Tel 0181-886 4231
Bengali quarterly. Editor: S Mazumdar

Punjab Mail
66 Dames Road, London E7 0DR
Fax 0181-519 5239   Tel 0181-519 5239
Monthly. Editor: Gurdip Singh Sandhu

Punjab Times International
30 Shaftesbury Street South, Derby DE23 8YH
Fax 01332 372833   Tel 01332 372851
Weekly. Editor: Daljit Singh Virk

The Punjabi Guardian
129 Soho Road, Birmingham B21 9ST
Fax 0121-567 1065   Tel 0121-554 3995
Monthly. Editor: Inder Jit Singh Sangha

Q News International
40/41 Conduit Street, London W1R 9FB
Fax 0171-734 4891   Tel 071-734 4887
Weekly. Editor: Fuad Nahdi

Ravi News Weekly
Unit E1, Legrams Lane, Bradford BD7 1NS
Fax 01274-721227   Tel 01274-721227
Urdu weekly. Editor: Farida Sheikh

Respect
PO Box 394, Reading RG6 2HH
Fax 01734-313818   Tel 01734 869283
Quarterly. Editor: Adrian Grant

Sagar Pare
5 Avondale Crescent, Iford, Essex 1GF 5JB
                          Tel 0181-550 4697
Bengali bimonthly. Editor: H Bhattacharya

Scottish Asian Voice
106 Tradestone Street, Glasgow G5 8EF
Fax 0141-429 6663   Tel 0141-429 6661
Fortnightly. Editor: Imran Muneer

Shang Ye Xian Feng
194 Old Brompton Road, London SW5 0AW
Fax 0171-370 6245   Tel 0171-835 2183
Chinese bimonthly. Editor: Emile Bekheit

The Sikh Courier International
88 Mollinson Way, Middlesex HA8 5QW
                          Tel 0181-952 1215
Quarterly. Editors: A S Chatwal/S S Kapoor

Sing Tao (UK)
46 Dean Street, London W1V 5AP
Fax 0171-734 0828   Tel 0171-287 1525
Chinese daily. Editor: S T Wan

Siyu
Chinese Information Centre, 16 Nicholas Street,
Manchester M1 4EJ
Fax 0161-228 3739   Tel 0161-228 0420
Chinese magazine. Editors: Jamie Kenny/Juliet Zhou

Surma
40 Wessex Street, London E2 0LB
Fax 0181-981 8829   Tel 0181-980 5544
Bengali weekly. Editor: Ayesha Ahmed

Ta Nea
8-10 Stamford Hill, London N16 8XS
Fax 0181-806 0160   Tel 0181-806 0169
Fortnightly. Editor: Louis Vrakas

Teamwork
WISC 5 Westminster Bridge Road, London SE1
7XW
Fax 0171-928 0343   Tel 0171-928 7861
Bimonthly. Editor: W Trant

La Voce Degli Italiani
20 Brixton Road, London SW9 6BU
Fax 0171-793 0385   Tel 0171-735 5164
Fortnightly. Editor: P Gaetano Parolin

The Voice
370 Coldharbour Lane, London SW9 8PL
Fax 0171-274 8994   Tel 0171-737 7377
Weekly for Black British. Editor: Winsome Cornish

Watan Wekend
Unit K, Middlesex Business Centre, Bridge
Road, Middlesex UB2 4AB
Fax 0181-831 8822   Tel 0181-893 5449
Urdu.

Weekly Des Pardes
8 The Crescent, Southall Middlesex
UB1 1BE
Fax 0181-571 2604   Tel 0181-571 1127
Weekly. Editor: Mr Virk

The Weekly Journal
370 Coldharbour Lane, London SW9 8PL
Fax 0171-924 0134   Tel 0171-737 7377
News for Black professionals. Editor: Richard Adeshiyan

The **Guardian**

arts
D I R E C T O R Y
1 9 9 6

This is the companion directory to The Media Guide packed with detailed information on the arts world: theatre, dance, classical music, jazz, museums, art galleries, photography, film, tv, architecture, literature – the what, the why, the who, the whereabouts – over 3,000 contact points. Indispensable.

Publication date: 1 January 1996

A **Guardian Book**

PUBLISHED BY FOURTH ESTATE LTD.   EDITED BY PAUL FISHER
PRICE £9.99 PAPERBACK

MAGAZINES

Over the past ten years the number of magazines being published has increased by nearly 75 per cent. There are, according to the Periodical Publishers Association, 7,792 magazines of which 5,362 it classifies as "business and professional" and 2,430 as consumer.

Among consumer magazines, some sort of TV connection is the surest circulation builder with five of the top-ten best selling mags based, being primarily listings of television programmes. BBC Publishing, much to the chagrin of other publishers, continues a lucrative trade in allying gardening, food, antiques and music broadcasts to its mags.

The growth of other parts of the magazine sector is due to several factors, most crucially that desk top publishing has brought down costs so that tiny niche markets yield profit from what would once have been impossibly small circulations and ad revenues. There are other reasons too and these were spelt out in a recent report the PPA commissioned from the Henley Centre. This claimed mags are sources of cohesion in an uncertain world and argued: "The traditional structures in society which segmented and distinguished between groups of individuals such as age, gender, class and religion are increasingly being overlaid by smaller groupings based on individual taste and interest." The Henley Centre reckons that when consumerism, the declining influence of authority figures and social mobility are factored in, the public is ripe for ever more specialist mags. Some of this is marketing fantasy dignified by sociology-speak. However, magazine publishers were the first in the media to systematically target particular audiences and, if it's true that society is becoming more fragmented, they could well profit by further fragmentation. Others too will get in on this act with "narrowcast" TV using the 500 digital channels to go for tightly specific audiences.

Trade magazines, the hidden underbelly of British journalism, have known the tricks of specialisation for years. They are places where many journalists serve excellent de facto apprenticeships at the beginning of their careers and where, amongst senior staff, there is often deep knowledge of specialist markets. And the obscure trade press has other claims to importance. Ian Locks, the PPA head, says: "Business magazines are uniquely placed to monitor economic confidence." He says their recruitment and advertising sales immediately reflect changes in business confidence and are a far swifter economic indicator than government statistics. It is part of magazine publishers' folklore that the Cabinet Office logs recruitment ads as a short-term economic predictor.

Magazine publishing, so the cliche has it, is a volatile business. Take Emap, Reed Elsevier's closest rival. As the Print Chronicle notes on pages 17 and 18, January was all gloom for Emap with the £8 million closure (or crash as every headline writer put it) of Carweek. But December had been all joy with the purchase of UK Press Gazette and the advertising directory Brad. Emap was already publisher of Broadcast and Media Week so it has now cornered the speicalist media market.

Emap, like so many other media owners, is diversifying out of print. It is already the second largest commercial radio operator in the UK and the relaxation of cross-media ownership rules make it likely the group will double its holdings. Reed Elsevier, the two year old Anglo Dutch company which is Britain's largest magazine publisher, has other tactics.

In mid-July Reed Elsevier put a for sale sign over the less profitable parts of its consumer publishing business. Although it will hang on to IPC Magazines, the group announced that it intends concentrating on what it calls "business-to-business publishing". These interests include some of the world's biggest medical, scientific and legal publishers. Reed, in the spirit of diversification into high tech, has also made a significant investment into on-line publishing with the £1.5 billion purchase of the American legal and business information service Lexis-Nexis.

For all the repositioning activities, confidence is high among magazine publishers. "The recession is over as far as we're concerned," said the IPC Magazines chairman John Mellon. He was reporting £600 million profits for Reed Elsevier during 1994 up 23 per cent in for consumer magazines and 60 per cent for business magazines.

Further details of magazines about the media start on pages 119 (the press) and 217 (broadcasting). This section continues with a chart of the best selling mags, then addresses and details of main magazine publishers and then the phone numbers of the most significant magazines.

Top selling magazines

1	Readers Digest	1,673,306
2	What's On TV	1,633,010
3	Take a Break *	1,508,000
4	Radio Times	1,463,942
5	TV Times	1,015,141
6	Bella *	981,000
7	Woman	812,211
8	Woman's Weekly	798,177
9	Woman's Own	795,293
10	TV Quick *	728,000
11	Prima	618,870
12	Viz	571,295
13	Best	564,233
14	Chat	541,423
15	Good Housekeeping	518,435
16	People's Friend	479,582
17	Hello	476,551
18	Candis	476,400
19	Cosmopolitan	460,582
20	BBC Good Food	438,715
21	Woman & Home	435,521
22	Marie Claire	430,622
23	My Weekly	423,812
24	More!	414,081
25	Essentials	383,676
26	Auto Trader	381,455
27	Cable Guide	351,795
28	Woman's Realm	351,164
29	Puzzler Collection	349,201
30	House Beautiful	325,915
31	Family Circle	313,512
32	Sainsbury's: The Magazine	312,440
33	The Economist	311,882
34	Company	305,592
35	Smash Hits	302,314
36	Weekly News	293,936
37	Homes & Ideas	285,378
38	Fiesta	283,690
39	She	281,109
40	Big	280,557
41	BBC Gardeners' World	275,185
42	Just Seventeen	269,513
43	Puzzler	263,086
44	New Woman	257,024
45	Elle (UK)	230,996
46	Looks	226,080
47	Ideal Home	215,659
48	Q	204,185
49	TV Hits	203,424
50	19	203,163
51	Yours	202,327
52	Mizz	195,191
53	Country Living	190,717
54	Vogue	186,555
55	Private Eye	186,124
56	Match	185,390
57	Homes & Gardens	183,561
58	The Garden	182,752
59	RTE Guide	182,133
60	TV & Satellite Week	179,051
61	OK! Magazine	172,150
62	NEXT Magazine	169,699
63	Slimming	160,538
64	Shoot	160,387
65	House & Garden	159,942
66	Options	158,315
67	Woman's Journal	157,391
68	Sky Magazine	155,133
69	Easy Finder	153,562
70	Hair	151,408
71	Clothes Show	150,256
72	Sayidaty	149,200
73	Top Sante Health & Beauty	148,064
74	Live & Kicking	146,627
75	Asharq Al Awsat Magazine	145,625
76	Computer Shopper	144,005
77	Empire	141,244
78	Shout	137,784
79	Top Gear	137,720
80	Moneywise	134,698
81	Motor Cycle News	132,852
82	Manchester UNITED Magazine	131,576
83	Living	131,296
84	Country Homes and Interiors	128,348
85	What Car?	127,041
86	Choice	126,799
87	GQ	126,227
88	Camping and Caravanning	121,576
89	Al Majalla	118,416
90	Garden Answers	118,365
91	BBC Wildlife	117,859
92	Inside Soap	116,734
93	New Musical Express	113,788
94	New Scientist	113,441
95	Practical Parenting	112,422
96	Vox	112,402
97	Maxpower	112,266
98	Times Educational Supplement	111,887
99	Angling Times	111,196
100	Esquire	110,583
101	Amiga Format	108,144
102	Time Out	107,745
103	BBC Homes and Antiques	107,344
104	Car	106,223
105	PC Plus	105,225
106	Knave	105,190
107	Word Search	105,033
108	Guardian Weekly	104,688
109	Mother and Baby	103,588
110	Soccer Stars	103,502
111	Shooting and Conservation	103,438
112	The Big Issue	102,142

ABC: July-December 1994/ * non-ABC audited H Bauer titles

MAGAZINE PUBLISHERS

Academy Group
42 Leinster Gardens, London W2 3AN
Fax 0171-423 9540   Tel 0171-402 2141
60 books and magazines, including:

Architectural Design	Art & Design
Journal of Philosophy and the Visual Arts	

Aceville Publications
97 High Street, Colchester, Essex CO1 1TH
Fax 01206-564214   Tel 01206-540621
Some 20 hobby and leisure magazines, including:

Classic Car Mart	Guns & Shooting
Model & Collectors Mart	Telecard Collector

Aim Publications
31 Beak Street, London W1R 3LD
Fax 0171-434 5383   Tel 0171-437 3493

You & Your Wedding	Dresses for Brides

Argus Press
2 Queensway, Redhill, Surrey RH1 1QS
Fax 01737-760510   Tel 01737-768611
One of Britain's large groups, with around 90 titles covering many topics. Divisions: Argus Business Publications with over 50 trade journals; and Argus Consumer Magazines with around 30 consumer publications.

Company Car	Exhibition Management
Fire/Fire International	Fish Trader
Frozen & Chilled Foods	Glass/Glazing Today
International Broadcast Engineer	International Security Review
Aeromodeller	Citizens Band
Ham Radio Today	Model Boats
Model Engineer	Model Railways
Popular Crafts	Practical Wargamer
Radio Control	Radio Modeller
Steam Classic	Woodworker

Attic Futura
4 Tottenham Mews, London W1P 9PJ
Fax 0171-580 8504   Tel 0171-636 5095

Hit Movies	Inside Soap
TV Hits	Sugar

Auto Trader
Unit 5, 50 Windsor Avenue, London SW19 2TJ
Fax 0181-540 6029   Tel 0181-543 7616
Publishes the 12 regional editions of Auto Trader. Owned 50 per cent by the Guardian Media Group.

H Bauer Publishing
Shirley House, 25/27 Camden Road, London NW1 9LL
Fax 0171-284 3641   Tel 0171-284 0909

Bella	TV Quick
Take a Break	Take a Puzzle

BBC Worldwide Publishing
Woodlands, 80 Wood Lane, London W12 0TT
Fax 0181-749 0538   Tel 0181-576 2000
BBC Magazines is a division of BBC Worldwide. It produces a variety of magazines including:

Gardeners World	Good Food
Wildlife	Homes & Antiques
Sports	Vegetarian Good Food
Clothes Show	BBC Music Magazine
Radio Times	Alive & Kicking
Wildlife Magazine	Toy Box

Benn Business Publishing
Sovereign Way, Tonbridge, Kent TN9 1RW
Fax 01732-361534   Tel 01732-364422
A subsidiary of the Miller Freeman section of United News and Media, Benn specialises in business, trade and professional magazines. Divisions include: Benn Business Information Services (annual directories), Benn Publications and Spotlight Publications. Its 70+ titles include:

Chemist and Druggist	DIY Week
Housewares	Leather
Music Business	Music Week
Packaging Week	Paper
Printing World	Studio Sound
Timber Trades Journal	Video Retailer

Blackwell Publishers
108 Cowley Road, Oxford, Oxon OX4 1J
Fax 01865-791347   Tel 01865-791100
Publisher of humanities and social science journals and learning materials.

Blackwell Scientific Publications
Osney Mead, Oxford, Oxon OX2 0EL
Fax 01865-721205   Tel 01865-206206
Specialists in technical, medical, scientific and academic journals.

BMJ Publishing Group
BMA House, Tavistock Square, London WC1H 9JR
Fax 0171-383 6668   Tel 0171-387 4499

BMA News Review	British Dental Journal
British Medical	Journal Health Visitor

British European Associated Publishers
Glenthorne House, Hammersmith Grove, London W6 0LG
Fax 0181-741 7762   Tel 0181-846 9922
BEAP is a subsidiary of VNU and publishes puzzle magazines, including:

Celebrity Crosswords	Cross Reference
Kriss Kross	Popular Crosswords
The Puzzler	Word Search

Builder Group
1 Millharbour, London E14 9RA
Fax 0171-537 6004   Tel 0171-537 2222
French-owned company, publishing construction and security
magazines including:

Building	Building Economist
Building Services	Electrical Contractor
OPUS	RIBA Journal

Butterworth-Heinemann
Linacre House, Jordan Hill, Oxford OX2 8DP
Fax 91865-310898   Tel 01865-310366
Part of Reed Elsevier and publisher of some 90 technical
journals.

Caledonian Magazines
Plaza Tower, East Kilbride, Glasgow G74 1LW
Fax 01355-263013   Tel 01355-246444
The former George Outram & Co, whose titles include:

Climber	The Great Outdoors
The Scottish Farmer	

Cambridge University Press
Edinburgh Building, Shaftesbury Road,
Cambridge, Cambs CB2 2RU
Fax 01223-315052   Tel 01223-312393
Publisher of over 120 academic journals.

Carfax Publishing Co
PO Box 25, Abingdon, Oxfordshire OX14 3UE
Fax 01235-553559   Tel 01235-555335
Publishes around 130 academic titles. One of the largest social
science publishers, now expanding into scietific, technical and
medical publishing.

Catholic Herald
Herald House, Lambs Passage Bunhill Row,
London EC1Y 8TQ
Fax 0171-256 9728   Tel 0171-588 3101

Catholic Herald	Catholic Standard

Centaur Communications
50 Poland Street, London W1V 4AX
Fax 0171-734 1120   Tel 0171-439 4222
Around 15 business titles, including:

Amusement Business	Creative Review
Design Week	The Lawyer
Leisure Week	Marketing Week
Precision Marketing	Televisual

Chapman and Hall
2 Boundary Row, London SE1 8HN
Fax 0171-522 9623   Tel 0171-865 0066
A subsidiary of the Thomson Corporation, producing specialist
technical and scientific journals, including:

Applied Economics	Evolutionary Ecology
Journal of Materials Science	Materials and Structures

Combined Service Publications
PO Box 4, Farnborough, Hants GU14 7LR
Fax 01252-517918   Tel 01252-515891
Military specialists, producing many British Army regimental
journals, plus:
Forces Weekly Echo

Conde Nast Publications
Vogue House, Hanover Square, London W1R
OAD
Fax 0171-493 1345   Tel 0171-499 9080
The US-owned publisherof lifestyle magazines such as:

Brides	GQ
House & Garden	Tatler
Vanity Fair	Vogue
World of Interiors	

Consumers Association
2 Marylebone Road, London NW1 4DX
Fax 0171-830 6220   Tel 0171-486 5544
The campaigning body for consumers. It produces five
magazines, including its flagship monthly Which?

Croner Publications
Croner House, London Road, Kingston-upon-
Thames, Surrey KT2 6SR
Fax 0181-547 2637   Tel 0181-547 3333
Publishes a range of reference guides on technical and business
topics. Owned by the Dutch company Wolters Kluwer (0171-603
4688).

Dennis Publishing
19 Bolsover Street, London W1P 7HJ
Fax 0171-636 5668   Tel 0171-631 1433
Specialises in consumer and business to business magazines,
also heavy metal, men's and one to one titles, with 16
publications, including:

Computer Shopper	Game Zone
Hi-Fi Choice	Home Entertainment
Mac User	Microscope
Windows Magazine	Zero

Economist Newspaper
25 St James's Street, London SW1A 1HG
Fax 0171-930 3092   Tel 0171-830 7000
Part of the Pearson Group.
Titles include:

Business Central	Europe Commmunicate
The Economist	

Elsevier Science Publishers
The Bouledvard, Langford Lane,Kidlington,
Oxon OX5 1GB
Fax 01865-843971   Tel 01865-843000
Part of Reed Elsevier, ESP works closely with the fellow
subsidiary of Pergamon Press and publishes over 400 technical
journals for industry, science and academia.

Emap
1 Lincoln Court, Lincoln Road, Peterborough,
Cambs PE1 2RF
Fax 01733-62636   Tel 0733-68900
Emap has two magazine divisions.

Emap Business Communications
21 John Street, London WC1N 2BP
Fax 0171-831 3540   Tel 0171-404 5513
About 100 titles are published by eight subsidiaries.
Architecture/Communications
0171-837 1212
Business/Sea fishing/Middle East
0171-404 5513
Computing
0171-388 2430
Fashion
0171-417 2800
Transport
01733-63100
Trade/Retail
0181-688 7788
Finance and Freight
0171-404 5513/071-837 1212/
0171-713 5569/0181-242 3000

Emap Consumer Magazines
Apex House, Oundle Road, Peterborough,
Cambs PE2 9NP.
Fax 01733-898100   Tel 01733-898100
About 90 British titles, are published from seven centres:
Bikes/Cars
01733-237111
Computers/Games
0171-972 6700
Gardens/Cameras/Rail
01733-898100
Health/Parenting/Lifestyle
0171-437 9011
Music/Entertainment
0171-436 1515
Retirement
01733-555123
Sport/Wildlife
01733-264666
Women
0171-957 8383
Emap titles include:

Angling Times	Big!
Elle	Garden News
Here's Health	Homes
Horse & Pony	Just 17
Kerrang!	More
Mother & Baby	Motor Cycle News
Parents	PC Review
Popular Classics	Practical Gardening
Practical Photography	Q
Rail	Sea Angler
Smash Hits	Steam World

Financial Times Group
1 Southwark Bridge, London SE1 9HL
Fax 0171-873 3076   Tel 0171-873 3000
A subsidiary of Pearson, it publishes numerous business
newsletters, plus financial magazines. Its publishing centres are:
Magazines
0171-405 6969
Newsletters
0171-411 4414
The magazines include:

The Banker	Financial Adviser
Investors Chronicle	Money Management

Fleetway Editions
25 Tavistock Place, London WC1H 9SU
Fax 0171-388 4020   Tel 0171-344 6400
A Danish-owned comic publisher with about 19 titles, including:

Buster	Disney Weekly
Judge Dredd	

Frank Cass and Co
890 Eastern Ave, Newbury Park, Ilford, Essex
IG2 7HH
Fax 0181-599 0989   Tel 0181-599 8866
Over 40 specialist academic journals and newsletters on a range
of topics, including: Environmental Politics; Intelligence &
National Security; Journal of Strategic Studies

Future Publishing
Beauford Court, 30 Monmouth Street, Bath,
Avon BA1 2BW
Fax 01225-460709   Tel 01225-442244
A pioneer of the "cover mount" freebie computer disc and (with
Classic CD) the sampler compact disc, Future was recently
bought by Pearson. Titles include:

Amiga Format	Amstrad Action
Commodore Format	Classic CD
Mac Format	MTB Pro
Mountain Biking	PC Answers/Format/Plus
Sega Power	Simply Crafts
Total	Ultimate Future Gamer

G & J of the UK
Portland House, Stag Place, London SW1E 5AU
Fax 0171-630 5509   Tel 0171-245 8700
Publishes the two women's magazines Best and Prima, and the
popular science title Focus.

Gordon and Breach Science Publishers
PO Box 90, Reading, Berks RG1 8JL
Fax 01734-568211   Tel 01734-560080
Publishes over 150 scientific and academic journals and
newsletters.

Gramophone Publications
177-179 Kenton Road, Harrow, Middlesex HA3
0HA
Fax 0181-907 0073   Tel 0181-907 4476
Publishes The Gramophone.

Harcourt Brace
24 Oval Road, London NW1 7DX
Fax 0171-482 2293   Tel 0171-267 4466
American-owned company, with the subsidiary Academic Press publishing over 90 technical journals, mainly medical and biological.

Haymarket Group
22 Lancaster Gate, London W2 3LY
Fax 0181-413 4503   Tel 0181-943 5000
Publishes 40 of the leading business, medical and consumer magazines, from offices at Lancaster Gate and Teddington (both on the same phone number).
Titles include:

Autocar	Business Express
Campaign	Four Four Two
General Practitioner	Horticulture Week
Management Today	Marketing
MIMS	Newspaper Focus
Planning Week	PrintWeek
PR Week	What Hi-Fi?
What Car?	

Hello!
Wellington House, 69-71 Upper Ground, London SE1 9PQ
Fax 0171-334 7411   Tel 0171-334 7404
Publishes Hello!

HMSO (Her Majesty's Stationery Office)
Publishing Division, PO Box 276, London SW8 5DT
Fax 0171-873 8200   Tel 0171-873 9090
Publishers of official magazines, reports and books. Magazines include:

Economic Trends	Employment Gazette
Hansard	London Gazette
Monthly Digest of Statistics	

Ian Allan
Coombelands House, Coombelands Lane, Addlestone, Surrey KT15 1HY
Fax 01932-854750   Tel 01932-855909
A publisher of popular transport magazines and books including:

Aircraft Illustrated	Buses
Light Rail & Modern Tramway	Modern Railways
Railway World	Steam Days

IDG Communications
99 Grays Inn Road, London WC1X 8UT
Fax 0171-414 0262   Tel 0171-831 9252
A publisher of computer titles including:

Acorn User	CD Rom Now
MacWorld	PC Works

Illustrated London News Group
20 Upper Ground, London SE1 9PF
Fax 0171-620 1594   Tel 0171-928 2111

Blue Riband	Natural World
Illustrated London News	Island Visitor

IML Group
184 High Street, Tonbridge, Kent TN9 1BQ
Fax 01732-770049   Tel 01732-359990
24 technical and business titles, including:
Business Equipment Digest   Electronic Product Design

International Business Communications
56 Mortimer Street, London W1N 7TD
Fax 0171-631 3214   Tel 0171-637 4383
Specialise in agriculture, business and technical magazines and newsletters. Its subsidiaries include Agra Europe and Fleet Street Publications. IBC's 50+ titles include:

Currency Confidential	Dairy Markets Weekly
Eurofood	Fleet Street Letter
Food Policy International	Penny Share Guide
Stockmarket Confidential	

IPC Magazines
King's Reach Tower, Stamford Street, London SE1 9LS
Fax 0171-261 6023   Tel.0171-261 5000
This subsidiary of Reed Elsevier and Britain's largest publisher of consumer and leisure magazines.
The weeklies include:

Amateur Gardening	Amateur Photographer
Angler's Mail	Country Life
Cycling Weekly	Horse and Hound
Me	Melody Maker
New Musical Express	New Scientist
Shoot	TV & Satellite Week
TV Times	What's on TV
Woman	Woman's Own
Woman's Realm	Woman's Weekly

IPC's monthly magazines include:

Chat	Classic Cars
Family Circle	Homes & Gardens
Ideal Home	Living
Marie Claire	Melody Maker
Motor Boat & Yachting	Options
Practical Boat Owner	Practical Parenting
Practical Woodworking	Railway Magazine
Soccer Stars	What's on TV
Woman & Home	Woman's Journal
Yachting Monthly	Yachting World
Your Garden	

John Brown Publishing
The Boathouse, Crabtree Lane, Fulham, London SW6 6LU
Fax 0171-381 6903   Tel 0171-381 6007
Titles include:

Classic FM - The Magazine	Gardens Illustrated
Hot Air	Viz

John Wiley & Sons
Baffins Lane, Chichester, West Sussex PO19 1UD
Fax 01243-775878   Tel 01243-779777
Publishes 120 technical and medical specialist journals.

Link House Magazines
Link House, Dingwall Avenue, Croydon, Surrey
CR9 2TA
Fax 0181-760 0973   Tel 0181-686 2599
Publishes consumer and leisure titles, including:

Camping	Caravan Sites
Car Trade	Country Music International
Hi-Fi News	Model Collector
Mountain Biker International	Prediction
Stamp Magazine	Superbike

Lloyd's of London
Sheepen Place, Colchester, Essex CO3 3LP
Fax 01206-46273   Tel 01206-772277
28 reference and listing titles including:

Business Risk	Lloyd's Ship Manager
Lloyd's List	Lloyd's List Maritme Asia
Internatioal Journal of Insurance Law	

Longman Group
Longman House, burnt Mill, Harlow, Essex
CM20 2JE
Fax 01279-431059   Tel 01279-426721
Subsidiary of Pearson, publishing journals, directories and year-
books, including:

Business Education Today	Company Lawyer
English Historical Review	Education
International Media Law	Solicitors Journal

Macmillan Magazines
Porters South, Crinan Street, London N1 9SQ
Fax 0171-379 4204   Tel 0171-833 4000
Publishes nearly 30 magazines and journals, mainly medical and
technical, including:

Community Outlook	Nature
Nursing Times	Therapy Weekly

The Magazine Business
8 Tottenham Mews, London W1P 9PJ
Fax 0171-436 5290   Tel 0171-436 5211
Titles include:
International Press Directory Magazine Business Weekly Report

Mark Allen Publishing
288 Croxted Road, London SE24 9BY
Fax 0181-671 1722   Tel 0181-671 7521
SMedical titles, including:

British Journal of Hospital Medicine	Hospital Magazine
British Journal of Nursing	Practice Nursing

Miller Freeman
30 Calderwood Street, London SE18 6QH
Fax 0181-854 7476   Tel 0181-855 7777
A subsidiary of United Newspapers, it publishes 100 business,
technical, trade, construction and farming titles, including:

Building Design	Cabinet Maker
Chemist & Druggist	DIY Week
Electronics Times	The Engineer
Estates Times	Farming News
Packaging Week	Printing World

Morgan-Grampian
see Miller Freeman

National Geogaphic Society
16 The Pines, Broad Street, Guildford, Surrey
GU3 3NX
Fax 01483-506331   Tel 01483-577235
Publishes National Geographic

National Magazine Company
72 Broadwick Street, London W1V 2BP
Fax 0171-437 6886   Tel 0171-439 5000
USA-owned company publishing 8 titles:

Company	Cosmopolitan
Country Living	Esquire
Good Housekeeping	Harpers & Queen
House Beautiful	SHE

Newsweek International
Key West, 53/61 Windsor Road, Slouth, Berks
SL1 2EH
Fax 01753-571617   Tel 01753-524552
Newsweek   Newsweek Atlantic

Nexus Media
Warwick House, Swanley, Kent BR8 8HY
Fax 01322 667633   Tel 01322 660070
A business publisher titles include:

Architects Actionfile	Cabling World
Network Europe	The Probe

Oxford University Press
Walton Street, Oxford OX2 6DP
Fax 01865-56646   Tel 01865-56767
Publishes 145 academic journals.

Paul Raymond Publications
2 Archer Street, London W1V 7HE
Fax 0171-734 5030   Tel 0171-734 9191
Britain's biggest publisher of sex magazines, including:
Mayfair   Men Only

Pearson
See: Financial Times and Longman Group

Pergamon Press
Headington Hill Hall, Oxford OX3 0BW
Fax 01865-60285   Tel 01865-843000
See Elsevier Science Publishers, above.

Reader's Digest Association
Berkeley Square, London W1X 6AB
Fax 0171-499 9751   Tel 0171-629 8144
Reader's Digest

Redwood Publishing
12 Lexington Street, London W1R 4HQ
Fax 0171-312 2601   Tel 0171-312 2600
From 1988 to 1994 Redwood was majority owned by the BBC,
publishing several leading BBC magazines. In July 1994 AMV

bought the company. Redwood is now a contract publisher, with clients including: AA, Abbey National, BSkyB, Boots,English Heritage, Harvey Nichols, Intercity, Marks & Spencer, PSION, Unisys, Volvo, Woolworths.

Reed Business Publishing
Quadrant House, The Quadrant, Sutton, Surrey SM2 5AS
Fax 0181-652 8932   Tel 0181-652 3500
Britain's largest business publisher with titles, including

Caterer & Hotel Keeper	Utility Week
Commercial Motor	Community Care
Computer Weekly	Construction
Electrical Times	Electronics Weekly
Flight International	Media International
The Motor Ship	Motor Trader
Optician	Poultry World
Railway Gazette International	Super Marketing
Surveyor	Television

Reed Elsevier
6 Chesterfield Gardens, London W1A 1EJ
Fax 0171-491 8212   Tel 0171-499 4020
In January 1993 Reed and the Dutch group Elsevier set up Reed Elsevier plc to create one of the world's biggest publishing companies employing over 25,000 people. The main UK magazine divisions (listed elswhere in this section) are:
   Butterworth-Heinemann
   Elsevier Science Publishers,
   IPC Magazines
   Reed Business Publishing,

Routledge
11 New Fetter Lane, London EC4P 4EE
Fax 0171-583 0701   Tel 0171-583 9855
A subsidiary of the Thomson Corporation. Journals include:

British Journal of Sociology	Feminist Review
Social History	World Archaeology

Saga Publishing
The Saga Building, Middleburg Square, Folkestone, Kent CT20 1AZ
Fax 01303-220391   Tel 01303-711527
Magazines for the retired.

Sage Publications
6 Bonhill Street, London EC2A 4PU
Fax 0171-374 8741   Tel 0171-374 0645
Publishes 100 academic/technical newsletters and journals.

Statesman and Nation Publishing Co
Foundation House, Perseverance Works, 38 Kingsland Road, London E2 8DQ
Fax 0171-739 9307   Tel 0171-739 3211
Publishes New Statesman & Society

Sterling Publishing Group
86 Edgware Road, London W2 2YW
Fax 0171-402 1468   Tel 0171-258 0066
Publishes 50 technical and business journals and directories.

Sweet and Maxwell
183 Marsh Wall, London E14 9FT
Fax 0171-538 8625   Tel 0171-538 8686
The legal publishing subsidiary of the Thomson Corporation

Civil Justice Quarterly	Criminal Law Review
Current Law	European Law Review
Housing Law Reports	Law Librarian
Law Teacher	Public Law

Taylor and Francis
4 John Street, London WC1N 2ET
Fax 0171-831 2035   Tel 0171-400 3500
Over 100 scientific and technical newsletters and journals.

Thomas Telford
1 Heron Quay, Isle of Dogs, London E14 4JD
Fax 0171-538 5746   Tel 0171-987 6999
Thomas Telford is wholly owned by the Institution of Civil Engineers and publishes technical magazines, including:
Magazine of Concrete Research

New Builder	New Civil Engineer
Water & Environmental Management	

DC Thomson and Co
2 Albert Square, Dundee, Tayside DD1 9QJ
Fax 01382-222214   Tel 01382-223131
Publishes 12 titles, including:

My Weekly	Beano
Bunty	Dandy
Shout	Peoples Friend

Thomson Corporation
180 Wardour Street, London W1A 4YG
Fax 0171-734 0561   Tel 0171-437 9787
The magazine publishing subsidiary of the Thomson Corporation of Canada. Its main UK divisions are:
   Sweet and Maxwell
   Chapman and Hall
   Routledge

Time Out
Universal House, 251 Tottenham Court Road, London W1P 0AB
Fax 0171-813 6001   Tel 0171-813 3000
Publishes Time Out

Time Life International
Brettenham House, Lancaster Place, London WC2E 7TL
Fax 0171-499 9377   Tel 0171-499 4080
publishes Time magazine

Times Supplements
66 East Smithfield, London E1 9XY
Fax 0171-782 3252   Tel 0171-782 3000
A subsidiary of Murdoch's News International, it publishes:
The Times Educational Supplement
The Times Higher Education Supplement
The Times Literary Supplement
The Times Scottish Education Supplement

Timothy Benn Publishing
244 Temple Chambers, Temple Ave, London
EC4Y 0DT
Fax 0171-353 6867   Tel 0171-583 6463
Publishes a dozen mainly-trade magazines and yearbooks,
including:
British Journal of Photography
Education Equipment   Post Magazine
Sports Retailing   Sports Trader

Tolley Publishing Co
2 Addiscombe Road, Croydon, Surrey CR9 5AF
Fax 0181-760 0588   Tel 0181-686 9141
A business publishing subsidiary of United Newspapers. Titles
include:
Charity World   Pensions World
Taxation   Wholesalers Gazette

TPD Publishing
Long Island House, 1/4 Warple Way, London
W3 0RG
Fax 0181-740 1741   Tel 0181-740 1740
Titles include:
AppleWorld   Dellware
Computer Marketing Intelligence   Open Systems

United News and Media
245 Blackfriars Road, London SE1 9UY
Fax 0171-928 2728   Tel 0171-921 5000
United News and Media (formerly United Newspapers) has a
total of about 120 magazines in Britain, and roughly 150 abroad.
Its main magazine subsidiaries are:
    Benn Business Publishing
    Miller Freeman (formerly Morgan-Grampian)
    Tolley Publishing

VNU Business Publications
32 Broadwick Street, London W1A 2HG
Fax 0171-316 9003   Tel 0171-316 9000
Netherlands-owned company, publishing over 20 magazines,
mainly on computing, including:
Accountancy Age   Computing
Personal Computer Magazine   Personal Computer World
What PC?

Voice Communications Group
370 Coldharbour Lane, London SW9 8PL
Fax 0171-274 8994   Tel 0171-737 7377
Pride   The Voice
The Weekly Journal

Wolters Kluwer (UK)
See Croner Publications, above.

Ziff-Davis UK
Cottons Centre, Hays Lane, London SE1
2QT
Fax 0171-403 0668   Tel 0171-378 6800
PC Direct   PC Magazine
Computer Life

MAGAZINE LISTINGS

Accountancy	0171-833 3291
Accountancy Age	0171-439 4242
Active Life	0171-262 2622
Aeromart	0181-699 9949
Aeroplane Monthly	0171-261 5849
Africa Confidential	0171-831 3511
Africa Events	0171-608 3454
African Affairs	01865-56767
African Review of Business	0171-834 7676
Air Forces Monthly	01780-55131
Air International	01780-55131
Air Mail	0181-994 8504
Air Pictorial	01424-720477
Aircraft Illustrated	01932-228950
Airflash	0114-279 5219
Airliners	01780-55131
Airports International	01892-784099
Airtrade	0181-242 3000
Al Aalam Magazine	0171-608 3454
Al Hawadeth	0181-740 4500
Al Majalla	0171-831 8181
Al Wasat	0171-602 9988
Amar Deep	0181-840 3534
Amateur Gardening	0171-261 2858
Amateur Photographer	0171-261 5020
Amiga Format/Power/Shopper	01225-442244
Amstrad Action	01225-442244
An Phoblacht	01232-624421
Angler's Mail	0171-261 5778
Angling Times	01733-264666
Animal Life/World	01403-264181
Animals	0181-302 1629
Annabel	01382-462276
Anti-Apartheid News	0171-387 7966
Antique	0171-434 9180
Antique Collector	0181-863 2020
Antique Dealer	0181-318 5868
Antiques Bulletin	0121-426 3300
Antiques Trade Gazette	0171-930 7192
Antiquity	01223-333512
Apollo	0171-235 1998
Appropriate Technology	0171-436 9761
Arable Farming	01473-241122
Architects Journal	0171-837 1212
Architectural Review	0171-837 1212
Architecture Today	0171-837 0143
Arena	0171-837 7270
Arguments & Facts International	01424-444142
Ariel	0171-780 4468
Art Business Today	0171-381 6616
Art Monthly	0171-240 0389

Art Quarterly	0171-821 0404	Boardroom Magazine	0171-262 5000
Art Review	0171-978 1000	Body Building Monthly	01482-668325
Artrage	0171-735 2062	Bonhams Auction Guide	0171-393 3900
ArtWork	01651-842429	Book & Magazine Collector	0181-579 1082
Asian Review of Business &Tech.	0171-834 7676	Books in the Media	01494-792269
Asian Times	0171-281 1191	Books in Wales	01970-624151
Asian Voice	0171-729 5453	The Bookseller	0171-836 8911
Asian Weekly	0181-813 9500	Boulevard	01942 31748
Astronomy Now	01908-377559	Bowls International	01780-55131
Atari ST Review/User	0625-878888	Boxing News	0171-734 4784
Athletics Weekly	01733-264666	Brides & Setting Up Home	0171-499 9080
Atom	01235 432520	British Archaeological News	01904-671417
Attitude	0171-987 5090	British Baker	0181-688 7788
Audio Visual	0181-688 7788	British Bike Magazine	01446-775033
Audiophile	0181-943 5000	British Birds	01767-40025
The Author	0171-373 6642	British Dental Journal	0171-387 4499
Auto Express	0171-928 8000	British Farmer	0171-235 5077
Auto Trader	0181-543 2323	British Horse	01203-696697
Autocar & Motor	0181-943 5000	British Journal of Photography	0171-583 3030
The Automobile	01932-864212	British Journalism Review	0171-839 4900
Automotive Management	0181-687 2340	British Medical Journal	0171-387 4499
Autosport	0181-943 5000	British Nationalist	0181-316 4721
Autotrade	0181-855 7777	British Naturism	01604-20361
Autoworld	0181-896 7653	British Printer	0181-242 3000
Aviation News	01908-377559	British Rail News	0171-387 4771
AWOL	01925-757874	Broadcast	0171-837 1212
Baby	0171-226 2222	The Budgerigar	01604-24549
Bad Attitude	0171-978 9057	Building	0171-537 2222
The Banker	0171-405 6969	Building Design	0181-855 7777
Banking World	0171-283 3355	Bunty	01382-23131
BAPLA Journal	0181-444 7913	Burlington Magazine	0171-430 0481
Baptist Times	01235-512012	Bus Fayre	01274-881640
Batman	0171-344 6400	Buses	01932-227399
BBC Gardener's World	0181-576 2000	Business Age	0171-4875057
BBC Good Food	0181-576 2000	Business Equipment Digest	01732-359990
BBC Music Magazine	0181-576 2000	Business Franchise	0181-742 2828
BBC Wildlife	0117 9732211	Business Traveller	0171-229 7799
Beano	01382-23131	Butterfly Conservation	01206-322342
Bedfordshire Magazine	01582-23122	Buy a Boat	01243-533394
Beekeeping & Development	01600-713648	Buying Satellite	0171-485 0011
Bella	0171-284 0909	**Cab Driver**	0171-493 5267
Best	0171-245 8700	Cable & Satellite Europe	0171-351 3612
Big!	0171-436 1515	Cable Television Engineering	0191-281 7094
The Big Issue	0181-741 8090	Cage & Aviary Birds	0171-261 6116
Big Shots	01733-264666	Cambridgeshire Life	01522-77567
Bike	01733-237111	Camcorder User	0171-485 0011
Billboard	0171-323 6686	Campaign	0181-943 5000
Birmingham Sketch Magazine	0121-327 4930	The Campaigner	0181-846 9777
Birmingham What's On	0121-626 6600	Camping & Caravanning	01203-694995
The Biochemist	0171-580 5530	Canal & Riverboat	01372-741411
Biologist	0171-581 8333	Candis	0151-632 3232
Bird Keeper	0171-261 5293	Candour	01730-892109
Bird Life	01767-680551	Canoeist	01235-847270
Bird Watching	01733-264666	Capital Gay	0171-738 7010
Birds	01767-680551	Car	0171-216 6200
Birdwatch	0181-983 1855	Car & Accessory Trader	0181-943 5000
Black Arts in London	0171-254 7295	Car Auction Magazine	01685-721933
Bliss	0131-555 6511	Car Boot Calendar	01734-402165
Blueprint	0171-486 7419	Car Choice	0181-943 5000
Blues & Soul	0171-402 6869	Car Classics	01279-465812

Car Hi-Fi	0181-943 5943		Class War	01272-870050
Car Mechanics	0181-658 3531		Climber & Hill Walker	01355-246444
Car Numbers Magazine	01380-818181		Clothes Show	0181-576 2000
Car Trade	0171-712 0550		Club Mirror	0181-681 2099
Caravan Life	01778-393652		Coastguard	0171-276 5082
Caravan Magazine	0181-686 2599		Coat of Arms	0171-430 2172
Caribbean Times	0171-281 1191		Comagazine	01895-444055
Caribbean World	0171-581 9009		Combat	0121-344 3737
Cars & Car Conversions	0181-686 2599		Combat & Survival	01484-435011
CarSport	01846-619099		Commercial Motor	0181-652 3500
The Cartoonist	0171-916 6760		Common Cause	01460-62972
Casablanca	0171-608 3784		Communications Africa	0171-834 7676
Cash & Carry Management	0181-688 2696		Community Care	0181-652 3500
The Cat	01403-261947		Community Transport Magazine	0161-351 1475
Cat World	01273-462000		Company	0171-439 5000
CataList	0171-381 6007		Company Car	01737-768611
Catch	01382-23131		Complete Car	0171-229 7799
Caterer & Hotelkeeper	0181-652 8680		Computer & Video Games	0171-972 6700
Catering	0181-855 7777		Computer Buyer/Shopper	0171-631 1433
Catholic Herald	0171-588 3101		Computer Weekly	0181-652 3500
Cats	0161-236 0577		Computing	0171-439 4242
Cats Magazine	01273-462000		Connexion	0171-439 4242
Caves & Caving	01278-691539		Conservative Newsline	0171-222 9000
Cage and Aviary Birds	0171 261 5000		Construction News	0171-410 6611
CD-ROM Magazine	0171-631 1433		Construction Today	0171-987 6999
CD-ROM Today	01225-442244		Construction Weekly	0181-652 4642
Central America Report	0171-631 4200		Containerisation International	0171-404 2763
Centrepoint	0181-539 3876		Contract Journal	0181-652 3500
Chat	0171-261 6565		Convenience Store	01293-613400
Checkout	0181-652 3500		Cornish Banner	01726-843501
Cheers	0191-284 2742		Cornish Life	0161-456 1818
Chemical Engineer	0171-987 6999		Cosmopolitan	0171-439 5000
Chemist & Druggist	01732-364422		Counter Culture	0171-373 3432
Chemistry in Britain	0171-437 8656		Country Homes & Interiors	0171-261 6451
Cheshire Magazine	0161-474 1758		Country Landowner	0171-928 1424
Chess	0171-388 2404		Country Life	0171-261 7058
Chic	01923-237799		Country Living	0171-439 5000
China Economic Review	0171-834 7676		Country Music International	0181-686 2599
China Now	01242-226625		Country Music People	0181-692 1106
Choice	01733-555123		Country Quest	01492-531188
Christian Democrat	0151-727 2712		Country Sports	0171-928 4742
Christian Herald	01903-821082		Country Walking	01733-264666
Christian Science Monitor	0181-543 9393		The Countryman	0181-686 2599
Christian Socialist	0181-520 4190		Countryside	01242-521381
Christian Week	0171-430 2572		Countryside Campaigner	0171-976 6433
Church of England News	0171-490 0898		Crafts	0171-278 7700
Church Times	0171-359 4570		Craftsman Magazine	01377-45213
Circle	0181-303 2730		Creative Review	0171-439 4222
Citizens' Band	01442-66551		Cricketer International	01892-740256
City Life	0161-839 1310		Crimesearch	0181-807 7676
City Life Magazine	0115-247 6122		Crops	0181-652 4080
Civil Protection Magazine	0171-273 3762		Crossbow	0171-727 9845
Clarinet and Saxophone	0115 9411699		CTN	0171-404 5513
Classic & Sportscar	0181-943 5000		CU Amiga	0171-972 6700
Classic Bike/Motor Cycle	01733-237111		Cultural Critique	01865-56767
Classic Boat	0181-686 2599		Current Archaeology	0171-435 7517
Classic Car Weekly	01733-237111		Custom Car	0181-686 2599
Classic Cars	0171-261 5858		Cuts	0171-437 0801
Classic CD	01225-442244		Cycle Sport	0171-261 5588
Classic FM - The Magazine	0171-381 6007		Cycle Touring & Campaigning	01483-417217

Cycling Plus	01225-442244	Elvis Monthly	0116 2537271
Cycling Weekly	0171-261 5791	Empire	0171-436 1515
Dairy Farmer	01473-241122	Employment Gazette	0171-226 2222
Dalton's Weekly	0181-949 6199	En Route	01342-326944
Dance & Dancers	0171-837 2711	Energy Management	0181-243 3000
Dance Gazette	0171-223 0091	The Engineer	0181-855 7777
Dancing Times	0171-250 3006	Engineering	01564-771772
Dandy	01382-23131	Engineering Professional	01284-763277
Darts World	0181-650 6580	English Churchman	01227-781282
Datacom	0171-837 1212	English Heritage Magazine	0171-973 3000
Day by Day	0181-856 6249	Environment City News	01522-544400
Y Ddraig Goch	01970-617492	Environment Digest	01223-568016
Defence Helicopter	01628-604311	Environmental Health	0171-928 6006
Defence Industry Digest	0171-242 2548	ES Magazine (free)	0171-938 6000
The Dentist	01483-304944	Escort	0171-734 9191
Deo	01903-821082	Esquire	0171-439 5000
Derbyshire Life & Countryside	01332-47087	Essentials	0171-836 0519
Design Engineering	0181-855 7777	Essex Countryside	01279-647555
Design Week	0171-439 4222	Estate Agency News	01253-722142
Devon Life	0161-456 1818	Estates Gazette	0171-437 0141
Dialogue	0171-388 3171	Estates Times	0181-855 7777
Diesel Car	01458-74447	Ethical Consumer	0161-237 1630
Y Dinesydd	01222-578772	Euroboy	0181-348 9963
Diplomat	0171-405 4874	Everywoman	0171-359 5496
The Director	0171-730 6060	Exchange & Mart	01202-445000
Disability Times	0171-258 1929	Executive Woman	0181-420 1210
Disco Club	01727-843995	Expression!	0171-331 8000
Disney & Me	0171-344 6400	Extra	0181-207 2757
Diver Magazine	0181-943 4288	**The Face**	0171-837 7270
DIY Radio	01707-659015	Fairplay International Shipping	0181-660 2811
DIY Week	01732-364422	Fairs & Markets Diary	01734-402165
DJ	0171-415 7113	Family Circle	0171-261 6195
Do It Yourself	0181-686 2599	Family Tree Magazine	01487-814050
Docklands Magazine	0171-537 3900	Farmers Guardian	01772-203800
The Doctor	0181-652 3500	Farmers Weekly	0181-652 3500
Doctor Who Magazine	0171-497 2121	Farming News	0181-855 7777
Dog World	01233-621877	Fashion Weekly	0181-688 7788
Dogs Monthly	01344-28269	Fast Car	01689-874025
Dogs Today	01344-875442	Fast Ford	01452-307181
Dorset Life	0929-551264	Fast Forward	0181-576 3254
Drapers Record	0181-688 7788	FHM · For Him Magazine	0171-247 5447
Dresses	0171-437 0796	The Field	01753-856061
Druglink	0171-430 1991	Fiesta	01376-510555
Earth Matters	0171-490 1555	Financial Adviser	0171-608 3471
Early Music Today	0171-333 1733	Financial Director	0171-439 4242
Eastern Eye	0171-702 8012	Financial Product Review	0171-439 4222
Echoes	0171-323 0178	Fire	01737-768611
The Ecologist	01258-73476	First	0171-439 1188
Economic Trends	0171-873 0011	Fish Trader	01737-768611
The Economist	0171-839 7000	Fishing News	0171-404 5513
Education Equipment	0171-583 3030	The Flag	0181-471 6872
Electrical Design	0171-537 2222	Fleet News	01733-63100
Electrical Products	01732-359990	Flight International	0181-652 3500
Electrical Times	0181-652 3115	Flying Angel News	0171-248 5202
Electronic Product Review	01322-277788	Flying Saucer Review	01923-779018
Electronics	01702-554155	FlyPast	01780-55131
Electronics & Wireless World	0181-652 3500	Focus	0171-245 8700
Electronics Times	0181-855 7777	Focus on Africa	0171-257 2792
Electronics Weekly	0181-652 3500	Folio	0171-407 7411
Elle	0171-957 8383	Folk Roots	0181-340 9651

Food Processing	01732-359990	Hairdressers' Journal	0181-652 3204
Food Worker	01707-260150	Hairflair	0171-493 1081
Football Monthly	0181-868 5801	Ham Radio Today	01442-66551
Football Referee	0161-766 4244	Hansard	0171-873 0011
The Footballer	01462-441068	Harpers & Queen	0171-439 5000
For a Change	0171-828 6591	Headlight	0181-660 2811
For Women	0171-538 8969	Headlines	01442-233656
Fore!	01733-264666	Health & Fitness	0171-388 3171
Fortean Times	0171-485 5002	Health & Safety at Work	0181-686 9141
Fortnight	01232-232353	Health Now	01483-426064
Fortune	0171-499 4080	Health Service Journal	0171-836 6633
Forum	0171-987 5090	Healthy Eating	01608-811266
Franchise Magazine	01603-620301	Heavy Horse World	01243-811364
Free Church Chronicle	0171-387 8413	The Heavy Stuff	01272-870050
Free Press	0171-278 4430	Helicopter International	01934-822524
Free Radical	0171-222 0861	Hello!	0171-334 7404
Freedom	0171-247 9249	Here's Health	0171-437 9011
The Friend	0171-387 7549	Here's How	0171-834 8534
Furnishing	01895-677677	Heritage Scotland	0131-226 5922
Future Music	01225-442244	Hi-Fi Choice	0171-631 1433
Games & Puzzles	0181-809 3063	Hi-Fi News	0171-686 2599
Gamesmaster	01225-442244	Hi-Fi World	0171-289 3533
Garage News	0181-943 5000	High Mountain Sports	01533-460722
Garavi Gujarat	0171-928 1234	Him	0171-482 2576
The Garden/Garden Answers	01733-898100	Hind Samachar Weekly	0181-575 8694
The Gardener	0171-261 5000	History Today	0171-439 8315
Gardeners World (BBC)	0171-331 3939	History Workshop Journal	01865-56767
Gas World	0171-251 3501	Holidays (BBC)	0171-331 3939
Gatelodge	0181-803 0255	Home & Country	0171-731 5777
Gatwick News	01293-545499	Home & Family	0171-222 5533
Gay Scotland	0131-557 2625	Home Cooking	01442-66551
Gay Times	0171-482 2576	Home Economics/Technology	0171-938 1035
Genealogists Magazine	0171-251 8799	Home Entertainment	0171-631 1433
General Practitioner	0181-943 5000	Homes & Antiques (BBC)	0171-331 3939
Geographical Magazine	0171-487 4284	Homes & Gardens	0171-261 5678
Geoscientist	01225-445046	Homes & Ideas	0171-261 5000
Geriatric Medicine	01322-222222	Horoscope	0181-679 1899
Girl About Town	0171-872 0033	Horse & Hound	0171-261 6315
The Gleaner	0171-733 7014	Horse & Pony	01733-264666
Golf Monthly	0171-261 7236	Horse & Rider	0181-390 8547
Golf World	0171-538 1031	Horse Review	01865-791006
Good Food (BBC)	0171-331 3939	Horticulture Week	0181-943 5000
Good Housekeeping	0171-439 5000	Hospital Doctor	0181-652 3500
Good Idea!	0171-331 8000	Hospital Equipment & Supplies	01322-277788
Good Motoring	01962-841772	Hospital Update	0181-652 3500
Good Vibrations	01733-370777	Hot Air	0171-381 6007
The Gospel Magazine	0171-228 5350	Hot Shoe International	0171-226 1739
GQ	0171-499 9080	Hotel & Restaurant Magazine	0181-681 2099
Gramophone	0181-907 4476	The House	0171-233 8283
Granta	0171-704 9776	House & Garden	0171-499 9080
Grapevine	01422-843785	House & Home	01622-688244
The Great Outdoors	01355-246444	House Beautiful	0171-439 5000
Greek Review	0171-272 2722	Housing	0171-837 8727
Green Drum	0121-445 2576	Howl	0115-959 0357
Green Line	01865-249949	**I-D Magazine**	0171-813 6170
Greenscene	0161-928 0793	Ideal Home	0171-261 6474
The Grocer	01293-613400	The Idler	0171-404 3095
The Guardian Weekly	0161-491 2505	Illustrated London News	0171-928 2111
Guiding	0171-834 6242	Image	0171-608 1441
Hair	0171-261 6974	Independent Grocer	0181-652 8754

Index on Censorship	0171-278 2313	Lifeguard	01527-853943
India Mail	0181-900 1781	Lifewatch	0171-722 3333
India Times	0181-843 1605	Lincolnshire Life	01522-77567
India Weekly	0171-377 9969	Line Up	01323-491739
Individual Homes	01527-36600	The List	0131-558 1191
Industrial Exchange & Mart	01202-445000	Literary Review	0171-437 9392
Inside Soap	0171-436 5220	The Little Ship	0171-236 7729
Inspirations	0171-836 0519	Living	0171-261 6281
Insurance Age	0171-837 1212	Living Marxism	0171-278 9908
Intelligence & National Security	0181-599 8866	Llafar Gwlad	01690-2261
InterMedia	0171-388 0671	Lloyd's List International	0171-250 1500
International Broadcasting	0171-837 1212	Loaded	0171-261 5000
International Defense Review	0181-763 1030	Lobster	01482-447558
International Express	0171-928 8000	Local Government Chronicle	0171-837 1212
International Management	0171-494 2008	Local Government News	0181-680 4200
International Power Generation	01737-768611	Local Historian	01243-787639
International Property	01708-450784	Local History Magazine	0115-970 0369
International Socialism	0171-538 5821	Locomotive Journal	0171-431 0275
Interzone Science Fiction	01273-504710	London Cyclist	0171-928 7220
Investors Chronicle	0171-405 6969	London Gazette	0171-873 8308
Irish Post	0181-561 0059	London Miscellany	0181-994 2285
Irish World	0171-836 9831	London Portrait	0171-261 7215
Issues in Focus	0171-430 2669	London Review of Books	0171-404 3338
IT	0171-485 0340	London Student	0171-580 7369
Jazz Journal	0171-608 1348	London Weekly Advertiser	0181-530 7555
Jagaran	0181-998 3876	Looks	0171-957 8383
Jane's Defence Weekly	0181-763 1030	Loot	0171-625 0266
Jane's Intelligence Review	0181-763 1030	**Mac Format**	01225-442244
Janomot Bengali Newsweekly	0181-767 1242	The Mac/MacUser	0171-631 1433
Jazz Journal International	0171-608 1348	MacWorld	0171-831 9252
Jewish Chronicle	0171-831 1100	Madam	0131-662 4445
Jewish Echo	0141-429 2034	Magazine News	0171-379 6268
Jewish Gazette	0161-740 5171	Mailout	01422-310161
Jewish Telegraph	0161-740 9321	Majesty	0171-436 4006
Jewish Tribune	0181-800 6688	Making Music	0171-251 1900
The Job	0171-490 8081	Management Today	0181-943 5000
The Journalist	0171-278 7916	Manchester United Magazine	0171-431 8104
Just Seventeen	0171-957 8383	Marie Claire	0171-261 5240
Kent Life	0171-973 6404	Marine Conservation	01989-566017
Kerrang!	0171-437 8050	Marketing	0181-943 5000
The Key Magazine	01734-697737	Marketing Week	0171-439 4222
Killers	0171-388 3171	Master Builder	0171-242 7583
Knave	01621-859242	Match	01733-264666
Kriss Kross	0181-846 9922	Materials Reclamation Weekly	0181-688 7788
Labour Briefing	0181-985 6597	Max Power	01733-237111
Labour Research	0171-928 3649	Mayfair	0171-734 9191
The Lady	0171-379 4717	Me	0171-836 0519
LAN Magazine	0171-837 1212	Mean Machines	0171-972 6700
The Lancet	171-436 4981	Mean Machines Sega	0171-972 6700
Land Rover Owner	01379-890056	Meat Trades Journal	0181-688 7788
The Landworker	0171-828 7788	Media & Marketing Europe	0171-837 1212
Law Society's Gazette	0171-242 1222	Media, Culture & Society	0171-374 0645
The Lawyer	0171-439 4222	Media International	0181-652 3500
Legal Action	0171-833 2931	Media Law & Practice	0181-686 9141
Legal Business	0171-286 1890	Media Monitor	0171-873 4082
Leisure Management	01462-431385	Media Week	0171-837 1212
Leisure Manager	01491-874222	Melody Maker	0171-261 6229
L'Express	0171-836 9831	Men Only	0171-734 9191
Library Association Record	0171-636 7543	Men's Wear	0181-688 7788
The Licensee	0171-836 9831	Metal Bulletin	0171-827 9977

Metal Hammer	0171-631 1433	New Builder	0171-987 6999
Methodist Recorder	0171-251 8414	New Civil Engineer	0171-987 6999
Metro Girl	0161-832 7200	New Cyclist	0171-250 1881
MicroScope	0171-631 1433	New European	0171-582 3996
Middle East Economic Digest	0171-404 5513	New Ground	0171-263 7424
Middle East International	0171-373 5228	New Humanist	0171-226 7251
Midweek Magazine	0171-636 3666	New Internationalist	01865-728181
Milap Weekly	0171-385 8966	New Law Journal	0171-400 2500
Militant	0181-533 3311	New Left Review	0171-734 8830
Military Hobbies	01202-512355	New Musical Express	0171-261 6472
Mims Magazine	0181-943 5000	New Scientist	0171-261 7301
Mind Body Soul	01908-377559	New Shetlander	01595-3816
Mind Your Own Business	0181-771 3614	New Statesman & Society	0171-739 3211
Mine & Quarry	01732-359990	New Times	0171-278 4451
The Miner	0114-276 6900	New Woman	0171-957 8383
Micro Computer Mart	0121-706 1433	Newspaper Focus	0181-943 5000
Miniature Wargames	01202-512355	Newsweek International	0171-629 8361
Mining Journal/Magazine	0171-377 2020	Next Step	0171-278 7699
MiniWorld	0181-686 2599	Nine to Five	0171-608 0800
Mizz	0171-261 6319	Nineteen	0171-261 6360
Model Engineer	01442-66551	Ninety Minutes	0171-261 7450
Model Railway Journal	01235-816478	Northamptonshire Image	01604-231122
Modern Churchman	01568-87271	Now	0171-261 6348
Modern Railways	0181-674 0227	Nuclear Times	01452-653700
Modern Review	0181-749 0593	Nursery Choice	0171-251 2505
Mojo	0171-436 1515	Nursery World	0171-837 7224
Money Management	0171-405 6969	Nursing Standard	0181-423 1066
Money Marketing	0171-439 4222	Nursing Times	0171-836 6633
Money Observer	0171-713 4188	**Observer Life Magazine** (free)	0171-278 2332
Moneywise	0171-629 8144	Off-Licence News	01293-613400
More!	0171-957 8383	Office Equipment News	01322-277788
Mother & Baby	0171-437 9011	Offshore Engineer	0171-987 6999
Motor Boat & Yachting	0171-261 5308	Offspring	0181-559 2015
Motor Cycle News	01536-411111	OK!	0171-987 5090
Motor Industry Management	01992-511521	Old Glory	01780-63063
Motor Ship	0181-652 8183	The Oldie	0171-636 3686
Motor Trader	0181-652 3276	On Target	01787-376374
Motor Transport	0181-652 3728	One World	0171-723 0721
Motorcaravan Monthly	01778-393313	Open Eye, Challenging Censorship	01956 250654
Motoring News	0171-628 4741	Opera	0171-359 1037
Mountain Biker International	0181-686 2599	Opera Now	0171-333 1720
Mountain Biking UK	01225-442244	Options	0171-261 6600
Movie International	0181-813 8183	Oral History	01206-873333
Moving Pictures International	0171-287 0070	Orbit	0181-780 2266
MS London Magazine	0171-636 3322	Organic Gardening	01984-623998
Municipal Journal	0171-973 6400	Oryx	01865-206206
Musclemag International	0121-327 7525	Our Dogs	0161-236 2660
Museums Journal	0171-250 1834	Outlook	0181-671 7920
Music (BBC)	0181-576 3693	**Packaging News**	0181-243 3000
Music Magazine	01733 370777	Packaging Week	01732-364422
The Musical Times	0181-863 2020	Parents	0171-437 9011
Music Week	0171-620 3636	Parentwise	0181-942 9761
My Weekly	01382-23131	Parikiaki	0171-272 6777
National Trust Magazine	0171-222 9251	Parkers Car Price Guide	0181-579 1082
Natural World	0171-928 2111	The Patient	01524-811260
Nature	0171-836 6633	PC Answers/Format/Plus	01225-442244
Navy News	01705-826040	PC Dealer/Week	0171-439 4242
Needlecraft	01225-442244	PC Direct/Magazine	0171-378 6800
Network	0171-439 4242	PC Review	0171-972 6700
New African	0171-713 7711	PC User	0171-837 1212

PC Zone	0171-631 1433
PCW Plus	01225-442244
Peace News	0171-278 3344
Pensioners' Voice	01254-52606
Pensions Management	0171-405 6969
Penthouse	0171-987 5090
People's Friend	01382-23131
Perfect Home	01895-677677
Performance Bikes/Car	01733-237111
Period House	01895-677677
Period Living	0171-437 9011
Personal Computer Magazine	0171-439 4242
Personal Computer World	0171-439 4242
Personnel Today	181-652 3500
Pharmaceutical Journal	0171-735 9141
Photo Answers	01733-898100
Photo Technique	0171-261 5000
The Photographer	01920-464011
Physics World	0117-929 7481
Pig Farming	01473-241122
The Pink Paper	0171-608 2566
Plain Truth	0181-207 2811
Planet	01970-611255
Planet News	0181-671 7920
Planning	01452-417553
Planning Week	0171-943 5000
Plastics & Rubber Weekly	0181-681 7788
Playdays	0181-576 2773
Plays and Players	0181-446 2282
Police	0181-399 2224
Police Review	0171-537 2575
Political Quarterly/Studies	0114-276 8555
Popular Classics	01733-237111
Popular Crafts	01442-66551
Popular Patchwork	01442-66551
Portfolio	0117-929 0158
Pot Black	0171-482 4596
PR Week	0171-413 4153
Practical Boat Owner	01202-680593
Practical Caravan	0181-943 5000
Practical Classics	01733-237111
Practical Coarse Fishing	0171-243 5000
Practical Electronics	01202-881749
Practical Fishkeeping	01733-264666
Practical Gardening	01733-898100
Practical Householder	0171-388 3171
Practical Motorist	01202-659910
Practical Musician	01905 420760
Practical Parenting	0171-261 5058
Practical PC	0171-388 3171
Practical Photography	01733-898100
Practical Wireless	01202-659910
Practical Woodworking	0171-261 6602
The Practitioner	0181-855 7777
Prediction	0181-686 2599
Premiere	0171-436 1515
Pride	0171-737 5599
Prima	0171-245 8700
Print Week	0181-943 5000
Printing World	01732-364422
Private Eye	0171-437 4017
Probation Bulletin	01943-602270
Production Journal	0171-636 7014
Professional Engineering	01284-7632777
Professional Nurse	0171-388 7676
Professional Printer	01892-538118
Property Confidential	0171-637 4383
Prospects	0171-2551278
Psychic News	0171-405 3340
The Psychologist	0116-254 9568
Public Administration	01865-791100
Public Service	0171-388 2366
Public Service & Local Govt	0181-688 7788
Publican	0181-681 2099
Publishing	0171-436 1673
Publishing News	0171-404 0304
Pulse	0181-855 7777
Punjab Times	0181-571 2751
Puzzle Compendium	0181-846 9922
Puzzle Monthly	0171-388 3171
Puzzle World	0171-388 3171
Puzzler Collection/Puzzler	0181-846 9922
Q	0171-4031790
Race and Class	0171-837 0041
Racing & Football Outlook	0171-608 1209
Radio Communication	01707-659015
Radio Control Models	01442-66551
Radio Magazine	01536-418558
Radio Times	0181-576 2000
RAF News	0171-305 8047
Rail	01733-898100
Railway Gazette International	0181-652 3500
Railway Magazine	0171-261 5821
Railway World	01256-469728
Rambling Today	01480-496130
The Raven	0171-247 9249
Raw	0171-436 1515
Readers Digest	0171-629 8144
Record Collector	0181-579 1082
Record Mirror	0171-620 3636
Red Pepper	0171-247 1702
Red Tape	0171-924 2727
Regiment	01442-66551
Reportage	0171-729 5155
Republican News	01232-624421
Resident Abroad	0171-405 6969
Restoration	01203-602777
Resurgence	01237-441293
Retail Jeweller	0171-404 2763
Retail Newsagent	0171-837 3168
Retail World	0117-925 1696
Riding	01400-82032
Right Start	0171-403 0840
Rock Power	0171-388 3171
Rock World	0181-748 1200
RPM	0181-874 3277
Rugby Monthly	01709-364721
Rugby World	01753-856061
Runners World	0171-972 9119
Runnymede Bulletin	0171-375 1496

RUSI Journal	0171-930 5854
Saga Magazine	01303-711523
Sainsbury's: The Magazine	0171-633 0266
Salisbury Review	0171-226 7791
Salmon & Trout	0171-243 5000
Satellite & Video Today	0171-351 3612
Satellite Guide	01268-710554
Satellite Times	181-677 7822
Satellite Trader	0171-351 3612
Sayidaty	0171-831 8181
Scenes	01520-2588
Scotland's What's On	0131-332 0471
Scots Law Times	0131-225 4879
Scots Magazine	01382-23131
Scottish Farmer	01355-246444
Scottish Field	01355-246444
Scottish Football Today	0141-248 8812
Scottish Memories	0141-204 3104
Scouting	0171-584 7030
Screen Digest	0171-580 2842
Screen International	0171-837 1212
Sea Angler	01733-264666
Sea Breezes	0151-236-3935
The Seaman	0171-622 5581
Searchlight	0171-284 4040
Seatrade Review	01206-45121
Secrets	0171-253 2445
Security Gazette	0181-688 7788
Security Management Today	0181-742 2828
Sega Power	01225-442244
Select	0171-436 1515
SFX	01225 442244
She	0171-439 5000
Shetland Life	01595-3622
Shoe & Leather News	0181-688 7788
Shoot!	0171-261 6287
Shooting & Conservation	01244-570881
Shooting Times	0171-243 5000
Shopping Centre	01293-613400
Short Wave Magazine	01202-659910
Shropshire Magazine	01743-362175
Sight & Sound	0171-255 1444
The Sign	01603-615995
The Singer	0171-333 1733
Skin Deep	01925-757874
Sky	0171-436 1515
Slimmer	01923-228577
Slimming	0171-437 9011
Smash Hits	0171-436 1515
Soccer Stars	0171-261 6269
Social Housing	0171-700 4199
Social Work Today	0171-836 6633
Social Market Review	0171-222 7060
Socialist Affairs	0171-627 4449
Socialist Lawyer	0171-404 1313
Socialist Standard	0171-622 3811
Socialist Worker	0171-538 0828
Soldier	01252-347355
Solicitors Journal	0171-242 2548
Solidarity	0181-552 3985
Somerset & Avon Life	01272-252052
Sound on Sound	01480-461244
Spare Rib	Closed 1993
The Spectator	0171-405 1706
Spectrum	0171-255 3000
Sport & Leisure	0171-388 3171
Sports Industry	0171-498 0177
Sri Lankans	0181-952 9527
Staffordshire Life	0161-427 7035
Stage, Screen & Radio	0171-437 8506
The Stage & Television Today	0171-403 1818
Statewatch	0181-802 1882
Steam Railway	01733-898100
Straight No Chaser	0171-613 1594
The Strad	0181-863 2020
Street Machine	01733-237111
Structural Engineer	0171-235 4535
Sunday Express Magazine (free)	0171-928 8000
Sunday Mirror Magazine (free)	0171-293 3000
Sunday Times Magazine (free)	0171-782 4000
Supermarketing	0181-652 8278
Surrey County Magazine	01483-898966
The Surveyor	0171-973 6400
The Tablet	0181-748 8484
Take a Break	0171-284 0909
Taking Liberties	0171-274 6655
Tatler	0171-499 9080
Taxation	0181-686 9141
Technical Review Middle East	0171-834 7676
Telegraph Magazine (free)	0171-538 5000
Television (Reed)	0181-652 3500
Television (Royal TV Soc)	0171-430 1000
Television Business Internat	0171-351 3612
Television Buyer	0171-837 1212
Television Week	0171-837 1212
Televisual	0171-439 4222
Theatreprint	0171-839 5355
Therapy Weekly	0171-836 6633
Third Text	0171-435 3748
Third Way	0171-373 3432
The Ticket	0181-686 2599
Timber Trades Journal	01732-364422
Time Life International	0171-499 4080
Time Out	0171-813 3000
Times Education Supplements	0171-782 3000
Times Literary Supplement	0171-782 3000
Titbits	0171-351 4995
Today's Golfer	01733-264666
Today's Runner	01733-264666
Toilers of the Deep	01482-23440
Top Banana	01253-596060
Top Car	01689-874025
Top Gear	0171-331 3939
Total	01225-442244
Townswoman	01635-278669
Toy Trader	01923-777000
Trade It	0181-686 2599
Trade Marks Journal	0171-405 8721
Traditional Homes	0171-437 9011
Transport	01494-678000

Transport Retort	0171-388 8386
Travel Weekly	0171-355 1600
Treasure Hunting	01245-381011
Trees	01342-712536
Trees are News	01342-712536
Tribune	0171-278 0911
Trout & Salmon	01733-264666
Truck	0171-224 9242
True Romances	0181-677 7538
True Story	0181-677 7538
Turning Point	0181-841 0503
TV & Satellite Week	0171-261 7956
TV Hits	0171-436 5565
TV Quick	0171-284 0909
TV Times	0171-261 7000
TV World	0171-837 1212
Twinkle	01382 223131
UFO Times	01924-444049
UK Press Gazette	0181-243 3000
Ulster Nation	0171-373 3432
Un-Common Sense	0181-856 6249
Under Five Contact	0171-833 0991
Undercover	0161-628 6566
Union Review	0181-462 7755
The Universe	0161-236 8856
Upbeat	0171-331 8000
Update	0181-652 3500
Vanguard	0181-471 6872
Vanity Fair	0171-499 9080
Vegetarian Good Food (BBC)	0171-331 3939
Vegetarian Living	0171-388 3171
Ventures	0171-378 6323
Veteran Car	01462-742818
Veterinary Record	0171-636 6541
Veterinary Times	01733-325522
Video Camera	0171-261 5633
Vintage Motor Cycle	01283-40557
Viz	0171-381 6007
Vogue	0171-499 9080
The Voice	0171-737 7377
Voice of the Listener	01474-463823
Vox	0171-261 6312
The War Cry	0171-236 5222
Watchout	01865-880505
Water & Environment	0171-987 6999
Water Bulletin	01923-777000
Water Gardener	01233-621877
Waterways	1283-790447
The Web	0171-831 9252
Wedding & Home	0171-261 7457
The Week	01296-89550
Weekly Journal	0171-924 0134
Weekly Law Digest	01243-783637
Weekly News	0171-242 5086
Weight Watchers	0171-243 5000
Welsh Nation	01222-231944
West Africa	0171-737 2946
What Camcorder	0171-485 0011
What Car?	0181-943 5000

What Diet & Lifestyle?	0171-437 0796
What Hi-Fi?	0181-943 5000
What Investment?	0171-638 1916
What Mortgage?	0171-638 1916
What PC?	0171-439 4242
What Personal Computer?	0171-837 1212
What Satellite?	0171-485 0011
What Video?	0171-485 0011
What's New in Farming	0181-855 7777
What's On TV	0171-261 7768
When Saturday Comes	0171-251 8595
Which Bike?	01733-237111
Which Car?	0181-943 5943
Which Computer?	0171-837 1212
Which Kit?	01737-249662
Which Mortgage?	0171-833 5566
Which Motorcaravan	01778-393652
Which?	0171-486 5544
Wild Cat	01438-716478
Wild London	0171-278 6612
Wildfowl and Wetlands	01453 890333
Wildlife (BBC)	0117-973 2211
Windows Magazine	0171-631 1433
Windows User	0181-652 3500
The Wire	0171-439 6422
Wired	0171-713 4465
Wisden Cricket Monthly	01483-570358
Woman	0171-261 7023
Woman & Home	0171-261 5423
Woman Alive	01903-821082
Woman's Journal	0171-261 6622
Woman's Own	0171-261 5500
Woman's Realm	0171-261 6033
Woman's Weekly	0171-261 6131
Woodworker	01442-66551
Woodworking News	01474-536535
Word Search	0181-846 9922
Workbox	01823-326561
Working Women	0181-947 3131
Works Management	01322-222222
World of Interiors	0171-499 9080
World Soccer	0171-261 6821
The World Today	0171-957 5700
World's Fair	0161-624 3687
Worldwide (BBC)	0171-240 3456
Writers Monthly	0181-342 8879
Writers News	01667-54441
Writers Newsletter	0171-723 8074
Writing Magazine	01667-454441
XYZ - Direction	0181-943 5000
Yachting Monthly	0171-261 6040
Yachting World	0171-261 6800
You and the Law	0171-242 1222
You Magazine (free)	0171-938 6000
Your Garden	01202-680586
Your Cat/Dog	01733-898100
Yours	01733-555123
Zionist Review	0181-343 9756
Zipper	0171-482 2576

This Guardian/Stop Press award winning photo for 1995 was taken by Thomas Nam Nguyen. The panel of judges had this to say about the picture: "Much of its power comes from its ambiguity, offering many different ways one can decode it. A child of uncertain gender stares at the photographer with uncertain eyes. Is it a look of reproach? If so, is it directed at the photographer or at a world which has failed to stem his/her msiery? Or is the child pleading for help, for food? Or is it, perhaps, a look of simple curiosity? The strength of the photograph is that it rewards sustained viewing; the callage of faces, expressions and eyes giving rise to innumerable meanings."

One of the judges was Eamonn McCabe, the Guardian picture editor. "There are no real rules to photography," he says. "If you like it, take it," is McCabe's advice. "Don't worry if the sun isn't over your left shoulder. If you have a sure shot, get in close. Frighten yourself a little. It doesn't matter if you cut off the odd leg, it might just make the picture memorable to someone else, which is the name of the game after all."

PRESS AWARDS 1995

If you want to win an award, the first rule is to enter everything going; the next is to feign utter indifference to the results. If you lose, everybody knows the judges are a spineless bunch who are being bullied by sponsors into awarding their gongs to the most undeserving no-hopers. If you win, it's a tribute to human wisdom, discretion and fair-mindedness. Your prize will be worth a pay rise and stay on the CV for longer than A level results. The third award rule applies to organisers. To ensure that hurt feelings are kept to aminimum, they must devise enough categories to let several people win the same race. A special prize, therefore, to the PPA for announcing six magazines of the year. And a booby prize to the wizened What The Papers Say awards.

Top newspaper awards

British Press Awards
UK Press Gazette, Chalk Lane, Cockfosters Road, Barnet, Herts EN4 OBU
Fax 0181-242 3088   Tel 0181-242 3081
Newspaper of the Year: Daily Mail
Reporter of the Year: Gary Jones, News of the World. Highly commended: David Hencke, the Guardian
Exclusive of the Year: Sunday Times Insight Team (Cash for Questions). Highly commended: Wayne Francis, the Sun (Camilla to Divorce)
Team Journalism Award: Sunday Times Insight Team (Cash for Questions). Highly commended: The Scotsman, Alan Huchison and Marcello Mega
Foreign Reporter: Robert Fisk, the Independent and Independent on Sunday. Highly commended: Ambrose Evans Pritchard, Sunday Telegraph; Patti Waldmeir, Financial Times
Foreign Stringer of the Year: Richard Shears, Daily Mail. Highly commended: Jonathan Freedland, the Guardian; Anatole Lieven, the Times
Columnist of the Year: Andrew Marr, the Independent. Highly commended: Simon Jenkins, The Times
Young Journalist of the Year: Peter Jinks, freelance. Highly commended: Victoria Harper, Daily Express; Ruaridh Nicoll, Scotland on Sunday
Industrial Report of the Year: Kevin Maguire, Daily Mirror
Headline of the Year: The Independent (4,000 moles in Blackburn, Lancashire, a story about the hunt for the first big lottery winner)
Photographer of the Year: Simon Townsley, Sunday Times. Highly commended: John Downing, Daily Express
Image of the Year: Charles Griffin, Daily Mirror. Highly commended: Alan Gililand, Daily Telegraph
Critic of the Year: Hugh Canning, Sunday Times. Highly commended: Jaci Stephen, Daily Mirror; Clement Crisp, FT

Interviewer of the Year: Mary Riddell, Today. Highly commended: Martyn Harris, Daily Telegraph; Deborah Ross, Daily Mail
Sports Feature Writer of the Year: Richard Williams, Independent on Sunday. Highly commended: James Lawton, Daily Express
Sports News Reporter of the Year: Simon Greenberg, Mail on Sunday. Highly commended: Neil Silver, Sunday Mirror
Chairman's Award: Marje Proops, for 41 years service at the Daily Mirror

UKPG Regional Press Awards
UK Press Gazette, Chalk Lane, Cockfosters Road, Barnet, Herts EN4 OBU
Fax 0181-242 3088   Tel 0181-242 3081
Joint Newspapers of the Year: The News, Portsmouth; Belfast Telegraph
Weekly Newspaper of the Year (circulation under 20,000): Southern Reporter, Selkirk. Highly commended: Yorkshire Gazette and Herald; Hampstead and Highgate Express
Weekly Newspaper of the Year (circulation over 20,000): Essex County Standard. Highly commended: Sheffield Telegraph; Westmoreland Gazette
Free Newspaper of the Year: Enfield Advertiser. Highly commended: Bognor Regis Observer; Redditch Advertiser
Morning/Sunday Paper of the Year: Sunday Sun, Newcastle. Highly commended: Yorkshire Post; Sunday Life, Belfast
Evening Newspaper of the Year (circulation under 50,000): Evening News, Norwich. Highly commended: Lancashire Evening Telegraph; Jersey Evening Post
Joint Evening Newspaper of the Year (circulation over 50,000): The News, Portsmouth: The Belfast Telegraph. Highly commended: Liverpool Echo; Evening Gazette, Middlesbrough
Reporter of the Year: David Charter, The News, Portsmouth. Highly commended: Caroline Storah, Liverpool Echo; Alan Hutchison and Marcello Mega, The Scotsman,
Specialist Writer of the Year: Nicola Barry, Evening News, Edinburgh,. Highly commended: Kate Taylor, Southern Daily Echo; Mike Amos, Northern Echo
Production Award: Southern Daily Echo. Highly commended: Yorkshire Evening Press; The News, Portsmouth
Columnist of the Year: Kenneth Roy, The Herald, Glasgow. Highly commended: Andrew Grimes, Manchester Evening News; Ian Bell, The Herald, Glasgow
Photographer of the Year: Ian Rutherford, The Scotsman. Highly commended: Crispin Rodwell, freelance; Rudi Gnoyke, Evening Argus, Brighton
Sports Photographer of the Year: Gareth Everett, South Wales Argus. Highly commended: Martin Brichall, Liverpool Post and Echo; Steve Ellis, Sheffield Star
Young Journalist of the Year: Steve Smith, Press and Journal, Aberdeen. Highly commended: Darren Parkin, Solihull Times; Stephen McGinty, The Herald, Glasgow
Sports Writer of the Year: Keith Newbery, The News,

Portsmouth. Highly commended: Stephen Brenkley, freelance: Tim Rich, Sunderland Echo
Sports Reporter of the Year: Brian McNally, Sunday Sun, Newcastle. Highly commended: Neil Squires, Yorkshire Post; Colin Farquharson, Press and Journal, Aberdeen
Trainee of the Year: Mike McCormack, Evening News, Edinburgh. Highly commended: Eloise Twisk, Eastern Counties Newspapers; Sara Naylor, Evening News, Edinburgh
Feature Writer of the Year: Anvar Khan, The Herald, Glasgow. Highly commended: Simon Freeman, The Scotsman; Reg Little, Oxford Times
Graphic Artist of the Year: Petra Stanton, Northern Echo. Highly commended: Mick Brady, Evening Times, Glasgow; Michael Stafford, The Journal, Newcastle

What the Papers Say
Granada, The London Television Centre, Upper Ground, London SE1 9LT
Tel 0171-620 1620
Magazine of the Year: The Spectator
Journalist of tthe Year: David Hencke, the Guardian
Scoop of the Year: News of the World
Investigation of the Year: Sunday Times
Columnist of the Year: Andrew Marr, the Independent
Award for Lifetime Achievement: Jane Bown, photographer for The Observer

Top magazine awards

Magazines '95 Awards: PPA
Periodical Publishers Association, 15 Kingsway, London WC2B 6UN
Fax 0171-379 5661   Tel 0171-379 6268
Consumer Magazine of the Year: Loaded
Business Magazine of the Year: Farmers Weekly
International Magazine of the Year (Consumer): Arena
International Magazine of the Year (Business): Nature
Customer Magazine of the Year: Sainsbury's: The Magazine
Consumer Specialist Magazine of the Year: BBC Top Gear Magazine
Editor of the Year (Consumer): James Brown, Loaded
Editor of the Year (Business): Juliet Warkentin, Drapers Record
News Designer of the Year (Consumer): Mike Clowes, Radio Times
News Designer of the Year (Business): Stuart Purcell, Checkout Fresh
Columnist of the Year (Consumer): Stephen Bayley, GQ
Columnist of the Year (Business): Bernard Ingham, PR Week
Writer of the Year (Consumer): Rian Malan, Esquire
Writer of the Year (Business): David Bradwell, What Personal Computer
Publisher of the Year (for companies with less than 25 employees): James Freedman, Zone
Publisher of the Year (Consumer): Liz Kershaw, Good Housekeeping
Columnist of the Year (Business): Trevor Barratt, Building
Editorial Campaign of the Year: Community Care

Top photography awards

British Picture Editors' Awards
UK PIcture Editors' Guild, c/o Gold Stag Public Relations, Victoria House, Consort Way, Horley, Surrey RH6 7AF
Fax 01293 821399   Tel 01293 822055
News Photographer of the Year: Ian Waldie, Reuter
Sport Photographer of the Year: Chris Cole, Allsport
Royal Photographer of the Year: Kent Gavin, Daily Mirror
Features Photographer of the Year: Paul Massey, Mail on Sunday You Magazine
Business and Industry Photographer of the Year: Stewart Goldstein, Eyecatchers
Technician of the Year: Larry Bartell, Daily Express
Awards for Technical Excellence: Roger Bamber, the Guardian; Gary Lodge, Yorkshire Post; Keith Taylor, Metro Photographic

Nikon
Nikon Uk Ltd, 380 Richmond Road, Kingston upon Thames, Surrey KT2 5PR
Fax 0181-541 4584   Tel 0181-541 4440
Press Photographer of the Year: Keith Bernstein
Regional Photographer of the Year: Crispin Rodwell
Royals Photographer of the Year: Brendan Beirne
Sports Photographer of the Year: Simon Bruty
Arts and Entertainments Photographer of the Year: Paul Massey
News Photographer of the Year: Jon Jones
Features Photographer of the Year: Gideon Mendel
Photo Essay Winner: Simon Townsley

Guardian awards

The two Guardian media awards go to gifted amateurs. However, many who win the student awards go on to make a career in journalism. Among the inspiring examples are: Andrew Culf, runner up 1982 and now Guardian media correspondent; Neil Bennett, winner 1985 and now Times deputy business editor; David Sharrock, winner 1983 and Guardian Northern Ireland correspondent; Marianne Macdonald, winner 1988, currently Independent arts reporter; James Wood, winner 1987 Guardian chief literary critic. The student awards are judged toward the end of October, which is too late for 1995 winners to be included in this directory.

Guardian/NUS Student Media Awards
National Union of Students, 461 Holloway Road, London N7 6LJ

Guardian/Stop Press
Guardian/Stop Press Competition, Room 4065, BBC Broadcasting House, London W1A 1AA

PRESS AGENCIES

Below are news agencies that find news items and sell them to all media, and feature and syndication agencies that supply fully written stories to the print sector. The top international news agencies are: Agence France Presse, Associated Press and Reuters. The main agency which gathers news inside the UK is the Press Association (PA) which is owned by the regional newspaper publishers.Most regional agencies belong to the National Association of Press Agencies whose details are in the Support Organisation section on page 113.

Advance Features
Clarendon House, Judges Terrace, East Grinstead, West Sussex RH19 3AD
Tel 01342-328562
Provides cartoons, crosswords and puzzles for newspapers, magazines and TV.

Agence France Presse
78 Fleet Street, London EC4Y 1HY
Fax 0171-353 8359   Tel 0171-353 7461
London office of the large international French news agency. Supplies international news and picture services to the UK media, and collects British material for foreign media.

AllScot News & Features Agency
PO Box 6, Haddington, East Lothian EH41 3NQ
Fax 01620-822578   Tel 01620-822578
Covers: All Scotland and includes specialist international Oil City news services.

Andes Press Agency
26 Padbury Court, London E2 7EH
Fax 0171-739 3159   Tel 0171-739 3159
Covers social, religious, political, economic and environmental issues around the world, especially in Latin America.

Anglia Press Agency
91 Hythe Hill, Colchester, Essex CO1 2NU
Fax 01206-797962   Tel 01206-797961
Covers: Essex, Suffolk and East Anglia.

Anglo-Danish Press Agency
Grosvenor Walks, Mount Pleasant Hill, London E5 9NE
Fax 0181-806 3236   Tel 0181-806 3232

ANSA
Essex House, 13-13 Essex Street, London WC2R 3AA
Fax 004471-2405518   Tel 004471-240 5514
ANSA is the leading Italian news agency.

AP-Dow Jones
10 Fleet Place, London EC4M 7RB
Fax 0171-823 9101   Tel 0171-832 9105
Business news section of Associated Press which reports economic, financial and market affecting political news.

Associated Press (AP)
12 Norwich Street, London EC4A 1BP
Fax 0171-353 8118   Tel 0171-353 1515
UK office of the giant American agency, co-operatively owned by US media companies. Supplies international news and picture services to the UK media, and collects British material for American and other clients. Also runs the AP-Dow Jones financial news service.

Australian Associated Press
12 Norwich Street, London EC4A 1EJ
Fax 0171-583 3563   Tel 0171-353 0153
Collects UK news for media outlets in Australia and the South Pacific.

Bellis News Agency
147 Marine Drive, Rhos-on-Sea, Colwyn Bay, Clwyd LL28 4HY
Fax 01492-543226   Tel 01492-549503
News reporters for most of north Wales for national and regional media.

Bloomberg Business News
39-45 Finsbury Square, London EC2A 1PQ
Fax 0171-256 5326   Tel 0171-330 7500
Business and financial service.

Bournemouth News & Picture Service
14 Lorne Park Road, Bournemouth, Dorset BH1 1JN
Fax 01202-553875   Tel 01202-558833
Covers: Hants, Dorset, Wilts.

Bristol & West News Agency
34 Dublin Crescent, Henleaze, Bristol, Avon BS9 4NA
Tel 0117-929 3266
Specialises in sports coverage of the region.

Britannia Press Features
Britannia House, 1 Pettits Close, Romford, Essex RM1 4EB
Fax 01708-727305   Tel 01708-761186
Provides wide range of feature services, travel a speciality.

Business News Service
28 Nottingham Place, London W1M 3FD
Tel 0171-581 2455
Specialises in company features and profiles.

Cambrian News Agency
37 Charles Street, Cardiff CF1 4EB
Fax 01222-372667   Tel 01222-395813
Covers: South Wales.

Canadian Press
12 Norwich Street, London EC4A 1EJ
Fax 0171-583 4238   Tel 0171-353 6355
The leading Canadian news agency.

Cassidy & Leigh (Southern News Service)
Exchange House, Hindhead, Surrey GU26 6AA
Fax 01428-606351   Tel 01428-607330
Covers: Surrey, Sussex, Hants and Kent.

Caters News Agency
43 Bartholomew Street, Birmingham B5 5QW
Fax 0121-616 2200   Tel 0121-616 1100
Covers: West Midlands.

Cavendish Press
17 Whitworth Street, Manchester M1 5WG
Fax 0161-237 5353   Tel 0161-237 1066
Covers: North west England.

Central News Network
30a Newmarket Street, Falkirk, FK1 1JQ
Fax 01324-630515   Tel.01324-630505

Central Office of Information (COI)
Hercules Road, London SE1 7DU
Fax 0171-928 5037   Tel 0171-928 2345
The government press and publicity agency.
  COI Eastern
  72-80 Hills Road, Cambridge CB2 1LL
  Fax 01223-316121   Tel 01223-311867
  COI Merseyside
  Graeme House, Derby Square, Liverpool L2
  7SU
  Fax 0151-236 1199   Tel 0151-227 4111
  COI Midlands
  Five Ways Tower, Frederick Road, Edgbaston,
  Birmingham B15 1SH
  Fax 0121-626 2041   Tel 0121-626 2017
  COI East Midlands
  20 Middle Pavement, Nottingham NG1 7DW
  Fax 0115-959 0316   Tel 0115-959 9177
  COI North Eastern
  Wellbar House, Gallowgate, Newcastle-upon-
  Tyne NE1 4TD
  Fax 0191-261 8571   Tel 0191-201 3300
  COI North Western
  Piccadilly Plaza, Manchester M1 4BD
  Fax 0161-236 9443   Tel 0161-952 4500
  COI South West
  The Pithay, Bristol BS1 2NF
  Fax 0117-929 8612   Tel 0117-927 3767
  COI Yorkshire & Humberside
  New Station Street, Leeds, W Yorks LS1 4JG
  Fax 0113-283 6586   Tel 0113-283 6596

Central Press Features
Unit 20, 32 Gordon House Road, London NW5
1LP
Fax 0171-284 4494   Tel 0171-284 1433
Specialists in reporting Parliament since 1863.

Chapman & Page
Denegate House, Amber Hill, Boston, Lincs
PE20 3RL
                          Tel 01205-290477
Syndication features agency, also crosswords and horoscopes.

Chester News Service
88-90 Watergate Street, Chester CH1
Fax 01244-326075   Tel 01244-345562
Covers: Chester, including local courts, sport and features

Chester Press Bureaux
Riverside House, River Lane, Saltney, Chester
CH4 8RQ
Fax 01244-678749   Tel 01244-678575
Offers press agency and contract publishing services.

Cotswold & Swindon News Service
101 Bath Road, Swindon, Wilts SN1 4AX
Fax 01793-485462   Tel 01793-485461
Specialist cover of magistates' and crown courts. Also research,
business profiles and features.

Coventry News Service
32 Butt Lane, Allesley Village, Coventry, West
Midlands CV5 9EZ
Fax 01203-407129   Tel 01203-402752

JW Crabtree & Son
36 Sunbridge Road, Bradford, West Yorks BD1
2AA
                          Tel 01274-732937
Covers: Bradford area.

Dee News Service
12 Chester Street, Mold, Clwyd CH7 1EG
Fax 01352-759009   Tel 01352-769009
Covers: Clwyd area of North Wales.

Derek Bellis
147 Marine Drive, Rhos-on-Sea, Colwyn Bay,
Clwyd LL28 4HY
Fax 01492-543226   Tel 01492-549503
Covers: North Wales.

Deutsche Presse Agentur
30 Old Queen Street, London SW1H 9HP
Fax 0171-233 3534   Tel 0171-233 2888
German national news agency, owned by the German media.

Devon News Agency
4 Clifton Road, Exeter, Devon EX1 2BR
Fax 01392-435248   Tel 01392-76338
Covers: Devon and Cornwall.

Dobson Photo Agency
39 Queen Street, Scarborough, North Yorks
YO11 1HQ
Fax 01262-67749   Tel 01723-363661
Covers: Yorkshire coast.

Dragon News & Picture Agency
21 Walter Road, Swansea, West Glamorgan
SA1 5NF
Fax 01792-475264   Tel 01792-464800
Covers: South and west Wales.

Eastern News Service
2 Clasketgate, Lincoln, Lincolnshire LN2 1JS
Fax 01522-560589   Tel 01522-533328
Covers Lincolnshire

East Kent News Services
130a Godinton Road, Ashford, Kent TN23 1LJ
Fax 01233-641816   Tel 01233-643574

EDIT UK
Suite 116-118, Imperial Centre, Grange Road,
Darlington, Co Durham DL1 5PE
Fax 01325-368824   Tel 01325-368823

Elliott News Service
1 Fisher Lane, Bingham, Nottingham NG13 8BQ
Fax 01949-836583   Tel 01949-836566

Essex News Service
121 High Street, Witham, Essex CM8 1BE
Fax 01376-521222   Tel 01376-521222

Ewan MacNaughton Associates
6 Alexandra Road, Tonbridge, Kent TN9 2AA
Fax 01732-771160   Tel 01732-771116
Syndication agents for the Telegraph newspaper group.

Extel Financial
13 Epworth Street, London EC2A 4DL
Fax 0171-251 2725   Tel 0171-825 5000
Extel is one of the biggest agencies, supplying financial information and business news around the world. Based in London.

Features International
Tolland, Lydeard St Lawrence, Taunton,
Somerset TA4 3PS
Fax 01984-623901   Tel 01984-623014
Syndicates internationally newspaper and magazine features.

Fentons Oxford Press Service
20 Beech Road, Headington, Oxford OX3 7RR
No fax.   Tel 01865-62791
Covers: Oxfordshire.

Ferrari Press Agency
Suite One, 4 Wellington Parade, Blackfen Road,
Sidcup, Kent DA15 9NB
Fax: 0181-301 6630   Tel 0181-301 6630

For pictures telephone 01634-373 572
Covers: South east London and Kent.

First Features Syndicate
39 High Street, Battle, East Sussex.
Fax 01424-870877   Tel 01424-870877
Supplies all types of feature material to press and TV.

Fleet News Agency
68a Stanfield Road, Bournemouth, Dorset
BH9 2NR
          Tel 01202-515151
Covers: Bournemouth, Dorset and surrounding area.

Fleet Street News Agency
68 Exmouth Market, London EC1R 4RA
Fax 0171-278 8480   Tel 0171-278 5661
Covers: London and Home Counties.

Fleetline News Service
1a Bedford Road, London N2 9DB
Fax 0181-444 2313   Tel 0181-444 9183
Covers: London and Home Counties.

Fourth Estate Press Agency
12 North Campbell Avenue, Milngavie, Glasgow
G62 7AA
          Tel 0141-956 1540
Covers: Glasgow and west of Scotland.

Fowlers Press Agency
65 Old Park View, Enfield, Middlesex EN2 7EQ
Fax 0171-236 8136   Tel 0171-248 6858
Nationwide bankruptcy and liquidation service.

Frank Ryan News Service
Cargenriggs, Islesteps, Dumfries DG2 8ES
Fax 01387-251121   Tel 01387-253700
Covers: South west Scotland- news, features, PR, photography.

Freemans Press Agency
Raleigh Mill, Lower Raleigh Road, Barnstaple,
Devon EX31 4JQ
Fax 01271-44922   Tel 01271-24000
Covers: News and pix from all SW England.

Gemini News Service
9 White Lion Street, London N1 9PD
Fax 0171-837 5118   Tel 0171-833 4141
International news and features.

Gloucester & County News Service
26 Westgate Street, Gloucester GL1 2NG
Fax 01452-300581   Tel 01452-522270

Great North News & Features
Woody Glen, How Mill, Carlisle, Cumbria CA4
9JY
Fax 01228-70381   Tel 01228-70381
News from the northern Lake District to southern Scotland.

Great Scot International
Camerons, Midton Road, Howwood (by Glasgow Airport), PA9 1AG
Fax 01505-702333   Tel 01505-705656
Newspaper, magazine, TV, radio, book design and research. They have Scottish experts and international medicine specialists.

Guardian/Observer News Services
119 Farringdon Road, London E1M 3LX
Fax 0171-837 1192   Tel 0171-278 2332
International syndication services of news and features from the Guardian and Observer. Most national daily and Sunday newspapers have similar syndication operations; contact via their main switchboards. See also London News Service and Solo Syndication, below, and Ewan MacNaughton, above.

Headline News Agency
249 Corn Exchange, Hanging Ditch, Manchester M4 3DH
Fax: 0161-839 2066   Tel 0161-832 8967

Hebridean Press Service
1 Maritime Buildings, Stornoway, Isle of Lewis HS1 2XU
Fax 01851-704270   Tel 01851-702737
Covers: Western Isles.

Hill's Welsh Press
93 St Mary Street, Cardiff CF1 1DW
Fax 01222-224947   Tel 01222-227606
A news and photographic agency specialising in news, sport, features, PR.

Humber Press Services
17 Cambridge Street, Cleethorpes, South Humberside DN36 8HD
                         Tel 01472-357533

INS Group
211a London Road, Reading, Berks RG1 3NU
Fax 01734-351232   Tel 01734-351234
Television Centre, Northam, Southampton, Hants SO14 0PZ
Fax 01703-230552   Tel 01703-330002
Covers: Southern England.

Inter-Continental Features
48 Southerton Road, London W6 0PH
Fax 0181-741 3819   Tel 0181-748 9722
Inter-Continental Features are agents for Universal Press Syndicate, Tribune Media Services and The Washington Post Writers Group.

International Fashion Press Agency
Mumford House, Mottram Road, Alderley Edge, Cheshire SK9 7JF
Fax 01625-583537   Tel 01625-583537
Monitors the international fashion collections.

Inter Press Service
44 Grays Inn Road, London WC1X 8LR
Fax 0171-831 7477   Tel 0171-404 5730

Islamic Republic News Agency
1st Floor, 390 High Road, Wembley, Middlesex HA9 6AS
Fax 0181-900 0705   Tel 0181-903 5531

Italian News Agency / ANSA
12 Essex Street, London WC2R 5AA
Fax 0171-240 5518   Tel 0171-240 5514

Jarrolds Press Agency
68 High Street, Ipswich, Suffolk IP1 3QJ
Fax 01473-218447   Tel 01473-219193
Covers: Suffolk and surrounding area and football coverage.

Jenkins Group
186 High Street, Rochester, Kent ME1 1EY
Fax 01634-830930   Tel 01634-830888

Jiji Press
76 Shoe Lane, London EC4A 3JB
Fax 0171-583 8353   Tel 0171-936 2847
Japanese news agency.

Joe Wood Agency
11 Village Way, Dulwich, London SE21 7AN
Fax 0171-236 8136   Tel 0171-248 6858
Covers: London courts, including Old Bailey.

John Connor Press Associates
43a High Street, Lewes, East Sussex BN7 2DD
Fax 01273-486852   Tel 01273-486851
Covers: Sussex.

Kett's News Service
19 Temple Road, Norwich, Norfolk, NR3 1ED
Fax 01603-415781   Tel 01603-403303

Knight Ridder Financial Europe
78 Fleet Street, London EC4Y 1HY
Fax 0171-583 01519   Tel 0171-353 4861

Kuwait News Agency
150 Southampton Row, London WC1B 5AL
Fax 0171-278 6232   Tel 0171-278 5445

Kyodo News Service
Suites 119-130, Bush House, Aldwych, London WC2B 4PJ
Fax 0171-438 4512   Tel 0171-438 4501
Covers: UK and Scandinavia.

Lakeland Press Agency
2 Lane Head, Windermere, Cumbria LA23 2DW
Fax 01539-445128   Tel 01539-445127
Covers: Lake District.

Leicester News Service
Epic House, Charles Street, Leicester LE1 3SH
Fax 0116-251 2979   Tel 0116-251 0255
Covers: Leicestershire

London At Large
36 Aybrook Street, London W1M 3JL
Fax 0171-224 4452   Tel 0171-224 4464
A forward planning press agency specialsing in arts and
entertainment.

London News Service
68 Exmouth Market, London EC1R 4RA
Fax 0171-278 8480   Tel 0171-278 5661
International news and feature service, allied to Sport and
General picture agency and agents for the News of the World.

M & Y News Agency
65a Osborne Road, Southsea, Hants PO5
3LS
Fax 01705-291709   Tel 01705-820311
Covers: Hants, West Sussex, IoW, Dorset. Specialists in sport,
particularly soccer and cricket.

Masons News Service
Unit 9, Chesterton Mill, French's Road,
Cambridge CB4 3NP
Fax 01223-361508   Tel 01223-366996
                        Tel 01733-314294
News, photographs and TV packages from eastern England for
national and international news outlets.

Mercury Press Agency
77 Victoria Street, Liverpool L1 6DE
Fax 0151-236 2180   Tel 0151-236 6707
Covers: Merseyside and surrounding areas, with news, features
and pictures.

Middle East News Agency
86 Eamont Court, Shannon Place, London NW8
7DN
Fax 0171-586 7187   Tel 0171-586 7187

Mike Ackroyd Press Agency
Hideaway Cottage, Rolley, Hull HU20 3XR
Fax 01482-848833   Tel 01482-846990

National Association of Press Agencies
See Support organisations

National News Press Agency
30 St Johns Lane, London EC1M 4BJ
Fax 0171-250 1204   Tel 0171-417 7707
Court and general news and features in London and the south
east.

New Zealand Press Association
12 Norwich Street, London EC4A 1EJ
Fax 0171-583 3563   Tel 0171-353 7040
The co-operatively owned national news agency.

News Team International
Manchester Evening News, 164 Deansgate,
Manchester M60 2RR
Fax 0161-839 8048   Tel 0161-839 8048
News, pictures and features from the West Midlands.and
Manchester areas. Also syndication agents for Midland
Independent Newspapers.

North Scot Press Agency
19 Adelphi, Aberdeen AB1 2BL
Fax 01224-212163   Tel 01224-212141
Covers; Grampian

North Wales Press Agency
157 High Street, Prestatyn, Clwyd LL19 9ES
Fax 01745-855534   Tel 01745-852262

North West News & Sports Agency
148 Meols Parade, Meols, Merseyside L47 6AN
Fax 0151-632 5484   Tel 0151-632 5261
Covers: Wirral and Merseyside.

Northants Press Agency
141-147 Clare Street, Northampton NN1 3JA
Fax 01604-38008   Tel 01604-38811
Covers: Northamptonshire, north Beds and north Bucks.

Northern Ireland Information Service
Stormont Castle, Belfast BT4 3ST
Fax 01232-528473   Tel 01232-520700
Government information service.

Nottingham News Service
8 Musters Road, West Bridgford, Nottingham
NG3 7PL
Fax 0115-982 2568   Tel 0115-982 1697

Novosti
See Russian Information Service

Orbit News Service
1 Froghall Lane, Warrington, Cheshire WA2 7JJ
                        Tel 01925-631592
News and picture service in Cheshire and South Manchester.

Parliamentary & EU News Service
19 Douglas Street, London SW1P 4PA
Fax 0171-821 9352   Tel 0171-233 8283
News on major developments in Parliament and the EU.

Press Agency Gatwick
Europe House, Station Road, Horley, Surrey
RH8 9HL
Fax 01293-820517   Tel 01293-822713
Covers: Gatwick Airport and surrounding area.

Press Agency (Yorkshire)
4 Peckitt Street, York YO1 1SF
Fax 01904-651642   Tel 01904-655777
Covers news, sport and pictures in Yorkshire.

PA (Press Association)

PA Newscentre, 292 Vauxhall Bridge Road,
London SW1V 1AA
Fax 0171·963 7192   Tel 0171·963 7000
             Picture: 0171·963 7191
             Teletext: 0171·963 7293
             Marketing: 0171·963 7594

The PA's three companies PA News, PA Sport and PA Data Design each day transmit over 400,000 words and 80 pictures to newspapers and broadcasters. It has 250 journalists and 1,000 stringers supplying news organisations with all types of services, using the latest satellite and computer technology. Other subsidiaries are: Tellex Monitors, monitoring and reporting on news and current events on radio and TV; and Two-Ten Communications, providing media information and press release distribution services. The PA, founded in 1868, is owned by the regional press. Its News Library holds over 14 million cuttings and its Photo Library more than five million images. Its regional offices are:

PA Belfast
4th Floor, Queen's Buildings, 10 Royal Avenue, Belfast, BT1 1DB
Fax 01232·439246   Tel 01232·245008

PA Glasgow
96 Warroch Street, Glasgow G3 8DB
Fax 0141·221 0283   Tel 0141·221 8521

PA Manchester:
26 Wood Street, Manchester M3 3EF.
Fax 0161·832 0788   Tel 0161·834 6511

Raymonds Press Agency
Abbots Hill Chambers, Gower Street, Derby DE1 1SD
Fax 01332·386036   Tel 01332·340404
Covers: Central and east Midlands. One of the largest regional agencies.

Reading News Agency
12a Castle Street, Reading, Berks RG1 7RD
Fax 01734·504340   Tel 01734·573636
Covers: Thames Valley.

Reg Hayter's Sports Agency
146 Clerkenwell Road, London EC1R 5DP
Fax 0171·837 2420   Tel 0171·837 7171
Specialises in sports features and statistics.

Reuters
85 Fleet Street, London EC4P 4AJ
Fax 0171·583 3769   Tel 0171·250 1122
The world's leading supplier of news and information to the print television and radio media and financial markets. Its flagship products are the Reuters World Reports, providing 24-hour global coverage of general, political, economic and sports news. Reuters specialises in business news, and produces five international financial news services. It also runs over 35 domestic news services, plus graphics, stills, database and library facilities. Reuters is an independent public company, founded in 1851. It has 128 news bureaux in 86 countries, with 1,639 journalists, photographers and camera operators. The company's turnover in 1994 was £2,309 million. Reuters took control of the international TV news agency Visnews in 1992, integrating its operations, and renaming it Reuters Television (see below). In early 1994 Reuters bought 85 Fleet Street from the Press Association.

Rex Features
See page 107

Russian Information Agency - Novosti
3 Rosary Gardens, London SW7 4NW
Fax 0171·244 7875   Tel 0171·370 1873
Russian news and information service, formerly the Novosti Information Agency.

Samuels News & Photo Service
71 Stafford Road, Uttoxeter, Staffs ST14 8DW
Fax 01889·567181   Tel 01889·566996

Saudi Press Agency
18 Cavendish Square, London W1M 0AQ
Fax 0171·493 7258   Tel 0171·495 0418

Scarborough News/Ridings Press Agency
77 Westborough, Scarborough, North Yorks YO11 1TP
Fax 01723·500254   Tel 01723·365535

Scase News Service
Little Congham House, Congham, Kings Lynn, Norfolk PE32 1DR
Fax 01485·600672   Tel 01485·600650
Covers: East Anglia and spcialises in royal news and features.

Scottish Office Information Directorate
New St Andrews House, Edinburgh EH1 3TD
Fax 0131·244 4785   Tel 0131·244 1111
Government information service.

Scottish News & Sport
74 York Street, Glasgow G2 8JY
Fax 0141·221 3595   Tel 0141·221 3602
Covers: West and central Scotland, news and showbusiness.

Seven Day Press
193 Bath Street, Glasgow G2 4HU
Fax 0141·248 1099   Tel 0141·226 2200
Covers: Scotland, the biggest sports agency in Scotland.

Shrewsbury Press Service
1a Victorian Arcade, Hills Lane, Shrewsbury, Salop SY1 1PS
Fax 01743·247701   Tel 01743·352710
Covers: Shropshire.

Sirius Media Services
237 London Road, Benfleet, Essex SS7 2RF
Fax 01702·556248   Tel 01702·551402
Provides a range of editorial features, including crosswords and horoscopes.

Skyport Communications
The Red House, 360 Cranford Lane, Hayes,
Middlesex UB3 5HD
Fax 0181-759 7739   Tel 0181-759 1235
Covers: Heathrow Airport and surrounding area.

Smith Davis Press
8 Westport Road, Stoke-on-Trent, Staffs ST6
4AW
Fax 01782-812428   Tel 01782-812311
Provides press agency and contract pubishing services.

Solent News & Photo Agency
21 Castle Way, Southampton SO1 0BW
Fax 01703-232983   Tel 01703-223217
Covers: Hants, IoW, Wilts and Dorset, specialist subjects include
yachting and shipping.

Solo Syndication
49 Kensington High Street, London W8 5ED
Fax 0171-938 3165   Tel 0171-376 2166
Features and news from Associated Newspapers, IPC women's
weeklies, News Limited of Australia and South African newspapers. Also archive library of three million photos including
12,000 Spanish images.

Somerset News Service
43 High Street, Taunton, Somerset TA1 3PW
Fax 01823-332862   Tel 01823-331789
Covers: Somerset. News and photo coverage for national and
regional TV, radio and newspapers.

South Bedfordshire News Agency
134 Marsh Road, Luton, Beds LU3 2NL
Fax 01582-493486   Tel 01582-572222
Covers: Herts, Beds and Bucks.

South Coast Press Agency
144 Old Christchurch Road, Bournemouth,
Dorset BH1 1NL
Fax 01202-297904   Tel 01202-290199
Covers: Dorset and surrounding counties.

South East News
7 Granary Buildings, Hope Sufferance Wharf, St
Mary Church Street, London SE16 4JE
                          Tel 0171-231 5258
Covers: South east London.

South West News Service
24 Hotwell Road, Clifton, Bristol BS8 4UD
Fax 0117-922 6744   Tel 0117-927 6661
Covers: West Country and South Wales.

Space Press
Bridge House, Blackden Lane, Goostrey,
Cheshire CW4 8PG
Fax 01477-535756   Tel 01477-533403
Covers: Cheshire and surrounding counties, news, features and
pictures.

Spanish News Agency
5 Cavendish Square, London W1M 0DP
Fax 0171-436 3562   0171-636 5226
The news agency for Spain and Latin America.

Stewart Bonney News Agency
26 Pudding Chare, Newcastle-on-Tyne NE1
1UE
Fax 0191-232 1710   Tel 0191-261 1517
Covers: North east England.

Strand News Service
226 The Strand, London WC2R 1BA
Fax 0171-936 2689   Tel 0171-353 1300

Tartan Tec News Agency
see Great Scot International

Tass/Itar
12-20, Second Floor, 320 Regent Street,
London W1R 5AB
Fax 0171-580 5547   Tel 0171-580 5543
London office of the Russian news agency.

Teespress Agencies
15 Baker Street, Middlesbrough, Cleveland TS1
2LF
Fax 01642-244595   Tel 01642-242522
Covers: Teesside, North Yorkshire, South Durham.

Thomson Features
100 Avenue Road, London NW3 3HF
Fax 0171-393 7461   Tel 0171-393 7000
Daily news/lifestyle features andpictures, planning and design
service, supplements and advertorials.

Torbay News Agency
45 Lymington Road, Torquay, Devon TQ1 4BG
No fax.   Tel 01803-214555
Covers: Torbay and south Devon.

UK News
St George Street, Leicester LE1 9FQ
Fax 0116-251 2151   Tel 0116-253 0022
Set up in 1993 by Northcliffe Newspapers and Westminster
Press. It provides national and international news, sport. and
pictures to 33 regional papers including those owned by its par-
ent companies.

United Press International (UPI)
408 The Strand, London WC2R 0NE
Fax 0171-333 1690   Tel 0171-333 0999
Covers: Middle East, business, sport, features, news and political events.

Wales News Service
Westgate House, Womanby Street, Cardiff CF1
2UD
Fax 01222-665650   Tel 01222-666366
Covers: Wales and the West.

Warwickshire News & Picture Agency
41 Lansdowne Crescent, Leamington Spa,
Warwickshire CV32 4PR
Fax 01926-424760   Tel 01926-424181
Covers: Warwickshire and West Midlands.
Specialists in features, investigations and a range of
photographic services.

Watson's Press Agency
103 Adelaide Street, Blackpool, Lancs FY1
4LU
Fax 01253-23996   Tel 01253-23996
Covers: Lancashire and South Cumbria.
The agency specialises in local news, sport and assorted feature
work.

Welsh Office -
Information Division
Cathays Park, Cardiff CF1 3NQ
Fax 01222-823807   Tel 01222-825111
Government communications agency.

Wessex News
108 High Street, Hungerford, Berkshire RG17
0NB
Fax 01488-686900   Tel 01488-686810
Covers: Berks, Wilts and the south.

West Riding News & Sports Service
Prospect House, Prospect Street, Huddersfield,
HD1 2NU
Fax 01484-530604   Tel 01484-530601
Covers: West Yorkshire.

White & Reed
12a Castle Street, Reading, Berkshire
RG1 7RD
Fax 01734-504340   Tel 01734-576628
Covers: Thames Valley.
Supplies news and feature pictures also public relations and
photography.

Wilkinsons of Bradford
200 Leeds Road, Bradford, West Yorkshire BD3
9PS
Fax 01274-720375   Tel 01274-731799
News, features and sports photography.

Xinhua News Agency of China
8 Swiss Terrace, Belsize Road, London NW6
4RR
Fax 0171-722 8512   Tel 0171-586 8437
Covers: foreign and domestic affairs.

Yaffa Newspaper Service
Suite 305-7, 29 Gt Pulteney Street, London
W1R 3DD
Fax 0171-439 7318   Tel 0171-437 5133
UK representatives of the US syndication service King
Features.

PICTURE AGENCIES & LIBRARIES

The British Association of Picture Libraries and
Agencies publishes an annual directory of its
320 members, See Print Support Organisations
for more details. The standard reference book to
picture sources is the Picture Researchers
Handbook, by Hilary & Mary Evans, published
by Chapman & Hall.

Ace Photo Agency
Satellite House, 2 Salisbury Road, London SW19
4EZ
Fax 0181-944 9940   Tel 0181-944 9944
Wide-ranging colour photo library.

Action Images
74 Willoughby Lane, London N17 0SP
Fax 0181-808 6167   Tel 0181-885 3000
Specialists in sports photos.

Action Plus
54 Tanner Street, London SE1 3LL
Fax 0171-403 1526   Tel 0171-403 1558
A specialist sports and action library covering 130 professional
and amateur sports worldwide.

Adams Picture Library
156 New Cavendish Street, London W1M 7FJ
Fax 0171-436 7131   Tel 0171-636 1468
General library with the work of more than 400 photographers.

The Advertising Archives
45 Lyndale Avenue, London NW2 2QB
Fax 0171-794 6584   Tel 0171-435 6540
Collection of US and British press ads and magazine covers

Alan Jones Photos
10 Pelwood Road, Camber, East Sussex TN31
7RU
Fax: 01797-225448   Tel 01797-225448
Covers: Sussex and Kent.

Aerofilms
Gate Studio, Station Road, Borehamwood, Herts
WD6 1EJ
Fax 0181-207 5433   Tel 0181-207 0666
Aerial photography, with a library dating back to 1919.

AKG London
10 Plato Place, 71 St Dionis Road, London SW6 4TU
Fax 0171-610 61250   Tel 0171-610 6103
London representative of the large Berlin picture library AKG and the Erich Lessing Archive of Fine Art and Culture, Vienna.

All African
9 Bury Street,Newport Pagnell, Milton Keynes Bucks MK16 ODS
Fax 01908-614721   Tel 01908-614721
Images covering all aspects of the various regions and countries.

Allsport (UK)
3 Greenlea Park, Prince Georges Road, London SW19 2JD
Fax 0181-648 5240   Tel 0181-685 1010
The world's largest specialist sports library, represented in 27 countries. Has over six million images, dating from 1880.

Andes Press Agency
26 Padbury Court, London E2 7EH
Fax 0171-739 3159   Tel 0171-739 3159
Covers social, religious, political, economic and environmental issues around the world, especially in Latin America.

Aquarius Picture Library
PO Box 5, Hastings, East Sussex TN34 1HR
Fax 01424-717704   Tel 01424-721196
Film stills dating from the earliest days and show business, TV opera and ballet.

Ardea London
35 Brodrick Road, London SW17 7DX
Fax 0181-672 8787   Tel 0181-672 2067
Wildlife and the environment, in colour and mono.

Assignments Photographers
31 Whiffler Road, Norwich, Norfolk NR3 2AW
Fax 01603-789175   Tel 01603-789234
Picture coverage of East Anglia for editorial use, PR shots.

Associated Sports Photography
21 Green Walk, Leicester LE3 6SE
Fax 0116-231 1123   Tel 0116-232 0310
National and international coverage.

Astra Picture Agency
8b St Vincent Street, Edinburgh
Fax 0131-557 3122   Tel 0131-556 4934

Autograph
13 Vine Hill, London EC1R 5DX
Fax 0171-278 2322   Tel 0171-278 2333

Barnaby's Picture Library
19 Rathbone Street, London W1P 1AF
Fax 0171-637 4317   Tel 0171-636 6128
A library of over 4 million colour transparencies, b/w prints. The coverage is worldwide and historic.

Barnardo's Photographic Archive
Tanners Lane, Barkingside, Essex IG6 1QG
Fax 0181-551 6870   Tel 0181-550 8822
400,000 photos dating from 1871 onwards, covering the social work of the UK's largest children's charity.

Barratts Photopress
68 Exmouth Market, London EC1R 4RA
Fax 0171-278 8480   Tel 0171-278 1223

BBC Picture Archives
TV Centre, Wood Lane, London W12 7RJ
Fax 0181-746 0153   Tel 0181-743 80000
Programme stills, mainly light entertainment and drama dating back to 1924, plus the News and Current Affairs collection.

BBC Photograph Library
see BBC Picture Archives

Beken Maritime Services
16 Birmingham Road, Cowes, Isle of Wight PO31 7BH
Fax 01983-291059   Tel 01983-297311
Reknown marine photographers and stock library, built around the Beken family's photos. Images from 1888 to the present.

Bernsen's International Press Service (BIPS)
see The Press Features Syndicate

British Association of Picture Libraries and Agencies (BAPLA)
see Support organisations

British Film Institute
21 Stephen Street, London W1P 1PL
Fax 0171-323 9260   Tel 0171-255 1444
Holds about 3 million pictures recording the history of cinematography and includes, film, TV and portait shots.

British Library Reproductions
British Library, Great Russell Street, London WC1B 3DG
Fax 0171-4127771   Tel 0171-412 7614
Photographic and reprographic material from BL collections.

Bruce Coleman
Unit 16, Chiltern Business Village, Arundel Road, Uxbridge, Middx UB8 2SN
Fax 01895-272357   Tel 01895-257094
Transparencies on natural history, agriculture and science.

Caledonian Newspapers Picture Library
195 Albion Street, Glasgow G1 1QP
Fax 0141-553 3587   Tel 0141 305 3209
6 million news photos from 1900 onwards, many of Scotland.

Calyx Photo-News
26 High Street, Swindon, Wilts SN1 3EP
Fax: 01793-513640   Tel 01793-520131
Covers: Mid-west, M4 corridor. Picture stories, features, PR.

Camera Press
21 Queen Elizabeth Street, London SE1 2PD
Fax 0171-278 5126   Tel 0171-378 1300
Long-established general picture library of over ten million items, covering more than a century of news. Famous photographers include Snowdon, Karsh, Lichfield and Cecil Beaton.

Capital Pictures
54a Clerkenwell Road, London EC1M 5PS
Fax 0171-253 1414   Tel 0171-253 1122
Specialises in pictures of famous people, especially showbusiness, sport and politics.

Cephas Picture Library
20 Bedster Gardens, West Molesey, Surrey KT8 1SZ
Fax 0181-224 8095   Tel 0181-979 8647
Specialises in the wine industry and vineyards of the world

Christian Aid Photo Library
35-41 Lower Marsh, London SE1 7RL
Fax 0171-620 0719   Tel 0171-620 4444
Social pictures on community programmes in Africa, Asia and Latin America.

Collections
13 Woodberry Crescent, London N10 1PJ
Fax 0181-883 9215   Tel 0181-883 0083
Collections on many aspects of life in the British Isles. Also child development from pregnancy to adulthood and the emergency services.

Colorific!
Innovation Centre, 225 Marsh Wall, London E14 9FX
Fax 0171-538 3555   Tel 0171-515 3000
Large colour photo library, covering wide range of current topics.

Colorsport
44 St Peters Street, London N1 8JT
Fax 0171-226 4328   Tel 0171-359 2714
Extensive library of sport photos, including football and cricket history. All other sports date from late 1960s to the present.

Comstock
28 Chelsea Wharf, 15 Lots Road, London SW10 0QQ
Fax 0171-352 8414   Tel 0171-351 4448
Access to about five million general images, mainly colour transparencies.

Council of Photographic News Agencies
See Support organisations

David Hoffman Photolibrary
21 Norman Grove, London E3 5EG
Fax 0181-980 2041   Tel 0181-981 5041
Documentary based library dating from late 1970s, with emphasis on social issues: policing, pollution, drugs, youth protest, race, housing etc.

David King Collection
90 St Pauls Road, London N1 2QP
Fax 0171-354 8264   Tel 0171-226 0149
Expert library covering the history of life and events in Russia, USSR and China. Also posters, maps and ephemera.

David Williams Picture Library
50 Burlington Avenue, Glasgow G12 0LH
Fax 0141-337 3031   Tel 0141-339 7823
Collections covering Scotland, Iceland, northern England.

David Woodfall Wild Images
14 Bull Lane, Denbigh, Clwyd LL16 3SN
Fax 01745-815903   Tel 01745-815903
Landscape, environment and wildlife collection that covers Britain, Europe and the Americas.

Ecoscene
The Oasts, Headley Lane, Passfield, Liphook, Hants GU30 7RX
Fax 01428-751057   Tel 01428-751056
Covers all aspects of natural history, especially the effects of people on the environment around the world.

Empics
26 Musters Road, West Bridgford, Nottingham NG2 7PL
Fax 0115-945 5243   Tel 0115-945 5885
International sports photo agency covering major sports events.

Environmental Investigation Agency
2 Pear Tree Court, London EC1R 0DS
Fax 0171-490 0436   Tel 0171-490 7040
Library following the charity's campaigns. Most pictures cover endangered subjects (wild birds, rhinos, whales, forests etc).

Environmental Picture Library
5 Baker's Row London EC1R 3DB
Fax 0171-833 1383   Tel 0171-833 1355
Specialists on all environmental isues and now holding the Greenpeace collection.

Farmers Weekly Picture Library
Quadrant House, The Quadrant, Sutton, Surrey SM2 5AS
Fax 0181-652 4005   Tel 0181-652 4914
Holds two and a half milion slides of farming and country life.

ffotograff
10 Kyveilog Street, Cardiff CF1 9JA
Fax 01222-229326   Tel 01222-236879
Photolibrary, specialising in travel, exploration and the arts and covering the Middle, Far East, and Wales.

Forest Life Picture Library
Forestry Commission, 231 Corstorphine Road, Edinburgh EH12 7AT
Fax 0131-334 4473   Tel 0131-334 0303
Official image bank of the Forestry Commission, Britain's biggest landowner. Covers forestry, nature, and recreation.

Format Photo Library
19 Arlington Way, London EC1R 1UY
Fax 0171-833 0381   Tel 0171-833 0292
All-women library representing over 20 photographers.

Francis Frith Collection
Old Rectory, Shaftesbury, Dorset SP7 8AT
Fax 01747-55065   Tel 01747-855669
4,000 British towns and villages taken between 1860 and 1970.

Frank Spooner Pictures
16 Baldwins Gardens, London EC1N 7US
Fax 0171-831 2483   Tel 0171-405 9943
News picture library and Gamma photos from NY and Paris.

Geonex UK
see National Remote Sensing Centre

GeoScience Features Picture Library
6 Orchard Drive, Wye, Kent TN25 5AU
Fax 01233-812707   Tel 01233-812707
Earth sciences and natural history worldwide.

George Outram Picture Library
see Caledonian Newspapers Picture Library

Greater London Record Office
40 Northampton Road, London EC1R 0HB
Fax 0171-833 9136   Tel 0171-332 3822
Half a million photos covering the history and topography of the
London area. Run by the Corporation of London.

Greenpeace Communications
see Environmental Picture Library

Greg Evans International Photo Library
91 Charlotte Sreet, London W1P 1LB
Fax 0171-637 1439   Tel 0171-636 8238
Comprehensive colour photo library.

Guardian/Observer Photo Service
119 Farringdon Road, London E1M 3LX
Fax 0171-837 1192   Tel 0171-278 2332
International syndication service for all Guardian pictures and
for the pre-1990 Observer archive library.

Headline Photo Agency
21 Green Walk Leicester LE3 6SE
Fax 0116-231 1123   Tel 0116-232 0310
World political leaders, British stage and TV personalities.

Hulton-Deutsch Collection
21 Woodfield Road, London W9 2BA
Fax 0171-289 6392   Tel 0171-266 2660
One of the world's greatest picture libraries, covering nearly all
topics and periods, with over 15 million images. Holds more than
50 special collections, including Picture Post, Keystone, Fox,
Central Press and the world's oldest news collection. Hulton-
Deutsch was formerly the Hulton Picture Library, owned by the
BBC from 1958-88, when it was bought by Brian Deutsch.

Hutchison Library
118b Holland Park Avenue, London W11 4UA
Fax 0171-792 0259   Tel 0171-229 2743
Half a million worldwide documentary colour transparencies.
Subjects include: agriculture, energy, environments, families,
festivals, industry, landscape, religion, transport and weather.

ICCE Photo Library
Cookbury Court, Cookbury, Holsworthy, Devon
EX22 7YG
Fax 01409 281302   Tel 01409-281302
The library of the International Centre for Conservation
Education, covers conservation worldwide.

Illustrated London News Picture Library
20 Upper Ground, London SE1 9PF
Fax 0171-928 8144   Tel 0171-928 2111
News images from 1842 onwards. Covers all aspects of history.

The Image Bank
17 Conway Street, London W1 P6EE
Fax 0171-391 9111   Tel 0171-312 0300
4 Jordan Street, Manchester M15 4PY
Fax 0161-236 8723   Tel 0161-236 9226
14 Alver Street, Edinburgh EH2 4QH
Fax 0131-225 1660   Tel 0131-225 1770
Possibly the world's largest picture agency, representing 450
photographers, 300 cinematographers and 350 illustrators
through 72 branches worldwide, holding over one and a half
million images in the UK, and 20 million worldwide.

Images of Africa
11 The Windings, Lichfield, Staffs WS13 7EX
Fax 01543-417154   Tel 01543-262898
Wide range of subjects covering 11 African countries from Egypt
to South Africa but particularly strong on Kenya.

Impact Photos
26 Great Sutton Street, London EC1V 0DX
Fax 0171-608 0114   Tel 0171-251 5091
People and places around the world, world editorial photography.

Imperial War Museum
Department of Photographs, Austral Street,
London SE11 4SJ
Fax 0171-416 5379   Tel 0171-416 5000
National archive of more than five million photos dealing with
20th century warfare, especially the two world wars.

Insight Photographers
24 Coronet Street, London N1 6HD
Fax 0171-729 5098   Tel 0171-739 1198
Photos covering a wide range of political and social issues,
including urban deprivation, pollution, ethnic tensions and
nationalism.

ISE Powerstock
9 College Terrace, London E3 5AN
Fax 0181-983 3846   Tel 0181-983 4222
The International Stock Exchange collection.

Janine Wiedel Photolibrary
8 South Croxted Road, London SE21 8BB
Fax 0181-761 1502   Tel 0181-761 1502
The photojournalist's coverage of contemporary society.

Jason Hawkes Aerial Collection
12 Thornton Place, London W1H 1FG
Fax 0171-486 6565   Tel 0171-486 2800
The library covers London, and the towns and cities of Britain together with industry and environment, in detail from the air.

John Frost Historical Newspaper Service
8 Monks Avenue, New Barnet , Herts EN5 1DB
Fax 0181-440 3159   Tel 0181-440 3159
Over 65,000 British and overseas newspapers, and 100,000 cuttings, relating to outstanding events from 1640 to the present.

Katz Pictures
13 Vine Hill, London EC1R 5DX
Fax 0171-814 9899   Tel 0171-814 9898
International photo agency and library covering many topics, including personalities, news, features and current affairs.

Kevin Fitzpatrick Photography
40 Woodville Drive, Sale, Cheshire M33 1NF
Fax 0161-962 9441   Tel 0161-969 2709
Covering the northwest from south Manchester.

Kobal Collection
184 Drummond Street, London NW1 3HP
Fax 0171-383 0044   Tel 0171-383 0011
It contains over 1 milion movie images including portraits and scene stills in colour and b&w, from 1895 to the present.

MacQuitty International Photographic Collection
7 Elm Lodge, River Gardens, Stevenage Road, London SW6 6NZ
Fax 0171-384 1781   Tel 0171-385 6031
Library of 250,000 photos on social life and culture in over seventy countries dating back to the 1920s. Also some archive fim.

Magnum Photos
2nd Floor, Moreland Buildings, 5 Old Street, London EC1V 9HL
Fax 0171-608 0020   Tel 0171-490 1771
International agency and library for leading photojournalists. Over one million photos cover all aspects of C20 life from the 1936 Spanish Civil War onwards.

Mary Evans Picture Library
59 Tranquil Vale, London SE3 0BS
Fax 0181-852 7211   Tel 0181-318 0034
Large photo library specialising in history, especially social.

Military Picture Library
45a Whitemore Road, Guildford, Surrey GU1 1QU
Fax 01483-573686   Tel 01483-573400
Military photos from Britain and countries around the world.

Mirror Syndication International
21 Woodfield Road, London W9 2BA
Fax 0171-266 2563   Tel 0171-266 1133
Picture agents for Mirror Group Newspapers and the British Tourist Authority. It includes the Picture Goer archive.

Monitor Syndication
17 Old Street, London EC1V 9HL
Fax 0171-250 0966   Tel 0171-253 7071
Large agency/library specialising in people.

Motoring Picture Library
John Montagu Building, Beaulieu, Brockenhurst, Hampshire SO42 7ZN
Fax 01590-612624   Tel 01590-612345
Extensive photo library covering motoring from 1884 until today.

Museum of London Picture Library
London Wall, London EC2Y 5HN
Fax 0171-600 1058   Tel 0171-600 3699
London views, daily life and events since prehistoric times illustrated through paintings, prints, drawings etc.

National Maritime Museum
Romney Road, Greenwich, London SE10 9NF
Fax 0181-312 6632   Tel 0181-312 6631
Holds library of photos and other visual material covering all maritime topics.

National Monuments Record Centre
Kemble Drive, Swindon, Wilts SN2 2GZ
Fax 01793-414606   Tel 01793-414600
The national collection of aerial photos, and pictures of historic buildings and archaeological sites and monuments.

National Museum of Photography
See: Science Museum, below.

National Railway Museum
Leeman Road, York, North Yorks YO2 4XJ
Fax 01904-611112   Tel 01904-621261
Extensive library of railway and transport photos.

National Remote Sensing Centre
Arthur Street, Barwell, Leicestershire LE9 8GZ
Fax 01455-841785   Tel 01455 844513
UK's largest archive of satellite imagery and colour aerial photography at varying scales.

Network Photographers
3 Kirby Street, London EC1N 8TS
Fax 0171-831 4468   Tel 0171-831 3633
Group of dedicated photojournalists, with extensive news collection. Represents Rapho, Paris and Bildeberg, Hamburg. It has an extensive personality file.

Newsfocus Press Photograph Agency
18 Rosebery Avenue, London EC1R 4TD
No fax.   Tel 0171-328 8759
Specialise in portraits of leading personalities.

Nunn Syndication Library
13b Limehouse Cut, 46 Morris Road, London
E14 6NT
Fax 0171-537 2661   Tel 0171-537 2660
Specialise in the British royal family.

Pacemaker Press International
787 Lisburn Road, Belfast, N Ireland BT9 7EX
Fax 01232-682111   Tel 01232-663191
All Ireland, covering news, sport, politics, current affairs and PR.

Panos Pictures
9 White Lion Street, London N1 9PD
Fax 0171-278 0345   Tel 0171-837 7505
Documentary library specialising in Third World and Eastern
European photography, with an emphasis on environment.

Parachute Pictures
1 Navarino Grove,London Fields, London E8 1AJ
Fax 0171-249 2751   Tel 0171-275 7066
Specialist Third World photo library, with coverage of narcotics,
human rights, development issues and 'World' music.

Photofusion
17A Electric Lane, London SW9 8LA
Fax 0171-738 5509   Tel 0171 738 5774
A collection of documentary images covering all aspects of
contemporary life in Britain.

Photonews Scotland
Suite 4, Pentagon Centre, 36 Washington
Street, Glasgow G3 8AZ
Fax 0141-248 2470   Tel 0141-248 4888
One of Scotland's leading picture, news and feature agencies,.

Picture House
200 Leeds Road, Bradford, West Yorks BD3
9PS
Fax 01274-720375   Tel 01274-731799

Pictor International
30-31 Lyme Street, London NW1 0EE
Fax 0171-267 1396   Tel 0171-482 0478
A prominent library, over 30 years old, with 3 million photos on a
variety of topics, especially travel, business and industry.

Popperfoto
The Old Mill, Overstone Farm, Overstone,
Northampton NN6 0AB
Fax 01604-670635   Tel 01604-670670
One of Britain's leading picture libraries, with more than 12
million images. Strong on history. Handles photos from Reuters,
UPI, European Pressphoto Agency and Agence-France Presse.

Press Association
292 Vauxhall Bridge Road, London SW1V 1AA
Fax 0171-963 7192   Tel 0171-963 7000
Photo section of the major national news agency (see entry
above), plus important library with six million items. Very strong
on British historical news photos.

The Press Features Syndicate
9 Paradise Close, Eastbourne, Sussex BN20
8BT
                          Tel 01323-728760
International photo-feature agency and picture library.

Production Design Co
Teddington Studios, Broom Road, Teddington,
Mddx TW11 9NT
Fax 0181-943 1198   Tel 0181-977 0181
Thames Television programme stills library dating back to the
mid-fifties, including ABC and Rediffusion archive material. Also
a production design book reference collection.

Professional Sport
8 Apollo Studios, Charlton Kings Road, London
NW5 2SA
Fax 0171-482 2441   Tel 0171-482 2311
Sport agency and library with specialism in tennis and football.

RAF Museum
Grahame Park Way, Hendon, London NW9 5LL
Fax 0181-200 1751   Tel 0181-205 2266
Records the history of military aviation.

Retrograph Archive / RetroTravel Archive
164 Kensington Park Road, London W11 2ER
Fax 0171-229 3395   Tel 0171-727 9378
Library and design source of worldwide nostalgia. Posters, packaging, magazine adverts from 1860 to 1960. RetroTravel has
international travel and tourism images from 1900 to 1960.

Reuters
See Popperfoto.

Rex Features
18 Vine Hill, London EC1R 5DX
Fax 0171-837 4812   Tel 0171-278 7294
Large international picture agency and photo library, strong on
news. Represents the work of over 1,500 photographers. Several
million images covering news, personalities and features. Also
handles most News International syndication.

Robert Harding Picture Library
58 Great Marlborough Street, London W1V 1DD
Fax 0171-631 1070   Tel 0171-287 5414
Over 2 million photos on all topics.

Royal Geographical Society Picture Library
1 Kensington Gore, London SW7 2AR
Fax 0171-584 4381   Tel 0171-584 4381
Archive specialising in geographical and explorational activity
from 1830 to the present day (including moving footage). For
commercial and academic use.

Royal Photographic Society
Milsom Street, Bath, Avon BA1 1DN
Fax 01225-448688   Tel 01225-462841
Covers the history and progress of photography. Photo collection
partiularly strong on Victorian and turn of the century prints.

Sabine Openlander
Number H, Welbeck Mansions, Inglewood Road,
London NW6 1QX
Fax 0171-431 5385   Tel 0171-794 4567

Sally and Richard Greenhill
357a Liverpool Road, London N1 1NL
Fax 0171-607 7151   Tel 0171-607 8549
Large library of social documentary photos.

Science Museum
Exhibition Road, London SW7 2DD
Fax 0171-938 9751   Tel 0171-938 9750
Pictures from the collections of three major museums: the
Science Museum, York's National Railway Museum and
Bradford's National Museum of Photography, Film and
Television. The latter's stock includes important collections
(Frith, Fox Talbot, Sutcliffe, Herschel, Daily Herald Archive, etc).

Scottish Highland Photo Library
Unit 5, Castle Avenue Industrial Estate,
Invergordon IV18 0PQ
Fax 01349-852144   Tel 01349-852144
Images of all aspects of the Highlands and Islands of Scotland.

Select Photo Agency
N5 Studio, Metropolitan Wharf, Wapping Wall,
London E1 9SS
Fax 0171-265 1421   Tel 0171-265 1422
Young agency specialising in environment and current affairs.

SIN
208 Upper Street, London N1 1RL
Fax 0171-359 2228   Tel 0171-359 0200
Specialises in mainsteam rock and pop, youth culture and new
and established rock stars.

Skyscan
Oak House, Toddington, Cheltenham, Glos
GL54 5BY
Fax 01242-621343   Tel 01242-621357
Aerial photos of Britain taken using a tethered helium-filled bal-
loon as a remotely controlled camera platform.

Sport & General Press Agency
68 Exmouth Market, London EC1R 4RA
Fax 0171-278 8480   Tel 0171-278 1223
One of Britain's oldest press photo libraries, specialising in
sport, also general news stock. Allied to London News Service.

Sporting Pictures (UK)
7A Lambs Conduit Passage, London WC1R 4RG
Fax 0171-831 7991   Tel 0171-405 4500
Comprehensive international library of over 3 million pictures

Sportsphoto Agency
20 Clifton Street, Scarborough, North Yorks
YO12 7SR
Fax 01723-500117   Tel 01723-367264
International sports events and politics, film and entertainment.

Still Moving Picture Co
67a Logie Green Road, Edinburgh EH7 4HF
Fax 0131-557 9699   Tel 0131-557 9697
Photo and film library with Sottish Tourist Board's collection.

Still Pictures Environmental Agency
199a Shooters Hill Road, London SE3 8UL
Fax 0181-858 2049   Tel 0181-858 8307
A leading source on environment, the Third World and nature.

Sygma
Paddock Suite, The Courtyard, 55 Charterhouse
Street, London EC1M 6HA
Fax 0171-608 3757   Tel 0171-608 3690
London office of the large French photographic agency,
specialising in news, showbusiness, history and personalities.

Syndicated Features
International Press Centre, 76 Shoe Lane,
London EC4A 3JB
Fax 0171-583 5901   Tel 0171-405 3515
An nternational agency with six million images.

Topham Picturepoint
PO Box 33, Edenbridge, Kent TN8 5PB
Fax 01342-850244   Tel 01342-850313
Also at Suite 5.1, International Press Centre, 76
Shoe Lane, London EC4A 3JB
Fax 0171-583 5901   Tel 0171-583 5900
General agency and library, with over seven million pictures.
Includes United Press International's collection 1932-70.

Tropix
156 Meols Parade, Meols, Merseyside L47 6AN
Fax 0151-632 1698   Tel 0151-632 1698
Specialise in the Third World and the environ-ment.

United Press International (UPI)
See Popperfoto.

Universal Pictorial Press & Agency
29-31 Saffron Hill, London EC1N 8FH
Fax 0171-421 6006   Tel 0171-421 6000
3 million pictures on all topics, dating back to 1944.

Waterways Photo Library
39 Manor Court Road, London W7 3EJ
Fax 0181-567 0605   Tel 0181-840 1659
Specialise in Britain's inland waterways.

Wellcome Centre for Medical Science
210 Euston Road, London NW1 2BE
Fax 0171-611 8577   Tel 0171-611 8348
Over 150,000 images covering the history of medicine and human
culture, from ancient times to the preset day.

Windrush Photos
99 Noahs Ark, Kemsing, Kent TN15 6PD
Fax 01732-763285   Tel 01732-763486
Specialises in the environment, particularly birds.

SUPPORT ORGANISATIONS

Amalgamated Engineering & Electrical Union
Hayes Court, West Common Road, Bromley,
Kent BR2 7AU
Fax 0181-462 4959   Tel 0181-462 7755
The AEEU was formed from the merger of the Amalgamated Engineering Union and EETPU, the Electrical, Electronic, Telecommunications and Plumbing Union. The EETPU section has members in newspaper production and broadcasting and publishes quarterly newspaper Contact.

Association of American Correspondents in London
AP, 12 Norwich Street, London EC4A 1BP
Fax 0171-936 2229   Tel 0171-353 1515
The association represents a broad spectrum of 200 American journalists. It was founded in 1919. and holds regular lunches.

Association of British Editors
49 Frederick Road, Birmingham, West Midlands B15 1HN
Fax 0121-454 6187   Tel 0121-455 7949
An organisation for editors and senior editorial executives. It .publishes the quarterly British Editor.

Association of British Science Writers
23 Savile Row, London W1X 2NB
Fax 0171-973 3051   Tel 0171-439 1205
Its aim is to improve standards of science journalism. The association organises meetings with scientists and policy makers, and arranges visits. It publishes a monthly newsletter The Science Reporter.

Association of Golf Writers
c/o Daily Express Sports (Frances Jennings),
245 Blackfriars Road, London SE1 9UX
Fax 0171-922 7974   Tel 0171-922 7118

Association of Illustrators
29 Bedford Square, London WC1B 3EG
Fax 0171-580 2338   Tel 0171-636 4100
Professional association promoting British illustration and supporting illustrators through membership services. Also campaigns and lobbies. Publishes guides and monthly newsletter. Runs annual competition Images, seeking the best of British illustration, with exhibition and national tour.

Association of Little Presses
30 Greenhill, Hampstead High Street, London NW3 5UA
                          Tel 0171-435 1889
Represents more than 300 small publishers and associates producing books and magazines on all topics, especially poetry. Publishes newsletter, magazine, Press and LittlePress Information bulletins and annual catalogue; organises bookfairs.

Association of Newspaper and Magazine Wholesalers
89 Kingsway, London WC2B 6RH
Fax 0171-405 1128   Tel 0171-242 3458

Association of Photographers
9 Domingo Street, London EC1Y 0TA
Fax 0171-253 3007   Tel 0171-608 1441
Trade association for professional fashion, advertising, design and editorial photographers. Publishes monthly magazine Image. Holds annual awards and runs own gallery at address above.

Association of Publishing Agencies
15 Kingsway, London WC2B 6UN
Fax 0171-379 5661   Tel 0171-379 6268
Trade association aiming to promote awareness and effectiveness of customer magazines as a marketing medium, to maintain high standards of business practice and to act as a central information source. Affiliated to the PPA.

Association of UK Media Librarians
News International Newspapers. 1 Virginia Street, London E1 9BD
Fax 0171-782 6370   Tel 0171-782 5230
A network of information professionals keeping pace with technological developments. Publishes quarterly journal Deadline.

Audit Bureau of Circulations (ABC)
Black Prince Yard, 207-209 High Street,
Berkhamsted, Herts HP4 1AD
Fax 01442-877407   Tel 01442-870800
Regulatory body for the publishing industry, providing certified international circulation data for newspapers and magazines (the ABC figures). Also runs Verified Free Distribution, checking distribution claims of publishers of free newspapers.

Authors' Licensing & Collecting Society
74 New Oxford Street, London WC1A 1EF-
Fax 0171-323 0486   Tel 0171-255 2034
Collects and distributes royalties to writers (books, television, radio and film) and campaigns for collective rights schemes and a just share for writers from those schemes.

Birmingham Press Club
Grand Hotel,Colmore Row, Birmingham B3 2DA
Fax 0121-233 1465   Tel 0121-236 7951

Book Trust
Book House, 45 East Hill, London SW18 2QZ
Fax 0181-874 479   Tel 0181-870 9055
The Trust organises and promotes literary prizes, including the Booker Prize, runs Children's Book Week. Its Book Information Service is the best around and it publishes author profiles plus guides to book selection.

Book Trust Scotland
Scottish Book Centre, 137 Dundee Street,
Edinburgh EH11 1BG
Fax 0131-228 4293   Tel 0131-229 3663
Publishes biographies, booklists, directories of authors and
guides. The Trust organises exhibitions and readership campaigns.

British Association of Communicators in Business
3 Locks Yard, High Street, Sevenoaks, Kent
TN13 1LT
Fax 01732-461757   Tel 01732-459331
Formerly the BAIE, the association is for editors of in-house journals. It publishes the monthly BAIE News, the quarterly
magazine Communicators in Business and the annual Editors'
Handbook. It runs training programmes and organises an annual
convention and awards.

British Association of Journalists
99 Fleet Street, London EC4Y 1DE
Fax 0171-353 2310   Tel 0171-353 3003
A small non-TUC trade union set up as a rival to the NUJ in 1992
by some Mirror Group journalists and former NUJ general
secretary Steve Turner.

British Association of Picture Libraries and Agencies (BAPLA)
13 Woodberry Crescent, London N10 1PJ
Fax 0181-883 9215   Tel 0181-444 7913
BAPLA is a trade association with over 320 members libraries
and agencies from commercial and non-commercial sectors.
Publishes annual directory (invaluable to all picture users),
twice-yearly journal, members newsletter, standard form
photographers' contract and other information. Runs a telephone
enquiry service giving advice on picture sources, copyright
clearances and general industry problems.

British Copyright Council
29 Berners Street, London W1P 4AA
Fax: Phone first. 0171-359 1895
Liaison committee for the organisations representing the owners
of copyright in literary, musical and artistic works. Not an advice
service, but will try to answer written queries. Publishes two
guides to the law.

British Guild of Travel Writers
90 Corringway, London W5 3HA
                          Tel 0181-998 2223
Association of writers, authors, broadcasters and photographers
specialising in travel. Publishes monthly internal newsletter The
Globetrotter and annual directory of members.

British Institute of Professional Photography
2 Amwell End, Ware, Herts SG12 9HN
Fax 01920-487056   Tel 01920-464011
Founded in 1901, this is the leading professional organisation for
photographers. It publishes the respected monthly magazine The
Photographer, and the annual Directory of Professional
Photography (with details of the 5,000 members).

British Printing Industries Federation
11 Bedford Row, London WC1R 4DX
Fax 0171-405 7784   Tel 0171-242 6904
Trade association for employers, representing over 3,000
companies. It publishes news pamphlet Action every three weeks
and the monthly magazine Printing Industries.

British Society of Magazine Editors
c/o PPA, 15-19 Kingsway, London WC2B 6UN
Fax 0171-379 5661   Tel 0171-379 6268
Professional association for magazine editors and senior
editorial staff. The Society organises annual editorial awards and
conference and publishes sets of guidelines.

Bureau of Freelance Photographers
497 Green Lanes, London N13 4BP
Fax 0181-886 5174   Tel 0181-882 3315
Gives advice and market information to freelance photographers
supplying publishing markets (magazines, newspapers, books,
picture agencies, etc). Publishes monthly Market Newsletter and
annual Freelance Photographers Market Handbook. Annual
membership £36.

Cartoon Art Trust
Baird House, 15-17 Saint Cross Street, London
EC1N 8UN
Fax 0171-405 4717   Tel 0171-405 4717
Aims to preserve and promote the art of cartooning. Runs an
appeal to establish a national museum of cartoon art, where the
best of cartoons, caricatures and comic strips can be available
for public enjoyment and research. Building up a library of
cartoon material. Publishes quarterly newsletter and exhibition
catalogues. In 1996 they start the Cartoon Art Trust Awards.

Cartoonists' Club of Great Britain/Cartoonists' Guild
46 Strawberry Vale, Twickenham, Middlesex
TW1 4SE
Fax 0181-891 5946   Tel 0181-892 3621
The Club is a social one for professional cartoonists. It meets on
the first Tuesday of every month at the Cartoonist pub, Shoe
Lane, London EC4, publishes the monthly magazine Jester and
holds regular exhibitions.

Central Criminal Court Journalists' Association
Press Room, Old Bailey, London EC4N 7EH
Fax 0171-248 0133   Tel 0171-248 3277
Represents media interests in court coverage.

Chartered Institute of Journalists
2 Dock Offices, Surrey Quays Road, London
SE16 2XU
Fax 0171-232 2302   Tel 0171-252 1187
Certificated independent trade union concerned with preserving
standards and protecting the pay and conditions of its members.
It publishes The Journal and maintains various charities.

Chartered Society of Designers
29 Bedford Square, London WC1B 3EG
Fax 0171-580 2338   Tel 0171-631 1510

Main professional body for designers in all fields, setting and maintaining standards. Promotes high standards of design. Organises events, seminars and awards. Publishes magazine, newsletter and practice documents.

Comics Creators Guild
7 Dilke Street, London SW3 4JE
                Tel 0171-228 5989
Formerly Society for Strip Illustration. Promotes comic strips as an exciting and modern art form, which can be used effectively in entertainment, education and marketing. Also represents professionals in this field. Publishes magazine Comics Forum 2x pa, Getting Started in Comics, Collected Submissions Guidelines, Sample Scripts for Artists and Guide to Contracts.

Commonwealth Journalists Association
17 Nottingham Street, London W1M 3RD
Fax 0171-486 3822   Tel 0171-486 3844
Fosters interest in Commonwealth affairs, undertakes training of journalists in Commonwealth countries and defends journalists' rights where these are threatened. Publishes newsletter 3x pa and holds international conference.

Commonwealth Press Union
184 Fleet Street, London EC4A 2DU
Fax 0171-831 4923   Tel 0171-242 1056
Association of Commonwealth newspapers, news agencies and periodicals, upholding the ideals and values of the Commonwealth. Activities include extensive training programmes throughout the Commonwealth, and biennial conferences. Publishes bi-monthly CPU News.

Copyright Licensing Agency
90 Tottenham Court Road, London W1P 0LP
Fax 0171-436 3986   Tel 0171-436 5931
Non-profit company looking after the interests of copyright owners in copying from periodicals and books. Collects copying fees and pays them to authors (via Authors Licensing and Collecting Society, 0171-255 2034) and publishers (via Publishers Licensing Society, 0171-436 5931).

Council of Photographic News Agencies
Oak Trees, Burrows Lane, Gomshall, Shere, Surrey GU5 9QF
FAx 01483-203378   Tel 01483-203378
Represents the UK's six largest press agencies/photo libraries.

Cricket Writers Club
2 Bobble Court, Little Rissington, Gloucestershire GL54 2ND
                Tel 01451-810435
Represents most cricket writers in newspapers, magazines, TV and radio. It celebrates its 50th anniversary in 1996.

Crime Reporters Association
c/o Peter Burden, Daily Mail, 2 Derry Street, London W8 5TT
Fax 0171-937 5287   Tel 0171-938 6094
Represents crime reporters in their dealings with the Home Office and police organisations.

Critics Circle
47 Bermondsey Street, London SE1 3XT
Fax 0171-403 141   Tel 0171-403 1818
Organisation of professional critics in theatre, film, music, dance and visual arts.

Defence, Press & Broadcasting Advisory Committee
Room 2235, Main Building, Ministry of Defence, London SW1A 2HB
Fax 0171-218 5857   Tel 0171-218 2206
Aka the D-Notice Committee. The Defence, Press and Broadcasting Advisory Committee oversees the voluntary code which operates between the media and those government departments with responsibilities for national security. The vehicle for this is the DA Notice system, where "advisory notices" are issued to the media at editor level describing sensitive areas. The notices were published openly for the first time in July 1993. Editors are invited to consult the committee secretary - currently Rear Admiral David Pulvertaft - where there may be doubt. Committee founded 1912.

Edinburgh Book Festival
137 Dundee Street, Edinburgh EH11 1BG
Fax 0131-228 4333   Tel 0131-228 5444
Organises the biennial festival, described by the Guardian as Europe's happiest and largest.

Edinburgh Press Club
19 Rutland Street, Edinburgh EH1 2AE
No fax.   Tel 0131-229 2800
Social club for the media in the Edinburgh area.

EETPU
See: Amalgamated and Electrical Union above.

Electronic Book Committee
104a St John Street, London EC1M 4EH
Fax 0171-490 4706   Tel 0171-490 1185
Independent and informal grouping of publishers, hardware and software manufacturers, developers, integrators, distributors, retailers and other companies and individuals interested in promoting closer working relationships for portable platforms including the Electronic Book.

European Society for News Design
28 Holden Road, London N12 8T
Fax 0181-446 7695   Tel 0181-445 4648
For anyone - not just designers - interested in design in newspapers and magazines, looking at all aspects of the subject.

Federation of Entertainment Unions
1 Highfield, Twyford, Hants SO21 1QR
Fax 01962-713134   Tel 01962-713134
Collective body of trade unions, representing the interests of 150,000 members in the broadcasting and entertainment industries. The unions are: BECTU, Equity, Musicians Union, NUJ, Writers Guild, AEEU and Film Artistes Association. It provides liaison, representation, lobbying and co-ordination services on issues of common concern.

Fleet Street Motoring Group
Merryweather, Abney Court Drive, Bourne End,
Bucks SL8 5DL
    Tel 01628-531346
Association of motoring correspondents, holding meetings to
entertain senior industry figures.

Football Writers Association
223 Great North Way, London NW4 1PN
Fax 0181-203 4067   Tel.0181-203 0360
Represents members' interests and liaises with football bodies to
improve working conditions at football grounds.

Foreign Press Association in London
11 Carlton House Terrace, London SW1Y 5AJ
Fax 0171-925 0469   Tel 0171-930 0445
Founded 1888. Helps London-based foreign correspondents in
their professional work, providing extensive facilities and
assistance at its headquarters. Arranges briefings and social
events. Publishes newsletter and members list.

Glasgow Press Club
94 West Regent Street, Glasgow G2 2QD
No fax   Tel 0141-332 1674
Social club for the media in the Glasgow area.

Graphical, Paper and Media Union
63 Bromham Rd, Bedford MK40 2AG.
Fax 01234-270580   Tel 01234-351521
GPMU is the print and paper workers trade union, formed from
the merger of SOGAT and the NGA. Covers printing,
papermaking, inkmaking, graphic arts, publishing, bookbinding
and all allied trades. Publishes GPMU Journal.

Guild of Editors
74 Great Russell Street, London WC1B 3DA
Fax 0171-637 2748   Tel 0171-636 7014
Professional association for all newspaper editors, editorial
directors and training editors. It provides a medium for
collective consultation and representation on matters of editorial
concern and interest. Publishes quarterly Guild Journal. Lobbies
in defence of press freedom.

Institute of Printing
8 Lonsdale Gardens, Tunbridge Wells, Kent TN1
1NU
Fax 01892-518028   Tel 01892-538118
The professional body for the printing industry. Holds lectures,
debates, seminars, conferences and local branch activities.
Publishes journal Professional Printer, and the Guide to
Educational Courses in the Printing Industry..

International Association of Women Sports Photographers
Wayside, White Lodge Lane, Baslow, via
Bakewell, Derbyshire DE45 1RQ
Fax 01246-582227   Tel 01246-582376
Aims to attract more women into the profession, help beginners
and raise standards. Produces videos, books, posters, calendars
and exhibitions.

International Federation of the Periodical Press
15 Kingsway, London WC2B 6UN
Fax 0171-379 3866   Tel 0171-379 3822
FIPP works through national associations to establish and
promote worldwide the optimum conditions for developing
periodical publishing. It fosters formal and informal alliances
between publishers to exploit successful publishing ideas,
marketing initiatives and technological opportunities. Publishes
quarterly Magazine World and holds biennial FIPP World
Congress (next: 13-15 May 1996, in Tokyo).

International Freelance Association
Mumford House, Mottram Road, Alderley Edge,
Cheshire SK9 7JF
Fax 01625-584344   Tel 01625-583537
Agency of freelance journalists and photographers.

JICNARS
See National Readership Surveys

Library Association
7 Ridgmount Street, London WC1E 7AE
Fax 0171-436 7218   Tel 0171-636 7543
Professional body for librarians which awards chartership status,
sets standards and lobbies government. It works for freedom of
access to information and against censorship and library cuts.
Publishes monthly magazine Library Association Record.

London International Press Centre
76 Shoe Lane, London EC4A 3JB
Fax 0171-583 3441   Tel 0171-353 2831
Offices and other facilities for the international media in London.

London Press Club
Wig & Pen, 229-30 Strand, London WC2R 1BA
Fax 0171-583 6608   Tel 0171-583 7255
Club for journalists and the media in general which makes annu-
al awards: News Scoop of the Year, and Edgar Wallace Trophy
for Outstanding Reporting.

London Writer Circle
49 Christchurch Street, London SW3 4AS
The oldest writing circle in Britain, formed 1924. Encourages
writers (published or unpublished) through monthly meetings
and workshops in central London, and through publishing the
news review magazine Within the Circle 3x pa.

Manchester Press Club
2 Queen Street, Manchester M2 5JB
No fax.   Tel 0161-834 9532
Social club for the media in the Manchester area.

Media Resource Service
Ciba Foundation, 41 Portland Place, London
W1N 4BN
Fax 0171-637 2127   Tel 0171-631 1634
This service gives journalists free and independent advice on
medicine, science and technology. It is run by the the Ciba
Foundation. A twice yearly newsletter contains news of the MRS
and the world of science communication.

Medical Journalists' Association
Barley Mow, 185 High Street, Stony Stratford,
Bucks MK11 1AP
Tel 01908-564623
Aims to improve understanding between medical journalists and
the health and medical professions. Organises awards and social
events and publishes directory of members and newsletter.

National Artists Association
PO Box 3005, London NW1 0SJ
Fax 0171-916 1509   Tel 0171-267 0280
It represents visual artists on UK national and European bodies.
Produces quarterly bulletin.

National Association of Press Agencies
41 Landsdowne Crescent, Leamington Spa,
Warwicks CV32 4PR
Fax 01926-424760   Tel 01926-424181
Trade association for regional news and photographic agenies. A
free handbook is available.

National Federation of Retail Newsagents
Yeoman House, Sekforde Street, London EC1R
0HD
Fax 0171-250 0927   Tel 0171-253 4225
Represents the interests of 28,500 independent retail
newsagents in the UK and Ireland. It publishes the weekly
journal Trade News and has 16 regional offices

National Readership Surveys
11-15 Betterton Street, London WC2H 9BP
Fax 0171-240 4399   Tel 0171-379 0344
The NRS measures newspaper and magazine readership in the
National Readership Survey. Formed in 1992 to replace JICNARS
(Joint Industry Committee for National Readership Surveys).

National Union of Journalists
314 Grays Inn Road, London WC1X 8DP
Fax 0171-837 8143   Tel 0171-278 7916
The leading trade union representing all editorial sectors of the
media, including photographers and freelancers. Membership
totals 29,000, including 1,800 student journalists. It provides
many services for members, including legal. Campaigns for journalists' rights and freedom of information, and against censorship. Publishes: the prominent and widely read bi-monthly magazine The Journalist; bi-monthly bulletin Freelance, with news
for freelancers; Freelance Directory; Freelance Fees Guide;
Careers in Journalism guide booklet; comprehensive annual
report; the NUJ Code of Conduct; and much other material. Holds
conferences, seminars and training sessions.

Newspaper Library (British Library)
Colindale Avenue, London NW9 5HE
Fax 0171-412 7379   Tel 0171-412 7353
The national collection of local, regional and national UK
newspapers, plus a large overseas holding. Has photocopying,
photographic and microfilm services. Open Monday-Saturday,
10am-5pm, admission free but only to persons over 18. Allow
plenty of time when visiting, and take proof of identity.
Publishes a series of Newsplan Reports, and a newsletter (2x pa)

Newspaper Press Fund
35 Wathen Road, Dorking, Surrey RH4 1JY
Tel 01306-887511
A charity set up in 1864 to assist member journalists and their
dependants in need. It runs residential homes for retired
journalists and dependants. Life membership is £50.

Newspaper Publishers Association
34 Southwark Bridge Road, London SE1 9EU
Fax 0171-928 2067   Tel 0171-928 6928
Trade association for the eight publishers of national
newspapers. The NPA monitors and lobbies on their behalf. It
promotes good relations with the advertising industry and
opposes government restraints on the press.

Newspaper Society
74 Great Russell Street, London WC1B 3DA
Fax 0171-631 5119   Tel 0171-636 7014
Trade association for publishers of the local press in England,
Wales and Northern Ireland. Founded in 1836, the society is the
oldest publishers' association. Its secretariat and committees
cover a wide range of activities, from advertisement control
advice to lobbying in Brussels and Whitehall on legislation.
Publishes newspapers Production Journal (monthly) and
Headlines (bi-monthly). Runs a series of conferences, seminars
and exhibitions throughout the year. PressAd is the commercial
arm of the society, housing the industry's database on the
regional and local press. The society administers JICREG - the
Joint Industry Committee for Regional Press Research - which
provides readership data for the industry. Helps run the Regional
Press Club, a business and social body for people involved in
selling and buying regional press advertising.

Paper Federation of Great Britain
Papermakers House, Rivenhall Road, Westlea,
Swindon, Wilts SN5 7BD
Fax 01793-886182   Tel 01793-886086
The employers federation for all sectors of the paper industry.
Runs the Pulp and Paper Information Centre, supplying data to
the media.

Paper Industry Technical Association
Randalls Road, Leatherhead, Surrey KT22 7RU
Fax 01372-377526   Tel 01372-376161
Provides a forum for people interested in the technology of the
paper industry.

Parliamentary Press Gallery/Lobby Journalists
House of Commons, London SW1A 0AA
Tel 0171-219 4700

PEN
7 Dilke St, London SW3 4JE
Fax 0171-351 0220   Tel 0171-352 6303
English centre of the International club for authors, with 119
centres in 87 countries. Fights for freedom of expression and
against censorship, and helps imprisoned writers worldwide.
Makes annual awards, holds regular meetings and publishes
newsletter. Hires out cassettes of meetings. PEN stands for
Poets, Playwrights, Editors, Essayists and Novelists.

Periodical Publishers Association
15 Kingsway, London WC2B 6UN
Fax 0171-379 5661   Tel 0171-379 6268
The trade association for magazine publishers, representing
nearly 200 companies generating 80% of the industry's revenue.
Lobbies on behalf of members, and organises conferences,
seminars and awards. Produces many publications, including the
journal Magazine News, annual Magazine Handbook with key
data on the industry, and industry overviews. The PPA provides
secretariats for the Association of Publishing Agencies (customer
magazines), the International Federation of the Periodical Press
(FIPP) UK Newsletter Publishers' Association and the British
Society of Magazine Editors (BSME). Also runs the Periodicals
Training Council - see below.

Periodicals Training Council
See Training, page 116

Pira International
Randalls Road, Leatherhead, Surrey KT22 7RU
Fax 01372-377526   Tel 01372-376161
Pira is the leading UK centre for research, consultancy, training
and information for the paper and board, packaging, printing and
publishing industries. Pira publishes books, directories, reviews
and newsletters.

Press Complaints Commission
see How to Complain, page 123

Press Standards Board of Finance
Merchants House Buildings, 30 George Square,
Glasgow G2 1EG
Fax 0141-248 2362   Tel 0141-221 3957
Co-ordinates and finances self-regulation in the newspaper and
magazine publishing industry.

PressWise
see Lobbyists, page 230

Publishers Association
19 Bedford Square, London WC1B 3HJ
Fax 0171-636 5375   Tel 0171-580 6321
Trade association for UK book publishers, offering a wide range
of services, and producing many of its own publications.

Publishers Licensing Society
See: Copyright Licensing Agency, above.

Publishers Publicity Circle
48 Crabtree Lane, London SW6 6LW
Fax 0171-385 3708   Tel 0171-385 3708
Provides a forum for book publicists to meet and share
information. Monthly meetings are held with members of the
media. Publishes directory and monthly newsletter.

Royal Photographic Society
Milsom Street, Bath, Avon BA1 1DN
Fax 01225-448688   Tel 01225-462841
A learned society founded in 1853 for the advancement and
promotion of the art and science of photography.

Provides an extensive range of services. Arranges many
exhibitions, lectures, seminars and workshops. The RPS runs its
own gallery, museum and archives. Publishes monthly
Photographic Journal and bi-monthly Journal of Photographic
Science.

St Bride Printing Library
St Bride Institute, Bride Lane, Fleet Street,
London EC4Y 8EE
Fax 0171-583 7073   Tel 0171-353 4660
A unique public reference library covering all aspects
of printing, with an extensive historical collection including
artefacts, archive material, photographs and patents. The
collection is particularly strong on newspaper history and is
housed in atmospheric surroundings just off Fleet Street. Hours:
9.30am-5.30pm, Monday-Friday. Also home of the Printing
Historical Society.

Scottish Daily Newspaper Society
30 George Square, Glasgow G2 1EG
Fax 0141-248 2362   Tel 0141-248 2375
The trade association for those connected with the Scottish
national papers.

Scottish Newspaper Publishers Association
48 Palmerston Place, Edinburgh EH12
5DE
Fax 0131-220 4344   Tel 0131-220 4353
Trade association and employers' organisation for the Scottish
weekly press.

Scottish Publishers Association
Scottish Book Centre, 137 Dundee Street,
Edinburgh EH11 1BG
Fax 0131-228 3220   Tel 0131-228 6866
Trade association working for 68 Scottish publishers. Publishes
Directory of Publishing in Scotland (annually) and new books
lists. Provides training, advice, marketing and promotion
services to members.

Small Press Group
c/o SKS, 20 Paul Street, Frome, Somerset BA11
1DX
Fax 01373-452888   Tel 01373-451777
Britain's largest organisation of small presses, autonomous
publishers and independent magazines. Holds annual fair
in late September and publishes members magazine and
yearbook with DIY guide. Runs Small Press Centre at
Middlesex University.

Society of Authors
84 Drayton Gardens, London SW10 9SB
Fax 0171-373 5768   Tel 0171-373 6642
An independent trade union, which was founded in 1884, to
promote the interests of authors and to defend their rights. The
Society gives a personal service to writers, with wide range of
facilities including advice on contracts. It arranges
conferences, meetings and social events. The Society publishes a
quarterly journal, The Author, plus numerous guides and has
over 5,500 members.

Society of Freelance Editors and Proofreaders
38 Rochester Road, London NW1 9JJ
Tel 0171-813 3113
Professional body representing editors, especially freelances, and working to improve editorial standards by providing training, information and advice. Publishes newsletter, directory, conference proceedings and other publications.

Society of Indexers
38 Rochester Road, London NW1 9JJ
No fax. Tel 0171-916 7809
Promotes indexing, the quality of indexing and the profession of indexers. Publishes quarterly newsletter, twice-yearly journal The Indexer, and ad hoc papers. Provides open learning course.

Society of Picture Researchers and Editors
BM Box 259, London WC1N 3XX
Phones: Admin 0171-405 5011
Register 01727-833676
Professional body promoting picture research as a profession. Encourages the use of trained researchers throughout the media, and runs a freelance register putting employers in touch with freelancers. Gives advice to members, organises meetings and publishes quarterly magazine.

Society of Typographic Designers
Chapelfield Cottage, Randwick, Stroud, Glos
GL6 6HS
Fax 01453-759311 Tel 01453-759311
Promotes high standards of typographic design.

Society of Women Writers & Journalists
110 Whitehall Road, Chingford, London
E4 6DW
Tel 0181-529 0886
Founded 1894. Encourages literary achievement and the upholding of professional standards. Organises competitions, social events and monthly meetings. Publishes magazine The Woman Journalist 3x pa.

Sports Writers Association of Gt Britain
c/o Sports Council, 16 Upper Woburn Place, London WC1H 0QP
Fax 0171-383 0273 Tel 0171-387 9415
Founded 1948 for sports journalists. Now has over 500 members. Organises meetings and social events. Makes awards for the Sportsman, Sportswoman and Sports Team of the Year. Organises the British Sports Journalism Awards in conjunction with the Sports Council. It appoints the Olympic press attache for the British media.

Talking Newspaper Association
National Recording Centre, Heathfield, East Sussex TN21 8DB
Fax 01435-865422 Tel 01435-866102
National subscription service transposing printed media on to audio cassettes for people with a visual handicap or other disability. A registered charity, with over 500 local groups, providing two million tapes of over 900 newspapers and magazines for 150,000 visually impaired people.

UK Picture Editors Guild
Bob Bodman, Daily Telegraph, 1 Canada Square, London E14 5DT
Tel 0171-538 6369
Formed 1971 for picture editors on national and provincial newspapers, and for those involved in organising pictures for pre-press publication. Provides mutual advice, and organises three meetings a year.

Women in Publishing
Information Officer, c/o 12 Dyott St, London
WC1A 1DF
Provides support and encouragement for women working in publishing and related fields through training courses and monthly meetings (with panels of speakers). Publishes monthly newsletter Wiplash, ad hoc reports, surveys and Women in Publishing Directory.

Women Writers Network
c/o 23 Prospect Road, London NW2 2JU
Helps women writers further their professional development by providing a forum for exchanging information and giving support. Holds monthly meetings, and publishes monthly newsletter and annual directory of members.

Worshipful Company of Stationers & Newspaper Makers
Stationers' Hall, Ave Maria Lane, London
EC4M 7DD
Fax 0171-489 1975 Tel 0171-248 2934
City livery company for stationers, printers and newspaper makers.

Writers Guild of Great Britain
430 Edgware Road, London W2 1EH
Fax 0171-706 2413 Tel 0171-723 8074
Trade union representing professional writers in film, TV, radio, theatre and books. Has scored many successes in improving terms and conditions. Holds regular meetings and publishes quarterly Writers' Newsletter.

Yachting Journalists' Association
Spinneys, Woodham Mortimer, Maldon, Essex
CM9 6SX
Fax 01245-223189 Tel 01245-223189
Promotes yachting - sail and power - in all its forms, and furthers the interests of its members. Open to writers, broadcasters, photographers and illustrators. Publishes annual directory of members, with media advice for event organisers. Organises awards: Yachtsman of the Year, and Young Sailor of the Year, both sponsored by BT.

Young Newspaper Executives' Association
Newspaper Society, 74 Great Russell Street, London WC1B 3DA
Fax 0171-631 5119 Tel 0171-636 7014
The regional newspaper industry's focal point for executives aged under 40. Members relish the word "executive", and are more pompous than former thirty-somethings who were content to be the Young Newspapermen's Association.

TRAINING FOR THE PRESS

Print journalism · the rushed and nervy business of getting words and pictures onto pages · is a trade for hustlers, idealists and the politically committed. Unlike real professions such as lawyering, doctoring, accounting and teaching in state schools, there are no compulsory qualifications. Job ads don't usually ask for the formally qualified and, as a rule, editors reinforce their self images as gifted amateurs by hiring on the basis of hunch and evidence of past work. The iron law of this trade is that you are as good as your last by-line.

This begs the question of how to get your first pieces published. Answers: school and university mags; better still, make a close study of the sort of stories your local paper runs and offer them something similar for nothing; ditto your favourite magazines. The beginner must do anything it takes to get into print and the paradox is that cheap (and maybe amateurish) copy will be accepted by the end of the market which says it is the keenest on training. The further up the hierarchy you look the less concern there is with formal training. The national papers attract the pushy and the bright and rarely even bother to pay lip-service to training. However they draw their talent from small magazines and papers and here, due to efforts of the Newspaper Society and the Periodical Publishers Association, there has been a growing commitment to training.

However, the training scene is one of muddle with many disparate schemes, qualifications and attempts at professionalisation. First is the in-company training offered by about half the local papers, particularly the ones belonging to the larger groups. The larger magazine companies also maintain training departments although, in general, their approach is less systematic than the local papers. Next come a plethora of courses accredited by the National Council for Training of Journalists (for newspapers) and by the PPA's training wing the Periodical Training Council (for magazines). Beyond these (and listed later in the guide from page 234 because they are not practical training) are the media studies courses which, it must be said, are more attractive to students than employers.

Magazines and local newspapers support the new National Vocational Qualifications which have introduced formal training mechanisms to places where none existed before. What was once called Sitting with Nellie or on-the-job training is now being dignified with certificates and the backing of the trade bodies. The Newspaper Society hopes that NVQs, which it says are a "guarantee of competence", will move the industry towards commonly agreed standards. Within the next two years, the likelihood is that the NCTJ's National Certificate will be amalgamated with NVQs.

Whether there is training or not, a first degree in any subject is more or less mandatory for any aspiring journalist. After that the ways into work are many and vague, usually mundane and ill-paid. Four out of five local paper trainees start on under £10,000 in offices that exploit the fact that a job in journalism is so fashionable. Apprenticeships, of one kind and another, must still be served. The rewards are unpredictable but there are good livings to be made. All it takes is a mixture of determination, talent, luck and (increasingly) a qualification. Having a parent in the business doesn't hurt either.

Training contacts

National Council for the Training of Journalists
Latton Bush Centre, Southern Way, Harlow, Essex CM18 7BL
Fax 01279-438008   Tel 01279-430009
The NCTJ is a charity which runs the most widely accepted independent training schemes for print journalists. It accredits courses at universities and colleges and should be the first point of contact for those who need to know more of the pre-entry, block and day release options for formal training. The NCTJ has three standard Textbooks - Essential Law for Journalists, published by Butterworths, Essential Local Government for Journalists, and Essential Central Government for Journalists published by LGC Communications - and provides a mail order service of recommended books on many aspects of journalism. The Council's short course department has provided over 500 open courses for more than 7,000 journalists.

National Union of Journalists
See Print Support Organisations, page 113
The NUJ's booklet Careers in Journalism is recommended.

Newspaper Society
See Print Support Organisations, page 113
The Society takes broad interest in local newspaper training and organises marketing, advertising and general management courses. It also promotes NiE, the Newspaper in Education scheme which oversees some 600 educational projects linking schools and newspaper companies. Although the Society leaves course accreditation to the NCTJ, it is a prime source of information on all aspects of newspaper training and its booklet Making the Decision is recommended.

The Periodicals Training Council
15-19 Kingsway, London WC2B 6UN
Fax 0171-836 8798   Tel 0171-379 5661
The PTC has been the training arm of the Periodical Publishers Association since 1992. It aims to enhance the performance of the UK magazine industry and act as a focus for training. It has recently been active in setting up magazine NVQs and has accredited the vocational courses in periodical journalism listed below. The Council publishes an annual Directory of Magazine Training.

RSA Examinations Board
Westwood Way, Coventry CV4 8HS
Fax 01203 468080   Tel 01203 470033
The NVQ awarding body.

Scottish Daily Newspaper Society/Scottish Newspaper Publishers Association
See PRINT support organisatons
Contact points for SVQ, the Scottish version of NVQs.

Accredited courses

The following institutions offer courses validated by the National Council for the Training of Broadcast Journalists (NCTJ) and the Periodicals Training Council (PTC).

Bell College of Technology
Almada Street, Hamilton, Lanarkshire ML3 0JB
                         Tel 01698-283100
NCTJ accredited two year Higher National Diploma.

Bournemouth University
Dorset House, Talbot Campus, Fern Barrow, Pool, Dorset BH12 5BB
                         Tel 01202 524111
NCTJ accredited degree course.

Calderdale College Further Education Corporation
The Percival Whitley Centre, Francis Street, Halifax, West Yorkshire HX1 3UZ
                         Tel 01422-358221
NCTJ accredited day-release course.

City of Liverpool Community College
Faculty of Adult & Continuing Education, Muirhead Centre, Muirhead Avenue East, Liverpool L11 1ES
                         Tel 0151-252 1515
NCTJ accredited day-release, degree and one year postgraduate courses.

College of Cardiff
University of Wales, 69 Park Place, Cardiff CR1 3AS
                         Tel 01222 874000
PTC accredited postgraduate diploma in journalism.

Cornwall College
Centre for Arts, Media & Social Sciences, Pool, Redruth, Cornwall TR15 3RD
                         Tel 01209 712911
NCTJ accredited pre-entry academic year and 20 week postgraduate courses.

Darlington College of Technology
Cleveland Avenue, Darlington, Co. Durham DL3 7BB
                         Tel 01325-503050
NCTJ accredited pre-entry academic year, pre-entry calendar year and block release courses.

Glasgow Caledonian University
Scottish Centre for Journalism Studies, Cowcaddens Road, Glasgow G4 0BA
                         Tel 0141-331 3000
NCTJ accredited post-graduate course.

Gloucestershire College of Arts & Technology
Brunswick Campus, Brunswick Road, Goucester GL1 1HU
                         Tel 01452-426549
NCTJ accredited pre-entry academic year course.

Graduate Centre of Journalism
City University, Northampton Square, London EC1V 0HB
                         Tel 0171-477 8000
PTC and NCTJ accredited periodical journalism diploma and one year postgraduate course.

Gwent Tertiary College
Pontypol and Usk Campus, Blaendare Road, Pontypool, Gwent NP4 5YE
                         Tel 01459-755141
NCTJ accredited pre-entry academic year course.

Handsworth College
Birmingham   Tel 0121-551 6031
An NCTJ approved college access course.

Harlow College
East Site, The Hides, Harlow, Essex CM20 1LT
                         Tel 01279-441288
NCTJ accredited block release, pre-entry academic year and two year HND courses and a 22 week postgraduate course.

Highbury College
Dovercourt Road, Portsmouth, Hants PO6 2SA
                         Tel 01705-383131
NCTJ and PTC accredited block release, pre-entry academic year, pre-entry calendar year courses and one year course in magazine journalism.

Journalism Training Centre
Mill Green Road, Mitcham, Surrey CR4 4HT
                         Tel 081-640 3696
PTC accredited course of 15 weeks, run three times a year,.

Lambeth College
Vauxhall Centre, Belmore Street, Wandsworth,
London SW8 2JY
Tel 0171-501 5424
NCTJ accredited pre-entry academic year course, for ethnic
minorities only.

The London College of Fashion
20 St John Prince's Street, London W1M 0DG
Tel 0171-514 7400
PTC accredited fashion degree with journalism and PR options.

The London College of Printing
School of Media, Herbal House, Back Hill,
Clerkenwell EC1 5EN
Tel 0171-514 6500
PTC accredited pre-entry certificate and graduate diploma in
periodical journalism.

Napier University of Edinburgh
Department of Print Media, Publishing and
Communications. 10 Colinton Road, Edinburgh
EH10 5DT
Tel 0131-4442266
NCTJ accredited block release course.

PMA Training
The Old Anchor, Church Street, Hemmingford
Grey, Camridgeshire PE18 9DF
Tel 01480-300653
PTC accredited postgraduate course in magazine journalism.

School of Communications
University of Westminster, 18-22 Riding House
Street, London W1P 7PD
Tel 0171-911 5000
PTC accredited one year diploma for ethnic minority
graduates.

Sheffield College
Stradbroke, Spinkhill Drive, Sheffield
S13 8FD
Tel 0114-2602700
NCTJ accredited block release, pre-entry academic year, pre-
entry calendar year and pre-entry Easter to Easter courses. Also
a course in photojournalism and press photography.

Strathclyde University
26 RichmondStreet, Glasgow G4 0BA
Tel 0141-553 4166
NCTJ accredited one year postgradute course.

Surrey Institute of Art & Design
Falkner Road, Farnham, Surrey GU9 7DS
Tel 01252-722441
NCTJ accredited two year HND course.

Swansea College
Tel 01792-206871
An NCTJ approved college access course.

University of Central Lancashire
Centre for Journalism, Preston, Lancs PR1 1HE
Tel 0772-201201
NCTJ accredited pre-entry academic year, degree and one year
postgraduate courses.

University of Wales see **College of Cardiff**

Yale College
Wrexham FE Centre, Grove Park Road,
Wrexham, Cywyd LL12 7AA
Tel 01978-311794
NCTJ accredited day release course.

Group training

Some local newspaper companies have their
own qualifications for reporters combining
competence and exam-based study. Details are
best obtained from the individual groups below.

EMAP Training Centre
4th Floor, 57 Priestgate, Peterborough PE1 1JW
Tel 01733 555111

Midland News Association
Rock House, Old Hill, Tettenhall Wolverhampton,
West Midlands WV6 8QB
Fax 01902-772415   Tel 01902-3742126

TRN Editorial Training Centre
Thomson House, Groat Market, Newcastle upon
Tyne NE1 1ED
Tel 0191-232 7500

Southern Newspapers
Journalism Training Centre, The Fountain, 1
High Street, Christchurch, Dorset BH23 1AE
Tel 01202-480180

Thomson Regional Newspapers
Hannay House, 39 Clarendon Road, Watford,
Hertfordshire WD1 1JA
Fax 01923-817020   Tel 01923-55588

Trinity International Holdings
6 Heritage Court, Lower Bridge Street, Chester,
Cheshire CH1 1RD
Fax 01244-341677   Tel 01244-350555

United Provinicial Newspapers
Wellington Street, Leeds, West Yorkshire LS1
1RF
Fax 0113-243 2701   Tel 0113-244 3430

Westminster Press Training Centre
Hanover House, Marine Court, St Leonards on
Sea, East Sussex TN38 0DX
Tel 01424-435991

PRESS MAGAZINES

The Author
84 Drayton Gardens, London SW10 9SB
Fax: 0171-373 5768   Tel 0171-373 6642
Publisher: Society of Authors.
Quarterly news magazine for society members and a twice yearly supplement: The Electronic Author.

The Bookseller
12 Dyott Street, London WC1A 1DF
Fax 0171-836 6381   Tel 0171-836 8911
Publisher: Whitaker Bibliographic Services.
The leading weekly trade paper of the book publishing and selling industry. Each year it publishes two huge guides (called Spring Books, and Autumn Books) with details of thousands of forthcoming books.

Books in the Media
15-Up, East Street, Lewins Yard, Chesham, Bucks HP5 1HQ
Fax 01494-784850   Tel 01494-792269
Publisher: Bookwatch.
Weekly resource newsletter keeping bookshops and libraries informed of books appearing in the media. Bookwatch carries out book-related research for newspapers, TV and radio.

British Journalism Review
13 Smiths Yard, Summerley Street, London SW18 4HR
Fax 0181-947 2664   Tel 0181-947 2777
Publisher: John Libbey & Co/BJR Publishing.
Scholarly quarterly, providing a critical forum for discussion of media topics.

British Printer
1a Chalk Lane, Cockfosters Road, Barnet, Herts EN4 0BU
Fax 0181-242 3154   Tel 0181-242 3000
Publisher: Emap Maclean.
Monthly news and features from around the printing industry.

Comagazine
Tavistock Road, West Drayton, Middx UB7 7QE
Fax 01895-445255   Tel 01895-444055
Publisher: Comag Quadraphic Design
Quarterly review of the magazine industry.

Comics Forum
7 Dilke Street, London SW3 4JE
Publisher: Comics Creators Guild.
Biannual magazine on the work of comic strip artists.

Financial Times Newsletters
Maple House, 149 Tottenham Court Road, London WC1P 9LL
Fax 0171-896 2256   Tel 0171-896 2222
Publisher: Financial Times Telecom & Media Publishing.
Produces the following newsletters: Asia-Pacific Telecoms Analyst; Business Computing Brief; Mobile Communications; Multimedia Business Analyst; Music & Copyright; New Media Markets; Screen Finance; Telecom Makets and related management reports.

Folio
PO Box 2029, Sturminster Newton, Dorset DT10 1YE
Fax 01258-821115   Tel 01258-821114
Publisher: Cowles Business Media
Magazine for magazine managers. 21x pa.

Free Press
8 Cynthia Street, London N1 9JF
Fax 0181-837 8868   Tel 0171-278 4430
Publisher: Campaign for Press and Broadcasting Freedom.
Members news magazine, with critical analysis of monopoly media ownership and control, and other issues. 6x pa.

Freelance Market News
Cumberland House, Lissadel Street, Salford, Greater Manchester M6 6GG
Fax: Phone first. 0161-745 8850
Monthly newsletter with details of markets for the work of freelance writers.

Freelance News
46 Ford End, Woodford Green, Essex IG8 0EG
Fax 0181-506 1011   Tel 0181-506 1011
Publisher: Stephen Webb & Co.
Bi-monthly journal of the Chartered Institute of Journalists freelance division, covering all matters of interest to freelancers.

Headlines
74 Gt Russell Street, London WC1B 3DA
Fax 0171-631 5119   Tel 0171-636 7014
Publisher: The Newspaper Society.
The Newspaper Society's news magazine for members, advertisers, agencies related companies and organisations. with much data on the regional press. 6x pa. The society also publishes Production Journal, a monthly review of newspaper technology.

Index on Censorship
33 Islington High Street, London N1 9BR
Fax 0171-278 1878   Tel 0171-278 2313
Publisher: Writers & Scholars International.
Comprehensive in-depth chronicle of the inter-national censorship of scholars, writers and the press, and the fight against it. Set up in 1972, the Index was redesigned and relaunched in 1994. 6x pa.

The Journalist
314 Grays Inn Road, London WC1X 8DP
Fax 0171-837 8143   Tel 0171-278 7916
Publisher: National Union of Journalists.
Two NUJ publications with the same title: a wide-ranging and lively magazine for all members, covering every aspect of media work, 6x pa; and a periodic tabloid newspaper concentrating on NUJ news, mainly delivered to members in offices. Together they provide Britain's biggest non-establishment view of journalism.

Journalists Handbook
2/7 Galt House, 31 Bank Street, Irvine KA12 0LL
Fax 01294-311322   Tel 01294-311322
Publisher: Carrick Publishing.
Quarterly journal with articles and a contacts list consisting of organisations which have paid for entries. Since 1993 Carrick has also published a small Media Yearbook.

Litho Week
See: Print Week, below.

The Magazine Business Weekly Report
8 Tottenham Mews, London W1P 9PJ
Fax 0171-436 5290   Tel 0171-436 5211
Publisher: The Magazine Business.
Weekly faxed newsletter with the latest information on what's happening in the magazine industry.

Magazine News
Imperial House, 15-19 Kingsway, London WC2B 6UN
Fax 0171-379 5661   Tel 0171-379 6268
Publisher: Periodical Publishers Association.
The update for people in media, with information of interest to advertisers and agencies. 5x pa.

Media Law & Practice
2 Addiscombe Road, Croydon, Surrey CR9 5AF
Fax 0181-686 3155   Tel 0181-686 9141
Quarterly legal journal.

Media Law Review
200 Aldersgate Street, London EC1A 4JJ
Fax 0171-600 5555   Tel 0171-600 1000
A quarterly newsletter which started in 1993. It is produced by law firm Clifford Chance and the Periodical Publishers Assoc..

New Media Age
50 Poland Street, London W1V 4AX
Fax 0171-439 1480   Tel 0171-287 9800
A mag for travellers on the information superhighway.

Newspaper Focus
60 Waldegrave Road, Teddington, Middlesex TW11 8LG
Fax 0181-943 5639   Tel 0181-943 5636
The newspaper publishers' monthly newspaper, with analysis, features, comment and data. Published by Haymarket.

PrePress News
3 Percy Street, London W1P 9FA
Fax 0171-436 1675   Tel 0171-436 1671
Pubisher: Forme Communications
News, reviews and features relating to the print production process.

Print Week
60 Waldegrave Road, Teddington, Middlesex TW11 8LG
Fax 0181-943 5639   Tel 0181-943 5000
Publisher: Haymarket.
Originally Litho Week, renamed in mid-1993. Widely-read weekly magazine, covering all the industry and its latest news.

Printing Industries
11 Bedford Row, London WC1R 4DX
Fax 0171-405 7784   Tel 0171-242 6904
Publisher: British Printing Industries Federation.
The printers management journal (also known as Pi), published 10x pa.

Printing World
Sovereign Way, Tonbridge, Kent TN9 1RW
Fax 01732-361534   Tel 01732-364422
Publisher: Benn Publications.
Large-circulation monthly covering all aspects of the printing industry and its personalities.

Private Eye
6 Carlisle Street, London W1V 5RG
Fax 0171-437 0705   Tel 0171-437 4017
Publisher: Pressdram
Independent fortnightly satirical magazine. An in-house journal for journalists and one of the few magazines which does not depend on advertising for its survival.

Production Journal
See: Headlines, above.

Professional Printer
8 Lonsdale Gardenns, Tunbridge Wells, Kent TN1 1NU
Fax 01892-538118   Tel 01892-538118
Publisher: Institute of Printing.
Journal of news and articles, published 6x pa.

The Publisher
Conbar House, Mead Lane, Hertford, Herts SG13 7AS
Fax 01992-500717   Tel 01992-584233
Publisher: Publishing Magazines
For publishers in the magazine business.

Publishing
3 Percy Street, London W1P 9FA
Fax 0171-436 1675   Tel 0171-436 1671
Publisher: Forme Communications.
Monthly coverage of issues affecting newspaper and magazine managers.

Publishing News
43 Museum Street, London WC1A 1LY
Fax 0171-242 0762   Tel 0171-404 0304
The weekly newspaper of the book trade.

Retail Newsagent
11 Angel Gate, City Road, London EC1V
2PT
Fax 0171-837 0821   Tel 0171-837 3168
Publisher: Newtrade Publishing (National
Federation of Retail Newsagents).
Weekly newspaper, established in 1888, covering the full CTN
business.

Secrets
88 Old Street, London EC1V 9AX
Fax 0171-608 1279   Tel 0171-253 2445
Publisher: Campaign for Freedom of
Information.
Produced irregularly the newspaper monitors unnecessary
official secrecy and its effects on the public and the
media. The campaign has 80 prominent national bodies
affiliated to it.

UK Press Gazette
Chalk Lane, Cockfosters Road, Barnet, Herts
EN4 0BU
Fax 0181-242 3088   Tel 0181-242 3000
Publisher: Emap.
The top weekly paper for all journalists with a concentration on
newspapers and magazines, though plenty of coverage about
television and radio.

Writers' Guide
11 Shirley Street, Hove, East Sussex
BN3 3WJ
Publisher: G Carroll.
Small, home-produced guide to outlets and publications for
freelance writers. 8x pa.

Writers Monthly
29 Turnpike Lane, London N8 0EP
Fax 0181-347 8847   Tel 0181-342 8879
Publisher: The Writer
Magazine for freelance writers.

Writers News
PO Box 4, Nairn, Highlands and Islands IV12
4HU
Fax 01667-54401   Tel 01667-54441
Independent subscription monthly for all writers and would-be
writers. Also publishes quarterly Writing Magazine, available on
news-stands.

Writers' Newsletter
430 Edgware Road, London W2 1EH
Fax 0171-706 2413   Tel 0171-723 8074
Publisher: Writers' Guild of Gt Britain.
Quarterly news from the writer's own trade union, full of useful
information and articles.

YEARBOOKS

Benn's Media
Benn Business Information Services
                                    Tel 01732-362666
Three vols £248, single vols £104.
Benn's has the most comprehensive listings amongst the general
media directories, and is also the most commonly stocked in
public libraries. It comes in three volumes, covering the UK,
Europe and the rest of the world. The UK volume lists around
19,000 organisations, publications and broadcasting stations.
Established 1846.

**Directory of Book Publishers, Distributors &
Wholesalers**
Booksellers Association   Tel 0171-834 5477
£41.
The leading ordering guide and reference book for the book
trade.

Directory of Publishing
Cassell & the Publishers Association
                                    Tel 0171-420 5555
£55.
The definitive guide to the book publishing business, with all
main publishers, organisations and agencies detailedin the UK
and the Commonwealth.

European Media Minibook Series
NTC Publications   Tel 01491-574671
£48 each.
Four books profiling the statistics of the main media
markets in Europe: TV, Radio, Cinema and Newspapers and
Magazines

Freelance Directory and Guide to Freelancing
National Union of Journalists   0171-278 7916
£20.
Biennial directory of 1,500 freelance reporters, writers,
photographers, broadcasters, editors, subs, cartoonists and
illustrators.

Freelance Fees Guide
National Union of Journalists
                                    Tel 0171-278 7916
free to members.
Freelancers' guide to fees in all media, plus advice on contracts
and copyright.

**Freelance Photographer's Market
Handbook**
Bureau of Freelance Photographers
                                    Tel 0181-882 3315
£9.95.
How to find possible markets for photographs, mainly with
magazines.

IPO Directory
Central Office of Information
Tel 0171-261 8534
£12 annual subscription.
The official directory of the information and press officers in government departments and public corporations. Published bi-annually.

Magazine Handbook
Periodical Publishers Association
Tel 0171-379 6268
£40.
Biennial listings of titles plus a statistical analysis of the magazine industry.

MDB Magazine Directory
The Magazine Business
Tel 0171-436 5211
£20.
Biannual advertising-oriented directory of magazines for sale in British newsagents. Its stablemate is the annual International Press Directory, £15, listing newsstand magazines and newspapers available for export. Also published is the bi-annual Complete ABC Report, £40 each, detailing and analysing the latest ABC circulation results and their implications.

The Media Guide
Fourth Estate, for The Guardian
Tel 0171-727-8993
£12.
You're reading it! We began in 1993 and publish in the autumn of each year. All suggestions for improvements are welcome.

Pims Media Directories
Pims International   Tel 0171-226 1000
Pims produces a range of detailed, loose-leaf guides to editorial media contacts, all regularly updated, aimed mainly at the public relations sector. Titles include: UK Media Directory (£298 pa), Townslist Directory (£160) and several USA/European directories (£140 each).

Media Industry in Europe
John Libbey & Co, for the Institute of Media Economics,
£24, mid-year.
Looks at the economic structure of the communications sector and its social effects.

Multimedia Yearbook
TFPL Publishing   Tel 0171-251 5522
A £135 directory of the 2,200 multi media companies.

PPA Annual Review
Periodical Publishers Association
Tel 0171-379 6268
Free annual report giving details of the industry, its members and their activities. The PPA publishes many other reports, including an annual List of Members, with details of the 1,500 magazines produced by the PPA's publishing houses.

Printing Trades Directory
Benn Business Information Services
Tel 01732-362666
£93.
The annual g listing more than 6,000 print related companies.

Publishers Handbook
Grosvenor Press
Tel 0171-278 7772
£49.95.
Classified guide to commercial services available for publishers.

Small Press Yearbook
Small Press Group, BM Bozo, London WC1N 3XX
£7.95.
Guide to the many small presses in the UK.

Studies in Newspaper & Periodical History
3 Henrietta Street, London WC2E 8LU
Fax 0171-379 0609   Tel 0171-240 0856
Publisher: Eurospan.
Scholarly look at press history. Formerly published as the Journal of Newspaper and Periodical History.

Two-Ten Media Directory
Two-Ten Communications
Tel 0171-490 8111
£239
Directory of editorial media contacts, updated six times a year, previously the PNA Directory.

UK Press Directory
UK Media Directories   Tel 01799 502665
Financial profiles of the 50 leading newspaper publishers.

Ulrich's International Periodicals Directory
Bowker-Saur
Tel 0171-493 5841
A five volume £330 American guide to the world's periodicals, detailing 130,000 titles.

Willings Press Guide
Reed Information Services   Tel 01342-326972
Two vols £152
Alphabetical list detailing over 26,000 news-papers and periodicals worldwide. The leading title in its field.

Writers' & Artists' Yearbook
A & C Black
Tel 0171-242 0946
£10.99.
Along-established handbook, mainly for writers and authors, with some sections for visual artists and musicians.

Writer's Handbook
Macmillan   Tel 0171-373 6070
£12.99
A directory for all writers covering publishers, publications, broadcasting, agents, services, prizes, etc.

HOW TO COMPLAIN ...

... about the press

Advertising Standards Authority
2 Torrington Place, London WC1E 7HN
Fax 0171-323 4339   Tel 0171-580 5555
For complaints about newspaper and magazine advertisements.

National Newspapers Mail Order Protection Scheme (MOPS)
16 Tooks Court, London EC4A 1LB
Fax 0171-404 0106   Tel 0171-405 6806
For mail order rip-offs.

Press Complaints Commission
1 Salisbury Square, London EC4 8AE
Fax 0171 353 8355   Tel 0171-3531248
For newspaper and magazine articles. Those who anticipate that the Council's Code of Practice will be breached in respect of their own affairs should use the 0171- 353 3732 Help-Line.

... and about broadcasting

BBC Viewer and Listener Correspondence
Villiers House, The Broadway, London W5 2PA
0181-743 8000 (for TV)
0171-580 4468 (for radio)
0181-576 8988 (Minicom number for the deaf)
For comments, queries or criticism of BBC broadcasts or policy.

BBC Programme Complaints Unit
BBC Broadcasting House, London W1A 1AA
If you think a programme has included specific and serious injustice, a serious invasion of privacy, a specific and serious inaccuracy or saerious breach of broadcasting standards write to Peter Dannheisser at the above address.

Broadcasting Complaints Commission
5 The Sanctuary, London SW1P 3JS
Fax 0171-828 7316   Tel 0171-630 1966
The BCC is for those complaining of a breach of privacy or of unjust or unfair treatment on radio or TV. Write to the Broadcasting Standards Council at the above address with complaints about the portrayal of violence and sex, and matters of taste and decency. See also Broadcasting Standards Council, page 208.

Independent Television Commission
33 Foley Street, London W1P 7LB
Fax 0171-306 7800   Tel 0171-255 3000
For complaints about ITV, Channel 4 and licensed cable or satellite services.

Radio Authority
Holbrook House, 14 Great Queen Street, London WC2B 5DG
Fax 0171-405 7064   Tel 0171-430 2724
For complaints about independent radio.

The rule about complaining is to make objections fast and then to be prepared for a long drawn out resolution. The more legalistic things get, the longer it takes.

For small complaints, write to the journalist or broadcaster who has caused offence. Ask them to answer the points you object to but lace the grizzles with praise. Journalists are prone to flattery and can be bamboozled into writing a follow up story when gently persuaded their wrong needs to be righted. More serious complaints warrant a phone call to the editor responsible for the article or broadcast. Editors, especially if they sense lawyers looming, will be cagey. However, they are unlikely to be openly hostile and will invariably ask for a letter. "Put it in writing," is how they will put it.

The complainant can either ask for a reply or, in the case of a press blunder, go for the letters page. A decently phrased letter will usually be printed and the smaller the offending newspaper or magazine, the more likely a letter is to get an airing. To editors letters prove there are readers out there and they provide free copy which lacks the whiff of paid for hackery. Lobbyists know this and use Dear Editor space to boost their causes.

With complaints about a TV or radio programme, contact the relevant broadcasting organisations listed in the column on the left. License paranoia means that the BBC and the independent companies take complaints seriously enough to have mechanisms built into their bureaucracies.Ask for producers to respond to your queries and, for those who reckon a complaints might be worth airtime, try the Biteback/Feedback/Points of View route.

If these direct routes do not settle matters and the complainant is dissatisfied with the responses, phone the Press Complaints Commission or the Broadcasting Complaints Commission. Before they go into action, both require complainants to have written to the editors. After that, they will send out free guidance notes and codes of practice. Adjudications in a complainant's favour result in judgements being printed in the press or the Radio or TV Times.

The alternative is to sue for libel. The best advice here is don't. It takes strong nerves and deep pockets and litigants will be entering a territory where the opponents know the by-ways. Publishing and TV lawyers are specialists and have the knowledge to out-manoeuvre expensive but non-specialist solicitors.Take things further and the libel courts are a lottery.

For better, for worse. Michael Grade, the chief executive of Channel 4 television

BROADCASTING CHRONICLE

Key events between August 1994 and July 1995

* By summer 1995 the BBC is equalling the ITV companies in the battle of the ratings
* A relaxation of rules governing cross-media ownership has newspaper bosses eyeing up TV stations
* Britain's streets are dug up for the rewiring of a nation; cable wins over a million subscribers
* Radio gets fashionable and the advertisers flock to the oldest form of broadcasting

Kelvin MacKenzie quits BSkyB

2 August: The former Sun editor Kelvin MacKenzie quits as managing director of satellite TV service BSkyB, after just six months in the job. Mr MacKenzie, aged 47, also leaves News International, the company controlling both the Sun and BSkyB. He had been editor of the Sun for 13 years, until the end of January 1994. On 19 October Mr MacKenzie becomes the Mirror Group Newspaper's executive director, in charge of all its television interests. He tries to arrange a deal with the cartoon giant Walt Disney to launch the Disney Channel in Britain on the cable system, in combat with satellite. But BSkyB sees it as a threat and in late November snatch the channel at the last moment. On 15 eptember MGN announces it is planning to launch the cable channel Live TV. [>15 February]

Radio ownership

2 August: The law governing the ownership of radio companies is redefined by the High Court when Emap is allowed to take control of Trans World Communications. Emap announced on 22 June it had arranged to boost its Trans World share-ownership to over 50 per cent, valuing the company at £71 million. But the 1990 Broadcasting Act says no company should own more than six radio stations covering populations over one million; this deal would give Emap eight. Emap says, however, that only six will be owned outright. The remainder will be "warehoused" in a company jointly owned by Emap and its merchant bank, Schroders. The Radio Authority says this device brings Emap within the law. This has been legally challenged by the Guardian Media Group, which owns 20 per cent of Trans World. The court's decision may open a loophole that could bring a concentration of broadcasting ownership in fewer hands. Harry Roche, the Guardian Media Group chairman, says: "This clearly rips up broadcast code arguments with regard to radio. We are all free to set up deadlocked companies along the lines of the blueprint now set up by Emap, and by making such arrangements you can legally now hold as many licences as you so desire. In my view, the decision has implications, not only for the radio industry, but for television as well." Emap chairman Sir John Hoskyns says the radio takeover gives the company the opportunity to "increase significantly its investment in the fastest growing advertising medium in the UK". Other companies decide to try similar takeovers. The first of these, by Bristol-based GWR, is blocked by the Radio Authority which awaits government decision on cross media ownership.

Radio 1 charm offensive

9 August: Public relations firm Lynne Franks is retained by the BBC after the release of the lowest-ever audience figures for Radio 1. In the second quarter of 1994, Radio 1 fell 21.7 per cent to 12.3 million listeners aged 15 and over, compared with the same period in 1993. The station has lost 3.4 million listeners in a year but Radio 1 says taking on the PR company is not a kneejerk reaction to the dwindling audiences: "This is not a panic attack," a spokeswoman insists. Matthew Bannister, who became Radio 1 controller late in 1993 has made several highly publicised changes, such as the departure of veterans Simon Bates and Dave Lee Travis. The spokeswoman says the problems have not been denied, "least of all by the controller, who has said it will take at least a year before things turn around". [>25 Oct]

Lord Archer's share deal

24 August: The Tory peer and millionaire author Lord Archer admits he made a "grave error" in buying 50,000 shares in Anglia TV, of which his wife, Mary, is a director, just as the board was agreeing a takeover by MAI. The shares were bought on behalf of a Kurdish associate, Mr Saib and sold at a profit of £77,219. Lord Archer publicly apologises for causing "needless embarrassment" to Mary. [>2 February]

Cable phones

24 August: The cable industry is boosted by an Oftel (Office of Telecommunications) decision allowing BT subscribers moving over to cable operators to take their old telephone number with them. The loss of their old number had held back many BT subscribers, especially in the business sector. Cable companies currently offer discounts over 10 per cent on telecommunications services.

Soaraway BSkyB

25 August: BSkyB's annual accounts reveal a rise in both profits and subscribers in the 12 months ending 30 June 1994. Shareholders profits jumped from £54.1 million to £176.8 million. The number of subscribers rose from 2.35 million to 3.45 million, with the upward trend continuing. The rate of people ending their subscriptions (the "churn") dropped from 15 per cent of total subscribers in 1992/3 to 12 per cent in 1993/4. BSkyB also says it is going to increase basic charges for its subscribers by £3 a month from October. This means that those buying BSkyB's basic package for £6.99 a month face a 43 per cent rise, boosting the company profits even further. BSkyB is now poised to become more profitable than all the ITV companies put together. The cable companies hope to follow down this success road early next decade, when their networks are completed. [>6 October]

Dyke warns of political meddling

26 August: The growth of a "dependency culture" in which broadcasters are constantly seeking favours from government is endangering the independence of television journalism, warns Greg Dyke, chief executive of London Weekend Television until its takeover by Granada in March 1994. He says the insidious threat from government poses a serious danger to current affairs programmes and television's right effectively to question decision-makers. Mr Dyke is delivering the keynote opening address to the Edinburgh International Television Festival, Britain's most influential annual TV conference. "At a time when the power of central government grows daily, the role of the fourth estate, the press and broadcasters, is more significant than ever ... I fear the relationship between broadcasters and government is becoming a dependent one, with broadcasters constantly wanting favours and legislative action from government - a position largely of government's making and which gives government far too much power." Mr Dyke condemns the 1990 Broadcasting Act as "a piece of legislation so flawed and so illogical that it's hard to find a Conservative MP who now admits to voting for it willingly." [>3 November]

Greg Dyke warns of threats to the independence to broadcaster and the press

Regional radio

1-16 September: Five regional radio stations are launched. They will reach a potential 12 million people and dwarf many local broadcasters covering a few towns or a city. Their arrival should boost commercial radio's 47.4 per cent share of total listening at the BBC's expense. But some wonder whether there are enough listeners and advertisers. On 1 September the launching stations are JFM 100.4 (the biggest of the five) in the north-west and Century Radio in the north-east. Galaxy Radio starts on 4 September for the Severn estuary area, Heart FM on 6 September for the West Midlands and Scot Radio on 16 September for central Scotland. The ITV company Border Television owns Century Radio and is a partner in Scot Radio. Border Television is setting up a joint venture with Luxembourg-based broadcasting group CLT to acquire UK radio licences. CLT is already the biggest shareholder of Atlantic 252.

Snobs vs slobs

6 September: The break-up of British television into a system of "telly for snobs and telly for slobs" is fast approaching, broadcaster Melvyn Bragg warns. He says there is an increasingly two-tier system of broadcasting where viewers without satellite or cable are being denied access to programmes. This is undermining the future of "the greatest comprehensive electronic newspaper the world has ever seen", Mr Bragg tells the launch of the South Bank Show. "It looks as if soon there will be a telly for snobs and a telly for slobs, a telly for cash and a telly for trash." He says "the cash and class system is about to uncouple British television: the more you can pay for, the more you will get."

Carlton/Central merger

6 September: A restructuring of the newly-merged Carlton and Central television companies is announced. The axing of 180 jobs to save £15 million prompts fears that regional ITV is in jeopardy. Carlton UK Television is now the UK's largest commercial TV company, after taking over Central in November 1993. Central's Birmingham HQ will be moved elsewhere in the city, but its 90 production staff will transfer to the company's main Nottingham studios. Critics say this is not honouring Central's franchise commitment to maintain TV production in the West Midlands, and that the region is becoming just an outpost of London-based Carlton. From 1 January Central Television will be Central Broadcasting, and Carlton Television will be Carlton Broadcasting.

Able cable

6 September: Cable television's availability throughout the country is continuing to expand by about 20 per cent every six months. Over a million more homes were passed by cable systems in the 12 months ending 30 June (up from 2.33 million to 3.37 million). The number of connected homes rose from 473,000 to 708,000. Installed telephone lines rose from 190,000 to 461,000. [>16 December]

Only connect...

NOTICE: TO VIDEOTRON CONTRACTORS PLEASE DO NOT CUT THE ROOTS OF THIS TREE

NATURE IS THE ROOT OF ALL LIFE
MY ROOTS ARE MY LIFE
PLEASE DIG ROUND THEM
AND LET ME LIVE

Channel 4 videos

12 September: Channel 4 launches its first video label, aiming to break into the big UK video market. Sixty million videos, worth £643 million, were sold in 1993, with 66 per cent of all households buying them. Channel 4 will release 24 videos in the first year. The BBC is particularly successful in selling classic material from its archives.

BBC tangles with BCC

12 September: The Broadcasting Complaints Commission (BCC) condemns an edition of Panorama as "unfair and unjust" to single parents. The BCC's attack is described as unsustainable and wrong by the BBC, which seeks leave for a High Court judicial review. The BBC's strong response fuels demands among broadcasters for abolition of the commission, whose future is currently under government review. In an unprecedented move the BBC broadcasts an on-air denunciation of the commission's decision on 26 September. A few days before this the BBC announces that Panorama editor Glenwyn Benson is soon to have the new role of head of BBC adult education. [> 10 October]

Channel 4 regional investment

13 September: Independent TV producers and Channel 4 hold a meeting discussing the company's investment in regional production, which is lagging behind BBC and ITV. A heated debate ends with an agreement to set up a C4 task force to expand regional production.

Survey of radio workers

Mid-September: A survey of 1,500 people in the radio industry shows that 64 per cent are paid under £20,000 a year, with 21 per cent below £11,000. Over half have a degree or diploma. Women have two-thirds of jobs in radio at the BBC, while the oppposite is the case in the independent sector, where men are in a similar majority. The survey is by the industry training body Skillset, sponsored by the Department of Employment. The workforce is found to be young, with an average age of 33, and only 6 per cent are older than 50. Some 96 per cent are white. [>23 September]

GMTV pulls its socks up

15 September: The threat of a large fine hanging over the breakfast station GMTV is removed after the ITC decides its quality has improved. The regulatory body - which has the power to fine GMTV up to £2 million - says there has been a "demonstrable improvement" in the past six months, particularly in news and current affairs. In July the commission issued a formal warning about GMTV's first year, describing its output as poor and unsatisfactory. It took over from TV-am in January 1993.

ITC licence awards

15 September: The ITC awards the second of its cable television local delivery licences. These are being given for areas not covered by the 127 cable franchises awarded by the old Cable Authority. The ITC says local delivery franchises are the new equivalent of a cable franchise, enabling a local operator to provide cable TV and telecommunications services within the area concerned. The licensee can use microwave frequencies in addition to or instead of installing cable. The first local licence was awarded for west Kent in May 1994. Today a subsidiary of SBC Cablecomms (UK) receives the franchise for the Blackpool and Fylde area. SBC, the only applicant, already holds franchises for much of the surrounding Lancashire area. But the third franchise to be made available - east Derbyshire - receives no applications by its deadline of 19 September. One is submitted for southern East Anglia by 17 October. On 19 October the ITC decides to invite applications for a local delivery licence covering the whole of Northern Ireland. This is the UK's biggest franchise, covering about 530,000 homes. Applicants can request only parts of the area if they wish. A deadline of 6 February is given. [>19 May]

Sinn Fein ban lifted

16 September: The government announces the immediate lifting of the broadcasting ban on Sinn Fein and Northern Ireland paramilitaries. The ban was introduced on 19 October 1988, triggered by an upsurge in IRA activity. Behind the order lay the imprint of Margaret Thatcher, who in 1985 had tried to have a television documentary banned on the grounds it indirectly furthered terrorism. In her famous phrase, she said: "We must not give them the oxygen of publicity." Though the broadcasters bowed to the censorship restrictions, in the early 1990s they became more confident in flouting its spirit. Actors were brought in to speak the words of Sinn Fein leaders and their imitations grew more precise. On 30 August 1994 the BBC director-general John Birt wrote to the government urging them to lift the rule. ITV leaders made similar requests.

TV more white than black

23 September: Trevor Phillips, the head of current affairs at LWT, complains that just four of the UK's top TV executives are non-white. He says: "Despite the growing number of black faces on screen, among the hundreds of TV programme executives who wield power in the BBC, ITV and Channel 4, there are only four non-whites and two of those executives deal exclusively with programmes for minorities." [<mid-September]

Big fast break

28 September: Chris Evans (right) quits as star of Channel Four's morning show Big Breakfast. It had replaced the disastrous news programme C4 Daily in October 1992, with Evans as the key personality. Big Breakfast saved C4's morning slot from total collapse. [> 22 April]

BBC sell-off

Late September: Privatising the BBC's transmission network does not make economic sense, concludes a confidential internal report. The government is currently examining the options. Consultants Coopers and Lybrand say the BBC would be forced to find another £35 million each year of licence payers' money. A commercial operator would take the £6 million annual commercial income the BBC gains from its masts, while pushing up the cost of beaming BBC services around the UK. A private network would also be more inefficient, say the consultants. The government has favoured privatising the network since 1988, but BBC chiefs are said to be strongly against it. The only interested company so far is NTL, the privatised arm of the old IBA, which transmits ITV and Channel 4. NTL says savings could be made if it ran the whole BBC/ITV/C4 operation. But it would also have monopoly power. [> 14 February]

All calm at the BBC

October: Journalists vote overwhelmingly for an end to the long-running pay and conditions dispute with the BBC. After fresh proposals from the corporation, National Union of Journalists members accept terms thrashed out at ACAS. Over 80 per cent of the 2,800 NUJ members vote for the peace deal. But broadcasting union BECTU votes in favour by only 51 per cent on 27 October.

Radio chief quits early

4 October: Radio Authority chief executive Peter Baldwin announces he has decided to leave the authority six months earlier than expected. Mr Baldwin's tenure was extended in 1992 from 31 December that year until 31 December 1995. Now he says he will leave by 30 June 1995.

LBC closes

5 October: Britain's oldest commercial radio station, LBC, goes off the air, being replaced at 6.00am today by London Radio. The news and talk station LBC was launched on 4 October 1974, a few days before music-dominated Capital. The Radio Authority stripped LBC of its two licences in September 1993. This sparked off many protests and a campaign to save it. LBC went into receivership in late March 1994 after failing to win one of that month's new INR licences. London News Radio took over LBC in late April. In May the landscape changed again, when London News Radio's two forthcoming licences were bought by Reuters, which had unsuccessfully bid against the company in September 1993. But under the 1990 Broadcasting Act, the Radio Authority is powerless to intervene in the takeover as long as it considers Reuters "fit and proper". London Radio from today provides chats, phone-ins and news on London News Talk 1152AM, while there is a 24-hour rolling news service on London News 97.3FM. At the end of October, Radio Authority chairman Lord Chalfont mildly criticises London News, saying its programming needs a "rethink". In early November James Morton, a former LBC director, attacks the authority for allowing London Radio to "loosen up" the FM rolling news format that had won it the licence instead of LBC. "This whole thing has been a disgrace from start to finish," says Mr Morton. By mid-January 1995 the number of London News listeners has fallen dramatically, forcing a revamp. "We want to make the station much more accessible and entertaining," says managing director Rory McLeod. [>7 October]

First new form of radio licence issued

6 October: The first Additional Service licence is issued by the Radio Authority. Additional Services make use of the spare capacity in an existing channel's signal which is not used by the programme service. This licence will utilise the RDS (Radio Data System) sub-carrier of the first Independent National Radio (INR1) service, Classic FM. Awarded the licence is the only applicant: US-owned company Differential Corrections Inc (DCI), bidding £1,000. DCI will provide a subscriber service telling receiving sets their precise location, to within a few metres. This is known as the Global Positioning System, using modified information from 24 US satellites. It will be of special value to transport companies and marine navigators.

BSkyB flotation ...

6 October: BSkyB announces details of its share flotation scheme. This is expected to give it more financial power to combat the expanding cable business, whose biggest British company, TeleWest, also announces flotation (see: 7 November). At present BSkyB is owned 50 per cent by Rupert Murdoch's News Corporation, 13.5 per cent by Granada, 17.5 per cent by the French media group Chargeurs and 17.5 per cent by Financial Times owners Pearson. These shareholdings will be diluted. The 7 October Financial Times says the flotation "is expected to involve the sale of up to £1 billion of new BSkyB shares, or 20 per cent of its enlarged equity, valuing the company at just under £5 billion". On 14 November a pathfinder prospectus is published saying shares are likely to cost between 233p and 268p, valuing the company at between £4 billion and £4.6 billion. Shares become available on 25 November without a firm price, with applications having to be in by 6 December. But leading stockbrokers Henderson Crosthwaite say on 30 November that the shares are overvalued. They believe BSkyB is worth about £2.6 billion. The shares reach 256p, however, and trading starts on 8 December. In early January the price dips by 11p because of some uncertainty, but it recovers soon after.

... BSkyB aggravation

7 October: BSkyB takes tough action in its long-running campaign to stamp out illegal viewing by satellite piracy in the UK. Pirates have been using a range of devices to get round BSkyB's scrambling system. The High Court today issues an order against a Buckinghamshire man, in a ruling which seems to prove beyond doubt that the new generation of pirate devices called "blockers" are illegal under the Copyright Act. This follows similar rulings in September. BSkyB has asked the government to tighten up the penalties, including imprisonment for ten years. Pirates say over 100,000 homes are watching satellite TV for free, although BSkyB says the figure is "nearer to 30,000". In early November the company says piracy could undermine confidence in its flotation unless tackled rigorously. It is granted a High Court injunction against a small electronics company after saying BSkyB would "suffer substantial and unquantifiable loss" unless piracy is stopped. [>Mid-February-satellite]

More London radio

7 October: Two days after LBC dies Capital FM and Capital Gold (on AM) are given eight-year renewed licences, starting on 16 October. Challenging Capital will be two new FM stations run by entertainment groups: Crystal FM, owned by Chrysalis; and Virgin Radio, broadcasting its Virgin 1215 AM service across London in FM, plus talk shows. The Radio Authority is criticised for giving these licences to stations that will be very similar to Capital, rather than encouraging fresh proposals. The Indy-music station XFM only lost out to Virgin by the casting vote of RA chairman Lord Chalfont. The other new licences are: London Christian Radio, on AM, with speech-based religious promotion; and the female-oriented magazine-style Radio Viva, also on AM. All four new licences will run for eight years from the start of their broadcasting, which will be in coming months. There were 41 applicants for the six licences. The Radio Authority says: "We do not envisage advertising any further London-wide licences in the forseeable future. However, we do intend to advertise more small-scale services for parts of the Greater London area over the next couple of years." But in following weeks the RA hints it could be more open-minded about London-wide FM licences. Then in mid-January 1995 the authority announces it will make another such regional ILR licence available by moving Melody Radio from 104.9FM, although it will not be advertised before early 1996. The RA also says it will be advertising at least three small-scale licences for parts of London. [<5 October, >28 October]

C4 tangles with BCC

10 October: Channel 4 is granted leave to seek judicial review against a decision by the Broadcasting Complaints Commission. At issue is a report from C4's legal series The Brief, which in March 1994 alleged that an Asian family had experienced racial abuse in their Derbyshire home village. Elmton Parish Council complained to the BCC that the report was an unfair portrayal of the local community. The station rejected the charge and argued that under the terms of the 1990 Broadcasting Act the commission is overstepping its powers in accepting a complaint from an organisation which was not directly involved in or affected by the programme. C4, like the BBC defending its Panorama case, believes the fairness and privacy watchdog is wrong to hear complaints lodged by interest groups, rather than wronged individuals. But in December Mr Justice Schiemann rules that the BCC was correct in deciding that it had a direct interest in the attitude of villagers to racial matters. [<12 September, 22 February]

Yorkshire-Tyne Tees gets heavy

11 October: Yorkshire-Tyne Tees Television starts issuing threats of dismissal notices to staff who have not accepted new employment conditions. The company is cutting its costs by scrapping premium rate overtime payments. About a fifth of the 800 staff are given warnings after refusing to sign new contracts. Members of the unions Bectu and NUJ vote to take resisting action. But most give in and agree the new terms by the deadline of 21 October.

Ealing tragedy

Mid-October: The famous Ealing Studio goes into receivership. It was bought just two years ago from the BBC by facilities group BBRK, which itself has just collapsed with debts of £6.5 million.

Channel 4 funding

17 October: The funding safety net scheme for Channel 4 is unlikely to be changed in the immediate future, the government says. Channel 4 has been trying to stop having to give ITV half its revenue above 14 per cent of total TV advertising. But National Heritage secretary Stephen Dorrell refuses to back the parliamentary private members bill that would be needed to change the formula, which gave ITV £38.2

million in 1993. On 3 November C4 leaders Michael Grade and Sir Michael Bishop claim that ITV company chiefs have urged the Treasury to privatise Channel 4, which could be worth £1 billion. Mr Grade says he will resign if privatisation takes place. ITV and the government initially deny the claim. In early December a campaign to overturn the funding formula is launched by Jeremy Isaacs, C4's founding chief executive. [>18 January]

Commercial radio beats BBC

25 October: For the first time in its 21-year history, commercial radio has taken a bigger audience share than the BBC. Figures for the third quarter of 1994 show commercial stations, including Virgin 1215 and Atlantic 252, have surged ahead at the expense of Radio 1, which lost another 1.25 million listeners in those three months. BBC Radio had 27.6 million listeners, compared with commercial radio's 27.7 million, according to the figures from Rajar. The Radio Advertising Bureau says the lead represents commercial radio's coming of age in its 21st year. The shift is described by the BBC as inevitable, with the number of commercial competitors doubling to more than 140 in the previous five years. At the end of October, the Henley Centre publishes a report predicting commercial radio will increase its share of all display advertising from its traditional 2 per cent to an unprecedented 6 per cent by the end of the decade. [<9 August, >13 January]

Cable Communications Association

25 October: The Cable Television Association changes its name to the Cable Communications Association, reflecting the cable TV companies growing involvement in telephone, multimedia and interactive services.

Mellor shuns publicity shock

27 October: Carlton TV bows to a request from former Tory cabinet minister David Mellor to remove film shot outside his home from tonight's documentary, The Big Story. The decision sparks a row with the independent production company Twenty Twenty Television. The programme examines the outside interests of MPs such as Mr Mellor, who refused to give an interview. He was therefore filmed outside his house, but this footage was given the axe by Carlton.

Radio Authority offers more licences

28 October: Four new regional radio licences and at least 28 local licences will be on offer from mid-1995, announces the Radio Authority. Most will be in FM frequencies in the 105-108 MHz sub-band which should become available at the end of 1995. The four regionals will cover southern and western Yorkshire, East Anglia, the East Midlands and the Solent/Bournemouth area. Twenty towns and small areas will be covered by local licences, which will generally be more localised in coverage than most existing ILR licences. A further eight districts - some of county size - will be eligible for small-scale local licences for one or more areas inside each district. In mid-November Capital Radio indicates that it may apply for all four of the regional licences. [<7 October]

IRN wins news deal

Late October: Independent Radio News wins a three year contract to supply the forthcoming Talk Radio station with a news operation. IRN defeated competition from Reuters and Network News.

New Labour media people

Late October: The Labour Party changes its two shadow media representatives. Mo Mowlam is replaced as shadow National Heritage Secretary by Chris Smith. Robin Corbett has to give way to Graham Allen. Critics believe this restyling by Labour leader Tony Blair is unnecessary and will weaken the party in complicated arguments.

ITC invites C5 bids

1 November: The ITC for the second time invites bids for the licence of Channel 5, the long delayed fifth terrestial television network. It is now hoped to reach 70 per cent of the UK population, despite earlier fears that it would reach only half the country. The ITC first invited applications for Channel 5 in April 1992. But in December that year the commission announced it would not award the licence to the single applicant company because of dissatisfaction with its business plan. The 1992 licence envisaged 74 per cent coverage of Britain, but the government in July 1994 earmarked one of the frequencies for digital television, reducing coverage to 50 per cent. This provoked much criticism, as it would make Channel 5 commercially unviable. The opposition forced the ITC to try to find more transmitter sites and

frequencies, hopefully pushing coverage back up to about 70 per cent of the UK. On 15 September the commission decided it would readvertise the licence on 1 November, despite continuing uncertainty about the coverage. The ITC says closing date for applications is 2 May 1995, with the licence being awarded by 31 July if possible. The licence will last for ten years and the service must start no later than 1 January 1997. Applicants may offer a national service, or city-based or regional services. Most of the South Coast counties will not be able to receive Channel 5. [>16 March]

Daily Mail's move into TV

3 November: Sir David English, chairman of Daily Mail publishers Associated Newspapers, tells a national conference: "I see now the beginning of a new professional relationship between newspapers and the electronic medium. The fusion between the immense

Sir David English

power of in-depth news gathering on the one hand and a broad band delivery capacity on the other. This will manifest itself in Britain [on 30 November] when Associated Newspapers launches Channel One for London. A 24-hour news and features service which in effect will be live video newspaper." The company directors wanted to move "into electronic journalism in parallel to our print activity". But they could not expand into terrestial TV because of "grossly unfair and stupid government regulations". [> 26 August, >11 January]

Digital TV plans

3 November: ITV company chief executives meet to discuss their plans for launching new channels when television's digital transmission technology becomes available. In a decade's time the companies could be running their own commercial channels alongside their ITV franchises. [>10 February]

TeleWest goes to market

7 November: TeleWest launches its revived plan to become the first of the mainly US-owned British cable TV companies to tap the UK stock market for funds. It is the UK's largest cable television operator, and hopes to raise finance for its British expansion by offering 26 per cent of its shares in London and New York. American parent companies US West and Tele-Communications Inc will retain the other shares. TeleWest's earlier scheme was abandoned in May 1994 because of unsettled US markets.. Trading starts on 22 November with a strong demand. Shares are priced at 182p, valuing Telewest at £1.8 billion. [>14 April]

ITN stakeholders

8 November: The deadline for Carlton and Granada to reduce their stake in ITN is postponed until the end of 1995. The Independent Television Commission rules that shareholders with more than a 20 per cent holding in ITN would no longer be required to reduce their percentage by 31 December 1994. Carlton, which took over Central, and Granada, which bought LWT, each now have 36 per cent stakes in ITN. Until today's 12 month deadline extension, under the terms of the 1990 Broadcasting Act no single shareholder was allowed to have more than 20 per cent beyond the end of 1994. The change has taken place because the government wants to consider ownership of ITN alongside the other cross-media ownership issues in the review being carried out. In December HTV and Yorkshire TV write to the ITC expressing "astonishment" that Carlton and Granada have not been forced to sell their excess shares.

Double vision

9 November: Two Thames TV productions are transmitted at the same time, 7.00pm. Take Your Pick has been on ITV since August, while This Is Your Life starts today on BBC 1. Broadcast magazines says: "It is the first time that two programmes from the same independent have been pitched against each other".

Sky News news

10 November: BSkyB for several months has been discussing having its 24-hour television news channel, Sky News, supplied under contract by ITN, reveals the Financial Times. The satellite company has been looking for a way of reducing the £30 million a year cost of the news service while improving its quality. Past talks with ITN and the BBC had come to nothing. But later in November Reuters emerges as a much more likely partner than ITN. This is expected to give Reuters its biggest opening so far in television. [<6 October, >2 February]

Radio profits up

Mid-November: London's Capital Radio reveals annual turnover has increased by 44 per cent, to £51.7 million. Pre-tax profits rose from £11.7 million to £22.2 million. Earnings per share went up from 11.3p to 22.8p. The company says it stations are the number one in all their markets. By late December five other radio companies report profit boosts. Newcastle-based Metro Radio says profits nearly doubled to £4.63 million. Scottish Radio has similar profit figures: up three-quarters to £4.2 million. The GWR group says its profits rose 241 per cent. Chiltern Radio Network turns a £246,000 loss the previous year into a £514,000 profit, while Allied Radio cuts its loss from £1.5 million down to £678,000.

BT video on demand

15 November: BT deals a blow to cable operators when it reveals that its planned video-on-demand service is being expanded to deliver services ranging from home shopping and banking to education over the telephone line. A six-month trial of Interactive TV will begin in mid-1995, announces BT. About 2,500 households in Ipswich and Colchester will be involved. Successful tests of the delivery technology have already been carried out. Although BT is banned under the regulatory rules from delivering broadcast television, Interactive TV is allowed because it delivers a signal direct to a specific user on request. Oftel, the regulator, welcomes the trial, but says it will look carefully at the effect on competition before allowing a more widespread introduction. [>22 November]

ITV aggro

17 November: ITV companies are asked by the Independent Television Commission to explain an increase in violence in programmes. The commission discovered the rise during a two week monitoring exercise in the spring. It reveals 36 per cent of all programmes on commercial channels between 6pm and midnight contained violence. A similar exercise in 1993 found 51 per cent of ITV drama contained violence, compared to 69 per cent in 1994, a rise of nearly 20 per cent. [>21 December]

Televised court

18 November: The first High Court trial to be broadcast nationally on British television starts as a five-part series on BBC 2. The Trial contains scenes in Scottish courts. These are not covered by section 41 of the 1925 Criminal Justice Act, which makes filming in English courts illegal. But it still took two years to obtain official permission and the co-operation of the participants. Series producer Nick Catliff says he hopes to gain similar access in England. Such a move would require legislation, and take at least four years.

National Lottery

19 November: Britain's first National Lottery begins on BBC 1. It is preceded by the most intensive advertising campaign for a decade, starting on 4 November, with the slogan: "It could be you". The lottery idea was launched by a government white paper in March 1992, proposing changes in gambling law. This was followed by the Lottery Act, given royal approval in October 1993. The seven-year lottery contract was won in May 1994 by Camelot. Twenty-eight per cent of the revenue - expected to reach £5.5 billion a year - will be given to five good causes. Camelot says the odds against winning the jackpot of £2 million or more are 13.98·1, and 57·1 against winning £10. The BBC won a battle with ITV over broadcasting rights. The corporation hopes to attract the biggest audience every Saturday evening by tele-vising the draw around 8pm. But the shows at first prove less popular than expected. ITV is legally able to broadcast the winning numbers almost simultaneously, removing the viewers' need to watch the BBC. The winner of the £18 million jackpot on 10 December has his identity revealed by the national press, despite having requested anonymity. After a three month inquiry, the National Lottery says this is not a matter of serious concern.

No TV for BT

22 November: The government surprises the telecommunication industry by confirming that the ban on BT and Mercury from offering wide-ranging national television and phone services will stay until 2001 at least. The Commons trade and industry select committee had called for changes. But today's government publication Creating the Superhighways of the Future says the ten-year ban that started in 1991 will stay in place, despite expectations of it being relaxed sooner. The 1991 rule stopped phone companies providing broadcast entertainment down their phone lines, but allowed cable companies to offer phone services as well as entertainment. This opened the door to the spending of £10 billion on the cable infrastructure now taking place. BT says: "The great leap in broadband communication we were hoping to provide has been postponed for several years." BT can carry on offering "on-demand" services, but is banned from a multimedia role. The company wants to spend £15 billion on its own information superhighway to compete directly against all the cable companies, rather than join them by applying for large existing franchises.
[<15 November, >mid-February]

Daytime yawn

23 November: Viewers deserve to be paid for having to watch daytime television says Andy Allan, chief executive of Carlton. He tells a meeting of the Broadcasting Press Guild that daytime output is "predictable, repetitive and unadventurous"and that watching it is "like being placed in a flotation tank and robbed of all sensory perception".

Granada profits

23 November: The Granada group announces record pre-tax profits of £265 million for the year ending 30 September 1994. This is a rise of 51per cent.

Labour hit the highway

27 November: The Labour leader Tony Blair appoints a commission to draw up plans for an information superhighway capable of entering every home, school, hospital and library in Britain. The chairman of the commission is the shadow national heritage secretary Chris Smith. His report is expected next May or June in time for publication and debate during the 1995 party conference.

A Channel 1 video-journalist

Channel One goes live

30 November: British television's first 24-hour local news station is launched. Channel One is a cable service exclusively for London. It is owned by the Associated Newspapers subsidiary of the Daily Mail and General Trust, whose Evening Standard is London's only non-free evening newspaper. The Standard says: "Made by Londoners for Londoners, Channel One offers a quick fix on the news and events of the day, all day and all night, mixed with updates on local weather, sport and travel, entertainment, quiz shows, holiday news, shopping information and competitions". Company chairman Sir David English promises: "Channel One is going to become as integral a part of London as Big Ben". Advertisements describe the channel as resembling an "electronic video-newspaper". The station's team of 30 one-person camera units - otherwise called "video-journalists" (VJs) - will be operating as highly mobile newsgathering units. The company is based in the former Channel 4 headquarters in Charlotte Street in central London. Channel One is exclusive to the 39 cable TV franchises in the London area, with about 285,000 subscribers. The station's model is the similar New York channel, New York One. Volunteer cable viewers are recruited to the Channel One Advisory Panel, giving suggestions fortnightly for improvements to the service. At the beginning of November Sir David announced that his company had acquired the cable TV business Arts and Entertainment Programming, which runs the Performance: Its Arts channel.

Sport up for grabs

Late November: The government refuses to ban satellite stations gaining exclusive TV coverage of top sporting events. The National Heritage secretary Stephen Dorrell rejects proposals from the members of the national heritage select committee that stations such as Sky Sports should be barred from exclusive access to the country's leading eight "listed" events. MPs had argued that occasions like the football World Cup should be available to all viewers. Mr Dorrell says sporting rights holders must decide how their events are televised. [>6 April]

Survey of attitudes to radio

7 December: Research shows there is great loyalty to particular radio services and little concern about radio violence or sex, reveals the Broadcasting Standards Council's survey. Radio and Audience Attitudes says its findings "support earlier research suggesting that the audience enjoys a more personal and individual relationship with radio than with television ... Listening to radio was perceived to be a singular activity, while television, while broadcasting pictures, was more social. Respondents who listened to radio developed a great loyalty to a station's style, presenters and schedules. They listened to the same station for many years and were familiar with its patterns. Listeners switched from one station to another only as their tastes changed. Alterations made to the station's style or scheduling created resentment, particularly when listening routine was affected. Change was highlighted as the most common criticism." Only 3 per cent of complaints recalled violence, 12 per cent sexual conduct and 18 per cent bad language. Council chairman Elspeth Howe says: "Our research shows what a popular medium radio is and listeners are happy with it". She says concern about radio is "nothing like that about TV".

Multi-media miracle

14 December: Children can watch up to four television programmes at one time and remember the plot and key incidents from all of them, according to Stephen Heppell of Anglia Polytechnic University.

Birmingham radio re-licensed

15 December: Birmingham Broadcasting Ltd is re-awarded its current two Independent Local Radio (ILR) licenses by the Radio Authority. Its stations, BRMB-FM/Xtra-AM, will have new eight-year licences from February 1996. There was no other applicant. The company is a subsidiary of Capital Radio, which had its London licences renewed on 7 October.

Ban on sneak advertising

15 December: The Independent Television Commission fines Granada Television £500,000 for repeated violations of the rules of "undue prominence" of products in the daily magazine programme, This Morning. The ITC issues a clear warning to all ITV companies that programmes should not be vehicles for selling products. This is the first fine to be imposed under powers in the 1990 Broadcasting Act.

Old TV stands up to cable

16 December: The terrestial channels - BBC, ITV and C4 - received in homes by cable have increased their audience shares, an ITC survey discovers. In October 1994 the combined channels took 65.1 per cent of all viewing, compared with 57.9 per cent in October 1993. ITV went up from 29.3 per cent to 30.3 per cent, BBC 1 from 19.9 per cent to 24.3 per cent, Channel Four from 5.4 per cent to 6.3 per cent and BBC 2 from 3.3 per cent to 4.2 per cent. [<6 September, >20 December]

BBC complaints

19 December: The BBC's new Programme Complaints Unit publishes its first report. The unit wholly or partially upholds 102 of the 590 complaints it investigated in its first eight months. Only three resulted in apologies on the air. The unit was set up in January 1994 following criticism that BBC executives were reluctant to appear on such programmes as Points of View to examine complaints. Most complaints were over poor taste and perceived bias or unfair treatment.

Radio renaissance, TV rut

20 December: Radio is undergoing a renaissance while television habits remain virtually unaltered despite the turmoil created by changes in the industry, says the Policy Studies Institute. The 1990 Broadcasting Act and the new ITV licensee companies had little impact, according to the institute's survey Cultural Trends No 21: Television and Radio. Editor Jeremy Eckstein says: "The only real change in viewer choice is coming from satellite and cable services ... In the context of a saturated market this is leading inevitably to an increasing fragmentation of viewing." The time people spent watching terrestial and satellite channels reached a peak of 3.9 hours per day in 1986, falling to 3.3 hours in 1991. It returned to 3.9 hours in 1992, since when it has fallen again. With TVs in most households, and viewers watching no more than a decade ago, opportunities for market growth are strictly limited, the report concludes. Viewers are either ignoring cable or satellite - only 12 per cent of households subscribe - or fragmenting their viewing. Mr Eckstein said: "Radio is undergoing something of a renaissance in the range and choice of programming on offer. However, the overall reach shows no sign of increasing as more stations come on air, nor does the total amount of listening." [<16 Dec, >3 January]

Children excluded from BBC Radio

20 December: "There isn't anyone in charge of children's radio programmes at Broadcasting House", says Sarah MacNiell, former editor of children's news magazines on BBC Radio 5. "The dismantling of the original Radio 5 marked an abject and dismal abdication by the BBC of its public service responsibility to provide radio for younger listeners." In the Independent she says children are basically excluded. "At the BBC, children's radio is simply an idea that does not have the support of the broadcasters. Controllers, editors, producers and presenters all condone the same unspoken "let's not" consensus. Short of legislation, there is small hope of anything for children appearing in the BBC Radio schedules." [>30 December]

Violence on TV

21 December: ITV and Channel 4 are accused of failing to achieve a reduction in violence and of being out of step with public concern on the issue. The ITC is to hold meetings in 1995 with the broadcasters to discuss what action they are planning to take to reduce violence in programmes. The commission expresses dissatisfaction that overall violence levels had not fallen despite demands made 18 months ago. Privately, broadcasters react with anger to the report, labelling ITC's research as flawed. 3 A month later the BBC publishes a poll saying that the public does not think TV violence is to blame for real-life violence. Unemployment, lack of discipline and poverty carry greater responsibility, says the survey of over 1,000 people. It is linked to a three-part Radio 4 series The Violence Files. [<17 November]

BBC drama flop

22 December: Seaforth, the wartime drama series which the BBC signalled as the highlight of its autumn schedule, is axed. The decision, after disappointing ratings and the departure of the lead actor, came even though the BBC had spent £200,000 on scripts for a second series.

TV is "incestuous flea market"

30 December: One of TV's most popular writers attacks heads of BBC and ITV for an entertainment policy of flogging "tired old job-lot shows" to death. Andrew Davies, speaking at the Royal Television Society's Huw Weldon Lecture, says the BBC is "turning itself into a vast, incestuous flea market". Mr Davies, whose work includes A Very British Coup, adds: "It's apparent to everybody - with the exception of the big nobs at the

head of the BBC - that the ITV network centre is a dreadful, embarrassing failure. The BBC is in the process of emulating the worst mistakes of the ITV network. The new pyramid structure concentrates all commissioning upwards into the hands of just two people [Alan Yentob and Michael Jackson]. They're arts features guys, with no comedy or drama experience" [<20 December, >18 January]

"Tired old job-lot shows." Andrew Davies bites the hands that feeds him.

Russell stays at ITC

31 December: Sir George Russell was due to stand down as ITC chairman today, but instead he has been given another two years in the position. This was agreed in early August. National Heritage secretary Stephen Dorrell wants to ensure leadership continuity at the commission. Sir George became chairman of the IBA, the ITC's predecessor, in 1990.

New Radio Authority chairman

1 January 1995: Sir Peter Gibbings takes over as chairman of the Radio Authority, succeeding Lord Chalfont. He pledges he will be a "listening chairman". Sir Peter, aged 65, a former chairman of the Guardian and Manchester Evening News and of Anglia Television, will hold the post for five years. He is currently a director of the Economist. Sir Peter says: "It is a very exciting time for commercial radio."

Christmas viewing down

3 January: Broadcasters dismiss suggestions that the Christmas television schedules were a turn-off, blaming increased competition for a slide in ratings. Audiences for Christmas editions of shows lime Casualty and Birds of a Feather, fell by up to 5.6 million compared to 1993. Average viewing on Christmas Day also declined 4.5 per cent, down from 5 hours 37 minutes per person in 1993 to 5 hours 22 minutes. ITV's performance improved compared with 1993. [<20 Dec, >24 January]

Euro dither over US TV

4 January: Sir Leon Brittan, the UK's senior European Commissioner, thwarts directive changes reducing the amount of American programmes on European television, by invoking a rarely used legal instrument that enables him to postpone the vote. The delay amounts to an early setback for the new French EU presidency, which has declared this issue as one of its priorities. The broadcasting directive is the 1989 Television Without Frontiers (89/552/EC), which requires at least 51 per cent of material shown by European channels to be of European origin "wherever practicable". The French want this tightened up, but trans-national business interests do not. The European Commission is deeply split. The proposed changes are part of an attempt by Brussels and Paris to safeguard European language and culture by protecting indigenous television producers from the competition of cheap imports from outside the EU, mainly from America. [>Mid-February]

Dyke back

11 January: Greg Dyke returns to the broadcasting scene as chairman and chief executive of Pearson plc's television interests. Pearson owns the Financial Times, which says the company "has in recent years been actively expanding its television division, as part of its long-term strategy of becoming a broadly based international media group." Mr Dyke, aged 47, takes charge of a business that includes Thames Television, a number of stakes in satellite services including BSkyB, and a joint European satellite venture with the BBC. [>26 January]

News at Ten

11 January: News at Ten was Britain's most popular news programme in 1994, according to figures published today. ITN's bulletin was watched by an average audience of 6.6 million, compared to 6.3 million for BBC 1's Six O'Clock News and 5.9 million for the Nine O'Clock News. [<10November, >27 January]

Junk journalism attacked

11 January: The Labour MP Chris Mullin unsuccessfully brings in a parliamentary Bill to "regulate ownership of the media". He wants to "reverse the growing trend towards monopoly ownership of most of what we see on our television screens and read in our newspapers. The purpose of the Bill is to protect our culture and democracy from the barbarism of the unregulated market." Mr Mullin believes that "every day, the frontiers that regulate the independence and quality of our television are pushed back a little further. The government are under enormous pressure to remove what restrictions remain and to let the market rip ... What I fear most is not political bias, but the steady growth of junk journalism - the trivialisation and demeaning of everything that is important in our lives, and its consequent effect on our culture."
[<3 November, >28 February]

Steve Wright quits Radio 1

13 January: BBC Radio 1 hits a fresh crisis when its popular DJ, Steve Wright, resigns. Mr Wright has spent 14 years at Radio 1, most recently presenting the key breakfast show. He has been one of the station's greatest assets, although that show's number of listeners has fallen. "Radio 1 is a Wright off" puns the Daily Star. Mr Wright, aged 40, resigns in a polite but surprise letter. This is a another personal set-back for Matthew Bannister, controller of Radio 1, who has been struggling in vain to stop its decline. The number of listeners fell 3.3 million in 1994. Mr Wright is widely reported to be join-ing Talk Radio UK, the third national commer-cial station, which starts on 14 February. He denies these rumours. After four weeks negotia-tions, Mr Bannister on 19 February signs up TV personality Chris Evans to take over the break-fast show. Mr Evans, aged 28, became popular nationally as presenter of C4's zany Big Breakfast. He starts an eight-month Radio 1 contract on 24 April.
[<25 October, >31 January]

Bart's ad banned

Mid-January: An advertisement defending the emergency service of London's Bart's Hospital is banned by television watchdogs for being too political. The Broadcasting Advertising Clearance Centre rules that the advert contravenes rule 10 of the Independent Television Commission code, which forbids any advertising for political ends. The casualty department is due to close by the end of January. The publicly-funded advert goes on cinema screens on 19 January.

Channel 4 funding

18 January: Channel 4's campaign to abolish the funding formula under which it will have to give ITV another large cash payment this year is scuppered by Stephen Dorrell, the National Heritage secretary. He says: "I do not believe that the supporters of change have demonstrated sufficient justification for this proposed course of action". Amending the funding formula before 1997 would also require a law change by Parliament, says Mr Dorrell. Last year C4 gave £38.2 million, a figure expected to be much higher in this year's payment, due on 14 February. C4 chairman Michael Bishop says the 1990 Broadcasting Act "is not working as Parliament intended and is creating unnecessary and distorting subsidies to ITV shareholders. As a result viewers are prevented from enjoying the full fruits of our commercial success. We will continue to press the compelling case for these rogue provisions to be removed."
[>17 October, >8 February]

BBC accused of wasting money

18 January: Allegations that BBC correspondents squandered licence fee money to ship grand pianos from South Africa to Europe and to run up a five-figure phone bills to sex lines are made by Michael Fabricant. The Conservative MP remarks are to the National Heritage Select Committee, and are protected by parliamentary privilege.
[<30 December, >3 February]

Even more Sunday politics

22 January: The debut of ITV's Jonathan Dimbleby programme boosts the number of Sunday TV and radio political shows to nine. All are interviews. What used to be a day of rest for politicians and journalists is now a day on which they have to wear their Sunday best. [<3 January, >27 February]

BBC and Pearson satellite channels

26 January: The BBC and Pearson jointly launch two new satellite television channels for continental Europe. Distribution is handled by European Channel Management (ECM), a new company established by BBC Worldwide Television and Pearson's wholly-owned subsidiary Thames Television. The 24-hour channels are: BBC World ("In Depth, In Focus, Informed"), described by the corporation as its "flagship news and information service"; and BBC Prime, a "quality entertainment channel". Neither are available in the UK. Pearson will meet the estimated £30 million cost of the venture, while the BBC supplies the programmes and expertise. This strategic alliance was formed in May 1994. BBC World, an advertising funded service, is a revamped version of the existing World Service TV, but is available in Europe for the first time. With over 150 journalists, its "worldwide news programmes are continually updated, combining the immediacy of television with the depth of newspapers". BBC Prime is a subscription funded service, replacing the BBC's existing European general programming channel. BBC Worldwide chairman Bob Phillis says: "This is a crucial development in the BBC's global strategy, and we are delighted to be making it with Pearson. It lays a firm foundation for a long and productive alliance." A few days later the US media group Cox Communications takes a 10 per cent stake in ECM. Its £5 million investment means Pearson will only have to pay costs of £25 million. Cox already has other partnerships with the BBC and Pearson. BBC World becomes available to cable operators in the USA on 1 February. [<11January, >15 March]

Beef inquiry journalist acquitted

27 January: Susan O'Keefe, a Granada journalist, is acquitted in Dublin of contempt of a tribunal following a documentary alleging scandals surrounding the Irish beef industry. She refused to tell Ireland's beef tribunal the names of any of the 120 people she spoke to when making the World in Action documentary Where's the Beef?, broadcast in May 1991. It accused one of Ireland's most prominent companies of forgery, reboxing old meat, selling substandard meat abroad and committing tax fraud. It is alleged that, while under oath at the tribunal, Ms O'Keefe, aged 34, was asked to disclose the people, but refused, saying "Yes, I am not willing to provide that list". After legal argument, judge Dominic Lynch rules that the words cannot be used against her. She had returned to Dublin for the trial voluntarily.

ITN chief quits

27 January: David Gordon, chief executive of ITN, suddenly resigns. Mr Gordon, aged 52,

joined ITN in May 1993 after 12 years as chief executive of the Economist Group. At that time he jokingly said about his new role at ITN: "I don't know much about telly, but I do know a man who does." On 28 March, ITN's editor-in-chief Stewart Purvis is appointed as Mr Gordon's successor as chief executive. Mr Purvis, aged 47, has been at ITN 22 years.

[<11 January, >2 February]

Radio audiences fall

31 January: People are now listening to the radio less than two years ago, the latest figures from Rajar reveal. Data for the fourth quarter of 1994 (19 September - 18 December) shows the total number of hours of adult listening in an average week was 842.1 million, down 3.8 per cent from the 875.6 million for the fourth quarter of 1992. This means the average hours per adult head per week were 17.9, compared with 18.8 in 1992. The "weekly reach" (the number of adults listening to radio for more than five minutes each week) was 40.4 million, down 2.8 per cent from the 41.6 million in 1992. But it is the BBC that is falling, while commercial radio is increasing. The BBC lost 13.9 per cent of its weekly reach, down from 32.3 million to 27.8 million. Most dramatic was the collapse of Radio 1, deserted by a third - 33.5 per cent - of the weekly reach: 16.5 million down to 11.0 million (in the last 12 months alone it lost 3.3 million).

[<20 December, >22 April]

Advertising radio advertising

Late January: The Radio Advertising Bureau launches a three-month advertising campaign using radio slots and a £2.5 million press campaign.

Porn channel go-ahead

Late January: David Sullivan, the owner of the tabloid papers Daily Sport and Sunday Sport, is given the go-ahead to launch Babylon Blue. Mr Sullivan tells the ITC that the channel will specialise in "adult entertainment, sport and feature films". The Labour Party says Mr Sullivan's arrival in the television market is a "matter of great concern". The ITC says it has no discretion to refuse a licence. The station will be encrypted and only available to people with a smart card.

New ITV health rules

1 February: The Independent Television Commission issues new rules imposing restrictions on the advertising of slimming products and pharmaceuticals, and on health claims made for food products. One of the regulations says advertisements "must not encourage or condone excessive consumption of any food." The ITC has been prompted by the government's Health of the Nation white paper.

Allied Radio loses licence

2 February: Allied Radio loses its local AM and FM licences for the Guildford area of Surrey. The Radio Authority re-advertised the licences and today announces the existing licensee County Sound plc (a subsidiary of Allied Radio plc, broadcasting as Radio Mercury) has re-applied unsuccessfully. The holder of the new eight-year licence starting in April 1996 is Surrey and North East Hampshire Radio Ltd. The RA says this company is offering a better local service. Mercury has been Allied's core business, broadcasting from Guildford and Crawley, in neighbouring West Sussex. The company's other significant operation is Fortune 1458 AM in Greater Manchester.

Reuters/BSkyB: news deal

2 February: Reuters and BSkyB announce their long-awaited television news partnership. For BSkyB, this cuts the annual £30 million costs of loss-making Sky News, boosts its information network and opens the door to going international. For Reuters, it is the biggest move so far into television. This Sky News/Reuters partnership could become a serious challenge to ITN and the new BBC World satellite channel that was launched on 26 January. Reuters will supply and manage all news for the 24-hour Sky News channel. The industry has expected an announcement on the partnership for several weeks. BSkyB initially discussed the deal with ITN for several months in 1994. But when news of this discussion was leaked in early November that year, BSkyB dropped the ITN idea and instead switched over to Reuters. By Christmas a scheme seemed likely. On 22 January 1995 Reuters announced a similar deal with another Rupert Murdoch-dominated company, the USA film and TV company Fox Television. Reuters and Fox will set up a television news service in the USA.

[<10 November]

Birt condemns BBC journalists

3 February: The BBC director-general John Birt (above) appears to suggest that some of his star interviewers are too big for their boots. Speaking at a lecture in Dublin he attacks the emphasis on "disputation" rather than "reflection" in "the picture of politics that emerges from the media". Concentration on personalities and short-term issues could mean that "rivalry between politicians, or differences within parties, are played out as a national soap opera". A spokeswoman says his remarks "have been taken out of context". His comments have revived arguments stirred in 1993 by a "courtesy drive" from corporation governors. [<18 January]

BSkyB's profits soar

7 February: BSkyB announces a 46 per cent rise in pre-tax profits to £55 million in the six months to 31 December 1994. And despite a rise in charges in October, the number of subscribers increased by 480,000 to 3.96 million, boosting turnover by 47 per cent. But despite the overall success of BSkyB, there are fears that sales of satellite dishes to the public are now plateauing out. In the last quarter of 1994 sales were much down on previous years. Total sales are now approaching the 20 per cent of population figure seen in other countries as the maximum market. [<2 Feb, >28 Feb]

Channel 4 attacks ITV subsidy

8 February: C4 must give £57.3 million of its 1994 profits to ITV companies, announces the ITC. The richest operator, Carlton UK Television, will acquire nearly £17 million. Michael Grade, C4 chief executive, condemns the decision, saying that instead of dividing the money amongst ITV shareholders the government should allow the money to be reinvested in British-made programmes. He speaks out after National Heritage secretary Stephen Dorrell refuses to allow changes in C4's annual funding formula. At present, all the surplus profits from advertising above a certain level are taken from C4 and shared between the ITV companies. They received £38 million last year. Mr Grade says they are embarrassed because they have taken £95 million from C4 in only two years, instead of the £100 million in ten years they expected. He demands an end to the "iniquitous" system, saying C4 will never need this "safety net" arrangement that only benefits the ITV companies. [<18 January, >20 March]

MPs debate BBC's future

9 February: The government's white paper The Future of the BBC is discussed by MPs in a debate that is lively, but much less emotional than in the past. The white paper came out in July 1994, announcing the plan to renew the BBC's charter for a 10-year period to the end of 1996. Included were details of how the government intends the BBC to develop in that period, especially as the corporation is now in a rapidly changing broadcast market place. Members of the public were given a deadline of 31 October 1994 for making comments on the white paper. National Heritage secretary Stephen Dorrell says it was "well received, both in the House and outside". He praises the BBC, unlike the Conservative government when Margaret Thatcher was prime minister. He says: "The BBC is a well-loved institution and the burden of proof lies firmly on those who want to change it."

Privatise BBC transmitters, says report

10 February: The BBC's extensive network of television transmitters should be privatised as a way of bringing competition and new capital into terrestrial broadcasting, says a report by the free-market Adam Smith Institute. It believes that only a future in the private sector will guarantee the BBC access to the substantial

investment needed to develop the new digital broadcasting technology that is set to revolutionise TV transmission over the next few years. "Today we are in the worst of all possible worlds", says author Keith Boyfield. "The successful private transmission company NTL is barred from seeking BBC business. Meanwhile the BBC cannot sell its transmission services to ITV companies because politicians fear it could be unfair competition, subsidised by licence-payers." The trade union Bectu says the Institute's report "masquerades as a reasoned study of all the options, but in reality merely adds up to a quest for a good enough excuse to privatise an efficient public service." On 22 February NTL says it is planning to build the UK's first digital terrestrial TV network between now and 1997. This should offer between 12 and 30 extra channels and improved picture quality, at moderate cost. [<3 November, >20 March]

New national radio station

14 February: Britain's first national commercial speech radio station goes on air at 6am. Talk Radio is widely seen as the UK version of American "shock jock" radio. The 24-hour station even attracts complaints before officially starting. There were 150 protest calls about pre-launch pilot transmissions, most of them involving presenter Caesar the Geezer, described by the station as "fat, rude, abusive, bigoted" etc. Talk Radio has the third national licence, lasting eight years. It is costing £8 million to launch and will have to pay the Radio Authority £3.82 million pa. Observers believe this annual bid by Talk Radio was too high to be met from income. Managing director John Aumonier says market research showed 76 per cent of people were dissatisfied with existing speech radio choices. Talk Radio has set itself a target of 20 million listening hours a year, overtaking Radio 5 Live. On AM 1053 and 1089, it is aiming at ages 25 to 45. Legally, it only has to be 51 per cent speech-based. [>7 March]

Mirror Group buys cable channel

15 February: Mirror Television, part of the Mirror Group, buys Wire TV, Britain's first nationwide cable channel. Selling it is CCP-1, the consortium of the largest UK cable companies. Mirror will replace Wire TV with its own long-planned service, Live TV, launching on 12 June. Live TV will be an entertainment-led, 24-hour channel, offering features,

information and news. It will be carried on nearly every cable system in Britain. The managing director is Janet Street-Porter, former head of BBC youth programming. [<2 August >12 June]

BBC's strategy review

15 February: The most radical overhaul of the BBC's radio and television programmes is outlined in order to redress criticism of stuffy elitism and metropolitan remoteness. The 18-month programme strategy review delivers a vote of confidence in much of the BBC's output, but identifies the young and ethnic minorities as groups poorly served. The 177-page document People and Programmes involved the largest public consultation exercise undertaken by the corporation, costing £500,000. It has resulted in 350 proposals and an £85 million investment in new programmes to reverse perceived deficiencies, mainly in drama, science and leisure. Fresh attempts are to be made to embrace the young, who find much of the output middle-aged, and those from ethnic minorities who think of the BBC as "remote, traditional and mainly white". Many were puzzled that the corporation had commissioned an 18-month review whose findings were so obvious. Sir Paul Fox, a former BBC TV managing director, says: "Six producers sitting in a room could have come up with the same conclusions more quickly."

European TV quotas

Mid-February: Europe's broadcasting ministers meet in Brussels to discuss the responsibility of their broadcasting companies to fill 51 per cent of schedules with European-origin programmes. This rule is mainly ignored, to the benefit of the USA. The French believe the regulations should be enforced, in order to protect European culture and production. But Britain - backing the US - wants a freer market. No conclusion is reached and the long-running debate is adjourned again. [<4 January, >20 February]

Satellite pirate sunk

Mid-February: A leading figure in satellite piracy is given a six-week prison sentence suspended for two years, a major step forward for BSkyB. David Lyons, who originally ran a well-known trade from Warrington and then Ireland, is convicted of trading in illegal "smartcards". He will also have to pay damages and all costs, possibly totalling more than £400,000. BSkyB welcomes the result, the first time courts impose a prison sentence for piracy. But at the same time a new type of smartcard is emerging, on sale by a Frankfurt-based company for £170. The smartcard can unlock the scrambled television signal and can be re-programmed by the user every time BSkyB brings in countermeasure codes. Previously cards had to be replaced. [<7 October]

Labour's ideas for the future

The shadow Heritage Secretary Chris Smith

Mid-February: Labour would consider lifting the ban on British Telecom broadcasting entertainment over its phone network before 1998, the earliest date under present legislation, says shadow trade secretary Jack Cunningham. BT has said it is not prepared to invest the estimated £15 billion needed to bring high capacity fibre optic cable to the home until it has a firm date for broadcasting. Separately, shadow National Heritage secretary Chris Smith criticises the Radio Authority, saying it should publish the minutes of its meetings. The authority does not reveal the reasoning behind its decisions. "I would hope for a greater system of openness at the RA in the future," he says. [<22 Nov. >15 March]

Cuts in BBC regions

17 February: Regional broadcasting will bear the brunt of the latest round of BBC spending cuts, it is announced · two days after the corporation says it is determined to become less biased to the Home Counties. Radio Berkshire will be merged with Radio Oxford. BBC CWR, the station serving Coventry and Warwickshire, is to be merged with the Birmingham-based BBC WM. These mergers will cut local radio, and there is much public dislike. Nearly a third of all MPs oppose them. The Bishop of Coventry is refused permission to address the BBC board of governors about CWR, but on 18 April National Heritage secretary Stephen Dorrell meets a delegation of protestors. Broadcasting unions believe the BBC is surreptitiously dismantling its local radio and replacing it with a cheaper sub-regional system. Radio Sussex was recently a victim, when it was "merged" with Radio Surrey to form Southern Counties Radio, run from Surrey. On 3 March, Broadcast magazine says it has been told that senior BBC managers are considering closing up to 20 more local stations over the next ten years, half the total. Management denies this figure. Over 130 jobs have been lost in the latest cuts in BBC local radio, about 10 per cent of the workforce. [>early April]

Birt fears EU digital plans

20 February: John Birt, director-general of the BBC, says the European Union is inadvertently preparing to give Rupert Murdoch and a handful of other satellite operators the chance to exert monopoly control over the coming revolution in information technology. He tells MEPs in Brussels that a technical directive approved by the EU's telecommunications ministers in November could allow a few powerful companies to determine which programmes and services reached people's homes. It could turn these firms into "digital gatekeepers" who would be able to restrict competition, limit choice and deny broadcasters fair access. Mr Birt wants the directive changed before it goes through the European parliament. [<mid-February, >26 February]

TV doorstepping guidelines

21 February: Broadcasters face tightened restrictions from today on "doorstepping" interviews, because of concern about invasions of privacy. The ITC has introduced new guidelines on interviews sought on private property. They are likely to have an impact on

investigative current affairs programmes such as ITV's The Cook Report. The guidelines say: "Interviews sought on private property without the subject's prior agreement should not be included in a programme unless they have a public interest purpose. Interviews in which criminal or other serious allegations are put to individuals should not be attempted without prior warning unless a previous request has been refused or received no response, or where there is good reason for not making a prior approach." There are other new guidelines in the ITC's first revised edition of the programme makers code since January 1993.

Court eases the pressure

22 February: Television journalists' freedom to tackle issues without interference from pressure groups is upheld in the High Court. It rules that the Broadcasting Complaints Commission acted beyond its powers in accepting a complaint from the National Council for One Parent Families against a BBC Panorama documentary (see 12 September). The decision is hailed as a victory by broadcast journalists who had feared the commission's decision to entertain the charity's complaint would open the floodgates to spurious protests from partisan pressure groups. The government is currently planning to merge the commission and the Broadcasting Standards Council, and this clarification of the law should be included in the fresh legislation. [<10 October]

Paris studio closes

26 February: Paris Studio, the BBC's studio home for radio comedy since 1940, closes. The lease of the Lower Regent Street building is expiring, and the owners plan to turn it into offices. It was the setting for classic series like Hancock's Half Hour and The Goons. Light entertainment is moving to the refurbished Concert Hall, at Broadcasting House, to be renamed the Radio Theatre.

Global superhighway green light

26 February: Europe agrees that market forces should be allowed to rule the development of the global information superhighway, in spite of the danger of heavy job losses in the short term and the risk of boosting the might of the US technology industry. The decision is made by the Group of Seven, the leading industrialised nations, meeting in conference in Brussels. This amounts to a green light for the emergence of mega-corporations operating in all the world's markets, subject only to as yet unspecified national regulations to prevent monopolistic abuse. The meeting agrees to 11 pilot projects to promote the use of information superhighways. The Financial Times says: "The hidden agenda was the speed at which countries · especially those in Europe · were prepared to liberalise their telecoms regimes by tearing down the protection around state-owned monopoly suppliers and allowing open competition in infrastructure and services." [<20 February]

Rise in cable subscriptions

27 February: The number of broadband cable subscribers rose in the last quarter of 1994 by nearly 130,000, by far the most substantial growth in the cable TV audience yet recorded. ITC statistics show the number of subscribers rose from 779,461 on 1 October 1994 to 909,043 on 1 January 1995, an increase of 16.6 per cent. On 1 January 1994 there were 611,423 subscribers, meaning the increase over the following 12 months was 48.7 per cent. This reflects the fast construction of new networks during 1994. The number of homes passed by cables rose from 2.79 million to 4.17 million, up 49.8 per cent. But the average penetration remains the same: at the beginning of the year 21.9 per cent of passed homes are connected, at the end 21.8 per cent. More good news for cablers is the 128 per cent rise in the number of phone lines installed by cable companies during 1994, up from 314,381 to 717,586. On 3 March Nynex CableComms says it will undercut by a quarter BT's standard prices for line rental and call charges. This roughly doubles the discounts by cable companies, and adds to the downward pressure on phone costs. [<24 January, >15 May]

Launch of BBC Radio Helpline

27 February: The BBC Radio Helpline is launched to provide a 24-hour telephone service linked to programmes on the five national networks. It will offer confidential advice on a range of issues raised in programmes, including crime, disability, relationships and education.

New Labour campaign director

27 February: Joy Johnson, the BBC political news editor, is confirmed as the Labour Party's new Director of Campaigns, Elections and Media. Ms Johnson, aged 44, has been a Labour member for 20 years. She started working for ITN in 1979, followed by the BBC in 1990.

Business channel

27 February: The cable channel European Business News (EBN) is launched. It aims to provide a full news, feature and information service to businesses, trades and markets across Europe. EBN is 70 per cent owned by Dow Jones, publisher of the financial bible The Wall Street Journal.

Associated attacks media law

28 February: Sir David English, chairman of Associated Newspapers, condemns the government's media ownership laws. "In the world of electronic publishing, you are certainly a second class citizen if you are a British newspaper company," he tells the Financial Times annual leading conference on satellite and cable TV. He believes that foreigners "can go into our national electronic supermarket with assured impunity and buy what they want." Sir David attacks the Conservative government which his newspapers have always supported: "There is little I can do because of the glass curtain which stands between newspaper publishers and the opportunities which government diktat has placed beyond our reach ... We stand with our noses pressed against the glass curtain bitterly resenting the arrogance and contempt with which our leaders are treating us." [<11 January, >21 March]

Floating cable firms

28 February: CableComms, one of Britain's biggest cable system operators, starts floating on the Stock Exchange in an attempt to raise £400 million for cable developments. The company is owned by New York-based Nynex. This is the biggest London-based flotation of a cable firm to date. Nynex CableComms has 16 franchise areas covering 2.7 million homes, many in the Manchester area. It employs 2,500 people. The French-owned group General Cable also floats in London, in March, hoping to raise about £200 million. On 16 March, the first cable company on the Stock Exchange, TeleWest, says it almost doubled its losses to £65 million in its 1994 financial year. But the deficit was in line with the expected results of its expansion, and its shares rise 4p. TeleWest floated in November 1994. But its "churn" rate (subscribers not renewing their annual connection) was 47.1 per cent. On 3 March another large operator, Bell Cablemedia, announces a loss of £26 million in 1994, resulting from its construction of cable networks. [<7 November, >19 April]

BSkyB market share

28 February: BSkyB's dominant position means there is not a free market in the UK's cable TV market for new channels, warns the Landmark Travel Channel. It tells a conference in London that it cannot reach three-quarters of the cable and satellite audience because of BSkyB's power. Negotiations between the two broke down in 1994. In early March BSkyB fends off an investigation by the Monopolies and Mergers Commission by agreeing to new conditions for supply of its programming to cable operators. [7 February, >5 May]

Talk Radio says: No crisis

7 March: Three weeks after going on air on 14 February, Talk Radio UK, the third national commercial station, is suffering a series of internal problems. But the "shockjock" station denies it is in crisis, despite 22 complaints and the departure of the sales director. Most complaints are about strong language and sexual references. Eventually the late-night DJ Wild Al Kelly is sacked because of complaints. A shake-up takes place in late April when it becomes clear that the audience has only been 1.5 million, instead of the predicted 3 million This is 0.9 per cent of radio listening. Programme director Jeremy Scott is sacked on 25 April. He is replaced by Jerry Thomas, who says he'll keep "ballsy irreverence" but drop obscenities. [<14 February >30 June]

Drive to end TV plugs

7 March: A crackdown on broadcasters who use programmes to plug products is launched by the ITC. It wants to stop brand-name goods being given undue prominence, contrary to the industry's code. A 30-second promotion, to be screened during commercial breaks, draws the rules about plugging products to viewers' attention. On 8 March Granada scraps a documentary when it is realised British Airways logos are emblazoned across clothing worn by children at the centre of the programme. In 1994 Granada was fined £500,000 in 1994 for plugs during its magazine show This Morning.

Two new ITV heads named

8 March: Appointments are made to the two most powerful posts in the ITV system. Marcus Plantin, aged 49, will take over as chief executive of the ITV Network Centre when Andrew Quinn steps down in October. Mr

Plantin, the former LWT director of programmes, will combine his new role with his present position as network director, presiding over a £570 million budget. Mr Plantin's former LWT colleague Barry Cox will take up the new post of ITV Association director, responsible for formulating ITV strategy. Former London Weekend Television employees include: the BBC director-general John Birt, Pearson's television organiser Greg Dyke and Channel 4 chief executive Michael Grade.

New Radio Authority chief

9 March: The Radio Authority announces the appointment of Tony Stoller as its chief executive from 1 July, to replace Peter Baldwin, who is retiring. Mr Stoller, aged 47, is currently managing a chain of John Lewis Partnership supermarkets from Southampton. From 1974-84 he had managerial roles in different sectors of the radio business, including the IBA. Nonetheless, the appointment creates some concern because of Mr Stoller's lack of involvement with commercial radio for over a decade. Mr Baldwin's deputy, Paul Brown, was the expected successor.

Is there life without television?

12 March: The Observer asks six households addicted to TV to voluntarily spend a week not watching the screen, as a prelude to America's first National TV-Turnoff Week at the end of April. "The results of the experiment ... were startling. Volunteers spoke of bereavement, of going 'barmy', of the worst week of their lives. They took to the bottle, tobacco and bed. Others discovered there were, after all, enough hours in the day: curtains were made, novels read, bread baked."

MPs debate BT

15 March: Is Britain making a strategic mistake of historic proportions in not allowing British Telecom to build a national network of high-capacity optical fibres? MPs hold a three-hour debate to answer this question about the future of the cable business. Some MPs argue that if British Telecom was given the go-ahead for its plans, Britain could catapult itself into the front of the global information revolution. But there is still no sign of the government changing the rules.
[<mid-February, >30May]

Thames TV head quits

15 March: Richard Dunn resigns as head of Thames Television, Britain's biggest independent TV production company, bought by Pearson in 1993. He is resigning two months after Greg Dyke was appointed over his head as chairman of Pearson's expanding television division. Mr Dunn, a former chairman of the ITV Association, was once the most senior TV executive within Pearson. On 30 March it is announced that he will become executive director of Rupert Murdoch's News International TV.
[<26 January]

Channel 5 boost

16 March: At least 66 per cent of the UK population will be able to receive Channel 5, says the ITC. When it invited bids for Channel 5 on 1 November 1994 it could only guarantee about 50 per cent. This means that the battle for the Channel 5 licence becomes more intense. Closing date is 2 May. In the weeks until then there is much speculation about which companies will make bids, and whether Rupert Murdoch's consortium would make a massive offer in order to guarantee his victory.
[<1 November, >24 April]

ITV leaders in dispute

20 March: Michael Green, chairman of Carlton Communications, warns that, unless broadcasters like Carlton are allowed to grow, then "our production base will shrink, and imports will grow". But C4 chief executive Michael Grade says ITV mergers "have been essentially financial events, providing healthy increases in profits for ITV companies, achieved by reducing employment, and doing nothing at all for competition or diversity of supply ... Mr Green has every right to want to run a bigger and better business, and to lobby hard to achieve it. But we shouldn't fall for the rhetoric that this is all done in the national interest, nor believe the disingenuous cry of the new licensee that inventing a Mark II ITV monopoly is the best way of stimulating competition."
[<8 February, >4 April]

Digital TV

20 March: The Royal Television Society holds a special conference on "what are likely to be the biggest changes in the history of the TV industry ... British television is facing a

revolution which will transform the industry in the next five years far more radically even than the Broadcasting Act and the BBC Charter Review in the last five. Digital technology is already offering low cost multi-channel television, transforming production methods, and eroding the boundaries between the television, computer and telecommunication industries." Digital TV lets six to 12 channels fill the space for just one available under the current analogue system. There could be 500 TV channels coming on stream over the next two years. Three all-digital Astra satellites are due for launching by mid-1997, the first in September 1995. On 28 March Astra's rival Eutelsat launches the first of its three Hot Bird satellites, which can be used for either digital or analogue channels. All Europe's leading subscription television companies now believe that digital satellite TV is the future. But viewers will need to buy "black box" to decode the pictures.
[<10 February, >1 May]

Cabinet minister condemns BBC

25 March: Fears of the strongest government attack on the BBC since 1986 are aroused when Jonathan Aitken, Chief Secretary to the Treasury, condemns Radio 4 presenter John Humphrys for alleged "open partisanship" and "ego-trip interviewing". This sparks a brief explosion of emotions on both sides. The BBC at all levels rallies round Mr Humphrys, defending him from further hostility. The government demands the BBC should be more "impartial", but at the same time the Cabinet back-pedals away from a 1986-style row. In the run-up to the 1987 general election the Tory chairman, Norman Tebbitt, launched a major long-term campaign against the BBC, attacking the "insufferable, smug, sanctimonious, naive, guilt-ridden, wet, pink, orthodoxy of that sunset home of that third-rate decade, the sixties". Mr Humphrys says that broadcasters have a responsibility to grill politicians.

Pearson buys TV production company

29 March: Financial Times owner Pearson invests £175 million in Grundy Worldwide, the independent TV production company best known for the Australian soap opera Neighbours. The deal, masterminded by Pearson's new head of television Greg Dyke, has been put together in less than five weeks and

snatches Grundy from the New York stock market, where it was planning a £186 million flotation. Pearson intends to exploit Neighbours and other mass-appeal soaps and game shows as part of the company's dream of becoming an international media player. Mr Dyke comments: "This purchase transforms us from a national to an international producer. We plan to expand our activities in all the major television territories around the world." News of the takeover follows two days after Pearson releases its accounts for 1994. There was a 43 per cent increase in pre-tax profits to £298 million. But there was also "a setback" over Pearson's £310 million purchase in May 1994 of the American interactive software company Mindscape. Its sales of video games have dropped 65 per cent.
[<26 January, >16 May]

Regional BBC in wonderland

Early April: The BBC's regional policy "is like something from Alice's Adventures in Wonderland", says the broadcasting union Bectu in its magazine Stage Screen & Radio. "As BBC management continues to announce further initiatives for the nations and regions of the UK, research by Stage Screen & Radio demonstrates that non-London programme making for the television network is substantially less than it was ten years ago." Between 1984 and 1994 "the huge gap between London, England, Scotland, Wales and Northern Ireland has actually widened and network production has dropped in every area. London dropped 27.7 per cent over the period; the English regions fell by 51 per cent; Scotland was reduced by 57.8 per cent; Wales by 77 per cent and Northern Ireland by a massive 89 per cent." At a media conference in Manchester in early April, Granada TV's ex-head of current affairs, Ray Fitzwalter, launches anattack on the BBC, ITV and C4 for their lack of commitment to regional production. He says: "There isn't anything to show that the strength of the ITV regional structure won't deteriorate further".
[<17 February, >3 April]

Court bans John Major on TV

3 April: The Court of Session in Edinburgh today twice bans the BBC from screening in Scotland a Panorama interview with prime minister John Major ahead of the local elections north of the border on Thursday 6 April. The three opposition parties in Scotland band

together for the court actions. They accuse the corporation of failing to meet standards of impartiality and balance in the run up to the local elections. Their QC says: "The BBC seems to have ignored, or perhaps been unaware of, the imminence of the local elections in Scotland". The ban is imposed just ten minutes before the start of the programme at 9.30. But it is broadcast in Wales and most of England, showing David Dimbleby carrying out a low-key 40-minute interview at Downing Street. The BBC suffers further humiliation on 4 April when the Scottish appeal court refuses the BBC leave to take its case to the House of Lords. The corporation had been hoping it could show the programme that night in Scotland. Many critics see the Panorama case as proof of the BBC's Home Counties prejudice. Gus MacDonald of Scottish TV says: "For years the BBC up here has been known as the London Broadcasting Corporation. It has not offered what Scottish viewers want." Lesley Riddoch, assistant editor of the Scotsman, says the "debacle was a source of enormous satisfaction to Scots · because at last, an example of everyday bias was made public".There is also speculation that the government quickly smothered the 25 March row because it was looking forward to the 3 April broadcast of Panorama. On 12 April the BBC's board of governors says: "We regret that overall the BBC showed insufficient regard to the Scottish dimensions."
[<early April]

C4 funding should change, say MPs
4 April: MPs call for a change in the funding formula that has forced C4 to give £95 million to ITV companies in just two years. The all-party National Heritage Select Committee proposes the overhaul, provided C4 meets two conditions. First, C4 must meet the shortfall of any ITV company failing to reach the cash income it predicted for 1993-97. Second, C4 must put the remaining revenue into programme-making, training and at least doubling its investment in British films.
[<20 March]

Murdoch's global sports plans
6 April: Plans by Rupert Murdoch to create an international rugby league "super-league" are unveiled. This comes straight after a deal securing TV rights in boxing involving certain key fighters. Sky Sports already has a five-year Premiership soccer deal and many other sports rights. Together, all these and other moves

under way could add up to a future dominance in world television sports coverage. Sport is a vital weapon in the battle to secure larger satellite audiences. Mr Murdoch's rugby proposals would revolutionise it, with a league competition involving the UK, Australia and New Zealand, later expanded to other continents. In Britain, the 35 league clubs would be shrunk to a super-league of only 14, playing for television. Many famous clubs would disappear, and this prospect arouses much grass-roots opposition. MPs investigate a legal challenge to the scheme. Ian McCartney, MP for Makerfield, says: "This is the first time a British sport has been bought lock, stock and barrel by an international media conglomerate. It will no longer be a game. It will be a media product."
[<late November, 23 June]

Minister sues Granada and Guardian
10 April: Jonathan Aitken, the Treasury minister denounces "wicked lies" told by the Guardian and Granada TV's World in Action about his business activities. Allegations about his relations with members of the Saudi royal family are the result of investigation by a joint team from the twoorganisations, both releasing the results today. Mr Aitken holds a press conference during the day, where he says he is starting "a fight to cut out the cancer of bent and twisted journalism in our country with the simple sword of truth and the trusty shield of fair play." He immediately issues writs against the Guardian and threatens similar action against World in Action if it goes on air in the evening. But it does. Alan Rusbridger, the new editor of the Guardian, dismisses Mr Aitken's attack, saying: "We stand by our story". The writ against Granada is not issued until 27 April. Mr Aitken's great-uncle was Max Aitken, the first Lord Beaverbrook, who bought the Express in 1916. In 1929 he launched a free trade campaign and created the paper's symbol: a crusader carrying a sword and shield.

Jonathan Aitken

Low cable bid

10 April: The ITC receives a tiny bid for a local cable licence: £1 pa. This is offered by Videotron for a small area west of Southampton. In contrast, CableTel bid £14.4 million pa for all Northern Ireland on 6 February.

ITV: "More remains to be achieved"

11 April: The 18 ITV licensees gave "generally strong performances" in 1994, "but more remains to be achieved", says the Independent Television Commission. In its second annual report for the 10-year licence period that started in 1993, the commission is not as critical of ITV as 12 months ago. But it thinks companies are still too cautious and should take more risks.

Radio slot closed to atheists

13 April: The BBC rejects the idea of allowing agnostics and atheists to present Radio 4's Thought for the Day. The decision is taken after a review of the 25-year old slot's format on the Today programme. It runs for three minutes at 7.50am. The BBC says the brief of Thought for the Day is to have a different, non-secular perspective on the daily news agenda. The National Secular Society says: "With at least a third of the population non-religious, and with many others non-Christian, it is a disgrace that about £10 million in licence-payer's money goes to support propaganda for the enormously wealthy Anglican, Catholic and non-Conformist Churches." On 10 June, Britain's first Christian commercial radio station opens. [>10 June]

General Cable cuts share price

19 April: A cable company floating its shares has to cut their price from the expected 220p-225p to 190p. The action means French-owned General Cable, the third largest UK cable operator, will raise about £170 million instead of the £200-230 million that had been expected. The flotation takes place in the US and Britain, with the cut price resulting from poor American interest. [<7 November >9 June]

Radio 1 launches £2m ad campaign

22 April: A £2 million advertising campaign, designed to recapture listeners who have deserted Radio 1, is launched by the BBC. The corporation, facing increased competition from commercial stations, has identified Radio 1 as its top priority for 1995. Although the network has lost five million listeners in two years, it is still Britain's largest station, with weekly audiences of 11 million. Chris Evans takes over the breakfast show from Steve Wright on 24 April. In early May the radio audience figures for January-March are released, showing Radio 1 has fallen again. Another 495,000 weekly listeners were lost, taking the total down to 10.5 million. [<31 January >late July]

Channel 5 "disaster"

24 April: The auction for the Channel 5 franchise is a "recipe for disaster", says Labour Party's national heritage spokesman Chris Smith. He tells a London conference he is "deeply worried" about the 2 May auction. But he does not explicitly condemn the involvement of Rupert Murdoch. This is done on 25 April by Channel 5 chief executive Michael Grade. He says: "A consortium backed by Murdoch stands a very good chance of putting in the highest bid, and winning. If it does, it will mark the final chapter of a sorry tale of government weakness, incompetence and opportunism in broadcasting policy. It will permanently remove all hope of fair and effective media ownership rules in the UK." Mr Grade believes "a Murdoch foothold in British terrestrial television will have enormous - and damaging consequences." He calls for an immediate change in the media ownership law to stop Mr Murdoch taking the Channel 5 licence. The following day, National Heritage secretary Stephen Dorrell rejects the demand. The government publishes its long-awaited white paper on media ownership on 23 May. [<16 March, >5 May]

ITV digital broadcasting proposals

1 May: The ITV Association describes its plans for the introduction of digital terrestrial broadcasting (DTB) in the UK. DTB will provide better pictures and sound, plus more channels, than the current analogue method. Until now the discussion has been about the European digital satellite services scheduled to start later in 1995. But with the government due to publish a policy statement on DTB soon, the ITV companies today issue their proposals. They suggest giving each of the existing UK broadcasters - the BBC, ITV, Channel 4 and the coming Channel 5 - a single UHF channel capable of running several digital programmes at the same time. As early a start date as possible is requested, probably late 1997. [<20 March, >5 May]

Virgin on the ridiculous. When Virgin made its Channel 5 bid to the ITC, the cameras were on hand to record the historic moment when the paperwork was delivered

Channel 5 deadline

2 May: The ITC receives four bids for the Channel 5 licence before the deadline of noon today. Rupert Murdoch astonishes his media rivals when his consortium New Century Television delivers the lowest offer. Also causing amazement is the fact that two of the other groups, Channel 5 Broadcasting and Virgin TV, make bids that are the same. The third shock is that the highest bid comes from a Canada-dominated consortium, UKTV. New Century Television bids £2 million. It has many owners, the most influential being BSkyB (the largest shareholder, with 20 per cent) and Granada (5 per cent). The chairman is Charles Allen, of Granada, and chief executive is David Elstein, of BSkyB. The reasons for Mr Murdoch's petty bid are widely debated. One theory is that he did not want to fall foul of the imminent changes in the law on cross-media ownership, while another says his ambitions are global, rather than UK regional. Channel 5 Broadcasting bids £22,002,000. It does not give details of its ownership, but the most influential companies are known to be Pearson and MAI. Its best-known personalities are chairman Frank Barlow, of Pearson, MAI's Lord Hollick and Pearson TV's Greg Dyke. Virgin TV also bids £22,002,000. It has six owners, four of them holding 20 per

cent: Virgin, Associated Newspapers, HTV and Paramount TV. Key players are Richard Branson of Virgin and Sir David English of Associated Newspapers. UKTV bids £36,261,158. It is internationally-owned, and masterminded by Canada's largest private media company CanWest (29.9 per cent). Its other owners are SelectTV (British, 20 per cent), Scandinavian Broadcast System (30 per cent) and The Ten Group (Australian, 19.9 per cent). ITC invites public comments on the applications, with a deadline of 13 June. It says it will award the licence by 30 November 1995, with the start-date being no later than 1 January 1997. Maximum coverage is now expected to be "around 69 per cent" of the UK population. Many commentators believe UKTV will not be given the ten-year licence because its annual bid may be too high to be sustained.
[<24 April, >4 May]

Channel 5 lifeline

4 May: Channel 5 Broadcasting discovers that its bid consultants Coopers & Lybrand had also been consultants for Virgin. The consortium organises an independent inquiry. Virgin thinks this is too narrow and calls on ITC to launch a more comprehensive one. On 18 May the ITC

says it will begin discussions with the consortia before deciding. They are asked to confirm in writing that they did not discuss the terms or the amount of their bids with outsiders. The ITC announces on 6 June that its inquiry has found no evidence of collaboration and decides to take no further action. In late May UKTV appoints appoints John Fairley, one of ITV's leading programme makers as its chief executive. UKTV says the competition, which suspect its bid is not going to be a sustainable one, is employing "distracting falsehoods" to discredit the application.
[2 May, >21 May]

BSkyB in cable deal

5 May: BSkyB looks set to win an unassailable position in British subscription television by making a 10-year "sweetheart" deal with two of the biggest UK cable communications companies. Nynex and TeleWest will pay low rates to carry BSkyB programmes, in exchange for which they have agreed not to transmit their own programmes in competition with satellite broadcasters. The deal is seen as a peace treaty between satellite and cable, effectively wiping out BSkyB's only serious competition in bidding for film and sporting rights. The ITV Association and Channel 4 call for an inquiry by the Monopolies and Mergers Commission. They say BSkyB has built a monopoly position in the pay-television market and is "picking off potential competitors one by one before the arrival of digital broadcasting". On 16 June the Department of Trade and Industry halts the deal by putting the agreement on the register of restrictive practices. The DTI examines the anti-competition elements of the agreement to see if any changes are needed.
[<28 February, >19 June]

Women's charter signed

5 May: European TV executives sign the Equal Opportunities for Women in Broadcasting Charter after a three-day conference hosted by the BBC in London. The charter seeks: fair and equal treatment in selection, recruitment and promotion procedures; freedom from harassment and intimidation; access to training; and participation in decision-making and the editorial process. In European broadcasting, women are 6 per cent of management, 11 per cent of senior executives and 7 per cent of technical staff.

Murdoch receives $2 billion in USA...

10 May: Rupert Murdoch's global media empire the News Corporation creates a new multimedia structure of worldwide significance by forming an alliance with MCI Corporation, the second biggest telecommunications company in the USA. They will share their strengths in media and telecoms to deliver information and entertainment around the world. MCI will invest $2 billion for 13.5 per cent equity stake in News Corporation. Both companies will put $200 million into the new venture.
[<5 May, >12 May]

... and bids $2 billion in Italy

12 May: News Corporation makes an offer of just under $2 billion for 51 per cent of the TV and advertising empire of Silvio Berlusconi, the former Italian premier. His company Fininvest owns three TV channels, with over 40 per cent of the national audience. Mr Berlusconi has put his media interests up for sale because of strong political opposition to major TV ownership in his hands. But on 11 June he wins a resounding victory in referendums aimed at curbing his control of Italian television. His conservative political bloc moves into a strong position. In July Mr Berlusconi rejects Mr Murdoch's bid for a controlling stake, instead going for foreign partners who will give him a high degree of management control. [<10 May, >21 May]

Cable telecoms continue strong growth

15 May: Figures from the ITC show that the number of new telephone lines installed by UK cable operators continues to rise rapidly. By 1 April, 872,573 lines had been installed, 132 per cent up in 12 months. In the first quarter of 1994, there were 62,400 lines installed; in the same period of 1995 the figure was 155,000.
[<27 February, >6 June]

Pearson pulls TV plug

16 May: Pearson announces the sale of its 14.8 per cent stake in Yorkshire-Tyne Tees Television to Lord Hollick's financial services and media group MAI for £41.3 million. Pearson Television chairman Greg Dyke says: "We have decided a 14 per cent stake in a regional broadcaster is no longer of any strategic interest to us." MAI already controls Meridian and Anglia, and now seems to be planning further expansion.
[<29 March]

Welsh TV to repay arts cash

16 May: The Welsh language television channel, S4C, is ordered to repay £53,500 to the Association for Business Sponsorship for the Arts after an inquiry by the National Heritage Department. A report found that the channel had set up a scheme enabling companies to receive sponsorship cash to which they were not entitled. The results of the inquiry are announced in the House of Commons by Stephen Dorrell. The scheme attempted to take advantage of arrangements whereby firms supporting the arts could have their grants matched pound-for-pound by the government. It was alleged that dummy companies were set up which did not trade, but into which S4C money was directed.

Increase in radio advertising

17 May: Commercial radio stations are now taking 3.8 per cent of the display advertising market of £5.8 billion, reports the Radio Advertising Bureau. Until the early 1990s the figure had been stuck for many years at 2 per cent. The launch of national stations has made radio the fastest-growing medium in the UK, up 23 per cent in 1994, and this could continue for several years. Its share of the total market could rise to five or six per cent by the end of the decade, believes RAB. On 18 May Capital Radio shows it has been successfully exploiting the advertising increase by pushing up its profits by 52 per cent, from £8.4 million to £12.7 million, in the first half of its current financial year. [<25 October]

Northern Ireland cable franchise

19 May: The new cable TV franchise for the whole of Northern Ireland is awarded by ITC to CableTel, making it the fourth largest UK cable operator. Its bid of £14.4 million a year is the highest of the four made in early February. CableTel will start construction in 1996 and offer TV and telecommunications services to at least 428,000 homes by the end of 2003. The US-owned company already has other cable operations in Greater Glasgow, South Wales, Yorkshire and other areas. It is considering floating on the Stock Exchange this year. [<15 September]

Murdoch: the empire strikes back

21 May: Rupert Murdoch accuses his detractors of paranoia and suggests there is something badly wrong with Britain. In a TV interview, on BBC2's Money Programme, he denies he is seeking global media domination and says he opposes imminent new ownership restrictions. "There is something awfully wrong with Britain when someone comes in and works hard and competes and they are successful and a catalyst for change ... Anybody could have set up Sky Television, anybody, and we started it and people are still free to start against us, but they'd rather write articles, bitch and moan, lay around and say: No we'd rather just keep our lazy way of life, we don't want to compete." Mr Murdoch rejects the need for tighter cross-media ownership rules. On his low Channel 5 bid, he says he has never been keen to apply for the channel, which he believes would not be commercially successful. The bid had been a "grudging compromise" with his London-based management. Asked whether his newspapers would support Labour at the general election, Mr Murdoch says: "We will have to find out what the difference is between Mr Blair and Mr Major before we make that decision. Right now, from this distance, it is rather confusing." [<4 May, >23 May]

Record High Court TV damages

23 May: Chris Brasher, the Olympic steeplechase champion who founded the London Marathon, wins his legal battle against allegations of improper dealings in financing the event. A High Court libel case ends when an out-of-court settlement offer of £380,000 is made by Channel 4, the New Statesman and journalist Duncan Campbell (not the Guardian's crime correspondent of the same name). They will also pay Mr Brasher's costs of over £1.1 million, and their own costs of £1 million. The settlement arises from an article by Mr Campbell in the New Statesman in 1990. The material was used by Channel 4 in a Dispatches programme in March 1991. The Campbell article was also carried in the Independent, but the newspaper was not sued.

New media ownership rules announced

23 May: The government's long-awaited new rules for regulating media ownership are announced. National Heritage secretary Stephen Dorrell lays out his blueprint to sweep away the existing "complex, myriad" rules. In a green paper, he outlines a two stage approach to liberalise ownership, which he says is consistent with diversity and plurality, while ensuring British media companies are able to flourish in a period of rapid technological change. At the heart of the green paper is a move to open

commercial television to newspaper owners, allowing print and electronic media to converge. But the government's long-term aim is to curb market domination by any single player. Some changes in secondary legislation can take place immediately. The first is in radio ownership, with the lifting of the permitted number of ILR licences from 20 to 35. The government forces this through on 18 July as a standing order, as a standing order, to Labour's protests. Alterations to primary legislation will be announced in the Queen's speech in November 1995. There will also be consultation about the creation of a limit on total media shares. [<21 May, >24 May]

Radio revolution begins

26 May: Just three days after the government's green paper, the reshaping of the British media industry begins - in the radio sector. Bristol-based GWR becomes the first company to take advantage of the proposed lifting of the limit on the number of ILR licences from 20 to 35. GWR, already at the old ceiling of 20, bids £20.5 million for Chiltern Radio and its nine stations. They are mainly in the south and west of England, geographically tying in with GWR. Chiltern opposes the offer, saying it is unsolicited, and there is suspicion that GWR is working with shareholders Capital Radio and the Daily Mail group to obtain control. On 20 July Chiltern gives up its struggle and GWR's bid is announced as successful, taking 63 per cent of shares for £19.3 million. Six days later Emap offers £97.5 million for Newcastle-based Metro Radio. If approved, Emap becomes the UK's second largest radio owner. Other media companies are turning their attention to radio, given the mushrooming of the industry and the new rules. [<23 May, >20 June]

Cablers plan video-on-demand

30 May: Three large British video companies are planning to launch video-on-demand and interactive television trials in London in the autumn of 1995. Nynex CableComms, TeleWest and Bell Cablemedia will be in direct competition to a similar trial being carried out by British Telecom with 2,500 people in Colchester and Ipswich. BT starts on 22 June, with a year-long experiment linking a central computer to an Apple Macintosh computer next to the viewer's TV. The viewer can watch a film at any time, costing £1.50-£3.99, or tap into the services on eight other channels. All three competitors are trying to assess the strength of consumer demand for new multimedia services. The three are cable operators, and their trials will involve 2000 London subscribers for up to two years. Olivetti's Acorn Computer group will also carry out a scheme, in Cambridge. [<15 March, >8 June]

Old white Oxbridge men

Early June: Old white Oxbridge men are the main regulators of TV and film standards, according to a study by the Institute of Public Policy Research. The members of the 10 media regulatory bodies are 96 per cent white, 57 per cent male and 25 per cent educated at Oxbridge. Their average age is 58. The institute says Britain needs a more representative range of decision-makers with better accountability to citizens and media users.

Murdoch minor becomes major

1 June: Lachlan Murdoch becomes one of the most powerful 23-year olds in the world when he is made deputy to his father Rupert at Star TV, the Asian satellite television operation with the potential to reach two-thirds of the world population. Lachlan was born in Britain in September 1971, but has spent much of his life in the US. He graduated from Princeton University in 1994 with a degree in philosophy. He is widely tipped as his father's chosen successor among his four children. [>4 July]

Spirits ban lifted

1 June: A 40-year voluntary agreement to ban spirits advertisements on UK television is lifted. It dates from the dawn of commercial TV, when the manufacturers feared competition amongst themselves. The ban is ending because of the advertising desires of one of the companies.

Porn channel's popular launch

2 June: A new porn television channel is launched, proving popular immediately. TVX - The Fantasy Channel goes out every night between midnight and 4am. Late in June, the government decides to try to block the hardcore porn channel Erotica, which started in February. Campaigners want the EU to allow the UK to stop the channel being beamed in from Sweden.

TV and radio audience surveys

5 June: A third of children aged 7 to 17 watch television after the 9pm watershed when programming becomes adult oriented. This is the finding of a survey carried out by the SMRC

market research agency. At weekends the proportion of children rises to almost 50 per cent. Two-thirds have a television in their bedroom, and a quarter of these have a video. The survey shows that many youngsters are watching what they want, when they want, despite public fears of the effects. A separate survey of adults, by MORI, shows that only 13 per cent of them listen to radio's main national news programme, Today, on Radio 4. But 80 per cent watch national news bulletins on television. The audience for Today is largely middle class, Conservative and living in southern England, while bulletin viewers are spread much more equally across all classes, parties and regions. World in Action is the most popular current affairs programme on TV, seen regularly by 45 per cent of the people surveyed, compared with Panorama's 39 per cent.

Channel 5 auction system a disaster?

5 June: The auction system to allocate the licence for Channel 5 is denounced by a leading bidder as a "disaster". Greg Dyke of Pearson TV, co-owner of Channel 5 Broadcasting, says at a Guardian meeting: "It is no way to allocate a scarce television resource like a national TV station. An auction was always a daft idea." David Elstein of New Century Television says Channel 5 is no stronger a business proposition now than three years ago. He defends New Century's bid as the only sustainable option. [<21 May]

Cable viewers almost a million

6 June: The steadily increasing size of the cable TV market is shown by the latest official figures from ITC. The number of cable subscribers reached 963,000 on 1 April, compared with 642,000 a year before, an increase of exactly 50 per cent. The number of homes passed by cables rose from 2.99 million to 4.49 million, also up 50 per cent in 12 months. But cable TV still cannot increase its penetration rate amongst the houses it passes. Only 21.4 per cent of homes with cables passing them were subscribing this April, even less than the 21.5 per cent in April 1994. This has been a long-term problem. Those homes with telephone lines installed went up from 377,000 to 873,000, a rise of 132 per cent. [<15 May]

Pearson expands into TV

7 June: Staff of Pearson are given details of the company's plans to expand into broadcasting. Greg Dyke, running Pearson Television, has re-organised the business group by creating three separate sectors specialising in production, broadcasting and international marketing. Also in June, Pearson reflects its rapidly changing media role by reshaping its local newspaper subsidiary Westminster Press.

Channel 4 in trouble

7 June: The Independent Television Commission imposes one of its most severe sanctions. Channel 4 has a formal warning issued against it for breaching its licence after a series of bad taste stunts on the late-night show The Word. The ITC wants C4 to exercise stricter controls over the five-year old series. But its chief exec Michael Grade disagrees, saying the ITC is again out of touch with desires of ordinary viewers. This is C4's second formal warning in C4's . In mid-July C4 says it is scrapping The Word.

Cable's consolidation begins

8 June: TeleWest extends its lead over its cable rivals by snapping up SBC Communications UK, the fifth largest operator, for £679 million. TeleWest will have potential coverage of 4.1 million homes, nearly 25 per cent of the cable market. This takeover is widely seen as the beginning of the consolidation of the cable industry. The number of operators could drop from over 50 to about ten. The Cable Communications Association believes that within two or three years four or five players will have 90 per cent of the market.[<30 May, >9 June]

Floating cable firms

9 June: Nynex CableComms, Britain's second biggest cable firm, starts floating on the Stock Exchange hoping to raise £400 million. Nynex has 16 UK franchise areas covering 2.7 million homes, many in the Manchester area and employs 2,500 people. The flotation price was lower than hoped, reflecting nervousness about the prospects of the cable business. The first cable company on the Stock Exchange was TeleWest, which floated in November 1994. In March 1995 it said it almost doubled its losses to £65 million in its 1994 financial year. But the deficit was in line with the expected results of its expansion, and its shares rose 4p, although its "churn" rate (subscribers not renewing their annual connection) was 47.1 per cent. The French-owned group General Cable floated in London in April, hoping to raise about £200 million, but falling short. On 3 March another large operator, Bell Cablemedia, announced a loss of £26 million in 1994, The company expected this loss and said it was in "good shape".[<19 April]

Christian radio station launched

10 June: Premier Radio, Britain's first Christian commercial radio station, goes on air. The 24-hour service for the Home Counties covers news, current affairs and lifestyle issues from a Christian perspective. The National Lottery has been banned from advertising with Premier because charities do not want their ads competing with it. The first British Christian cable television station should start in the spring of 1996. Organisers hope the 12-hour channel, Ark2, will be carried by 95 per cent of national cable operators.

Live TV born

Janet Street-Porter, Live TV's boss

12 June: The Mirror Group's £30 million Live TV is launched. Calling itself "Britain's first national live cable exclusive channel", Live TV is going to about 90 per cent of cable homes. It is the only provider of live programming 24 hours a day, from its Mirror home on the 24th floor of the Canary Wharf tower. It has a magazine-style output, with nothing lasting more than ten minutes. The Guardian's review of the first day says: "There's more intellectual stimulation printed on the paper napkins at Burger King. Can British TV sink any lower?" [<15 February]

First woman TV news editor

12 June: ITN appoints the first woman to become editor of a British network's television news service. Sara Nathan, aged 39, becomes editor of Channel 4 News, the 7pm weekday programme. She moves over from BBC Radio.

US media unleashed

15 June: The United States Senate approves a major shake-up of the media industry, even more deregulatory than Whitehall's 23 May proposals for Britain. Almost all restrictions on the big media companies will be lifted. Broadcasters currently restricted to owning 12 television stations will now be able to own as many as they like. Also removed is the limit of 40 radio stations. The term of local television station licences will be doubled, making them harder to challenge. The ceiling on cable TV prices will be eliminated. The whole package gives enormous power to the media companies which lobbied hard for it and which also helped fund the Republican party.

BSkyB and Radio Authority attacked

15 June: Andrew Neil, formerly one of Rupert Murdoch's most trusted lieutenants, warns of the dangers of BSkyB achieving overwhelming power in the TV marketplace. He says Sky is poised to dominate British digital broadcasting with potentially dangerous consequences for diversity. Mr Neil, who helped launch Sky, says the market is currently stacked in Sky's favour. On 19 June, Mr Neil attacks the Radio Authority while giving the opening lecture at the Radio Academy's annual festival. He calls the RA an "interfering, busybodying quango", and condemns its decision in 1994 not to renew LBC's licence. Mr Neil believes the media rulers see radio as an insignificant "poor sister" of TV and national newspapers. He believes the BBC has too much power over national radio. The BBC's uncontroversial formula stops the development of a dynamic business that could speak out against the feudal establishment that covertly controls most of the British media.

BBC journalists disciplined

16 June: Two BBC journalists are disciplined after allegations that they reconstructed scenes of urban decay while filming a report in Italy. The pair, who were filming a report on drugs for BBC World, the corporation's international news channel, are said to have used a condom and syringe as props to represent slum conditions in the Mafia-dominated town of Reggio Calabria.

BSkyB programme deal

19 June: The Office of Fair Trading increases the pressure on BSkyB to remove "significantly anti-competitive restrictions" from its recent 10-year deals to provide programmes for the TeleWest and Nynex cable TV operators. The OFT, which recently placed the deals on the register of restrictive trading agreements, tells the three companies they have 30 days to reconsider the restrictions or face action in the Restrictive Trade Practices Court. Three cable companies · Videotron, CableTel and General Cable · form the new Campaign for Media Choice to oppose BSkyB's monopoly action. In their first self-defence move, they protest to the European Commission, which on 29 June issues a formal complaint against BSkyB. On 10 July BSkyB gives the OFT a revised rate card for the sale of its programmes and says it is revising TeleWest and Nynex contracts. [<5 May · BSkyB, >25 July]

Producers agree separation

19 June: The two main producers' organisations in the broadcasting industry agree to stay separate. Members of IARP (the Independent Association of Radio Producers) have worried for several months that PACT (the Producers Alliance for Cinema and TV) may set up a rival radio arm. This would given radio interests an inferior position to television in the rapidly changing market. But now the two groups have agreed to remain autonomous, while working closely together. IARP, recently suffering from other internal problems and personality clashes, will relaunch in a more professional framework.

Radio licence unwanted

20 June; For the first time ever, the Radio Authority does not receive an application for a licence it has advertised. The community radio group that had been planning to apply for the new local licence for Southwold in Suffolk is unable to do so.

Media ownership changes welcomed

20 June: Sir Peter Gibbings, chairman of the Radio Authority, says the RA is "very pleased" with the government's proposals for changing the media ownership rules. "We hope that the end result will be sound financial investment in the industry, which will create stability, whilst the retention of the 15 per cent limit will continue to ensure diversity of ownership." [<26 May]

The public's view of TV

22 June: Television is catching up local papers in providing the public with local news, reveals the ITC's annual survey Television: The Public's View. Ten years ago over half of people consulted their paper first when looking for local news, compared with only 18 per cent citing TV. Today television lures twice as many people (36 per cent), while papers are down to 42 per cent. The survey uncovers many other facts: 94 per cent of homes with children have a video recorder; 36 per cent of cable subscribers were attracted more by the cheap telephone service than the different TV channels; and 37 per cent over-45 believe TV standards have declined.

Murdoch scores in rugby deal

23 June: News Corporation announces it has secured the rights to international rugby union in the southern hemisphere for £366 million. The 10-year deal buys Mr Murdoch rights to a southern hemisphere version of the Five Nations championship, involving Australia, New Zealand and South Africa. News Corp is already providing the finance for "super leagues". The last shadow of amateurism in rugby union is expected to disappear. On 3 July the head of sport at the ITV Network Centre, Trevor East, tries to immediately resign and switch over to BSkyB, dominated by News Corp. But the network is so angry at the sudden move that it takes legal action to force Mr East to serve out his six months notice. [<6 April, >18 July]

ITV's wobbly spring

26 June: ITV senior executives agree to take action to combat the rising cost of television advertising at a time of falling audiences. In the last week of May ITV had a 35.4 per cent share of the audience, compared to BBC1's 33.1 per cent. A year ago ITV had a lead of nearly 10 per cent. ITV has already revamped its schedule with emergency plans. Today an ITV meeting agrees to add an extra £10 million to the autumn rating's budget to fend off the competition from the revitalised BBC. On 10 July a contingency fund of £20 million is added, with network director Marcus Plantin saying ITV has suffered a "wobbly" spring. He denies there is a crisis, although that is the feeling of advertisers, who are paying more money for fewer customers. They have been demanding not only more spending on programmes, but also the increase of the average advertising time per hour from 7 minutes to eight minutes. In June ITV's audience share increases significantly.

BBC internal unhappiness

27 June: Internal problems at the BBC are highlighted in a staff survey. BBC managers pledge to reduce bureaucracy after its survey singles out red tape as one of the worst failings. Replies from 40 per cent of staff (10,078) show employees remain frightened to say what they think about the BBC and do not believe what they are told about its workings. The staff assessment of John Birt and senior executives is broadly negative, but is mainly positive about programmes. The management is quietly pleased with the survey, because it shows the staff are not quite as unhappy as they were in 1993.

A separate NUJ survey finds specialist journalists in the BBC regions are working an average 57.3 hours per week, and are suffering "gross overwork, stress and confused management". On 9 July the Sunday Times reveals: "The BBC has quietly increased the combined salaries of its senior management by more than 27 per cent, amid accusations of excessive secrecy about finances, and boardroom profligacy at the expense of licence-fee payers ... By contrast, most of the BBC's 25,000 staff were forced to accept a 4.5 per cent settlement in the last financial year, and have had a 3 per cent increase imposed for this year. Last week the corporation axed 73 staff from its factual programme department to save money." On 11 July the Independent says: "The BBC has paid up to £2,500 a day for managers to be given media training by former BBC staff, even though its own broadcasters are banned from giving such instruction."

Talk Radio flop

30 June: The managing director of Talk Radio UK, which had a troubled launch in February, parts company with the station. The departure of John Aumonier means Britain's newest commercial station has lost all three of its senior staff in its first five months. The sales director left in March, followed by the programme director early in April. The new programme director, Jerry Thomas, said on 21 June that the station's launch had been a "flop ... It was unpalatable to a British listener - they are too educated, informed and discerning to buy into the simplistic demagogery of shock-jocks". He believes some of the swearing in early weeks was "infantile". He is now seeking new presenters jockers.[<7 March]

Local TV experiment

Mid-June: Bradford's annual arts festival carries out a experiment in local television. For three weeks the festival broadcasts 12 hours a day of locally-made programmes across the screens of Yorkshire Cable subscribers.

BBC radio to leave Broadcasting House

Late June: The BBC's board of management approves a plan to move all of its radio journalists from their traditional home of Broadcasting House in central London to a £40 million extension being built onto BBC Television Centre in west London. Radio staff strongly oppose the scheme, fearing the interests of radio will be subsumed to those of TV and that Broadcasting House will lose its heart. BBC news and current affairs bosses estimate annual savings of up to £8 million over five years will be achieved by bringing all 800 radio and TV journalists together on one site. The decision must be sanctioned by the board of governors. [>27 June]

Women's radio station launched

3 July: The first British radio station for women, Viva! 963AM, goes on air. Broadcasting to London and the south-east, with a 50:50 split between music and speech, it aims to appeal mainly to women aged 25-45 in the ABC1 socio-economic groups. It expects 30 per cent of its 400,000 target audience to be male. Viva! characterises itself as a cross between Marie Claire and She magazines, and claims to be the world's only women's service. Most of its staff are women. It is being operated by Golden Rose Communications, which runs JFM 102.2 (formerly Jazz FM) in London and JFM 100.4 in Manchester.

Lords ban political radio adverts

4 July: A bar on the human rights pressure group Amnesty International advertising on radio is upheld as lawful in a High Court test case. In a decision likely to hit many other campaigning bodies, two judges rule that broadcasting regulators are entitled to conclude that the organisation's objectives are "mainly political" and that it should be denied access to the UK's commercial airwaves. Amnesty says TV as well as radio could now become a "no go" area for its commercials. It is planning to appeal, if necessary taking its case to the European Court of Human Rights. The veto was imposed in October 1994 by the Radio Authority, under section 92(2)(a)(i) of the 1990 Broadcasting Act. Amnesty says it is not a political body, and

the ban is an unacceptable, irrational interference with freedom of speech. Lord Justice Kennedy says listeners deserve "freedom from being virtually forced to listen to unsolicited information of a contentious kind". He also believes the public have to be protected against the danger of the wealthy buying access to the media and "distorting the democratic process". Mr Justice McCullough agrees, saying the ruling means Amnesty "cannot even advertise that it is holding a concert".

Court warrant against Murdoch

4 July: Rupert Murdoch, owner of Star TV, has a warrant issued against him by an Indian magistrate after a programme refers to Mahatma Gandhi as a "bastard trader". One of Gandhi's great-grandsons says this is defamation. India's parliament strongly attacks the programme. Star withdraws it and apologises.

BBC annual report

4 July: BBC chiefs round on their critics to declare the success of their changes to the corporation's management and programming. The message comes with the publication of the BBC's annual report where the director general John Birt pledges to tackle bureaucracy and to promote management skills.

More TV complaints

11 July: The number of complaints about television rose 31 per cent in the year April 1994 to March 1995, says the Broadcasting Standards Council in its sixth annual report. There were 2,247 complaints, compared with 1,711 in 1993/4. Specific programmes were the subject of 76 per cent of the complaints, while another 15 per cent were about advertisements. The majority of complaints (46 per cent) were about taste and decency. Of the complaints taken to a finding, 20 per cent were upheld. The BSC claims that mainstream satellite channels are regularly transmitting pornographic films. Chairman Lady Howe says there is a detectable trend of stations, including Sky, screening late night soft porn. The BSC will merge with the Broadcasting Complaints Commission in 1996. Mark Jones, media editor of the Evening Standard, voices a widely held scepticism abut the role of BSC: "Very few people actually complain. Such bodies as BSC are reliant on a tiny, tiny minority of complainants; and those complainants are simply not reliable."

Millionth cable viewer

16 July: The cable TV industry signs up its one millionth subscriber. In reward, a south London family is given a free telephone line for a year and a million minutes of free cable rental. The Cable Communications Association says the number of connections has more than doubled in 18 months. Cable television now seems more popular than satellite. Research by GfK Marketing Services shows a declining interest in satellite viewing, with only 22,000 new dishes in May, the lowest monthly increase since July 1994. Price cuts in dishes to below £100 have failed to boost sales. The number of homes with dishes is now 3,076,000. [<6 June]

Labour pledges superhighway

17 July: A Labour Party policy document, Communicating Britain's Future, sets out plans for a national communications infrastructure · an information superhighway · to which everyone would have access. British Telecom would be allowed to participate in this through the gradual removal between 1998 and 2002 of the regulations which prevent it from broadcasting entertainment over its phone network. In return, BT and other network operators would be expected to link all schools, hospitals, libraries and health centre to the network at no cost.

Murdoch in Asia

18 July: Rupert Murdoch's News Corporation buys the 36.4 per cent interest in the Asian satellite broadcaster Star TV that it did not already own. It pays $346 million to Hong Kong magnate Li Ka-Shing and his company Hutchison Whampoa. Murdoch's empire has controlled Star since buying the other shares for $825 million in July 1993. The five-channel service is beamed to 53 countries across Asia, the area seen as the most profitable future market for all the media. Asia already had 368 million homes with TV in 1994, with 484 million forecast by 2003. Big media owners are currently trying to ensure they have sectors of the Asian business staked out as soon as possible. On 13 June Murdoch signed a pioneering deal with China's most prominent newspaper see Print Chronicle. Asia's broadcasters are awaiting the launch of the AsiaSat2 satellite in September 1995, covering two-thirds of the world's population. Also in mid-July, Murdoch moves into Latin America with a partnership with the Globo Organisation to develop a direct-to-home satellite service for Latin America and the Caribbean, starting in 1996. [<23 June, >28 July]

Channel 4 chief's pay rise

25 July: Michael Grade, chief executive of Channel 4, is given a five-year contract and a near-20 per cent pay rise, taking him from £377,000 to £450,000 pa. The rise is his reward for the continuing success of C4. Mr Grade is now £185,000 ahead of the BBC's John Birt, and almost the same amount behind Michael Green, the chairman of Carlton.

Pearson to sell BSkyB stake

25 July: Media group Pearson announces it is ready to sell a "substantial part" of its 9.7 per cent direct stake in BSkyB, netting a windfall of around £500 million before tax. Pearson says its stake is now regarded merely as an investment since it does not provide significant management control. Rupert Murdoch's News Corporation owns 40 per cent of the company and has day-to-day control. Pearson, which also indirectly owns another 4.3 per cent, will ask shareholders for permission to sell at least 8 per cent of its direct stake. [<19 June]

First libel by government department

28 July: In what is thought to be the first successful libel case against a government department, £40,000 damages and £15,000 costs are given to Martin Gregory, producer, director and reporter on the Channel 4 television programme The Torture Trail. The Department of Trade and Industry agrees to make the payment over allegations by Michael Heseltine which it admits were untrue. The programme, broadcast last January, was named best documentary by Amnesty International in its media awards in June. It centred on the supply of torture equipment overseas by three British companies. Mr Heseltine made several allegations about Mr Gregory, including scaremongering. The DTI "sincerely apologises" in the High Court. Mr Gregory says: "This is an important victory for investigative journalism over a government that seems to have lost its moral authority".

TV doesn't make us more violent

31 July: Television is not to blame for crime and violence, but has been used as a scapegoat for deep-rooted social problems, according to the University of Leeds report Moving Experiences, published by Faber. It challenges conventional assumptions of a causal link between screen and real life violence, and criticises researchers for creating a moral panic about the effects of television violence. Author David Gauntlett says it is irresponsible to blame television for complex social problems. "The causes of violence and crime seem much more likely to be found in poverty, unemployment, homelessness, abuse, frustration, personality traits and psychological background". On 27 July the Department of Heritage secretary Virginia Bottomley said the government will crackdown on TV violence by inserting a taste and decency clause in the BBC's new charter. Early in July the BBC governors decided they would hold an autumn seminar on the subject. John Birt has said it is one of the most difficult issues facing the BBC. In August the University of Sheffield published a study which found the level of violence on terrestrial TV has fallen.

Jazz FM name revived

31 July: The radio station Jazz FM, which spent £350,000 on a name change to JFM in 1994, switches back after having lost 100,000 listeners.

Major mergers in US

31 July: The world's biggest entertainments company is created in the US by Walt Disney's takeover of Capital Cities/ABC, owner of ABC television, for $19 billion. The deal makes sense in that the companys' activites fit together, but do not overlap. ABC is rivalling NBC for top position among US networks. The new company will be called simply Walt Disney. The next day, the third biggest US TV network CBS agrees to be bought by Westinghouse for $5.4 billion, although a higher bid is rumoured. The combined group called Westinghouse CBS will be able to broadcast to a third of all US households. NBC says it is not for sale, and itself buys three TV stations in August.

Radio 1 revival

Late July: Radio 1 has reversed months of falling ratings with a 600,000 surge in listeners, according to official figures. The station, which has lost 5 million listeners over the last two years, increased its total weekly audience to 12.9 million in the second quarter of 1995, compared with 12.3 million the first quarter. The recovery has been spearheaded by the April relaunch of the breakfast show with Chris Evans, who recently signed up until the end of 1996. Another landmark in the figures is the achievement of commercial radio in taking more than 50 per cent of the audience for the first time. It now has 28.6 million listeners a week, up 895,000 on the first quarter. [<22 April]

TELEVISION

Television is the ubiquitous medium. All bar 5 per cent of households have a TV set and people turn themselves into viewers for an average of three and a half hours a day. The most popular programmes are watched by a quarter of the population. BBC and ITV soaps rule. Viewing figures for the week ending 28 May, 1995 were:

1	Eastenders (Thu/Sun)	17.42m
2	Coronation Street (Mon/Wed)	16.97m
3	Eastenders ((Tue/Sun)	16m
4	National Lottery Live	15.83m
5	Coronation Street (Fri)	14.84m
6	Eastenders (Mon/Sun)	14.74m
7	Neighbours (Wed)	13.32m
8	Neighbours (Thu)	12.82m
9	Neighbours (Mon)	12.28m
10	Neighbours (Fri)	11.76m
11	Home and Away	11.27m
12	Neighbours (Tue)	11.25m
13	Fawlty Towers	11.16m
14	The Bill	11.13m
15	Emmerdale	11.09m

That week the BBC had 33.1 per cent of the audience against ITV's 35.4 per cent. The year before ITV had a 40.9 per cent share to the BBC's 31.5 per cent.

Two public bodies have the main responsibility for television. The BBC broadcasts radio as well as television and the Independent Television Commission licenses and regulates non-BBC television including cable and satellite. The ITC, however, does not make programmes. The Department of National Heritage oversees broadcasting.

The green paper on cross media ownership maintained the two license limit on ITV companies but allowed so-called terrestrial broadcasters to take controlling interests in satellite and cable companies. It also promises more scope to newspaper companies wanting to diversify into broadcasting. The proposals are likely to become law by summer 1996. At the beginning of 1996 much attention will go to the company awarded the Channel 5 licence in November. First broadcasts are by 1 January 1997, the day the BBC charter is renewed.

Share of television audience

		licence area	audience share
1	BBC1	national	33.6%
2	BBC2	national	11%
3	Channel 4/S4C	national	10%
4	Central	East, West and South Midlands	6%
5	Granada	North West England	4.6%
6	Yorkshire	Yorkshire	4%
7	BSkyB	national	4%
8	Carlton	London weekday	3.4%
9	Meridian	South and South East England	3.1%
10	Other	not applicable	3.2%
11	HTV West and Wales	Wales and West of England	2.8%
12	Scottish Television	Central Scotland	2.6%
13	London Weekend Television	London weekend	2.6%
14	Anglia	East of England	2.3%
15	GMTV	national breakfast time	1.6%
16	Tyne Tees	North East England	1.9%
17	Ulster	Northern Ireland	1.1%
18	Westcountry	South West England	1%
19	Grampian	North of Scotland	0.7%
20	Border	Borders and Isle of Man	0.5%

Source: ITC/BARB

BBC TELEVISION

Though the BBC has come to describe its activities using managerial language, it is more like a minor nation state than a business. The Corporation has its own distinct ethos, employs over 22,000 people and has an annual budget of £1.75 billion.

During 1995 the BBC stopped being so much of a news story in its own right. The corporation settled down after winning a battle for its indepedence and, it seemed, its survival. The 1990 Broadcasting Act had threatened to transform the BBC into a commercial organisation with a much-reduced public role. The years that followed saw it become more commercial. Various painful and long overdue efficiency drives were eventually rewarded with a guarantee that the licence fee will be the main source of income until at least the end of the year 2001.

The 1994/95 annual report says: "For the third successive year, the BBC has injected more money into programmes as a result of efficiency savings, beating its own target of £60 million. In the region of £80 million went into new and better programmes and services

Marmaduke Hussey, the BBC chairman, reasserts the BBC's traditional role: "In Britain there must be a place for a powerful media influence in the pocket of no individual proprietor or interest group, whose journalism is acknowledged as the hallmark of accuracy and responsibility. These are the principles at the heart of the BBC's public service ethos and the justification for it."

during the year to 31 March 1995." Four out of every five peak-time programmes on BBC 1 and BBC 2 were new programmes made by the BBC. There were 300 fewer repeats. John Birt, the BBC director general, used the report to praise the adapatation of Martin Chuzzlewit, David Attenborough's Private Life of Plants, and coverage of the Proms centenary and the D-Day half centenary.

The BBC began life in 1922 as a cartel of radio equipment manufacturers licensed by the government. It became a public body in 1927 when it was granted a royal charter defining its objects, powers and obligations. The charter is the primary constitutional document of the BBC and it outlines the public and state obligations the corporation must fulfil. The BBC's first object is defined as "to provide as public services, broadcasting services". In strict legal terms the granting of the charter is an act of the royal prerogative, issued by the Privy Council on behalf of the Crown, on the petition of the House of Commons. In practice the charter is granted by the government and at the end of 1995 a new royal charter goes before parliament. For the first time it will set out the range and nature of programmes the BBC should offer and the stanadards it should meet. "It will," says Mr Birt, "renew the historic charge to educate, inform and entertain."

The charter has been reissued five times, most recently in 1981. This, the sixth charter, expires on 31 December 1996. Attached to the charter is the licence and agreement which details the terms and conditions of the BBC's operations. This subsidiary agreement is one which is made between the BBC and the National Heritage Department.

The relationship between the government of the day and the BBC has always been tetchy. During the eighties tetchiness became an hostilty to the licence fee, though much of the heat went out of the argument with Mrs Thatcher's departure from office. The BBC was allowed to reassert itself at the centre of national life. However the notion of public sector broadcasting will need a continual defence now that the airwaves are open to so many private interests. Douglas Hurd, one of the old breed of one nation Tories, put it well (and harshly) in 1988 when he was home secretary. "As choice multiplies and the average viewer has more and more channels to choose from, it will become less and less defensible that he should have to pay a compulsory license fee to the BBC."

BBC main offices

The BBC lays great stress on its regionalism and an increasing amount of programming is being devolved beyond the Home Counties. Regional TV offices are listed on page 165 and BBC local radio contacts from 188 to 189. However, the BBC's main offices remain in London and the activities they direct are covered in the next three pages.

BBC Corporate Headquarters & BBC Network Radio
Broadcasting House, Portland Place, London W1A 1AA
Fax 0171-637 1630   Tel 0171-580 4468
See page 187 for Radio
The hub of the BBC and the HQ of network radio (Radios 1FM, 2, 3, 4 and 5 Live), with main radio studios.

BBC Network Television
Television Centre, Wood Lane, London W12 7RJ
Fax 0171-637 1630   Tel 0181-743 8000
Headquarters of network TV (BBC-1 and BBC-2) and World Service TV, with the main television production facilities.

BBC Worldwide Television & BBC Worldwide Publishing
Woodlands, 80 Wood Lane, London W12 0TT
                          Tel 0181-743 5588
Headquarters of BBC commercial activities.

BBC World Service
Bush House, PO Box 76, London WC2B 4PH
                          Tel 0171-240 3456
See pages 164 and 187

BBC White City
201 Wood Lane, London W12 7TS
                          Tel 0181-752 5252
New offices of several departments, including regional broadcasting HQ, educational broadcasting, some current affairs production, personnel, finance and resources.

BBC Written Archives
Caversham Park Reading, Berks RG4 8TZ
                          Tel 01734-472742

Press offices

The main BBC press office is at Television Centre. Its working hours are 8.30am to midnight on weekdays, and 10am to 11pm at the weekend. For specific enquiries, try the Publicity numbers after the addresses on the following three pages.

Main press office   0181-576 1865
International press office 0171-257 2941

Management structure

The 12 BBC governors lay down broad policy guidelines, select the director-general and other senior staff, and are responsible for maintaining programme standards. They are appointed by the Queen in theory, but in reality the prime minister makes the decision. Appointments are for five years. The governors' responsibility for programmes is shared in Wales, Scotland and Northern Ireland with National Broadcasting Councils. The councils control the policy and content of broadcasting provided primarily for their principalities. The BBC also has a General Advisory Council, regional advisory councils in England, and local radio advisory councils. While the governors give general advice on policy the day-to-day decisions are taken by the Board of Management.

BBC BOARD OF GOVERNORS
Chairman: Marmaduke Hussey, former director of Times Newspapers (to 5.11.96)
Vice chairman: the Rt Hon Lord Cocks of Hartcliffe, former Labour chief whip (31.7.98)
National Governor for Scotland: the Rev Norman Drummond, former head teacher (31.9.99)
National Governor for Northern Ireland: Sir Kenneth Bloomfield KCB, former head of N Ireland civil service (31.7.96)
National Governor for Wales: Dr Gwyn Jones, former chairman of Welsh Development Agency (31.12.96)
Bill Jordan CBE, former president of Amalgamated Engineering Union (31.7.98)
Lord Nicholas Gordon Lennox KCMG KCVO, former ambassador to Spain (31.7.2000)
Mrs Margaret Spurr, former head teacher (31.7.98)
Mrs Janet Cohen, director of Charterhouse Bank (28.2.99)
Three positions currently vacant.

BBC BOARD OF MANAGEMENT
Director-General: John Birt
Deputy director-general & chairman, BBC Worldwide: Bob Phillis
Managing director, Network Television: Will Wyatt
Managing director, Network Radio: Liz Forgan
Managing director, Regional Broadcasting: Ronald Neil
Managing director, News & Current Affairs: Tony Hall
Managing director, World Service: Sam Younger
Director of Education: Jane Drabble
Managing director, Resources: Rod Lynch
Director of Personnel: Margaret Salmon
Director of Policy & Planning: Patricia Hodgson
Director of Finance & Information Technology: Rodney Baker-Bates
Director of Corporate Affairs: Colin Browne
Managing director, BBC Worldwide TV: Dr John Thomas
Managing director, BBC Worldwide Publishing: Nick Chapman

News and Current Affairs

News and Current Affairs · aka NCA · began as a merger between BBC Lime Grove current affairs and the Television Centre newsroom. It has a £180 million a year budget and employs over 2,000 staff. When other parts of the BBC were getting the financial squeeze during the early nineties, News and Current Affairs was protected. All that has changed and it now has to rein in on expenditure. Nonetheless NCA has staff budgets unmatched elsewhere in the media with 13 national political correspondents, 19 regional ones at Westminster and eight reporters in North America. Plans to launch a 24 hour television news channel have been deferred to autumn 1996 and could well be scuppered altogether.

Television is the prime way most people learn of the news and there is a continuing tussle about who sets the agenda: the government, management or the broadcasters themselves. A fair chunk of television news coverage is a hall of mirrors where the coverage concerns the organisations doing the coverage. On page 128 of the Broadcasting Chronicle, for two examples, are criticisms of a Panorama programme described as "unfair and unjust" to single parents and news of the ban on Sinn Fein ban being lifted. Both became news items in the press and across television. So was the attempt to broadcast the Panorama interview with John Major on the eve of Scottish local elections. The coverage of coverage grew more incestuous with the subsequent encounter between Jeremy Paxman and his boss, the NCA managing director Tony Hall. That too was a newspaper article and one which earned nearly the same prominence as the director general John Birt's earlier criticisms of his own "overwhelming and sneering interviewers".

BBC News and Current Affairs
Television Centre, Wood Lane, London W12 7RJ
Fax 0171-637 1630   Tel 0181-743 8000
                    Publicity: 0181-576 7726
Managing director, News & Current Affairs: Tony Hall
Assistant Director: Eric Bowman
Head of Resources: Tom Wragg
Head of Communication & Information: Richard Peel
Head of Newsgathering: Chris Cramer
Managing editor, Newsgathering: Ray Gowridge
News editor: Richard Sambrook
Ceefax editor: Graham Norwood

Network TV

The scope of BBC Network Television allows the BBC to claim itself as Britain's largest cultural patron. It splits into the following divisions: Drama; Entertainment; Factual Programmes; Music and Arts; Children's Television; and Sport.

The 1994/95 annual report says: "BBC Television's mix of programmes has been richer than for many years, with more newly originated output, a sharp decline in repeats of our programmes and ambitious productions winning wide acclaim. The BBC became the first international broadcaster to win five Emmys in a single year, and the first to win the top prize in all three categories of the Prix Italia. Alone amongst terrestrial broadcasters, the BBC has increased its overall share of viewing. BBC2 has, in contrast to all other terrestrial channels, had a growing audience. The proportion of people who watched BBC2 each week went up from 72 to 73 per cent."

BBC Network Television
Television Centre, Wood Lane, London W12 7RJ
Fax 0171-637 1630   Tel 0181-743 8000

General Publicity: 0181-576 7789
Drama Publicity: 0181-576 1861
Entertainment Publicity: 0181-576 7797/7786
Sports Publicity: 0181-576 1871
Documentary Publicity: 0181-576 1859
Features Publicity: 0181-576 7702
Science Publicity: 0181-576 7854
Music and Arts Publicity: Tel 0181-576 7737
Children's Publicity: 0181-576 1860
Feature Films Publicity: 0181-576 1868
Purchased Programmes: 0181-576 1539
Youth Publicity: 0161-200 2229/2354
Religious Publicity: 0161-200 2353
Managing director, Network Television: Will Wyatt
Controller, BBC 1: Alan Yentob
Controller, BBC 2: Michael Jackson
Controller, Pubicity & Public Relations: Keith Samuel
Head of Drama Group: Charles Denton,
Head of Entertainment Group: (vacant)
Head of Sport and Events Group: Jonathan Martin
Head of Factual Group: Mark Thompson
Head of Music & Arts: Kim Evans
Head of Children's Programmes: Anna Home
Head of Programme Acquisition Group: Alan Howden
Head of Presentation: Pam Masters
Head of Rights: Colin Campbell
Head of Youth & Entertainment Features: John Whiston

BBC Worldwide

The Future of the BBC white paper included the phrase "Competing Worldwide" in its subtitle. The government directive was that the BBC should develop its commercial activities and expand sales of its programme, and further develop international TV services, with the private sector. By the time this was published in mid-1994 BBC Worldwide was up and delivering what the government intended it should. BBC magazine and book publishing, most of which is ifor British consumption, put the BBC second to Penguin in 1994 best-seller lists. With TV, the BBC has reorganised to cover 140 countries At the beginning of 1995 BBC World (formerly BBC World Service Television) and BBC Prime went into Europe in partnership with Pearson and Cox Communications. Revenues increased from £256 million in 1993 to £305 million.

BBC Worldwide Television
Woodlands, 80 Wood Lane, London W12 0TT
Tel 0181-743 5588
Publicity: Tel 0181-576 2719
Chairman: Bob Phillis
Strategy & marketing director: Richard Emery
Finance & commercial director: Mark Young
Managing director: Dr John Thomas
Director of broadcasting: Hugh Williams
Director of sales and marketing: (vacant)
Commercial director: Tony Kay
Director, co-prods. & business development: Juliet Grimm
Chief exec. officer, BBC Worldwide Americas: Sarah Frank
Director, Europe, Middle East, Africa: (vacant)
Director, Asia, Australasia: (vacant)
Director of channels development: Jeff Hazell
Head of business development (channels): Alan Macdonald
Head of business affairs: Sarah Cooper
Head of press & public relations: Phil Johnstone
Head of human resources: Anne Knights

BBC Worldwide Publishing
Woodlands, 80 Wood Lane, London W12 0TT
Publicity: Tel 0181-576 2208
Chairman: Bob Phillis
Strategy & marketing director: Richard Emery
Finance & commercial director: Mark Young
Managing director: Nicholas Chapman
Finance director: Ken Wright
Director, magazine publishing: Peter Phippen
Director, book and audio publishing: Chris Weller
Director, home video: (vacant)
Director, BBC Multimedia: David Lee
Director, internationl sales & licensing: Ben Lenthall
Director, strategy & new development: Jeremy Mayhew
Director, BBC English: Charles Hyde

BBC Education

The BBC's Education Directorate comprises: School Programmes; Continuing Education and Training; the Publishing Division; Open University Production Centre; and Education Policy and Services. It produces 90 per cent of the most-watched primary school programmes and seven of the top ten in secondary school programmes. BBC Education anticipates growing markets in the new technologies with, for example, Shakespeare CD-ROMs from the Open University and much material posted on the Internet.

BBC Education
White City, 201 Wood Lane, London W12 7TS
Publicity: 0181-752 5152
Director of education: Jane Drabble
Chief adviser, policy: Lucia Jones
Head of commissioning (schools): Frank Flynn
Head of education for adults: Glenwyn Benson
Head of publishing division: David Mortimer
Head of Open University productiion centre: Colin Robinson
Managing editor, BBC Select: Paul Gerhardt
Financial & business affairs controller: Jim Buckle
Chief officer personnel: Bob Cross

Resources

BBC Resources is the market-oriented technical arm of the BBC and a product of Producer Choice. According to the annual report: "Resources is a £650 million turnover business, trading very close to break-even for the first time. A systematic programme of change has resulted in production resources, services and engineering being streamlined, refocused and given a new identity and price in serving the customer ... BBC progamme makers." It does 86 per cent of BBC programmes and sold £33 million of services to other broadcasters.

BBC Resources
White City, 201 Wood Lane, London W12 7TS
Publicity: 0181-752 5401
Managing director: Rod Lynch
Financial controller: Robin Moulson
Controller, personnel: Rob Murdoch
Controller, London production resources: Mike Lumley
Controller, regional resources: John Lightfoot
Controller, technical resources: Ian Jenkins
Contoller, services: Stephen Reid
General manager, marketing: Robert Bruce
Directorate secretary: Paula Carter

BBC Regional TV

More than a quarter of network television and radio programmes are made outside London and the south east; the aim, by 1998, is for a third of the BBC's output to come from the regions. The BBC divides Britain into six regions, three in England (Midlands/East, South and North) and Wales, Scotland and Northern Ireland. The HQ is in London. Below are regional HQs and TV centres; local radio stations are from page 188.

BBC White City (London HQ)
201 Wood Lane, London W12 7TS
    Tel 0181-752 5252

BBC Midlands and East, Birmingham (Regional HQ)
Broadcasting Centre, Pebble Mill Road, Birmingham B5 7QQ
    Tel 0121-414 8888
Daily news programme: Midlands Today

BBC Midlands and East, Nottingham
York House, Mansfield Road, Nottingham NG1 3JB
    Tel 0115-955 0500
Daily news programme: East Midlands Today

BBC Midlands and East, Norwich
St Catherine's Close, All Saint's Green, Norwich, Norfolk NR13ND
    Tel 01603-619331
Daily news programme: Look East

BBC South, Bristol (Regional HQ)
Broadcasting House, Whiteladies Road, Bristol BS8 2LR
Fax 0117-974 4114   Tel 0117-973 2211
Daily news programme: News West

BBC South, Elstree
Clarendon Road, Borehamwood, Herts WD6 1JF
Fax 0181-207 8765   Tel 0181-953 6100
Daily news programme: Newsroom South East

BBC South, Southampton
Broadcasting House, Havelock Road, Southampton, Hants SO14 7PU
Fax 01703-339931   Tel 01703-226201
Daily news progamme: South Today

BBC South, Plymouth
Broadcasting House, Seymour Road, Mannamead, Plymouth, Devon PL3 5BD
Fax 01752-234595   Tel 01752-229201
Daily news programme: Spotlight

BBC North, Manchester (Regional HQ)
New Broadcasting House, PO Box 27, Oxford Road, Manchester M60 1SJ
Fax 0161-236 1005   Tel 0161-200 2020
Daily news programme: North West Tonight

BBC North, Leeds
Broadcasting Centre, Woodhouse Lane, Leeds, West Yorks LS2 9PN
Fax 0113-243 9387   Tel 0113-244 1188
Daily news programe: Look North

BBC North, Newcastle
Broadcasting Centre, Barrack Road, Newcastle-upon-Tyne NE99 2NE
Fax 0191-221 0112   Tel 0191-232 1313
Daily news programme: Look North.

BBC Scotland, Glasgow (National HQ)
Broadcasting House, Queen Margaret Drive, Glasgow G12 8DG
Fax 0141-334 0614   Tel 0141-339 8844
Controller: John McCormick.

BBC Scotland, Edinburgh
Broadcasting House, 5 Queen Street, Edinburgh EH2 1JF
Fax 0131-469 4220   Tel 0131-225 3131

BBC Scotland, Aberdeen
Broadcasting House, Beechgrove Terrace, Aberdeen AB9 2ZT
Fax 01224-642931   Tel 01224-625233

BBC Scotland, Dundee
66 The Nethergate, Dundee DD1 4ER
Fax 01382-202188   Tel 01382-202481

BBC Wales, Cardiff (National HQ)
Broadcasting House, Llantrisant Road, Llandaff, Cardiff CF5 2YQ
Fax 01222-552973   Tel 01222-572888
Controller: Geraint Talfan Davies.

BBC Wales, Swansea
Broadcasting House, 32 Alexandra Road, Swansea SA1 5DT
Fax 01792-468194   Tel 01792-654986

BBC Wales, Bangor
Broadcasting House, Bryn-Meirion Road, Bangor, Gwynedd LL57 2BY
Fax 01248-352784   Tel 01248-370880

BBC Northern Ireland, Belfast (National HQ)
Broadcasting House, Ormeau Ave, Belfast BT2 8HQ
Fax 01232-338800   Tel 01232-338000
Controller: Robin Walsh.

INDEPENDENT TELEVISION

In 1951 Sir William Beveridge, the architect of the welfare state, chaired a committee which vetoed suggestions for a commercial television channel. It was a short-lived reprieve for the BBC's monopoly because ITV soon won parliamentary approval and its first broadcast was in 1955. By 1962 the Royal Commission on Broadcasting was huffing: "The disquiet about television is mainly attributal to independent television and largely to its entertainment programmes."

Television is far too influential to be left to the market and has been subjected to government regulation since its inception. First came the Independent Television Authority, then the Independent Broadcasting Authority and, as a result of the 1990 Broadcasting Act, the Independent Television Commission.

The ITC is a statutory corporation, with a board of members appointed for five years by the National Heritage Secretary. It is responsible for licensing and regulating all commercially-financed television services in the UK. These include ITV, Channel Four, public teletext and cable and satellite services. Excluded are the BBC and S4C.

The 1990 Act forced a separation of powers so that the new ITC does not, as before, double up as licensing authority plus a broadcaster of ITV, Channel Four and teletext. These non-licensing functions were taken away from the ITC on 1 January 1993. What it is left with, in response to memories of fifties' moral panics about the spread of mass commercial culture, is a regulatory role, for it is now directed to monitor independent broadcasts. According to the ITC's 1995 Factfile: "One of the ITC's most important functions is to see that the programmes and advertisements it regulates maintain proper standards. The ITC publishes programme, advertising and sponsorship codes applying to all channels, a technical performance code applying to the terrestrial channels and a public teletext code." Penalties it can make range from the issuing of warnings and demands for apologies, to the revoking of licences.

Arbitrating on taste and decency is a hard task likely to be made harder by the impending relaxation of regulations on cross-media ownership. As newspapers become more financially tied into television companies, so their reporting of TV's programming controversies and office politics will become increasingly tinged by the tedium of profit-motivated moral outrage. The ITC will need the wisdom of several Solomons.

Meanwhile the old post-war Beveridge-style consensus, which ITV played its part in fracturing, will continue breaking up. In the short term the ITC will be in there dispensing yet more TV licences to cable and satellite companies and for the new Channel Five. Longer term, with hundreds of channels coming on line and computers merging into TV sets, television will move beyond effective regulation. It will become what some commentators would call a supermarket of local and global style and what others might call a flickering dustbin.

ITC Head Office

33 Foley Street, London W1P 7LB
Fax 0171-306 7800   Tel 0171-255 3000
Engineering: Kings Worthy Court, Kings Worthy, Winchester, Hants SO23 7QA
Fax 01962-886141   Tel 01962-848600
See Broadcast Support Organisations on page 210 for ITC regional offices
Chief executive: David Glencross
Deputy: Peter Rogers
Director of programmes: Clare Mulholland

ITC BOARD OF MEMBERS

Sir George Russell, chairman, also chairman of Marley and 3i Group and of the Northern Development Company.
Jocelyn Stevens, deputy chairman, also chairman of English Heritage.
Dr John Beynon, member of the British Library Advisory Council.
Earl of Dalkeith, member for Scotland, also director of Buccleuch Estates.
Roy Goddard, business consultant, chairman of the Dyslexia Institute and a Freeman of the City of London.
Jude Goffe, venture capitalist and non-executive director of Moorfields Eye Hospital
Eleri Wynne Jones, member for Wales, and a lecturer in psychotherapy.
Pauline Mathias, also a schools' governor.
Dr Maria Moloney, member for Northern Ireland, also general manager with Harland and Wolff and member of the Industrial Development Board for Northern Ireland.
John Ranelagh, former Channel 4 commissioning editor.

ITV Network Centre

The ITV Network Centre was established to meet the competition requirements of the 1990 Broadcasting Act. It is owned by the ITV companies to commission, purchase and schedule the programmes which are shown across the ITV network. That amounts to over 4,000 hours of programming a year. It also provides a range of services to the ITV companies where a common approach is required.

Network Centre policy is decided by two committees. The first, which forms the governing body of the Centre, is the Council of the ITV Association. It creates policy in areas of common cause and considers and agrees financial and cost sharing arrangements between ITV licensees. Such costs include the funding of the Centre. The Broadcast Board of the ITV Association works with the Council to agree the broad details of the network schedule and its cost for approval by the Council. Once this has been agreed the Centre acts independently to buy in the programmes. Material for the network is commissioned

Marcus Plantin, the new director of the ITV Network Centre. The man whose first television work was wrapping parcels for the Generation Game conveyor belt is now one of the most powerful figures in British television. He is in charge of a commissioning budget which was £530 million in 1994, £550 million in 1995 and will be at least £600 million in 1996.

from the ITV companies and independent producers, who answer to the network director and a team of controllers. As the Centre has no legal status as a broadcaster, successful commissions must then be contracted jointly with one of the ITV companies, to achieve compliance with broadcasting licence conditions. The scheduling of all networked programmes is decided by the network director, as approved by the Broadcast Board.

Network Centre started in earnest when the last round of ITV franchises began, at the beginning of 1993. In March 1995 a review of 1994 activities noted that in 1994 27 of the 30 top-rating dramas were on ITV; that 16 of the top 20 light entertainment shows were ITV; and it claimed a "well resourced and uncompromising record in current affairs". Leslie Hill, the chairman, wrote in the report: "The ITV network is a complex commercial structure, answerable to a constituency that includes shareholders, regulators and advertisers. Above all, we must continue to satisfy viewers."

By June both the advertising and viewing parts of Mr Hill's "constituency" were not at all satisifed. The viewers were turning off and the advertisers compared May 1994 with May 1995 to find ITV had lost 5 per cent of national viewing having dropped from 40.9 per cent to 35.4 per cent of ratings. ITV was almost on a par with the BBC and the Incorporated Society of British Advertisers said: "The number of eye-balls we're hitting for our money is down. We are the customers and we are singularly unhappy. Somebody has got to take notice of what we are saying.".

Somebody did. The logic of an advertiser-led market dictated that more money was immediately committed to the autumn schedule when the £570 million 1996 budget was reviewed and set for an increase of up to £630 million.

ITV Network Centre
200 Grays Inn Road, London WC1X 8HF
Fax 0171-843 8158   Tel 0171-843 8000
Council of ITV Association chairman: Leslie Hill
Broadcast Board chairman: Gus McDonald
Chief executive: Barry Cox

NETWORK PROGRAMME CONTROLLERS
Network director: Marcus Plantin
Children's programmes: Vanessa Chapman
Drama/entertainment: Vernon Lawrence
Factual/religion: Stuart Prebble
Sport: Trevor East

ITV (CHANNEL 3)

The 1990 Broadcasting Act used the phrase "independent televison" to cover all advertising-funded UK television. The act also labelled the former ITV regional services as "Channel 3", though the companies have preferred to stick with the old ITV title.

There are 15 regional Channel 3/independent television/ITV licencees plus another which provides national breakfast-time programmes. For the purposes of Channel 3, the UK is divided into 14 regions, all but one of which has a single Channel 3 company monopolising regional broadcasting rights. The exception is the biggest market in London where there is a split between two licensees: Carlton for weekdays and LWT for weekends.

The bulk of ITV programmes emanate from ITV Network Centre (see previous page). The news is provided by Independent Television News (see Broadcast News Organisations). ITN has a weekly output of 18 hours which includes News at Ten, Early Evening News and Channel Four News.

Channel 3 licences came into force on 1 January 1993 and are valid for ten years. An application for renewal may be made by the current licence holder any time after six years from the start of the licence. The terms of renewal will be set by the ITC.

Anglia Television
Anglia House, Norwich, Norfolk NR1 3JG
Fax 01603-631032   Tel 01603-615151
London office: 48 Leicester Square, WC2H 7FB
Fax 0171-930 8499   Tel 0171-321 0101
Regional newsrooms:
Norwich	01603-619261
Cambridge	01223-467076
Chelmsford	01245-357676
Ipswich	01473-226157
Luton	01582-29666
Milton Keynes	01908-691660
Northampton	01604-24343
Peterborough	01733-346677

Owner: MAI, which bought the company Anglia TV Group in March 1994; see Meridian, below.
Chairman: David McCall.
Covers: East Anglia and the East Midlands.
Regional news Programme: Anglia News East/West.
1993-2002 licence fee: £17.8 million pa.
ITC 1994 Performance Review: "the company exceeded the amount of regional material specified."

Border Television
Durranhill, Carlisle, Cumbria CA1 3NT
Fax 01228-41384   Tel 01228-25101
Newsroom: 01228-21222
Owner: Border Television; largest shareholder Cumbrian Newspapers Group (18%).
Chairman: Melvyn Bragg.
Covers: Scottish borders, Lake District and the Isle of Man. Also has local radio involvement.
Regional news programme: Lookaround, Border News.
1993-2002 licence fee: £52,000 pa.
ITC 1994 Performance Review: "improved its close identification with this diverse region ... Main disappointment was the rejection of its programme offers to the network."

Carlton Broadcasting
101 St Martins Lane, London WC2N 4AZ
Fax 0171-240 4171   Tel 0171-240 4000
Newsroom (LNN): 0171-827 7700
Owner: Carlton Communications (100%).
Chairman: Nigel Walmsley.
Covers: London area from 01600 Monday until 1715 Friday.
Regional news programme: London Tonight.; After 5.
1993-2002 licence fee: £43.17 million pa.
Carlton took over the London weekday licence - the biggest in the UK - from Thames Television in January 1993. In early 1994 Carlton Communications bought Central Television. Carlton Communications also owns 36 per cent of ITN and 20 per cent of GMTV and 20 per cent of Meridian.
ITC 1994 Performance Review: "... more remains to be achieved ... ITC expects the improvement seen in 1994 to be continued further."

Central Broadcasting
Broad Street, Birmingham B1 2JP
Fax 0121-634 4766   Tel 0121-643 9898
Regional newsrooms:
West (Birmingham)	0121-643 9898
East (Nottingham)	0115-986 3322
South (Abingdon)	01235-554123

Other news studios:
Gloucester	01452-309666
Peterborough	01733-331113
Swindon	01793-617002

Owner: Carlton Communications.
Chairman: Leslie Hill.
Covers: English Midlands.
Regional news programme: Central News East/South/West.
1993-2002 licence fee: £2,000 pa.
ITC 1994 Performance Review: " maintained its reputation for popular, well produced network programmes ... there was little progress in expanding non-news sub-regional programmes."

Channel Television

Television Centre, La Pouquelaye, St Helier,
Jersey, Channel Islands JE2 3ZD
Fax 01534-59446   Tel 01534-68999
Regional newsrooms:
  Guernsey   01481-723451
  Jersey   01534-34040
Owner: Channel Islands Communications (TV), whose largest shareholders are Bois Trustees (8.9%) and 3i Capital (8.5%).
Chairman: John Riley.
Covers: Channel Islands.
Regional news programme: Channel Report.
1993-2002 licence fee: £1,000 pa.
ITC 1994 Performance Review: "The regional service contained a range of material and was of high quality."

GMTV

London Television Centre, Upper Ground,
London SE1 9TT
Fax 0171-827 7002   Tel 0171-827 7000
Owners: Walt Disney (25%), the Granada Group (20%), Scottish TV (20%), Carlton Communications (20%), Guardian Media Group (15%).
Chairman: Nigel Walmsley.
1993-2002 licence fee: £34.61 million pa.
Took over the ITV network breakfast-time service from TV-am in January 1993. On air from 6.00 am to 9.25 am seven days a week. Offers a programme of news and entertainment including The Sunday Programme.
News programme: News Hour.
ITC 1994 Performance Review: " There was a marked improvement on 1993... but the quality of the service in children's programmes was still disappointing in certain respects."

Grampian Television

Queen's Cross, Aberdeen, Grampian AB9 2XJ
Fax 01224-635127   Tel 01224-646464
Regional newsrooms:
  Dundee   01382-739363
  Inverness   01463-242624
Owner: Grampian Television, whose largest shareholder is Abtrust Scotland Investment Co (7.8%).
Chairman: Dr Calum MacLod.
Covers: North and north-east Scotland.
Regional news programme: North Tonight.
1993-2002 licence fee: £720,000 pa.
ITC 1994 Performance Review: "high quality news and current affairs output...new regional programmes introduced."

Granada Television

Quay Street, Manchester M60 9EA
Fax 0161-832 7211x 3405   Tel 0161-832 7211
London office: 36 Golden Square, W1R 4AH
Fax 0171-287 8566   Tel 0171-734 8080
Regional newsrooms:
  Blackburn   01254-690099

Chester   01244-313966
Lancaster   01524-60688
Liverpool   0151-709 9393
Manchester   0161-832 7211
Owner: Granada Group, whose largest shareholder is SG Warburg Group (16.4%).
Chairman: Gerry Robinson.
Covers: North-west England.
Regional news programme: Granada Tonight.
1993-2002 licence fee: £9.0 million pa.
Granada bought LWT (Holdings) in early 1994. Granada owns 18% of ITN. In mid-1994 Granada said it was interested in taking over Yorkshire TV if the rules on TV ownership be changed by cross media legislation.
ITC 1994 Performance Review: "continued to provide a high quality service...some innovative new styles of programming."

HTV

Wales: Television Centre, Culverhouse Cross, Cardiff CF5 6XJ
Fax 01222-592134   Tel 01222-590590
West: Television Centre, Bath Rd, Bristol, Avon BS4 3HG
Fax 0117-972 2400   Tel 0117-977 8366
Regional newsrooms:
  Cardiff   01222-590754
  Carmarthen   01267-236806
  Colwyn Bay   01492-534555
  Newtown   01686-623381
  Taunton   01823-270293
Owner: HTV Group; largest shareholder Flextech (19.9%).
Chairman: Louis Sherwood.
Covers: Wales and Avon/Glocs/Somerset.
Regional news programme: Wales Tonight, HTV News.
1993-2002 licence fee: £20.53 million pa.
Cable giant Flextech moved into HTV in early 1994.
ITC 1994 Performance Review: "ITC was concerned about the rescheduling of a significant number of regional programmes.....However quality improving in both Wales and the West."

London Weekend Television (LWT)

London Television Centre, Upper Ground,
London SE1 9LT
Fax 0171-261 1290   Tel 0171-620 1620
Newsroom (LNN)   0171-827 7700
Owner: Granada Group .
Chairman: Gerry Robinson.
Covers: London area, from 1715 Friday until 0600 Monday.
Regional news programme: London Today.
1993-2002 licence fee: £7.59 million pa.
Its local news service is provided by London News Network, jointly owned with Carlton.
ITC 1994 Performance Review: "There were certain aspects of the regional service which were not up to the same high standards of the previous year."

Meridian Broadcasting

Television Centre, Northam, Southampton, Hants
SO14 0PZ
Fax 01703-335050   Tel 01703-222555
London office: 48 Leicester Square, WC2H 7LY
Fax 0171-925 01665   Tel 0171-839 2255
Regional centres:
  New Hythe   01622-882244
  Newbury, Berks   01635-522322
  Southampton   01703-712006
Owner: MAI (owns 61%), Carlton Communications (20%),
SelecTV (15%). MAI has no large single shareholder.
Chairman: Lord Hollick.
Covers: South and south east England, with separate news
services for each of its three regions.
Regional news programme: Meridian Tonight.
1993-2002 licence fee: £36.52 million pa.
Took over from TVS in January 1993.
ITC 1994 Performance Review: " ...built on its succesful first
year of operation....although some arts programming did not come
up to expectation."

Scottish Television

Cowcaddens, Glasgow G2 3PR
Fax 0141-332 6982   Tel 0141-332 9999
Regional newsrooms:
  Glasgow   0141-332 9274
  Edinburgh   0131-557 4554
Owner: Scottish Television, whose largest shareholder is Mirror
Group Newspapers (19.99%).
Managing director: Gus Macdonald.
Covers: Central Scotland and south-west Highlands.
Regional news programme: Scotland Today.
1993-2002 licence fee: £2,000 pa.
Owns 20% of GMTV and 5% of ITN.
ITC 1994 Performance Review: "..sustained a strong Scottish
identity...substantial amounts of local programming...increased
its already high audience shares."

Tyne Tees Television

Television Centre, City Road, Newcastle-upon-
Tyne NE1 2AL
Fax 0191-261 2302   Tel 0191-261 0181
London office: 15 Bloomsbury Square, London
WC1A 2LJ
Fax 0171-242 2441   Tel 0171-405 8474
Regional newsrooms:
  Newcastle   0191-261 0181
  Billingham   01642-566999
  York   01904-610066
Owner: Yorkshire-Tyne Tees Television Holdings since mid-1992
Chairman: Sir Ralph Carr-Ellison.
Covers: North-east England and north Yorkshire.
Regional news programmes: Tyne Tees Today/Network North.
1993-2002 licence fee: £17 million pa.
ITC 1994 Performance Review: "..complied with the licence
conditions, providing a strong regional and sub-regional service."

UTV (Ulster Television)

Havelock House, Ormeau Road,
Belfast BT7 1EB
Fax 01232-246695   Tel 01232-328122
Derry newsroom   01504-366611
Owner: Ulster Television,.No single shareholder over 6%.
Chairman: John McGuckian.
Covers: Northern Ireland.
Regional news programme: UTV Live at Six.
1993-2002 licence fee: £1.03 million pa.
ITC 1994 Performance Review: "political developments ..were
reported wih impartiality and authority ... arts programmes ...
... showed considerable improvement."

Westcountry Television

Western Wood Way, Langage Science Park,
Plymouth, Devon PL7 5BG
Fax 01752-333030   Tel 01752-333333
Owner: Westcountry Television, whose main shareholders are
Associated Newspapers (19.42%), South West Water (22.56%)
and Britanny Ferries (16.92%).
Chairman: Sir John Banham.
Covers: Cornwall, Devon and adjacent area.
Regional news programme: Westcountry Live.
1993-2002 licence fee: £7.82 million pa.
Took over the south-west England licence from Television
South-West in January 1993.
ITC 1994 Performance Review: "Westcountry's regional service
was considered sufficiently diverse and of generally high
quality."

Yorkshire Television

Television Centre, Kirkstall Road, Leeds, West
Yorks LS3 1JS
Fax 0113-244 5107   Tel 0113-243 8283
Regional news rooms:
  Grimsby   01472-357026
  Hull   01482-24488
  Lincoln   01522-530738
  Sheffield   0114-272 7772
  York   01904-610066
Owner: Yorkshire-Tyne Tees Television Holdings , whose largest
shareholders are Granada Group (14.2%) and Pearson plc
(14%).
Owner's Chairman: Ward Thomas.
Covers: Yorkshire, Humberside, Derbyshire, Nottinghamshire,
Lincolnshire.
Regional news programme: Calendar.
1993-2002 licence fee: £37.7 million pa.
ITC 1994 Performance Review: "Regional news output was
high quality...scope exists to expand non-news sub-regional
programmes."

CHANNEL 4 AND S4C

Channel 4 is a compromise between public sector and commercial television and has thus always been a minority channel. This minority status was made explicit when the 1990 Broadcasting Act said Channel 4 programmes should "appeal to tastes and interests not generally catered for by ITV ... encourage innovation and experiment [and] be distinctive." The Act also talked of quality, education, a Euro commitment and that Channel 4 should operate as a TV publisher by its reliance on independent producers.

Channel 4 has done all this and more. Its co-financing of blockbuster Middle England movies like Four Weddings and a Funeral and The Madness of King George has made it the dominating influence over what remains of the British film industry. Its commissioning from over 600 production companies has been successful enough to attract a tenth of the TV audience ... plus a fair portion of right-wing criticism asserting that TV is driving moral standards down. According to the Daily Telegraph, Channel 4 represents "the yob culture, aimed at the illiterate and the impervious, trading in filth and humiliation".

"There is no comparable channel worldwide operating without public funding," says the Channel 4 chairman Sir Michael Bishop. He was reporting 1994 pre-tax profits of £83.6 million, to more than double the £38.9 million of 1993. Jubilation was muted due to the funding formula which requires Channel 4 to pay ITV half of any revenue it earns over and above 14 per cent of the UK's total terrestrial earnings. By this arcane calculation, Channel 4 forfeited £57.3 million of its profits.

"With that money," says the channel's programme director John Willis, "we could fund more than 400 hours of British production. A thousand more jobs, more exports, better quality, wider choice. Perhaps before we have to start yet more re-runs of I Love Lucy, Stephen Dorrell [then the Heritage Secretary] will put the viewer first."

Thus far the Heritage Department has not yielded to Channel 4's lobbying and the likelihood is that the government will refuse to tinker with legislation until 1997 or 1998. The system has its roots in Channel 4's early history when it relied on subsidies from Channel 3. When it was founded in 1982 finance came from a 13.6 per cent levy on the advertising revenue of the ITV companies. In return the companies sold Channel 4's advertising time and kept the proceeds. The 1990 Act enabled Channel 4 to sells its own advertising and reversed the subsidy with the carrot (never felt necessary by Channel 4 insiders) that Channel 3 would provide a safety net should ad sales not cover the costs. The price of success is that for the next couple of years Channel 4 will have to subsidise far richer companies which are free to chase larger audiences.

The Welsh fourth channel frequencies are used by S4C or Sianel Pedwar Cymru (Channel Four Wales). It began in 1982 alongside Channel Four and broadcasts about 30 hours of Welsh language programmes. The BBC supplies 10 hours of them with the remainder coming from HTV and independent producers. S4C has been directly funded by the Treasury since 1993.

Channel 4
124 Horseferry Road, London SW1P 2TX
Fax 0171-306 8351   Tel 0171-396 4444
Chief executive: Michael Grade
Director of programmes: John Willis
Controller of arts/entertainment: Andrea Wonfor
Head of drama: David Aukin

THE CHANNEL 4 BOARD
Chairman: Sir Michael Bishop, chairman of British Midland Airways.
Deputy Chairman: David Plowright, former chairman of Granada Television.
Bert Hardy, managing director of Associated Newspapers.
Anne Lapping, a director of Brook Productions.
Mary McAleese, of Queens University, Belfast.
John McGrath, independent producer and writer.
Sir David Nicholas, former chairman of ITN.
Usha Prashar, past director of the NCVO.
The executive directors are Michael Grade (chief executive), Stewart Butterfield, Colin Leventhal, Frank McGettigan, David Scott and John Willis.

S4C (Sianel Pedwar Cymru)
Parc ty Glas, Llanishen, Cardiff CF4 5DU
Fax 01222-754444   Tel 01222-747444
Chairman: Prys Edwards
Chief executive: Huw Jones
Director of programmes: Deryk Williams

CHANNEL 5

Channel 5 will be the long-awaited offspring of the 1990 Broadcasting Act. The expected mid-nineties birth never happened because the ITC rejected the single company that offered to parent it. Four consortia came forward for the next auction and, such has been the recent fascination with Rupert Murdoch, the main news was that the outfit he was with only bid £2 million. Though Murdoch didn't use these words, he doubted that TV audiences wanted yet more schlock around the clock.

Channel 5's gestation has been elephantine because the risks of nurturing it beyond a demanding infancy are considerable. Start up costs in the region of £200 million will burden a channel that faces growing rivalry from cable and satellite channels and later from up to 500 digital TV channels; athough Channel 5 offers TV companies something approaching a national audience, transmission restrictions will in fact limit it to a maximum 70 per cent of the population; and millions must be spent if the Channel 5 signal is not to disrupt video players.

Nonetheless one of the bidders listed below will be pressing ahead during 1996 to ensure the channel starts no later than 1 January 1997. See also Broadcasting Chronicle, page 150.

Four bid for 5

ITC announces the winning bidder by 30 November, 1995, shortly after this book has been published. However, details are worth noting here because the backers, if not the companies specifically formed to make the bids, will definitely remain in the TV marketplace.

UKTV
12-13 Henrietta Street, London WC2
Fax 0171-240 7434   Tel 0171-240 7433
Bid: £36,261,158
Backers: CanWest Global, Mirror Group, Scandinavian Broadcast System, SelecTV, The Ten Group

Channel 5 Broadcasting
Cavendish House, 128-134 Cleveland Street, London W1P 5DN
Fax 0171-916 6556   Tel 0171-911 0055
Bid: £22,002,000
Backers: Pearson, MAI, CLT, Warburg Pincus Ventures

Virgin Television
Virgin Communications, 186 Campden Hill Road, London W8 7TH
Fax 0171-229 1889   Tel 0171-2297344
Bid: £22,002,000
Backers: Associated Newspapers, HTV, Paramount, Philips, Virgin, Electra

New Century Television
19 Buckingham Gate, London SW1E 6LD
Fax 0171-931 8010   Tel 0171-931 8368
Bid: £2,000,000
Backers: Granada Group, TCI, BSkyB, PolyGram, Really Useful Group, Kinnevik, Goldman Sachs, Hoare Govettt

TELETEXT

Teletext is the name for written copy receivable on TV sets fitted with decoders. There are two main services: Ceefax on BBC and Teletext on ITV. The latter is a consortium 45 per cent owned by the Daily Mail and General Trust whose other main partners are Philips Electronics and Media Ventures.

Unlike its predecessor Oracle, regional news is at the heart of Teletext's operation. It was awarded a ten year licence on condition it supplied a 24-hour service with at least 30 pages of national and international news. The news is supplied by the Press Association. Each region has about 3,000 pages available.

In addition to providing a similar amount of news and information, BBC Ceefax operates a BBC1 and BBC 2 subtitling service for the hard of hearing.

About 10.5 million homes · half of all households · have access to teletext and the weekly audience approaches 16 million.

Ceefax
Room 7013, BBC Television Centre, Wood Lane, London W12 7RJ
Fax 0181-749 6734   Tel 0181-576 1801

Teletext UK
101 Farm Lane, Fulham, London SW6 1QJ
Fax 0171-386 5002   Tel 0171-386 5000

NEW TV: THE MARKET

The number of households with a satellite dish is over three million and there are a million households connected to cable. New TV has already shattered the broadcasting's status quo for, once cable or satellite is installed, it accounts for a third of the average viewing time. The success of the satellite station BSkyB in capturing 4 per cent of the television audience has paved the way for the cable operators by proving beyond doubt that people are prepared to pay directly for their television viewing.

Melvyn Bragg, the chairman of Border TV as well as a broadcaster, put the new establishment line that the multiplicity of low quality programmes will be socially divisive. His headline phrase is that the break-up of British television is creating "telly for snobs and telly for yobs".

Virtually all channels on satellite are also available on cable, but not all cable channels are on satellite. Therefore cable is increasing its spread at a faster rate than satellite and the expansion is threatening more than the vested interests at the BBC and Channel 3. A newly cabled Britain lays British Telecom open to more competition as 40,000 of its phone customers a month switch to cable phones. While the cable companies, which are predominantly American owned, are using their cables for discounted phone calls as well as TV, anti monopoly legislation prevents BT from delivering live TV down its phone lines. All British Telecom can do is put down a marker with trials of a video on demand service. In a parliamentary debate some MPs claimed that were BT to be allowed a broadcaster's role, it would rewire Britain more thoroughly and allow "the nation to catapult itself to the front of the global information revolution". The government declined to change the rules.

Therefore, in yet another spin on the complexities of cross media ownership, Britain's privatised telephone company is now aching to join the ranks of broadcasters although, now that we grow used to the idea of communication technologies converging, that seems less and less of an oddity. The real oddity is that British Telecom, a creation of free market policy, is tied up in central government legislation that is allowing American-owned cable companies to take over an entire industry. So perhaps it's not so much a free market more a strategy free zone.

The top channels

By mid-1995 1,109,771 households were able to receive cable *and* satellite transmissions. Of these the vast majority, a total of 963,132 were connected to broadband cable networks. The ITC figures below show the number of cabled homes receiving the various channels available from satellites or otherwise

Sky One	1,091,436
Sky News	1,028,176
Children's Channel	996,860
UK Gold	970,714
NBC Super Channel	969,061
Eurosport	965,333
MTV Europe	965,119
Discovery	956,671
Parliamentary Channel	919,508
Bravo	918,888
TNT/Cartoon Network	909,942
TLC (Learning Channel)	906,970
CNN Inernational	901,444
QVC	870,054
Nickelodeon	858,022
VH-1	837,632
Wire TV	835,089
Performance	811,590
The Channel Guide	811,180
CMT Europe	782,764
Landscape Channel	778,647
Travel Channel	766,844
The Box	726,049
UK Living	701,468
Euronews	581,192
Sky Sports	516,786
Sky Movies	499,637
Sky Sports 2	496,707
The Movie Channel	452,561
Family Channel	431,401
Sky Movies Gold	407,903
Sky Soap	387,790
Vision	323,718
Channel One	287,131
Identity TV	233,322
Sky Travel	203,224
Asianet	198,223
The Adult Channel	63,635
Home Video Channel	62,970
Namaste Asian Television	48,022
Zee TV	21,107

NEW TV: CABLE

The millionth cable user signed up in July 1995 and joined the ranks of those paying between £30 and £50 connection charges plus a further £15 a month subscriptions to hook into cable. The money buys them nearly 40 channels and another subscription buys access to BSkyB.

The cable television business is turning over nearly £250 million a year, and is just starting to pay back the £10 billion invested in digging up the roads and rewiring Britain. By 1 April 1995 there were 86 broadband cable franchises operational and the cabling passed the doors of 4.5 million homes. As of June 1995, there were 963,132 houses connected to cable compared with 642,000 a year earlier. They form 4.26 per cent of TV homes. Northampton is where cable is most popular with 50.4 per cent of the homes passed by cables being connected. And the cabling isn't just being used for telly; by 1 April 1995 there were 872,573 phone lines installed, up from 376,795 a year before.

According to the Cable Communications Association (which dropped the word "Television" from its name in favour of "Communications"), the burgeoning industry will have created 25 jobs a day throughout 1995. A few of these will be a new species of one-person-with-a-camera video journalist.

A promise (or banal threat) of cable television is that broadcasting will become ever more local. Narrowcasting is another name for it and London's Channel One is one of the pioneers. It was opened in November 1994 by Associated Newspapers, the owner of the Daily Mail and London Evening Standard. It is billed as London's video newspaper and is the Daily Mail's screen equivalent.

Among the cable companies, a rapid commercial consolidation is taking place. In November 1994 the market leader Telewest went to the UK stock market for extra funds. By June it had taken over a major rival when it paid £679 million for SBC Cablecomms. The odds are that, before the big profits start to be made, the current 20 or so large operators will shrink to a handful.

The Independent Television Commission provides the regulatory framework, though cable operators face a looser regime than that imposed on the old broadcasters. The crucial difference is that there is no need to ensure that cable channels carry anything remotely educational. The patrician contract that TV should both entertain and inform has been broken and in its place is niche TV; the closest media comparison is with the magazine market.

The ITC, which gives licences to cable operators and progamme providers (often one and the same), also gives definitions to a complex arena. Its description of a cable service is as follows: "A cable system is a network of cables. In Britain these are almost always installed in ducts below roads or footpaths. They radiate from a central control point (called the headend) to homes and businesses in a town or group of towns or, in London, a group of boroughs. The systems use mainly coaxial cable but usually employ optical fibre in the trunks.A cable system is primarily a means of delivering television to the home. The cable is connected to viewers' existing TV sets, usually through a set-top box provided by the cable operator. The TV channels carried by cable systems include those from a number of satellites, as well as from other sources. Because a cable connection avoids the need for individual viewers to have satellite dishes, receivers and decoders, cable provides an easy and cost-effective way of delivering the new TV choices now developing. The cable systems currently being designed and built can carry between 30 and 45 channels."

Cable companies are also known as Multiple System Operators and, according to ITC data released immediately before Telewest bought out SBC, the market is as follows:

MSO	homes connected	homes passed
Telewest	189,875	873,484
Comcast	151,293	547,710
Nynex	130,377	687,923
SBC	111,927	530,647
Videotron	95,558	446,966
Bell	75,873	340,460
Telecentenial	64,813	254,826
Gen. Cable	56,574	275,318
CableTel	20,735	134,766

Cable operator companies

What follows are the main companies holding most of the operator franchises for the broadband cable systems, that is the physical cabling rather than the programmes it transmits. The cable business has dozens of companies and many apparent rivals often either share the same parent or have complex and shifting franchise relationships with each other.

The companies listed here are nearly all owned or dominated by North American organisations. In ITC language they are the franchised cable operators and their licences are granted after a competitive process which gives the winners the right to broadcast multi channel television over a large scale purpose built network for 15 years. The licence, which comes from the Department of Trade and Industry, also allows them to sell telecommunications services.

Included below are details of the most prominent franchises the franchised operators control, often through subsidiary companies with different names. These companies have a controlling interest in and management control of the cable system operators.

For further information consult Who's Who in Cable and Satellite (available from WOAC Communications on 01582-873001) or contact the Cable Communications Association on 0800-300750.

Bell Cablemedia
Bell Cablemedia House, Upton Road, Watford, Herts WD1 7EL
Fax 01923-444004   Tel 01923-444000
Franchises: London and surrounding areas, Leeds, Norwich and East Anglia, Harrogate and York, worcester, Wearside.
Subsidiaries: Encom Cable TV and Telecommunictions, Fenland Cablevision, Jones Cable Group, Norwich Cablevision, Peterborough Cablevision.
30 per cent investor in Videotron.
Owner: Bell Canada, Canada.

BT Cable TV Services
Euston Tower, 286 Euston Road, London NW1 3DG
Fax 0171-728 5265 Tel 0171-728 7145
Franchises: Westminster and parts of London, Milton Keynes, Washington.
Subsidiaries: BT New Towns Systems; Westminster Cable, Barbican Cable, Irvine Cable, Milton Keynes Cable.
Owner: BT

Cable Corporation
see General Cable

CableTel
CableTel House, Guildford Business Park, Guildford, Surrey GU2 5AD
Fax 01483-254100   Tel 01483-254000
Franchises: Glasgow, Cardiff, Swansea, Guildford, south Bedfordshire, Hampshire, Huddersfield, Northern Ireland.
Subsidiaries: CableTel Bedfordshire, CableTel Glasgow, CableTel Kirklees, CableTel Northern Ireland, CableTel South Wales, CableTel Surrey.
Owner: International Cable Tel Inc, USA, with Comcast (41.25 per cent) and Singapore Telecom (41.25 per cent). The third largest franchise holder.

Comcast Cable
Network House, Bradfield Close, Woking, Surrey GU22 7RE
Fax 01483-763005   Tel 01483-722000
Franchises: Managing partner in franchises in many parts of London, plus Cambridge, Harlow, Birmingham, Teeside, Darlington.
Subsidiaries: Anglia Cable, Birmingham Cable, Cable London, Cambridge Cable, East Coast Cable.
Owner: Comcast, USA.

Devanha Group
303 King Street, Aberdeen, Grampian AB2 3AP
Fax 01224-644601   Tel 01224-646644
Franchises: Aberdeen, Coventry, Medway towns, Salford.
Subsidiaries: Aberdeen Cable, Coventry Cable, Medway Cablevision, Multichannel Television, Salford Cable Television.

Diamond Cable
Regency House, 2a Sherwood Rise, Nottingham NG7 6JN
Fax 0115-952 2211   Tel 0115-952 2222
Franchises: Nottingham, Newark, Mansfield, Grantham, Melton, Grimsby, Lincoln.
Owner: Diamond Cable, USA with European Cable Partners (72.4 per cent) and Macdonld Family Trust (20 per cent).

Eurobell
Multimedia House, Lloyds Court, Manor Royal, Crawley RH10 2PT
Fax 01293-400440   Tel 01293-400444
Franchises: Parts of Surrey, south Devon and west Kent.
Subsidiaries: Devon Cablevision, Eurobell (South West), Eurobell (Sussex), Eurobell (West Kent).
Owner: Orbis Trust, European Broadband Systems (54 per cent), Detecon and Transon (46 per cent).

General Cable
37 Old Queen Street, London SW1H 9JA
Fax 0171-393 2800   Tel 0171-393 2828
Franchises: Windsor, Hillingdon, Birmingham, Bradford, Sheffield, Doncaster, Wakefield, Barnsley.
Subsidiaries: Cable Corporation, Middlesex Cable Communications, Windsor Television, GC and Singapore Telecom both own 45.5 per cent of Yorkshire Cable Group.
Owner: Compagnie Generale des Eaux, France.

IVS Cable Holdings
3 Colomberie, St Helier, Jersey JE2 4QB
Fax 01534-66681   Tel 01534-66477
Franchises: Andover, Oxford, Stafford, Salisbury.
Subsidiaries: Andover Cablevision, Stafford Communications, Wessex Cable, Oxford Cable, Jersey Cable.
Owner: Flextech, USA.

Jones Cable Group
9 Greycaine Road, Watford, Herts WD2 4JP
Fax 01923--444004   Tel 01923-444000
Franchises: Leeds, south Herts, Aylesbury, plus stake in several east London franchises.
Owner: Jones Intercable, USA, Bell Cablemedia.

LCL Cable Communications
28-29 Owin Road, Leicester LE3 1HR
Fax 0116-233 4050   Tel 0116-233 4100
Franchises: Leicester, Loughborough, Shepshed.
Subsidiaries: Tamworth Cable Communications, Lichfield Cable Communications, Burton-upon-Trent Cable Communications, Hinckley Cable Communications.
Owner: SaskTel (56 per cent), Fundy Cable (23 per cent).

Metro Cable Television
Bentalls, Basildon, Essex SS14 3BY
Fax 01268-527797   Tel 01268-526841
Owner: Metro Cable TV

Nynex Cablecomms
1 Hartfield Road, Wimbledon, London SW19 3RU
Fax 0181-544 0811   Tel 0181-540 8833
Franchises: Portsmouth, north and east Surrey, Hants, Stoke, Oldham, Manchester, Derby, Teesside, Wirral, Brighton, Darlington, Bromley, Bournemouth, Stockport, Macclesfield, Bury, Derby, Warrington, Blackburn.
Subsidiaries: Nynex Cablecomms Midlands Region, Nynex Cablecomms North West Region, Nynex Cablecomms Southern Region.
Owner: Nynex, USA.
One of the two largest franchise holders in the UK, alongside TeleWest.

SBC Cablecomms
Hollywood House, Church Stret East Woking, Surrey GU21 1HJ
Fax 01483-740922   Tel 01483-751756

Franchises: South and north Liverpool, Preton, Wigan, Bootle, Black Country, Blackpool, Telford, St Helens.
Subsidiaries: Cable Midlands, Cable North West.
Owner: Southwestern Bell USA (50 per cent) and Cox International (50 per cent) until June 1995 when they were bought out, for £679 million by Telewest.

Telecential Communications
Link 2, Beacontree Plaza, Gillette Way, Basingstoke Road, Reading, Berks RG2 0BS
Fax 01734-753025   Tel 01734-756475
Franchises: Swindon, Thames Valley, Warwick, Nuneaton, Rugby, Corby, Kettering, west Herts, Northampton, Stratford, Coventry.
Subsidiaries: Bracknell Cable, Swindon Cable, Telecential Communications Northants, Telecential Communications Thames Valley, Telecential Communications West Herts, Telecential Commnications Warwickshire.
Owners: 50 per cent CUC Broadcasting, Canada (Shaw Communications) ; 50 per cent Telus Corporation, Canada.

TeleWest Communications
Unit 1, Genesis Business Park, Albert Drive, Woking, Surrey GU21 5RW
Fax 01483-750901   Tel 01483-750900
Franchises: One of the two largest operators in UK, with franchises in north Kent, south Essex, Avon, Merton, Kingston, Croydon, Edinburgh, Cheltenham and Gloucester, Tyneside, Dundee, Perth., Motherwell, Falkirk, Cumbernauld.
Companies: United Artists.
Subsidiaries: United Artists Communications (Avon), UAC (Cotswolds), UAC (London South), UAC (North East), UAC (Scotland), UAC (South East).
Owners: Joint venture of TeleCommunications Inc and US West TeleWest is one of the two largest franchise holders in the UK, alongside Nynex.

Videotron Corporation
76 Hammersmith Road, London W14 8UD
Fax 0181-244 1599   Tel 0181-244 1234
Franchises: London boroughs of Greenwich, Wandsworth, Lambeth, Thamesmead, Ealing, Kensington, Barnet, Brent, Hammersmith and Harow also Southampton, Winchester.
Owner: Le Groupe Videotron, Canada (64 per cent) and Bell Cablemedia (30 per cent).

Yorkshire Cable Group
Communications House, Mayfair Business Park, Broad Lane, Bradford BD4 8PW
Fax 01274-828400   Tel 01274-828282
Franchises: Bradford, Sheffield, Doncaster, Barnsley, Wakefield, Halifax.
Subsidiaries: Doncaster Cable Communications, Barnsley Cable Comunications, Halifax Cable Communications, Sheffield Cable Communications.
Ownership: General Cable (45.5 per cent), Singapore Telecom (45.5 per cent), Yorkshire Water (9 per cent).

Cable franchise holders

Below is a guide to cable operator areas. Phone the CCA on 0800-300750 for fuller details.

Aberdeen area:
Aberdeen Cable (Devanha)   01224-649444
Andover:
Andover Cablevision (IVS)   01264-334607
Avon:
United Artists (TeleWest)   01454-612290
Bedfordshire: south, Luton:
Cablevision Beds (CableTel)   01582-401044
Birmingham, Solihull:
Birmingham Cable (Comcast)   0121-628 1234
Bolton:
Nynex CableComms   0161-946 0388
Bradford:
Yorkshire Cable   01274-828282
Brighton, Hove, Worthing, Shoreham:
Nynex CableComms   01273-880000
Burton-upon-Trent, Swadlincote, Ashby-de-la-Zouch
LCL Cable   0116-233 4100
Cambridge, Ely, Newmarket, Huntingdon:
Cambridge Cable (Comcast)   01223-567200
Coventry:
Coventry Cable (Devanha)   01203-505345
Derby:
Nynex CableComms   01332-200002
Dundee, Perth area:
United Artists (TeleWest)   01382-322220
Edinburgh:
United Artists (TeleWest)   0131-539 0002
Gatwick, Crawley:
Eurobell   01293-400444
Glasgow area:
CableTel   0141-221 7040
Guildford, W Surrey, E Hants:
CableTel   01483-254000
Hampshire: east, Portsmouth, Gosport:
Nynex CableComms   01705-266555
Harlow, Bishops Stortford, Stansted:
Anglia Cable (Comcast)   01279-867000
Hertfordshire: south:
Jones Cable   01923-464000
Hertfordshire: west:
Telecential   01442-230444
Hinckley, Bosworth
LCL Cable   0116-233 4100
Lancashire: central/south, Merseyside:
Cable North West (SBC)   01772-832888
Lancashire: east:
Nynex CableComms   0161-946 0388
Leeds:
Jones Cable   0113-293 2000

Leicester, Loughborough:
LCL Cable   0116-233 4100
Lichfield, Burntwood, Rugeley
LCL Cable   0116-233 4100

London:
  Barking, Bexley, Dagenham, Havering, Newham, Tower Hamlets:
  Encom Cable (Bell)   0171-363 2000
  Barnet, Brent, Ealing, Fulham, Greenwich, Harrow, Hammersmith, Kensington, Lambeth, Lewisham, Southwark, Thamesmead, Wandsworth:
  Videotron   0181-244 1234
  Bromley:
  Nynex CableComms   0181-446 9966
  Camden, Enfield, Hackney, Haringey, Islington:
  Cable London (Comcast/TeleWest)
                                   0171-911 0911
  Croydon, Kingston, Merton, Richmond, Sutton:
  United Artists (TeleWest)   0181-760 0222
  Hillingdon, Hounslow:
  Middx Cable (Gen Cable)   01753-810810
  Westminster:
  Westminster Cable (BT)   0171-935 4400
Motherwell, Hamilton, East Kilbride:
United Artists (TeleWest)   01698-322332
Northampton:
Telecential   01604-643619
Northern Ireland
CableTel Northern Ireland   01483-254000
Norwich:
Norwich Cable (Bell)   01603-787892
Nottingham, Grimsby, Lincoln, Mansfield:
Diamond Cable   0115-952 2240
Peterborough:
Peterborough Cable (Bell)   01733-371717
Southampton, Eastleigh:
Videotron   01703-315000
Surrey: north, north east:
Nynex CableComms   01372-360844
Swansea, Neath, Port Talbot:
CableTel   01222-456644
Swindon:
Swindon Cable (Telecential)   01793-480483
Tamworth, north Warwicks and Meriden
Tamworth Cable (LCL)   0116-233 4100
Thames Valley, Basingstoke, Wycombe:
Telecential   01734-756868
Tyneside:
United Artists (TeleWest)   0191-420 2000
Windsor, Slough, Maidenhead, Heathrow:
Windsor TV (Gen Cable)   01753-810810
Wolverhampton, Walsall, Dudley, Telford:
Cable Midlands (SBC)   01384-838483

Cable channels

Or what the ITC calls licensable progamme operators. The label describes services provided nationally to cable systems other than by satellite and includes community TV.

Aberdeen Channel	01224-649444
African Channel	0171-252 3296
Afro-Caribbean Channel	0181-802 4576
Airport Television	01753-580233
Andover Now	01264 334607
Arabic Channel	0171-935 6699
Arcade	01753-810810
Asianet	0181-572 0527
BVTV	0181-884 0966
Black Music Television	0181-740 5505
Box	0171-376 2000
British Greek Community Channel	0181-807 6035
Cable North West Channel	01772 832888
Cable Video Store	0181-964 1141
Cable 10	01639 899999
Capital Network	0181-424 0383
The Channel Guide	01902-469238
Channel One	0171-209 1234
Channel Seven	01384-482448
Channel 9 Stevenage	0181-961 6776
Channel 17	01483-750900
Clyde Cablevision	0141-221 7040
Colt TV	01203-505345
Commuity Channel	01442 231311
EZTV	01375-392025
Ebony Television	0181-961 5637

Education & Training Channel	0191-515 2070
Education Channel	01254-55144
GPTV	0181-550 7711
Grapevine	0171-911 0911
Havering Community Channel	0171-363 2000
Hellenic Television	0171-485 8822
Home Video Channel	0181-964 1141
Identity Television	0181-960 3338
Interactive Channel	0181-244 1234
Interactive London News	0171-827 7700
International Shopping Network	01483-747700
Leicester Community Channel	0116-233400
Local 8	01603-787892
MK-LTV	01203-422042
Metrovision	0171-935 6699
Mind Extension University	01923-444000
Multi-Screen Channel	01483-750900
NCTV	01273-413021
NCTV Community Television	0161-834 4902
Network 021	0121-628 1234
PTV	0131-220 1110
Performance - Arts Channel	0181-961 0011
Redbridge Community Channel	0171-895 9910
Royal Opera House Channel	0171-240 1200
Shakti Vision	0171-359 6464
Skelmersdale Local Channel	01695-510000
Swindon ocal	01793-615601
TellyWest	01483-750900
Tower Hamlets	0171-895 9910
Videotron Channel	0181-244 1234
Videotron Home Shopping	01730-895640
Vision	01793-511244
Westscan	0171-935 6699

NEW TV: SATELLITE

The story of satellite TV broadcasting is largely the story of BSkyB. It began as Sky TV in 1989 and was financed with profits from Rupert Murdoch's newspapers. Within a year Sky TV had absorbed BSB, its only significant rival. Half a decade later and BSkyB was declaring six monthly profits of over £50 million and repaying the original investment by covering the losses accrued during the round of newspaper price cutting.

BSkyB has earned itself 3 million satellite dish owners and a 4 per cent of the TV audience largely by upping the stakes in sports coverage. No true sports nut can exist without Sky. The channel will further shrug off a reputation for junk TV by becoming a significant news provider. In February 1995 BSkyB announced a deal whereby Reuters is to supply and manage the coverage for a round-the-clock news channel. The partnership will challenge both Channel 3's Independent Television News and the BBC World satellite channel that had been anounced just a month earlier.

BSkyB
6 Centaurs Business Park, Grant Way, Isleworth, Middlesex TW7 5QD
Fax 0171-705 3030   Tel 0171-705 3000
Sky channels: Sky Movies, Sky Movies Gold, Sky News, Sky One, Sky Soap, Sky Sports, Sky Sports 2, Sky Travel
Chief executive: Sam Chisholm.
Head of programming: David Elstein.

Satellite owners

There are hundreds of channels being beamed down from dozens of geo-stationary satellites above Europe. Listed here are the three main TV satellites and then the main channels.

Astra
Societe Europeenne des Satellites, L-6815
Chateau de Betzdorf, Luxemburg.
Fax 00-352 71725324   Tel 00-352 717251
Astra UK Marketing   01442-235540

Eutelsat
Tour Maine-Montparnasse, 33 Avenue du Maine, 75755, Paris Cedex 15, France
Fax 00-331 45383700   Tel 00-331 45384747

Intelsat
3400 International Drive, North West
Washington DC, 20008
Fax 001-202 9447898   Tel 001-202 9446800

Satellite channels

Adult Channel	0181-964 1141
AMC	0116-233 5599
Asian TV Network	0181-202 6304
ASTV	0171-229 1048
Bravo	0171-482 4824
Cartoon Network	0171-637 6700
Chand Televsion	01384-291854
Children's Channel	0171-240 3422
China News Europe	0171-610 3880
Discovery Channel	0171-482 4824
Dragon	0161-236 3557
EDTV	01273-455557
Euronet Television	0171-351 3612
European Family Christian Network	01442-219525
Family Channel	0171-976 7199
GSTV	0171-404 8444
International Shopping Network	01483-747700
Intershop	0171-722 0242
Japan Satellite TV	0171-607 7677
Kindernet	0171-637 8566
Landscape Channel	01424-830688
Learning Channel	0171-482 4824
London Live TV	0171-353 0246
MED TV	0171-275 7010
Media Shop TV	0171-722 0242
Middle East Broadcasting	0171-371 9597
Movie Channel	0171-705 3000
MTV Europe	0171-284 7777

Muslim TV Ahmadiyya	0181-870 8517
Namaste Asian Television	0181-523 1442
NBC Super Channel	0171-418 9418
Nickleodeon	0171-782 3116
Outlook TV	0181-959 5469
Parliamentary Channel	0171-482 4824
Quantum Home Shopping	0171-465 1234
QVC Shopping Channel	0171-705 5600
Regal Shop	0171-434 0567
Reise TV	0171-255 3000
Satellite Information Services	0171-696 8002
Sell-a-Vision Shopping	0171-465 1234
Setanta Sport	0171-930 8926
Sky (all channels)	0171-705 3000
STEP UP	01752-233635
Supersell	0171-824 7909
Supershop	0171-465 1243
TNT	0171-637 6700
Travel Channel	0171-636 401
TV Asia	0181-381 2233
TV Shop	0171-722 0242
TV1000	01895-420421
TV3 Denmark	01895-433327
TV3 Norway	01895-433433
TV3 Sweden	01895-433327
UK Channel	0171-439 3000
UK Gold	0171-306 6100
UK Living	0171-306 6100
VH1	0171-284 7777
VT4	0171-638 1111
Visual Arts	0171-439 3000
What's in Store	0171-465 1234
Wire TV	0171-284 1570
World Health Network	01256-600230

DIGITAL TV

Digital broadcasting is the future for TV and radio. The technique converts sound and pictures into computer digits which can be transmitted in compressed form. This opens the way for wide-screen TVs and CD sound. New channels will be created and existing one split. At leat 18 new TV channels and over 40 radio stations could be created the government said in August 1995. The first digital broadcasting license will be advertised early in 1987 and viewers will need new set-top decoding boxes, costing from £300 to £500.

Astra and Eutelsat (see above!) have both recently launched satellites designed to transmit digital signals and BSkyB reckons satellite transmission of digital TV could start before the earth-bound terrestrial competition.

INDEPENDENT PRODUCERS

Independent television production companies have been part of the media landscape since 1982 when Channel 4 began as a publisher-contractor. The arrangement was successful enough to be used as a model for standard practice when the 1990 Broadcasting Act required Channel 3 stations and the BBC to meet a 25 per cent UK independent production quota.

At the BBC the 25 per cent quota has been backed up by Producer Choice and then a Charter for Independent Producers which aimed to establish "fair and open negotiation on rights, ownership and exploitation". Independents were guaranteed the same access to production facilities as the BBC's in-house staff.

The ITC monitors ITV's observance of its obligations to independent producers. The producers are represented by the Producers Alliance for Cinema and Television (Pact) whose chief executive, John Woodward, says: "The federal network of 15 ITV licensees has by no means stabilised following changes wrought by the 1990 legislation. The creation of an independent ITV Network Centre to commission and acquire all ITV network programming from UK independents as well as ITV licensee broadcaster/producers has created an unresolved struggle between the ITV licensees and regulation. As the ITV licensees struggle to merge and acquire each other, it will be the independents who will remain best placed to supply programmes via the Network Centre, precisely because they are able to operate outside the corporate politics of ITV."

According to Pact estimates, the 1994 output and value of network programming was:

Channel 4: 1,575 hours of production, value £133 million;
ITV Network: 1,276 hours of production, value £169 million
BBC: 1,150 hours of production, value £82 million.

Pact says: "It is now a matter of fact that the independent sector is the largest TV production force in the UK." The expansion of satellite and cable TV is expected to stimulate yet more business for the independent sector. Pact's radio equivalent is the Independent Association of Radio Producers. In 1994 IARP members were responsible for around £4 million of BBC Radio's £8.2 million in commissions. Both Pact and IARP are listed in the Support Organisations at the end of the Broadcasting section on page 206.

Production companies

A19 Film & Video	0191-565 5709
Aardman Animations	0117-984 8485
Absolutely Productions	0171-734 9824
Abu-Tele	01471-833200
Acacia Productions	0181-341 9392
Action Time	0161-236 8999
Adventure Pictures	0171-613 2233
Afro Wisdom Films	0171-490 8386
After Image	0171-737 7300
Agenda Television	01792-470470
Agran Barton TV	0171-351 7070
Aimimage Productions	0171-482 4340
Air-Edel Associates	0171-486 6466
Air-Time Productions	0171-734 9304
Aisling Films (NI)	01232-666631
Alive Productions	0171-384 2243
Allied Vision	0171-224 1992
Amazing Productions	0171-602 5355
Amirani Films	0171-624 4669
Amy Hardie Productions	0171-263 1541
Amy International Productions	01784-483131
Andor Films	0171-602 2382
Anglia Films	0171-321 0101
Anglia TV Entertainment	0171-389 8555
Anglo/Fortunato Films	0181-840 4196
Animation City	0171-580 6160
Animation Partnership	0171-636 3300
Annalogue	0181-743 3630
Antelope	0171-209 0099
Apex TV	01223-872900
Apt Film & TV	0171-248 1695
Arena Films	0181-392 9161
Argo Productions	0171-485 9189
Ariel Productions	0171-437 7972
Armac Films	0141-337 2322
Arts Council Films	0171-973 6443
ASM London Productions	0181-341 1222
Aspect Productions	0171-434 0672
Atticus TV	0181-977 3252
Avalon TV	0171-434 3888
AVL Broadcast	0181-961 9500
Back 2 Back TV	0171-916 2529
Bamboo Film & TV	0171-916 9353
Bandung	0171-482 5045
Barony TV Productions	0131-558 3275
Barraclough Carey	0181-741 4777
Barrass Company	0181-749 3527
Basilisk Communications	0171-580 7222
BBC Enterprises - Wildvision	0117-923 8221
BBC Projects Office	0171-927 4415
Bedford Productions	0171-287 9928
Berwick Universal Pictures	0171-923 1998
Bevanfield Films	0171-487 4920

BFI Production	0171-636 5587	Christmas TV & Film Co	0171-924 1404
Big Star in a Wee Picture	0141-204 3435	Christopher Swann Assocs	0181-749 9056
BJE	01761-471055	Christopher Sykes Production	0181-748 8748
Black Star Films	01232-643399	Christopher Young Films	0171-708 0820
Black Star Productions	01238-561107	Chrysalis Sport	0171-284 2288
Blackbird Productions	0171-352 4882	Chrysalis Television	0171-221 2213
Blackstone Pictures	0181-563 2223	Cicada Films	0171-266 4646
Blue Heaven Productions	0171-404 4222	Cine Century Productions	0171-376 3498
Bob Godfrey Films	0171-278 5711	Cine Electra	0171-287 1123
Bordeaux Films International	0181-959 8556	Cinecontact	0171-434 1745
Box Clever Productions	0171-607 5766	Cinecosse	01358-722150
Box Productions	0171-240 4900	Cinema Verity	0181-749 8485
Brain Waddell Productions	01232-427646	Cinemation	0181-398 7307
Breakout Productions	01235-835226	Clandestine Productions	0171-735 1275
Brian Lapping Associates	0171-482 5855	Clarioncall Film & TV	01943-607553
Brighter Pictures	0171-738 4048	Clark Television Production	0171-388 7700
British Film Institute	0171-636 5587	Class Productions	0171-387 0915
British Lion	01753-651700	Clear Idea Television	0171-284 1442
Britt Allcroft Group	01703-331661	Clement Le Frenais	0171-355 2868
Broadcast Communications	0171-240 6941	Colstar International	0171-437 5725
Broadsword TV	01603-762211	Compact TV	0171-387 4045
Brodeaux Films International	0181-959 8556	Compass Film Productions	0171-734 8115
Brook Productions	0171-482 6111	Connaught Films	0171-240 4808
Brookside Productions	0151-722 9122	Contrast Films	0181-472 5001
Buena Vista	0171-605 2400	Convergence Productions	0171-721 7531
Bumper Films	01934-418961	Cori	0171-493 7920
Burrill Productions	0171-736 8673	Corporate Vision	0171-734 2335
Buxton Films	0171-931 9875	Cosgrove Hall Productions	0161-881 9211
Cabachon Film Productions	0171-373 6543	Countrywide Films	01703-230286
Cafe Productions	0181-567 6655	Courtyard Productions	01732-700324
Caledonia, Sterne & Wyld	0141-353 3153	Covent Garden Pioneer FSP	0171-371 6191
Caledonian TV	01698-845522	Cowboy Films	0171-287 3808
Cambrensis	01222-813733	Creative Law	01732-460592
Cambridge Video	01223-553416	Crystalvision	0181-781 6444
Capron Productions	0181-871 5107	Csaky	0171-794 1574
Carlyle TV	0171-439 8967	CSL Films	0171-221 8318
Carnival Films	0181-968 1818	CST Productions	0117-923 7733
Carrie Britton	0181-969 5372	CTVC	0181-950 4426
Cartwn Cymru	01222-575999	Cyrus Productions	01444-415097
Case TV	0171-383 3845	**Dakota Films**	0171-287 4329
Catalyst TV	0171-603 7030	Dancelines Productions	0171-352 6261
Ceddo Film	0181-889 7654	Darlow Smithson Productions	0171-428 0270
Celador Productions	0171-240 8101	David Bellamy Associates	0191-386 4429
Celtic Films	0171-637 7651	David Wickes Productions	0171-225 1382
Celtic Productions	0171-221 2681	Day-Lewis Productions	01278-671334
Central Films	0171-486 6688	DBA Television	01232-231197
CFX	0171-734 3155	DBF Television	0171-232 0491
Chain Production	0171-937 1981	Deco Films & TV	0181-746 0448
Chameleon Television	0113-244 4486	Denham Productions	01752345444
Channel X	0171-436 2200	Dennis Woolf Productions	0161-442 8175
Chapman Clarke Films	0117-929 7744	DG Film & Video	0181-977 6677
Chapter One	0171-580 8636	Diamond Time	0171-433 3355
Charisma Films	0171-603 1164	Dibb Directions	0181-748 1579
Charlotte St Productions	0171-486 4478	Distant Horizon	0171-734 8690
Chatsworth Television	0171-734 4302	Diverse Production	0171-603 4567
Cheerleader Productions	0171 240 5389	Document Films	0171-437 4526
Children's Film/TV Foundation	0181-953 0844	Domaine	0171-437 3084
Children's Film Unit	0181-871 2006	Domino Films	0171-582 0393
Childsplay Productions	0171-328 1429	Double E Productions	0181-993 2394
Chistera Productions	01232-615573	Double Exposure	0171-490 2499

Double-Band Films	01232-243331	Fulmar Television and Film	0171-437 2222
Dove Productions	0171-262 0063	**Gabriel Productions**	01225-311194
Drama House	0171-388 9140	Gainsborough Productions	0171-409 1925
Dreamworld Productions	0191-438 4667	Gallus Besom Productions	0131-556 2429
Driftwood Films	0181-332 6365	Garfield Kennedy Co	0141-353 0456
Eala Bhan	01369-82319	General Entertainment	0171-221 3512
Earth Images Associates	0181-894 2262	Geofilms	01235-555422
Eastwest Productions	0181-964 3433	Glasgow Film Fund	0141-337 2526
Ecosse Films	0171-371 0290	Global Features	0171-937 1039
Eden Productions	0171-435 3242	Goldcrest Films & TV	0171-437 8696
Edinburgh Film	01968-672131	Goldhawk Film & TV	0171-284 2238
Edinburgh Film Worshop	0131-557 5242	Goldwyn Associates	0181-743 3223
Educational & TV Films	0171-226 2298	Granada Film	0171-734 8080
Educational Broadcasting	0171-765 5023	Granada LWT International	0171-620 1620
EFS TV Production	0181-950 8393	Grand Slam	0171-839 4646
Elephant Productions	01932-562611	Grant Naylor Productions	0171-412 0404
Elgin Productions	0171-727 9174	Grasshopper Productions	0171-229 1181
Ella Communications	0171-379 8449	Green Umbrella	0117-973 1729
Elmgate Productions	01932-562611	Greenpoint Films	0171-437 6492
Endboard Productions	0121-429 9779	Greg Angel (Film & TV)	01734-794607
English & Pockett	0171-287 1155	Greystoke Productions	0171-388 8561
English Channel	0171-494 1090	Griffin Productions	0171-636 5066
Enigma Productions	01753-630555	Gruber Brothers	01932-572274
Entertainment Film Production	0171-439 1606	**Half Way Production House**	0181-673 7926
Eolas	01851-705638	Hammer Film Productions	0181-207 4011
Eon Productions	0171-493 7953	Hand Pict Independent	0131-558 1543
EPA International	0171-267 9198	HandMade Films	0171-584 8345
Equal Media	01801-5268	Hardcourt Films	0171-267 0882
Esta's TV Company	0181-741 2843	Hartswood Films	0181-977 3252
Euan Lloyd Productions	01753-651700	Hasan Shah Films	0171-722 2419
Euston Films	0181-614 2800	Hat Trick Productions	0171-434 2451
Excalibur Productions	01422-843871	Hauer Rawlence Productions	0171-493 1022
Excelsior Group Productions	01737-812673	Havahall Pictures	0171-792 8318
Faction Films	0171-608 0654	Hawkshead	0171-255 2551
Fairwater Films	01222-640140	HD Thames	0181-614 2965
Felgate Productionst	0171-794 0909	Healthcare Productions	0171-267 8757
Festival Film & TV	01622-684546	Helen Langridge Associates	0171-833 2955
Figment Films	0171-602 7101	Hemdale Holdings	0171-724 1010
Film Four Productions	0171-794 6967	Hibbert Ralph Entertainment	0171-494 3011
FilmFair Animation	0171-935 1596	Hightimes Productions	0171-482 5202
Filmit	0171-738 4175	Hindi Picture	0171-284 3617
FilmNOVA	0191-222 0733	Holmes Associates	0171-637 8251
First Film Company	0171-439 1640	Horntvedt Associates	0171-731 8199
First Freedom Productions	0171-482 7307	Hot Shot Films	01232-313332
First Take	0171-328 8765	Hourglass Productions	0181-858 6870
Flamingo Pictures	0171-607 9958	Hummingbird Films	0117-923 8887
Flashback Productions	0171-727 9904	Humphrey Barclay Production	0171-482 1992
Flashback Television	0171-490 8996	Hyndland Television	0141-332 1005
Flying Brick Films	0171-249 7440	Hyphen Films	0171-734 0632
Flying Fox Films	01232-244811	**Iambic Productions**	0117-923 7222
Focus Films	0171-435 9004	Icon Films	0117-924 8535
Focus Productions	01753-831522	Illuminations (Television)	0171-226 0266
Forum Television	0117-974 1490	Illustra TV	0171-437 9611
Fourth Wall Productions	0171-437 2222	Images First	0181-579 6848
Freeway Films	0131-225 3200	Imagicians	0171-287 5211
Friday Productions	0171-730 0608	InCa	0181-748 0160
Front Page Films	0171-329 6866	Independent Image	0171-387 9525
Frontroom Films	0181-653 9343	Initial Film & Television	0181-741 4500
Fugitive Features	0171-383 4373	Insight Productions	01647-432686
Fulcrum Productions	0171-253 0353	Interesting Television	01564-783958

Intermedia	0115-950 5434	Medialab	0171-351 5814
International Broadcast Trust	0171-482 2847	Meditel Productions	0171-836 9216
Intrepid Film & TV	0171-736 8226	Melanie Chait Productions	0171-722 7903
InVision Productions	0171-371 2123	Mentorn Films	0171-287 4545
IPCA	0117-922 1342	Merchant Ivory Productions	0171-437 1200
IPH Westhall	0171-437 4055	Merlin Films	0191-264 1019
Isis Productions	0171-602 0959	Mersey Television	0151-722 9122
Island World Productions	0171-734 3536	Mersham Productions	0171-589 8829
Jacaranda Productions	0181-741 9088	Metrodome Films	0171-723 3494
Jane Balfour Films	0171-267 5392	Michael Cole Productions	0181-994 4821
Jane Walmsley Productions	0171-494 3061	Michael Hurll Television	0171-465 0103
Jim Henson Productions	0171-431 2818	Michael Weigall Productions	0171-229 5725
Jo Lustig	0171-937 6614	Michael White Productions	0171-839 3971
Jo Manuel Productions	0181-964 1888	Middlemarch Films	0171-229 0605
John Gau Productions	0181-788 8811	Midlantic Films Inc UK	0181-455 4481
Jon Blair Film Co	0171-287 1254	Mike Mansfield TV	0171-494 3061
Julian Seddon	0171-831 3033	Miracle Pictures	0181-960 7429
Juniper	0171-722 7111	Mirus Production	0181-740 5505
Just Television	0171-404 6744	Mixpix	0181-742 1188
Kai Productions	0181-673 4550	Mogul TV	01344-22140
Kazan River Productions	0181-893 3743	Molehill Productions	01703-615688
Kelso Films	0181-746 1566	Momentum Productions	0181-985 8823
Kilroy Television Company	0181-943 3555	Montage Films	0171-439 8113
King Rollo Films	01404-45218	Moore TV	0181-929 8339
Kohler	0171-734 4943	Mosaic Pictures	0171-437 3769
Kudos Productions	0171-287 0097	Moving Picture Productions	0171-434 3100
Lambeth Productions	0181-892 4477	Multilingual Productions	0171-820 9577
Landmark Productions	01962-734227	Music Box	0171-387 9808
Landseer Film & TV	0171-485 7333	Music House (International)	0171-434 9678
Langham Productions	0181-675 3326	**NCTV**	01224-283545
Lara Globus International	01594-530708	Nebraska Productions	0181-444 5317
Large Door	0171-439 1381	Nelvana Enterprises	0171-408 1734
Last Ditch TV	01986-892549	New Era Productions	0171-236 5532
Lauderdale Productions	0181-742 7852	New Media	0171-916 9999
Laurel Productions	0171-267 9399	Newsflash	0171-287 1616
Learning Media	0181-948 5166	NFH	0171-584 7561
Leda Serene	0171-733 2861	Nirvana Films	0171-439 8113
Lifetime Group	0171-387 9808	Noel Gay Television	0171-412 0400
Lightyears Films	0191-259 5408	North South Productions	0171-388 0351
Line TV	0171-792 8480	Northland Film Productions	01504-267616
Link Entertainment	0181-995 5080	Northlight Productions	01224-210007
Little Bird Co	0171-434 1131	Nub Television	0171-485 7132
Lityville Productions	0171-371 5940	NVC Arts	0171-388 3833
Living Tape Productions	0171-439 6301	**Observer Films**	0171-713 4343
Lochran Media	01851-703676	October Films	0171-916 7198
London Films	0171-323 5251	OG Films	01753-651700
Lucida Productions	0171-437 1140	Open Mind Productions	0171-437 0624
Lumiere Pictures	0171-413 0838	Orbit Films	0171-221 5548
Lusia Films	0171-240 2350	Orchid Productions	0171-379 0344
Luther Pendragon	0171-353 1500	Orlando TV Productions	01608-683218
Malachite Productions	01790-763538	Oxford Film Company	0171-483 3637
Malone Gill Productions	0171-287 3970	Oxford Independent Video	01865-250150
Manhattan Films	0171-581 2408	Oxford Scientific Films	0171-494 0720
Marble Arch Productions	0181-892 4477	**Pacesetter Productions**	01306-70433
Mark Forstater Productions	0181-964 1888	Palace Gate Productions	0171-584 3025
Mars Productions	0171-792 8584	Paladin Pictures	0181-740 1811
Marshall Healey Productions	0181-992 2666	Palindrome Productions	0181-659 4676
Martin Gates Productions	0171-486 9626	Panoptic Productions	0171-287 3931
Mary Evans Productions	0181-740 5319	Parallax Pictures	0171-836 1478
Maya Vision	0171-836 1113	Paramount British Pictures	0171-287 6767

Paramount Revcom	0171-636 5066	Richard Taylor Cartoon Films	0181-444 7547
Paravision	0171-351 7070	Richmond Films & TV	0171-734 9313
Partners in Production	0171-490 5042	Ritefilms	01303-252335
Partridge Films	0117-972 3777	Riverfront Pictures	0171-481 2939
Pathway Productions	0131-447 3531	RM Arts	0171-439 2637
Paul Berriff Productions	01482-641158	Roach & Partners	01753-650007
Pavilion International	0171-636 9421	Roadshow Productions	0171-584 0542
Pearl Catlin Associates	01483-67932	Rob Walker Productions	0181-964 3226
Pelicula Films	0141-945 3333	Robert Stigwood	0171-437 2512
Peninsula Films	0181-964 2304	Roberts & Wykeham Films	0171-602 4897
Pennies from Heaven	0171-580 3172	Rodney Read	0181-891 2875
Pentagon Communications	01482-226298	Roger Bolton Productions	0171-636 4330
Penumbra Productions	0171-328 4550	Rose Bay Film Productions	0171-412 0400
Persistent Vision	0171-639 5596	Rosso Productions	0171-281 4709
Persona Films	01222-231680	Saffron Productions	01440-785200
Peter Batty Productions	0181-942 6304	Samuelson Productions	0171-236 5532
PHI Television	0171-351 4160	Sands Films	0171-231 2209
Photoplay Productions	0171-722 2500	Sankofa Film & Video	0171-485 0848
Picture Music International	0171-486 4488	Sarah Radclyffe Productions	0171-911 6100
Picture Palace Films	0171-734 6630	Saturn Films	0171-284 4104
Picture Parade	0181-964 1500	Scala Productions	0171-734 7060
Pictures of Women	0171-249 9632	Science Pictures	01462-421110
Pineapple Productions	0171-323 3939	Scimitar Films	0171-603 7272
Piranha Productions	0171-607 3355	Scorer Associates	0117-946 6838
Planet 24	0171-712 9300	Scottish Film Production Fund	0141-337 2526
Platinum Film & TV	0171-267 9947	Scottish TV E	01825-712034
Portman Productions	0171-224 3344	Screen Ventures	0171-580 7448
Portobello Pictures	0171-379 5566	Screenlife	0181-878 7826
Poseidon Productions	0171-734 4441	See More Productions	0171-434 9869
Pozzitive	0171-734 3258	SelecTV	0171-355 2868
Praxis Films	01472-398547	September Films	0171-494 1884
Premiere Productions	0181-785 2933	Sered Films	0171-286 3655
Pretium	0171-636 0366	Sevenday Productions	0171-798 4498
Primal Pictures	0181-348 4161	Seventh Art Productions	01273-777678
Primetime Television	0171-935 9000	Seventh House Films	01603-749068
Principal Film Company	0171-494 4348	SFTV	0181-780 0678
Producers Creative Partnership	0171-439 1966	Shadowlands Productions	0181-892 4477
Projectile Productions	0171-609 3873	Shepperton Productions	01932-562611
Prometheus Productions	01768-898334	Shoebox Productions	0181-747 8747
Prominent Features & TV	0171-284 0242	Shooting Star	0171-409 1925
Propeller Productions	01222-377128	Sindibad Films	0171-499 2424
Prospect Cymru Wales	01222-667444	Siriol Productions	01222-488400
Prospect Pictures	0171-636 1234	Skreba	0171-437 6492
Psychology News	0171-404 8648	Skyline TV Productions	0171-631 4649
Ragdoll Productions	01789-262772	Smith & Watson Productions	01803-863033
Rapide Productions	0171-371 1777	Soho Communications	0171-637 5825
Rapido TV	0171-229 9854	Songbird Film Productions	0171-586 9656
Ray Fitzwalter Associates	0161-832 3337	Soul Purpose Productions	0181-960 7987
Real Life Productions	0113-234 7271	South Productions	0171-240 4565
Really Useful Picture Co	0171-240 0880	Spafax	0171-706 4488
Recorded Picture Co	0171-439 0607	Specific Films	0171-580 7476
Red Flannel Films	01222-229239	Speedy Films	0171-437 9313
Red Rooster Film	0171-379 7727	Spidercom Films	0171-287 5589
Red Snapper Productions	0171-287 3267	Spitting Image Productions	0171-375 1561
Redwing Film Co	0171-734 6642	Spoken Image (Broadcast)	0161-236 7522
Reg Grundy Productions	0171-928 8942	St Pancras Films	0171-631 0163
Regent Productions	0181-789 5350	Stagescreen Productions	0171-497 2510
Remote Films	0171-738 2727	Stand & Deliver Productions	0171-255 2755
Renegade Films	0171-732 6922	State Screen Productions	0181-961 1717
Replay	01276-857040	Steel Bank Films	0114-272 1235

Stephens Kerr	0171-916 2124	**UBA**	0171-402 6313
Straight Forward Film & TV	01232-427697	Uden Associates	0171-351 1255
Strawberry Vale Film & TV	0181-747 4783	Unicorn Organisation	0171-229 5131
Studio Nine	0121-444 4750	Unicorn Productions	0181-748 2149
Studio Z	01622-684544	Union Pictures	0171-287 5110
Supervision (West)	01403-274488	United Television Artists	0171-287 2727
Swanlind Communication	0121-616 1701	Vanson Wardle Productions	0171-223 1919
Taft TV Associates	0171-223 0906	Victoria Real	01903-851243
Talbot Television	0171-284 0880	Video Visuals	0171-731 0079
Talisman Films	0171-603 7474	Videotel Productions	0171-439 6301
Talkback	0171-631 3940	Visage Productions	0171-487 2641
Tartan TV	0171-323 3022	Vision Group	0171-431 9153
Telegram	0171-483 3031	Visual Music	01222-641511
Telemagination	0171-828 5331	Viz	01383-412811
Television History Workshop	0171-405 6627	Volcano Films	0171-600 0481
Television Sport & Leisure	0171-820 0700	**Wall to Wall Television**	0171-485 7424
Teliesyn	01222-667556	Walnut Partnership	0113-245 6913
Tempest Films	0181-340 0877	Wark, Clements & Co	0141-339 6087
Tern Television Productions	01224-631000	Warner Sisters Film	0171-836 0134
Testimony Films	0117-925 8589	Waterfront Productions	0191-261 0162
Thames	0181-614 2800	Waterloo Films	0171-494 4060
The Comedy House	0171-437 4551	Watershed TV	0117-973 3833
The Filmworks	0181-741 5631	Waterside Productions	0121-633 3545
The Grade Company	0171-409 1925	Westbourne Films	0171-221 1998
The Ideas Factory	0161-406 6685	White City Films	0181-994 6795
The Television Company	0171-354 3414	Wide Vision Productions	0171-439 4177
Third Eye Productions	0181-969 8211	Wilcox Bulmer Productions	0171-602 9811
Tiger Aspect	0171-434 0672	Wild & Fresh Productions	0171-609 6465
Tiger Bay Productions	01222-492321	Wildcard	01752-262968
Tigervision	0171-383 2267	Windfall Films	0171-379 5993
Time & Light Productions	0181-692 0145	Woodfilm Productions	0171-243 8600
TKO Communications	01273-550088	Word-Pictures	01494-481629
Topaz Productions	0181-749 2619	Workhouse TV	01962-863449
Topical TV	01703-712233	Working Title Films	0171-911 6100
Touch Productions	0171-287 5520	World Film Services	0171-734 3536
Trade Films	0191-477 5532	World Wide International TV	0171-434 1121
Trans World International	0181-233 5400	Worldmark Productions	0181-960 3251
TransAtlantic Films	0171-727 0132	WTTV	0171-911 6100
Triple Vision	0171-388 5375	XYTV	0113-237 1199
TV Cartoons	0171-388 2222	Year 200 Productions	01253-395403
TV Choice	0171-379 0873	Yo Yo Films	0171-735 3711
TV21	0171-734 7067	Yorkshire Film Co	0113-244 1224
Twentieth Century Vixen	0171-359 7368	ZED	0171-494 3181
Twenty Twenty Television	0171-284 2020	Zenith North	0191-261 0077
Two Four Productions	01752-406922	Zenith Productions	0171-224 2440
Ty Gwyn Films	01286-881235	Zooid Pictures	0171-281 2407
Tyburn Productions	01753-651700	Zoom Production Co	0171-434 3895

RADIO

As with TV, British radio is divided between the non-commercial BBC and the profit making independents. Again like TV, radio is governed by legislation designed to stimulate the independent sector. For radio, the 1990 Broadcasting Act Act replaced a tight regulatory system with a "lighter touch" which, crucially, removed obligations to provide such a wide range of programmes. Expansion was further aided by making local radio licences easier to obtain, and by permitting the start of the three new national channels and five regional ones which are listed in the Independent Radio section in the following pages.

Further commercial liberalisation is following the government's Media Ownership green paper. It said there was an immediate need to relax radio ownership rules by raising the limit on holding radio licences from 20 to 35. Previous restrictions on television companies owning radio stations will be abolished by legislation in 1996, except in areas of significant population overlap.

There are currently some 180 commercial radio stations. Figures released in mid 1995 by the Radio Advertising Bureau supported its claim that commercial radio was "the fastest growing advertising medium for the second year running". In 1994 advertising revenue was £220.1 million, up from £178.3 million in 1993. This amounts to 3.8 per cent of the total national display advertising market of £5.8 billion. Small wonder that newcomers crowd in and that established companies declare record profits. Fewer restrictions in a profitable market inevitably stimulate takeover bids, notably with Emap taking over Metro Radio and GWR paying £21 million for Chiltern Radio.

Radio's money-politicing now belongs on the financial pages. Another result of the expansion is that the airwaves are filled with ever more middle of the road pop in a limbo where the word "gold" is used to distinguish old dross from the new. When the British Media Industry Group came to calculate radio influence · what it called "share of the national voice" · it estimated that radio was precisely half as influential as TV or newspapers. "This," explained the BMIG, "is because of radio's perceived lower impact on diversity of view issues caused by, for example, the prevalence of music-based radio formats. In other words, 1 per cent of newspaper circulation or TV viewing is deemed to have more impact on diversity of view issues than 1 per cent of radio listening."

The government goes along with this novel numerological approach. The Radio Authority, though delighted at most of the green paper's contents, felt a sleight to its sense of importance and argued "there are some areas which need clarification, for instance, the calculation of the share of total voice".

Tuning in

UK radio is broadcast in four wavebands:
Short Wave (SW) 3956 KHz · 26.1 MHz
Medium Wave (MW) 525 KHz · 1605 KHz
Long Wave (LW) 148.5 KHz · 283.5 KHz
VHF/FM88 MHz · 105 MHz

Listening figures

All BBC	27.90m	47.9%
BBC Radio 1	11.06m	11.7%
BBC Radio 2	8.43m	12%
BBC Radio 3	2.39m	1%
BBC Radio 4	8.39m	10.4%
BBC Radio 5 Live	4.98m	2.9%
All Commercial	28.64m	50.1%
Classic FM	4.75m	2.9%
Virgin 252	3.53m	3.2%
Talk Radio UK	2.07m	1.4%
Atlantic 252	4.6m	3.8%

Source: Rajar, 27 March to 25 June 1995. Figures show the number of adults who listen to a station for at least five minutes in the course of an average week. Percentages show the share of listening time per station.

Tuning in to FM

88.1 · 90.2	BBC Radio 2
90.3 · 92.4	BBC Radio 3
92.5 · 95.9	BBC Radio 4
93.1 · 95.4	BBC Radio Ulster
94.6 · 96.1	BBC local radio
96.1 · 97.6	Independent local
97.7 · 99.8	BBC Radio 1
99.8 · 102	Independent nat.
99.9 · 101.9	Classic FM
102 · 103.5	Independent local
103.5 · 105	BBC local radio.
103.6 · 104.9	Radio 4 (in parts of Wales and Scotland)
105 · 108	Up to 33 new locals

The Radio Listener's Guide has fuller details of local frequency variations. Its publisher is PDQ Publishing (01865-820387).

BBC RADIO

Nineteen ninety four was a stinker of year for BBC Radio. In the three months to Christmas its share of the national listening audience fell beneath the psychological barrier of 50 per cent. It therefore dipped under what had once been generally accepted as justifying funding by licence fee. But what is deemed acceptable changes with time and even laissez faire Visigoths didn't complain when the BBC said its lower ratings were an inevitable consequence of it being in a deregulated market.

There were many changes during BBC Radio's traumatic year. Radio 1 cleared out its elderly DJs; Radio 2 chugged on; Radio 3 went for new listeners with an oldies' guide to rap; Radio 4 dumped the unfortunate Gerry Anderson and messed up Gardener's Question Time; and Radio 5 dispensed with its education brief, became Radio 5 Live and recast itself as the news and sporty Radio Bloke.

Nineteen ninety five has sounded better. Radio 4's Today programme remains the institutionalised slot where politicians prefer to repeat their soundbites. The BBC has concentrated its drive for higher ratings on Radio 1 which has lost five million listeners during the past two years. The new controller, Matthew Bannister, hired a PR firm to spruce up the image, spent £2 million on advertising and £500,000 on an eight month contract securing Chris Evans' morning DJ-ing services. The payoff came by June with 500,000 listeners returning to the station.

The received wisdom is that Radio 1 always was a naff replacement for the sixties pirate stations. There's a counter-intuitive line which starts from the statistic that Radio 1's eleven million listeners make it by far and away Britain's most popular station. Popular *and* good according to George Michael who says Radio 1's eclectic approach to pop has been responsible for the multiracial sound of English bands. The contrast must be made with American stations which segment audiences by race as well as age and class.

From September 1995 the five national BBC radio services will also be broadcast in digital form. Digital audio broadcasting gives CD-quality reception and reduces the pressure on overcrowded frequencies. More a marker for the future than a way of grabbing back a majority slice of the audience, the new service demands that listeners buy new receivers costing several hundred pounds. Transmission will reach 60 per cent of Britain within four years of launch.

International radio

The BBC World Service broadcasts radio in English and 38 other languages. News bulletins, current affairs, political commentaries and magazine programmes are supplemented by sports, music, drama and general entertainment. Regular listeners are estimated at 130 million, twice as many as the nearest competitor. News bulletins and some other programmes are rebroadcast by some 900 radio and cable stations in 100 countries.

BBC World Service - HQ
Bush House, The Strand, London WC2B 4PH.
Publicity Office   0171-257 2941
Chairman: Bob Phillis
Managing director: Sam Younger
Resources controller: Barry Whitehall

BBC Monitoring
Caversham Park, Reading, Berks RG4 8TZ
Fax 01734 463823   Tel 01734 469289
BBC Monitoring reports on foreign broadcasts to the BBC and the government. This information is also sold to the press, businesses, academic staff and public bodies.

BBC national radio

BBC Network Radio
Broadcasting House, Portland Place, London W1A 1AA
Publicity Office: 0171-765 2265
Managing director: Liz Forgan

Radio 1
Publicity office: 0171-765 4575
Controller: Matthew Bannister

Radio 2
Publicity office: 0171-765 5712
Controller : Frances Line

Radio 3
Publicity office: 0171-765 4934
Controller: Nicholas Kenyon

Radio 4
Publicity office: 0171-765 5337
Controller: Michael Green

Radio 5 Live
Publicity office: 0171-765 2139
Controller: Jenny Abramsky

BBC local radio: South

BBC Radio Berkshire
42a Portman Road, Reading, Berks RG3 1NB
Fax 01734-503393:   Tel 01734-567056

BBC Radio Bristol
PO Box 194, Bristol BS99 7QT
Fax 0117-973 2549   Tel 0117-974 1111

BBC Radio Cornwall
Phoenix Wharf, Truro, Cornwall TR1 1UA
Fax 01872-75045   Tel 01872-75421

BBC Radio Devon
Broadcasting Hosue, Seymout Road,
Mannamead, Plymouth, Devon PL3 5DB
          Tel 01752-260323

BBC Radio Gloucestershire
London Road, Gloucester GL1 1SW
Fax 01452-309491   Tel 01452-308585

BBC Radio Guernsey
Commerce House, Les Banques, St Peter Port,
Guernsey, Channel Islands
Fax 01481-713557   Tel 01481-728977

BBC Radio Jersey
18 Parade Road, St Helier, Jersey, Channel
Islands.
Fax 01534-32569   Tel 01534-870000

BBC Radio Kent
Sun Pier, Chatham, Kent ME4 4EZ
Fax 01634-830573   Tel 01634-830505

BBC Radio Oxford
269 Banbury Road, Summertown, Oxford
OX2 7DW
Fax 01865-311996   Tel 01865-311444

BBC Radio Solent
Broadcasting House, Havelock Road,
Southampton, Hants SO1 7PW
Fax 01703-339648   Tel 01703-631311

Dorset FM
PO Box 900, Portfolio House, Princes Street,
Dorchester DT1 1TP
Fax 01305-250910   Tel 01305-269654
Off-shoot of BBC Radio Devon.

GLR (Greater London Radio)
35c Marylebone High Street, London W1A 4LG
Fax 0171-487 2908   Tel 0171-224 2424

Somerset Sound
14 Paul Street, Taunton, Somerset TA1 3PF
Fax 01823-332539   Tel 01823-252437

Southern Counties Radio
Broadcasting House, Guildford, Surrey
GU2 5AP
Fax 01483-304952   Tel 01483-306306

Wiltshire Sound
56 Prospect Place, Swindon, Wilts SN1 3RW
Fax 01793-513650   Tel 01793-513626

Midlands and East

BBC CWR
25 Warwick Road, Coventry, West Midlands
CV1 2WR
Fax 01203-520080   Tel 01203-559911

BBC Radio Cambridgeshire
104 Hills Road, Cambridge CB2 1LD
Fax 01223-460832   Tel 01223-259696

BBC Radio Derby
PO Box 269, 56 St Helens Street, Derby DE1
3HL
Fax 01332-290794   Tel 01332-361111

BBC Radio Essex
198 New London Road, Chelmsford, Essex
CM2 9XB
Fax 01245-492983   Tel 01245-262393

BBC Hereford & Worcester
Hylton Road, Worcester WR2 5WW
Fax 01905-748006   Tel 01905-748485
43 Broad Steet, Hereford HR4 9HH
Fax 01432-356446   Tel 01432-355252

BBC Radio Leicester
Epic House, Charles Street, Leicester LE1
3SH
Fax 0116-251 1463   Tel 0116-251 6688

BBC Radio Lincolnshire
PO Box 219, Radion Buildings, Newport, Lincoln
LN1 3XY
Fax 01522-511058   Tel 01522-511411

BBC Radio Norfolk
Norfolk Tower, Surrey Street, Norwich, Norfolk
NR1 3PA
Fax 01603-633692   Tel 01603-617411

BBC Radio Northampton
Abington Street, Northampton NN1 2BE
Fax 01604-230709   Tel 01604-239100

BBC Radio Nottingham
York House, Mansfield Road, Nottingham NG1
3HZ
Fax 0115-948 1482   Tel 0115-955 0500

BBC Radio Shropshire
PO Box 397, 2 Boscobel Drive, Shrewsbury,
Shropshire SY1 3TT
Fax 01743-271702   Tel 01743-248484

BBC Radio Stoke
Conway House, Cheapside, Hanley, Stoke-on-
Trent, Staffs ST1 1JJ
Fax 01782-289115   Tel 01782-208080

BBC Radio Suffolk
Broadcasting House, St Matthews Street,
Ipswich, Suffolk IP1 3EP
Fax 01473-210887   Tel 01473-250000

BBC Three Counties Radio
PO Box 3CR, Hastings Street, Luton,
Bedfordshire LU1 5XL
Fax 01582-401467   Tel 01582-459111
Covers Beds, Herts and Bucks.

BBC Radio WM
PO Box 206, Broadcasting Centre, Pebble Mill
Road, Birmingham B5 7SD
Fax 0121-472 3174   Tel 0121-414 8484

BBC local radio: North

GMR (Greater Manchester Radio)
PO Box 951, New Broadcasting House, Oxford
Road, Manchester M60 1SJ
Fax 0161-236 5804   Tel 0161-200 2000

BBC Radio Cleveland
PO Box 95FM, Broadcasting House, Newport
Road, Middlesbrough, Cleveland TS1 5DG
Fax 01642-211356   Tel 01642-225211

BBC Radio Cumbria
Annetwell Street, Carlisle, Cumbria
CA3 8BB
Fax 01228-511195   Tel 01228-592444

BBC Radio Cumbria, Furness Service
Broadcasting House, Hartington Street, Barrow-
in-Furness, Cumbria LA14 5FH
Fax 01229-870008   Tel 01229-836767
Local service opting out of BBC Radio Cumbria.

BBC Radio Humberside
9 Chapel Street, Hull, North Humberside HU1
3NU
Fax 01482-226409   Tel 01482-23232

BBC Radio Lancashire
20 Darwen Street, Blackburn, Lancashire BB2
2EA
Fax 01254-680821   Tel 01254-262411

BBC Radio Leeds
Broadcasting House, Woodhouse Lane, Leeds,
West Yorks LS2 9PN
Fax 0113-242 0652   Tel 0113-244 2131

BBC Radio Merseyside
55 Paradise Street, Liverpool L1 3BP
Fax 0151-708 5356   Tel 0151-708 5500

BBC Radio Newcastle
Barrack Road, Newcastle-upon-Tyne NE99 1RN
Fax 0191-232 5082   Tel 0191-232 4141

BBC Radio Sheffield
Ashdell Grove, 60 Westbourne Road, Sheffield
South Yorks S10 2QU
Fax 0114-266 4375   Tel 0114-268 6185

BBC Radio York
20 Bootham Row, York, North Yorks YO3 7BR
Fax 01904-610937   Tel 01904-641351

Wales, Scotland & N Ireland

BBC Radio Wales: National HQ
Broadcasting House, Llantrisant Road, Llandaff,
Cardiff CF5 2YQ
Fax 01222-552973   Tel 01222-572888
Editor Radio Wales: Gaynor Vaughan-Jones

Radio Clwyd
The Old School House, Glanrafon Road, Mold,
Clwyd CH7 1PA
Fax 01352 759821   Tel 01352 700367

Radio Gwent
Powys House, Cwmbran,Gwent NP44 1YF
                        Tel 016333 872727

BBC Radio Scotland: National HQ
Broadcasting House, Queen Margaret Drive,
Glasgow G12 8DG
Fax 0141-334 0614   Tel 0141-330 8844
Head of Radio: James Boyle

Radio nan Gaidheal
Clydesdale Bank Buildings, Portree, Skye IV51
9EH
Fax 01478-2792   Tel 01478-612005

BBC Radio Northern Ireland: National HQ
Broadcasting House, Ormeau Ave, Belfast
BT2 8HQ
Fax 01232-338800   Tel 01232-338000
Controller: Robin Walsh.

BBC Radio Foyle
8 Northland Road, Derry BT48 7NE
Fax 01504-260067   Tel 01504-262244

INDEPENDENT RADIO

The Radio Authority was set up by the 1990 Broadcasting Act to take over from the Independent Broadcasting Authority. It has three main tasks: planning frequencies; awarding licences; and regulating via obligatory codes covering programmes, advertising, sponsorship and engineering.

The Radio Authority has issued three national licences, five regional licences, 47 new local licences and over 900 restricted service licences for temporary low-powered stations. In 1994 the authority granted 262 licences allowing stations to broadcast for 28 days covering a town or a two mile radius in a city. By September 1995 the authority completed the re-advertisement of the 125 existing licences which were originally awarded by the IBA. Despite the officially sanctioned activity, illegal pirate stations still go on air. In 1994 the Radio Investigation Service of the Department of Trade and Industry carried out 570 raids on 164 pirate stations. The raids resulted in 61 prosecutions, all of which brought a conviction.

From Autumn 1995, the Radio Authority began advertising licences for stations to use the FM frequencies between 105 and 108 MHz. Around two licences a month will be on offer and, on this basis, the allocation process will take 18 months. Community radio hopes to be a major beneficiary with over a hundred groups wanting to run non-profit making local stations. Only a small number of community stations have long licences at present, because they received no special treatment in the 1990 Broadcasting Act. There are over 100 groups around the country seeking a chance to start.

Commercially, the future of independent radio seems assured with predictions that by the end of the decade it will be attracting 5 per cent of total national advertising budgets and 56 per cent of listeners.

Radio Authority
Holbrook House, 14 Great Queen St, Holborn, London WC2 5DG.
Fax 0171-405 7064   Tel 0171-430 2724
Chairman: Sir Peter Gibbings
Deputy chairman: Michael Moriarty
Chief executive: Tony Stoller
Head of development: David Vick
Head of finance: Neil Romain
Press officer: Tracey Mullins

Independent National Radio

Until 1992 the only national radio channels belonged to the BBC. The Broadcasting Act changed all that and gave the Radio Authority power to issue licenses for three new Independent National Radio (INR) networks. Only INR1 could be on an FM frequency and the other two had to be on AM. The Act also said that INR1 should concentrate "wholly or mainly, in the broadcasting of music which ... is not pop music" and that the first AM service could offer any programming that did not duplicate INR1. INR3 would have to be primarily speech-based. Hence the arrivals of Classic FM, Virgin 1215 and, since February 1995, Talk Radio UK.

Classic FM's populist alternative to Radio 3 has earned it twice the audience and, given its programming of light classics, the unlikely status of being the country's largest commercial station. Virgin, despite the disadvantage of broadcasting on AM, gets hefty audiences for its diet of adult rock. The mild shock about Talk Radio and its over-hyped shock jocks, is that relatively few have tuned in to be shocked or even amused. The most interesting talk from Talk Radio has been about who will be replacing the next bunch of departing executives.

Classic FM - INR1
24 Oval Rd, London NW1 7DJ.
Fax 0171-713 2630   Tel 0171-284 3000

Virgin 1215 - INR2
1 Golden Square, London W1R 4DJ.
Fax 0171-434 1197   Tel 0171-434 1215

Talk Radio UK - INR3
76 Oxford Strfeet, London W1N 0TR
Fax 0171-636 1053   Tel 0171-636 1089

Atlantic 252
Mornington House, Trim, County Meath
Fax 010-353 4636688   Tel 010-353 4636655
Atlantic 252 broadcasts from across the Irish Sea in Southern Ireland. It operates without a British government licence, but is effectively a national station due to a 10 per cent national audience share garnered from two-thirds of the UK, north and west of a line from the Wash to Dorset.
Dial: 252 LW

Local radio: main owners

Capital Radio
Euston Tower, Euston Road, London NW1 3DR
Fax 0171-387 2345   Tel 0171-608 6080
Subsidiaries: Midland Radio plc, Southern Radio
plc, 50% of West Country Broadcasting.
Stations: BRMB-FM, Capital FM, Capital Gold,Invicta FM,
Invicta Supergold, Ocean FM, Power FM, S Coast, Southern FM.

Chiltern Radio Network
Chiltern Road, Dunstable, Beds LU6 1HQ
Fax 01582-661725   Tel 01582-666001
Shareholders: The GWR Group bought 63% of the shares in July
1995.
Stations: Chiltern, Chiltern Supergold, Galaxy, Horizon,
Northants, Northants Supergold, Severn Sound/Supergold.

Emap Radio
127-131 The Piazza, Manchester M1 4AW
Fax 0161-228 1503   Tel 0161-236 9913
Shares: Emap owns over 50% of Radio City (Sound of
Merseyside), 19% of East Anglian Radio and 10% of Essex
Radio.
Stations: Kiss 100 FM, Key 103FM, Piccadilly Gold, Radio Aire
FM, Magic 828 AM, Red Dragon FM, Touch AM, Red Rose.

GWR Group
PO Box 2000, Swindon, Wiltshire SN4 7EX
Fax 01793-853929   Tel 01793-440300
Subsidiaries: Mid-Anglia Radio . Chiltern Radio Network
Stations: Beacon, Brunel Classic Gold, CN FM, Gem-AM, GWR
FM, Hereward, Isle of Wight, KL FM, Leicester Sound, Mercia
FM/Classic Gold, Ram FM, 1332, Trent FM, 2CR FM/Classic
Gold, 210 FM/Classic Gold, WABC.

Metro Radio Group
Long Rigg, Newcastle-upon-Tyne, NE99 1BB
Fax 0191-496 0174   Tel 0191-488 3131
Stations: Hallam FM, Great North, Great York-shire, Metro FM,
The Pulse, TFM, Viking FM.

Scottish Radio Holdings
Clydebank Business Park, Glasgow G81 2RX
Fax 0141-306 2265   Tel 0141-306 2200
Stations: Clyde 1 FM, Clyde 2, Forth RFM, Max AM, Tay,
Northsound, Borders 51%, Carlisle 40%, Moray Firth 30%.

Sunrise Radio Group
Sunrise House, Southall, Middlesex UB2 4AV
Fax 0181-813 9800   Tel 0181-574 6666
Stations: Sunrise, Sunrise East Midlands, Sunrise FM.

Trans World Communications
130 Broadway, Salford, Manchester M5 2UW
Fax 0161-848 9255   Tel 0161-848 9055
Shareholders: Emap increased its shareholding to over 51% in
August 1994, making it the owner; Guardian Media Group 20%.
Stations: Aire FM, Magic 828, Piccadilly Gold/Key 103, Red
Dragon FM, Red Rose Gold/Rock FM, Touch AM.

Regional radio

The Radio Authority has granted five regional
radio licences with the stipulation that the
stations should "broaden the range of audience
choice". They therefore steer clear of straight
pop which goes some way to explaining why
none has as large an audience as the biggest
London local stations.

Century Radio
Century House, PO Box 100, Gateshead NE8
2YY
Fax 0191-477 5660   Tel 0191-47 6666
Parent company: Border Media
Policy: Speech, easy listening and country music.
Starting date: 1.9.94
Area: North East
Dial: 100.7, 101.8 & 96.2 MHz

Galaxy Radio
The Broadcast Centre, Portland Square, Bristol
BS2 8RZ
Fax 0117-924 5589   Tel 0117-924 0111
Parent company: Chiltern Radio Network
Policy: Classic and contemporary dance music, regional news
and information.
Starting date: 4.9.94
Area: Severn eastuary
Dial: 101 MHz & 97.2 MHz

Heart FM
1 The Square, 111 Broad Street, Birmingham
B15 1AS
Fax 0121-696 1007   Tel 0121-626 1007
Parent company: Chrysalis Group
Policy: Soft adult contemporary music
Starting date: 7.9.94
Area: West midlands
Dial: 100.7 MHz

JFM 100.4
The World Trade Centre, Exchange Quay,
Manchester M5 3EJ
Fax 0161-877 1005   Tel 0161-877 1004
Parent company: Golden Rose Communications
Policy: Jazz, blues, R&B and soul, international, national and
regional news.
Area: The north west
Dial: 100.4 MHz

Scot FM
Number 1 Shed, Albert Quay,
Leith EH6 7DN
Fax 0131-554 2266   Tel 0131-554 6677
Starting date: 16.9.94
Policy: Speech and adult contemporary music
Area: Central Scotland
Dial: 100.3 & 101.1 MHz

Local radio

A1 FM
34 Carmel Road, Darlington DL 38DJ
Tel 01325-467558
Starting date: to be advised
Area: Darlington and Newton Aycliffe. Dial: 103.2 MHz

The Bay
PO Box 969, Street George's Quay, Lancaster,
Lancs LA1 3LD
Fax 01524-848787   Tel 01524-848747
Starting date: 1.3.93
Area: Morecambe, S Lakeland. Dial: 96.9, 102.3 & 103.2 MHz

Beacon/WABC
267 Tettenhall Road, Wolverhampton, West
Midlands WV6 0DQ
Fax 01902-7755163   Tel 01902-757211
Parent company: GWR Group
Starting date: 12.4.76; Shrewsbury & Telford 14.7.87
Area: Wolverhampton & Black Country, Shrewsbury & Telford
Dial: 97.2 & 103.1 MHz

Borders
Tweedside Park, Galashiels, Borders TD1 3TD
Fax 01896-759494   Tel 01896-759444
Parent company: Scottish Radio Holdings
Starting date: 22.1.90
Area: Scottish Borders. Dial: 96.8, 97.5 & 103.4 MHz

Boss 603
Churchill Studios, Churchill Road, Cheltenham,
Glos GL53 7EP
Fax 01242-228938   Tel 01242-255023
Starting date: 3.3.93
Area: Cheltenham. Dial:603 kHz

Breeze AM/Essex
Radio House, Clifftown Road, Southend-on-Sea,
Essex SS1 1SX
Fax 01702-345224   Tel 01702-333711
Parent company: Essex Radio
Starting date: 16.7.89
Dial: 1431 kHz (Southend), 1359 kHz (Chelmsford)

96.4 BRMB
Aston Road North, Birmingham B6 4BX
Fax 0121-359 1117   Tel 0121-359 4481
Parent company: Capital Radio
Starting date: 19.2.74
Area: Birmingham. Dial: 96.4 MHz

Broadland
47 Colegate, Norwich, Norfolk NR3 1DB
Fax 01603-666353   Tel 01603-630621
Parent company: East Anglian Radio. Group
Starting date: 1.10.84
Area: Norwich and Great Yarmouth. Dial:102.4 MHz, 1152kHz

Brunel Classic Gold
PO Box 2020, Bristol BS99 7SN
Fax: 0117-983 3202   Tel 0117-983 3201
Parent company: GWR Group
Starting date: 25.11.88
Dial: 1260 kHz (Bristol), 936 kHz (west Wilts), 1161 kHz
(Swindon)

Capital FM/Capital Gold
Euston Tower, Euston Road, London NW1 3DR
Fax 0171-387 2345   Tel 0171-608 6080
Parent company: Capital Radio
Starting date: 16.10.73 (Capital FM), 28.11.88 (Capital Gold)
Area: London. Dial: 95.8 MHz (Capital FM), 1548 kHz (Capital
Gold)

Central FM
Kerse Road, Stirling, Central Scotland FK7 7YJ
Fax 01786-461883   Tel 01786-451188
Starting date: 4.6.90
Area: Stirling an Falkirk. Dial: 103.1 MHz

Ceredigion
Yr Hen Ysgol Gymraeg, Ffordd Alexandra,
Aberystwyth, Dyfed SY23 1LF
Fax 01970-627206   Tel 01970-627999
Bilingual community station
Starting date: 14.12.92
Area: Ceredigion. Dial: 103.3 & 96.6 MHz

CFM
PO Box 964, Carlisle, Cumbria CA1 3NG
Fax 01228-818444   Tel 01228-818964
Starting date: 14.4.93
Area: Carlisle. Dial: 96.4 (Penrith), 102.5 MHz

Channel 103 FM
6 Tunnel Street, St Helier, Jersey, Channel
Islands JE2 4LU
Fax 01534-887799   Tel 01534-888103
Starting date: 25.10.92
Area: Jersey. Dial: 103.7 MHz

Channel Travel Radio
PO Box 2000, Folkestone, Kent CT18 8XY
Fax 01303-272292   Tel 10303-272222
Starting date: 20.4.95
Area: along the M20 towards the Kent Channel ports

**Chiltern Radio/Chiltern Radio East/ Chiltern
Radio SuperGold/Chiltern Radio SuperGold
East**
Chiltern Road, Dunstable, Beds LU6 1HQ
Fax 01582-661725   Tel 01582-666001
Parent company: Chiltern Radio Network
Starting dates: 15.10.81 (Chiltern Radio), 1.3.82 (Chiltern East),
15.7.90 (Chiltern Radio SuperGold, 15.7.90 (SuperGold East)
Area: Bedford, Luton. Dial: 97.6 MHz (Chiltern Radio), 96.9 MHz
(Chiltern Radio East), 828 kHz (Chiltern Radio SuperGold), 792
kHz (Chiltern Radio SuperGold East).

Choice FM
16 Trinity Gardens, London SW9 8DP
Fax 0171-738 6619   Tel 0171-738 7969
Starting date: 31.3.90
Area: Brixton. Dial: 96.9 MHz

Choice FM - Birmingham
95 Broad Street, Birmingham B15 1AU
Fax 0121-616 1011   Tel 0121-616 1000
Starting date: 1.1.95
Area: Birmingham. Dial: 102.2 MHz

City FM
8-10 Stanley Street, Liverpool LI 6AF
Fax 0151-471 0330   Tel 0151-227 5100
Parent company: Emap
Starting date: 21.10.74
Area: Merseyside. Dial: 96.7 MHz

Classic Gold 1332
PO Box 2020, Queensgate Centre, Peterborough
PE1 1LL
Fax 01733-28145   Tel 01733-460460
Parent company: GWR Group
Starting date: 14.4.92
Area: Peterborough. Dial: 1332 kHz

Classic Gold 1431
PO Box 210, Reading, Berks RG31 7RZ
Tel 01734-254456   Tel 01734-254400
Parent company: GWR Group
Starting date: 8.3.76
Area: Reading. Dial: 1431 kHz

Clyde 1 / Clyde 2
Clydebank Business Park, Glasgow G81 2RX
Fax 0141-306 2265   Tel 0141-306 2200
Parent company: Scottish Radio Holdings
Starting date: 31.12.73
Dial: Clyde 1, 102.5 MHz (Glasgow), 97.0 MHz (Vale of Leven), 103.3 MHz (Firth of Clyde). Clyde 2, 1152 kHz

Coast FM
41 Conway Road, Colwyn Bay, Clwyd
Fax 01492-535248   Tel 01492-534555
Starting date: 27.8.93
Area: north Wales coast. Dial: 96.3 MHz

Cool FM
PO Box 974, Belfast BT1 1RT
Fax 01247-814974   Tel 01247-817181
Starting date: 7.2.90
Area: Belfast. Dial: 97.4 MHz

Country 1035
Hurlingham Business Park, London SW6 3DU
Fax 0171-384 1177   Tel 0171-384 1175
Country music
Starting date: 1.9.94
Area: Greater London. Dial: 1035 kHz

Downtown Radio/
Newtownards, Co Down, N Ireland BT23 4ES
Fax 01247-818913   Tel 01247-815555
Starting date: 16.3.76
Dial: 1026 kHz (Belfast), 102.4 MHz (Londonderry), 96.4 MHz (Limavady), 96.6 MHz (Enniskillen)

eleven SEVENTY AM
PO Box 1170, High Wycombe, Bucks HP13 6YT
Fax 01494 445400   Tel 01494 446611
Starting date: 31.12.93
Area: High Wycombe. Dial: 1170 kHz

Essex FM
Clifftown Road, Southend, Essex SS1 1SX
Fax 01702-345224   Tel 01702-333711
Parent company: Essex Radio
Starting date: 12.9.81
Dial: 96.3 MHz (Southend), 102.6 MHz (Chelmsford)

Forth FM/Max AM
Forth House, Forth Street, Edinburgh EH1 3LF
Fax 0131-558 3277   Tel 0131-556 9255
Parent company: Scottish Radio Holdings
Starting date: 22.1.75
Area: Edinburgh. Dial: 97.3/97.6 Hz (Forth FM, 1548 kHz (Max AM)

Fortune 1458
Quay West, Trafford Park Manchester M17 1FL
Fax 0161-872 0206   Tel 0161-872 1458
Starting date: 20.6.94
Area: Greater Manchester. Dial: 1458 kHz

Fox FM
Brush House, Pony Road, Horspath Estate,
Cowley, Oxford OX4 2XR
Fax 01865-748721   Tel 01865-748787
Starting date: 15.9.89
Area: Oxford, Banbury. Dial: 102.6 & 97.4 MHz

Gem-AM
29-31 Castle Gate, Nottingham NG1 7AP
Fax 0115-958 8614   Tel 0115-952 7000
Parent company: GWR Group
Starting date: 4.10.88
Area: Nottingham and Derby. Dial: 999 & 945 kHz

Gemini AM/Gemini FM
Hawthorn House, Exeter Business Park, Exeter,
Devon EX1 3QS
Fax: 01392-444433   Tel 01392-444444
Starting date: 1.1.95
Area: Exeter, east Devon and Torbay. Dial: 666 & 954 kHz

Gold Radio
Longmead, Shaftesbury, Dorset SP7 8QQ
Fax 01747-855722   Tel 01747-855711
Starting date: 25.6.95
Area: Shaftesbury. Dial: 97.4 MHz

Great North Radio (GNR)
Newcastle-upon-Tyne NE99 1BB
Fax 0191-488 0933   Tel 0191-420 3040
Parent company: Metro Radio Group
Starting date: 8.4.89
Area: Tyne & Wear, Teesside. Dial: 97.4 MHz

Great Yorkshire Gold
900 Herries Road, Sheffield, S Yorks S6 1RH
Fax 0114-285 3159   Tel 0114-285 2121
Parent company: Metro Radio Group
Starting date: 13.9.93
Dial: 1548, 1305, 990 kHz (south Yorkshire, north Midlands), 1278, 1530 kHz (west Yorkshire), 1161 kHz (Humberside)

GWR FM
PO Box 2000, Bristol, Avon BS99 7SN
Fax 0117-984 3202   Tel 0117-984 3200
Parent company: GWR Group
Starting date: 27.10.81 (Bristol), 22.5.87 (Bath)
Dial: 96.3 MHz (Bristol), 103.0 MHz (Bath)

GWR-FM Wiltshire
PO Box 2000, Swindon SN4 7EX
Fax 01793-440302   Tel 01793-440300
Parent company: GWR Group
Starting date: 12.10.82
Dial: 97.2 MHz (Swindon), 102.2 MHz (west Wilts), 96.5 MHz (Marlborough)

Hallam FM
900 Herries Road, Sheffield S6 1RH
Fax 0114-285 3159   Tel 0114-285 3333
Parent company: Metro Radio Group
Starting date: 1.10.74
Dial: 97.4 MHz (Sheffield), 96.1 MHz (Rotherham), 102.9 MHz (Barnsley), 103.4 MHz (Doncaster)

Heart 106.2
The Chrysalis Building, Bramley Road, London W10 6SP
Fax 0171-470 1062   Tel 0171-468 1062
Parent company: Chryalis Group
Starting date: summer 1995
Area: Greater London. Dial: 106.2 MHz

Heartland FM
Lower Oakfield, Pitlochry, Perthshire PH16 5DS
Fax 01796-474007   Tel 01796-474040
Some Gaelic and mixed language output.
Starting date: 21.3.92
Area: Pitlochry and Aberfldy. Dial: 97.5 MHz

102.7 Hereward FM
Queensgate, Peterborough, Cambs PE1 1XJ
Fax 01733-281445   Tel 01733-460460
Parent company: GWR Group
Starting date: 20.7.80
Area: Peterborough
Dial: 102.7 MHz

Horizon
Broadcast Centre, Crown Hill, Milton Keynes, Bucks MK8 0AB
Fax 01908-564893   Tel 01908-269111
Parent company: Chiltern Radio Network
Starting date: 15.10.89
Area: Milton Keynes. Dial: 103.3 MHz

Invicta FM / Invicta SuperGold
Radio House, John Wilson Business Park, Whitstable, Kent CT5 3QX
Fax 01227-771558   Tel 01227-772004
Parent company: Capital Radio
Starting date: Invicta FM: 1.10.84, Invicta SuperGold 27.3.89
Dial: Invicta FM 103.1 MHz (Maidstone & Medway), 102.8 MHz (Canterbury, 95.9 MHz (Thanet), 97.0 MHz (Dover), 96.1 MHz (Ashford). Invicta SuperGold 1242 kHz (west Kent), 603 kHz (east Kent)

Island FM
12 Westerbrook, St Sampson, Guernsey GY2 4QQ
Fax 01481-496768   Tel 01481-42000
Starting date: 15.10.92
Dial: 104.7 MHz (Guernsey), 93.7 MHz (Alderney)

Isle of Wight
Dodnor Park, Newport, Isle of Wight PO30 5XE
Fax 01983-821690   Tel 01983-822557
Parent company: GWR Group
Starting date: 15.4.90
Area: Isle of Wight.
Dial: 1242 kHz

JFM 102.2
26 Castlereagh Street, London W1H 6DJ
Fax 0171-723 9742   Tel 0171-706 4100
Jazz, blues R & B
Parent company: Golden Rose Communications.
Starting date: 4.3.90
Area: Greater London.
Dial: 102.2 MHz

KCBC
PO Box 1548, Kettering, Northants NN16 8PU
Fax 01536-517390   Tel 01536-412413
Parent company: Radio Investments
Starting date: 6.4.90
Area: Kettering, Corby.
Dial: 1548 kHz

KFM
1 East Street, Tonbridge, Kent TN9 1AR
Fax 01732-369201   Tel 01732-69200
Starting date: 8.7.95
Area: Tonbridge, Tunbridge Wells and Sevenoaks
Dial: 96.2 Hz (south)
101.6 MHz (north)

Kiss 100FM
80 Holloway Road, London N7 8JG
Fax 0171-700 3979   Tel 0171-700 6100
Parent company: Emap
Starting date: 1.990
Area: Greater London. **Dial:** 100.0 MHz

Kiss 102
PO Box 102, Manchester M60 1GJ
Fax 0161-228 1020   Tel 0161-228 0102
Parent company: Emap
Starting date: 16.10.94
Area: Greater Manchester. **Dial:** 102 MHz

Kix 96
Ringway House, Hill Street, Coventry CV1 4AN
Fax: 01203-551744   Tel 01203-525656
Starting date: 28.8.90
Area: Coventry. **Dial:** 96.2 MHz

KL-FM
18 Blackfriars Street, Kings Lynn, Norfolk
PE30 1NN
Fax 01553-767200   Tel 01553-772777
Parent company: GWR Group
Starting date: 1.7.92
Area: Kings Lynn. **Dial:** 96.7 MHz

Lantern Radio
The Lighthouse, Market Place, Bideford, Devon
EX39 2DR
Fax 01237-423333   Tel 01237-424444
Starting date: 19.10.92
Area: North Devon. **Dial:** 96.2 MHz

Leicester Sound
Granville House, Granville Road, Leicester LE1
7RW
Fax 0116-256 1303   Tel 0116-256 1300
Parent company: GWR Group
Starting date: 7.9.84
Area: Leicester. **Dial:** 103.2 MHz

Lincs FM
Witham Park, Waterside South, Lincoln, Lincs
LN5 7JN
Fax 01522-549911   Tel 01522-549900
Starting date: 1.3.92
Area: Lincolnshire

London Greek Radio
Florentia Village, Vale Road, London N4 1TD
Fax 0181-800 8005   Tel 0181-800 8001
Music, news and info for Greek speaking listeners
Starting date: 13.11.89
Area: Haringey. **Dial:** 103.3 MHz

London News/London News Talk
72 Hammersmith Road, London W14 8YE
Fax 0171-973 2300   Tel 0171-973 1152

London and world news, comment and analysis, with phone-ins
on London News Talk
Parent company: Reuters
Starting date: 5.10.94
Area: Greater London
Dial: 97.3 MHz (London News), 1152 kHz (London News Talk).

London Turkish Radio
185 High Road, Wood Green London N22 6BA
Fax 0181-881 5151   Tel 0181-881 0606
Music for the Turkish community
Starting date: summer 1995
Area: north London, Haringey. **Dial:** 1584 kHz

Magic 828
PO Box 2000, 51 Burley Road, Leeds LS3 1LR
Fax 0113 2421830   Tel 0113 2452299
Parent company: Emap
Starting date: 17.7.90
Area: Leeds. **Dial:** 828 kHz

Radio Maldwyn
Studios, The Park, Newtown, Powys SY16 2NZ
Fax 01686-623666   Tel 01686-623555
Starting date: 1 .7.93
Area: Montgomeryshire. **Dial:** 756 kHz

Manx
PO Box 1368, Broadcasting House, Douglas,
Isle of Man IM99 1SW
Fax 01624-661411   Tel 01624-661066
Area: Isle of Man.

Marcher Gold
Studios, Mold Road, Wrexham, Clywd LL11 4AF
Fax 01978-759701   Tel 01978-752202
Starting date: 5.9.83
Area: Wrexham, Chester, Deeside and Wirral. **Dial:** 1260 kHz

Mellow 1557
21 Walton Road, Frinton-on-Sea, Essex CO13
OAA
Fax 01253-678585   Tel 01253-675303
Starting date: 7.10.90
Area: NE Essex, south Suffolk. **Dial:** 1557 kHz

Melody
180 Brompton Road, London SW3 1HF
Fax 0171-581 7000   Tel 0171-581 1054
Starting date: 9.7.90
Area: Greater London. **Dial:** 105.4 MHz

Mercia FM/Classic Gold 1359
Hertford Place, Coventry, West Midlands
CV1 3TT
Fax 01203-868202   Tel 01203-868200
Parent company: GWR
Starting date: 7.3.94 (Mercia Classic Gold), 23.5.80 (Mercia FM)
Area: Coventry, Warwickshire. **Dial:** 1359 kHz (Mercia Classic
Gold), 97.0 & 102.9 Hz (Mercia FM)

Radio Mercury FM East/Mercury Extra AM
Broadfield House, Brighton Road, Crawley, West Sussex RH11 9TT
Fax 01293-565663   Tel 01293-519161
Parent company: Allied Radio
Starting date: 20.10.84 (Mercury FM East), 4.5.92 (Mercury xtra AM)
Area: Reigate, Crawley, Guildford, Haslemere
Dial: 102.7 MHz (Mercury FM East), 1476 & 1521 kHz (Mercury Extra AM)

Radio Mercury FM West
The Friary, PO Box 964, Guildford, Surrey
Fax 0483-31612   Tel 01483-451964
Parent company: Allied Radio
Starting date: 4.5.92 (from 4.4.96 it will be Surrey & N E Hampshire Radio)
Area: Guildford & Haslemere
Dial: 96.4 MHz (Guildford)
97.1 MHz (Haslemere)

Metro FM
Long Rigg Road, Swalwell, Newcastle-upon-Tyne NE99 1BB
Fax 0191-488 9222   Tel 0191-420 0971
Parent company: Metro Radio
Starting date: 15.4.74
Areas: Tyne & Wear
Dial: 97.1 MHz (Tyne & Wear)
103.0 MHz (Tyne Valley)

MFM
The Studios, Mold Road, Wrexham, Clwyd LL11 4AF
Fax 01978-759701   Tel 01978-752202
Starting date: 31.8.89
Area: Wrexham, Chester, Deeside and Wirral
Dial: 97.1 & 103.4 MHz

Minster FM
PO Box 123, Dunnington, York YO1 5ZX
Fax 01904-488878   Tel 01904-488888
Starting date: 4.7.92
Area: York.
Dial: 104.7 MHz

Mix 96
Friars Square Studios, 11 Bourbon Street, Aylesbury, Bucks HP20 2PZ
Fax 01296-398988   Tel 01296-399396
Starting date: 15.4.94
Area: Aylesbury
Dial: 96.2 MHz

Moray Firth
PO Box 271, Inverness, IV3 6SF
Fax 01463-243224   Tel 01463-224433
Starting date: 23.2.82
Area: Inverness
Dial: 97.4 & 96.6 MHz, 1107 kHz

Nevis Radio
Inverlochy, Fort William, Inverness PH33 6LU
Fax 01397 701007   Tel 01397-700007
Starting date: 1.8.94
Area: Fort William
Dial: 96.6 MHz

96.7 BCR (Belfast Community Radio)
Claremont Street, Lisburn Road, Belfast BT9 6JX
Fax 01232-230505   Tel 01232-438500
Starting date: 6.9.90
Area: Belfast
Dial: 96.7 MHz

North East Community Radio
Town House, Aberdeenshire AB51 0US
Fax 01467-632969   Tel 01467-632878
Starting date: 6.6.94
Area: Inverurie
Dial: 102.1 MHz

Northants/Northants Supergold
Enterprise Park, Boughton Green Road, Northampton NN2 7AH
Fax 01604-721934   Tel 01604-792411
Parent company: Chiltern Radio Network.
Starting date: 1.10.86 (Northants), 25.6.90 (SuperGold)
Area: Northampton
Dial: 96.6 MHz (Northants), 1557 kHz (Supergold)

NorthSound One/Two
45 Kings Gate, Aberdeen, Grampian AB2 6BL
Fax 01224-637289   Tel 01224-632234
Parent company: Scottish Radio Holdings
Starting date: 27.7.81
Area: Aberdeen. Dial: 96.9, 97.6, 103 MHz (One),1035 kHz (Two)

Oasis
The Broadcast Centre, 7 Hatfield Road, St Albans AL1 3RS
Fax 01727-834456   Tel 01727-831966
Parent company: Chiltern Radio Group
Starting date: 22.10.94
Area: St Albans and Watford. Dial: 96.6 MHz

Ocean FM
Radio House, Whittle Avenue, Segensworth West, Fareham PO15 5SH
Fax 01489-589453   Tel 01489-589911
Parent company: Capital Radio
Starting date: 12.10.86
Area: Portsmouth, Soton and Worcester. Dial: 96.7, 97.5 MHz

Orchard FM
Haygrove House, Shoreditch, Taunton, Somerset TA3 7BT
Fax 01823-321044   Tel 01823-338448
Starting date: 26.11.89
Area: Yeovil and Taunton. Dial: 97.1, 102.6 MHz

Piccadilly Gold / Piccadilly Key 103
127 The Piazza, Piccadilly Plaza, Manchester
M1 4AW
Fax 0161-228 1503   Tel 0161-236 9913
Parent company: Emap
Starting date: 2.4.74 (Gold), 3.9.88 (Key 103)
Area: Manchester
Dial: 1152 kHz (Gold), 103 MHz (Key 103)

Pirate FM
Carn Brae Studios, Wilson Way, Redruth,
Cornwall TR15 3XX
Fax 01209 314345   Tel 01209-314400
Starting date: 3.4.92
Area: Cornwall
Dial: 102.2 MHz (east Cornwall, west Devon), 102.8 (west
Cornwall, Isle of Scilly)

Plymouth Sound AM/FM
Earls Acre, Plymouth, Devon PL3 4HX
Fax 01752-670730   Tel 01752-227272
Starting date: 19.5.75
Area: Plymouth
Dial: 1152 kHz (AM), 97.0, 96.6 MHz (FM)

Power FM
Radio House, Whittle Ave, Fareham, Hampshire
PO15 5PA
Fax 01489-589453   Tel 01489-589911
Parent company: Capital Radio
Starting date: 4.12.88
Area: Portsmouth, Southampron and Winchester
Dial: 103.2 MHz

Premier Radio
Glen House, Stag Place, London SW1E 5AG
Fax 0171-233 6706   Tel 0171-233 6705
News and lifestyle issues reflecting beliefs of the Christian faith
Starting date: 10.6.95
Area: Greater London
Dial: 1305, 1332 & 1413 kHz

The Pulse
Forster Square, Bradford, West Yorks BD1 5NE
Fax 01274-307774   Tel 01274-731521
Parent company: Metro Radio
Starting date: 31.8.91
Area: Bradford, Halifax, Huddersfield
Dial: 97.5 MHz (Bradford)
102.5 MHz (Huddersfield & Halifax)

Q103-FM
Vision Park, Chivers Way, Histon, Cambridge
CB4 4WW
Fax 01223-235161   Tel 01223-235255
Parent company: GWR Group
Starting date: 12.2.89
Area: Cambridge, Newmarket
Dial: 103.0 MHz (Cambridge)
97.4 MHz (Newmarket)

Q96 FM
26 Lady Lane, Paisley, Strathclyde PA1 2LG
Fax 0141-887 0963   Tel 0141-887 9630
Starting date: 1.9.92
Area: Paisley. Dial: 96.3 MHz

Q102 FM
Old Waterside Station, Duke Street, Waterside,
Londonderry BT46 1DH
Fax 01504-311177   Tel 01504-44449
Starting date: 21.10.93
Area: Londonderry
Dial: 102.9 MHz

Q103 FM
PO Box 103, Vision Park, Chivers Way, Histon,
Cambridge CB4 4WW
Fax 01223-235161   Tel 01223-235255
Parent company: GWR Group
Area: Cambridge, Newmarket

Radio Aire FM
51 Burley Road, Leeds, West Yorks LS3 1LR
Fax 0113-242 1830   Tel 0113-245 2299
Parent company: Emap
Starting date: 1.9.81
Area: Leeds
Dial: 96.3 MHz

Radio City Gold
8/10 Stanley Street, Liverpool L1 6AF
Fax 0151-471 0330   Tel 0151-227 5100
Starting date: 21.10.74
Area: Merseyside
Dial: 1548 kHz

Radio XL 1296 AM
KMS House, Bradford Street,Birmingham B12
0JD
Fax 0121-53 3111   Tel 0121-753 5353
For the Asian community in the West Midlands
Starting date: 30.5.95
Area: Birmingham
Dial: 1296 kHz

Ram FM
The Market Place, Derby DE1 3AA
Fax 01332 292229   Tel 01332 292945
Parent company: GWR Group
Starting date: 3.3.87
Dial: 102.8 MHz

Red Dragon FM
Radio House, West Canal Wharf, Cardiff CF1
5XJ
Fax 01222-384014   Tel 01222-384041
Parent company: Emap
Starting date: 11.4.80 (Cardiff), 13.6.83 (Newport)
Area: Cardiff, Newport
Dial: 103.2 MHz (Cardiff), 97.4 (MHz (Newport)

Red Rose Gold/Red Rose Rock FM
St Pauls Square, Preston, Lancashire PR1 1XS
Fax 01772-201917   Tel 01772-556301
Parent company: Emap
Starting date: 1.6.90
Area: Blackpool, Preston
Dial: 999kHz (Gold),
97.4 Hz (Rock FM)

RTM
Harrow Manor Way, Thamesmead, London SE2 9XH
Fax 0181-312 1930   Tel 0181-311 3112
Starting date: 18.3.90
Area: Thamesmead
Dial: 103.8 MHz

Sabras Sound
63 Melton Road, Leicester LE4 6PN
Fax 0116-266 7776   Tel 0116-261 0666
24 hour Asian programming
Starting date: 7.9.95
Area: Leicester
Dial: 1260 kHz

Severn Sound/Severn Sound SuperGold
Broadcast Centre, Southgate Street, Gloucester GL1 2DQ
Fax 01452-529446   Tel 01452-423791
Parent company: Chiltern Radio Network
Starting date: 23.10.80
Area: Gloucester and Cheltenham
Dial: 102.4 & 103 MHz (Severn Sound),
774 kHz (SuperGold)

SGR FM Bury
PO Box 250,Bury St Edmunds, Suffolk IP33 1AD
Fax 01473-741200   Tel 01284-702622
Parent company: East Anglian Radio
Starting date: 6.11.82
Area: Bury St Edmunds
Dial: 96.4 MHz, 1251 kHz

SGR FM Ipswich
Radio House, Alpha Business Park, Whitehouse Road, Ipswich, Suffolk IP1 5LT
Fax 01473-741200   Tel 01473-461000
Parent company: East Anglian Radio
Starting date: 28.10.75
Area: Ipswich
Dial: 97.1 MHz, 1170 kHz

SGR Colchester
9 Whitewell Road, Colchester CO2 7DE
Fax 01206-561199   Tel 01206-575859
Parent company: East Anglian Radio
Starting date: 17.10.83
Area: Colchester
Dial: 96.1 MHz

SIBC
Market Street, Lerwick, Shetland ZE1 0JN
Fax 01595-695696   Tel 01595-695299
Starting date: 19.10.91
Area: Shetland Islands
Dial: 96.2 MHz

Signal Cheshire
Regent House, Heaton Lane, Stockport, Greater Manchester SK4 1BX
Fax 0161-474 1806   Tel 0161-480 5445
Parent company: Signal Radio
Starting date: 17.2.90
Area: Stockport and Congleton

Signal Gold / Signal One
Studio 257, Stoke Road, Stoke-on-Trent, ST4 2SR
Fax 01782-744110   Tel 01782-747047
Parent company: Signal Radio
Starting date: 14.9.92 (Gold), 5.9.83 (One)
Area: Cheshire, Staffordshire
Dial: 1170 kHz (Gold), 102.6 & 96.9 MHz (One)

South Coast Radio
PO Box 2000, Brighton BN14 2SS
Fax 10273-430098   Tel 01273-430111
Radio Whittle Avenue, Segensworth West,
Fareham PO15 5SH
Fax 01489-589453   Tel 01489-589911
Parent company: Capital Radio
Starting date: 29.8.83 (Brighton), 10.3.91 (Portsmouth & Southampton)
Area: Brighton, Southampton, Portsmouth
Dial: 1323 kHz (Brighton), 1170, 1557 kHz (Portsmouth, Southampton)

South West Sound
Campbell House, Bankend Road, Dumfries DG1 4TH
Fax 01387-65629   Tel 01387-50999
Parent company: West Sound Radio
Starting date: 21.5.90
Area: Dumfries and Galloway
Dial: 97.2 MHz

South West Sussex Radio
1 Argyle Road, Bognor Regis PO21 1DY
                        Tel 01243-828488
Starting date: to be advised
Area: Chichester, Bognor Regis, Littlehampton
Dial: 96.6 & 102.3 MHz

Southern FM
Radio House, PO Box 2000, Brighton, East Sussex BN41 2SS
Fax 01273-430098   Tel 01273-430111
Parent company: Capital Radio
Starting date: 12.2.88
Area: Brighton, Newhaven, Eastbourne and Hastings

Dial: 103.5 MHz (Brighton),
96.9 MHz (Newhaven),
102.4 MHz (Eastbourne),
102.0 MHz (Hastings)

Spectrum International
Endeavour House, Brent Cross, London
NW2 1JT
Fax 0181-209 1029   Tel 0181-905 5000
Music, news and information for ethnic communities
Starting date: 25.6.90
Area: London
Dial: 558 kHz

Spire FM
City Hall Studios, Malthouse Lane, Salisbury,
Wilts SP2 7QQ
Fax 01722-415102   Tel 01722-416644
Starting date: 20.9.92
Area: Salisbury
Dial: 102.0 MHz

Star FM
Observatory Shopping Centre, Slough, Berks
SL1 1LH
Fax 01753-512277   Tel 01753-551016
Starting date: 21.5.93
Area: Windsor, Slough, Maidenhead
Dial: 106.6 MHz

Stray FM
PO Box 972, Station Parade, Harrogate HG1
5YF
Fax 01423-522922   Tel 01423-522972
Starting date: 4.7.94
Area: Harrogate
Dial: 97.2 MHz

Sunrise Radio
Sunrise House, Sunrise Road, Southall,
Middlesex UB2 4AU
Fax 0181-813 9800   Tel 0181-574 6666
Music, news and information for the Asian community
Parent company: Sunrise Group
Starting date: 5.11.89
Area: Ealing, Hounslow area of London
Dial: 1458 kHz

Sunrise East Midlands
see Sabras Sound

Sunrise FM
30 Chapel Street, Little Germany, Bradford BD1
5DN
Fax 01274-728534   Tel 01274-735043
Music, news and information for the Asian community
Parent company: Sunrise Group
Starting date: 9.12.89
Area: Bradford
Dial: 103.2 MHz

Sunshine 855
Sunshine House, Waterside, Ludlow, Shropshire
SY8 1GS
Fax 01584-875900   Tel 01584-873795
Starting date: 18.1092
Area: Ludlow, south Shropshire
Dial: 855 kHz

Swansea Sound
Victoria Road, Gowerton, Swansea, West
Glamorgan SA4 3AB
Fax 01792-898841   Tel 01792-893751
Some Welsh language broadcasting
Parent company: Enterprise Radio Holdings
Starting date: 30.9.74
Area: Swansea
Dial: 96.4 MHz, 1170 kHz

Tay FM/Radio Tay AM
6 North Isla Street, Dundee, Tayside DD3 7JQ
Fax 01382-24549   Tel 01382-200800
Parent company: Scottish Radio Holdings
Starting date: 17.10.80 (Tay FM), Radio Tay AM (to be advised)
Area: Dundee, Perth
Dial: 102.8 MHz (Dundee), 96.4 MHz (Perth) Tay FM/
1161 kHz (Dundee), 1584 kHz (Perth), Radio Tay AM

Ten 17
Latton Bush Centre, Harlow, Essex CM18 7BU
Fax 01279-445289   Tel 01279-432415
Parent company: Essex Radio
Starting date: 1.5.93
Area: Harlow. **Dial:** 101.7 MHz

TFM
Yale Crescent, Stockton-on-Tees, TS17 6AA
Fax 01642-674402   Tel 01642-615111
Parent company: Metro Radio
Starting date: 24.6.75
Area: Teesside. **Dial:** 96.6 MHz

Touch AM
PO Box 99, Cardiff CF1 5YJ
Fax 01222-384014   Tel 01222-384041
Parent company: Emap
Starting date: 15.7.90
Dial: 1359 kHz (Cardiff), 1305 kHz (Newport)

Townland Radio
PO Box 828, Cookstown, Co. Tyrone BT80 9LQ
Fax 016487-63828   Tel 016487-64828
Starting date: 15.4.95
Area: Mid Ulster. **Dial:** 828 kHz

Trent FM
29 Castle Gate, Nottingham NG1 7AP
Fax 0115-958 8614   Tel 0115-952 7000
Parent company: GWR Group
Starting date: 3.7.75
Area: Nottingham. **Dial:** 101.7 MHz

2CR FM / Classic Gold 828
5 Southcote Road, Bournemouth, Dorset BH1 3LR
Fax 01202-299314   Tel 01202-294881
Parent company: GWR Group
Starting date: 15.9.80
Area: Bournemouth
Dial: 102.3 MHz (2CR FM)
828 kHz (Classic Gold)

2-Ten FM
PO Box 210, Reading, Berks RG31 7RZ
Fax 01734-254456   Tel 01734-254400
Parent company: GWR Group
Starting date: 8.3.76
Area: Reading, Basingstoke, Andover
Dial: 97.0 & 102.9 MHz

Viking FM
Commercial Road, Hull, North Humberside HU1 2SG
Fax 01482-587067   Tel 01482-325141
Parent company: Metro Radio
Starting date: 17.4.84
Area: Humberside
Dial: 96.9 MHz

Virgin Radio London
1 Golden Square, London W1R 4DJ
Fax 0171-434 1197   Tel 0171-434 1215
Parent company: Virgin Communications
Starting date: 10.4.95
Area: Greater London
Dial: 015.8 MHz

Viva!
26-27 Castlereagh Street, London W1H 6DJ
Fax 0171-723 9742   Tel 0171-706 9963
Starting date: 3.7.95
Area: Greater London
Dial: 963 kHz

WABC
See: Beacon Radio.

Wave
965 Mowbray Drive, Blackpool, Lancashire FY3 7JR
Fax 01253-301965   Tel 01253-304965
Starting date: 25.5.92
Area: Blackpool
Dial: 96.5 MHz

Wear FM
39 Holmeside, Sunderland
Fax 0191-567 0777   Tel 0191-567 3333
Parent company: Minster Sound Radio
Starting date: 1.7.95
Area: Sunderland
Dial: 103.4 MHz

Wessex FM
Radio House, Trinity Street, Dorchester, Dorset DT1 1DJ
Fax 01305-250052   Tel 01305-250333
Starting date: 4.9.93
Area: Dorset
Dial: 97.2 MHz & 96.0 MHz

West Sound
Radio House, Holmston Road, Ayr, Strathclyde KA7 3BE
Fax 01292-283665   Tel 01292-283662
Starting date: 16.10.81
Area: South west Scotland
Dial: 96.7 & 97.5 MHz, 1035 kHz

Wey Valley Radio
Prospect Place, Mill Lane, Alton, Hants GU34 2SY
Fax 01420-544044   Tel 01420-544444
Starting date: 22.11.92
Area: Alton
Dial: 101.6 & 102 MHz

Wyvern
5 Barbourne Terrace, Worcester WR1 3JZ
Fax 01905-612212   Tel 01905-612212
Area: Hereford, Worcester
Dial: 97.6 Mhz & 954 kHz (Hereford), 102.8 MHz & 1530 kHz (Worcester)

Yorkshire Coast Radio
PO Box 962, Scarborough, Yorkshie YO12 5YX
Fax 01723-501050   Tel 0173-500962
Parent company: Minster Sound Radio
Starting date: 7.11.93
Area: Scarborough
Dial: 96.2 & 103.1 MHz

Radio news services

BBC Radio News
Broadcasting House, Portland Place, London W1A 1AA
Tel 0171-580 4468   0171-580 4468
All BBC local radio stations have their own news staff; see list below under BBC: Regional.

FT Business News
50 Lisson Street, ondon NW1 5DF
Fax 0171-723 6132   Tel 0171-402 1011
Business and personal finance news for comercial radio stations. Service provided by Unique Broadcsting, Financial Times and ABC Radio.

Independent Radio News (IRN)
1 Euston Centre, London NW1 3JG
Fax 0171-388 4449   Tel 0171-388 4558
Newsroom: 200 Grays Inn Road, London

WC1X 8XZ
Fax 0171-430 4834   Tel 0171-430 4814
IRN is Britain's main radio news agency, supplying bulletins and services to over 90 per cent of the commercial radio stations. The news is provided to IRN by ITN Radio, using the resources of ITN at its headquarters in 200 Grays Inn Road. IRN is effectively a commissioning agency acting on behalf of its customers. Its owners are the major radio groups and individual stations within the ILR network.

Network News
Chiltern Road, Dunstable, Beds LU6 1HQ
Fax 01582-661725   Tel 01582-666884
National agency for Independent Radio, main rival to IRN. Supplies world, national and local news, sport, entertainment, traffic and weather to national and 40+ ILR stations.Formed in 1991, and owned mainly by individuals, plus 25 per cent by Chiltern Radio, at whose studios it is based.

Reuters Radio News
85 Fleet Street, London EC4 4AJ
Fax 0171-333 2525   Tel 0171-333 2500
Reuters offers its news service to all IRN stations.

Sportsmedia Broadcasting
51a Victoria Road, London NW6 6TA
                          Tel 0171-625 6581
The sports news provider for INR and ILR.

Satellite and cable radio

Asda FM
PO Box 100, Tydesley, Manchester M29 7TT
Fax 01942-884397   Tel 01942-889100
Starting date: 7.93
Area national in-store radio
Satellite

Birmingham's BHBN
Dudley Road, Birmingham B18 7QH
Fax 0121-554 7863   Tel 0121-554 5522
Hospital and health care information, local news and features
Starting date: 5.9.94
Cable

CMR (Country Music Radio for Europe
PO Box 42, Alton, Hampshire GU32 4YU
Fax 01253-724312   Tel 01253-724891
Satellite

CRMK
14 Vincent Avenue, Crown Hill, Milton Keynes MK8 0AB
                          Tel 01908-265266
Starting date: 9.90
Area: Milton Keynes
Cable

Eclipse FM
Unit 31, Times Square Shopping Centre, High Street, Sutton, Surrey SM1 1LF
Fax 0181-395 3334   Tel 0181-395 3388
Starting date: 23.10.93
Area: Sutton, Croydon, Merton, Richmond, Kingston
Cable

Fashion FM
214 Oxford Street, London W1N 9DF
                          Tel 0171-927 0226
In-store radio
Starting date: 4.87
Cable

Music Choice Europe
16 Harcourt Street, London W1H 1DS
Fax 0171-724 0404   Tel 0171-724 9494
Cable

Radio Phoenix
Neath General Hospital, Neath, West Glamorgan SA11 2LQ
                          Tel 01639-641161
Cable

Sunrise Radio - Europe
Sunrise House, Sunrise Road, Southall, Middlesex UB2 4AU
Fax 0181-813 9800   Tel 0181-574 7777
Parent company: Sunrise Radio Group
Starting date: 1.7.91
Satellite

UCB (United Christian Broadcasters)
Hanchurch Christian Centre, PO Box 255, Stoke-on-Trent, Staffs ST4 2UE
Fax 01782-202278   Tel 01782-202466
Starting date: 4.93
Satellite

Virgin Radio
1 Golden Square, London W1R 4DJ
Fax 0171-434 1197   Tel 0171-434 1215
Parent company: Virgin Communications
Starting date: 30.4.93
Satellite

WRN (World Radio Network)
Wyvil Court, 10 Wyvil Road, London SW8 2TY
Fax 0171-896 9007   Tel 0171-896 9000
Starting date: 10.93
Satellite

BROADCAST AWARDS 1995

BAFTA Performance Awards (TV Section)
British Academy of Film and Television Arts,
195 Piccadilly, London W1V 0LN
Fax 0171- 734 1792   Tel 0171-734 0022

Best Single Drama: Skallagrigg, Screen 2
Best Drama Series: Cracker, ITV
Best Drama Serial: Takin' Over the Asylum, BBC2
Best Factual Series: Beyond the Clouds, Channel 4
Best Light Entertainment: Don't Forget Your Toothbrush, C4
Best Comedy: Three Fights,Two Weddings and a Funeral, BBC2
Best News Coverage, Rwanda, ITV
Best Sports Event: Grand National, BBC1
Best Actress: Juliet Aubrey, Middlemarch, BBC2
Best Actor: Robbie Coltrane, Cracker, ITV
Best Light Entertainment Performance: Rory Bremner, C4
Best Comedy Performance: Joanna Lumley, Absolutely
Fabulous, BBC1
Best Arts Programme: An Interview with Dennis Potter: C4
Best Children's Factual Programme: As Seen on TV
Best Children's Entertainment: Coping with Grown-ups
Best Documentary: Silent Twin Without My Shadow, BBC1

Broadcasting Press Guild Awards
Tiverton, The Ridge, Woking, Surrey GU22 7EQ
                    Tel 01483 764895

Radio Programme of the Year: Today, Radio 4
TV Journalist of the Year: George Alagiah, BBC South Africa
correspondent
Best Single Documentary: Melvyn Bragg's interview with
Dennis Potter for LWT Arts
Best TV Documentary Series: Beyond the Clouds, produced by
Phil Agland for DJA River Films Productions
Outstanding Contribution Award: Richard Dunn, former chief
exec of Thames Television

The Indies
Single Market Events, 23-24 George Street,
Richmond, Surrey TW9 1HY
Fax 0181-332 0495   Tel 0181-948 5522

Indie Award: Beyond the Cloud, River Films
Indie Pioneer: Hat Trick Productions
Drama and Film: The Crying Game, Palace Pictures
Light Entertainment: Drop the Dead Donkey, Hat Trick
Music and Arts: Plague and the Moonflower, Ecosse Films
Factual: The Good Sex Guide, Prospect Pictures
News and Current Affairs:
Children and Youth: Byker Grove, Zenith North
Sports: Tour de France, TV Sport and Leisure
Regional: Shops and Robbers, Hart Ryan Productions
Radio Times Readers': Drop the Dead Donkey, Hat Trick

Royal Television Society Awards
100 Grays Inn Road, London WC1X 8AL
Fax 0171-430 0924   Tel 0171-430 1000

TV Journalist of the Year: Fergal Keane, BBC Southern Africa
correspondent
Regional Daily News Magazine: East Midlands Today, BBC
Regional Current Affairs: Spotlight: Cockfighting, BBC NI
News (Home): News at Ten for Baby Abbie, ITN/Central News
News (International): Chinese Prisons, BBC Breakfast News
Current Affairs (Home): Getting Away with Rape, Channel 4
Current Affairs (International): Panorama, Journey Into
Darkness, BBC
Special Commendation: Algeria's Hidden War, BBC
Television Camera Operator: Ian Robbie, Sky News
News Event: John Smith's death, ITV
Sports Coverage: Graham Taylor: an Impossible Job, Channel 4
Sports News: ITN for Andy Norman reports
Regional Sports: International North West 200, Ulster TV
Sports Presenter: Desmond Lynam, BBC
Special Award: Peter Taylor, for 25 years Ulster reporting

Sony Radio Awards
Sony, The Heights, Brooklands, Weybridge,
Surrey KT13 0XN
                    Tel 01932 816000
UK Station of the Year: Radio 2
UK Broadcaster of the Year: Neil Fox, Network Chart Show
Reporter of the Year: John Waite, Radio 4
Radio Academy Award: Jenny Abramsky, Radio 5 Live
Sony Special Award: Peter Baldwin
Gold Award: Alistair Cooke
Breakfast Shows (Music): Chris Tarrant Breakfast Show, 95.8
Capital FM; Sarah Kennedy Early Show, Radio 2
Popular Music Programme: It Was Thirty Years Ago Today,
BBC Radio Humberside
Comedy Show: Sorry I Haven't a Clue, Radio 4
News and Current Affairs: Eye on Wales, BBC Radio Wales
Breakfast Show (Speech): Today, Radio 4
Response to News Event: IRA Ceasefire, Radio 5 Live
Short Feature/Documentary: The Fly, BBC Radio Wales
Documentary Feature : CSA: Making Daddy Pay, City FM
Topical Debates: Talkback, Bullying, BBC GMR
Sports Award: Tour de France, Southern FM
Arts or Music Feature: Leonard Cohen, Tower of Song, Radio 1
Specialist Music: Music of Madagascar, Radio 3
Drama Production: Mr McNamara, BBC World Service
Dramatic Performances: Bernard Hepton in Elgar's Third,
Radio 3; Christine Lahti in Three Hotels, BBC World Service
Creatived Writing: Ronan Bennett for Fire and Rain, Radio 4
Original Drama: Elgar's Third, Radio 3
Service to the Communikty: Man Matters, Radio 2
Local/Regional Broadcaster: Liz Green, BBC Radio Leeds
Local Station of the Year: BBC Radio Gloucester
Regional Station of the Year: 95.8 Capital FM

NEWS ORGANISATIONS

ABC News Intercontinental
8 Carburton Street, London W1P 8JD
Fax 0171-631 5084   Tel 0171-637 9222
London office of the American news network.

CBS News
68 Knightsbridge, London SW1X 7LL
Fax 0171-581 4431   Tel 0171-581 4801
London office of the American news network.

CNN International
19 Rathbone Place, London W1P 1DF
Fax 0171-637 6868   Tel 0171-637 6800
Cable News Network is the world's only global network. Distributing 24-hour news via 13 satelites CNN and CNNI are seen by 156 million households in more than 210 countries. and now have 29 international news bureaux and nearly 600 affiliated TV stations around the world. CNN was started by Ted Turner in Atlanta, Georgia, in 1980. CNNI was launched in 1985 and has production cenres in Atlanta, London and Hong Kong. The European Regional News Centre in London is the largest ouside the U.S. CNNI is a subsidiary of Turner Broadcasting.

IRN - Independent Radio News
Euston Centre, London NW1 3JG
Fax 0171-388 4449   Tel 0171-388 4558
News desk   Tel 0171-430 4814
IRN is Britain's main radio news agency, supplying bulletins and services to over 90 per cent of the commercial radio stations. The news is provided to IRN by ITN, using the resources of ITN at its headquarters in 200 Grays Inn Road. IRN is effectively a commissioning agency acting on behalf of its customers. Its owners are ITN the main radio groups.

ITN
200 Grays Inn Road, London WC1X 8XZ
Fax 0171-430 4016 (news) Tel 0171-833 3000
Press office   0171-430 4700
ITN provides national and international news to ITV, Channel 4 and IRN. ITN's UK television programmes have a total weekly output of 18 hours; they include News at Ten, Early Evening News and Channel 4 News. News at Ten is Britain's most popular main evening news programme. ITN was owned by all the ITV companies from its formation in 1955 until April 1993. Then it was bought by a new consortium: Carlton Communications, Central Independent TV, Granada, LWT and Reuters, each with 18 per cent; and Anglia TV and Scottish TV, both with 5 per cent.

London News Network
London Television Centre, Upper Ground, London SE1 9LT
Fax 0171-827 7721   Tel 0171-827 7700
Jointly set up and run by the London ITV companies Carlton and LWT to provide their local news. Began in January 1992. Also supplies news to breakfast ITV station GMTV.

NBC News Worldwide
8 Bedford Avenue, London WC1B 3AW
Fax 0171-636 2628   Tel 0171-637 8655
London office of the American network.

Network News
Broadcast Centre, Chiltern Road, Dunstable, Beds LU6 1HQ
Fax 01582-661725   Tel 01582-666884
National radio news agency formed in 1991 as a rival to IRN, supplying news to commercial radio stations. 25 per cent owned by Chiltern Radio, at whose studios it is based.

Parliamentary Channel
16 Bonny Street, London NW1 9PG
Fax 0171-911 0146   Tel 0171-482 4824
Provides unedited live coverage of daily proceedings in the House of Commons and recorded coverage of the Lords and Parliamentary committees.The channel is a cable-exclusive service, run as a non-profit organisation.

Press Association
292 Vauxhall Bridge Road, London SW1V 1AA
Fax 0171-963 7192   Tel 0171-963 7000
See Press agencies, page 100.

Reuters Television
200 Grays Inn Road, London WC1X 8XZ
Fax 0171-570 4970   Tel 0171-250 1122
Reuters, one of ITN's owners and tenants, has expanded its media operations. In late 1992, Reuters bought out its minority partners in Visnews, the international TV news supplier. The revamped organisation was named Reuters Television.

Sky News
6 Centaurs Business Park, Grant Way, Isleworth, Middlesex TW7 5QD
Fax 0171-782 9902   Tel 0171-705 3000
24-hour rolling newschannel on satellite and cable, providing national, international, business and parliamentary coverage.

TV News London
22-23 Gayfere Street, London SW1P 3HP
Fax 0171-222 0832   Tel 0171-222 0807
London news agency supplying stories about events in the capital to regional broadcasting companies. Started in 1992.

Worldwide Television News (WTN)
Interchange, Camden Lock, London NW1 7EP
Fax 0171-413 8303   Tel 0171-410 5200
WTN provides a 24-hour satellite service from camera crews in 90 cities to more than a thousand broadcasters. WTN also has one of the most comprehensive film and video archives. Owned by ITN, ABC (USA) and Nine Network (Australia). WTN HQ is in London, with bureaux in 55 other cities around the world.

FILM LIBRARIES

The list below concentrates on collections with a news, current affairs or documentary content. A fuller list of film libraries is the Researcher's Guide to British Film and TV Collections from British Universities Film and Video Council, 55 Greek St, London W1V 5LR. 0171-734 3687.

A19 Film and Video
21 Foyle Street, Sunderland, SR1 1LE
Fax 0191-565 6288   Tel 0191-565 5709
Documentary makers, focussing on the north-east.

Archive Film Agency
21 Lidgett Park Avenue, Roundhay, Leeds, West Yorkshire LS8 1EU
Fax 0113-266 4703   Tel 0113-266 2454
Specialists in early news reel, documentary, fiction.

BBC Worldwide Television Library Sales
Woodlands, 80 Wood Lane, London W12 0TT
Fax 0181-576 2939   Tel 0181-576 2861
The BBC has Britain's largest library of film and videotape, with over 400 million feet of film. The archive contains over 45 years of recorded BBC TV programmes, across all subject genres.

British Film Institute
21 Stephen Street, London W1P 2LN
Fax 0171-436 7950   Tel 0171-255 1444
The BFI archive, founded in 1935, has 250,000 titles, from 1895 on. Research and access are dealt with by the Cataloguing Department, Viewing Service and Production Library. The BFI also has an extensive stills, posters and designs collection and a library and database about film and television.

British Movietone News
N Orbital Road, Denham, Middlesex UB9 5HQ
Fax 01895-834893   Tel 01895-833071
A library based on the 1929-79 newsreel output and raw material of Movietone, including the Look at Life collection.

British Pathe News
46 Great Titchfield Street, London W1P 7AE
Fax 0171-436 3232   Tel 0171-323 0407
Also at Pinewood Studios, Iver, Bucks, SLO 0NH
Fax 01753-655365   Tel 01753-630361
Holds more than 50 million feet of historical film footage from 1895 to 1970, covering world events, as reported by Pathe.

Chameleon Film Library
Folded in 1995

COI Footage File
Hercules Road, London SE1 7DU
Fax 0171-261 8555   Tel 0171-261 8951
The COI holds film, going back over 60 years.

East Anglian Film Archive
University of East Anglia, Norwich NR4 7TJ
Fax 01603-58553   Tel 01603-592664
Non-profit archive of film showing life and work in East Anglia.

Educational & Television Films
247a Upper Street, London N1 1RU
Fax 0171-226 8016   Tel 0171-226 2298
Filmed history of the 20th century, with emphasis on the former Soviet Union, Eastern Europe, China, Vietnam and Cuba.

Environmental Investigation Agency
2 Pear Tree Court, London EC1R 0DS
Fax 0171-490 0436   Tel 0171-490 7040
Video library of EIA campaigns for endangered species.

Film Archive Management & Entertainment
PO Box 608, Hailsham, East Sussex BN27 3UN
Fax 01323-840756   Tel 01323-849186
Film library with social and industrial documentary footage from the 1930s onwards, 50 per cent about railways.

Film Images London
184 Drummond Street, London NW1 3HP
Fax 0171-383 2333   Tel 0171-383 2283
Represents: (1) Archive Films, the London end of the top US library, with 1896-1970 holdings including the March of Time and Universal newsreels; (2) Timescape Image Library of contemporary generic shots of cities, skies and landscapes.

Film Research
177-183 Regent Street, London W1R 8LA
Fax 0171-734 8017   Tel 0171-734 1525
Provides a research service for the sourcing, supply and clearance of moving footage for all media purposes.

Greenpeace Communications Video Library
5 Baker's Row, London EC1R 3DB
Fax 0171-837 6606   Tel 0171-833 0600
Footage of Greenpeace campaigns.

Huntley Film Archives
78 Mildmay Park, London N1 4PR
Fax 0171-241 4929   Tel 0171-923 0990
Documentary film dating from 1895 to c1960, including social history, shipping, transport, industry, the arts and media.

The Image Bank Film
17 Conway Street, London W1P 6EE
Fax 0171-391 9100   Tel 0171-312 0300
4 Jordan Street, Manchester M15 4PY
Fax 0161-236 8723   Tel 0161-236 9226
Holds material from 450 photographers, 300 cinematographers and 350 illustrators, including the MGM Library and Turner Broadcasting. Worldwide network of 70 offices.

Imperial War Museum Film and Video Archive
Lambeth Road, London SE1 6HZ
Fax 0171-416 5379   Tel 0171-416 5291
Holds the British "official" war film shot since 1914, plus news-reels and other material. Totals about 70 million feet of film.

Index Stock Shots
12 Charlotte Mews, London W1P 1LN
Fax 0171-436 8737   Tel 0171-631 0134
Stock footage of transport, animals, industry and space.

International Video Network
107 Power Road, Chiswick, London W4 5PL
Fax 0181-995 7871   Tel 0181-742 2002
Travel and documentary videos covering most countries.

ITN Archive
200 Grays Inn Road, London WC1X 8XZ
Fax 0171-430 4453   Tel 0171-430 4480.
Holds footage covering most news since 1955. The collection is on 14 million feet of film and over 70,000 hours of video tape.

ITV
All ITV companies have libraries of material:
Anglia	01603-615151
Central	0121-643 9898
Channel Four	0171-396 4444
Granada	0161-832 7211
HTV	01222-590590
LWT	0171-261 3690
Meridian	01703-222555
Scottish	0141-332 9999
Thames (1968-92)	0181-614 2800
Ulster	01232-328122
Yorkshire · Tyne Tees	0113-243 8283

London Stockshots Library
London News Network, London TV Centre,
Upper Ground, London SE1 9LT
Fax 0171-827 7710   Tel 0171-827 7700
LNN library of London coverage during the nineties.

Moving Image Research & Library Services
21 Goldhawk Road, London W12 8QQ
Fax 0181-749 6142   Tel 0181-740 4606
TV-am material 1983-92 and wide-ranging British history.

National Film Archive
See British Film Institute.

North West Film Archive
Manchester Metropolitan University, 47
Chorlton Street, Manchester M1 3EU
Fax 0161-247 3098   Tel 0161-247 3097
Non-commercial archive recording the life of north west England

Oxford Scientific Films
Lower Road, Long Hanborough, Oxon OX8 8LL
Fax 01993-882808   Tel 01993-881881
Natural history films, commercials and non-broadcast film.

Polygram Film and Television Library
2nd Floor, 10 Livonia Street, London W1V 3PH
Fax 0171-800 1337   Tel 0171-800 1339
The ATV/ITV libraries from 1955-1981.

Reuters Television
40 Cumberland Avenue, London NW10 7EH
Fax 0171-542 8568   Tel 0181-965 7733
The world's largest TV news archive, with material dating from 1896. Holds more than 26,000 hours of material, including collections of Gaumont, Empire News, British Paramount and Visnews.

Ronald Grant Archive
The Old Fire Station, 46 Renfrew Road, London SE11 4NA
Fax 0171-793 0849   Tel 0171-820 9991
Images of cinema and film from 1896 to the present day.

RSPB Film Library
The Lodge, Sandy, Beds SG19 2DL
Fax 01767-692365   Tel 01767-680551
More than a million feet of natural history footage (not just birds).

Scottish Film Archive
74 Victoria Crescent Road, Glasgow G12 9JN
Fax 0141-334 8132   Tel 0141-334 4445
Covers Scottish social, cultural and industrial history.

Sports Video Library
Transworld International, The Axis Centre,
Hogarth Business Park, London W4 2TH
Fax 0181-233 5301   Tel 0181-233 5500
One of the largest European sports libraries

Survival Anglia
Anglia House, Norwich, Norfolk NR1 3JG
Fax 01603-765887   Tel 01603-615151
Large collection of natural history material.

Wales Film & Television Archive
Cefn Llan, Aberystwyth, Dyfed SY23 3AH
Fax 01970-626007   Tel 01970-626007
Non-commercial archive governed by the Wales Film Council.
Holdings include the National Library of Wales film collection.

Wessex Film & Sound Archive
Hampshire Record Office, Sussex Street,
Winchester, Hants SO23 8TH
Fax 01962-878681   Tel 01962-847742
Set up in 1988 by the Hampshire Archives Trust

WTN - Worldwide Television News
The Interchange, Oval Road, London NW1 7EP
Fax 0171-413 8327   Tel 0171-410 5270
WTN claims to have the largest group of newsreel archives in the world. Covers worldwide events since 1963. WTN also represents the ABC News Library, which chronicles day-to-day American history.

SUPPORT ORGANISATIONS

Amsat-UK
94 Herongate Road, London E12 5EQ
Fax 0181-989 3430   Tel 0181-989 6741
National society specialising in amateur radio satellite matters.
Publishes Oscar News 6x pa.

Association of Broadcasting Doctors
PO Box 15, Sindalthorpe House, Ely, Cambridge
CB7 4SG
Fax 01353-688451   Tel 01353-688456
Represents practising doctors who also broadcast, providing
training, data and media liaison. Publishes monthly newsletter
and briefings. Contact point for broadcasters seeking medical
contributors.

Association of Independent Radio Companies
46 Westbourne Grove, London W2 5SH
Fax 0171-229 0352   Tel 0171-727 2646
The trade association for independent radio broadcasting
companies, it co-ordinates initiatives, acts as a representative to
government and generally promotes independent radio interests.

Audio Visual Association
156 High Street, Bushey Heath, Hertfordshire
WD2 DD
Fax 0181-950 7560   Tel 0181-950 5959
Special interest group of the British Institute of Professional
Photography representing people working to
sub-broadcast standard in audio visual and multi-media. The
association evolves with new technical developments.

British Academy of Film and Television Arts
195 Piccadilly, London W1V 0LN
Fax 0171-734 1792   Tel 0171-734 0022
BAFTA promotes high creative standards in film and television
production, and encourages experiment and research. Formed in
1946, it organises the main TV awards ceremony every April.

British Academy of Songwriters, Composers & Authors
34 Hanway Street, London W1P 9DE
Fax 0171-436 1913   Tel 0171-436 2261
BASCA was founded in 1947 and is the largest trade association
for songwriters and composers. It lobbies for developments in
copyright legislation, produces BASCA News, holds a regular
forum for legal advice and administers various awards. The
academy is represented on all the major music industry boards.

British Amateur Television Club
Fern House, Church Road, Harby, Notts NG23
7ED
Fax 01522-703348   Tel 01522-703348
Founded in 1948 to inform, instruct, co-ordinate and represent
the activities of television enthusiasts in the UK and worldwide.
Publishes quarterly technical magazine CQ-TV

British Board of Film Classification
3 Soho Square, London W1V 5DE
Fax 0171-287 0141   Tel 0171-439 7961
The official body responsible for ensuring that publicly shown
films conform to certain standards, it classifies films into the
following categories:
U (Universal)
PG (Parental Guidance)
12 (age 12 and over only)
15 (age 15 and over only)
18 (age 18 and over only)
R18 (restricted distribution on premises barred to under 18s)

British Film Commission
70 Baker Street, London W1M 1DJ
Fax 0171-224 1013   Tel 0171-224 5000
Bath Film Office   01225-477711
Cardiff Media City   01222-388002
Central England   0121-643 9309
Eastern Screen   01603-767077
Edinburgh Screen Industries   0131-228 5960
Highland Regional Council   01463 702552
Gwynedd Film Office   01248-670007
Isle of Man Film Commission   01624-686841
Liverpool Film Office   0151-225 5446
Northern Screen Commission   0191-469 1000
Scottish Screen Locations   0131-229 1213
Screen Wales   01222-578370
South West Fim Commission   01752-841199
South West Scotland Film Commission
                                          01387-263666
Yorkshire Film Commission   01142-799115
Set up by the government in 1991, the BFC is funded through the
National Heritage Department. It promotes the UK as an
international production centre and provides support to those
filming in the UK. BFC publications include Check Book, a UK
production guide for overseas film-makers and the newsletter
Framework. The commission runs FIND, the Film Information
National Database covering personnel, facilities and locations.
The BFC works regionally through the bodies listed above.

British Film Institute
21 Stephen Street, London W1P 2LN
Fax 0171-436 7950   Tel 0171-255 1444
The BFI is Britain's leading moving image resource. It
encourages the development of film, TV and video, both as an art
and as a medium of record. The institute runs the London Film
Festival, Museum of the Moving Image , National Film Archive
and National Film Theatre . The BFI helps in film production,
runs a library and information services, provides training advice
and organises events. It publishes many books and periodicals
(including the annual BFI Film Handbook and the monthly mag
Sight and Sound). The institute supports regional and local film
theatres and societies. BFI funding comes partly from its
commercial activities and partly from the government.

British Interactive Multimedia Association
6 Washingley Road, Folksworth, Peterborough
PE7 3SY
Fax 01733-240020   Tel 01733-245700
The trade body for the multimedia industry. Publishes directory
of members and newsletter. Meets ten times a year.

British Kinematograph, Sound and Television Society
M6-M14 Victoria House, Vernon Place, London
WC1B 4DJ
Fax 0171-405 3560   Tel 0171-242 8400
BKSTS was founded in 1931 and is the only European society
covering all technical aspects of film, television, sound and
associated industries. It plays a leading role in the development
and implementation of technical standards. The main aim is to
keep members abreast of the continually changing technology in
the industry and its implications. The society achieves this
through its newsletter Images (10x pa), journals and
programmes, and by holding seminars and conferences. Many
training courses are held.

British Library National Sound Archive
29 Exhibition Road, London SW7 2AS
Fax 0171-414 7441   Tel 0171-412 7430
The national collection of sound recordings, covering all topics
since the 1890s. Provides library, information, listening and
transcription services. Publishes newsletter Playback and range
of print and audio titles.

British Screen Advisory Council
93 Wardour Street, London W1V 3TE
Fax 0171-734 5122   Tel 0171-413 8009
Independent, industry-funded advisory body to government and
the screen media industry, providing a forum for senior
management of the audio-visual industry to discuss major
issues. The Council publishes reports of these managerial
deliberations.

British Radio & Electronic Equipment Manufacturers' Association
19 Charing Cross Road, London WC2H 0ES
Fax 0171-839 4613   Tel 0171-930 3206
BREMA is the trade association for the television and radio
manufacturing industry.

British Screen Finance
14 Wells Mews, London W1P 3FL
Fax 0171-323 0092   Tel 0171-323 9080
A company dependent on government funding, it provides loans
to film makers for developing and producing commercial feature
films.

British Society of Cinematographers
11 Croft Road, Chalfont St Peter, Gerrards
Cross, Bucks SL9 9AE
Fax 01753-891486   Tel 01753-888052
Society of motion picture cinematographers. Arranges technical
meetings, social events, film shows etc. Publishes directory
biennially.

Broadcasters Audience Research Board
Glenthorne House, Hammersmith Grove,
London W6 0ND
Fax 0181-741 1943   Tel 0181-741 9110
BARB is a provider of information to all elements of the TV
industry, broadcasters, advertising/media buying agencies and
advertisers. BARB uses professional research suppliers to
conduct and report on audience research. It produces statistical
research on TV audiences for its subscribers. Audiences for TV
programmes are measured by electronic meters attached to
television sets in 4,435 homes. This panel, which is the largest
of its kind in the world, includes some 10,500 people. The
meters record the state of each TV set or video. The information
is transmitted automatically each night by telephone into a
central computer and is used to calcualte the size of the
audience. Since 1991, the meters have been able to record video
playbacks.

Broadcasting Complaints Commission
5 The Sanctuary, London SW1P 3JS
Fax 0171-828 7316   Tel 0171-630 1966
The BCC was set up by Act of Parliament to investigate
complaints against broadcasters. It looks into allegations of
unjust or unfair treatment and at infringements of privacy. As of
January 1996 the BCC shares premises with the Broadcasting
Standards Council. See How to Complain, page 123.

Broadcasting Consortium
National Council of Voluntary Organisations, 8
All Saints Street, London N1 9RL
Fax 0171-713 6300   Tel 0171-713 6161
Coalition of national charities working to protect and enlarge
voluntary organisations' access to radio and television nationally
and locally. Publishes leaflet The Good Radio Guide, explaining
how to influence the outcome of the current re-advertising of
local radio services, and booklet The Good Franchise Guide,
showing voluntary bodies how to get involved with ITV.

Broadcasting, Entertainment, Cinematograph and Theatre Union
111 Wardour Street, London W1V 4AY
Fax 0171-437 8268   Tel 0171-437 8506
Midlands office   Tel 0121-632 5372
North west office   Tel 0161-274 3174
Scottish office   Tel 0141-332 4620
Wales office   Tel 01222-465574
BECTU is the largest trade union in broadcasting, with 55,000
members. It represents non-performing staff and freelancers in
TV, radio, film, theatre and leisure. Offers employment,
financial, legal and training advice. Publishes monthly journal
Stage, Screen and Radio, with news from around the industry
(available to non-members).

Broadcasting Press Guild
Tiverton, The Ridge, Woking, Surrey GU22 7EQ
Fax: 01483-764895   Tel.01483-764895
Association of 80-90 journalists writing about the media in the
national and trade press. Holds monthly lunches addressed by
top broadcasting executives. Each spring it presents the BPG TV
and Radio Awards.

Broadcasting Research Unit
c/o Voice of the Listener and Viewer, 101 King's Drive, Gravesend, Kent DA12 5BQ
Fax: Phone first.01474-352835
Independent trust researching all aspects of broadcasting, development and technologies, operating from 1980-1991.

Broadcasting Standards Council
7 The Sanctuary, London SW1P 3JS
Fax 0171-233 0397   Tel 0171-233 0544
Established under the 1990 Broadcasting Act , the BSC is concerned with the broadcast portrayal of violence, sexual conduct and matters of taste and decency, such as bad language or the treatment of disasters.The BSC has produced a code of practice, conducts research and monitoring and considers complaints. It publishes a monthly bulletin, an annual report and research into public attitudes. Chairman is Lady Howe. The July 1994 government white paper on the future of the BBC proposed merging the BSC with the Broadcasting Complaints Commission.

Cable Communications Association
5th Floor, Artillery House, Artillery Row, London SW1P 1RT
Fax 0171-799 1471   Tel 0171-222 2900
Formerly the Cable Television Association, this trade body for the cable TV companies promotes the development of the industry. It has a freephone telephone line for consumers wanting to find out about their local cable operator: 0800-300750. The CCA publishes Cable Companion, a book/database available by subscription, and Case for Cable, a free summary of statistics and industry changes.

Celtic Film and Television Association
The Library, Farraline Park, Inverness IV1 1LS
Fax 01463-716368   Tel 01463-226189
Organises the annual International Celtic Festival of Film and Television, peripatetic in Scotland, Wales, Cornwall, Ireland and Brittany, including awards and conference. It supports development of TV and film in Celtic nations and indigenous languages.

Children's Film & Television Foundation
Elstree Studios, Borehamwood, Herts WD6 1JG
Fax 0181-207 0860   Tel 0181-953 0844
Non-profitmaking organisation which funds script development for quality television projects aimed at 5-12 year old children. Holds an extensive film library, with a wide range of films made for children/family viewing. Founded 1951.

Churches Advisory Council for Local Broadcasting
PO Box 124, Westcliffe-on-Sea, Essex SS0 0QU
Fax 01702-348369   Tel 01702-348369
A charity bringing together the main Christian churches for the advancement of Christianity through radio and TV. Has an Association of Christian broadcasters, quarterly news bulletin, annual conference and awards.

Cinema and TV Benevolent Fund
22 Golden Square, London W1R 3PA
Fax 0171-437 7186   Tel 0171-437 6567
Trade charity for retired and serving employees and their dependents needing caring help, support and financial aid.

Communication Workers Union
150 Brunswick Road, London W5 1AW
Fax 0181-991 1410   Tel 0181-998 2981
The largest trade union in posts, telecommunications and financial services. The CWU Voice is published monthly.

Community Radio Association
Head office: 15 Paternoster Row, Sheffield, South Yorkshire S1 2BX
Fax 0114-279 8976   Tel 0114-279 5219
London Development Unit: The Resource Centre, 356 Holloway Road, London N7 6PA
Fax 0171-700 8108   Tel 0171-700 0100
UK membership body, developing and campaigning for community-based radio. It offers information, advice, training and consultancy, holds conferences and events and publishes the quarterly journal Airflash.

Confederation of Aerial Industries
Fulton House Business Centre, Fulton Road, Wembley Park, Middlesex HA9 0TF
Fax 0181-903 8719   Tel 0181-902 8998
Trade association for makers and erectors of broadcasting aerials and satellite dishes. Publishes newsletter and codes of practice, and holds training courses and an annual exhibition.

CSV Media
237 Pentonville Road, London N1 9NJ
Fax 0171-278 7912   Tel 0171-278 6601
CSV Media, part of the national charity Community Service Volunteers, specialises in social action broadcasting, media support services and media training. Services range from TV and radio programme production, broadcast back-up , including telephone helplines and training in TV and radio production.

Deaf Broadcasting Council
70 Blacketts Wood Drive, Chorleywood, Rickmansworth, Herts WD3 5QQ
Fax 01923-283127
An umbrella organisation to which all the major national bodies for and on behalf of deaf, deafened and hard of hearing people are affiliated. Ensures that TV companies and broadcasters are aware of their needs. Publishes newsletter Mailshot 3-4x pa.

Directors Guild of Gt Britain
15-19 Great Titchfield Street, London W1P 7FB
Fax 0171-436 8646   Tel 0171-436 8626
Union for directors in all media, including TV, film, theatre and radio. Issues an advised schedule of rates, code of practice and model contracts. Gives contractual advice and holds workshops and social events. Publishes a quarterly newsletter Direct and annual directory of all members.

Edinburgh International Television Festival
24 Neal Street, London WC2H 9PS
Fax 0171-836 0702   Tel 0171-379 4519
Britain's biggest and liveliest international forum for the television industry attracts prominent speakers, many delegates and widespread interest. Usually held for three days, in late August, during the Edinburgh Festival. Publishes the annual Television Book.

Edinburgh Television Trust
13 Bellevue Place, Edinburgh
EH7 4BS
Fax 0131-557 8608   Tel 0131-557 8610
Local charity set up to provide training for access and community television services.

Equity
Guild House, Upper St Martins Lane, London
WC2 9EG
Fax 0171-379 7001   Tel 0171-379 6000
British Actors' Equity Association is the trade union for actors, stage managers, opera singers, dancers, directors, designers, choreographers, variety artistes and stunt performers working in theatre, film, television, radio and variety venues. The union publishes the quarterly magazine Equity which is distributed to the membership of 45,000.

European Satellite User Group
Rio House, Stafford Close, Ashford, Kent
TN23 2TT
Fax 01233-610106   Tel 01233-610040
Supplies satellite data to end users, TV and radio broadcasters and prospective broadcasters. Publishes monthly newsletter Footprint and supplies information to other publications, plus teletext and radio services.

Federation Against Copyright Theft
7 Victory Business Centre, Worton Road,
Isleworth, Middlesex TW7 6ER
Fax 0181-560 6364   Tel 0181-568 6646
Fact is the industry funded body dedicated to preventing copyright piracy.

Federation of Commercial Audio Visual Libraries
PO Box 422, Harrow, Middlesex HA1 3YN
Fax 0181-423 5853   Tel 0181-423 5853
FOCAL is the international trade association for audio visual libraries, researchers and producers. It promotes the use of library footage in programming and holds regular seminars and meetings.

Federation of the Electronics Industry
10 Russell Square, London WC1B 5AE
Fax 011-331 2040   Tel 0171-331 2000
Trade association for the telecoms, radio and satellite communications industries.

Federation of Entertainment Unions
1 Highfield, Twyford, near Winchester, Hants
SO21 1QR
Fax 01962-713134   Tel 01962-713134
Collective body of trade unions, representing the interests of 140,000 members in the broadcasting and entertainment industries. The unions are: BECTU, Equity, Musicians Union, NUJ, Writers Guild, AEEU and Film Artistes Association. It provides liaison, representation, lobbying and co-ordination services on issues of common concern.

Film Artistes Association
61 Marloes Road, London W8 6LE
Fax 0171-937 0790   Tel 0171-937 4567
The trade union representing crowd artistes, stand-ins and doubles.

405-Line Group
71 Falcutt Way, Northampton NN2
8PH
Fax 01604-821647   Tel 01604-844130
Promotes the study of television history. Publishes quarterly magazine 405 Alive and holds occasional displays of old television equipment. In 1996 it celebrates 60 years of real TV in the UK.

Gaelic Television Committee
4 Harbour View, Cromwell St Quay, Stornoway,
Isle of Lewis HS1 2DF
Fax 01851-706432   Tel 01851-705550
Statutory body grant-funding Gaelic television programmes, development and training.

Guild of British Animation
26 Noel Street, London W1V 3RD
                          Tel 0171-434 9002
The Guild represents the interests of the growing number of British animation companies.

Guild of British Camera Technicians
5 Taunton Road, Metropolitan Centre,
Greenford, Middlesex UB6 8UQ
Fax 0181-575 5972   Tel 0181-578 9243
The Guild represents motion film camera technicians working in the UK entertainment industry. It publishes the bimonthly news magazine Eyepiece.

Guild of British Film Editors
Travair, Spurlands End Road, Great Kingshill,
High Wycombe, Bucks HP15 6HY
Fax 01494-712313   Tel 01494-712313
The Guild of British Film Editors organises film shows and technical visits for its members. It presents awards for film and sound editing. The Guild also maintains a dialogue with other technical guilds at home and abroad and publishes regular newsletters.

Guild of Local Television
16 Fountain Road, Edgbaston, Birmingham B17 8NL
Fax 0121-429 3706   Tel 0121-429 3706
Promotes locally-originated TV, and supports groups and individuals involved in local TV. Organises conferences, seminars, workshops and publications. Promotes the skills of its members and undertakes research on their behalf. Aims to identify and accredit training opportunities. Lobbies in support of cable.

Guild of Television Cameramen
1 Churchill Road, Whitchurch, Tavistock, Devon PL19 9BU
Fax 01822-614405   Tel 01822-614405
Professional association aiming to preserve the working status of TV camera operators. Publishes bi-annual Zerb Magazine and newsletter. Holds regular workshops.

Independent Association of Radio Producers
29 Foley Street, London W1P 7LB
Fax 0171-436 0132   Tel 0171-323 2770
A recently-formed trade body representing independent radio producers. It is a lobbying organisation that negotiates with the radio network, government and the unions. One of its aims is to increase the BBC's quota of independently produced programmes from around 10 per cent to some 25 per cent of its total output.

Independent Television Commission (ITC)
HQ: 33 Foley Street, London W1P 7LB
Fax 0171-306 7800   Tel 0171-255 3000
Kings Worthy Court, Kings Worthy, Winchester, Hants SO23 7QA.
Fax 01962-886141   Tel 01962-848600
National and regional offices:
Northern Ireland   01232-248733
Scotland   0141-226 4436
Wales   01222-384541
East of England   01603-623533
Midlands - Birmingham   0121-693 0662
Midlands - Nottingham   0115-952 7333
North East England   0191-261 0148
North of England   0114-276 9091
North West England   0161-834 2707
South of England, Winchester   01962-883950
South of England, Plymouth   01752-663031
West of England   0122-384541
The ITC is the public body responsible for licensing and regulating commercially funded television services provided in and from the UK. These include Channel 3 (ITV), Channel 4, public teletext and a range of cable, local delivery and satellite services. They do not include services provided by the BBC or by S4C, the fourth channel in Wales. The ITC replaced the Independent Broadcasting Authority and the Cable Authority in 1991. It publishes the quarterly magazine Spectrum.

Institute of Broadcast Sound
27 Old Gloucester Street, London WC1N 3XX
Fax 0181-887 0167   Tel 01753-646404
Professional body for people responsible for the sound broadcast on TV and radio. Publishes the industry's bi-monthly trade magazine Line Up.

Institute of Local Television
13 Bellevue Place, Edinburgh EH7 4BS
Fax 0131-557 8608   Tel 0131-557 8610
Aims to increase local programme availability and maintain high quality through conferences, research and publications about cable and Channel Five.

International Broadcasting Trust
2 Ferdinand Place, London NW1 8EE
Fax 0171-284 3374   Tel 0171-482 2847
An independent TV company with charitable status specialising in making programmes on development, environment and human rights issues. Its aim is to promote a wider understanding of these issues through the use of the media. IBT is backed by a consortium of 70 aid and development agencies, educational bodies, churches and trade unions. It publishes the bi-annual newsletter Fast Forward and a range of back-up material.

International Institute of Communications
Tavistock House South, Tavistock Square, London WC1H 9LF
Fax 0171-380 0623   Tel 0171-388 0671
Promotes the open debate of issues in the communications field worldwide, in the interest of human and social advancement. Specialises in broadcasting, telecommunications and communications policy. It publishes books, bimonthly journal Intermedia, newsletter, reports, etc.

International Visual Communications Association
5 Clipstone Street, London W1P 8LD
Fax 0171-436 2606   Tel 0171-580 0962
A trade association representing the users and suppliers of the corporate visual communications industry. It publishes magazine and guides and organises regular professional and social events. Provides legal and information help.

ITV Network Centre
200 Grays Inn Road, London WC1X 8HF
Fax 0171-843 8158   Tel 0171-843 8000
Represents the interests of the regional ITV companies. Set up in late 1992 to commission and schedule ITV's networked programmes from 1 January 1993, as required by the 1990 Broadcasting Act. Also responsible for research, programme acquisitions and financial, legal and business matters for ITV. The Centre also clears advertisements prior to transmission. Grew out of the ITV Association, the trade body of the pre-1993 ITV companies.

JICRAR (Joint Industry Committee for Radio Audience Research)
See RAJAR

Mechanical-Copyright Protection Society
41 Streatham High Road, London SW16 1ER
Fax 0181-769 8792   Tel 0181-664 4400
Organisation of music publishers and composers, collecting and distributing royalties from the recording of copyright music onto CDs, cassettes, audio-visual and broadcast material. The society's National Discography, a comprehensive database of commercial music and records, offers wide range of music information. Also publishes On the Right Track (a guide to starting in the music business) and the quarterly magazine For the Record

Museum of the Moving Image
South Bank, Waterloo, London SE1 8XT
Fax 0181-815 1419   Tel 0171-815 1331
The national museum of TV and cinema including pre-cinema film, TV, video and new technologies. It is run by the British Film Institute. It hosts regular screenings, press previews and photocalls. Special events celebrate the centenary of cinema in 1996.

Musicians'.Union
60 Clapham Road, London SW9 0JJ
Fax 0171-582 9805   Tel 0171-582 5566
The trade union which looks after the interests all styles of musician. It publishes the quarterly journal Musician plus a range of leaflets on the music biz.

NTL
Crawley Court, Winchester, Hants SO21 2QA
Fax 01962-822378   Tel 01962-823434
The privatised engineering division of the former Independent Broadcasting Authority, set up in 1991. Owns and operates the transmitters used by the independent TV and radio stations. Also manufactures high-tech broadcasting products and provides telecommunications services. The full name is National Transcommunications Ltd.

National Association of Hospital Broadcasting Organisations
PO Box 2481, London W2 1JR
                    Tel 0171-402 8815
Charity umbrella organisation for over 320 hospital radio stations nationwide, who provide local radio programmes to 90 per cent of patients. It publishes the On Air magazine bi-monthly.

National Communications Union
see Communication Workers Union

National Film and Television Archive
21 Stephen Street, London W1P 1PL
Fax 0171-580 7503   Tel 0171-255 1444
Founded in 1935 and now a part of the British Film Institute. It

selects, acquires, preserves, catalogues and makes permanently available for study, research and screening a national collection of moving images of all kinds. Now holds 200,000 titles, starting from 1895. Covers TV, documentary and feature films.

National Film Theatre
South Bank, Waterloo, London SE1 8XT
Fax 0171-633 9323   Tel 0171-928 3535
Three cinemas owned by the British Film Institute (cf) showing the widest possible range of film and television from around the world

National Sound Archive
see British Library National Sound Archive

National Viewers and Listeners Association
All Saints House, High Street, Colchester, Essex CO1 1UG
No fax   Tel 01206-561155
Organisation founded by Mary Whitehouse seeking to uphold high moral standards in the media. It campaigns to make the Obscene Publications Act 1959 and 1964 effective, and encourages discussion and debate about the effects of the media on individuals, family and society. Publishes magazine The Viewer & Listener three times a year, plus reports of programmes and media issues.

Networking
Vera Productions, 30 Dock Street, Leeds, West Yorks LS10 1JF
Fax 0113-245 1238   Tel 0113-242 8646
European organisation for women involved in any way, or hoping to work in film, video or TV. It publishes newsletter and a contacts index, organises events and provides information and advice.

PACT (Producers Alliance for Cinema & TV)
Gordon House, Greencoat Place, London SW1 1PH
Fax 0171-233 8935   Tel 0171-233 6000
Trade association and employers' body for feature film and independent TV producers. Formed in 1991 from the Independent Programme Producers Association and the British Film and TV Producers Association. Provides a range of services, including information and production advice. Publishes monthly newsletter, The Pact magazine, an annual members directory and specialist guides.

Production Managers Association
Gordon House, Greencoat Place, London SW1P 1PH
Fax 0171-233 8935   Tel 0171-931 9671
Offers a professional voice for both freelance and permanently employed production managers. Provides regular workshops, training courses and an employment register. Publishes bi-monthly newsletter and directory of members. Affiliated to PACT.

Radio Academy
64 Great Titchfield Street, London W1A
Fax 0171-255 2029   Tel 0171-255 2010
Professional membership organisation for the radio industry. Organises the industry's annual conference, the Radio Festival plus seminars and workshops. Regional centres organise their own programme of events. Makes a number of awards for outstanding contributions to the radio industry.

Radio Advertising Bureau
74 Newman Street, London W1P 3LA
Fax 0171-636 6995   Tel 0171-636 5858
The RAB is the marketing arm of the commercial radio industry. It aims to increase the levels of familiarity and favourability towards commercial radio as an advertising medium.

Radio Amateurs Emergency Network
4 North End, Bedale, North Yorkshire DL8 1AB
National body of radio amateurs who provide communications in times of emergency and disaster, as a community service.

Radio Authority
14 Great Queen Street, London WC2B 5DG
Fax 0171-405 7064   Tel 0171-430 2724
Statutory body licensing and regulating independent radio (all non-BBC services). Started in 1991, replacing part of the Independent Broadcasting Authority (see also Independent Television Commission). Publishes the invaluable annual Radio Authority Pocket Book, detailing the independent radio industry, and The Radio Authority and the Consumer, explaining how to make complaints.

Radio Joint Audience Research (RAJAR)
Collier House, 163-169 Brompton Road, London SW3 1PY
Fax 0171-589 4004   Tel 0171-584 3003
Joint body involving the BBC and commercial radio, implementing and controlling a system of audience research for radio in the UK.

Radio Society of Great Britain
Lambda House, Cranborne Road, Potters Bar, Herts EN6 3JE
                        Tel 01707-659015
The leading national organisation for amateur radio enthusiasts, offering a range of services to members. The society publishes: the monthly magazine Radio Communication, full of news, features, etc; and the annual Amateur Radio Call Book and Information Directory, a comprehensive guide to all organisations and the holder of every G call-sign.

Radiocommunications Agency
Waterloo Bridge House, Waterloo Road, London SE1 8UA
Fax 0171-928 4309   Tel 0171-215 2150
An executive agency of the Department of Trade and Industry, responsible for the management and licensing of the civil use of the radio spectrum. Approves plans proposed by the Radio Authority. Publishes an annual report and many useful information sheets on radio-related topics.

RAJAR
see Radio Joint Audience Research

Reel Women
57 Holmewood Gardens, London SW2 3NB
No fax.   Tel 0181-678 7404
Brings together women working in television, film and video for discussions, seminars, screenings and workshops.

Right to Peace and Quiet Campaign
PO Box 968, London SE2 9RL
Fax 0181-312 9997   Tel 0181-312 9997
An anti-noise lobby, campaigning to see an improvement to noise control, and to raise awareness. Gives help to noise victims.

Royal Television Society
100 Grays Inn Road, London WC1X 8AL
Fax 0171-430 0924   Tel 0171-430 1000
Promoting the art and science of television broadcasting. The society is at the heart of the British television world. It provides a unique forum where all branches of the industry can meet and discuss major issues. Organises conferences, lectures, workshops, masterclasses and awards ceremonies. The RTS has 15 regional centres each running their own programme of events. Publishes journal Television eight times a year, annual handbook, various monographs and educational leaflets. Membership £49 pa, students £10.

Satellite & Cable Broadcasters' Group
34 Grand Avenue, London N10 3BP
Fax 0181-444 6473   Tel 0181-444 4891
Association of cable and satellite TV programme channel providers. Formerly called the European Programme Providers Group.

Satellite Media Services
24 Euston Centre, London NW1 3JH
Fax 0171-388 4858   Tel 0171-387 3232
SMS uses its dedicated lines, digital satellite and ISDN networks to distribute commericals, programmes, IRN, PA and Reuters radio news services.

Scottish Association of Smallscale Broadcasters
13 Comely Bank Row, Edinburgh EH4 1EA
No fax.   Tel 0131-332 8270
Co-operative umbrella for all individuals and organisations concerned with smallscale broadcast operations, RSLs (restricted service licences), training workshops, etc. Publishes quarterly newsletter. Formerly called the Scottish Community Broadcasting Group, set up in 1985.

Scottish Film Council
74 Victoria Crescent Road, Glasgow G12
9JN
Fax 0141-334 8132   Tel 0141-334 4445
Government-backed body encouraging all aspects of film
development and education in Scotland. Provides wide range of
information and support services. Runs the Scottish Film
Archive, preserving Scotland's moving image heritage. Founded
1934.

Scottish Film Production Fund
74 Victoria Crescent Road, Glasgow G12 9JN
Fax 0141-337 2562   Tel 0141-337 2526
Fosters and develops the Scottish film and video industries
by the provision of financial and other assistance to
appropriate productions, events and individuals. Also
runs the Glasgow Film Fund, with investment for
feature films made in the Glasgow area or for films
made by Glasgow based companies.

Services Sound and Vision Corporation
Chalfont Grove, Gerrards Cross,
Buckinghamshire SL9 8TN
Fax 01494-872982   Tel 01494-874461
Official supplier to the British armed forces of radio and
television broadcasts, audiovisual training, education and
entertainment. Now a private company and charity. Broadcasts
over 18 hours of TV a day. Has TV and radio studios around the
world. Its radio branch is the British Forces Broadcasting
Service.

Society of Cable Telecommnication Engineers
Fulton House Business Centre, Fulton Road,
Wembley Park, Mdx HA9 0TF
Fax 0181-903 8719   Tel 0181-902 8998
Technical body aiming to raise the standards of cable TV
engineering, improve the status of cable engineers and offer
members opportunities to attain further skills. Publishes journal
Cable Television Engineering.

Television History Centre
27 Old Gloucester Street, London WC1N
3AF
Fax 0171-242 1426   Tel 0171-405 6627
Provides resources, materials, information and assistance to
help people record their own history. Produces books, pamphlets
and leaflets, and sells/rents videos.

Television & Radio Industries Club
2 Duckling Lane, Salbridgeworth, Herts
CM21 9QA
Fax 01279-723100   Tel 01279-721100
Founded 1931 to promote goodwill amongst those engaged in the
audio, visual and allied industries. Its primary role is arranging
social events and it also publishes a yearbook and organises
annual Celebrity Awards.

3WE (Third World & Environmental Broadcasting Project)
2 Ferdinand Place, London NW1 8EE
Fax 0171-284 3374   Tel 0171-482 2847
3WE works for sustained and imaginative coverage of global
affairs on UK TV on behalf of Oxfam, WWF, Amnesty
International and a consortium of other leading voluntary
agencies.

UK Media Antenna Scotland
74 Victoria Crescent Road, Glasgow G12 9JN
Fax 0141-334 8132   Tel 0141-334 4445
A European Community funded film initiative run through the
Scottish Film Council.

UK Media Antenna Wales
Screen Wales Screen Centre, Llandaff, Cardiff
CF5 2PU
Fax 01222-578654   Tel 01222-578370
A European Community funded film initiative.

Voice of the Listener and Viewer
101 King's Drive, Gravesend, Kent DA12 5BQ
Fax: Phone first.01474-352835
Non-profit making, independent society working to support high
quality and diversity in broadcasting. The only consumer body
speaking for viewers and listeners on all broadcasting issues.
Publishes quarterly newsletter, reports and briefing papers on
broadcasting developments. Arranges public seminars, debates
and conferences.

Wireless Preservation Society
52 West Hill Road, Ryde, Isle of Wight PO33
1LN
Fax 01983-564708   Tel 01983-567665
The society and the linked Communications and Electronics
Museum preserve a reference collection of radio, TV and other
electronic equipment in Museums at Arreton Manor and
Puckpool on the Isle of Wight and at Bletchley Park, near Milton
Keynes.

Women in Film and Television
11 Betterton Street, London WC2H 9BP
Fax 0171-379 1625   Tel 0171-379 0344
Professional membership organisation for women with a
minimum three years experience in the film and TV industry.
Provides information and support to members and promotes
equal opportunity. Publishes quarterly magazine and runs
comprehensive programme of events: seminars, workshops,
screenings, lunches and an annual awards ceremony.

The Writers' Guild of Great Britain
430 Edgware Road, London W2 1EH
Fax 0171-706 2413   Tel 0171-723 8074
The union for writers in film, television, radio and theatre. The
Guild has an agreement with PACT covering higher and lower
budget feature films, single TV movies, TV series and serials. It
also has agreements with the BBC and ITV.

BROADCAST TRAINING

A recent survey of undergraduates showed that half of them want to be a journalist. The strong probability is that a large proportion of them would prefer to be broadcasters and the absolute certainty is that most will be disappointed. Best estimates are that less than 5,000 people make a full time living as broadcast journalists, a figure that includes everyone from local radio reporters to Jeremy Paxman.

Unlike print, broadcasting demands specific technical skills which are not taught in the course of a normal secondary education. The training structure, therefore, is less chaotic than for print journalism. Nonetheless broadcast training is still somewhat of a muddle with three separate organisations accrediting the various journalistic and production courses listed below. Efforts have been made to pull things together and in Skillset - the Industry Training Organisation for Broadcast, Film and Video - there is something approaching a strategic body. Formed in 1992 to promote National and Scottish Vocational Qualifications, it is managed and funded by broadcasting organisations.

A degree by itself won't secure a job in broadcast journalism. It takes further training, either through in-house courses run by the BBC or the ITV companies, or on postgraduate courses accredited by the National Council for the Training of Broadcast Journalists. As local radio is where most broadcasters begin their careers, these NCTBJ courses tend to concentrate on radio journalism although, television being the greatest lure, most of the courses contain a TV component.

Competition for all kinds of places, especially at the BBC and ITV, is high. Companies have postive recruitment and training policies and there are initiatives to develop the skills of women (especially in technical and craft areas), black and disabled people. For the most widely quoted example half of the places on BBC's annual TV production training scheme are reserved for those from under-represented ethnic groups.

The demand for information about getting into broadcasting has stimulated a minor branch of the publishing industry. Two books are recommended: the Skillset Careers Pack covers much ground, though its tumble of looseleaf pages demands a determined seeker after information; and the best introduction to the business is Josephine Langham's Light Camera Action, published by the BFI.

Training guides: books and...

Skillset Careers Pack
Skillset   Tel 0171 30666 8585

Media Courses UK 96
BFI   Tel 0171 255 1444
£9.95 including post and packing
A full listing of further education, undergraduate, postgraduate and short courses.

Short Courses in Film, Video, TV and Radio
BFI   Tel 0171 255 1444
£3 including post and packing
Updated three times a year.

Lights, Camera, Action!
BFI   Tel 0171 255 1444
A look at what's going on in the industry with case studies and advice for newcomers.

The Way In
BBC (See next page)

The Official ITV Careers Handbook
ITV (See next page)

...software

The BFI and Skillset training database can, by appointment, be scanned at the Arts Council Regional Arts Boards. Contact:

London Arts Board	Tel 0171-240 1313
South East Arts Board	Tel 01892 515210
Southern Arts Board	Tel 01962 855099
South West Arts Board	Tel 01392 218188
Eastern Arts Board	Tel 01223 215355
East Midlands Arts Board	Tel 01509 218292
West Midlands Arts Board	Tel 0121-631 3121
Yorkshire and Humberside Arts Board	
	Tel 01924 4555
North West Arts Board	Tel 0161-228 3062
Northern Arts Board	Tel 0191-281 6334
Scottish Arts Council	Tel 0131-226 6051
Welsh Arts Council	Tel 01222 394711
Arts Council of Northern Ireland	
	Tel 01232 381591

Association of Independent Radio Companies
46 Westbourne Grove, London W2 5SH
Fax 0171-229 0352 Tel 0171-727 2646
AIRC maintains the best kept database of courses in radio training.

Training contacts

BBC Corporate Recruitment Services
PO Box 7000, London W12 7ZY
Tel 0181-752 5252
The door to the Beeb. Ask for a copy of The Way In: Job Opportunities in the BBC. Otherwise go to page 696 of Ceefax for information on current BBC vacancies.

Broadcasting, Entertainment, Cinematograph and Theatre Union
See Support Organisations, page 207
BECTU accredits film, video and TV courses and operates a Student Link Up scheme.

British Kinematograph Sound and Television Society
See Support Organisations, page 207
The BKSTS publishes a regularly updated collection of documents called Education, Training and Working in Film, Television and Broadcasting, 1993, £5. It accredits training courses, runs its own courses and student membership is a good way to make contacts in the industry.

British Film Institute
See Support Organisations, page 206
The BFI has an education section which publishes the career books recommended aboved. Also helpful is the BFI library at its central London headquarters.

British Universities Film & Video Council
55 Greek Street, London W1V 5LR
Fax 0171-287 3914   Tel 0171-734 3687
Promotes the study, production and use of television, film and related media for research and higher education. Runs information service, has viewing and editing facilities, organises conferences and courses and provides research facilities. Publishes the invaluable Researcher's Guide to British Film and TV Collections, the Researcher's Guides to British Newsreels, other books and magazine Viewfinder. Maintains the Slade Film History Register which holds copies of British newsreels from 1896-1979.

Cyfle
Gronant, Penrallt Isaf, Caernarfon, Gwynedd LL55 1NW
Fax 01286-678890   Tel 01286-671000
Training for the Welsh film and TV industry.

Educational Television Association
37 Monkgate, York, YO3 7PB
Fax 01904-639212   Tel 01904-639212
Brings together organisations and individuals using TV and other media for education and training. Holds annual conference and video competition. Publishes newsletter and academic-oriented Journal of Educational Television.

Film Education
41 Berners Street, London W1P 3AA
Fax 0171-637 9996   Tel 0171-637 9932

A film industry sponsored non profit-making body promoting the use of film in the school curriculum and the use of cinema by schools. It organises workshops, screenings, lectures and seminars and publishes a variety of teaching material: guides to current and classic films and concept guides. Most are free.

FT2 - Film and Television Freelance Training
Fourth Floor, 5 Dean Street, London W1V 5RN
Fax 0171-287 9899   Tel 0171-734 5141
Provides two year, full-time new entrant technical training programmes enabling young people to become freelance grade assistants in film and television. It is funded by the industry and managed by representatives from PACT, AFVPA, BECTU, ITVA and Channel 4.

First Film Foundation
222 Kensal Road,London W10 5BN
Tel 0181-969 5195
A charity that works with first-time filmmakers in TV and feature film prodcution.

Gaelic Television Training Trust
Tel 01471-4373
Helping Gaelic-speaking people gain access to the television industry.

Institute of Communications Studies
University of Leeds, Leeds, West Yorkshire LS2 9JT
Fax 0113-233 5805   Tel 0113-233 5805
Britain's oldest academic media research body, originally the Television Research Unit. Mainly looks at the role of TV in political communication.

ITV Network Centre
200 Gray's Inn Road, London WC1X 8HF
Fax 0171-843 8158   Tel 0171-843 8077
It publishes the £7.95 Official ITV Careers Handbook. Otherwise contact the ITV companies direct.

National Association for Higher Education in Film & Video
24 Shelton Street, London WC2H 9HP
Fax 0171-497 3718   Tel 0171-836 9642
Forum for debate on all aspects of film, video and TV education. Fosters links with industry, the professions and government. Represents all courses offering a major practical study in film, video or TV at higher education level.

National Council for the Training of Broadcast Journalists
188 Lichfield Court, Sheen Road, Richmond, Surrey TW9 1BB
Fax and tel 0181-940 0694
The NCTBJ is a voluntary organisation made up of representatives from all sides of the radio and TV industry, the NUJ and colleges which offer courses in broadcast journalism. Its role is to advise and cooperate with the colleges to maintain standards. The Council has worked on the NVQs and is represented on Skillset.

Scottish Broadcast and Film Training
74 Victoria Crescent Road, Dowanhill, Glasgow
G12 9JN
Tel 0141-332 2201
The major training co-ordinator and provider in Scotland.

Skillset
124 Horseferry Road, London SW1P 2TX
Fax 0171-306 8372   Tel 0171-306 8585
The industry training organisation for broadcasting, film and video. Operates at a strategic level, working to improve training and education policy and provision. Publishes an invaluable free careers pack, the best guide available for anyone wanting to enter the industry, plus book lists, a guide to the business and much more. Set up in 1992, Skillset is managed and funded by leading bodies including the BBC, ITV and the independent producers trade body PACT.

Women's Audio Visual Education Scheme
c/o London Women's Centre, 4 Wild Court, London WC2B 5AU
Fax 0171-430 2036   Tel 0171-430 1076
Runs practical and theoretical training courses for women in film, video and radio.

Accredited courses

The BBC and ITV companies run their own in-house courses and should be contacted for further details. Listed below are the institutions running courses accredited by: British Kinematograph Sound and Television Society (BKSTS); Broadcasting Entertainment Cinematograph and Theatre Union (BECTU); National Council for the Training of Broadcast Journalists (NCBTJ)

Bell College of Technology
Hamilton, Lanarkshire
NCTBJ recognised postgraduate diploma in radio journalism.

Bournemouth and Poole College of Art and Design
Wallisdown, Poole, Dorset BH12 5HH
Tel 01202-538204/533011
BKSTS and BECTU accredited HND in film and TV and diplomas in media production and AV design.

Bournemouth University
Talbot Campus, Fern Barrow, Dorset BH12 5BB
Tel 01202-524111
BKSTS validated college, NTCBJ recognised multi-media journalism degree.

Bradford University
Richmond Road, Bradford BD7 1DP
Tel 01274-384001
BKSTS accredited course covering electronic imaging and media.

City University
Graduate Centre for Journalism, St John Street, London EC1V 0HB
Tel 0171-477 8229
NCTBJ recognised courses.

Darlington College of Technology
Cleveland Avenue, Darlington, Durham DL3 7BB
Tel 01325-486643
NCTBJ recognised courses.

Falmouth School of Art and Design
Woodlane, Falmouth, Cornwall TR11 4RA
Tel 01326 211077
NCTBJ recognised courses.

Goldsmiths' College
New Cross, London SE14 6NW
Fax 0181-691 4490   Tel 0181-692 7171
NCTBJ recognised postgraduate course in radio journalism.

Gwent Tertiary College
Blaendare Road, Pontypool, Gwent NP4 5YE
Tel 01495-755141
BECTU accredited courses.

Highbury College of Technology
Cosham, Portsmouth, Hants PO6 2SA
Tel 01705-383131
NCTBJ recognised courses.

London College of Printing
6 Back Hill. Clerkenwell, London EC1R 5EN
Tel 0171-278 7445
BECTU accredited and NCTBJ recognised courses.

London International Film School
24 Shelton Street, London WC2H 9HP
Tel 0171-836 9642
BECTU accredited courses.

National Film and Television School
Beaconsfield Studios, Bucks HP9 1LG
Tel 01494-671234
BECTU accredited courses.

North East Media Training Centre
Stonehills, Gateshead, Tyne & Wear NE10 0HW
Tel 0191-438 4044
BECTU accredited courses.

Nottingham Trent University
Clifton Lane, Nottingham NG11 8NS
Tel 0602-418418
NCTBJ recognised degree in broadcast journalism.

Plymouth College of Art and Design
Tavistock Place, Plymouth PL4 8AT
Tel 01752-385987
BKSTS accredited HND course in film and TV.

Ravensbourne College
Walden Road, Chislehurst, Kent BR7 5SN
Tel 0181-295 8128
BECTU accredited courses.

Salisbury College of Art and Design
Southampton Road, Salisbury, Wilts
Tel 01822-323711
BKSTS accredited HND in film and TV.

South Thames College
Wandsworth High Street, London SW18 2PP
Tel 0181-870 2241
BKSTS accredited HNDs in TV production and AV.

Sunderland University
Chester Road, Sunderland, Tyneside SR1 3SD
Tel 0191-545 2103
NCTBJ recognised postgrad diploma in broadcast journalism.

Trinity and All Saints College
University of Leeds, Leeds LS18 5HD
Tel 01532-584341
NCTBJ recognised one calendar year postgraduate diploma in broadcast journalism.

University of Bristol
29 Park Row, Bristol BS1 5LT
Tel 017 930 3204
BECTU accredited courses.

University of Central England in Birmingham
Perry Bar, Birmingham B42 2SU
Tel 0121-331 5719
NCTBJ recognised 25 week postgraduate course.

University of Central Lancashire
Department of Journalism, Preston PR1 2HE
Tel 01772-201201
NCTBJ recognised journalism degree with a broadcasting option and a postgraduate diploma.

University of Wales
Centre for Journalism Studies, 69 Park Place, Cardiff CF1 3AS
Tel 01222-394069
NCTBJ recognised courses.

University of Westminster
Centre for Communication and Information Studies, 235 High Holborn, London WC1V 7DN
Tel 0171-911 5157
BECTU accredited courses and NCTBJ recognised postgraduate diploma in broadcast journalism.

Vauxhall College
Lambeth College, Vauxhall Centre, London SE1
Tel 0171-498 1234
NCTBJ recognised modular course in radio journalism.

West Surrey College of Art and Design
Falkner Road, Farnham, Surrey GU9 7DS
Tel 01252-722441
BECTU and BKSTS accredited degrees in film and video andin animation. NCTBJ recognised 2 year HND course with radio option and a degree course in journalism.

West Herts College
Hempstead Road, Watford, Herts WD1 3EZ
Tel 01923-257661
BKSTS accredited course in media production.

BROADCAST MAGAZINES

Airflash
15 Paternoster Row, Sheffield S1 2BX
Fax 0114-279 8976   Tel 0114-279 5219
Publisher: Community Radio Association,
Quarterly journal with all that's new in community radio.

Ariel
Room 123, Henry Wood House, 3 Langham Place, London W1A 1AA
Fax 0171-765 3646   Tel 0171-765 3623
Publisher: BBC
Internal weekly staff magazine of the BBC.

Audio Media
Media House, 3 Burrell Road, St Ives, Cambs PE17 4LE
Fax 01480-492422   Tel 01480-461244
Publisher: AM Publishing

A monthly publication aimed at audio professionals in the fields of recording, broadcast, post-production, live sound and multi-media.

Audio Visual
19 Scarbrook Road, Croydon, Surrey CR9 1QH
Fax 0181-681 1672   Tel 0181-688 7788
Publisher: Emap MacLaren
Monthly news on the audio-visual business.

BAPLA Journal
13 Woodberry Crescent, London N10 1PJ
Fax 0181-883 9215   Tel 0181-444 7913
Publisher: British Association of Picture Libraries and Agencies
Essential twice yearly news and information for all picture libraries, agencies and researchers, produced by the leading association in the field.

BBC Worldwide
Bush House, The Strand, London WC2B 4PH
Fax 0171 240 4899   Tel 0171-257 2875
Publisher: BBC World Service.
Monthly programme journal of the World Service, incorporating London Calling.

Better Satellite
57 Rochester Place, London NW1 9JU
Fax 0171-482 6269   Tel 0171-485 0011
Publisher: WV Publications
Quarterly magazine for satellite TV programme consumers.

Books in the Media
15-East Street, Lewins Yard, Chesham, Bucks HP5 1HQ
Fax 01494-784850   Tel 01494-792269
Publisher: Bookwatch.
Weekly resource newsletter keeping bookshops and libraries informed of books appearing in the media. Bookwatch carries out book-related research for newspapers, TV and radio.

Braille Radio/TV Times
Orton Southgate, Peterborough, Cambs PE2 0XU
Fax 01733-371555   Tel 01733-370777
Publisher: Royal National Institute for the Blind.
Two weeklies summarising programmes.

British Journalism Review
13 Smiths Yard, Summerley Street, London SW18 4HR
Fax 0181-947 2664   Tel 0181-947 2777
Publisher: John Libbey & Co/BJR Publishing.
Scholarly quarterly, providing a critical forum for discussion of media topics.

British Journal of Photography
58 Fleet Street, London EC4Y 1JU
Fax 0171-583 4068   Tel 0171-583 3030
Publisher: Bouverie Publishing.
The leading weekly photographic magazine, established 1854.

Broadcast
33 Bowling Green Lane, London EC1R 0DA
Fax 0171-837 8250   Tel 0171-837 1212
Publisher: Emap Media.
The leading weekly newspaper on the TV and radio industry, with news, features and comments; essential reading. Also on broadcasting Emap publishes: International Broadcasting, a specialist monthly for technical equipment managers and engineers; International Broadcasting Asia and Business Video, TV World, 10x pa, on international television; and Television Buyer, a monthly for buyers of the technical equipment.

Cable Guide
5 Factory Lane, Croydon, Surrey CR9 3RA
Fax 0181-681 2340   Tel 0181-681 1133
Publisher: Cable Guide .
Free monthly programme guide, for cable subscribers.

Cable & Satellite Communications International
463 Bethnal Green Road, London E2 9QY
Fax 0171-729 7723   Tel 0171-613 5553
Publisher: View Cable & Satellite
Monthly magazine aimed at management.

Cable & Satellite Europe
531-533 Kings Road, London SW10 0TZ
Fax 0171-352 4883   Tel 0171-351 3612
Publisher: 21st Century Publishing.
Other 21st Century titles include: 5x p.a. Cable and Satellite Express newsletter; 4x p.a., Cable and Satellite Asia; monthly Advanced Television Markets newsletter; monthly Satellite Trader newsletter/magazine, for equipment dealers; Television Business International magazine, 10x pa, for executives; consumer monthly lisitngs guide Satellite TV Europe and consumer monthly entertainment guide, Home Cinema.

Cable Television Engineering
26 Monksdene Gardens, Sutton, Surrey SM13BY
Fax 0181-715 2406   Tel 0181-641 5818
Publisher: WOAC Comms   Tel 0582-873001
Quarterly journal of the Society of Cable Television Engineers.

Convergence
13 Smiths Yard, Summerley Street, London SW18 4HR
Publisher: John LIbbey & Co
Fax 0181-947 2664   Tel 0171-947 2777
Biannual journal of research into new media technologies.

Crosstalk
PO Box 124, Westcliff on Sea, Essex SS0 0QU
Fax 01702-348369   Tel 01702-348369
Publisher: Church Advisory Council
Quarterly news bulletin.

CTE
35 Piccadilly, London W1V 9PB
Fax 0171-734 1737   Tel 0171-734 6143
Publisher: David Sheppard & Associates.
Society of Cable Telecommunication Engineers journal.

Cuts
50 Frith Street, London W1V 5TE
Fax 0171-437 3259   Tel 0171-437 0801
Publisher: Sound & Vision Publishing.
Europe-oriented TV production and post-production monthly.

Digital Media
Nestor House,Playhouse Yard,London EC4V 5EX
Fax 0171-779 8525   Tel 0171-779 8888
Publisher: Euromoney Publications
Business guide to the new media.

Eyepiece
5 Taunton Road, Greenford, Mdx UB6 8UQ
Fax 0181-575 5972   Tel 0181-578 9243
Publisher: Guild of British Camera Technicians.
Magazine covering events around the film industry. 6x pa.

Financial Times Newsletters
Maple House, 149 Tottenham Court Road,
London WC1P 9LL
Fax 0171-896 2256   Tel 0171-896 2222
Publisher: Financial Times Telecom & Media
Publishing.
Produces the following newsletters: Asia-Pacific Telecoms
Analyst; Business Computing Brief; Mobile Communications;
Multimedia Business Analyst; Music & Copyright; New Media
Markets; Screen Finance; Telecom Makets and related manage-
ment reports.

Free Press
8 Cynthia Street, London N1 9JF
Fax 0181-837 8868   Tel 0171-278 4430
Publisher: Campaign for Press and
Broadcasting Freedom.
Members news magazines. 6x pa.

Historical Journal of Film, Radio & Television
PO Box 25, Abingdon, Oxon OX14 3UE
Fax 01235-553559   Tel 01235-555335
Publisher: Carfax Publishing Co.
Quarterly academic journal.

Hot Shoe International
35 Britannia Row, London N1 8QH
Fax 0171-226 1540   Tel 0171-226 1739
Publisher: Creative Magazines.
Covers the visual communications industry: photography, video
and film.

Image
9 Domingo Street, London EC1Y 0TA
Fax 0171-253 3007   Tel 0171-608 1441
Publisher: Association of Photographers.
High quality, monthly magazine, with news, reviews, events and
ads. They also ppublish The Awards Book, an annual of top
advertising and editorial photography.

Image Technology
M6-14 Victoria House, Vernon Place, London
WC1B 4DJ
Fax 0171-405 3560   Tel 0171-242 8400
Publisher: BKSTS.
Monthly technical journal for members of the British
Kinematograph Sound and TV Society.

Information World Review
Woodside, Hinksey Hill, Oxford OX1 5AU
Fax 01865-736354   Tel 01865-730275
Publisher: Learned Information.
Monthly newspaper on the information industry, for users and
producers of electronic information services.

Inside Cable
PO Box 5 Church Stretton, Shropshire SY6 6ZZ.
Fax 01694-724195   Tel 01694-722504
Gives coverage of UK cable industry with a focus on service
development in the context of the 'information super highway'.

InterMedia
Tavistock House South, Tavistock Square,
London WC1H 9LF
Fax 0171-380 0623   Tel 0171-388 0671
Publisher: International Institute of
Commun-ications.
Discussion journal covering issues affecting international
telecommunications, broadcasting and media. 6x pa.

International Broadcast Engineer
2 Queensway, Redhill, Surrey RH1 1QS
Fax 01737-760564   Tel 01737-768611
Publisher: International Trade Publications Ltd.
Looking at broadcast technology, for senior engineering and
operational staff. 6x pa.

International Broadcasting
See: Broadcast, above.

Journal of Educational Media
37 Monk Gate, York YO3 7PB
Fax: 01904-639212   Tel 01904-639212
Publisher: Carfax Pubishing Co..
Academic journal, published 3x pa, providing forum for
discussing developments in TV and related media in education.

Kagan World Media
524 Fulham Road, London SW6 5NR
Fax 0171-371 8715   Tel 0171-371 8880
Kagan is an international company specialising in analysis of the
media and communications industries. It publishes a range of
Europe-oriented monthly newsletters, covering topics around TV,
cable, video and radio, and annual reports.

Line Up
27 Old Gloucester Street, London WC1N 3XX
Fax 01323-491739   Tel 01323-491739
Publisher: Institute of Broadcast Sound.
Journal mixing technical information, news and articles by prac-
titioners in sound. 6x pa.

London Calling
See: BBC Worldwide, above.

MED-MEDIA
TVE, Prince Albert Road, London NW1 4RZ
Fax 0171-586 7719   Tel 0171-483 3848
Publisher: MED-MEDIA Programme (EU).
Twice-yearly bulletin launched in 1994 under the European
Union's New Mediterranean Policy, to explain MED MEDIA pro-
gramme which aims to increase understanding between the EC
and non-member countries in the Mediterranean.

Media Action UK
21 Stephen Street, London W1P 1PL
Fax 0171-636 6568   Tel 0171-255 1444
Publisher: UK Media Desk, BFI
Internal newsletter of the Media Desk, keeping members
informed about the Media Programme of the EC countries, plus
other film media news.

Media, Culture & Society
6 Bonhill Street, London EC2A 4PU
Fax 0171-374 8741   Tel 0171-374 0645
Publisher: Sage Publications.
Wide-ranging, academic journal,.

Media Education Journal
c/o Scottish Film Council, 74 Victoria Crescent
Road, Glasgow G12 9JN
                              Tel 0141-334 4445
Publisher: Media Education in Scotland.
Two journals p.a. for media teachers. They also publish teaching
packs and newsletters.

Middle East Broadcast & Satellite
Chancery House, St Nicholas Way, Sutton ,
Surrey SM1 1JB
Fax 0181-642 1941   Tel 0181-6421117
Publisher: Icom Publications Ltd.
Quarterly on the broadcasting scene in the Middle East and India
with a bi-annual suplement Middle East Satellite Today. They
also publish Middle East Satellite Today for satellite buyers,
distributors and resellers and Middle East Communications.

Moving Pictures International
1 Richmond Mews, London W1V 5AG
Fax 0171-287 9637   Tel 0171-287 0070
Publisher: Moving Pictures International Ltd.
Weekly coverage of the international film, TV and video industry.

MultiMedia
19 Scarbrook Road, Croydon, Surrey CR9 1QH
Fax 0181-688 9300   Tel 0181-688 7788
Publisher: Emap MacLaren.
Quarterly review of the expanding multimedia technology, aimed
at the large organisations.

Pact
PACT, Gordon House, Greencoat Place, London
SW1P 1PH
Fax 0171-233 8935   Tel 0171-233 6000
Publisher: Producers Alliance for Cinema and
TV.
Monthly internal magazine for independent prod-ucers, examin-
ing key topical issues.

The Photographer
Fox Talbot House, Amwell End, Ware, Herts
SG12 9HN
Fax 01920-487056   Tel 01920-464011
Publisher: Icon Publications, for British Institute
of Professional Photography,
The BIPP's "journal of images and imaging technology", with
news from the industry.

Programme News
19 Hackford Walk, London SW9 0QA
Fax 0171-587 1373   Tel 0171-793 8220
Independent broadcast listings. The guide to who is making what
for broadcast where. 6x pa.

Radio
PO Box 4SZ, London W1A 4SZ
Fax 0171-765 4992   Tel 0171-323 3837
Publisher: The Radio Academy.
Quarterly magazine of the radio industry's leading professional
society.

The Radio Magazine
Crown House, 25 High Street, Rothwell,
Northants NN14 2AD
Fax 01536-418539   Tel 01536-418558
Publisher: Goldcrest Broadcasting.
Weekly, glossy magazine; small, but packed with snippets of
information on the radio world.

Radio Times
Woodlands, 80 Wood Lane, London W12 0TT
                              Tel 0181-576 2000
Publisher: BBC Magazines.
The BBC's key magazine, detailing all TV programmes, including
those of ITV and satellite, plus radio. Is now part of BBC
Worldwide Publishing.

Reportage
PO Box 2029, London W1A1GD
Fax 0171-287 4767   Tel 0171-439 2409
Independent quarterly magazine of photo-journalism,
in large format, telling stories in black-and-white
photos, and allowing photographers to talk about what
they see and do. Started 1993.

Satellite Guide
Business Centre, 11 Capper Street, London
WC1E 6JA   Tel 0171-436 8383
Publisher: MCA
Monthly consumer guide to satellite viewing.

Satellite TV Europe
531 Kings Road, London SW10 0TZ
Fax 0171-352 9657   Tel 0171-351 3612
Publisher: 21st Century Consumer Publishing.
Consumer guide to all European satellite TV channels.
Monthly.

Satellite Times
23 Mitcham Lane, London SW16 6QL
Fax 0181-677 8223   Tel 0181-677 7822
Publisher: Everpage
Prominent monthly consumer magazine for the satellite and
cable television viewers.

Satellite Trader/Satellite Today
See: Cable & Satellite Europe, above.

Screen Digest
37 Gower Street, London WC1E 6HH
Fax 0171-580 0060   Tel 0171-580 2842
Publisher: Screen Digest.
Monthly round-up of internaional news, research and statistics
on film, video and television, aimed at executives.

Screen International
33 Bowling Green Lane, London EC1R 0DA
Fax 0171-837 8305   Tel 0171-837 1212
Publisher: Emap Media.
Prominent weekly magazine on the international cinema business.

Short Wave Magazine
Enefco House, The Quay, Poole, Dorset BH15 1PP
Fax 01202-659950   Tel 01202-659910
Publisher: PW Publishing.
The monthly magazine for enthusiasts of short wave broadcasting.

Sight & Sound
21 Stephen Street, London W1P 1PL
Fax 0171-436 2327   Tel 0171-255 1444
Publisher: British Film Institute.
Leading monthly magazine for the film world.

Spectrum
33 Foley Street, London W1P 7LB
Fax 0171-306 7738   Tel 0171-255 3000
Publisher: Independent Television Commission.
The quarterly news magazine of the ITC.

Stage, Screen & Radio
111 Wardour Street, London W1V 4AY
Fax 0171-437 8268   Tel 0171-437 8506
Publisher: BECTU.
Monthly journal of the largest trade union in broadcasting, with news from around the industry. Available on subscription to non-members.

The Stage & Television Today
47 Bermondsey Street, London SE1 3XT
Fax 0171-403 1418   Tel 0171-403 1818
The independent weekly newspaper of the theatre world, with a special section on TV. They also publish Showcall, a light entertainment directory.

Summary of World Broadcasts Media
BBC Monitoring, Caversham Park, Reading, Berks RG4 8TZ
Fax 01734-463823   Tel 01734-469289
Weekly BBC newsletter, also on the Internet, for broadcasters with news of industry developments around the world as obtained by the monitoring of overseas broadcasters. The newsletter is available in two parts: World Broadcasting Information (£383 pa) and Broadcasting Schedules (£104 pa); or together they cost £435 pa. Accompanying the newsletter is the WBI Directory, a loose-leaf guide to the broadcasting stations covered in the weekly service.

Television
100 Grays Inn Road, London WC1X 8AL
Fax 0171-430 0924   Tel 0171-430 1000
Publisher: Royal Television Society.
Bi-monthly journal.

Television
Quadrant House, The Quadrant, Sutton, Surrey SM2 5AS
Fax 0181-652 8956   Tel 0181-652 8120
Publisher: Reed Business.
Specialist monthly news for the television electronics engineer.

Television Asia
81 Leonard Street, London EC2A 4QS
Fax 0171-739 1089   Tel 0171-739 1134
Publisher: Partners in Media
Bi-monthly glossy magazine looking at the TV business across Asia. Launched in 1993.

Television Business International
See: Cable & Satellite Europe, above.

Television Buyer
See: Broadcast, above.

TV Quick
25 Camden Road, London NW1 9LL
Fax 0171-284 0593   Tel 0171-284 0909
Publisher: H Bauer Publishing
Weekly witty TV listings magazine geared to women's interests.

TV & Satellite Week
Kings Reach Tower, Stamford Street, London SE1 9LS   Tel 0171-261 7534
Publisher: IPC Magazines.
A weekly consumers guide to what's on satellite and terrestial TV.

TV Times
Kings Reach Tower, Stamford Street, London SE1 9LS   Tel 0171-261 5000
Publisher: IPC Magazines.
Weekly details of television programmes. After it began in 1968 it was the ITV rival to the BBC's Radio Times. Sales of the TV Times have now been overtaken by IPC's mass-market magazine What's On TV, operating out of the same offices.

Television Today
See: The Stage & Television Today, above.

Television Week
Incorporated into Broadcast (cf, above) in 1993.

TV World
See: Broadcast, above.

TV Zone
9 Blades Court, Deodar Road, London SW15 2NU
Fax 0181-875 1588   Tel 0181-875 1520
Publisher: Visual Imagination Ltd.
Monthly news and features on cult television programmes, like Doctor Who.

Televisual
50 Poland Street, London W1V 4AX
Fax 0171-287 0768   Tel 0171-439 4222
Publisher: Centaur Communications Ltd.
Monthly business magazine for independent producers, facility providers and the TV industry.

UK Press Gazette
Emap Business Communications, Chalk Lane, Cockfosters Road, Barnet, Herts EN4 OBU
Fax 0181-242 3088   Tel 0181-242 3000
Publisher: Emap.
The weekly paper for all journalists, covering newspapers, magazines, television and radio.

Vertigo
7 Earlham Street, London WC2H 9LL
Fax: 0171-497 0446   Tel 0171-240 2350
New independent film, video and television quarterly providing a focus for debate about the media industries and their products.

Viewfinder
55 Greek Street, London W1V 5LR
Fax 0171-287 3914   Tel 0171-734 3687
Publisher: British Universities Film/Video Council.
News and features published 3x pa by the British Universities Film/Video Council, which exists to promote the production, study and use of film, TV and related media for higher education and research.

Voice of the Listener & Viewer
101 Kings Drive, Gravesend, Kent DA12 5BQ
Fax: Phone first.01474-352835
Publisher: Voice of the Listener and Viewer.
Quarterly journal of the independent watchdog, which bills itself as "the only consumer body speaking about the full range of broadcasting issues".

What Satellite TV
57 Rochester Place, London NW1 9JU
Fax 0171-482 6269   Tel 0171-485 0011
Publisher: WV Publications.
Monthly consumer magazine for the mass market, with news on "the equipment to buy and the programmes to watch". In 1993 WV launched the consumer magazine Buying Satellite, a guide to equipment on the market.

What's On TV
See: TV Times, above.

Zerb
1 Churchill Road, Whitchurch, Tavistock, Devon PL19 9BU
Fax 01822-614405   Tel 01822-614405
Publisher: Guild of TV Cameramen.
The Guild of Television Cameramen's half-yearly glossy journal.

YEARBOOKS

BAPLA Directory
British Association of Picture Libraries & Agencies   Tel 0181-444 7913
£10.
An invaluable guide to picture sources by Britain's leading association. With full details of all members, a description of their stock, a subject index and hints for library users.

BBC Broadcasting Research
John Libbey & Co   Tel 0181-947 2777
The BBC produces two annual audience research surveys. The Annual Review of BBC Broadcasting Research (£17.50) presents a digest of the corporation's main studies over the previous year. Global Audiences: Research for Worldwide Broadcasting (£24) by the World Service focuses on the international audience.

Benn's Media
Benn Business Information Services   Tel 01732-362666
Three vols £248, single vols £104.
Benn's has the most comprehensive listings amongst the general media directories. It comes in three volumes, covering the UK, Europe and the rest of the world.

Blue Book of British Broadcasting
Tellex Monitors   Tel 0171-490 1447
£45
The most comprehensive contacts book for radio and TV, containing thousands of names,addresses and phone numbers.

Bowkers Complete Video Directory
Bowker-Saur   Tel 01732-884567
£200, two vols.
Lists virtually every video in every format.

British Film Institute Film & TV Handbook
BFI   Tel 0171-255 1444
£14.95.
Combines hundreds of useful film and broadcasting facts and figures with an extensive directory of thousands of contacts and addresses. The best value book in its field.

British Media Guide
Media Guide   Tel 0171-938 2222
Annual directory of companies that have paid to be included. Distributed free to certain outlets.

Broadcast Diary
See: Broadcast Production Guide, next page

Broadcasting Standards Council Annual Reviews
John Libbey & Co   Tel 0181-947 2777
A themed annual review by the BSC. Recent topics have included Violence in Factual TV, Sex & Sexuality, and Taste & Decency.

Broadcast Production Guide
Emap Media   Tel 0171-837 1212
£45
Annual details of technical contacts, services and equipment, from the publishers of the prominent weekly magazine Broadcast. Also available: International Broadcasting Directory, £40, guide to international broadcasting hardware and services; Broadcast Diary, £40, desk diary with extensive industry information; Screen International Film & TV Directory, three volumes of data on companies, people and countries, £60; and TV Buyer Handbook, £40, the producers guide to the global TV market.

Cable & Satellite Yearbook
21st Century Publishing   Tel 0171-351 3612
£75
Comprehensive details of the industry in all European countries, covering manufacturers, distributors and broadcasters, plus a breakdown of each nation. Also published are: TV Business International, £140, with all the world's TV stations and prices; Co-Production International, £160, a guide to co-producing programmes.

Cable TV & Telecom Yearbook
See: Who's Who in Cable & Satellite, below.

The Creative Handbook
Reed Information Services   Tel 01342-326972
£104
Large, glossy bible for anyone working in the commercial creative arts. New in 1993 was the first edition of a partner publication, the European Creative Handbook, now£90

Directors Guild Directory
Directors Guild of Gt Britain Tel 0171-383 3858
A-Z of Britain's broadcasting directors.

Directors and Producers Directory
BECTU   Tel 0171-437 8506
£9.95 (members £5).
Contains the names and addresses of over 1,000 producers and directors who are members of the London Production Division of the main broadcasting trade union BECTU.

Directory of British Film & TV Producers
Pact (Producers Alliance for Cinema and Television,   Tel 0171-233-6000
£25.
Full details of PACT members.

Directory of International Film & Video Festivals
British Film Institute   Tel 0171-255 1444
£10.20.
Details of over 300 international festivals.

European Media Minibook Series
NTC Publications   Tel 01491-574671
£48 each.
Four books profiling the statistics of the main media markets in Europe: TV, Radio, Cinema and Newspapers & Magazines

European Multimedia Yearbook
Interactive Media Publications,
£95.
Guide to the new multimedia industry, with articles and listings of companies, products, suppliers, services, etc. A free CD-ROM version accompanies the book. First published 1992.

Film and TV Handbook
See: British Film Institute, above.

International Broadcasting Directory
See: Broadcast Production Guide, above.

IPO Directory
Central Office of Information
     Tel 0171-261 8534
£12 annual subscription.
The official directory of the information and press officers in government departments and public corporations. Published bi-annually.

Kays UK Production Manual
Kays Publishing   Tel 0181-749 1214
£55.
With its Crew Directory, this is one of the most comprehensive and reliable manuals of people and organisations in the production side of the film, TV and broadcast industry. Contains 15,000 names and addresses in over 250 classifications. Also available is its European equivalent the European Production Manual (£75), plus the Art Diary (£25) listing the art business.

Kemps Film, TV & Video Yearbook
Reed Information Services   Tel 01342-335889
£65
Long-established directory of the film and television production industries in nearly every country. Recently taken over by Reed and revamped.

The Knowledge
Benn Business Information Services
     Tel 01732-362666
£63.50
The leading guide to the products and services of the UK film, TV and video industry. Over 10,000 A-Z listings of equipment, technicians and specialist services, plus features on codes of conduct, procedures, specifications, and more.

The Media Guide
Fourth Estate, for The Guardian
     Tel 0171-727-8993
£12
You're reading it.

Pims Media Directories
Pims International   Tel 0171-226 1000
Pims produces a range of detailed, loose-leaf guides to editorial media contacts, all regularly updated, aimed mainly at the public relations sector. Titles include: UK Media Directory (£298 pa), Townslist Directory (£160) and several USA/European directories (£140 each).

RADAD
Radio Advertising Bureau Tel 0171-636 5858
Free
Pocket handbook of radio advertising, providing an overview of the independent radio industry, with masses of data and listings information.

Radio Authority Pocket Guide
Radio Authority Tel 0171-430 2724
Free
Regularly updated reference booklet to the independent radio business. The authority also produces a free video called "The Radio Authority - What It Is, What It Does", aimed at students.

Radio Listener's Guide
PDQ Publishing Tel 01865-820387
£3.95.
Pocket guide to all the UK radio stations, detailing which wavelengths they are on, and explaining clearly how to tune in. This is an invaluable aid to those trying to find their way around the radio dial.

Radio Times Yearbook
Ravette Books, 0171-344 6400
£14.95.
A review of the television and radio events and programmes of the previous year, aimed at the popular market.

Reporters Sans Frontieres Report
John Libbey & Co Tel 0181-947 2777
£18.
An annual report published by the independent France-based body Reporters Sans Frontieres of the state of freedom in the world's press. The 1995 report showed that at 103 working journalists died in 1994, the highest number since records were started.

Royal Television Society Handbook
RTS Tel 0171-430 1000
£6.50
Guide to the society, with directory of its many members, leading figures in the TV world.

Satellite Broadcasting Guide
Billboard Tel 0171-323 6686
£16.95
Details of installation methods, satellite global coverage and satellite broadcasters.

Screen International Film & Television Directory
See: Broadcast Production Guide, above.

The Television Book
Edinburgh International Television Festival
  Tel 0171-379 4519
£9.99.
Published to tell people of the profusion of programmes and programme-making issues arising at the annual August festival in Edinburgh.

Television Business International Yearbook
21st Century Publishing Tel 0171-352 3211
£150.
Handbook for international TV executives, with facts, statistics and contact details.

Television: The Public's View
John Libbey & Co Tel 0181-947 2777
£16.
Annual wide-ranging survey by the Independent Television Commission of the public's use of TV and their views on what they see. Libbey also publish the ITC's occasional monographs.

TV World Handbook
See: Broadcast Production Guide, above.

TV World Very Useful Handbook
See: Broadcast Production Guide, above.

University of Manchester Broadcasting Symposia
John Libbey & Co Tel 0181-947 2777
Each year all sides of the broadcasting industry meet for a symposium organised by the University of Manchester. The proceedings, usually lively, are published later by John Libbey in book form.

WBI Directory
BBC Monitoring Tel 01734-472742
£58.
The World Broadcasting Directory details international broadcasting stations around the world. It supplements the weekly newsletter WBI (see under Periodicals heading below). Produced by the BBC's monitoring unit.

The White Book
The White Book Tel 01784-464441
£43.
The key international production directory.

Who's Who in Cable & Satellite
WOAC Communications Tel 01582-873001
£10.95.
Biannual pocket directory of the organisations and people in the cable and satellite worlds (mainly cable). WOAC also publishes the Cable TV and Telecom Yearbook (£14.95)..

Who's Who in Commonwealth Broadcasting
£10 Commonwealth Broadcasting Assocation
Pocketbook with main Commonwealth broadcasters.

World Radio & TV Handbook
Billboard Tel 0171-323 6686
£18.95.
World broadcasting stations, by frequency, time and language.

World Satellite Yearly
Baylin Publications Tel 01734-414468
£59.
American technical manual and guide to satellites

GUIDE THIS GUIDE ...

... and perhaps win a case of champagne

Your answers to the questions below will help us update the next edition. The questions are in order of importance and we don't need you to answer every one if you don't want to. The questionnaires with a phone number on them will go into an office hat at the end of February 1996. The first to be pulled out wins a case of champagne

Job title ....

Media sector ....

Which town or city are you based in? ....

Where did you buy the 1996 Guardian Media Guide? ....

How did you find out about the Media Guide? ....

Employer ....

Your name ....

Daytime phone number ....

Are there other categories or contacts you'd put in the book?

CROSS MEDIA OWNERSHIP

At the beginning of June United Newspapers rechristened itself United News and Media. Rather than being mere image tinkering, the name change is a reflection that we are moving into a realm of generalised media. Convergence is the word for it and it is a term that enthrals media owners. They must diversify or die and deal in TV as well as newspapers, in magazines as well as radio. Some of the urgency is a hankering after greater profit and influence, some a bending to the winds of techno-change.

Technology is blurring the obvious demarcations between newspapers and TV. As newspapers convert to digital editing, so computerised delivery of their digitised pages surely follows. Examples proliferate. The Guardian, for one example, siphons off its digitised text and recasts it in the terms of a computer database. The entire editorial is transferred on to CD ROMs. and also converted into a megabyte of data for nightly broadcast to the computers of the blind. It is distributed in exactly the same way as a TV signal and reconstituted as a synthesised voice. This computerised version of The Guardian can also be read on screen by the sighted and is consumed in a way that allows the users to treat what started as a conventional newspaper as they would any other database. To lapse into computer jargon, they access the information by key words. It is, in fact an extension of scanning a paper for headlines and is something which can't be done with TV. Yet.

Convergence is causing a rush towards cross media ownership with newspapers buying slices of TV stations and vice versa. When the majority of newspaper owners (although not the two largest) united to lobby for a relaxation of cross media ownership rules, the government found itself being asked a straightforward question: what are the maximum shares of which markets that any one media company should control? A digest of the suggestions provided in the June 1995 Media Ownership green paper are at the top of the next column. Most await primary legislation, probably by summer 1996, although the increase in the limit of radio licenses and doubling the newspaper circulation thresholds for MMC referral were made law at the end of July 1995.

The green paper resulted in clear winners and losers. The winners were Associated

New ownership rules

Newspaper companies with under 20 per cent of national newspaper circulation can control radio and TV companies with up to a 15 per cent market share within any given locality

Regional newspaper companies can't own local TV or radio licences if they control 30 per cent of an area's newspaper circulation

The two licence limit on ITV companies remains and terrestrial broadcasters will be allowed controlling interests in satellite and cable companies, provided they do not exceed 15 per cent of audience share

An end to the 50 per cent limit on combined Channel 3 holdings in ITN

An increase in the limit of radio licenses from 20 to 35

Doubling, to 50,000, of the minimum circulation for newspaper mergers to be referred to the Monopolies and Mergers Commission

Newspapers, the Guardian Media Group, The Telegraph and Pearson. They funded the British Media Industry Group which, in a copybook lobbying operation, persuaded the Department of National Heritage to accept its "share of voice" equation of media power and to include itsliberalising suggestions in the green paper. The BMIG has switched lobbying efforts to ensure the proposals become law.

The losers are News Corporation (aka News

What the winners said ...

The FT: "A reasonable compromise."
The Guardian: "A fair fist of a potentially contradictory remit."
Daily Mail: "An enlightened balance between regulation and freedom."
Daily Telegraph: "Radical proposals and welcome ones."

Share of the national voice

		national press	local press	TV	radio	total
1	Other media owners	1.3%	47.8%	16.%	31.6%	**23.2%**
2	BBC	-	-	43.6%	50.3%	**19.7%**
3	News Internatiional	35.3%	-	1.9%	-	**10.6%**
4	Mirror Group	26.1%	-	0.5%	-	**7.6%**
5	Daily Mail & Gen. Trust	12.4%	14.3%	0.2%	0.9%	**7.8%**
6	United News and Media	14.4%	5.7%	-	-	**5.7%**
7	Carlton Communications	-	-	10.9%	-	**3.1%**
8	Thomson Newspapers	-	10.2%	-	-	**2.9%**
9	ITC	-	-	10.1%	-	**2.9%**
10	Granada Goup	-	-	8.9%	-	**2.5%**
11	Pearson	1.0%	5.7%	1.5%	-	**2.3%**
12	Guardian Media Group	2.9%	3.6%	0.7%	-	**2.0%**
13	Daily Telegraph	6.6%	-	-	-	**1.9%**
14	Emap	-	3.7%	-	4.8%	**1.7%**
15	Trinity Holdings	-	6.%	-	-	**1.7%**
16	Capital Radio	-	-	-	9.0%	**1.3%**
17	MAI	-	-	4.1%	-	**1.2%**
18	Reed Elsevier	-	3.%	-	-	**0.9%**
19	GWR Group	-	-	-	3.4%	**0.5%**
20	DCI/Cox/TCI/Flextech	-	-	1.6%	-	**0.5%**

The British Media Industry Group devised "share of national voice" as a way of accounting for the influence of cross media ownership and of calculating the influence of the modern media companies. It is defined as any one company's overall share of the combined consumption of national and paid for regional papers, of radio listening and of TV viewing. The share of voice percentages combines figures from ABC, the Newspaper Society, Rajar and Barb. Because most of radio is music (and thus has less effect on diversity of view) radio listening figures are down-weighted by 50 per cent. The main criticism of the share of voice approach is that including the BBC and C4 underestimates the way the rest of Britain's media ownership is concentrated in so few private hands.

International aka Rupert Murdoch) and Mirror Group Newspapers. Murdoch howled the loudest, as well he might. Having led the way into this brave new world, the new rules will mean that his 36 per cent share of national newspapers and 40 per cent share of BSkyB leaves News Corporation with no room to expand. During a series of uncharacteristic interviews and press releases Murdoch implied he might shut loss making papers and withdraw support for the Conservatives at the next election. Other potential losers are the larger local newpapers owners, resentful that the 30 per cent circulation threshhold would restrict them from buying into local radio and TV. And the PPA complained that magazine owners are still banned from converting their titles into TV programmes. A fair point when so much TV is made into magazines whilst ITC sponsorship rules prevent mag-to-prog routes to profit.

... and the losers

Rupert Murdoch: "Is this really the government of enterprise and competition?"
The Times: "...muddle, weakness and defeatism ... fear, favour and misplaced philosophy ..."
The Sun: The Tories want to penalise success and reward the also-rans."
Sunday Times: "A scheme to punish success and reward indolence in the name of media pluralism."
Lord Hollick, managing director of MAI: "The government should follow the logic of its own proposals and sweep away the artificial rule which restricts ITV ownership to two licences and instead measure by share of audience or revenue."

Tom O'Malley of the Campaign for Press and Broadcasting Freedom predicted a reduction in the number of titles and he wrote to the Guardian saying: "The proposals open the door for an increase in the concentration of media ownership. They grant a few companies the possibility of wielding immense, and relatively unaccountable, power over our cultural and political agenda. These proposals make little sense to those concerned about the quality and accountability of our media."

As the What the winners said ... panel on the previous page reveals, members of the BMIG lobby welcomed the changes and the consensus here is that liberalisation will encourage plurality among newspaper and TV companies while simultaneously encouraging building businesses large enough to take on American competitors. But whether a newspaper company will actually get hold of a television station is another matter. As of writing the green paper had stimulated radio owners to the most activity and otherwise had fuelled speculation that: Carlton will buy the Daily or Sunday Express; that the newly named United News and Media will sell the Daily or Sunday Express to finance radio and TV ventures; that the Daily Mail and General Trust may sell local papers in order to buy an ITV company or Capital Radio; that the Telegraph might snap up some Murdoch cast offs like Today or The Times; that Pearson will continue its expansion into TV. The permutations are infinite and the only sure thing is that changes in ownership will render bits of this book way out of date before it's even printed. We'll have to go digital.

Cross-media ownership: Key contacts

British Media Information Group
7 The Sanctuary, Parliament Square, London SW1P 3JS
Fax 0171-222 5872   Tel 0171 799 1500

Campaign for Press and Broadcasting Freedom
8 Cynthia Street, London N1 9JF
Fax 0171-837 8868   Tel: 0171-278 4430

Department of National Heritage (Broadcasting Policy Division)
2-4 Cockspur Street, London SW1Y 5DH
Tel 0171-211 6466

Media Ownership: The Government's Proposals
A £6.75 green paper from HMSO

INTERNET

Originally the Internet was a dispersed computer network built by the American military to be nuke proof. It is now a global network linking individuals' computers to each other and into countless databases. Uses are twofold: first, electronic mail which merges into membership of informal newsgroups that swap information in ways conventional media can't match. Secondly, surfing the World Wide Web to browse or
plunder the contents of computer databases wherever they exist. Estimates of the number connected vary between 20 and 40 million and by early in the next century linkage will be as common as phone or TV ownership is now.

Fans of the Internet - and here's a subject to unhinge normal journalistic scepticism - claim it is every bit as revolutionary as the invention of printing. They say the widespread linkage of computers will alter power balances by enabling everybody with a computer modem and phone line to be a publisher, radio station and TV studio. Disintermediation is the clumsy word describing an emerging media landscape where there are no controllers of information. Should this comes to pass, it means that the dictum about freedom of the press being guaranteed only to those who own a press no longer stands.

Media owners are well aware of possible losses and profits in a less structured media and are quickly getting involved. News International has bought the American on-line company Delphi. Reed Elsevier has bought Mead Data which manages the US Library of Congress. The BBC has its own networking club and has put programme listings on line. The Liverpool Daily Post and Daily Telegraph are the first newspapers to put their contents online and every alert newspaper management has plans to do likewise. Magazine publishers have been swift to spot a new hobby with The Internet from Emap, .Net (spoken Dot net) from Future Publishing and the Guardian Media Group's co-ownership of Wired. "The authentic voice of the Internet world view," wrote John Gray in The Guardian. "It is cool and postmodern and at the same time innocently Utopian."

Whether the Internet makes the earth move or not, it is part of a technolgical shift that could make the craft of journalism unrecognisable within a few years. Any journalist who is Internet illiterate could soon be as useless as one who

Internet gateways

Getting wired to the world requires an account with one of the gateway companies selling access to the Internet. The typical connection charge is £25 plus around £10 monthly charges and, assuming the gateway is within range, local phone bills for global computer linkage.

BBC Networking Club
Tel: 0181-576 7799
E-Mail: info@bbcncc.org.uk
Web page: http://www.bbcnc.org.uk/

CityScape/IP GOLD
Tel: 01223 566950
E-Mail: sales@cityscape.co.uk
Web page: http://www.cityscape.co.uk/

CIX
Tel: 01492 641961
E-Mail: Webmaster@compulink.co.uk
Web page: http://www.compulink.co.uk

CompuServe
Tel: 0800 289378
E-Mail: 70006.101@compuserve.com

Delphi Internet
Tel: 0171-757 7080
E-Mail: ukservice@delphi.com
Web page: http://www.delphi.com

Demon Internet
Tel: 0181-371 1234
E-Mail: sales@demon.net
Web page: http://www.demon.co.uk

Easynet
Tel: 0171-209 0990
E-Mail: admin@easynet.co.uk
Web page: http://www.easynet.co.uk

Pavilion Internet
Tel: 01273 607072
E-Mail: info@pavilion.co.uk
Web page: http://www.pavilion.co.uk

PC User Group
Tel: 0181-863 1191
E-Mail: info@win-uk.net
Web page: http://www.ibmpcug.co.uk

Pipex Dial
Tel: 01223 250120
E-Mail: sales@pipex.net
Web page: http://www.ws.pipex.com

Media web sites

Below are Internet sites already being operated by conventional media owners.

BBC Networking Club
http://www.bbcnc.org.uk/

FutureNet
http://www.futurenet.co.uk/

Guardian OnLine
http://www.gold.net/online/

Press Association
http://www.padd.press.net/

Daily Telegraph - Electronic Telegraph
http://www.telegraph.co.uk/

Time Out
http://www.timeout.co.uk

Other web sites

A list of sites most commonly accessed by the Guardian's Jack Schofield.

BARD (Bodleian Access to Remote Databases)
http://www.rsl.ox.ac.uk/bardhtml

Best of British
http://www.,vnu.co.uk/vnu/pcw/bob.html

Cerberus Sound+Vision
http://www.cerberus.co.uk/cdj/

Edinburgh Microsoft Windows Academic Centre
http://emwac.ed.ac.uk/

Hypermedia Research Centre
http://www..wmin.ac.uk/media/HRC/

Imperial College London
http://src.doc.ic.ac.uk/

Internet Movie Database
http://www.cm.cf.ac.uk/Movies/

State 51
http://www.state51.co.uk/state51/

UK Web-Server Guide
http://src.doc.ic.ac.uk/all-uk.html

World Conservation Monitoring Centre
http://www.wcmc.org.uk/

MEDIA LOBBYISTS

All Party Media Group
c/o Nicholas Winterton MP, House of
Commons, London SW1A 0AA
Tel 0171-219 3585
Cross party forum of 100 MPs and peers with an interest in
media issues. See Government Relations Unit, below.

Amnesty International Journalists' Network
Queen Street, Derby DE1 3DX
Fax 01332-290852   Tel 01332-290852
Campaigns on behalf of media workers who have disappeared,
been imprisoned, tortured or threatened with death. Holds
meetings and publishes quarterly newsletter.

Article 19, the International Centre Against Censorship
33 Islington High Street, London NN1 9LH
Fax 0171-713 1356   Tel 0171-278 9292
International human rights organisation campaigning for the
right to freedom of expression and information. Promotes
improved legal standards for freedom of expression and defends
victims of censorship. Publishes regular newsletter and a range
of country and theme reports, with emphasis on media freedom.

Broadcasting Consortium
8 All Saints Street, London N1 9RL
Fax 0171-713 6300   Tel 0171-713 6161
Coalition of national charities working to protect and enlarge vol-
untary organisations' access to radio and TV. It publishes The
Good Radio Guide, explaining how to influence the outcome of
the re-advertising of local radio services, and The Good
Franchise Guide, showing charities how to get involved with ITV

Campaign for Freedom of Information
88 Old Street, London EC1V 9AX
Fax 0171-608 3325   Tel 0171-253 2445
The campaign is pressing for a Freedom of Information Act
which would create a general right of access to official records
subject to exemptions protecting information whose disclosure
would cause real harm to essential interests such as defence,
law enforcement and privacy. Campaigns for a public interest
defence under the Official Secrets Act. It also seeks disclosure
in the private sector on issues of public interest. It publishes the
newspaper Secrets, plus briefings and other publications.

Campaign for Press and Broadcasting Freedom
8 Cynthia Street, London N1 9JF
Fax 0171-837 8868   Tel 0171-278 4430
Campaigns for a democratic, diverse and accountable media,
accessible to all. The CPBF opposes monopoly ownership of the
press and seeks a Freedom of Information Act. It organises
events and publishes bi-monthly journal Free Press, occasional
pamphlets and the Media Catalogue of mail order books, videos
and postcards. The wall chart Britain's Media shows the ways
British media companies are connected.

Government Relations Unit (Media Division)
3 Goodwins Court, London WC2N 4LL
Fax 0171-379 6095   Tel.0171-240 7172
The only specialist source of advice and assistance to all
sections of the media industries about how best to identify,
approach and influence key decision-makers in Westminster,
Whitehall and Brussels. The unit offers guidance on
Parliamentary procedure, amending legislation and contesting
European regulations. Chairman: Nicholas Winterton MP. It
services the programme of the All Party Media Group (see
above).

Media Research Group
c/o Nick Hiddleston, 36 Howard Street, London
W1
Fax 0171-915 2165   Tel 0171-580 6690
Provides forum for debating issues relating primarily to media
planning and research. Holds bi-annual conference.

Media Society
PO Box 124, East Rudham, Kings Lynn, Norfolk
PE31 8TT
Fax 01485-528155   Tel 01485-528664
Forum for discussing topical issues in the media, usually in the
form of luncheons and dinners in London addressed by
prominent figures (summaries of the speeches available). Also
submits evidence to appropriate select committees, commissions and enquiries.

Media Workers Against the Nazis
PO Box 3739, London E5 8EJ
Campaigns among media workers to: (1) stop Nazis (members
of the British National Party and National Front) using the press,
TV and radio to propagate fascist news; and (2) encourage
media workers to expose the Nazi's racist violence and anti-
democratic aims. Launched in April 1994.

National Viewers and Listeners Association
All Saints House, High Street, Colchester, Essex
CO1 1UG
Tel 01206 561155
The right wing TV monitoring body.

PressWise
Enderby House, Chester CH1 4AH
Fax 01244-390914   Tel 01244-390681
Charitable trust promoting high standards of journalism and
aiming to empower those ordinary people who become victims of
unfair media intrusion and inaccurate or irresponsible reporting.
Set up in 1993 by Clive Soley MP.

Voice of the Listener and Viewer
101 King's Drive, Gravesend, Kent DA12 5BQ
Tel 01474 352835
A "consumer body for listeners and viewers".

THINK TANKS

There are two reasons for think tanks to exist: the first is to feed journalists with ready made phrases and attitudes and the second is to give political parties somewhere to turn when they cast round for new manifesto ideas. The Adam Smith Institute, which views the widespread aceptance of privatisation as its great success, has direct links with Downing Street and has already sent the prime minister a list of 50 policy suggestions for possible inclusion in the next election campaign. Demos is equally busy on behalf of Labour.

Adam Smith Institute
23 Great Smith Street, London SW1P 9XX
Fax 0171-222 7544   Tel 0171-222 4995
Chairman: Sir Austin Bide
It explores new ways of extending choice, competition and quality into public services. It formulates practical policy strategies and leads public debate on new solutions for economic problems.

Centre for Policy Studies
52 Rochester Row, London SW1P 1JU
Fax 0171-828 7746   Tel 0171-828 1176
Director: Gerald Frost
It was set up in 1974 by Margaret Thatcher and Sir Keith Joseph. The CPS runs conferences and produces publications.

Demos
9 Bridewell Place, London EC4V 6AP
Fax 0171-353 4481   Tel 0171-353 4479
Director: Geoff Mulgan
Demos was launched in March 1993 to help reinvigorate public policy and political thinking which was felt to have become too short term, partisan and out of touch. As well as looking for practical policy solutions it also looks for new forms of democracy and governance fit for the 21st century.

Employment Policy Institute
Southbank House, Black Prince Road, London SE1 7SJ
Fax 0171-793 8192   Tel 0171-735 0777
Director : John Philpott
The EPI researches causes of unemployment, exploration of policy options for reducing unemployment and the dissemination of results. It has a programme of conferences and reports.

Fabian Society
11 Dartmouth Street, London SW1H 9BN
Fax 0171-976 7153   Tel 0171-222 8877
General Secretary: Simon Crine
A research organisation in social policy, philosophy, women, race, housing, youth and international issues. It runs conferences, meetings and publications.

Henley Centre for Forecasting
9 Bridewell Place, London EC4V 6AY
Fax 0171-353 2899   Tel 0171-353 9961
Chairman: Bob Tyrrell
A strategic market consultancy, rather than a think tank. Useful for all sorts of information on people and markets.

Institute of Economic Affairs
2 Lord North Street, London SW1P 3LB
Fax 0171-799 3745   Tel 0171-799 2137
General Director: John Blundell
The IEA aims to extend the public understanding of economic principles in their application to practical problems. It has a library and publishes information.

Institute for Employment Studies
Mantell Building, University of Sussex, Falmer, Brighton BN1 9RF
Fax 01273-690430   Tel 01273-686751
Director: Richard Pearson
Employment research.

Institute for Fiscal Studies
7 Ridgmount Street, London WC1E 7AE
Fax 0171-323 4780   Tel 0171-636 3784
Director: Andrew Dilnot
It promotes research and understanding of the economic and social implications of existing taxes and different fiscal systems. It has a programme of conferences and publications.

Institute for Public Policy Research
30-32 Southampton Street, London WC2E 7RA
Fax 0171-497 0373   Tel 0171-379 9400
Director: James Cornford
The IPPR promotes research into economic, social and political sciences and the effects of moral, social, political and scientific factors on public policy.

Policy Studies Institute
100 Park Village East, London NW1 3SR
Fax 0171-388 0914   Tel 0171-387 2171
Director: Pamela Meadows
It contributes to effective planning and policy making by government and industry by studying selected problems and publishing the results. It produces a journal and other publications.

Social Market Foundation
20 Queen Anne's Gate, London SW1H 9AA
Fax 0171-222 0310   Tel 0171-222 7060
Chairman: Professor Lord Skidelsky
Established in 1989 and relaunched in 1992 as a non-libertarian free market think tank. Its director, Daniel Finkelstein espouses gradualism and accepts that "society does exist". The foundation has a programme of seminars and conferences.

ADS, MARKETING AND PR

Advertising Association
Abford House, 15 Wilton Road, London SW1V 1NJ
Fax 0171-931 0376   Tel 0171-828 2771
The only association speaking for all branches of advertising: agencies, advertisers, the media and support services. Promotes the value of advertising, defends it against unwarranted attack and is the industry's principle source of statistics. Publishes and co-publishes a wide range of leaflets, pamphlets and books covering all aspects of advertising

Advertising Film & Videotape Producers Association
26 Noel Street, London W1V 3RD
Fax 0171-434 9002   Tel 0171-4342651
Trade association representing the television commercials production companies.

Advertising Standards Authority
2 Torrington Place, London WC1E 7HW
Fax 0171-323 4339   Tel 0171-580 5555
Promotes and enforces high standards in all non-broadcast advertisements. It ensures that everyone who commissions, prepares and publishes advertisements observes the British Codes of Advertising and Sales Promotion by making them legal, decent, honest and truthful. The Authority acts independently of both the government and industry. It is financed by a levy on advertising space.

Association of Media and Communications Specialists
Woodgate Studios, 2-8 Games Road, Cockfosters, Herts EN4 9HN
Fax 0181-446 6794   Tel 0181-343 7779
AMCO was formerly the Association of Media Independents and is the trade association for independent companies buying advertising media.

Broadcast Advertising Clearance Centre
200 Grays Inn Road, London WC1X 8HF
Fax 0171-843 8154   Tel 0171-843 8265
Ensures that TV commercials comply with ITC codes and guidelines. BACC does this on behalf of the ITV and satellite companies. Also responsible for the clearance of radio commercials on behalf of the Association of Radio Companies.

Direct Marketing Association
1 Oxendon Street, London SW1Y 4EE
Fax 0171-321 0191   Tel 0171-321 2525
The trade association for direct marketers, carrying out lobbying, setting standards, running many events and publishing leaflets, members' directory and code of practice.

History of Advertising Trust
Raveningham, Norwich, Norfolk NR14 6NU
Fax 01508-548478   Tel 01508-548623
Archive of advertising material from 1800 to present day, containing over one million items. Research source for social and economic historians with items available for exhibitions and publications.

Institute of Practitioners in Advertising
44 Belgrave Square, London SW1X 8QS
Fax 0171-245 9904   Tel 0171-235 7020
Trade and professional body for advertising agencies in the UK. Publishes extensive range of material (list available).

Institute of Public Relations
15 Northburgh Street, London EC1V 0PR
Fax 0171-490 0588   Tel 0171-253 5151
Professional association for all working in PR. Publishes monthly journal and annual handbook with register of members.

Market Research Society
15 Northburgh Street, London EC1V 0AH
Fax 0171-490 0608   Tel 0171-490 4911
Professional body for those individuals who have an interest in, or are involved in, compiling or using marketing, social or economic research. It publishes a monthly magazine called the Journal of Market Research Society and runs training courses and seminars, and holds an annual conference every March.

National Newspapers Mail Order Protection Scheme (MOPS)
16 Tooks Court, London EC4A 1LB
Fax 0171-404 0106   Tel 0171-405 6806
Reimburses readers of member newspapers who lose money when approved mail order advertisers enter liquidation or bankruptcy, or cease to trade.

Radio Advertising Bureau
74 Newman Street, London W1P 3LA
Fax 0171-636 6995   Tel 0171-636 5858
Marketing company set up by the commercial radio industry to provide advice and planning services on commercial radio to advertisers and advertising agencies. The bureau publishes regular papers on commercial radio buying and listening.

Society of County & Regional PR Officers
7 Greenlands, South Road, Taunton, Somerset TA1 3EB
Fax 01823-325721   Tel 01823-251604
Professional society for PR exces.

MAGAZINES

Campaign
22 Lancaster Gate, London W2 3LY
Fax 0171-413 4507   Tel 0181-943 5000
Publisher: Haymarket.
Leading weekly news magazine for the advertising industry.

Creative Review
50 Poland Street, London W1E 6JZ
Fax 0171-734 6748   Tel 0171-439 4222
Publisher: Centaur Communications.
Monthly looking at the best in advertising and design, including TV, film, and photography. Centaur also publishes: Design Week, the weekly news magazine for the design industry; and Marketing Week, covering marketing, media and advertising.

Marketing
22 Lancaster Gate, London W2 3LY
Fax 0171-413 4504   Tel 0181-943 5000
Publisher: Haymarket.
The weekly business newspaper for marketing.

Media International
Quadrant House, The Quadrant, Sutton, Surrey SM2 5AS.
Fax 0181-652 8961   Tel 0181-652 4943
Publisher: Reed Business Publishing.
Monthly for advertising executives.

Media & Marketing Europe
33 Bowling Green Lane, London EC1R 0DA
Fax 0171-837 2034   Tel 0171-837 1212
Publisher: Emap Media.
Monthly magazine aimed at Euro advertising and marketing execs.

Media Week
33 Bowling Green Lane, London EC1R 0DA
Fax 0171-837 3285   Tel 0171-837 1212
Publisher: Emap Media.
Leading weekly news magazine linking media and advertising .

PR Week
22 Lancaster Gate, London W2 3LP
Fax 0171-413 4509   Tel 0171-413 4520
Publisher: Haymarket.
The weekly news magazine for the public relations industry.

YEARBOOKS

Advertisers Annual/Blue Book
Reed Information Services   Tel 01342-326972
Three vols £180, single vols £104.
An ad directory from the same stable as Willings Press Guide. Covers: Agencies/advertisers; UK media; Overseas media.

Benn's Media
Benn Business Information Services
                            Tel 01732-362666
Three vols £248, single vols £104
Benn's has the most comprehensive listings amongst the general media directories, and is also the most commonly stocked in public libraries. It comes in three volumes, covering the UK, Europe and the rest of the world. Established 1846.

Brad (British Rate & Data)
Emap   0181-242 3116
Leading advrtising directory of all print media. with ABC figures, ad rates and mechanical data. In two monthly volumes: Brad Newspapers, £245 pa covering 900 papers; and Brad, £300 pa listing 7,500 other publications. Also published: Agencies and Advertisers, monthly; £250 pa; Direct Marketing, £75; Publishing Companies Portfolio, £150 (updated regularly); Glossary of European Media Terms, £30.

Editors
PR Newslink   Tel 0171-251 9000
£415 pa.
Six-volume directory of media contacts for the PR industry.

Hollis Press & PR Annual
Hollis Directories   Tel 01932-782054
£65.
Media and public relations contacts book.

Institute of Public Relations Handbook
Kogan Page   Tel 0171-278 0433
£9.95.
List of 3,500 IPR members, plus other information and articles.

Media Pocket Book
Advertising Association   Tel 01491-574671
£24, each May.
Key facts and figures on the media and advertising, from newspaper circulations to TV ownership. Other titles in this series, are the Marketing, Retail and Lifestyle Pocket Books.

PR Planner
Romeike Group   Tel 0181-882 0155
Loose-leaf guide to thousands of contacts in all media. The UK edition is updated monthly and costs £275 pa. The European edition is updated every other month and costs £315 pa.

UK Media Yearbook
Saatchi & Saatchi Advertising
                            Tel 0171-636 5060
£160.
An analysis, for advertisers, of media data and recent developments.

World Advertising Trends
NTC Publications   01491-411000
£95
Statistical analysis of ad spends from 57 countries.

MEDIA STUDIES

Media studies is the most fashionable subject of the mid-1990s. According to the Universities and Colleges Admissions Service (UCAS), it is more popular than mathematics, physics, chemistry and civil engineering. Nearly 35,000 sixth formers finishing their A levels applied in 1995.

The courses they have been flocking to should come with the health warning that a media studies qualification no more guarantees a job in journalism than an English degree qualifies a person as a novelist. Course content tends to the theoretical and earns the contempt of practitioners, most of whom did what they regard as more rigorous liberal arts degrees in the 1970s and 1980s. Then there's the School of Hard Knocks line which was well expressed by an unnamed editor quoted in a Guild of Editors training survey: "I want trainees who have shorthand and know what we can and cannot report on in court, not theorists who can argue at length on the role of the press and the judiciary of the 20th century," he said.

The most complete listing of media studies courses is in the British Film Institute's book Media Course UK 96 (see the Broadcast training section starting page 214 for more detail). The listing below concentrates on higher education and is from the Media Studies section of the UCAS Official Guide to University and College Entrance. A copy should be available in every careers offices and it costs £15 from UCAS which is on 01242- 222444.

Anglia Polytechnic University
Fax 01223-352973   Tel 01223-63271
Communication studies.

Bangor Normal College
Fax 01248-370461   Tel 01248-30171
Communications.

Barnsley College
Fax 01226-298514   Tel 01226-730191
Media.

University of Birmingham
Fax 0121-414 3850   Tel 0121-414 3697
Media and Cultural Studies.

Bournemouth University
Fax 01202-13292   Tel 01202-504152
Media/Advertising/PR.

University of Bradford
Fax 01274-305340   Tel 01274-383081
Communications/Technology.

Bradford & Ilkley Community College
Fax 01274-741060   Tel 01274-753026
Communications.

University of the West of England, Bristol
Fax 0117-976 3804   Tel 0117-965 6261
Media/Publishing/Society.

Brunel: The University of West London
Fax 01895-230883   Tel 01895-274000
Communications/Information/Sociology.

Bucks College
Fax 01494-524392   Tel 01494-522141
Media/Arts/Culture.

Cardiff University of Wales
Fax 01222-874130   Tel 01222-874404
Comunication/Language/Journalism.

Univesity of Central England in Birmingham
Fax 0121-331 6358   Tel 0121-331 5595
Media/Communication.

University of Central Lancashire
Fax 01772-892946   Tel 01772-201201
AV/Journalism.

Cheltenham and Glos College of Higher Ed
Fax 01242-250762 Tel 01242-532825/543477
Media Communications.

Chichester Institute of Higher Education
Fax 01243-828351   Tel 01243-865581
Media Studies.

City University
Fax 0171-477 8559   Tel 0171-477 8028
Media Studies/Journalism.

Colchester Institute
Fax 01206-718299   Tel 01206-718000
Communications/Media Studies

Coventry University
Fax 01203-838638   Tel 01203-838352
Communications.

Cumbria College of Art & Design
Fax 01228-514491   Tel 01228-25333
Media.

De Montfort University
Fax 0116-255 0307   Tel 0116-255 1551
Media Studies

University of Derby
Fax 01332-294861   Tel 01332-622289
Visual Communication.

University of East Anglia
Fax 01603-58596   Tel 01603-592216
Media Studies.

University of East London
Fax 0181-590 7799   Tel 0181-590 7722
Communication Studies/IT/Media Studies.

Edge Hill College of Higher Education
Fax 01695-579997   Tel 01695-575171
Communication Studies.

Falmouth College of Arts
Fax 01326-211205   Tel 01326-211077
Advertising/Broadcasting/Journalism.

Farnborough College of Technology
Fax 01252-547496   Tel 01252-391212
Media Production/Publishing and Design.

University of Glamorgan
Fax 01443-480558   Tel 01443-480480
Comunication Studies/Media Studies.

Glasgow Caledonian University
Fax 0141-331-3005   Tel 0141-331 3000
Comunication/Marketing.

Goldsmiths College
Fax 0181-691 4490   Tel 0181-692 7171
Communication Studies.

University of Greenwich
Fax 0181-316 8145   Tel 0181-316 8590
Media/Communication/Production.

Gwent College of Higher Education
Fax 01633-432306   Tel 01633-430088
Media Studies.

University of Huddersfield
Fax 01484-516151   Tel 01484-422288
Communication Arts.

University of Humberside
Fax 01482-586692   Tel 01482-440550
Communication Processes
Media Production.

King Alfred's College
Fax 01962-842280   Tel 01962-841515
Combined Studies.

Lancaster University
Fax 01524-846243   Tel 01524-65201
Comunication.

University of Leeds
Fax 0113-233 2334   Tel 0113-233 2332
Communications/Broadcasting Studies.

Leeds, Trinity & All Saints
Fax 0113-283 7200   Tel 0113-283 7123
Communication/Cultural Studies/Media.

Leeds Metropolitan
Fax 0113-283 3114   Tel 0113-283 2600
PR/Media Technology.

University of Leicester
Fax 0116-252 2447   Tel 0116-252 2295
Comunications.

University of Liverpool
Fax 0151-708 6502   Tel 0151-794 3212
Communication Studies.

Liverpool John Moores University
Fax 0151-707 1938   Tel 0151-231 2121
Media/Cultural Studies/Journalism.

London Guildhall University
Fax 0171-320 3462   Tel 0171-320 1000
Comunication Studies/AV.

London Institute
Fax 0171-514 6131   Tel 0171-514 6000
Marketing/Media/Journalism.

Loughborough University
Fax 01509-265687   Tel 01509-263171
Communication/Media/Publishing Studies.

University of Luton
Fax 01582-418677   Tel 01582-34111
Media Practices/Media Production/Media
Technology/Journalism.

Manchester Metropolitan University
Fax 0161-236 7383   Tel 0161-247 1035
Human Communication

Middlesex University
Fax 0181-362 6878   Tel 0181-362 5000
Communication/Media/Publishing/Journalism.

Napier University
Fax 0131-455 7209   Tel 0131-455 4330
Communication/Publishing/Journalism.

North East Wales Institute of Higher Education
Fax 01978-290008   Tel 01978-290666
Media Studies.

University of North London
Fax 0171-753 5075   Tel 0171-753 5066
Communication/Information Studies.

University of Northumbria
Fax 0191-227 4017   Tel 0191-227 4064
Information Management.

Nottingham Trent University
Fax 01602-484266   Tel 01602 418418
Communication Studies/Broadcast Journalism.

Oxford Brookes University
Fax 01865-483983   Tel 01865-483039
Publishing.

University of Plymouth
Fax 01752-232141   Tel 01752-232158
Media/Photomedia.

Queen Margaret College
Fax 0131-317 3256   Tel 0131-317 3240
Communication Studies.

University College of Ripon & York St John
Fax 01904-612512   Tel 01904-616851
Communication Arts.

Robert Gordon University
Fax 01224-263000   Tel 01224-262000
Communication/Publishing Studies.

University of Salford
Fax 0161-745 5885   Tel 0161-745 5000
Media.

University College of Salford
Fax 0161-745 8386   Tel 0161-736 6541
Media/TV and Radio.

University of Sheffield
Fax 0114-272 8014   Tel 0114-276 8555
Journalism Studies.

Sheffield Hallam University
Fax 0114-253 2161   Tel 0114-272 0911
Communication/Media.

Southampton Institute of Higher Education
Fax 01703-222259   Tel 01703-229381
Commnication/Media/Journalism.

South Bank University
Fax 0171-815 8155   Tel 0171-815 6109
Media Studies.

College of St Mark & St John
Fax 01752-761120   Tel 01752-777188
PR/Media Studies
Information Technology.

Staffordshire University
Fax 01782-745422   Tel 01782-744531
Media Studies.

University of Stirling
Fax 01786-466800   Tel 01786-467044
Film & Media Studies.

Suffolk College
Fax 01473-230054   Tel 01473-255885
Media Studies/Information Technology.

University of Sunderland
Fax 0191-515 2423   Tel 0191-515 2082
Communication/Media Studies.

Surrey Institute of Art & Design
Fax 01252-718313   Tel 01252-732232
Media Studies/Journalism.

University of Sussex
Fax 01273-678545   Tel 01273-678416
Media Studies.

Swansea Institute of Higher Education
Fax 01792-208683   Tel 01792-481000
Multi-Meia Technology

University of Teesside
Fax 01642-432067   Tel 01642-218121
Journalism.

Thames Valley University
Fax 0181-231 2900   Tel 0181-231 2902
Media/Publishing & Information.

Trinity College Carmarthen
Fax 01267-230933   Tel 01267-237971
Media Studies.

University of Ulster
Fax 01265-44141   Tel 01265-40927
Communication
Media Studies.

Warrington College Institute
Fax 01925-816077   Tel 01925-814343
Media Studies.

West Herts College
Fax 01923-257556   Tel 01923-257500
Advertising/Graphic Media.

University of Westminster
Fax 0171-911 5118   Tel 0171-911 5000
Media Studies.

University of Wolverhampton
Fax 01902-322528   Tel 01902-321000
Multimedia Communication.

MEDIA READING LIST

There is no library devoted solely to the media and journalism. But there are public and private libraries which either hold a range of media material as part of their general stock or are solely devoted to one aspect of the media.

Amongst the publicly owned libraries there is the British Library's Newspaper Library at Colindale in north west London, which has the UK's national historical collection of newspapers, plus a general reference library on them. The Corporation of London's St Bride Printing Library, off Fleet Street in London, is given over to the history of printing. Barking Public Library in east London holds a regional specialist collection on journalism, as do some other public libraries in other regions. Oxford University Modern Languages Faculty Library has a collection of European newspapers in their original form.

In broadcasting, the BBC has several collections, the most useful general one being in the Reference Library in Broadcasting House. Access is limited and at the discretion of the BBC librarians; contact via the Data Enquiry Service. The Independent Television Commission has a valuable library, near Broadcasting House. It is open to the public by appointment. The British Film Institute in central London has the world's largest collection about film and television, and also runs an information and enquiry service. The Home Office library in Westminster has a section on broadcasting, which researchers can consult.

Institutions running media courses have libraries holding a variety of stocks of books and periodicals. In London, for example, there are the London College of Printing, the University of Westminster and City University. Public access to the academic libraries is often allowed, by arrangement. Trade associations, pressure groups and trade unions are worth contacting, as they often have collections. Examples are: BKSTS, Pact, Royal Television Society and the Voice of the Listener and Viewer. National papers have their own libraries, but members of the public are rarely allowed in, and phone enquiries are not always welcome.

The most useful source books commonly stocked in public libraries are: Benn's Media (covering all media), Brad (for advertisers), the Blue Book (broadcasting), British Film Institute Film & TV Handbook, Hollis (public relations), Willing's (newspapers and periodicals) and the Writer's Handbook (mainly for book authors).

Also recommended, are: BAPLA Directory (for picture libraries, agencies and researchers), The Knowledge (TV and film production directory) and Pims (for personal contacts in all sectors).

The leading periodicals, which are in this book's specialist sections from page 119 and page 217, are: UK Press Gazette (for all press and broadcasting journalism, but with a leaning towards the press), Print Week, Broadcast (on general broadcasting), Cable and Satellite Europe, Media Week (connecting media and advertising) and Campaign (advertising).

Many newspapers have media sections. The Guardian every Monday has the most media job adverts. Also try the Independent on Tuesdays and Times on Wednesdays. The Financial Times has no specific media section, but carries in-depth news of the media industry. Details of any current book or publisher are published on CD-ROM by Whitakers, and stocked by most public reference libraries.

The first section starting page 238 has books giving advice and information. This lists titles published from 1992 onwards. Following that are books shedding light on the workings of the media world either by analysis or memoir. This is a more selective section. Books are listed by alphabetical order of authors.

Selected libraries

Barking Public Library
0181-517 8666

BBC Data Enquiry Service
0171-927 5998.

British Library's Newspaper Library
0171-323 7353

British Film Institute
0171-255 1444

Home Office Library
0171-273 3398

Independent Television Commission
0171-584 7011

Oxford University Modern Languages Faculty Library
01865-278152

St Bride Printing Library
0171-353 4660

Manuals and guides

Publishers phone numbers are on page 249.

A - Z of Film, TV and Video Terms
Alex Bushby. Blueprint. 1993, £12.95.
A complete glossary of broadcast media terms.

A for Andromeda to Zoo Time
Simon Baker & Olwen Terris. British Film Institute. 1994, £35.
An illustrated catalogue of the television holdings of the National Film and Television Archive, from 1936-79. With around 10,000 entries, arranged alphabetically by series and title.

The Actor and the Camera
Malcolm Taylor. A&C Black. 1994, £10.99.
A description of the practicalities of the camera acting technique, covering TV and film.

The Advertising Handbook
Sean Brierley. Routledge, 1995, £12.99.
Unravels the how-and-why of advertising and places the industry in its social, historical and political context. Part of Routledge's Media Practice Series, aimed at teachers and students.

The Art of Digital Audio
John Watkinson. Focal Press, 1994, £49.50.
An industry bible, giving a detailed description of the technalities of the increasingly important new form of radio.

Basic TV Technology
Robert L Hartwig. Focal Press, 1993, £12.99.
Teaches prospective and curent media professionals the technical basics, in a simple but detailed style.

Baylin Publications
Swift TV Publications
Baylin is an American publisher specialising in satellite books, nearly all with a technical orientation. Titles include: The Satellite Book (3rd edition), World Satellite Yearly, International Satellite Directory, Hidden Signals on Satellite TV and Scrambling Methods. Contact for catalogue.

BBC Charter Review Series
British Film Institute. 1993/4, £5.95 each.
Six titles with contributions by various authors, experts and politicians, looking critically at different aspects of the review of the BBC's charter, due in 1996.

BBC TV Training
The BBC's TV Training Centre at Borehamwood produces over 20 books and 30 videos covering a wide range of the technical and journalistic sides of broadcasting. It is the only internal section of the BBC publishing specialist media material. Titles include: Television and Children, tracing the evolution of BBC kiddies' programmes; Teletalk, a dictionary of broadcasting terms; High Definition Television for Programme Makers; Video Documentary Making, giving a guide to creating videos at home; News! News!, outlining how the BBC News operation works; The TV Researchers Guide; Television - An Introduction to the Studio; High Definition TV for Programme Makers; Television Stage Management; Video Documentary Making; and The Production Assistant's Survival Guide. Contact above for lists. BBC Books (0181-576 2000) publishes BBC general interest titles. BBC Direct (0800-258259) markets the books and videos.

Best Practices Guidelines
Periodical Publishers Association. 1993, £5.
Short guide designed to assist editors in dealing with editorial and photographic contracts with contributors. Contains draft letters for commissioning freelancers and illustrators, plus draft photo agreement, interviewee disclaimer and release form.

Beyond the Lens
Jill Anthony (ed). Association of Photographers, 1994, £15.
Wide-ranging guide to the rights, ethics and business practices of professional photography (except trade unions are not included). Supported by the Arts Council, Kodak and BTEC.

BKSTS Training Manuals
British Kinematograph, Sound & Television Society
Publishes a series of helpful introductory leaflets about the industry, aimed at new entrants. Also booklets, including: Education, Training and Working in Film, Television and Broadcasting (1993 edition, £5), an invaluable guide to courses, qualifications and organisations.

British Film Institute
The BFI, a charity, produces an extensive range of valuable titles on film, TV and the media, including education. Many are listed on these pages. Contact them for catalogues.

British Printing Industries Federation
The BPIF is the printers' trade body. It publishes many books and pamphlets on aspects of printing and print production. Examples are: Introduction to Printing Technology, £50; Desktop Publishing, £25; Journal Production - Principles and Practice, £12; Customs of the Trade for the Production of Periodicals, £3; Multilingual Dictionary of Printing and Publishing Terms, £50; and Print Buyers' Guide, £15. Catalogue available.

British Television
Tise Vahimagi. British Film Institute, 1994. £12.99.
Laishly illustrated definitive guide to over 1,100 programmes since 1936, chronologicaly arranged.

Broadcast Journalism
Andrew Boyd. Butterworth-Heineman. 1994, 3rd edition, £17.95.
Well-illustrated textbook aimed at students and newcomers, on techniques of TV and radio news.

Broadcasting It!
Keith Howes. Mansell. 1993, £14.99.
A1,000 page encyclopedia of homosexuality in British broadcasting since 1923.

Broadcasting Law: A Comparative Study
Eric Barendt, Oxford University Press. 1993, £30.
The first comparative study of the regulation of radio and television, discussing the law in the UK, USA and Europe. One subject is the way British broadcasters are less legally protected than many European countries.

Broadcasting in the UK
Barrie MacDonald. Mansell. 1994, revised, 2nd edition, £20.
Indispensable reference guide to the British broadcasting industry. A key book, packed with essential contemporary and historical data.

Campaign for Freedom of Information
The Campaign has produced a range of reports on secrecy in British society, especially its legal structure, and on proposals to make information more freely available. Also published is the Campaign's regular newspaper Secrets (see Press Magazines, page 121). For details of all these, ask for a copy of the Publications List.

Campaign for Press and Broadcasting Freedom
The CPBF produces an annual Media Catalogue detailing the many books, videos and postcards available on campaign atters. As well as its regular Free Press, CPBF's wn publications include the book Britain's Media: How They Are Related, by Granville Williams, and a wall chart with the same title, both produced mid-1994. The Full-colour chart is the only graphic portrayal of the complex ways in which the main British TV, radio and publishing businesses are connected. Other recent publications include Media Monopoly: A Human Rights Issue. The CPBF regularly radical contributiions to the national debate over the power and role of the media.

Careers in Journalism
Peter Medina, Vivien Donald. Kogan Page. 1992 edition, £5.99
Concise, useful guide and overview of the industry.

Copy-Editing
Judith Butcher. Cambridge University Press. 1992, 3rd edition, £19.95.
The classic handbook for editors, authors and publishers.

Cross-Media Ownership Chart
see Campaign for Press and Broadcasting Freedom

Current British Journals
Turpin Distribution, for the British Library. 1992, 6th edition, £70
Authoritative guide to 10,000 periodicals published in Britain.

Desktop Design
Brian Cookman. Blueprint. 1993, 2nd edition, £19.95.
Describes the basics of producing pages on DTP systems, with creative ideas for designs.

Desktop Publishing
Ron Strutt et al. Blueprint. 1992, 4th edition, £25.00.
Basic introductiion for beginners, with guide to hardware and sofware.

Dictionary for Writers & Editors
Bill Bryson. Penguin. 1994, £6.99.
A guie to the most commonly encountered problems of English spelling and usage.

Dictionary of Communication & Media Studies
James Watson & Anne Hill. Edward Arnold 1993, 3rd edition, £10.99.
An unusual mixture of entries, almost like an encyclopedia.

Editing, Design & Book Production
Charles Foster. Journeyman. 1993, £10.95.
Complete guide to book production, from manuscript to bound copies.

Editor's Handbook
British Association of Industrial Editors. Free to members.
Comprehensive loose-leaf manual of practical editorial advice for all people working in corporate communications. Regularly updated.

Effective TV Production
Gerald Millerson. Focal Press 1993, £12.95.
Provides an overview of the production process.

Encyclopedia of the British Press
Dennis Griffiths, Macmillan 1992, £49.50
A 694 page book with a big interest in minor personalities.

English for Journalists
Wynford Hicks. Routledge. 1993, £5.99.
A guide to basic English, plus special journalist concerns such as spelling, punctuation, style, reporting speech and jargon.

Essential Finance for Journalists
Brian O'Kane. Oak Tree Press. 1993, £12.95.
A unique and invaluable guide to British finance, company law, city institutions, accounts, regulation and taxation. This has been written for the practical benefit of journalists (including students), and published with the Periodicals Training Council and Price Waterhouse.

Essential Law for Journalists
See: McNae's Essential Law for Journalists, below.

European Institute for the Media
The EIM is the European centre for policy-orientated research in the fields of radio, TV and the press. John Libbey & Co co-publishes their monographs covering issues under discussion in the European media. Details are in John Libbey's EIM catalogue.

Financial Times Style Guide
Financial Times. 1993, £12.
Informative and entertaining A-Z guide to the problems of the English language, designed to help writers improve their skills and avoid mistakes. With glossaries and explanations.

Focal Encyclopedia of Photography
Focal Press. 1993, 3rd edition, £75.
One of the main reference sources for professional photographers for over 35 years, with 1500 pages of detail.

Focal Press
Focal is the media division of publishers Butterworth-Heineman, specialising most notably in practical books. Its extensive annual catalogue includes sections covering audio, broadcasting, cinematography, journalism, photography, radio, scripting, TV and video. Many of the technical broadcasting books have not been included in this Media Guide, but are in the catalogue. Many Focal titles are included in the series called Media Manuals, giving basic introductions.

Freelance Writing for Newspapers
Jill Dick. A & C Black. 1991, £9.99.

Get Mediawise
Mediawise Communications. 1994, £6.95.
Subtitled "The essential guide for maximising your publicity potential", this has been produced by several journalists, with the aim of explaining how to get a message across to the media.

Getting into Advertising
Advertising Association. £5.
Description of the advertising business and guide to careers in it, by the industry trade association.

Getting the Message Across
Sue Ward. Journeyman. 1993, £12.95.
Practical guide for members of the public seeking media coverage for their event, campaign or publication.

Great Advertising Campaigns
Nicholas Ind. Kogan Page. 1993, £25.
Examines what makes an advertising campaign inspired and successful, drawing on memorable examples from the recent past.

Guide to Editorial Practice
Periodicals Training Council. £49.
Extensive loose-leaf guide to magazine production, by the experts.

The Guinness Book of Classic British TV
Paul Cornell et al. Guinness Publishing. 1993.
Looks in some detail at some of the most-loved programmes since the 1950s.

Hands On!
Roy Stafford. British Film Institute. 1993, £19.95.
A teacher's guide to media technology, including photography, audio and video recording, keyboards and computers.

High Definition Television for Programme Makers
Brendan Slamin, BBC Television Training 1993, £17.50.
Explains in simple language the differences between the new wide screen technologies and how they and HDTV affect programme makers.

Hitting the Headlines
Stephen White et al. British Psychological Society. 1993, £8.99.
Subtitled "A practical guide to the media", this is an invaluable aid to persuading journalists or broadcasters to accept one of your stories.

How to Get Publicity for Free
David Northmore. Bloomsbury. 1993, £9.99.
Handbook for fundraisers, event organisers and campaigners on writing press releases, contacting the media and gaining airtime.

How to Get Into Films & TV
Robert Angell. How To Books. 1995, £8.99.
Succinct but comprehensive guide to careers, describing the range of available jobs and how to set about obtaining one. With glossary and useful addresses and publications.

Interviewing for Journalists
Joan Clayton. Piatkus Books. 1994, £16.
An in-depth practical guide for journalists, explaining how to research and conduct good interviews that can be sold.

Introduction to Electronic News Gathering
B Hesketh & I Yorke. Butterworth-Heinemann 1993, £16.95.
Covers all aspects of ENG, from cameras, sound, lighting and interviewing, to getting the material back to base.

Introduction to Printing Technology
Hugh Speirs. British Printing Industries Federation. 1992, 4th edition, £50, students £30.
Comprehensive guide to every aspect of the printing industry, from typesetting to distribution, by the experts.

Journalism Workbook
Brendan Hennessy and FW Hodgson. Focal Press, 1995, £14.99.
This "manual of tasks, projects and resources" is aimed at NVQs and other vocational courses. It covers simply but carefully all the basic aspects of journalism: reporting, feature writing, photojournalism, subediting, page planning, design etc.

Journalism for Beginners
Joan Clayton, Piatkus Books 1992, £15

Law & the Media
Tom Crone. Focal Press. 1994, 3rd edition, £16.95.
Answers legal queries across all areas of the media.

Lights, Camera, Action!
Josephine Langham. British Film Institute 1993, £9.95.
Detailed description and analysis of careers available in film, television and video, with a useful analysis of the industry today. The BFI also regularly publishes Media Courses UK, the valuable practical guide to all media education. It details every further education, undergraduate and postgraduate course on the media.

McNae's Essential Law for Journalists
Tom Welsh & Walter Greenwood. Butterworths 1995, 13th edition, £14.95.
The leading outline description of the law affecting journalism. Used on most training courses and in many newspaper offices.

Magazine Writers Handbook 1995/6
Gordon Wells. Allison & Busby, 1994, £7.99.
Practical guide for people wanting to write magazine articles and short stories. Details of 70 magazines, plus comments on others.

Making it as a Radio or TV Presenter
Peter Baker. Piatkus Books, 1995, £7.99.
Practical detailed analysis of the skills needed to become a presenter and reporter. "How to get into the business and to stay there". 220pp.

Marketing for Small Publishers
Bill Godber et al. Jorneyman. 1992, 2nd edition, £8.99.
Revised version of Inter-Action's 1980 manual, recommended by many in the trade.

Measuring Media Audiences
Raymond Kent (ed). Routledge. 1994, £12.99.
A description for students and companies of the ways media audiences - TV, radio, press, magazines, cinema - are assessed, in terms of quantity and quality.

Media Law
Rhonda Baker. Blueprint, 1994, £39.
This is a user's guidebook with a misleading title: it is only aimed at film and programme makers. It claims to be "the first book which covers all the major legal aspects of film and television production to be written specifically for people working in the industry".

Media Manual Series
Imprint of Butterworth-Heinemann
Titles include: Local Radio Journalism, Modern Newspaper Practice, Newspaper Language, Practical Newspaper Reporting, Practical Photojournalism, Subediting and Writing Feature Articles (all cf). Butterworth also publish many other media books; contact them for details.

Media Studies
Stuart Price. Pitman Publishing, 1993, £15.99.
Claimed by Pitmans to be "the first, fully comprehensive A Level text", these 450 pages focus mainly on academic theories.

Modern Newspaper Practice
FW Hodgson. Butterworth-Heinemann. 1993, 3rd edition, £14.99.
Leading introduction to the world of newspapers and newspaper journalism, covering everything from technicalities to ethics.

National Council for the Training of Journalists
The NCTJ retails some of the key books listed here, and also sells its own publications and videos covering the basics of journalism, including shorthand and Teeline.

News and Journalism in the UK
Brian McNair. Routledge. 1993, £10.99.
Student textbook introducing the political, economic and regulatory environments of the British press and broadcast journalism.

Newspaper Language
Nicholas Bagnall. Focal Press. 1993, £14.95.
Journalists' guide to words and how to use them.

The Newspapers Handbook
Richard Keeble, Routledge. 1994, £12.99.
Routledge say this is "the first comprehensive guide to the job of a newspaper journalist", with wide-ranging advice, plus a challenging look at the theoretical, ethical and political dimensions of the work.

1,000 Markets for Freelance Writers
Robert Palmer. Piatkus. 1993, £9.99.
A-Z guide to general and specialist magazines and journals, with much basic data.

Periodical Publishers Association
The PPA and its linked organisations (including the Periodicals Training Council) publish many useful reports, newsletters, pamphlets and other material on all the different aspects of magazine production. Details are in the PPA's 36-page Publications List, available on request.

Picture Researchers Handbook
Hilary & Mary Evans. Blueprint. 1992, 5th edition, £35.
Indispensable detailed guide to picture sources and their use; the industry bible. Blueprint also publish a companion volume by Mary Evans: Practical Picture Research (£29.50), covering the skills, procedures and techniques of commercial picture research.

Practical Newspaper Reporting
Geoffrey Harris & David Spark. Focal Press 1993, 2nd edition, £16.95.
Updated edition of one of the classic handbooks on journalism, covering all aspects of the job. Produced in association with the National Council for the Training of Journalists.

Practical Photojournalism
M Keene. Focal Press. 1993, £17.95.
Well-illustrated textbook, explaining professional work from camera handling to the electronic picture desk.

Practical Picture Research
See: Picture Researchers Handbook, above.

PressWise Media Handbook
PressWise, 1995, £16.
New pocket-size handbook listing the media and related organisations. Also describes PressWise, the non-profit body promoting higher standards in the press.

Print: How You Can Do It Yourself!
Jonathan Zeitlyn. Journeyman. 1992, 5th edition, £7.95.
First published in 1974, this is still one of the best DIY printing handbooks for anyone wanting to produce posters, leaflets, pamphlets and magazines.

The Print & Production Manual
Chapman & Hall. 1992, 7th edition, £95.
Just about everything you need to know, from copy preparation to despatch.

The Printing Ink Manual
RH Leach & RJ Pierce (eds). Blueprint. 1993, £75.
Latest developments in ink technology, new UK and US standards and environmental issues.

A Production Handbook
Peter Jarvis, Focal Press. 1993, £17.50.
A guide for TV programme producers, helping them hit targets and dodge pitfalls. It explains many of the legal and organisational problems that producers are likely to encounter.

Professional Magazine Journalism
Jill Baker. Chapman & Hall. 1992, £25.
Practical, accessible manual designed for all trainee magazine journalists.

Public Relations: An Introduction
Shirley Harrison. Routledge, 1995, £12.99.
Textbook for students of PR, linking theory and practice, and focusing on the principles that underpin successful practice of the chameleon career.

The Radio Handbook
Peter Wilby & Andy Conroy. Routledge. 1994, £12.99.
Comprehensive guide to the theory, history and practice of radio broadcasting, with much production information, plus help for radio students and trainees.

Radio Production
R McLeish. Focal Press, 1994, £19.95.
Easy-to-follow guide describing the strengths and weaknesses of radio, including how studios operate and how to use them.

The Radio Station
Michael Keith. Focal Press. 1993, £28.50.
A blueprint of the modern radio station, detailing the functions performed.

Research for Writers
Ann Hoffman. A & C Black. 1992, 4th edition, £10.99.
Invaluable guide for journalists and authors, covering both research methods and sources.

Researcher's Guide to British Film & TV Collections
British Universities Film & Video Council (BUFVC). 1993, 4th edition, £18.95.
The definitive guide to sources of film and television archive material in Britain. It has details of collections in the UK that are not normally available for viewing outside the premises where they are held.

Researcher's Guide to British Newsreels
British Universities Film & Video Council 1993, vol III, £13.50.
The last volume in an authoritative series charting the development and decline of newsreels, from 1910 to 1979. With many articles, abstracts, details of newsreel staff and a chronological wall-chart of company activity.

Reuters Handbook for Journalists
Ian Macdowall & FW Hodgson. Butterworth-Heinemann. 1992, £14.95.
Style guide for journalists which is based on the one used by Reuters.

RSI - It Can Be Prevented
National Union of Journalists. 1993.
A special pack of information on the epidemic of Repetitive Strain Injuries (RSI) that in recent years has hit many journalists using computer terminals. Compiled by the National Union of Journalists for its chapels.

The Satellite Book
Swift Television Publications. 1994, 3rd edition, £32.
Extensive practical guide to satellite theory and practice, aimed at the technical market.

Skillset
Skillset is the industry training organisation for broadcasting, film and video. In June 1993 it published a comprehensive free careers pack explaining how the industry works and how to find training opportunities. This is the best starting point for anyone seeking employment in this field.

Society of Freelance Editors and Proofreaders
The SFEP publishes several useful small guides, including Copy into Print - The Shape of the Next 20 Years (£4.50), Standing up for Standards (£5.60) and The Tax Wo/man Cometh, with valuable tax advice, (£2.90)

Studying the Media
Tim O'Sullivan et al. Edward Arnold. 1994, £13.99.
Aimed at 16+ students. Written from a media/cultural studies perspective.

Subediting
FW Hodgson. Focal Press. 1993, 2nd edition, £14.95.
The complete guide for subs working in today's computerised environment, explaining all aspects of editing and production.

Surviving the Media
Diana Mather. Harper Collins. 1995, £7.99.
Simple handbook for anyone putting their message across the media, subtitled "How to appear successfully on TV, radio or in the press".

Teach Yourself Journalism
Michael Bromley. Hodder & Stoughton. 1994, £6.99.
Lightweight introduction.

Teaching Media in the Primary School
Adrian Emerson. Cassell. 1993, £12.99.
Entertaining guide for primary teachers on showing ways of giving young children an understanding of the important role the media play in their lives.

The Technique of Special Effects in Television
Bernard Wilkie. Focal Press. 1993, 2nd edition, £19.95.
In-depth reference book for people making special effects, whether professionals or students.

Television's Greatest Hits
Paul Gambaccini & Rod Taylor. Network Books, 1993, £14.99.
A large package of data on the most-watched TV programmes in the UK every week since 1960.

The Twentieth Century Newspaper Press in Britain - An Annotated Bibliography
David Linton, Mansell. 1994, £70.
Companion volume to the Linton and Ray Boston's 1987 classic bibliography The Newspaper Press in Britain, covering all eras. The new publication focuses on the present century, with a preliminary listing of basic reference works. More than 3,700 extensively annotated entries, covering books, articles, theses and special issues. Chronology appended.

Typesetting & Composition
Geoff Barlow & Simon Eccles. Blueprint 1992, 2nd edition, £27.50.
Clear, comprehensive and readable guide to typesetting and its surrounding mysteries.

Video Camera Operator's Handbook
Peter Hodges. Focal Press. 1994, £19.99.
Useful, easily-understood explanation of all the details of video operation, aimed at every kind of camera user.

The Video Studio
Alan Bermingham. Focal Press. 1994, £12.99.
Manual for anyone setting up a professional installation of roughly 150 square metres or less, either studio or location based.

Writing Feature Articles
Brendan Hennessy. Focal Press. 1993, 2nd edition, £14.95.
Practical guide to methods and markets, particularly aimed at novices.

Your Message & the Media
Linda Fairbrother. Nicholas Brealey Publishing and the Industrial Society. 1993, £19.95.
Wide-ranging and detailed handbook for media relations officers.

Other media books

The News of the World Story
Bainbridge, Cyril, & Roy Stockdill. Harper Collins, 1993.
This is the official history of the News of the World, celebrating its 150th birthday in 1993. An entertaining tale, although superficial in parts.

Media Freedom
Barbrook, Richard. Pluto Press, 1995.
A scholarly examination of the "contradictions of communications in the age of modernity".

The Battle for the BBC - A British Broadcasting Conspiracy?
Barnett, Steven & Andrew Curry. Aurum Press, 1994.
A factual account of the many conflicts between the BBC management and journalistic principles.

New Directions - Media Education Worldwide
Bazalgette, Cary, et al. British Film Institute, 1993.
Uniquely combines accounts of media education policy and practice from around the world.

In Front of the Children - Screen Entertainment and Young Audiences
Bazalgette, Cary, et al. British Film Institute, 1995.
Lively description by various media academics of TV's varied effects (sometimes surprisingly beneficial) on youngsters.

Murdoch: The Great Escape
Belfield, Richard, & Christopher Hird. Warner, 1994.
Revised and updated edition of the 1991 book, a hard-hitting attack on Rupert Murdoch.

Disasters, Relief and the Media
Benthall, Jonathan. IB Tauris & Co, 1993.
This is believed to be the first detailed study of the way natural and human disasters are represented in the broadcast media. The central topic is the relationship between relief agencies and the media which itself can often appear arbitrary and ruthless.

It Ain't as Easy as It Looks
Bibb, Porter. Virgin Publishing, 1994.
Biography of the American billionaire Ted Turner, founder in 1980 of CNN (Cable News Network), the world's dominant news system.

News on a Knife - Edge
Bourne, Richard. John Libbey & Co, 1995.
The history of the brave London-based news feature agency Gemini, born in 1967, which specialised in trying to improve the news flow between the North/South Worlds.

Tiny Rowland
Bower, Tom. Heinemann, 1993.
Another revealing biography of a tough media tycoon, the owner of the Observer until 1993.

Women's Magazines - The First 300 Years
Braithwaite, Brian. Peter Owen, 1995.
Factual description of the history of women's mags, starting with the Ladies Mercury three centuries ago.

History of Broadcasting in the UK Vol 5: Competition 1955-74
Briggs, Asa. Oxford University Press, 1995.
Final volume of Lord Briggs' mammoth official history of the BBC. This definitive series, which began publication in 1963, is essential reading for students and anyone with a serious interest in broadcasting. Unfortunately it is expensive, but libraries should have it.

The Tele - A History of the Belfast Telegraph
Brodie, Malcolm. Blackstaff Press, 1995.
Detailed and well-illustrated history the prominent regional paper, known locally as "The Tele". From the birth in 1870, this story also reflects much of the history of Northern Ireland since then.

Exposed!
Brown, Gerry. Virgin, 1995.
"The Sensational True Story of a Fleet Street Reporter" - a veteran News of the World front-liner describes how he unearthed many top sleaze stories. An enlightening description of the painstaking work of a fiercely professional man of the People (or NoW).

Reading Audiences: Young People and the Media
Buckingham, David (ed). Manchester University Press, 1993.
Eight prominent academics ask children about the programmes they watch, the print they read, and the effect it has on them.

The BBC: 70 Years of Broadcasting
Cain, John. BBC Books, 1992.
Well-illustrated and informative history, aimed at the general public as a valuable reference book.

... and there was television
Cashmore, Ellis. Routledge, 1994.
Why is there so much fuss over the profound social effects of TV? The author argues that much of the panic is unjustified. He believes TV is the central apparatus of consumer society.

The Sky Barons
Clarke, Neville, & Edwin Riddell. Methuen, 1992.
Analysis of the men who control the global media, from Berlusconi to Turner.

Paper Tigers
Coleridge, Nicholas. Heinemann, 1993.
A unique in-depth book profiling many of the world's leading newspaper tycoons. It is based on personal interviews with these characters, some of whom are strangely shy about personal publicity. Descriptive rather than revealing.

Broadcasting and Audio - Visual Policy in the European Single Market
Collins, Richard. John Libbey, 1994.
A new technical study of the complex evolution of these policies in the EC.

Satellite Television in Western Europe
Collins, Richard. John Libbey & Co, 1992, 2nd edition.
Pioneering study of the history of satellite television, also looking at its future and asking how much it will destroy national cultures.

Paying for Broadcasting - The Handbook
Congdon, Tim, et al. Routledge, 1992.
Commissioned by the BBC to take forward the national debate on its funding options.

TV News, Urban Conflict & the Inner City
Cottle, Simon. Leicester University Press, 1993.
A study of how a major TV company presents inner city conflict to viewers

Pioneering Television News
Cox, Geoffrey. John Libbey & Co, 1995.
The story of the rise of television news to its position as the main source of news for the general public, told by one of those who led this revolution in journalism.

Understanding Radio
Crisell, Andrew. Routledge, 1994, 2nd edition.
A radio textbook, exploring how radio processes genres such as news, drama and comedy in distinctive ways, and how the listener's use of the medium has significant implications for audience studies.

Interference on the Airwaves - Ireland, the Media and the Broadcasting Ban
Curtis, Liz, & Mike Jempson. Campaign for Press and Broadcasting Freedom, 1993.
A wide-ranging critical analysis of the British government's pressures on media reporting of Ireland, especially the 1988 legal ban on broadcasting Sinn Fein material.

Communication and Citizenship - Journalism and the Public Sphere

Dahlgren, Peter, & Colin Sparks (eds). Routledge, 1993.
Can the media play a role in the formation of a "public sphere" at a time when public service broadcasting is under attack?

Under the Hammer - Greed & Glory Inside the Television Business

Davidson, Andrew. Mandarin, 1993.
The gripping and at times bizarre story of the auctioning of the ITV regional franchises in 1991, told by a former business journalist on the Sunday Times.

Broadcasting and the BBC in Wales

Davies, John. University of Wales Press, 1994.
Traces in detail the history of the BBC in Wales, from the opening of Cardiff's radio station in 1923 to the early 1990s.

The Media and Disasters: Pan Am 103

Deppa, Joan, et al. David Fulton Publishers, 1993.
Major disasters, such as the destruction of aircraft Pan Am 103 by a terrorist bomb, have become a major attraction for the media. Deppa shows what this means for reality, detailing the case's investigation by 1,000 journalists.

The Executive Tart and Other Myths - Media Women Talk Back

Dougary, Ginny. Virago, 1994.
Revealing and critical analysis of the inferior role forced on women in the media world for many years.

Channels of Resistance - Global Television and Local Empowerment

Dowmunt, Tony (ed). British Film Institute, 1993.
Essays from around the world examining how television influences, affects and reflects diff-erent cultural identities. The collection particularly illuminates the colonising effects of TV.

National Identity and Europe

Drummond, Phillip et al. British Film Institute, 1993.
Essays looking at the processes by which collective identities in the new Europe are being defined and changed by television.

Getting the Message - News, Truth and Power

Eldridge, John (ed). Routledge, 1993.
Glasgow University Media Group has been a prominent feature of media studies for many years, and this book provides an introduction to its recent work.

The Media in Western Europe

Euromedia Media Research Group. Sage, 1992.
This Euromedia handbook gives a descriptive, rather than factual, guide to each country's media system.

Good Times, Bad Times

Evans, Harold. Phoenix, 1994.
In 1983 the former editor of the Sunday Times and Times wrote his powerful history of life under Rupert Murdoch. This 1994 edition of that book adds a new chapter, re-assessing Murdoch's role and political influence.

CNN World Report - Ted Turner's International News Coup

Flournoy, Don. John Libbey, 1992.
Academic study of the origins of Ted Turner's pioneering global satellite TV news programme, CNN World Report.

Television and Sponsorship

Ford, Bianca and James. Focal Press, 1993.
Pioneering book examining the immense influence that programme commercial sponsors have had over the political, economic and cultural rise of television. Sponsorship's power cannot be under-estimated, they say.

Packaging Politics

Franklin, Bob. Edward Arnold, 1994.
The increasingly feeble role of investigative journalism has produced a superficial coverage of politics, graphically described by this Reader in Journalism at the University of Sheffield.

Media Education Across Europe

French, David, & Michael Richards (eds). Routledge/Broadcasting Standards Council, 1994.
Compares the practice of university media education in several European countries, and explores the potential for collaboration.

Moving Experiences

Gauntlett, David. John Libbey & Co, 1995.
The author examines the effects of television on behaviour and concludes that the links cannot be found. He argues that TV is just one of hundreds of influences touching people every day, and it should be put in a much wider social context.

Paper Dreams

Glover, Stephen. Penguin, 1994.
A candid, funny and critical account of the early life of the Independent and its Sunday stablemate, by one of the founding trio. First published 1993, updated to March 1994.

Seeing is Believing - Religion and Television in the 1990s

Gunter, Barrie, & Rachel Viney. John Libbey/Independent TV Commission, 1994.
ITC research monograph giving the most comprehensive analysis to date of public opinion about religious television.

A Northern Star

Harcup, Tony. Campaign for Press and Broadcasting Freedom, 1994.
Subtitled "Leeds Other Paper and the Alternative Press 1974-94", this pamphlet tells the history of the radical Leeds magazine Northern Star and chronicles the rise and fall of the British alternative press, arguing for a more democratic way of owning and running the media.

Sharper Vision - The BBC and the Communications Revolution
Hargreaves, Ian. Demos, 1993.
The former director of news and current affairs at the BBC argues that the corporation needs radical change to prepare for the harsher environment it will face in the next millenium.

Good and Faithful Servant
Harris, Robert. Faber. 1991
Disturbing account of how th media were manipulated by Margaret Thatcher's press secretary Bernard Ingham.

Social Scientists Meet the Media
Haslam, Cheryl, & Alan Bryman (eds). Routledge, 1994.
A personal account by many social scientists of the problems they have encountered in persuading the media to publicise their research. Plus advice on overcoming the difficulties.

The Broadcast Century - A Biography of American Broadcasting
Hilliard, Robert and Michael Keith. Focal Press, 1992.
A vibrant chronicle of the events and people that made broadcasting a primary source of commun-ication in the US.

Into the Box of Delights
Home, Anna. BBC Books, 1993.
Well-illustrated history of children's television, from the days of Muffin the Mule in 1946.

Behind the Screens - The Structure of British Television in the Nineties
Hood, Stuart (ed). Lawrence & Wishart, 1994.
BBC TV's former Controller of Programmes and a group of academics raise important questions about what is now happening to television's core.

Fuzzy Monsters - Fear and Loathing at the BBC
Horrie, Chris, & Steve Clarke. Heinemann, 1994.
A lightweight sensationalist account of how the BBC survived recent chaos and threats to overthrow it, and now faces the future with confidence.

Inside Outside Broadcasts
Hudson, Rober. R&W Publishing, 1993.
Lightweight memoirs of one of the BBC's top post-war commentators. Amusing at times but hardly revealing. An opportunity missed.

The People's Voice
Jankowski, Nick, et al. John Libbey & Co, 1992.
Overview of the current status and anticipated trends of local radio and television across Europe. Looks at the history of community broadcasting, the position in 11 countries and future issues.

Press, Politics and Society
Jones, Aled. University of Wales Press, 1993.
Study of the origins, history and impact of journalism in Wales.

Parallel Lines - Media Representations of Dance
Jordan, S, & D Allen (eds). John Libbey/Arts Council, 1993.
Accounts of how dance and dancing, in a variety of roles, have been represented on television.

Treacherous Estate - The Press After Fleet Street
Leapman, Michael. Hodder & Stoughton, 1992.
Critical look at the condition and morals of the national press since the mid-1980s.

All My Yesterdays
Lewis, Cecil. Element Books, 1993.
The lively personal memoirs of the BBC's Deputy Director of Programmes at a crucial time in the corporation's history, 1922-26.

Talk on Television - Audience Participation and Public Debate
Livingstone, Sonia, & Peter Lunt. Routledge, 1993.
Examines the value and significance of televised public discussion and debate, analysing a wide range of programmes.

Media Communication, Culture - A Global Approach
Lull, James. Polity Press, 1995.

Public Service Broadcasting - A Reader
McDonnell, James. Routledge. 1991
Looks at the history of public service broadcasting, providing useful background to the current ebate on the future of the BBC.

The Expense of Glory
McIntyre, Ian. HarperCollins, 1993.
The former Controller of Radio Four has written this detailed biography of the BBC's dominating controller John Reith, in charge from 1922 to 1938. Reith's diaries have been used.

Media Policy and Music Activity
Malm, Krister, & Roger Wallis. Routledge, 1993.
Looks at how people make music, and how this activity relates to the policies of governments and the music industry.

A Mind of My Own
Maxwell, Elisabeth. Sidgwick & Jackson, 1994.
Robert Maxwell's widow describes life with Mr M.

Media Law and Regulation in Europe
Meinel, Wulf. British Film Institute, 1994.
Examines the development of media legislation in Europe and argues for the adoption of an EC broadcasting constitution to avoid conflict.

Inside the BBC - British Broadcasting Characters
Miall, Leonard. Weidenfeld & Nicholson, 1994.
Lightweight sketches of 25 of the key figures who have shaped the BBC (22 of them men), starting with John Reith.

Don't Mention the War - Northern Ireland, Propaganda and the Media

Miller, David. Pluto Press, 1994.
Examines the way different groups from all sides devised media strategies, how news was produced and the impact news content had on public understanding of the conflict.

Broadcasting Enters the Marketplace

Miller, Nod, & Rod Allen (eds). John Libbey, 1994.
Transcript of the 1993 annual University of Manchester Broadcasting Symposium, looking at the consequences for choice and quality of the 1990 Broadcasting Act.

The Enemy Within - MI5, Maxwell and the Scargill Affair

Milne, Seamus. Verso, 1994.
Meticulous, detailed account of the secret state's vicious manoeuvring during the 1984/5 miners' strike, and the critical role played on their behalf by Robert Maxwell and his Daily Mrror.

The Media Audience

Moore, Shaun. Sage, 1994.
A critical overview of recent research.

Television and the Gulf War

Morrison, David. John Libbey. 1992.
A survey of public opinion on tv reporting of the Gulf War.

The Stalker Affair and the Press

Murphy, David. Unwin Hyman. 1991.
Uses the 1986 Stalker affair to discuss the interaction between journalists, their sources and the way news is produced.

Politics and the Mass Media in Britain

Negrine, Ralph. Routledge, 1994.
Second edition, looking at the role of mass communications in politics at all levels.

Hippie Hippie Shake

Neville, Richard. Bloomsbury, 1995.
"The Dreams, the Trips, the Trials, the Love-ins, the Screw-ups ... the Sixties." A vivid, fascinating account of the alternative 1960s magazine Oz and the dynamic young world in which it was born - and then died.

Selling the Beeb?

O'Malley, Tom, & Jo Treharne. Campaign for Press and Broadcasting Freedom, 1993.
With the BBC's current charter due for renewal in 1996 this pamphlet looks at changes in the corporation since the last renewal in 1981, and ways of protecting public service broadcasting.

Closedown? - The BBC and Government Broadcasting Policy 1979-92

O'Malley, Tom. Pluto Press, 1994.
Revealing and controversial study of the impact of government policies towards the BBC following the arrival of the Tory government in 1979.

Hidden Agendas - The Politics of Religious Broadcasting in Britain 1987-91

Quicke, Andrew, & Juliet Quicke:
Detailed account of a key period in the history of religious broadcasting.

Media, Crisis and Democracy

Raboy, Marc, & Bernard Dagenais (eds). Sage Publications, 1992.
An exploration of the way in which crises highlight the problematic issues of media performance in democratic states.

Making the News

Raymond, Joad. Windrush Press, 1993.
Subtitled as An Anthology of the Newsbooks of Revolutionary England 1641-1660, this looks in detail at the first time in English history when news material was published uncensored. Included are examples of the leading products.

The Power of News - The History of Reuters 1849-1989

Read, Donald. Oxford University Press, 1992.
Detailed authorised history of one of the world's most influential news organisations, drawing on the company's extensive records. Includes new material on the controversial relationship between Reuters and the British government.

Who Stole the News?

Rosenblum, Mort. John Wiley, 1993.
Subtitled "Why we can't keep up with what happens in the world - and what we can do about it", this analyses the international media's overall failure to provide in-depth reportage of the true news, as seen by this leading correspondent with Associated Press.

Citizen Television

Rushton, Dave (ed). John Libbey & Co, 1993.
Pioneering investigation into the hidden public demand for a more democratic approach to the expansion of broadcasting. Draws on four years work by the Institute of Local Television monitoring the introduction of cable TV into Britain. Argues for more local TV content.

Mediawatch - The Treatment of Male and Female Homosexuality in the British Media

Sanderson, Terry. Cassell, 1995.
Until the mid-1960s homosexuality was almost never mentioned in British broadcasting, but now broadcasters are falling over themselves to redress the balance, as described and analyzed here.

Culture and Power

Scannell, Paddy, et al (eds). Sage Publications, 1992.
An introduction to the issues recently central to media studies, drawn from major articles published in the journal Media, Culture and Society in the period 1985-91. Scannell is also editor of the 1991 book Broadcast Talk, which shows the relevance of talk and its analysis to understanding the communicative process in radio and television.

Reporting Crime - The Media Politics of criminal Justice

Schlesinger, Philip, & Howard Tumber. OUP, 1994.

Critical and in-depth analysis of the way journalists cover crime - and the ways they are themsleves managed by the police.

Battling for News - The Rise of the Woman Reporter

Sebba, Anne. Hodder & Stoughton, 1994.

Women have played a key role in the rise of journalism over the past 150 years. This book provides an invaluable history, and also gives powerful backing for critics of the way women are forced into a lower media status and role than men. Recommended.

Hello Mrs Butterfield

Sidey, Phil. Kestrel Press,1995.

The story of the setting up of a pioneering local radio station, BBC Radio Leeds, in 1968, by the man who was in charge of the operation.

Television and Everyday Life

Silverstone, Roger. Routledge, 1994

Explores the way TV has found its way so profoundly into the fabric of people's everyday lives. The author constructs an academic theory which locates TV centrally within multiple realities and discourses of everyday life.

Pop Went the Pirates

Skues, Keith. Lambs Meadow Publications, 1994.

Comprehensive, detailed history of the British offshore pirate radios that had a revolutionary impact on BBC broadcasting in the mid/late 1960s. Skues' definitive and graphic book includes lists of all stations and DJs, plus 230 illustrations. The author was himself a pirate DJ in the 1960s, and drafted the book then. This is a unique record of one of the very few British media systems which have accurately and sympathetically mirrored public culture and emotion of the time.

Television - An International History

Smith, Anthony (ed). Oxford University Press, 1995.

"The first authoritative illustrated international history of this most influential cultural phenomenon ... written by a distinguished team of experts ... a major contribution to media studies." With 180 pictures, many in colour.

The Good, the Bad and the Unacceptable

Snoddy, Raymond. Faber, 1993.

A critical examination of the British press, by the Financial Times's media correspondent. Essential background reading for understanding the debate on privacy and new press laws.

Mass-Media

Sorlin, Pierre. Routledge, 1994.

A short, thought-provoking sociological guide to the mass media in today's society.

A Night in at the Opera - Media Representations of the Opera

Tambling, Jeremy (ed). John Libbey/Arts Council, 1994.

A range of accounts of how the popular arts have represented opera, written by specialists in music, media and popular culture.

Changing Faces - A History of the Guardian 1956-88

Taylor, Geoffrey. Fourth Estate, 1993.

Continues the official history, following on from the books written by Ayers and Hetherington.

Television Producers

Tunstall, Jeremy. Routledge, 1993.

A survey of the spectrum of TV broadcasting, looking at seven programming areas, including news and documentaries.

A Frenzy of Indifference

Turner, Harry. Lutterworth Press, 1993.

Independent TV company TSW lost its broad-casting franchise in the 1991 auction. Managing director Harry Turner tells what happened.

Feminist Media Studies

Van Zoonen, Liesbet. Sage, 1994.

Provides a critical introduction to the relations between gender, media and culture.

Arts TV - A History of Arts Television in Britain

Walker, John. John Libbey/Arts Council, 1993.

The first detailed systematic history of the "plastic" visual arts in British television programmes, focusing on the years 1950-90.

Picture Post Britain

Weightman, Gavin. Collins & Brown. 1991

The best photos from Britains famous news magazine.

Britain's Media: How They Are Related

Williams, Granville. Campaign for Press and Broadcasting Freedom, 1994.

A topical and critical analysis of the issues behind the current multimedia revolution. Evidence is presented of the damage to democracy caused by excessive media concentration, and proposed media policies that are designed to serve people rather than powerful media corporations.

Local Television - Finding a Voice

Wilson, Roger. Dragonflair Publishing, 1994.

Local television has a long history in the cable industry, but there are few local channels at present. If the cable sector expands, however, local TV could become the "third force".

Claiming the Real - The Documentary Film Revisited

Winston, Brian. British Film Institute, 1995.

A slashingly revisionist history of the documentary, portraying all the film-makers as bewitched by a delusion of "objectivity". This could become essential reading for media students. broadcasting in World War Two and the Cold War.

PUBLISHERS

Allen Lane	0171-416 3000
Andre Deutsch	0171-580 2746
Arrow Books	0171-973 9700
Aurum Press	0171-379 1252
Bantam	0181-579 2652
BT Batsford	0171-486 8484
Baylin Publications	01734-414468
BBC Books	0181-576 2639
Bedford Square Press	0171-636 4066
Benn	01732-362666
Billboard	0171-323 6686
A&C Black	0171-242 0946
Blackwell	01865-791100
Blandford Press	0171-839 4900
Bloomsbury	0171-494 2111
Blueprint	0171-865 0066
Bodley Head	0171-973 9730
Booksellers Association	0171-834 5477
Bowker-Saur	0171-493 5841
Boxtree	0171-379 4666
British Film Institute	0171-636 3289
Broadcast Books	0181-769 3483
Butterworth & Co	01732-884567
Butterworth-Heinemann	01865-310366
Cassell	0171-839 4900
CBD Research	0181-650 7745
Century Publishing	0171-973 9670
Chapman & Hall	0171-865 0066
Chatto & Windus	0171-973 9740
Collins	0181-741 7070
Constable	0181-741 3663
Corgi	0181-579 2652
Coronet	0171-636 9851
Demos	0171-353 4479
JM Dent & Sons	0171-240 3444
Diamond Books	0181-307 4406
Directory Publishers Assoc	0171-221 9089
Dorling Kindersley	0171-836 5411
Dragonflair Publishing	01694-722504
Ebury Press	0171-973 9690
Element Books	01747-51339
Emap Media Information	0171-837 1212
Euromonitor	0171-251 8024
Eyre & Spottiswoode	01223-312393
Faber & Faber	0171-465 0045
Focal Press	01865-310366
Fontana	0181-741 7070
Fourth Estate	0171-727 8993
Frank Cass	0181-530 4226
Frederick Warne	0171-416 3000
George Philip	0171-581 9393
Grafton	0181-741 7070
Guinness Publishing	0181-367 4567
Hamish Hamilton	0171-416 3000
Hamlyn	0171-581 9393
HarperCollins	0181-741 7070
Harrap	0181-313 3484
Heinemann	0171-581 9393
HMSO Books	0171-873 0011
Hodder Headline	0171-636 9851
How To Books	01752-705251
Hutchinson Books	0171-973 9680
Interactive Media Publications	0171-490 1185
John Libbey & Co	0181-947 2777
John Wiley & Sons	01243-779777
Jonathan Cape	0171-973 9730
Journeyman Press	0181-348 2724
Kogan Page	0171-278 0433
Ladybird Books	01509-268021
Lawrence & Wishart	0171-820 9281
Longman Group	01279-426721
Lutterworth Press	01223-350865
Macdonald & Co	0171-334 4800
McGraw-Hill	01628-23432
Macmillan Publishers	0171-836 6633
Mandarin	0171-581 9393
Mansell Publishing	0171-839 4900
Marion Boyars	0181-788 9522
Marshall Cavendish	0171-734 6710
Methuen	0171-581 9393
Michael Joseph	0171-416 3000
Mills & Boon	0181-948 0444
Mitchell Beazley	0171-581 9393
Network Books	0181-576 2538
New English Library	0171-636 9851
Nicholas Brealey Publishing	0171-713 7455
NTC Publications	01491-574671
Oak Tree Press	00-3531 8723923
Octopus Publishing	0171-581 9393
Open University Press	01280-823388
Oxford University Press	01865-56767
Paladin Books	0181-741 7070
Pan Books	0171-373 6070
Pandora Press	0181-741 7070
PDQ Publishing	01865-820387
Penguin Books	0171-416 3000
Pergamon Press	01865-794141
Piatkus Books	0171-631 0710
Picador	0171-373 6070
Pitman Publishing	0171-379 7383
Pluto Press	0181-348 2724
Polity Press	01223-324315
Publishers Assoc	0171-580 6321
Puffin	0171-416 3000
Quartet Books	0171-636 3992
Random House	0171-973 9000
Ravette Books	0171-344 6400
Readers Digest	0171-629 8144
Reed Information Services	01342-335832
Reed International Books	0171-581 9393
Routledge	0171-583 9855
Royal Television Society	0171-430 1000
Sage Publications	0171-374 0645
Salamander Books	0171-267 4447
Secker & Warburg	0171-581 9393
Shire Publications	01844-44301
Sidgwick & Jackson	0171-373 6070
Simon & Schuster	0171-724 7577
Sweet & Maxwell	0171-538 8686
Thames & Hudson	0171-636 5488
Thames Publishing	0181-969 3579
Thomas Nelson & Sons	01932-246133
Tolley Publishing	0181-686 9141
Transworld Publishers	0181-579 2652
Usborne Publishing	0171-430 2800
VCH/Academy Group	01223-321111
Verso	0171-437 3546
Victor Gollancz	0171-836 2006
Viking	0171-416 3000
Virago Press	0171-383 5150
Virgin Publishing	0181-968 7554
Ward Lock	0171-839 4900
Weidenfeld & Nicolson	0171-240 3444
J Whitaker & Sons	0171-836 8911
William Heinemann	0171-581 9393
Windrush Press	01608-652012
WOAC Communications	01582-873001
Womens Press	0171-251 3007
Zed Books	0171-837 4014

1996 ANNIVERSARIES

On this day - the media's numerological obsession either shows primitive superstition or a prudent anticipation of how to fill space on dull news days. All events listed here happened a multiple of five years ago. 1996 is the:

75th anniversary of 1921

50th anniversary of 1946

25th anniversary of 1971

January

1 First British trademark is registered, for Bass Pale Ale, 1876. China and North Korea launch major offensive in 1950-53 Korean War, 1951. BBC radio's Light Programme launches The Archers, billed as "The daily events in the lives of country folk", 1951. Channel Four Television Company comes into official being, as a wholly-owned subsidiary of the IBA, 1981. Spain and Portugal join Common Market, 1986. Independent Television Commission and the Radio Authority replace the IBA and the Cable Authority as regulatory bodies, 1991; Broadcasting Standards Council assumes full statutory status.

2 Crowd barriers collapse at Glasgow's Ibrox Park football stadium, killing 66 people and injuring hundreds, 1971. BBC Radio Newcastle is launched, 1971.

3 Three armed anarchists fight troops in the Siege of Sydney Street, in London's East End, 1911. USA severs its diplomatic and consular relations with Fidel Castro's Cuba, 1961. Open University programmes begin on radio and TV, 1971. Last issue of The Listener is published, 1991.

4 American magazine Billboard publishes the first pop music chart based on national sales, 1936.

5 German physicist Rontgen gives the first demonstration of X-rays, 1896. Ten Protestant workers shot dead when their works minibus is ambushed at a bogus road block at Kingsmills, South Armagh, 1976.

6 First widow's pensions are paid out at post offices, 1926. Start of ITV's long running current affairs programme This Week, 1956.

7 Television inventor John Logie Baird gives TV its first demonstration to the press, at 23 Frith Street in Soho, 1926; followed by first public demonstration there on 27 January. Launch of ITV fantasy series The Avengers, 1961.

8 Britain occupies the former Dutch colony the Cape of Good Hope (Cape Town, South Africa), 1806. USA launches its biggest-ever offensive in Vietnam War, 1966. ITV begins first regular Sunday evening religious programmes, 1956.

9 First British X Certificate is awarded to the film La Vie Commence Demain, 1951. Cabinet defence secretary Michael Heseltine resigns in bitter dispute with Downing Street over Mrs Thatcher's style of government, 1986; Leon Brittan resigns as trade and industry secretary on 24 January.

11 Steamship London sinks in gale off France, killing 220 people, 1866. Radio Authority advertises the first Independent National Radio licence, 1991; it is awarded to Classic FM on 19 August.

12 The Angry Brigade claims responsibility for bombing the home of Cabinet minister Robert Carr, 1971. The death at the age of 85, of the crime fiction author Agatha Christie, 1976.

15 Death of Matthew Brady, American Civil War photographer, 1896.

16 Former MP Bernadette McAliskey (née Devlin) is shot and wounded by three loyalist gunmen, 1981. USA launches Western military onslaught - Operation Desert Storm, lasting until 28 February - on Iraq to retake invaded Kuwait, 1991.

17 An American B-52 plane with four hydrogen bombs on board is in an air collision over Spain, 1966.

19 Birth of Scottish engineer James Watt, who developed the steam engine, 1736. Government announces closure of West India and Millwall Docks in London, 1976; A fire sweeps through a house in Deptford South London, killing 13 black people at a party, 1981.

20 Hong Kong is occupied by the British, 1841. Death of King George V after 26 years on the throne, 1936. John F Kennedy becomes president of the USA, 1961. Postal workers go on strike for the first time ever, 1971. Britain and France agree to build today's Channel Tunnel, 1986. A Luton woman is the first person to bring a private prosecution for manslaughter to a Crown Court trial, 1986.

21 Birth of the News Chronicle (as Daily News, with Charles Dickens as editor), and the Church of England's weekly magazine the Guardian, both 1846. Communist newspaper Daily Worker is suppressed by government, 1941. Emley Moor, Britain's highest TV broadcasting tower, begins operation on UHF aerials, 1971. Concorde makes its first commercial flight, London to Bahrain, 1976.

22 Death of Queen Victoria, after a 64-year reign, 1901.

23 Death of USA's leading radical black singer Paul Robeson, 1976.

24 The 270,000 ton oil tanker Olympic Bravery runs aground off France, being the world's largest shipwreck until then, 1976. News International unveils its plan to move the Sun, Times, Sunday Times and Sunday Times from Fleet Street to a new print plant at Wapping, near Limehouse, 1986; print workers go on strike, but printing starts on 25 January.

SDP: 15 YEARS AGO ON 25 JANUARY
No left turn as Rodgers, Jenkins, Williams and Owen leave Labour to form the SDP.

25 Limehouse Declaration by four former Labour cabinet ministers (the "Gang of Four"), including David Owen, leads to the formation of the Social Democratic Party, 1981.

26 A local radio first when BBC Radio Blackburn is launched in 1971.

27 Birth of Austrian composer Wolfgang Mozart, 1756; died 1781. Sunday opening of cinemas is declared illegal, 1931.

28 Death off Panama of Sir Francis Drake, first Englishman to sail round the world, 1596. First speeding fine is given to a British motorist, for driving at 8 mph, 1896. The space shuttle Challenger blows up after lift-off from Cape Canaveral, killing seven astronauts, 1986. TUC supports unions striking against News International moving to Wapping, the electrical union EETPU supplies the labour force, 1986.

29 Patenting of first successful petrol-driven car, by Karl Benz, 1886.

30 United Nations General Assembly meets for first time, London, 1946. Contraceptive pills go on sale in Britain, 1961. Joint US/UK naval force routs flotilla of Iraqi vessels off Kuwait, 1991.

31 Guy Fawkes, the man who tried to blow up the Houses of Parliament in 1605, is executed, 1606. The Daily News is created, with novelist Charles Dickens as editor, 1846. All US "red indians" are ordered to move onto reservations or be declared hostile, 1876. Death of author AA Milne, creator of Winnie-the-Pooh, 1956.

February

1 Test flying begins at the new civilian airport Heathrow, 1946. Death of film comedian Joseph "Buster" Keaton, 1966. Licences for radios abolished, 1971.

2 Idi Amin declares himself the absolute ruler of Uganda, 1971.

3 Birth in Bristol of Elizabeth Blackwell, who in the US became the first woman doctor in the world, 1821. A Soviet spacecraft makes the first controlled landing on the Moon, 1966.

4 The car makers Rolls Royce commissions its famous figurehead "The Spirit of Ecstasy", 1911.

5 Launch of Sunday Telegraph, at the time the first new national Sunday paper for 43 years, 1961.

6 Britain's first police motor-cycles equipped with radio telephones go on duty in London, 1951. Spurs captain Danny Blanchflower becomes first person to say "no" on air to This is Your Life show, 1961. In the Northern Ireland Troubles which began in 1969, the first British soldier is killed, 1971.

7 The Liberal party wins the general election and brings in legislation to start many of the 20th century's welfare services. On the same day, Labour wins its first significant number of seats, 1906. The hated Haiti dictator Baby Doc Duvalier flees an uprising, taking £100 million with him to France, 1986. The IRA fires a mortar bomb into the garden of 10 Downing Street while the Cabinet is meeting inside the building, 1991.

8 Peaceful demonstration by unemployed people in Trafalgar Square is broken up by armed forces, 1886. BBC announces it is dropping its Children's Hour radio programme because of the increasing popularity of television, 1961. Freddie Laker forms his cut-price trans-Atlantic airline, 1966.

9 Confederate States of America are formed, 1861. Death of American pioneer rock-and-roll singer Bill Haley, 1981.

10 Britain completes the conquest of India, with battle on this day at Sobraon in 1846. Britain's pioneer battleship Dreadnought is launched, 1906. High Court judge orders sequestration of the £17 million assets of trade union SOGAT '82 for defying court orders to stop blacking distribtion of News International papers, 1986; but on 24 April Court of Appeal overturns decision and on 8 May Sogat retrieves its money after apologising.

12 First inter-club football match is held, at Sheffield, 1861.

13 Rupert Murdoch buys Times and Sunday Times, 1981. During the Gulf War, American bombers kill hundreds in Baghdad bunker,1991.

14 IBM begins operating its computer, using 18,000 electronic valves, at Pennsylvania University, 1946. Fire inside a Dublin disco kills 49 young people, 1981.

15 Decimal currency replaces Britain's pounds, shillings and pence, 1971.

16 ITC advertises the 16 ITV channels (due to start on 1 January 1993), 1991. Trade unionists protesting against News International's move to its new plant at Wapping are in major clash with police outside the building, 1986.

17 ATV starts the first commercial TV service for the Midlands, 1956, on weekdays; ABC Television begins Midlands weekend service tomorrow.

19 Another Cod War involving Britain and Iceland starts, 1976; it ends 1 June.

23 Death in Rome of John Keats, aged 25, of consumption, 1821. Military coup tries to restore the Spanish monarchy, 1981.

25 BBC Radio Humberside is launched, 1971.

26 Birth of Buffalo Bill (also known as Colonel William Frederick Cody), the Wild West showman, 1846. Hitler launches Volkswagen motorcar, 1936.

27 British defeated by Boers at Battle of Majuba, South Africa, 1881.

28 Oswald Mosley leaves Labour Party to launch the fascist New Party, 1931.Swedish prime minister Olaf Palme is assassinated, 1986.

March

1 Bank of England is nationalised, 1946. Wearing car seat belts is made compulsory 1976. IRA prisoners in Northern Ireland begin seven-month hunger strike, 1981. Oracle Teletext starts, 1986. End of BBC/ITV monopoly of their programme details, 1991.

4 Start of Housewives' Choice, the record request programme for women at home, 1946; ended 1967. Eddie Shah's Today newspaper published for first time, the first national daily in Britain to carry colour pictures, 1986.

5 First flight takes place of prototype Spitfire fighter aircraft, 1936. Winston Churchill coins phrase "Iron Curtain" to describe the hostile Russian presence in Europe, 1946. Government white paper on telecommunications allows cable TV operators and telephone companies to diversify dramatically, 1991.

6 End of legendary Battle of the Alamo (Texans lose to Mexicans), 1836. Death of English comedian George Formby, 1961. Women's liberation march is held, showing the spreading support for the movement, 1971.

TODAY: 10 YEARS AGO ON 4 MARCH
Here today, gone tomorrow. Eddie Shah fails to make the grade as a press baron

7 Alexander Bell patents the first telephone capable of carrying sustained speech messages, 1876.

8 British empire nowcovers a fifth of the Earth's land surface, says a government survey, 1906. Death of English conductor Sir Thomas Beecham, founder of Royal Philharmonic orchestra, 1961. East End gangster Ronnie Kray, one of the Kray twins, carries out a murder in a Whitechapel pub, 1966. Launch of Radio 210, ILR station for Reading area, 1976.

9 Accident at Bolton Wanderers football ground kills 33 people and injures 500 others in FA cup-tie, 1946. Harold Evans becomes editor of Times, 1981.

10 The first Cruft's Dog Show took place in London, 1886.

11 Birth of Labour prime minister Harold Wilson, 1916. Birth in Australia of media mogul Rupert Murdoch, 1931. BBC World Service TV News service begins, 1991.

13 The planet Uranus is discovered, 1781. Republic of Cyprus is formed, following the 1959 civil war, 1961.

14 First telephone cable laid across English Channel, 1891. New Liberal government approves starting old age pensions, 1906. Six men wrongly jailed for IRA bombing of a Birmingham pub in 1974 are freed, 1991.

16 Labour prime minister Harold Wilson announces his surprise resignation, 1976. House of Commons gives go-ahead for radio broadcasting of its proceedings, 1976. Launch of Downtown Radio, ILR station for Belfast area, 1976.

17 British are forced to evacuate Boston by George Washington, 1776. Britain's first birth control clinic, created by Marie Stopes, opens in north London, 1921.

18 The Communards start their uprising in Paris, eventually creating world's first socialist government, 1871.

19 Married couple Princess Margaret and Earl of Snowdon announce separation plans, 1976.

21 Information on betting odds is broadcast before a horse race for first time, by BBC, 1961. British government announces end of its poll tax, after public opposition, 1991.

23 London's first tram cars begin operating, 1861. Pakistan is declared a republic, 1956. For first time in 400 years, the heads of the Roman Catholic and Anglican churches meet officially, 1966.

24 Argentina's president Isabel Peron is deposed in military coup, 1976.

26 East Pakistan is declared the independent republic of Bangla Desh, starting nine-month war, 1971.

27 Labour Party rejects Communist Party's application for affiliation, 1946.

28 British novelist Virginia Woolf commits suicide, 1941.

29 Opening of London's Royal Albert Hall, 1871. Nazis win 99 per cent of the vote in German elections, 1936. Government announces Independent Television Authority will have responsibility for Independent Local Radio (ILR), 1971. Birth of first test-tube quintuplets, 1986.

30 President Ronald Reagan is shot and wounded in Washington, 1981.

31 Coal miners launch a three-month national strike, unsuccessfully trying to stop the government giving the mines back into private hands after First World War state control, 1921. Labour wins general election, with bigger majority, 1966. Labour-controlled GLC (the world's largest local authority) comes to an end, 1986. Hampton Court Palace is severely damaged by fire, 1986. Trade unions are forced to agree Express Newspapers cutting its workforce by 2,500, just hours before a deadline which would have closed all its papers, 1986.

April

1 All BBC commercial activities are brought together in a single organisation, BBC Enterprises, 1986.

5 James Callaghan replaces Harold Wilson as Labour's prime minister following his sudden resignation on 16 March, 1976.

6 Opening of innovatory new railway up Snowdon mountain, with serious accident, 1896. First modern Olympic Games are held, in Athens, 1896. Germany invades Yugoslavia and Greece, with both countries surrendering 11 days later, 1941.

9 Birth of Isambard Kingdom Brunel, pioneering engineer, 1806.

11 Germany carries out a heavy air raid on Coventry, 1941. Soviet Union puts the first man into space, Major Yuri Gagarin, in a single satellite orbit, 1961. Bobby Sands is elected Sinn Fein MP for Fermanagh in by-election, 1981; he is on hunger strike in the Maze Prison, where he dies on 5 May, prompting widespread rioting in Northern Ireland.

12 Start of American Civil War, with Confederate forces bombarding Fort Sumter, South Carolina, 1861. Launch of Beacon Radio, ILR station for Wolverhampton and Black Country area, 1976. Summer of inner-city rioting around UK begins in London's Brixton area, 1981.

14 Ministry of Transport issues the Highway Code, 1931.

15 USA unsuccessfully carries out its "Bay of Pigs" military invasion of Cuba, 1961. USA attacks Libya, 1986. BBC World Service Television begins, 1991.

16 The Jacobite highlanders suffer a military defeat by Duke of Cumberland, at Culloden Moor, 1746. Submarine HMS Affray sinks in English Channel, killing 75 crew, 1951.

17 Prize-paying premium bonds are launched by government, 1956.

18 Severe earthquake in San Francisco kills over 500 people, 1906.

19 First Miss World beauty contest is held, 1951. Vietnam Veterans Against the War stage week-long series of demonstrations in Washington, USA, 1971.

21 Birth of Jane Eyre author Charlotte Brontë, 1816. Birth of Elizabeth II, 1926.

22 A revolt by right-wing generals in Algeria, who threaten to invade France, but it is crushed in four days, 1961.

23 Death of William Shakespeare, 1616. Charles II crowned King, 1661.

24 Five-day Easter Rising takes place in Dublin, with nationalists unsuccessfully challenging British imperialism in Ireland, 1916; about 450 people die in the city and the leaders surrender following violent action by 5,000 British troops. Bradford lorry-driver Peter Sutcliffe admits he is the "Yorkshire Ripper" who murdered 13 women, 1981.

GENERAL STRIKE: 50 YEARS AGO ON 3 MAY
Bus queues in Manchester during the nine day General Strike in 1926.

26 World's worst ever nuclear accident takes place when a fire at Chernobyl nuclear power station in the Ukraine contaminates much of Europe with radioactive fall-out, 1986.

29 Westward Television launches TV service for south-west England, 1961. BBC Radio Derby launched, 1971.

30 The hovercraft begins its first regular service across English Channel, 1966.

May

1 Opening of New York's Empire State Building, then the world's tallest building, 1931. TV Ad Duty imposed by government, bringing temporary switch of ads to newspapers, 1961. Betting shops legalised, 1961.

3 The nine-day General Strike begins, the most significant industrial dispute in British history, 1926; Times is only national newspaper to continue appearing; BBC broadcasts five radio news bulletins daily. Granada TV launches the weekday service for north of England, 1956; ABC Television starts the north's weekend service on 5 May. Times is redesigned to print front page news, 1966.

4 Launch of Alfred Harmsworth's Daily Mail, immediately becoming the first of today's popular tabloids, 1896. Festival of Britain opens on London's South Bank, 1951.

5 Birth of the Liberal newspaper Manchester Guardian (now The Guardian), 1821; leading article said "We are enemies of scurrility and slander". Italy takes over Ethiopia after militarily defeating native people following October 1935 invasion, 1936.

6 The birth of the sexual psychologist Sigmund Freud, 1856. The Moors murderers Myra Hindley and Ian Brady are jailed for life for killing two children and a teenager, 1966.

7 German troops reoccupy Rhineland area which they had lost after First World War, 1936.

8 Birth of the leading natural history broadcaster and dramatiser of the life of plants, Sir David Attenborough, 1926.

9 The Horseless Carriage Show opens its doors to the motor trade for the first time, 1896. The German terrorist Ulrike Meinhof, co-founder of Baader Meinhof, is found dead in her prison cell, 1976.

10 House of Commons is destroyed by Germany's most devastating bombing raid on London in World War Two, 1941. Jeremy Thorpe, MP, quits as leader of Liberal Party, 1976.

12 Fifteen leaders of Ireland's Easter Rising are executed by the British, becoming the martyrs of the Irish War of Independence that soon begins, 1916. Frightened TUC leadership calls off General Strike, Britain's biggest ever industrial conflict, despite the possible success by trade unionists, 1926.

13 John Osborne's pioneering and highly controversial play Look Back in Anger opens at London's Royal Court theatre, 1956. Pope John Paul II shot and wounded in Vatican City, 1981.

14 Founding of the Newspaper Society, 1836.

16 British government unveils its plans for Indian independence, 1946. Britain's seamen go on strike, 1966; government declares State of Emergency 23 May; strike ends 1 July.

18 BBC acquires its first female announcers, 1936.

20 USA explodes its first hydrogen bomb onto the Pacific's Bikini atoll, 1956.

21 Clocks are put forward an hour to save more daylight for the first time, 1916.

23 The pirate Captain Kidd is hanged at London's Execution Docks, 1701.

24 In the Battle of the Atlantic, leading German warship Bismarck sinks Royal Navy's pride HMS Hood, 1941; in retaliation, Bismarck is sunk on 27 May. First Eurovision Song Contest is held, in Switzerland, 1956.

25 Parliament passes Bank Holiday Act, creating the now-familiar national annual holidays, 1871. Diplomats Donald Maclean and Guy Burgess disappear, and are soon revealed as major Soviet spies, 1951. Bob Geldof's "Race Against Time" has 30 million people running in Sport Aid to raise funds for starving population of Africa, 1986.

26 News International makes £50 million offer to trade unions to end the 18-week dispute over moving to Wapping, 1986; but this is refused on 6 June.

27 Start of Southampton-New York maiden voyage of liner Queen Mary, 1936.

28 BBC radio broadcasts first Goon Show, 1951.

29 BBC broadcasts the first TV interview with a member of the Royal Family (Duke of Edinburgh), 1961.

31 Launch of the Titanic, in Belfast, 1911. Britain defeats Germany at the Battle of Jutland, 1916. South Africa becomes a republic, 1961.

June

1 First electric trolley buses begin running, in Leeds and Bradford, 1911. Birth of actress Marilyn Monroe, 1926. World's first scheduled experimental colour television service begins (by CBS, in New York), 1941. British television licences issued for the first time, costing £2, including radio service, 1946; estimated 7,500 sets. End of third Cod War between Britain and Iceland, 1976. Broadcasting Complaints Commission comes into operation, 1981.

2 Broadcasting is born in the UK when Guglielmo Marconi patents his wireless system using electromagnetic waves, 1896; it is first publicly demonstrated on 27 July that year, with a transmission from GPO's London head-quarters. First live TV pictures from the Moon, 1966.

3 First bikini bathing suit is unveiled in Paris, 1946. British Railways abolishes its Third Class seating on trains, 1956.

4 Summer of serious rioting in Belfast begins with loss of life, 1886.

5 HMS Hampshire, with Lord Kitchener aboard, sinks after striking a mine, 1916.

6 Launch of Cunard liner Lusitania, then world's largest passenger vessel, 1906. First publication of John Bull, a prominent news weekly magazine for many years, 1906. Gatwick Airport opens, 1936. Sitcom Till Death Us Do Part first televised by the BBC, 1966.

7 BBC re-opens its television service, closed since 1 September 1939, within range of about 40 miles from Alexandra Palace, 1946. Britain's national economic crisis forces the Labour government to borrow £3,000 million from abroad and adopt right-wing policies ordered by International Monetary Fund, 1976. Israeli bombers attack and destroy an Iraqi nuclear reactor, 1981.

THE OZ TRIAL: 25 YEARS AGO ON 23 JUNE
The Oz editors James Anderson, Richard Neville and Felix outside the Old Bailey.

8 First post-war outside television broadcast shows victory parade through London, 1946.

12 Derek Hatton, deputy leader of Liverpool Council, is expelled from Labour Party for membership of Militant Tendency, 1986.

13 Wat Tyler leads the Peasants' Revolt, the first popular rebellion in English history, 1381; he is beheaded two days later. Football's first European Cup is won by Real Madrid, 1956.

14 Death of John Logie Baird, the inventor of the television, 1946.

15 USA and Canada agree the 49th parallel is the border between them, 1846. House of Lords votes in favour of televising itself, excluding Commons, 1966; but full coverage does not begin until January 1985. Margaret Thatcher, the government's education secretary, decides to end free school milk, 1971.

16 Death of BBC's first director-general, Lord Reith, 1971; aged 81. At least 176 people are killed in South Africa's worst-ever rioting, which starts today in Soweto near Johannesburg, 1976.

17 Breakfast-time television will start in May 1983, announces the IBA, 1981.

20 In India, 123 people die in the Black Hole of Calcutta, 1756. A former Kenyan man becomes first black British police officer, 1966.

21 Foundation stone of Tower Bridge laid by Prince of Wales, 1886. Police seize the cartoon magazine Nasty Tales, 1971.

22 Coronation of King George V, 1911. Hitler launches "Operation Barbarossa" invasion of Soviet Union, 1941.

23 Start of trial of three leading creators of Oz magazine, over alleged obscenity of its Schoolkids issue, 1971; they are found guilty and jailed, then bailed.

24 English Civil War ends with Royalists surrendering to Parliamentarians, Oxford, 1646. Britain agrees terms to join the Common Market 1971.

25 Sioux indians kill all 264 soldiers of the US 7th Cavalry at Custer's Last Stand, 1876. The world's first regular commercial colour TV service begins (by CBS in New York), 1951. Croatia and Slovenia declare independence from USSR, 1991.

26 First Grand Prix motor race takes place at Le Mans, 1906.

29 Britain carries out its first official census, 1801. Hampstead Heath in north London is purchased by Metropolitan Board of Works, 1871. First British credit card (the Barclaycard) is introduced, 1966.

30 The Queen, riding her horse during the Trooping of the Colour, has blank shots fired at her by a protestor against unemployment, 1981.

July

1 Start of Battle of the Somme, an unsuccessful British/French attack, leaving over 420,000 men dead when it ends on 13 November, 1916. World's first TV commercial (for a Bulova watch) is shown on NBC's WNBT station in New York, 1941. Home Secretary announces he has authorised purchase of 24 bullet-proof vehicles and 80 personnel carriers for police use in dealing with future rioting in London, 1986.

2 Author Ernest Hemingway commits suicide, 1961.

3 Launch of magazine Tatler, 1901. Israeli commandos rescue 103 hostages held on an airplane by Palestinian hijackers in Entebbe Airport, Uganda, 1976. Government Report of the Committee on Financing the BBC recommends a radical reorganisation of British television, sparking many of the major changes in coming years, 1986.

4 American Congress votes for independence from Britain, 1776. Philippine islands are given their independence from USA, 1946. Britain's worst week of rioting in living memory begins in Toxteth, Merseyside, 1981; a number of copy cat riots follow.

6 First broadcast on TV of Hancock's Half Hour (radio began 2 November 1954), 1956; Tony Hancock committed suicide 1968. Death of jazz musician Louis Armstrong, 1971.

7 Start of BBC's first children's TV programme For the Children, 1946.

9 Second World War comes to an official end nearly 12 years after its 1939 start, 1951.

10 A week of serious rioting culminates in "Britain's night of anarchy" in many inner-city areas, 1981.

11 British newspapers are banned from printing extracts from Peter Wright's book Spycatcher, about Soviet penetration of the security service, 1986.

14 Home Secretary authorises a further 25 new locations for ILR stations (bringing total up to 69), 1981.

17 First edition of Punch magazine published, 1841. This day in 1936 was the start of the three-year Spanish Civil War, when the right-wing military attacks the Republican government which had been elected in 1931; Germany and Italy support the fascists, the Soviet Union then organises the International Brigades and anarchists create their own volunteer bodies.

20 Football Association proposes start of FA Challenge Cup competition, 1871. The "V for Victory" campaign is launched in Britain, 1941. Government tries to halt rise in inflation by freezing all pay and dividends, 1966. US spacecraft lands on Mars and sends back pictures, 1976.

21 Birth of Paul von Reuter, creator of news communication company Reuters, 1816. British ambassador to Dublin, Sir Christopher Ewart-Biggs, is killed by an IRA bomb under his car, 1976. Setting up of new joint BBC/ITV system of audience research BARB 1981.

23 Dog licences are being abolished, announces government, 1986. Prince Andrew marries Sarah Ferguson, 1986.

25 USA starts using Bikini Atoll island in the Pacific for its nuclear bombs tests, 1946.

26 Birth of Irish playwright George Bernard Shaw, 1856. Launch of London newspaper Evening News, 1881. Egypt seizes control of Anglo-French Suez Canal, 1956.

27 Jim Laker becomes first cricketer to take all ten wickets in a test innings, against Australia, 1956. Launch of NorthSound Radio, ILR station for Aberdeen area, 1981. Death of cartoonist Sir Osbert Lancaster, 1986. A second bridge will be built over River Severn, announces government, 1986.

28 Potatoes arrive in Britain for first time, from Columbia, 1586. Birth of children's author Beatrix Potter, 1866. Government publishes its Marine Broadcasting (Offences) Bill that will make popular pirate radio illegal, 1966.

29 Prince Charles marries Lady Diana Spencer in St Paul's Cathedral, 1981.

30 Britain wins football World Cup for first time, defeating West Germany 4-2, 1966.

31 BBC Lime Grove studios close, 1991.

August

1 BBC Royal Charter expiring at the end of 1996 comes into force, 1981.

3 Irish nationalist and British diplomat Sir Roger Casement is hanged for high treason, at Pentonville Prison, 1916. First British traffic lights are installed at Piccadilly Circus, 1926. US comedian Lenny Bruce dies from drug overdose, 1966.

4 Government applies for Britain to join Common Market, 1961.

6 An American woman becomes first female to swim English Channel, 1926.

7 First British motoring Grand Prix is run, at Brooklands, 1926.

8 Women launch a major, well-supported campaign to bring peace to Northern Ireland after three children are killed, 1976.

9 Internment without trial is introduced in Northern Ireland, sparking violent reaction by its Republican opponents, 1971.

10 Britain applies to join EEC, 1961. Launch of first US moon satellite Orbiter One, 1966.

11 Westward Television goes off the air after losing its ITV licence, 1981.

12 Three plain-clothes London policemen shot dead in street near Wormwood Scrubs, 1966.

13 Fierce rioting in Liverpool, 1911; part of the widespread and militant industrial unrest this year, aimed at creating a socialist society. Death of author HG Wells, 1946. East Germany closes frontier between East and West Berlin, and soon erects the Berlin Wall, 1961.

14 Death of US newspaper giant Randolph Hearst, 1951.

15 Birth in Scotland of first Labour Party leader James Keir Hardie, 1856.

17 A Croydon woman becomes first pedestrian to be killed by a car, 1896. The discovery of gold at Bonanza Creek in Canada's Yukon Territory leads to 1898 gold rush, 1896.

18 Australia and New Zealand withdraw their armed forces from the South Vietnam War, 1971.

19 France and Spain form alliance against Britain, 1796. Thousands die in India during rioting between Hindus and Moslems over Britain's plans for the country's independence, 1946. The Soviet premier Mikhail Gorbachev is arrested while on holiday in Crimea in unsuccessful coup attempt, 1991; in following months the USSR disintegrates.

23 Death of great screen lover Rudolf Valentino, aged 31, 1926.

24 Labour government falls because of severe economic crisis hitting Britain, 1931; Ramsay MacDonald forms coalition National Government to replace it.

25 British and Russian forces invade Iran, 1941.

26 England defeats France at Battle of Crécy, 1346. BBC experimentally transmits its first high definition television pictures, from Alexandra Palace to the Radio Show at Olympia, 1936; its first announcer is Leslie Mitchell.

27 Francis Chichester sets off from Plymouth, to become first old-age pensioner to sail around the world alone, 1966.

28 King Edward of England takes control of Scotland (temporarily) when 2,000 Scottish leaders submit to him, at Berwick, 1296.

29 The first electrical transformer is demonstrated, by Michael Faraday, at London's Royal Institute, 1831. Beatles play their last live concert, in San Francisco, 1966.

30 Germans lay siege to Leningrad, 1941.Traffic wardens are born, 1956.

31 One of Britain's worst ever (but popular) sun-baked summer droughts is interrupted by the first showers, 1976. Death of world-famous British sculptor Henry Moore, 1986. Start of BBC TV NICAM stereo sound services, 1991.

September

1 London's Cannon Street railway station opens, 1866. Twenty five councillors from Poplar are jailed for refusing to levy rates, 1921. Britain's first supermarket opens, in Earls Court, London, 1951. Borders Television launches the commercial television service for the England/Scotland border, 1961. Launch of Aire Radio, ILR station for Leeds area, 1981.

2 Great Fire of London starts in a bakery in Pudding Lane, lasting four days, 1666.

3 Two British servicemen row across the Atlantic, 1966.

4 Surrender of Geronimo, leader of the last American Indian resistance, 1886.

5 Following the Parliamentary victory in the English Civil War, the offices of Archbishop of Canterbury and other bishops are abolished, 1646. World's first high-definition (240-line) TV outside broadcast made in Britain, from Alexandra Palace, 1936.

6 TUC condemns the widespread use of troops to quash widespread industrial unrest this summer, 1911. South African prime minister Hendrik Verwoerd assassinated by a white extremist, 1966. Launch of top BBC 1 series Casualty, 1986.

7 Birth of US pop star Buddy Holly (killed aged 23 in an air crash), 1936.

8 Giant Japanese car makers Nissan open a plant at Sunderland, 1986.

9 Inaugural rally at Westminster's Central Hall of Festival of Light, campaigning against the moral depravity of the time, 1971. Death of Chinese Communist leader Mao Tse-tung, 1976. Launch of Rediffusion's Starview pioneering cable TV service, in five towns, 1981; first subscriber TV service in Britain.

11 Installation of first TV set in a house, at Green Gables, Harrow, 1926. Death of former Soviet premier Nikita Kruschev, 1971.

12 Nobel prize winner Bertrand Russell is jailed for his active role in the Campaign for Nuclear Disarmament, 1961. Launch of Essex Radio, ILR station for Southend/Chelmsford area, 1981.

13 The Gold Coast will be Britain's first black colony in Africa to get independence, announces the government, 1956.

15 Tanks go into action for the first time for British Army, in the Somme, 1916. Royal Navy "mutiny" at Invergordon, 1931. The BBC produces first televised church service, 1946. Royal Navy's first nuclear submarine is launched, at Barrow, 1966.

17 A fleet of 100 fishing boats sails up Thames in protest at Britain joining EEC, 1971. Death of actress Pat Phoenix, Elsie Tanner in Coronation Street, 1986.

18 First publication of New York Times, 1851. About 800 people are arrested in Britain's biggest ban-the-bomb CND demonstration so far, 1961. Dag Hammarskjold, head of UN, is killed in a mysterious air crash, 1961. France abolishes guillotine, 1981.

19 England defeats France at Battle of Poitiers, 1356.

20 Britain comes off gold standard, causing much industrial unrest, 1931. An Argentinian man becomes first person to swim non-stop across English Channel and back again, 1961.

21 Ninety Russian diplomats are expelled from Britain for spying, 1971.

23 The planet Neptune is discovered, 1846.

29 The Third Programme begins on BBC radio, joining Home Service and Light Programme, 1946. Death of Bill Shankly, Liverpool Football Club manager who made it one of finest teams in world, 1981.

30 Opening of Hollywood-rival Pinewood Studios, near Iver in Buckinghamshire, 1936. Grampain Television launches a commercial TV service for north-east Scotland, 1961. Times is bought by Lord Thomson, already owner of the Sunday Times, 1966. Bechuanaland becomes independent nation of Botswana, 1966.

October

1 General Franco takes over as head of Nationalist Government in Spain, 1936. Disney World opens in Florida, 1971. Launch of Northants Radio, ILR station for Northampton area, 1986. Marmaduke Hussey named as new chairman of BBC by government, 1986.

2 First Royal Navy submarine launched. at Barrow, 1901.

3 Death of William Morris, aged 62, the pioneering socialist artist, writer and designer, 1896. IRA hunger strike that began on 1 March ends after ten deaths, 1981.

4 Earls Court Underground station switches on Britain's first escalator, 1911.

6 President Sadat of Egypt assassinated in Cairo by Muslim extremists, 1981.

7 Woman's Hour and Dick Barton, Special Agent begin on BBC radio, 1946. Launch of first satellite dish aerial for domestic use in Britain, at demonstration in a shop's roof garden in Kensington, 1981. First issue of Independent newspaper, 1986.

10 Anti-European rioting in Kowloon, the mainland area of Hong Kong, results in 51 people being killed, 1956.

11 British anti-Fascist demonstrations reach a climax, with 100,000 people trying to stop Sir Oswald Mosley marching through London's East End, 1936.

12 Opening of Holme Moss transmitter, bringing TV to the north of England, 1951. Launch of Ocean Sound, ILR station for Southampton/Portsmouth area, 1986.

14 Victory at Battle of Hastings allows the Normans to take over England, 1066. Launch of the underground magazine IT, 1966. BBC World Service TV launches Asian Service, which later becomes first BBC 24-hour TV channel, 1991.

15 Birth of English novelist PG Wodehouse, 1881. Nazi war criminal Herman Goering commits suicide in Nuremberg Prison, 1946. First British party-political broadcast televised by the BBC (for the Liberals), 1951. Launch of Chiltern Radio, ILR station for Luton/Bedford area, 1976. Start of BBC World Service's news and information channel, 1991.

16 A medical anaesthetic is used successfully for the first time, in Massachussets Hospital, 1846. First issue of Sunday newspaper the People, 1881. World's first birth control clinic opens, in New York, 1916. Express owner Lord Beaverbrook arranges with King Edward VIII there will be press silence about his affair with Mrs Simpson, 1936. Launch of West Sound, ILR station for Ayr area, 1981. ITC awards the 1993 ten-year ITV licences, 1991; four existing licensees are losers.

17 Queen opens Britain's first nuclear power station, at Calder Hall, Cumbria, 1956.

18 Birth of US rock and roll pioneer Chuck Berry, 1926. Death of American Thomas Edison, world's leading electronics inventor, 1931. Pardon granted to Timothy Evans, hanged in 1950 for apparent murder at 10 Rillington Place, London, 1966.

19 Launch of SIBC, the ILR station for Shetland Islands, 1991.

20 Setting up of the Audit Bureau of Circulations (ABC), 1931.

21 A coal tip engulfs a school in the Welsh village of Aberfan, killing 116 children and 28 adults, 1966. Two Tory MPs successfully sue the BBC over Panorama allegations that they had close links with right-wing racist groups, 1986.

22 Tit Bits magazine launched, 1881. George Blake, Soviet spy, escapes from prison and goes to East Berlin, 1966.

23 Start of the Hungarian revolt against Soviet control of the country, 1956.

24 Eleven militant suffragettes are jailed after holding a demonstration at the House of Commons, 1906. National Transcommunications, the privatised engineering arm of former IBA, is sold to Mercury Asset Management, 1991.

25 Birth of Pablo Picasso, 1881. Last horse-bus service in London, 1911. Post-war Labour government loses general election to Tories, with Winston Churchill becoming prime minister for first time, 1951. Launch of Private Eye magazine, 1961. New National Theatre on London's South Bank is opened by Queen, 1976.

26 Jeffrey Archer resigns as chairman of Tory Party after unproved allegations of prostitute payment, 1986.

27 First publication of short-lived radical news magazine Seven Days, 1971. Launch of Radio West (later GWR), ILR station for Bristol area, 1981. Stock Exchange's "Big Bang" deregulation day creates new computer-based dealing system, 1986. The BBC's Daytime Television service launches, 1986.

28 Statue of Liberty presented to USA by France, 1886. House of Commons votes in favour of UK's entry into the European Communities, 1971; UK officially joins 1 January 1973.

29 The new coalition National Government is re-elected at a general election, 1931.

31 Anglo-French forces invade Egypt to take control of Suez Canal, 1956; a ceasefire begins on 8 November after USA condemns Britain's action. IRA bomb explodes at top of London's Post Office Tower, 1971.

November

1 BBC English Regional reorganisation announced, 1986.

2 World's first public high-definition TV service begins, with BBC television formally launched from Alexandra Palace in North London, using 405-line service, 1936 (first transmission was on 26 August 1936); only 400 receiving sets in early days.

4 Soviet Army invades Hungary, crushing its liberation movement, 1956.

5 BBC Radio Essex is launched, 1986. Three London boroughs ordered by High Court to stop banning News International newspapers from their public libraries, 1986. Media magnate Robert Maxwell, owner of Mirror newspapers, is mysteriously found dead in the sea near Tenerife, 1991.

10 American scientists discover the secrets of the atomic nucleus, 1931.

11 Jarrow Crusade of 200 unemployed workers marching from Tyneside to London ends with prime minister Stanley Baldwin refusing to meet them, 1936. Stevenage is designated first new town in Britain, 1946. Special leaflet on Aids will be distributed to 23 million homes, decides government, 1986.

13 Scottish explorer Dr David Livingstone is found in central African jungle after going missing four years earlier, 1871. A television viewer undertaking a stunt for Noel Edmonds's Late Late Breakfast Show killed during rehearsals, 1986; BBC cancels the show.

14 Speed limit for horseless carriages raised from 4 mph (2 mph in towns) to 14 mph, 1896. An international agreement cuts the number of BBC radio wavelengths, forcing it to turn local broadcasting into regional, 1926. BBC Radio Surrey is launched, 1991.

15 NBC (National Broadcasting Corporation) is inaugurated in US, 1926.

19 Coal miners end their unsuccessful six month strike that had started the General Strike, 1926.

20 Rolls Royce car company formed by Charles Stewart Rolls and Frederick Henry Royce, 1906. Rolls Royce buys Bentley Motors, 1931.

24 The pop star Freddie Mercury, lead singer with Queen, dies of Aids, 1991.

29 Publication of first weekly newspaper/magazine, called The Heads of Severall Proceedings in this Present Parliament, London, 1641

30 Crystal Palace, built 1851, is destroyed by fire, 1936; almost all John Logie Baird's pioneering TV equipment is lost there.

December

1 Opening of world's first purpose-built picture palace, the Cinema Omnia Pathé, in Paris, 1906.

2 Fidel Castro and a small band of revolutionaries land in Cuba, beginning 1956-59 Cuban Revolution, 1956.

4 Britain's oldest Sunday newspaper, the Observer, is first published, 1791. Birth control pill becomes available on NHS, 1961. Fifteen people killed in Ulster Volunteer Force bomb attack on McGurk's Bar in north Belfast, 1971. Death of English composer Benjamin Britten, 1976.

5 Death of French Impressionist painter Claude-Oscar Monet, 1926. Britain's first woman judge is appointed, in Burnley, 1956.

6 The historic treaty creating Irish Free State is signed, 1921, ending the War of Independence, but creating the 1921-22 Irish Civil War.

7 Lloyd George becomes prime minister of coalition government, 1916.

8 Britain and USA declare war on Japan the day after it attacks Pearl Harbour, 1941.

9 A cookery demonstration is televised for the first time, by BBC, 1936. British colony Tanganyika becomes independent Tanzania, 1961.

10 Death of dynamite inventor Alfred Nobel, founder of Nobel prizes, 1896. Britain's new king, Edward VIII, abdicates because of his love affair with American divorcee Wallis Simpson, 1936; he is succeeded by George VI.

11 USA declares war on Germany and Italy, 1941. New rules mean television can be broadcast between 6pm and 7pm, 1956. British

Satellite Broadcasting (BSB) is awarded the government's first contract for a British satellite TV service, 1986. Controversial Treaty of Maastricht emerges in EC long-term integration planning, 1991.

12 Explosion in Oaks Colliery, near Barnsley, kills 340 men, 1866. Guglielmo Marconi gives the first large-scale public demonstration of radio, at London's Toynbee Hall, 1896; he makes the first transAtlantic radio transmission, from Cornwall to Newfoundland, this day in 1901.

14 Norwegian explorer Roald Amundsen leads first team to reach South Pole, 35 days ahead of Britain's Captain Scott, 1911.

15 Death of US cartoonist film producer Walt Disney, 1966.

17 Cease-fire ends successful struggle to set up independent Bangla Desh, following India's support over recent days in India-Pakistan War, 1971.

18 End of ten-month Battle of Verdun, with a million casualties following Germany's unsuccessful attack on part of France, 1916. Nationalisation plans for ports, railways and road haulage are agreed by MPs, 1946.

20 The eight crew of the Penlee lifeboat are killed while carrying out a ship rescue off Lands End, 1981.

24 Radio telephone broadcasting is first demonstrated, in Massachusetts, 1906.

25 William the Conqueror is crowned King of England, 1066. First Welsh eisteddford takes place, in Cardigan Castle, 1176. An American vessel is winner of first transAtlantic yacht race, 1866. Hong Kong surrenders to Japanese, 1941.

29 Launch of long-running BBC radio series Down Your Way, 1946. Death of 92-year old former Tory prime minister Harold Macmillan, 1986.

30 Murder of Russian "Mad Monk" Gregory Rasputin, 1916.

31 British Broadcasting Company Ltd (formed 18 October 1922) is dissolved, 1926; it becomes the BBC by Royal Charter tomorrow. Southern Television and ATV go off the air after losing their ITV licences, 1981.

PARLIAMENT & POLITICS

House of Commons

The last general election was on 9 April 1992. The resulting House of Commons had 651 MPs of whom there were:

Conservative 336
Labour 271
Liberal Democrat 20
Plaid Cymru (Welsh Nationalist) 4
Scottish Nationalist 3
Ulster Unionist 9
SDLP 4
Democratic Unionist 3
Ulster Popular Unionist 1

The election of the Labour MP Betty Boothroyd to become Speaker of the House of Commons reduced the number of voting Labour MPs to 270. As a result, the Conservatives had the initial majority of 22 over all other parties combined. The by-elections from then until August 1995 reduced the Tory majority from 22 to eight:

Conservative 329
Labour (but minus the Speaker in votes) 273
Liberal Democrat 24
Plaid Cymru 4
Scottish Nationalist 4
Ulster Unionist 9
SDLP 4
Democratic Unionist 3
UK Unionist 1

At the 1992 general election the turnout was 77.8 per cent with 33.6 million of the 43.2 million registered electors actually voting. Up to a million potential electors failed to register because the poll tax was a disincentive to revealing where they lived. Percentage results are as follows:

Conservatives
51.6% of the seats
14.1 million votes
41.9% of the turnout, or 32.6% of the electorate
Labour
41.6% of the seats
11.6 million votes
34.4% of the turnout, or 26.7% of the electorate
Liberal Democrats
3% the seats
6 million votes
17.8% of the turnout, or 13.7% of the electorate

The next general election must be held before the fifth anniversary of the last one, that is by early April 1997. The Labour Party could only win outright by achieving its biggest swing in any post-war election. The number of seats will be increased from 651 to 659 following the 1995 report of the Boundary Commissioners. This said the average constituency size should be 69,281.

House of Commons:	
Main number (all MPs)	0171-219 3000
Night line/Information Office	0171-219 4272
Library	0171-219 3838
Journal office	0171-219 3361
Official report (Hansard)	0171-219 5293
Press Gallery/Lobby:	
Secretary	0171-219 4700
Superintendent	0171-219 5371
Private bill office	0171-219 3250
Public bill office	0171-219 3251
Records	0171-219 3074
Select committees office	0171-219 4300
Serjeant at Arms	0171-219 3083
Vote office	0171-219 3631
Whips offices: Government	0171-219 3131
Opposition (Labour)	0171-219 3237
Liberal Democrat	0171-219 3114

House of Lords

In mid-1995 the House of Lords had 1,195 members of whom there were:
476 Conservatives
115 Labour
53 Liberal Democrat
284 cross-benchers
There were also 109 with no allegiance and 158 who never attended.

Main number	0171-219 3000
Information Office	0171-219 3107
Committees office	0171-219 5791
Journal office	0171-219 5317
Library	0171-219 5242
Official report (Hansard)	0171-219 3031
Private bills	0171-219 3231
Public bills	0171-219 3153
Records	0171-219 3074
Serjeant at Arms (Black Rod)	0171-219 3100
Whips offices: Government	0171-219 3131
Opposition (Labour)	0171-219 3237
Liberal Democrat	0171-219 3114

Parliamentary parties

Conservative Party	0171-222 9000
Press	0171-222 0151
MEPs, London	0171-222 1720
Scottish Conservative Party	0131-555 2900
Primrose League	0171-976 7158
National Society of Conservative Agents	01954 211444
Labour Party	0171-701 1234
Press	0171-234 3394
Regional offices:	
London	0171-490 4904
South east	01473-255668
South and west	01249-460011
Central	01159-462195
West midlands	0121-553 6601
North	01924-291221
North west	01925-574193
Wales	01222-398567
Scotland	0141-332 8946
MEPs, London	0171-222 1719
Liberal Democrats	0171-222 7999
Welsh Lib Dems	01222-382210
Scottish Lib Dems	0131-337 2314
Alliance Party of N Ireland	01232-324274
Plaid Cymru	01222-231944
Scottish National Party	0131-226 3661
Social Democratic & Labour Party	01232-668100
Ulster Democratic Unionist Party	01232-471155
Ulster Unionist Party	01232-324601

Other parties

British National Party	0181-316 4721
Campaign for an Independent Britain	0181-340 0314
Charter 88	0171-833 1988
Class War Federation	01850-393975
Communist League Political Party	0171-401 2293
Communist Party of Britain	0171-275 8162
Co-operative Party	0171-439 0123
Democratic Left	0171-278 4443
Electoral Reform Society	0171-928 1622
English National Party	0171-278 5221
Fabian Society	0171-222 8877
Freemasons	0171-831 9811
Green Party	0171-272 4474
GROT (Get Rid of Them)	0171-378 6320
Hansard Society	0171-955 7478
Irish Freedom Movement	0171-278 9908
Islamic Party of Britain	01908-671756
Labour Campaign for Electoral Reform	0117-924 5139

Liberal Party (not Lib-Dems)	0171-233 2124
Militant Labour	0181-533 3311
Monster Raving Loony Party	01364-652205
National Front (aka National Democratic Party)	0181-471 6872
New Britain	0171-600 4282
Republic	0181-875 9854
Revolutionary Communist Party	0171-278 9908
Sinn Fein	01232-323214
Socialist Action Research	0114-266 5063
Socialist Movement	0800-581611
Socialist Party of Gt Britain	0171-622 3811
Socialist Society	0171-700 3853
Socialist Workers Party	0171-538 5821
Third Way	0171-373 3432
Voting Reform Group	0171-928 9322
Workers Revolutionary Party	0171-928 3218

Essential guides

Britain: An Official Handbook
HMSO   Tel 0171-873 9090
An annual guide outlining the workings of the British government system

Civil Service Yearbook
HMSO   Tel 0171-873 9090
The leading Whitehall directory describes the ministries, civil service bodies and Next Steps agencies, with addresses, contact numbers and top personnel.

IPO Directory
COI   Tel 0171-261 8534
A twice-yearly journalists' guide listing press officers in the ministries and public corporations.

Public Bodies
HMSO   Tel 0171-873 9090
Contains details of the largest 1,400 quangos plus nationalised industries, public corporations and some NHS bodies.

Register of Members' Interests
HMSO   Tel 0171-873 9090
Many MPs have financial interests outside parliament and these may be recorded in the Register of Members' Interests, published every January by HMSO, The Register was set up in 1974 to "provide information of any pecuniary or other material benefit which a Member receives which might reasonably be thought by others to inlufence his or her actions, speeches or votes in parliament, or actions taken in his or her capacity as a Member of Parliament." MPs write their own entries. Between HMSO editions, updated information can be inspected in the House of Commons by making an appointment with the Committee Office.

DEPARTMENTS OF STATE

Cabinet Office

Main number	0171-270 1234
Press: General	0171-270 0393
Citizens' Charter/Next Steps	0171-270 0375
Prime Minister	John Major
Deputy Prime Minister and First Secretary of State	
	Michael Heseltine

Department of Agriculture

Main number	071-270 3000
Press: General	0171-270 8973
Eves	0171-20 8080
Animal welfare/fisheries	0171-270 8434/8
Food safety	0171-270 8435/46
Agriculture/pesticides	0171-270 8094/8436
Information office	0171-270 8489
Secretary of State	Douglas Hogg
Minister of State	Tony Baldry

Ministry of Defence

Main number	0171-218 9000
Press: Head of news	0171-218 3250
Policy/procurement	0171-218 2906
Armed forces	0171-218 2661
Navy	0171-218 3257
Army	0171-218 3255
RAF	0171-218 3253
Eves	0171-218 7907
Press/Broadcast.Committee	0171-218 2206
Secretary of State	Michael Portillo
Ministers of State	James Arbuthnot
	Nicholas Soames

Education and Employment

Main number	0171-925 5000
Press	0171-925 5135
Eves	0171-925 5096
Information office	0171-925 5189
Secretary of State	Gillian Shephard
Minister of State	Eric Forth
	Lord Henley

Department of Environment

Main number	0171-276 3000
Press: General enquiries	0171-276 0900
Eves	0171-873 1966
Countryside/green issues	0171-276 0929
Housing/planning	0171-276 0920
Local govt/urban issues	0171-276 0935/6
Secretary of State	John Gummer
Ministers of State	David Curry
	Robert Jones
	Earl Ferrers

Foreign Office

Main number	0171-270 3000
Press	0171-270 3100
Information Dept	0171-210 6148
Secretary of State	Malcolm Rifkind
Minister for Overseas Development	Baroness Chalker
Ministers of State	Jeremy Hanley
	Sir Nicholas Bonsor

Department of Health

Main number	0171-210 3000
Eves	0171-210 5368
Press	0171-210 5224/8
Public enquiry office	0171-210 4850
Secretary of State	Stephen Dorrell
Minister of State	Gerald Malone

Home Office

Main number	0171-273 3000
Eves	0171-273 4595
Press: Chief press officer	0171-273 4117
Police/fire/emergencies	0171-273 4610
Immigration/coroners/animals	0171-273 4620
Crime/drugs/young offenders	0171-273 4600
Elections/shops/race/privacy	0171-273 4640
Prisons	0171-217 6633
Secretary of State	Michael Howard
Ministers of State	Baroness Blatch
	David Maclean
	Ann Widdecombe

Law Officers

Secretariat	0171-828 7155
Attorney Genera	Sir Nicholas Lyell
Solicitor General	Sir Derek Spencer
Lord-Advocate	Lord Rodger

Lord Chancellor's Dept.

Main number	0171-210 8500
Press	0171-210 8512/3
Lord Chancellor and Speaker of the Lords	
	Lord Mackay of Clashferne

Lord Privy Seal

Office	0171-270 0501
Lord Privy Seal & Leader Houseof Lords	Viscount Cranborne

Minister without Portfolio
(Also the Conservative Party chairman)

Party office	0171-222 9000
Minister/chairman	Brian Mawhinney

Dept of National Heritage

Main number	0171-211 6000
Public inquiries	0171-211 6200
Eves	0181-840 7000
Press	0171-211 6269
Arts	0171-211 6269
Heritage	0171-211 6271
Media/sport/lottery	0171-211 6273
Secretary of State	Virginia Bottomley
Minister of State	Iain Sproat

Northern Ireland Office

Main numbers: Belfast	01232-520700
London	0171-210 3000
NI Information Service	01232-520700
London press office	0171-210 6470-3
Secretary of State	Sir Patrick Mayhew
Ministers of State	Michael Ancram
	Sir John Wheeler

Prime Ministers Office

Main number	0171-270 3000
Press	0171-930 4433
Prime Minister	John Major
Press Secretary	Christopher Meyer

Privy Council Office

Office	0171-270 0472
Judicial Committee	0171-270 0485
Lord President of the Council	Tony Newton
Lord Privy Seal	Viscount Cranbourne

Scottish Office

Main number, London	0171-270 3000
Main number, Edinburgh	0131-244 5600
Eves	0131-556 8400
Press	0131-244 4943
Agriculture/fisheries	0131-244 4975
Environment/arts/sport	0131-244 4944
Health/home affairs	0131-244 4976
Housing/transport/tourism	0131-244 4950
Industry	0131-244 4966
London office	0171-270 6744
Secretary of State	Michael Forsyth
Minister of State	Lord James Douglas-Hamilton

Dept of Social Security

Main number	0171-210 3000
Press	0171-210 5968
Benefits Agency	0113-232 4136
Disabled	0171-210 5239
Family issues	0171-210 5242
Pensions/insurance	0171-210 5240
Public enquiry office	0171-210 5983
Secretary of State	Peter Lilley
Minister for Social Security	Alistair Burt
	Lord Mackay of Ardbrecknish

Dept of Trade and Industry

Main number	0171-215 5000
Eves	0171-215 4657
Press: Head of news	0171-215 5954
Company law/insolvency	0171-215 5971
Consumer/small business	0171-215 5969
Energy	0171-215 6405
Industry	0171-215 5967
Technology	0171-215 5962
Trade	0171-215 5970
Secretary of State	Ian Lang
Ministers of State	Tim Eggar
	Anthony Nelson
	Lord Fraser of Carmyllie

Department of Transport

Main number	0171-276 3000
Press	0171-276 0888
Eves	0171-873 1985
London transport	0171-276 5189
Other public transport	0171-276 5175
Roads	0171-276 5182
Road safety	0171-276 5183
Sea/air/Channel Tunnel	0171-276 5172
Secretary of State	Sir George Young
Ministers for Public Transport	John Watts

HM Treasury

Main number	0171-270 3000
Press	0171-270 5238
Chancellor of the Exchequer	Kenneth Clarke
Chief Secretary	William Waldegrave
Financial Secretary	Micahel Jack
Economic Secretary	Angela Knight
Paymaster General	David Heathcoat-Amory

Welsh Office

Main numbers: Cardiff	01222-825111
London	0171-270 3000
Press: Cardiff	01222-825648
London	0171-270 0565
Secretary of State	William Hague

QUANGOS

Quangos have multiplied as welfare state institutions have been dismantled and power has been shifted from local authorities. In 1994 nearly a third of public expenditure · about £50 billion · went through 5,521 quangos; there are 25,000 elected local councillors and 75,000 unelected quango appointees.

The word quango is an abbreviation of "quasi-autonomous non-governmental organisation" and describes any unelected body carrying out public functions with public money. Government people never say "quango" but refer to Non-Departmental Public Bodies or Next Steps Agencies. Whitehall defines NDPBs as: "A body which has a role in the process of national government, but is not a department or part of one, and accordingly operates to a greater or lesser extent at arm's length from ministers". Next Steps Agencies are less autonomous than the Public Bodies. They are defined as semi-independent organisations performing executive functions of government, while still remaining part of the civil service.

Both NDPBs and Next Step Agencies are quangos. A characteristic they share is that public accountability is hard to define, often being merely a personal one where chief execs are responsible to the minister of the sponsoring government department. In NDPBs government departments appoint the members of managing boards and monitor accounts. Most quangos cannot be investigated by ombudsmen or audited by the National Audit Office. A guide to seekers after Quango truths is published by the Local Government Information Unit (Tel 0171-608 1051). Secret Services: a Handbook for Investigating Local Quangos, bills itself as "a guide to what local authorities and others can do to investigate and expose the activities of non-elected service providers in their areas".

The white paper on the civil service (The Civil Service: Continuity and Change) outlines government plans to make all sectors of the civil service work within a quango-style framework and culture. Each minister will have powers similar to those of a company managing director, top officials will have individual contracts and central pay bargaining will end. The business of government will become more opaque. Already many quangos are difficult to locate and where no phone number is given in the list, inquiries should be made to the sponsoring department.

Official bodies

This initial list is of government bodies which are still part of the traditional civil service and thus not part of the generalised quangocracy. The government is considering some form of privatisation for as many as possible by redefining them as Next Steps Agencies.

British Standards Institution	01908-220022
Charity Commission	0171-210 4477
Press	0171-210 4433
Commission for Local Authority Accounts	
in Scotland	0131-477 1234
Commonwealth Secretariat	0171-839 3411
Crown Estate	0171-210 4210
Crown Prosecution Service	0171-273 8000
Eves	01459-138467
Press	0171-273 8106
European Community:	
Commission UK Office	0171-973 1992
Parliament Info Office	0171-222 0411
Export Credits Guarantee Dept	0171-512 7000
Forestry Commission	0131-334 0303
Government Actuary's Dept	0171-242 6828
Law Commission: England	0171-453 1220
Scotland	0131-668 2131
National Audit Office	0171-798 7000
Press	0171-798 7400
National Savings Department	0171-605 9300
Office of Population Censuses and	
Surveys (OPCS)	0171-242 0262
Overseas Development	
Administration	0171-917 7000
Press	0171-917 0950
Post Office	0171-490 2888
Press 24 hrs	0171-320 7443
Queen's Awards Office	0171-222 2277
Registry of Friendly Societies	0171-437 9992
Royal Commission on Environmental	
Pollution	0171-276 2109
Royal Mail	0171-250 2888
Press 24 hrs	0171-320 7443
Royalty · Buckingham Palace	0171-930 4832
Clarence House	0171 930 3141
Duchy of Cornwall	0171-834 3346
Duchy of Lancaster	0171-836 8277
Serious Fraud Office	0171-239 7272
Eves	0171-239 7050
Trade Unions & Employers Associations	
Certification Office	0171-210 3734
United Nations	0171-630 1981
Welsh Development Agency	01222-222666
	01345-775577

UK and English quangos

The initials after each name below are those of the sponsoring government departments which are listed on pages 266 and 267. Where the quango appears to have no phone number of its own, contact it via the sponsor department.

ACAS - Advisory, Conciliation &Arbitration
Service - ED	0171-396 0022
Accounts Services Agency - DTI	0181-672 4117
ADAS - MAFF	01865-842742
Advisory Committees on:	
Advertising	via CO
Business & the Environment	via DOE
Business Appointments	via CO
Conscientious Objectors	via MOD
Hazardous Substances	via DOE
Historic Wreck Sites	via DNH
Justices of the Peace	via LCD
NHS Drugs	via DOH
Novel Foods	via DOH
Pesticides	via MAFF
Telecommunications	via DTI
Advisory Councils on:	
Public Records - LCD	0171-210 8810
Race Relations	via HO
Science & Technology	via CO
The Misuse of Drugs	via HO
Agricultural Land Tribunals	via MAFF
Agricultural Wages Board	via MAFF
Aids Action Group	via DOH
Alcohol Education & Research Council	via HO
Armed Forces Pay Review Body	via HMT
Army Base Repair Organisation - MOD	01264-383148
Arts Council - DNH	0171-333 0100
Audit Commission for Local Authorities & the NHS - DOE	0171-828 1212
Press	0171-930 6077
Bank of England - HMT	0171-601 4444
Press	0171-601 4411
BBC - DNH Radio	0171-580 4468
TV	0181-743 8000
Press	0181-576 1865
Benefits Agency - DSS	0113-232 4000
Press	0113-232 4139
Biotechnology, Biological Research Council - CO	01793-413200
Boards of Visitors to Penal Establishments	via HO
Boundary Commissions - Local Government:	
England	0171-430 8400
Wales	01222-395031
Scotland	0131-244 4061
Boundary Commissions - Parliamentary:	
England & Wales	0171-242 0262
Scotland	0131-244 2196
Northern Ireland	01232-311210

British Antarctic Survey	01223-61188
British Coal - DTI	0171-201 4141
British Council - FCO	0171-930 8466
Press	0171-389 4878
British Film Institute - DNH	0171-255 1444
British Library - DNH	0171-636 1544
Press	0171-323 7111
British Museum - DNH	0171-636 1555
Press	0171-323 8779
British National Space Centre	0171-215 0960
British Nuclear Fuels - DTI	01925-832000
Sellafield (press)	01946-728333
British Overseas Trade Board - DTI	0171-215 5660
British Railways Board - DOT	0171-928 5151
British Shipbuilders - DTI	0171-581 1393
British Technology Group - DTI	0171-403 6666
British Tourist Authority - DNH	0181-846 9000
British Waterways Board - DOE	01923-226422
Broadcasting Complaints Commission - ` DNH	0171-630 1966
Broadcasting Standards Council - DNH	0171-233 0544
Building Regulations Advisory Committee	via DOE
Building Research Establishment - DOE	01923-894040
Building Societies Commission	0171-437 9992
Buying Agency - DOE	0151-227 4262
Central Fire Brigades Advisory Council	via HO
Central Office of Information - CDL	0171-928 2345
Eastern	01223-311867
Midlands	0121-626 2017
Midlands East	0115-959 9177
North East	0191-201 3300
North West	0161-832 9111
South East	0171-261 8795
South West	0117-927 3767
Yorkshire/Humberside	0113-283 6591
Central Railusers Consultative Committee - DOT	0171-839 7338
Central Science Laboratory - MAFF	01753-534626
Central Statistical Office - HMT	0171-270 3000
Central Veterinary Laboratory - MAFF	01932-341111
Chemical & Biological Defence Establishment - MOD	01980-613000
Child Support Agency - DSS	0171-217 3000
Citizen's Charter Unit - CO	0171-270 6303
Civil Aviation Authority - DOT	0171-379 7311
Civil Service College - CO	01344-634000
Commission for Racial Equality - HO	0171-828 7022
Commission for the New Towns -DOE	0171-828 7722
Commissioner for the Rights of Trade	

Union Members · ED	01925-415771
Committee for Monitoring Agreements on	
Tobacco Advertising and Sponsorship	via DOH
Committees on:	
Carcinogenicity of Chemicals	via DOH
Medical Aspects of Food Policy	via DOH
Safety of Medicines · DOH	0171-273 0451
Toxicity of Chemicals in Food etc	via DOH
Commons Commissioners ·	
DOE	0171-210 4584
Commonwealth Development Corporation ·	
FCO	0171-828 4488
Commonwealth Institute · FCO	0171-603 4535
Community Development Foundation ·	
HO	0171-226 5375
Companies House · DTI	01222-388588
Consultative Panel on Badgers	
& Tuberculosis	via MAFF
Copyright Tribunal	0171-438 4776
Council on Tribunals · LCD	0171-936 7045
Countryside Commission	01242-521381
Crafts Council · DNH	0171-278 7700
Criminal Injuries Compensation	
Board · HO	0171-842 6800
Crown Agents · FCO	0171-834 3644
Customs & Excise · HMT	0171-620 1313
Eves	0171-696 7000
Press	0171-865 5469
VAT Central Unit	01702-348944
Data Protection Registrar · HO	01625-535711
Defence Accounts Agency ·	
MOD	01225-828106
Defence Operational Analysis	
Centre · MOD	01932-341199
Defence Research Agency ·	
MOD	01252-392000
Design Council · DTI	0171-839 8000
Doctors and Dentists Review Body	via HMT
Driver & Vehicle Licensing Agency ·	
DOT	01792-782318
Driving Standards Agency ·	
DOT	0115-955 7600
Economic and Social Research	
Council · CO	01793-413000
Press	01793-413120
Education Assets Board	via DE
Electricity Consumers Committee ·	
via OFFER	0121-456 2100
Employment Appeal Tribunal ·	
ED	0171-273 1041
Employment Service · ED	0171-389 1377
English Heritage · DNH	0171-973 3000
English Nature · DOE	01733-340345
English Tourist Board · DNH	0181-846 9000
Equal Opportunities Commission ·	
ED	0161-833 9244
Press	0171-222 1110
Farm Animal Welfare Council ·	
MAFF	0181-330 8031

Fire Service College · HO	01608-650831
Food Advisory Committee ·	
MAFF	0171-238 6267
Food From Britain · MAFF	0171-720 2144
Football Licensing Authority ·	
DNH	0171-491 7191
Forensic Science Service · HO	0171-273 4610
Further Education Funding	
Council · DE	01203-530300
Gaming Board · HO	0171-306 6200
Government Centre for Information	
Systems	0171-217 3800
Government Property Lawyers	01823-345275
Health & Safety Commission &	
Executive · ED	
Press	0171-717 6000
Health Advisory Service	via DOH
Health Education Authority ·	
DOH	0171-383 3833
Highways Agency · DOT	
Historic Royal Palaces · DNH	0181-781 9750
HMSO · CDL	01603-622211
Publications info	0171-873 8787
Press	01603-695255
Housing Corporation · DOE	0171-393 2000
Hydrographic Office · MOD	01823-337900
Immigration Appellate Authority ·	
LCD	0171-353 8060
Independent Television Commission ·	
DNH	0171-255 3000
Industrial Development Advisory Board	via DTI
Industrial Injuries Advisory	
Council · DSS	0171-962 8065
Industrial Tribunals Central	
Office · ED	01284-762300
Press	0171-236 0116
Information Technology Advisory Board	via DTI
Inland Revenue · HMT	0171-438 6622
Press	0171-438 6692
Innovation Advisory Board ·	
DTI	0171-215 1705
Insolvency Practitioners Tribunal ·	
DTI	0171-326 1002
Insolvency Rules Advisory Committee	via DTI
Insolvency Service · DTI	0171-323 3090
Interception of Communications	
Tribunal · HO	0171-273 4096
Intervention Board · MAFF	01734-583626
Joint Nature Conservation	
Committee · DOE	01733-62626
Laboratory of the Government	
Chemist · DTI	0171-215 5000
Land Registry · LCD	0171-917 8888
Lands Tribunal · LCD	0171-936 7200
Landscape Advisory Committee	via DOT
Law Commission · LCD	0171-453 1220
Legal Aid Advisory Committee ·	
LCD	0171-405 6991
Legal Aid Board · LCD	0171-813 1000

Library & Information Services	
Council	via DNH
London Docklands Urban Development	
Corporation - DOE	0171-512 3000
London Transport - DOT	0171-222 5600
London Residuary Body - DOE	0171-938 4028
Meat & Livestock Commission -	
MAFF	01908-677577
Medical Practices Committee -	
DOH	0171-972 2930
Medical Research Council - CO	0171-636 5422
Medicines Commission/Control	
Agency - DOH	0171-273 0392
Mental Health Act Commission	via DOH
Mental Health Review Tribunal	via DOH
Meteorological Office - MOD	01344-420242
Press	01344-856655
Enquiries/complaints	01344-854455
Military Survey - MOD	0181-890 3622
Misuse of Drugs Advisory Body	via HO
Monitoring Committee on Misleading Price	
Indications	via DTI
Monopolies and Mergers Commission -	
DTI	0171-324 1467
Press	0171-324 1407
Museums & Galleries Commission -	
DNH	0171-233 4200
National Consumer Council -	
DTI	0171-730 3469
National Council for Vocational	
Qualifications - ED	0171-387-9898
National Curriculum Council - DE	0171-229 1234
National Food Survey Committee -	
MAFF	0171-270 8563
National Health Service Tribunal	via DOH
National Heritage Memorial Fund -	
DNH	0171-930 0963
National Physical Laboratory -	
DTI	0181-977 3222
National Radiological Protection	
Board - DOH	01235-831600
National Research Development	
Corporation - DTI	0171-403 6666
National Rivers Authority - DOE	01454-624400
Press	0171-820 0101
National Weights & Measures	
Laboratory - DTI	0181-943 7272
National Youth Agency	via DE
Natural Environment Research	
Council - CO	01793-411500
Natural Resources Institute -	
FCO	01634-880088
NHS Estates - DOH	0113-254 7000
Nuclear Electric plc - DTI	01452-652222
Press	01452-652793
Nuclear Powered Warships Safety	
Committee	via MOD
Nuclear Weapons Safety Committee	via MOD
Occupational Health Service -	

CDL	0131-220 4177
Occupational Pensions Board -	
DSS	0191-225 6414
Ordnance Survey - DOE	01703-792000
Parliamentary Boundary	
Commission	0171-396 2805
Parole Board - HO	0171-217 3000
Passport Agency - HO	0171-799 2290
Patent Office - DTI	01633-814000
Paymaster General	01293-560999
Pesticides Safety Directorate -	
MAFF	01904 640500
Planning Inspectorate - DOE	0117-921 8811
Poisons Board	via HO
Police Advisory Board	via HO
Police Complaints Authority -	
HO	0171-273 6450
Political Honours Scrutiny Committee -	
CO	0171-210 5058
Post Office - DTI	0171-490 2888
Press 24 hrs	0171-320 7443
Post Office Users National Council -	
DTI	0171-928 9458
Prescription Pricing Authority	via DOH
Prison Service - HO	0171-217 6633
Property Services Agency	0181-256 4000
Public Health Laboratory - DOH	0181-200 1295
Public Record Office - LCD	0181-876 3444
Radio Authority - DNH	0171-430 2724
Radioactive Waste Management Advisory	
Committee	via DOE
Radiocommunications Agency -	
DTI	0171-215 2352
Railway Inspectorate - ED	0171-215 5000
Recruitment & Assessment Services -	
CDL	01256-29222
Registrar of Public Lending Right	via DNH
Renewable Energy Advisory Committee	via DTI
Royal Commission on Environmental	
Pollution - DOE	0171-276 2109
Royal Commission on Historical	
Monuments - DNH	0171-973 3500
	0171-208 8200
Royal Commission on Historical	
Manuscripts - DNH	01793-414600
Royal Fine Art Commission -	
DNH	0171-839 6537
Royal Mint - HMT	01443-222111
Royal Parks - DNH	0171-298 2000
Rural Development Commission -	
DOE	0171-276 6969
School Curriculum Assessment	
Authority - DE	0171-229 1234
Science and Engineering Research	
Council - CO	01793-444000
Sea Fish Industry Authority -	
MAFF	0131-558 3331
Securities & Investments Board	0171-638 1240
Security Commission	via CO

Security Facilities Executive ·
   DOE   0171-921 4813
Security Services Tribunal   via HO
Social Security · DSS:
   Advisory Committee   0171-412 1506
   Benefits Agency   0113-232 4000
   Contributions Agency   0191-225 7665
   Resettlement Agency   0171-388 1188
Sports Council · DNH   0171-388 1277
Standing Advisory Committee on Trunk
   Road Assessment   via DOT
Street Works Advisory Committee   via DOT
Top Salaries Review Body   via HMT
Traffic Director for London ·
   DOT   0171-222 4545
Transport Research Laboratory ·
   DOT   01344-773131
Trinity House · DOT   0171-480 6601
UK Atomic Energy Authority -
   DTI   01235-821111
   Press   01235-432852
UK Nirex   01235-825500
Valuation Office · HMT   0171-324 1033
Value Added Tax Tribunals ·
   LCD   0171-631 4242
Vehicle Certification Agency ·
   DOT   0117-951 5151
Vehicle Inspectorate · DOT   0117-954 3274
Veterinary Medicines Directorate ·
   MAFF   01932-336911
Warren Spring Laboratory · DTI   01235 463040
Wilton Park Conference Centre ·
   FCO   01903-815020
Women's National Commission ·
   ED   0171-273 5486

Welsh quangos

Agriculture Advisory Panel   01222-825111
Ancient Monuments Board   01222-465511
Arts Council   01222-394711
Cadw: Welsh Historic
   Monuments   01222-465511
Countryside Council   01248-370444
Development Agency   01345 775537
Development Board for Rural
   Wales   01222-825111
Fourth Channel Authority   01222-825111
Health Promotion Authority   01222-752222
Hill Farming Advisory Cttee   01222-823623
Historic Buildings for Wales   01222-465511
Housing for Wales   01222-747979
Industrial Development Advisory
   Board   01686 626965
Land Authority   01222-223444
Local Government Boundary
   Commission   01222-395031
Medical Committee   01222-825111

National Library   01970-623816
National Museum   01222-397951
Parliamentary Boundary
   Commission   0171-242 0262
Place Names Advisory
   Committee   01222-825111
Royal Commission on Ancient & Historical
   Monuments   01222 465511
Sports Council   01222-397571
Tourist Board   01222-499909
Welsh Language Board   01222-224744
Youth Agency   01222-616123

Scottish quangos

Agricultural Consultative Panel   0131-244 4999
Ancient Monuments Board   0131-662 1456
Boundary Commission   0131-244 2196
Commission for Local Authority
   Accounts   0131-477 7234
Community Education Council   0131-313 2488
Consultative Council on the
   Curriculum   01382-455053
Crofters Commission   01463-663450
Economic Council   0131-244 4999
Examination Board   0131-244 4999
Film Council   0141-334 4445
Health Education Board   0131-244 4999
Health Board   0131-244 4999
Health Service Professional Advisory
   Committee   0131-244 2750
Highlands & Islands Enterprise   01463-234171
Hill Farming Advisory Cttee   0131-244 6374
Historic Buildings Council   0131-244 4999
Historic Scotland   0131-668 8600
Lands Tribunal   0131-225 7996
Law Commission   0131-668 2131
Legal Aid Board   0131-226 7061
Local Government Boundary
   Commission   0131-244 4182
Mental Welfare Commission   0131-225 7034
National Galleries   0131-556 8921
National Health Service Tribunal   0131-244 4999
National Library   0131-226 4531
National Museums   0131-225 7534
Parliamentary Boundary
   Commission   0131-244 2196
Parole Unit   0131-244 8528
Pensions Appeal Tribunal   0131-220 1404
Police Advisory Board   0131-244 2143
Red Deer Commission   01463-231751
Register of Scotland   0131-659 6111
Royal Commission on Ancient &
   Historical Monuments   0131-662 1456
Royal Fine Art Commission   0131-229 1109
Scottish Agricultural Science
   Agency   0131-244 8843
Scottish Arts Council   0131-226 0051

Scottish Fisheries Protection Agency	0131-244 6059	Fishery Harbour Council	01232-520000
Scottish Enterprise	0141-248 2700	Health Promotion Agency	01232-520700
Scottish Homes	0131-313 0044	Health & Safety Agency	01232-520700
Scottish Nuclear	01355-262000	Historic Monuments Council	01232-235000
Scottish Natural Heritage	0131-447 4784	Housing Executive	01232-240588
Scottish Prison Service	0131-244 8660	Independent Commission for Police Complaints	01232-520700
Scottish Record Office	0131-556 6585	Industrial Court	01232-520700
Sports Council	0131-317 7200	Industrial Development Board	01232-233233
Tourist Board	0131-332 2433	Law Reform Advisory Committee	01232-520700

Northern Ireland quangos

Parliamentary Boundary Commission	01232-311210
Police Authority	01232-230111
Probation Boardvia	01232-520700
Arts Council	01232-381591
Boundary Commission	01232-311210
Citizen's Charter Advisory Panel	01232-520700
Compensation Agency	01232-249944
Construction Industry Advisory Council	01232-520700
Curriculum Council	01232-381414
Driver & Vehicle Testing Agency	01232-681831
Economic Council	01232-520700

Schools Examination & Assessment Council	01232-704666
Sports Council	01232-381222
Standing Advisory Committee on Human Rights	01232-243987
Tourist Board	01232-231221
Transport Holding Company	01232-243456
Ulster Museum	01232-381251
Water Council	01232-520700

LOCAL GOVERNMENT

Local government in the UK takes varying forms in different areas. In **England and Wales**, excluding London, there are 53 counties, divided into 369 districts. The counties are responsible for major functions such as education, fire brigades, consumer protection, social services, police, refuse disposal, libraries, strategic planning and highways. The districts look after environmental health, local planning, housing, parks, cemeteries, tourism, refuse collection, museums etc. Forty seven of the counties · the "non-metropolitan" or "shire" counties · and all the districts have elected councils overseeing their affairs. The other six counties · the "metropolitan counties" · used to have elected councils, but these were abolished in 1986, along with the Greater London Council. Now the 36 district councils in the metropolitan counties and the 32 London boroughs are responsible for most services in their areas, with some co-ordination provided by ad hoc bodies. In Wales some local government functions are exercised by the Welsh Office, based in Cardiff.

Mainland **Scotland** is split into nine regions, in turn divided into 53 districts, almost mirroring the county/district arrangement in England and Wales. There are also three virtually all-purpose authorities covering the remote island groups of Orkney, Shetland and the Western Isles. These 65 authorities all have elected councils. The Scottish Office in Edinburgh acts as the local arm of the Westminster government. In **Northern Ireland** there are no county authorities. Instead services are provided by government departments. The only directly elected authorities are 26 district councils, with less powers than their British namesakes. Between councils and government departments is a system of area boards providing social services, education and libraries.

Exceptions to all the above are: the Isle of Man, with its own government and parliament (the Tynwald); the Channel Island bailiwicks of Guernsey and Jersey, with limited autonomy; the Isles of Scilly, a separate local authority, but dependent on Cornwall for many services; and the independent City of London Corporation.

The structure of local government in Britain is currently being changed. The 1992 Local Government Act set up the Local Government Commission to review the structures of the English counties and their equivalents in Wales and Scotland. The aim was to replace the present two-tier system described above with a single tier of "unitary authorities."

The commission's restructuring of Wales and Scotland takes place on 1 April 1996. In Wales, the government replaces the eight counties and 37 districts with 22 unitary authorities. In May 1995 the first elections for these were held. Labour won control of 14 councils, Plaid Cymru one, Independents four and the Tories and Liberals none. In Scotland, the three island councils are remaining unchanged, while the nine regional and 53 district councils are being succeeded by 29 of the single-tier councils. Their first elections took place in April 1995, with Labour winning 20 of the 29, the Scottish National Party three, Independents three and the Tories and Liberals none. In England, the Commission's proposals provoked much opposition, requiring several rethinks. It was unable to come up with an acceptable overall plan for unitary authorities in every county. There will be a confusing mixture of two-tier and unitary bodies. By the time of the May 1995 local elections only 14 new authorities had been scheduled to start in April 1996. The only outright winners were Labour, scoring nine, and the Liberals, with one.

Councillors are elected for four years. In England and Wales, county council seats are all polled at the same time. In that year there are no district council elections. The most recent of these county elections were in May 1993. In district councils each authority can choose whether to elect all seats together once every three years, or ballot a third of seats every year, except in the year of county council elections.

Municipal Yearbook

Municipal Journal	Tel 0171-973 6400

Of the many directories and guides to local government, this annual publication is the most comprehensive

Local government bodies

Assoc of County Councils	0171-235 1200
Assoc of District Councils	0171-233 6868
Assoc of London Government	0171-222 7799
Association of Metropolitan Authorities	0171-222 8100
Audit Commission for Local Authorities	0171-828 1212
Convention of Scottish Local Authorities	0131-346 1222
Local Government Commission for England	0171-430 8400
Local Government Boundary Commissions:	
Scotland	0131-556 8400
Wales	01222-395031
Local Government Management Board	0171-235 6081
National Assoc Local Councils	0171-637 1865
Welsh Counties Assembly	01222-780094

Regionalism

In April 1994 the government created ten Government Office for the Regions in England, though none in Wales, Scotland and Northern Ireland because therse already had established statelet systems. The purpose of the GORs is to work with private businesses and local government to "maximise the sompetitiveness, prosperity and quality of life of their region".

East Midlands	0115-950 6181
Eastern	01234-363131
London	0171-211 4193
Merseyside	0151-227 4111
North-east	0191-2013300
North-west	0161-832 9111
South-east	0171-605 9000
South-west	0117-927 3710
West Midlands	0121-212 5000
Yorkshire and Humberside	01532 836300

English local authorities

Counties have their names in **bold**. If the county does not have a county council authority, there is no phone number alongside.

Avon	0117-987 4447
Bath	01225-477000
Bristol	0117-922 2000
Kingswood	0117-960 1121
Northavon	01454-416262
Wansdyke	01761-417510
Woodspring	01934-631701
Bedfordshire	01234-363222
Luton	01582-31291
Mid Bedfordshire	01525-402051
Bedfordshire Borough	01234-267422
South Bedfordshire	01582-472222
Berkshire	01734-875444
Bracknell Forest	01344-424642
Newbury	01635-42400
Reading	01734-575911
Slough	01753-523881
Windsor & Maidenhead	01628-798888
Wokingham	01734-786833
Buckinghamshire	01296-395000
Aylesbury Vale	01296-555555
Chiltern	01494-729000
Milton Keynes	01908-691691
South Bucks	01753-533333
Wycombe	01494-461000
Cambridgeshire	01223-317111
Cambridge	01223-358977
East Cambridgeshire	01353-665555
Fenland	01354-54321

Huntingdonshire	01480-388388
Peterborough	01733-63141
South Cambs	01223-351795
Channel Islands	
Guernsey	01481-717000
Jersey	01534-603000
Cheshire	01244-602424
Chester	01244-324324
Congleton	01270-763231
Crewe & Nantwich	01270-537777
Ellesmere Port & Neston	0151-356 6789
Halton	0151-424 2061
Macclesfield	01625-500500
Vale Royal	01606-862862
Warrington	01925-444400
Cleveland	01642-248155
Hartlepool	01429-266522
Langbaurgh-on-Tees	01642-231212
Middlesbrough	01642-245432
Stockton-on-Tees	01642-670067
Cornwall	01872-322000
Caradon	01579-341000
Carrick	01872-78131
Kerrier	01209-712941
North Cornwall	01208-812255
Penwith	01736-62341
Restormel	01726-74466
Cumbria	01228-23456
Allerdale	01900-604351
Barrow-in-Furness	01229-825500
Carlisle	01228-23411
Copeland	01946-693111
Eden	01768-64671
South Lakeland	01539-733333
Derbyshire	01629-580000
Amber Valley	01773-570222
Bolsover	01246-240000
Chesterfield	01246-277232
Derby City	01332-293111
Derbyshire Dales	01629-580580
Erewash	0115-944 0440
High Peak	01663-751751
North East Derbyshire	01246-231111
South Derbyshire	01283-221000
Devon	01392-382000
East Devon	01395-516551
Exeter	01392-77888
Mid Devon	01884-255255
North Devon	01271-327711
Plymouth	01752-668000
South Hams	01803-861234
Teignbridge	01626-61101
Torbay	01803-296244
Torridge	01237-476711
West Devon	01822-615911
Dorset	01305-251000
Bournemouth	01202-552066
Christchurch	01202-486321
East Dorset	01202-886201
Poole	01202-633633
Purbeck	01929-556561
West Dorset	01305-251010
Weymouth & Portland	01305-761222
Durham	0191-386 4411
Chester-le-Street	0191-387 1919
Darlington	01325-380651
Derwentside	01207-580580
Durham City	0191-386 6111
Easington	0191-527 0501
Sedgefield	01388-816166
Teesdale	01833-690000
Wear Valley	01388-765555
East Sussex	01273-481000
Brighton	01273-710000
Eastbourne	01323-410000
Hastings	01424-781066
Hove	01273-775400
Lewes	01273-471600
Rother	01424-216321
Wealden	01892-653311
Essex	01245-492211
Basildon	01268-533333
Braintree	01376-552525
Brentwood	01277-261111
Castle Point	01268-792711
Chelmsford	01245-490490
Colchester	01206-282222
Epping Forest	01992-564000
Harlow	01279-446611
Maldon	01621-854477
Rochford	01702-546366
Southend-on-Sea	01702-215000
Tendring	01255-425501
Thurrock	01375-390000
Uttlesford	01799-510510
Gloucestershire	01452-425000
Cheltenham	01242-262626
Cotswold	01285-643643
Forest of Dean	01594-810000
Gloucester City	01452-522232
Stroud	01453-766321
Tewkesbury	01684-295010
Hampshire	01962-841841
Basingstoke	01256-844844
East Hampshire	01730-266551
Eastleigh	01703-614646
Fareham	01329-236100

Gosport	01705-584242	Rochester	01634-727777
Hart	01252-622122	Sevenoaks	01732-741222
Havant	01705-474174	Shepway	01303-850388
New Forest	01703-285000	Swale	01795-424341
Portsmouth	01705-822251	Thanet	01843-225511
Rushmoor	01252-516222	Tonbridge & Malling	01732-844522
Southampton	01703-223855	Tunbridge Wells	01892 526121
Test Valley	01264-364144		
Winchester	01962-840222	**Lancashire**	01772-254868
		Blackburn	01254-585585
Hereford & Worcester	01905-763763	Blackpool	01253-25212
Bromsgrove	01527-873232	Burnley	01282-425011
Hereford City	01432-268121	Chorley	01257-265611
Leominster	01568-611100	Fylde	01253-721222
Malvern Hills	01684-892700	Hyndburn	01254-388111
Redditch	01527-864252	Lancaster	01524-582000
South Herefordshire	01432-346300	Pendle	01282-617731
Worcester	01905-723471	Preston	01772-254881
Wychavon	01386-565000	Ribble Valley	01200-25111
Wyre Forest	01562-820505	Rossendale	01706-217777
		South Ribble	01772-421491
Hertfordshire	01992-555555	West Lancashire	01695-577177
Broxbourne	01992-631921	Wyre	01253-891000
Dacorum	01442-60161		
East Hertfordshire	01279-655261	**Leicestershire**	0116-232 3232
Hertsmere	0181-207 2277	Blaby	0116-275 0555
North Hertfordshire	01462-474000	Charnwood	01509-263151
St Albans	01727-866100	Harborough	01858-410000
Stevenage	01438-356177	Hinckley & Bosworth	01455-238141
Three Rivers	01923-776611	Leicester City	0116-254 9922
Watford	01923-226400	Melton	01664-67711
Welwyn Hatfield	01707-331212	North West Leicestershire	01530-833333
		Oadby & Wigston	0116-288 8961
Humberside	01482-867131	Rutland	01572-722577
Beverley	01482-882255		
Boothferry	01405-765141	**Lincolnshire**	01522-552222
Cleethorpes	01472-200200	Boston	01205-357400
East Yorkshire	01262-679151	East Lindsey	01507-601111
Glanford	01652-652441	Lincoln	01522-511511
Great Grimsby	01472-242000	North Kesteven	01529-414155
Holderness	01964-562333	South Holland	01775-761161
Kingston upon Hull	01482-223111	South Kesteven	01476-591591
Scunthorpe	01724-280444	West Lindsey	01427-615411
Isle of Man	01624-685685	**London**	
		Barking & Dagenham	0181-592 4500
Isle of Wight	01983-821000	Barnet	0181-202 8282
Medina	01983-520000	Bexley	0181-303 7777
South Wight	01983-402175	Brent	0181-904 1244
		Bromley	0181-464 3333
Kent	01622-671411	Camden	0171-278 4444
Ashford	01233-637311	Corporation of London	0171-606 3030
Canterbury	01227-763763	Croydon	0181-686 4433
Dartford	01322-343434	Ealing	0181-579 2424
Dover	01304-821199	Enfield	0181-366 6565
Gillingham	01634-281414	Greenwich	0181-854 8888
Gravesham	01474-564422	Hackney	0181-986 3123
Maidstone	01622-602000	Hammersmith & Fulham	0181-748 3020

Haringey	0181-975 9700
Harrow	0181-863 5611
Havering	01708-772222
Hillingdon	01895-250111
Hounslow	0181-570 7728
Islington	0171-226 1234
Kensington & Chelsea	0171-937 5464
Kingston-upon-Thames	0181-546 2121
Lambeth	0171-926 1000
Lewisham	0181-695 6000
Merton	0181-543 2222
Newham	0181-472 1430
Redbridge	0181-478 3020
Richmond-upon-Thames	0181-891 1411
Southwark	0171-237 6677
Sutton	0181-770 5000
Tower Hamlets	0171-512 4200
Waltham Forest	0181-527 5544
Wandsworth	0181-871 6000
Westminster	0171-828 8070

Greater Manchester	0161-234 5000
Bolton	01204-22311
Bury	0161-705 5000
Manchester	0161-234 5000
Oldham	0161-624 0505
Rochdale	01706-47474
Salford	0161-794 4711
Stockport	0161-480 4949
Tameside	0161-342 8355
Trafford	0161-872 2101
Wigan	01942-44991

Merseyside	
Knowsley	0151-489 6000
Liverpool	0151-227 3911
St Helens	01744-24061
Sefton	01704-533133
Wirral	0151-638 7070

Norfolk	01603-222222
Breckland	01953-452884
Broadland	01603-31133
Gt Yarmouth	01493-856100
Kings Lynn & West Norfolk	01553-692722
North Norfolk	01263-513811
Norwich	01603-622233
South Norfolk	01508-533633

Northamptonshire	01604-236236
Corby	01536-402551
Daventry	01327-71100
East Northants	01933-412000
Kettering	01536-410333
Northampton	01604-233500
South Northants	01327-350211
Wellingborough	01933-229777

Northumberland	01670-533000
Alnwick	01665-510505
Berwick-upon-Tweed	01289-330044
Blyth Valley	01670-542000
Castle Morpeth	01670-514351
Tynedale	01434-652200
Wansbeck	01670-814444

North Yorkshire	01609-780780
Craven	01756-700600
Hambleton	01609-779977
Harrogate	01423-568954
Richmond	01748-850222
Ryedale	01653-600666
Scarborough	01723-372351
Selby	01757-705101
York	01904-613161

Nottinghamshire	0115-982 3823
Ashfield	01623-755755
Bassetlaw	01909-475531
Broxtowe	0115-925 4891
Gedling	0115-967 0067
Mansfield	01623-656656
Newark & Sherwood	01636-605111
Nottingham	0115-948 3500
Rushcliffe	0115-981 9911

Oxfordshire	01865-792422
Cherwell	01295-252535
Oxford	01865-249811
South Oxfordshire	01491-835351
Vale of White Horse	01235-520202
West Oxfordshire	01993-702941

Scilly Isles	01720-422537

Shropshire	01743-251000
Bridgnorth	01746-765131
North Shropshire	01939-232771
Oswestry	01691-654411
Shrewsbury & Atcham	01743-232255
South Shropshire	01584-874941
The Wrekin	01952-202100

Somerset	01823-333451
Mendip	01749-343399
Sedgemoor	01278-435435
South Somerset	01935-75272
Taunton Deane	01823-335166
West Somerset	01984-632291

South Yorkshire	
Barnsley	01226-770770
Doncaster	01302-734444
Rotherham	01709-382121
Sheffield	0114-272 6444

Staffordshire	01785-223121
Cannock Chase	01543-462621
East Staffs	01283-508000
Lichfield	01543-414000
Newcastle-under-Lyme	01782-717717
South Staffs	01902-696000
Stafford	01785-223181
Staffs Moorlands	01538-399181
Stoke-on-Trent	01782-744241
Tamworth	01827-311222
Suffolk	01473-230000
Babergh	01473-822801
Forest Heath	01638-719000
Ipswich	01473-262626
Mid Suffolk	01449-720711
St Edmundsbury	01284-763233
Suffolk Coastal	01394-383789
Waveney	01502-562111
Surrey	0181-541 8800
Elmbridge	01372-474474
Epsom & Ewell	01372-732000
Guildford	01483-505050
Mole Valley	01306-885001
Reigate & Banstead	01737-242477
Runnymede	01932-845500
Spelthorne	01784-451499
Surrey Heath	01276-686252
Tandridge	01883-722000
Waverley	01483-861111
Woking	01483-755855
Tyne & Wear	
Gateshead	0191-477 1011
Newcastle-upon-Tyne	0191-232 8520
North Tyneside	0191-257 5544
South Tyneside	0191-427 1717
Sunderland	0191-567 6161
Warwickshire	01926-410410
North Warwicks	01827-715341
Nuneaton & Bedworth	01203-376376
Rugby	01788-533533
Stratford-on-Avon	01789-267575
Warwick	01926-450000
West Midlands	
Birmingham	0121-235 9944
Coventry	01203-833333
Dudley	01384-456000
Sandwell	0121-569 2200
Solihull	0121-704 6000
Walsall	01922-650000
Wolverhampton	01902-27811
West Sussex	
Adur	01273-455566

Arun	01903-716133
Chichester	01243-785166
Crawley	01293-528744
Horsham	01403-215100
Mid Sussex	01444-458166
Worthing	01903-239999
West Yorkshire	
Bradford	01274-752111
Calderdale	01422-357257
Kirklees	01484-422133
Leeds	0113-234 8080
Wakefield	01924-290900
Wiltshire	01225-713000
Kennet	01380-724911
North Wiltshire	01249-443322
Salisbury	01722-336272
Thamesdown	01793-526161
West Wiltshire	01225-776655

Welsh local authorities

Clwyd	01352-752121
Alyn & Deeside	01244-525000
Colwyn	01492-515271
Delyn	01352-762345
Glyndwr	01824-702201
Rhuddlan	01745-345000
Wrexham-Maelor	01978-292000
Dyfed	01267-233333
Carmarthen	01267-234567
Ceredigion	01970-617911
Dinefwr	01558-822521
Llanelli	01554-741100
Preseli	01437-764551
South Pembrokeshire	01646-683122
Gwent	01633-838838
Blaenau Gwent	01495-350555
Islwyn	01495-226622
Monmouth	01495-762311
Newport	01633-244491
Torfaen	01495-762200
Gwynedd	01286-672255
Aberconwy	01492-592000
Arfon	01286-673113
Dwyfor	01758-613131
Meirionnydd	01341-422341
Ynys Mon (Anglesey)	01248-750057
Mid Glamorgan	01222-820820
Cynon Valley	01685-878888
Merthyr Tydfil	01685-723201
Ogwr	01656-643643

Rhondda	01443-434551	East Lothian	0162-082 4161
Rhymney Valley	01443-815588	Edinburgh	0131-225 2424
Taff-Ely	01443-407811	Mid Lothian	0131-663 2881
		West Lothian	01506-637000
Powys	01597-826000		
Brecknock	01874-624141	**Strathclyde**	0141-204 2900
Montgomeryshire	01938-552828	Argyll & Bute	01546-602127
Radnorshire	01597-823737	Bearsden & Milngavie	0141-942 2262
		Clydebank	0141-941 1331
South Glamorgan	01222-872000	Clydesdale	01555-661331
Cardiff	01222-822000	Cumbernauld & Kilsyth	01236-722131
Vale of Glamorgan	01446-700111	Cumnock & Doon Valley	01290-422111
		Cunninghame	01294-274166
West Glamorgan	01792-471111	Dumbarton	01389-65100
Lliw Valley	01792-893081	East Kilbride	01355-271200
Neath	01639-641121	Eastwood	0141-638 6511
Port Talbot	01639-875200	Glasgow	0141-221 9600
Swansea	01792-301301	Hamilton	01698-282323
		Inverclyde	01475-24400

Scottish local authorities

Borders	01835-823301	Kilmarnock & Loudoun	01563-21140
Berwickshire	01361-882600	Kyle & Carrick	01292-281511
Ettrick & Lauderdale	01896-745451	Monklands	01236-441200
Roxburgh	01450-375991	Motherwell	01698-266166
Tweeddale	01721-720153	Renfrew	0141-889 5400
Central	01786-442000	Strathkelvin	0141-776 7171
Clackmannan	01259-450000	Tayside	01382-23281
Falkirk	01324-624911	Angus	01307-465101
Stirling	01786-479000	Dundee	01382-434000
		Perth & Kinross	01738-39911

Dumfries & Galloway	01387-261234		
Annandale & Eskdale	01461-203311		

Northern Ireland authorities

Nithsdale	01387-253166	Antrim	01849-463113
Stewartry	01557-330291	Ards	01247-812215
Wigtown	01776-702151	Armagh	01861-524052
		Ballymena	01266-44111
Fife	01592-754411	Ballymoney	01265-662280
Dunfermline	01383-722711	Banbridge,	01820-662991
Kirkcaldy	01592-645000	Belfast City	01232-320202
North East Fife	01334-653722	Carrickfergus	01960-351604
		Castlereagh	01232-799021
Grampian	01224-682222	Coleraine	01265-52181
Aberdeen	01224-276276	Cookstown	01648-762205
Banff & Buchan	01261-812521	Craigavon	01762-341199
Gordon	01467-620981	Down	01396-610800
Kincardine & Deeside	01569-762001	Dungannon	01868-725311
Moray	01343-543451	Fermanagh	01365-325050
		Larne	01574-272313
Highland	01463-702000	Limavady	01504-722226
Badenoch & Strathspey	01540-661555	Lisburn	01846-682477
Caithness	01955-603761	Londonderry	01504-365151
Inverness	01463-239111	Magherafelt	01648-32151
Lochaber	01397-703881	Moyle	01265-762225
Nairn	01667-455523	Newry & Mourne	01693-65411
Ross & Cromarty	01349-863381	Newtownabbey	01960-352681
Skye & Lochalsh	01478-612341	North Down	01247-270371
Sutherland	01408-633033	Omagh	01662-245321
Lothian	0131-229 9292	Strabane	01504-382204

EUROPEAN UNION

The European Parliament has 567 members (MEPs) of whom 87 are British. The last election, in June 1994, had the following UK result (figures in brackets are from the 1989 election):

Labour - 62 members (45)
Conservative - 18 members (32)
Liberal-Democrat - 2 members (0)
Scottish Nationalist Party - 2 members (1)
In Northern Ireland one each to SDLP, Democratic & Labour Party, Democratic Unionist Party and Official Unionist Party as in 1989).

In the European Parliament the MEPs sit in political groupings rather than country ones. The largest are:

European Socialists 213 (inc UK Labour)
European People's Party 148 (inc UK Tories)
Liberal Democratic and Reformist Group 44

The European Union (EU) was set up in 1957, and was then called the European Economic Community (EEC) or Common Market. The original members were Belgium, France, Germany, Italy, Luxembourg and the Netherlands. Denmark, Ireland and the UK joined in 1973, Greece in 1981, and Spain and Portugal in 1986. The unification of Germany in 1990 brought in the former East Germany. Austria, Finland, and Sweden joined in 1995, bringing the total to 15

Though the original aims of the EU were primarily economic, its powers were extended into broader political, social and environmental areas by the Single European Act of 1986. The act aimed to turn the EU into a single market without internal trade barriers. This came into force at the beginning of 1993.

The 1991 Maastricht Treaty - aka the Treaty on European Union - continued the process of integrating member states. It came into force in November 1993. with a proposal for an intergovernmental conference on European Union to be held in 1996. This will consider changing many of the key portions of the treaty.

The major decision-making body in the EU is the **Council of Ministers** which consists of government ministers from each state. It meets regularly, mainly in private. The presidency rotates every six months. France and Spain

presided in 1995 and 1996 has Italy and Ireland. The UK's turn is the first half of 1998.

The European Council, comprising heads of state of each member country, sets guidelines for the Council of Ministers. The European Council should not be confused with the Council of Europe. This is a political institution outside the EC, set up by ten states in 1949, and today having 26 member countries. The council drew up the European Convention on Human Rights, violations of which the council examines through its European Court of Human Rights. The council is based in the European Parliament building in Strasbourg.

The **European Parliament** only participates in drawing up new law, rather than initiating it. Its main role is to scrutinise the activities of the Council of Ministers and the staff-run Commission. Critics say this means the Parliament is ineffective and an illusion of democratic control over the European super-state. The 56.5 per cent turnout across Europe in the 1994 election was the lowest ever in a Euro-vote.

The main driving force of the EU is the **European Commission**, being both the EU's executive civil service and its legislature. The commission drafts proposals, which are looked at by the Parliament and decided by the Council of Ministers. The commission has 17 commissioners, nominated by member states for four-year renewable terms. The current British commissioners are Sir Leon Brittan and Bruce Millan. The commission's work is carried out by its 23 Directorates-General which employ and 17,000 officials. Other major EU bodies are: the Court of Justice, which makes final rulings on European law; the Court of Auditors, monitoris the EU's financial activities; the Economic and Social Committee is consulted about draft law changes; and the Committee of the Regions must be consulted about regional interests.

A confusing aspect of the EU is the absence of a central headquarters. Brussels performs the role in many respects, but there are exceptions. The Council can meet in any country and has its HQ in Strasbourg. The Council of Ministers meets mainly in Brussels, but sometimes in Luxembourg; its staff is based in Brussels. Most full sessions of the European Parliament take place in Strasbourg, while committees meet in Brussels and staff are in Luxembourg.

Council of Ministers

Secretariat, Brussels	00-322 234 6111
UK Representation, Brussels	00-322 287 8211

European Parliament

UK Information Office	0171-222 0411
Secretariat, Luxembourg	00-352 43001
Parliament, Strasbourg	00-338 817 4001
Parliament, Brussels	00-322 284 2111

European political parties

European Democratic Alliance:	
Brussels	00-322 284 2111
Luxembourg	00-353 43001
European People's Party:	
Brussels	00-322 284 2111
Luxembourg	00-352 43001
Tory MEPs, London	0171-222 1720
Green Group, Brussels	00-322 284 2111
Left Unity, Brussels	00-322 284 2111
Luxembourg	00-352 43001
Liberal & Democratic Reformist Group:	
Brussels	00-322 284 2111
Luxembourg	00-352 43001
Non-Attached, Brussels	00-322 284 2579
Rainbow Group, Brussels	00-322 284 2111
Socialist Group, Brussels	00-322 284 2111
Luxembourg	00-352 43001
Labour MEPs, London	0171-222 1719
Technical Group of the European Right:	
Brussels	00-322 284 2111
Paris	00-331 455 03411

European Commission

Headquarters, Brussels, & all directorates-general	00-322 299111
UK offices: London	0171-973 1992
Cardiff	01222-371631
Edinburgh	0131-225 2058
Belfast	01232-240708
Economic/Social Committee	00-322 5199011
Publications Office	00-352 49928
Statistical Office	00-352 43011

European Court of Auditors

Secretariat, Luxembourg	00-352 4398

European Court of Justice

Secretariat, Luxembourg	00-352 43031

European Investment Bank

Luxembourg	00-352 4379
London	0171-839 3351

Other Euro bodies

America-European Community Association (in London)	0171-497 0335
Anti-Common Market League	0181-337 2533
Association of European Air lines (Brussels)	00-322 640 3175
Banking Federation of the EC (Brussels)	00-322 508 3711
Bureau of European Consumer Organisations (Brussels)	00-322 735 3110
Campaign for an Independent Britain	0181-340 0314
Centre for the Development of Industry (Brussels)	00-322 679 1811
Centre for European Policy Studies (Brussels)	00-322 513 4088
CERN (Geneva)	00-4122 767 6111
College of Europe	00-325 033 5334
Committee of Agricultural Organisations in the EC (Brussels)	00-322 287 2711
Committee of the Regions	00-322 519 9243
Council of the Bars & Law Societies of the EC (Brussels)	00-322 640 4274
Council of Europe	00-352 88412000
Economic & Social Committee	00-322 519 9011
Euro Institute for the Media	00-492 119 0104
Euro Space Agency (Paris)	00-331 42737654
European Aid Intelligence Unit	0171-588 7070
European Bank for Reconstruction & Development (London)	0171-338 6000
European Broadcasting Union (Geneva)	00-22 717 2111
European Business Link	0171-734 6617
European Committee for Standardisation Brussels	00-322 519 6811
European Centre for the Development of Vocational Training (Berlin)	00-4930 884120
European Foundation for Improvement of Living/Working Conditions (Dublin)	00-3531 82688
European Free Trade Association - EFTA (Geneva)	00-4122 749 1111
European Links Research	0114-266 5063
European Movement (London)	0171-824 8388
European Policy Forum	0171-222 0733
European Sports Network	0171-439 1177
European Trade Union Confederation	00-322 209 2411
GATT (Geneva)	00-4122 739 5111
House of Commons Select Committee on European Legislation	0171-219 5467
Kangaroo Group - Movement for Free Movement (London)	0171-588 9755
NATO (Brussels)	00-322 728 4111
New Britain	0171-600 4282
OECD (Paris)	00-331 45248200
United Nations New York	00-212 963 1234
London	0171-630 1981

THE LEGAL SYSTEM

The Lord Chancellor's Department oversees the courts system. The Lord Chancellor is a government minister and head of the judiciary, responsible for administering civil courts, considering reforms, appointing magistrates, and advising on the appointment of judges. The Attorney General, assisted by the Solicitor General, is the government's chief legal adviser and prosecutor. The Home Secretary has many legal responsibilities, especially concerning criminal law and the administration of justice.

There are two kinds of law: criminal (offences against state laws) and civil (disputes between individuals or organisations). In **England and Wales** every criminal case starts in juryless magistrates courts, where most are also settled. Serious crimes move on to the 93 crown courts, where they are heard in front of a judge and jury. Appeals are heard by the Criminal Division of the Court of Appeal or the Queens Bench Division of the High Court. Civil actions start in: the many local county courts; the Queen's Bench, Chancery or Family Divisions of the High Court in more complicated cases; or the magistrates courts in certain limited actions. Most appeals go to the Civil Division of the Court of Appeal. From the Court of Appeal, criminal and civil appeals involving important points of law can ask to be heard by the House of Lords.

In **Scotland** district courts are the equivalent of the magistrates courts. Above them are the sheriff courts, arranged in six sheriffdoms. They hear both criminal and civil cases, combining the roles of the crown and county courts south of the border. The final criminal court is the High Court of Justiciary, which is both a trial and appeal court, with no appeal to the House of Lords. The supreme civil court is the Court of Session, but subject to the House of Lords.

The **Northern Ireland** legal system is similar to England and Wales, with magistrates, crown and county courts. The fundamental difference is that terrorism cases are usually heard before judges without juries. Crown court appeals go to the Northern Ireland Court of Appeal, and then the House of Lords. The superior civil court is the High Court of Justice, with appeals to the Court of Appeal and House of Lords.

The lists below focus on the supreme, crown and sheriff courts. The magistrates and county courts are too numerous to include, but the county court administrators' offices are given.

Lord Chancellor's Dept.

Main number	0171-210 8500
Press	0171-210 8512/3
Lord Chancellor's Clerk	0171219 3232

The Lord Chancellor is a government minister and head of the judiciary, responsible for administering civil courts, considering reforms, appointing magistrates, and advising on the appointment of judges.

Home Office

Main number	0171-273 3000
Eves	0171-273 4595
Chief press officer	0171-273 4117
Crime/drugs/young offenders	0171-273 4600
Prisons	0171-217 6633

Law officers

Attorney General and Solicitor General	0171-828 7155
Scotland: Lord Advocate and Solicitor General	0171-276 3000
Privy Council Judicial Committee	0171-270 0485

Crown Prosecution Service

Headquarters (London EC4)	0171-273 8000
Eves	0171-273 8341
Press	0171-273 8105/6
Anglia	01480-432333
East Midlands	0121-629 7200
Hull	01482-228816
London	0171-915 5700
Mersey/Lancashire	0151-236 7575
North	0191-201 2390
North West	0161-837 7402
Severn/Thames	01905 793763
South East	01483-573255
South West	01392-422555
Yorkshire	01904-610726
Wales	01222-783002
West Midlands	0121-629 7200

The Crown Prosecution Service takes over many of the criminal prosecution cases started by the police. It reviews the evidence and decides whether the case should be continued.

Supreme courts

England/Wales

Old Bailey (Central Criminal Court)	0171-248 3277
Royal Courts of Justice	0171-936 6000
Central office	0171-936 6621
Lord Chief Justice's clerk	0171-936 6001
Master of the Rolls' clerk	0171-936 6371
Companies Court	0171-936 6294
Court of Appeal:	
Criminal	0171-936 6817
Civil	0171-936 6916

Scotland

Court of Session and High Court of Justiciary	0131-225 2595

Northern Ireland

Royal Courts of Justice	01232-235111
Court Service	01232-328594

Crown courts

The Crown Courts of England and Wales are divided into six circuits. Each is under the control of a circuit administrator who is eventually responsible to the Lord Chancellor's Department.

Midland and Oxford Circuit

Circuit Administrator (B'ham)	0121-681 3000
Birmingham	0121-681 3000
Coventry	01203-536166
Derby	01332-622600
Grimsby	01472-345816
Hereford	01432-276118
Leicester	0116 265 3400
Lincoln	01522-521500
Northampton	01604-250131
Nottingham	0115-979 3500
Oxford	01865-264200
Peterborough	01733-346342
Shrewsbury	01743-355775
Stafford	01785-55217
Stoke-on-Trent	01782-215076
Warwick	01926-495428
Wolverhampton	01902-481000
Worcester	01905-27006

North Eastern Circuit

Circuit Administrator (Leeds)	0113-251 1200
Bradford	01274-840274
Doncaster	01302-322211
Durham	0191-386 6714
Hull	01482-586161
Leeds	0113-283 0040
Newcastle-upon-Tyne	0191-232 7102
Sheffield	0114-273 7511
Teeside	01642-340000
York	01904-645121

Northern Circuit

Circuit Administrator (Manchester)	0161-833 1005
Barrow-in-Furness	01772-823431
Bolton	01204-392881
Burnley	01282-416899
Carlisle	01228-20619
Lancaster	01772 823431
Liverpool	0151-473 7373
Manchester	0161-954 1800
Preston	01772-823431

South Eastern Circuit

Circuit Administrator (London)	0171-936 7232
Aylesbury	01296-434401
Bury St Edmunds	01284-762676
Cambridge	01223-64436
Canterbury	01227-819200
Chelmsford	01245-358222
Chichester	01243-786151
Guildford	01483-506808
Ipswich	01473-213841
King's Lynn	01553-760847
Lewes	01273-480400
London:	
Old Bailey	0171-248 3277
Croydon	0181-681 2533
Harrow	0181-424 2294
Inner London Sessions, SE1	0171-234 3100
Isleworth	0181-568 8811
Kingston-upon-Thames	0181-549 5241
Knightsbridge	0171-922 5800
Middlesex Guildhall, SW1	0171-799 2131
Snaresbrook	0181-982 5500
Southwark	0171-522 7200
Wood Green	0181-881 1400
Woolwich	0181-312 7020
Luton	01582-488488
Maidstone	01622-754966
Norwich	01603-761776
Reading	01734-595934
St Albans	01727-834481
Southend	01702-351681

Wales and Chester Circuit

Circuit Administrator (Cardiff)	01222-396925
Caernarfon	01286-675686
Cardiff	01222-345931
Carmarthen	01267-236071
Chester	01244-317606

Dolgellau	01341-423307
Haverfordwest	01437-765741
Knutsford	01565-755486
Merthyr Tydfil	01685-721322
Mold	01244-317606
Newport	01633-266211
Swansea	01792-459621
Warrington	01925-572192
Welshpool	01938-553144

Western Circuit

Circuit Administrator (Bristol)	0117-974 3763
Barnstaple	01271-73286
Bournemouth	01202-556461
Bristol	0117-976 3030
Devizes	01793-614848
Dorchester	01305-778684
Exeter	01392-210655
Gloucester	01452-529351
Newport	01983-526821
Plymouth	01752-674808
Portsmouth	01705-822281
Salisbury	01722-325444
Southampton	01703-228586
Swindon	01793-614848
Taunton	01823-335972
Truro	01872-222340
Winchester	01962-841212

County courts

The County Courts in England and Wales are part of the Crown Court circuits. To find one, contact either the areas' Circuit Administrators offices in that list, or the Court Administrators offices below. The latter oversee courts within each circuit, including the County Courts.

Midlands/Oxford County Courts

Birmingham	0121-2681 3000
Nottingham	0115 979 3500
Stafford	01785-55219

North Eastern County Courts

Leeds	0113-2283 0040
Newcastle-upon-Tyne	0191-232 7102
Sheffield	0114-275 5866

Northern County Courts

Liverpool	0151-236 5211
Manchester	0161-833 0110
Preston	01772-823431

South Eastern County Courts

Chelmsford	01245-287974
Kingston-upon-Thames	0181-335 3090
London	0171-936 6000
Maidstone	01622-754966

Wales & Chester County Courts

Cardiff	01222-396483
Chesterfield	01352-754562

Western County Courts

Bristol	0117-925 0296
Exeter	01392-74876
Winchester	01962-841212

Scottish Sheriff courts

Grampian, Highlands & Islands

Aberdeen	01224-648316
Banff	01261-812140
Dingwall	01349-863153
Dornoch	01862-810224
Elgin	01343-542505
Fort William	01397-702087
Inverness	01463-230782
Kirkwall	01856-872110
Lerwick	01595-693914
Lochmaddy	01876-500340
Peterhead	01779-476676
Portree	01478-612191
Stonehaven	01569-762758
Stornoway	01851-702231
Tain	01862-892518
Wick	01955-602846

Tayside, Central & Fife

Alloa	01259-722734
Arbroath	01241-876600
Cupar	01334-652121
Dundee	01382-226513
Dunfermline	01383-724666
Falkirk	01324-620822
Forfar	01307-462186
Kirkcaldy	01592-260171
Perth	01738-620546
Stirling	01786-462191

Lothian & Borders

Edinburgh	0131-225 2595
Haddington	0162-082 2936
Jedburgh	01835-863231
Linlithgow	01506-842922
Peebles	01721-720204
Selkirk	01750-21269

Glasgow & Strathkelvin	0141-429 8888

North Strathclyde

Campbeltown	01586-552503
Dumbarton	01389-763266
Dunoon	01369-704166

Greenock	01475-787073
Kilmarnock	01563-520211
Oban	01631-562414
Paisley	0141-887 5291
Rothesay	01700-502982

South Strathclyde, Dumfries and Galloway

Airdrie	01236-751121
Ayr	01292-268474
Dumfries	01387-262334
Hamilton	01698-282957
Kirkcudbright	01557-330574
Lanark	01555-661331
Stranraer	01776-702138

N Ireland crown courts

Armagh	01861-522816
Ballymena	01266-49416
Belfast	01232-754741
Craigavon	01762-341324
Derry	01504-362834
Newtownards	01247-814343
Omagh	01662-242056

Legal bodies

Inquest gives advice to people seeking justice through the coroner's inquest system. The Law Society is the professional organisation for lawyers. The Legal Action Group works to improve legal services for poorer people and deprived areas. Release provides advice on drug-related legal problems. Rights of Women gives legal help on women and the law.

Children's Legal Centre	01206 873820
Coroners Society	0171-371 9935
Inquest	0181-802 7430
Justice (British Section of International Commission of Jurists)	0171-329 5100
Law Centres Federation	0171-387 8570
Law Society	0171-242 1222
Solicitors Complaints Bureau	01926-820082
Press office	01926-822043
Legal Action Group	0171-833 2931
Liberty (aka National Council for Civil Liberties)	0171-403 3888
Magistrates Association	0171-387 2353
Registry of County Court Judgements	0171-380 0133
Release	0171-729 9904
Rights of Women	0171-251 6577

PRISONS

The UK has over 52,000 prisoners in almost 160 prisons. The prisons on the British mainland were taken out of direct public control in 1993 with the setting up of two quangos: the Prison Service (Executive Agency), covering England and Wales, and the Scottish Prison Service Agency, for Scotland. Until then prisons had been run by the Home Office and the Scottish Office Home and Health Department. The two new services now own the prisons and are independent, except that their directors are responsible to the Home Secretary and Scottish Secretary respectively. The Northern Ireland prison service remains under the Northern Ireland Office.

Also in 1993 the government started a scheme to privatise the staffing of up to 10 per cent of prisons in the near future. Three new prisons have been given to security companies to run: the Wolds remand centre on Humberside, and Blakenhurst in Hereford and Worcester, both in 1993; plus Doncaster in South Yorkshire in 1994. Only prisons with secure units are likely to remain in the public sector in the long run.

Prison services

Prison Service (Executive Agency):

Main number	0171-217 3000
Press	0171-217 6633
Scottish Prison Service	
Agency	031-244 8401

Home Office

Main number	0171-273 3000
Press	0171-217 6633
Parole Board	0171-217 5314
Prison Inspectorate	0171-273 3702

Scottish Office

Main number	0131-556 8400
Press	0131-244 1111
Parole Board	0131-244 8755
Prison Inspectorate	0131-244 8481

Northern Ireland Office

Main number	01232-520700

Prison support agencies

The Apex Trust helps ex-offenders find jobs. The Howard League analyses and reports on the working of the criminal penal system. NACRO campaigns for the care and resettlement of offenders in the community. The Prison Officers Association is the trade union for prison staff, which has campaigned against the privatisation of prison management. The Prisoners Families and Friends Service gives help to the families and friends of serving prisoners.

Apex Trust	0121-411 2929
Howard League for Penal Reform	0171-281 7722
NACRO	0171-582 6500
National Assoc of Prison Visitors	01234-359763
National Association of Probation Officers	0171-223 4887
Prison Governors Association	0171-217 8591
Prison Officers Association	0181-803 0255
Prison Reform Trust	0171-251 5070
Prisoners Advice and Information Network	0181-542 3744
Prisoners Families and Friends Service	0171-403 4091

Male prisons (Eng & Wales)

O = open prison.

Acklington, Northumberland	01670-760411
Albany, Isle of Wight	01983-524055
Aldington, Kent	01233-720436
Ashwell, Leics	01572-756075
Bedford	01234-358671
Belmarsh, London SE28	0181-317 2436
Blakenhurst, Worcs	01527-543348
Blantyre House, Kent	01580-211367
Blundeston, Suffolk	01502-730591
Brinsford, Wolverhampton	01902-791118
Bristol	0117-942 6661
Brixton, London SW2	0181-674 9811
Brockhill, Worcs	01527-550314
Bullingdon, Oxon	01869-322111
Camp Hill, Isle of Wight	01983-527661
Canterbury, Kent	01227-762244
Cardiff	01222-491212
Channings Wood, Devon	01803-812361
Chelmsford, Essex	01245-268651
Coldingley, Surrey	01483-476721
Dartmoor, Devon	01822-890261
Dorchester, Dorset	01305-266021
Downview, Surrey	0181-770 7500
Durham	0191-386 2621
Elmley, Kent	01795-880808
Erlestoke, Wilts	01380-813475
Everthorpe, North Humberside	01430-422471
Exeter, Devon	01392-78321
Featherstone, Wolverhampton	01902-790991
Feltham, Mdx	0181-890 0061
Ford (O), West Sussex	01903-717261
Frankland, Co Durham	0191-384 5544
Full Sutton, York	01759-372447
Garth, Lancs	01772-622722
Gartree, Leics	01858-410234
Glen Parva, Leics	0116-277 2022
Gloucester	01452-529551
Grendon, Bucks	01296-770301
Guernsey, Channel Islands	01481-48376
Haslar, Hants	01705-580381
Haverigg, Cumbria	01229-772131
Highpoint (O), Suffolk	01440-820611
Hindley, Lancs	01942-866255
Hull, N Humberside	01482-320673
Isle of Man	01624-621306
Jersey, Channel Islands	01534-44181
Kirkham (O), Lancs	01772-684343
Lancaster	01524-68871
Latchmere House, Surrey	0181-948 0215
Leeds, West Yorks	0113-263 6411
Leicester	0116-254 6911
Lewes, East Sussex	01273-477331
Leyhill (O), Glos	01454-260681
Lincoln	01522-533633
Lindholme, South Yorks	01302-846600
Littlehey, Cambs	01480-812202
Liverpool	0151-525 5971
Long Lartin, Worcs	01386-830101
Low Newton, Co Durham	0191-386 1141
Maidstone, Kent	01622-755611
Manchester	0161-834 8626
Moorland, South Yorks	01302-351500
Morton Hall (O), Lincs	01522-868151
The Mount, Herts	01442-834363
North Sea Camp (O), Lincs	01205-760481
Norwich	01603-37531
Nottingham	0115-962 5022
Oxford	01865-721261
Parkhurst, Isle of Wight	01983-523855
Pentonville, London N7	0171-607 5353
Portsmouth, Hants	01705-829561
Preston, Lancs	01772-257734
Ranby, Notts	01777-706721
Reading, Berks	01734-587031
Risley, Cheshire	01925-763871
Rochester, Kent	01634-830300
Rudgate (O), West Yorks	01937-844844
Send, Surrey	01483-223048
Shepton Mallet, Somerset	01749-343377
Shrewsbury, Salop	01743-352511
Spring Hill (O), Bucks	01296-770301
Stafford	01785-54421
Standford Hill (O), Kent	01795-880441
Stocken, Leics	01780-410771
Sudbury (O), Derbys	01283-585511
Swaleside, Kent	01795-880766
Swansea	01792-464030

Wealston, West Yorks	01937-844241
Usk, Gwent	01291-672411
The Verne, Dorset	01305-820124
Wakefield, West Yorks	01924-378282
Wandsworth, London SW18	0181-874 4377
Wayland, Norfolk	01953-884103
Wellingborough, Northants	01933-224151
Whatton, Notts	01949-850511
Whitemoor, Cambs	01354-660653
Winchester, Hants	01962-854494
Winson Green, Birmingham	0121-554 3838
Wolds, Humberside	01430-421588
Woodhill, Bucks	01908-501999
Wormwood Scrubs, W12	0181-743 0311
Wymott, Lancs	01772-421461

Female prisons (Eng & Wales)

Askham Grange (O), York	01904-704236
Bullwood Hall, Essex	01702-202515
Cookham Wood, Kent	01634-814981
Drake Hall (O), Staffs	01785-850621
Durham	0191-386 2621
East Sutton Park (O), Kent	01622-842711
Exeter, Devon	01392-78321
Holloway, London N7	0171-607 6747
Low Newton, Co Durham	0191-386 1141
New Hall, West Yorks	01924-848307
Pucklechurch, Bristol	0117-937 2606
Risley, Cheshire	01925-763871
Styal, Cheshire	01625-532141

Scottish prisons

Aberdeen	01224-876868
Barlinnie, Glasgow	0141-770 2000
Cornton Vale, Stirling	01786-832591
Dungavel, Lanarkshire	01357-40371
Edinburgh	0131-444 3000
Friarton, Perth	01738-625885
Glenochil, Clackmannanshire	01259-760471
Inverness	01463-233320
Longriggend, Lanarkshire	01236-830392
Low Moss, Glasgow	0141-762 4848
Noranside, Angus	01356-650217
Penninghame, Wigtownshire	01671-402886
Perth	01738-622293
Peterhead, Aberdeenshire	01779-479101
Shotts, Lanarkshire	01501-822622

Northern Ireland prisons

Belfast: Crumlin Road	01232-741100
Hydebank (young offenders)	01232-253666
Magilligan, Co Londonderry	01504-763311
Maze, Co Antrim	01846-683111
Maghaberry, Co Antrim	01846-611888

EMBASSIES

Afghanistan: London Em	0171-589 8891
Algeria: London Em	0171-221 7800
UK Em, Algiers	00-2132 622411
Angola: London Em	0171-495 1752
UK Em, Luanda	00-2442 334582
Antigua: London HCom	0171-486 7073
UK HCom, St Johns	00-1809 4620008
Argentina: London Em	0171-584 6494
UK Em, Buenos Aires	00-541 8037070
Australia: London HCom	0171-379 4334
UK HCom, Canberra	00-616 2706666
UK Con, Melbourne	00-613 6504155
UK Con, Perth	00-619 2215400
UK Con, Sydney	00-612 2477521
Austria: London Em	0171-235 3731
UK Em, Vienna	00-431 7131575
Azerbaijan: London Em	0171-938 2222
Bahamas: London HCom	0171-408 4488
UK HCom, Nassau	00-1809 3257471
Bahrain: London Em	0171-370 5132
UK Em, Bahrain	00-973 534404
Bangladesh: London Em	0171-584 0081
UK HCom, Dhaka	00-8802 882705
Barbados: London HCom	0171-631 4975
UK HCom, Bridgetown	00-1809 4366694
Belgium: London Em	0171-235 5422
UK Em, Brussels	00-322 2876211
Belize: London HCom	0171-499 9728
UK HCom, Belmopan	00-5018 22146
Bolivia: London Em	0171-235 4248
UK Em, La Paz	00-5912 357424
Botswana: London HCom	0171-499 0031
UK HCom, Gaborone	00-267 352841
Brazil: London Em	0171-499 0877
UK Em, Brasilia	00-5561 2252710
UK Con, Rio	00-5521 327788
Brunei: London HCom	0171-581 0521
UK HCom, Begawan	00-6732 226001
Bulgaria: London Em	0171-581 3144
UK Em, Sofia	00-3592 885361
Burma: London Em	0171-499 8841
UK Em, Rangoon	00-951 81700
Burundi: UK Con, Bujumbura	00-2572 23711
Cameroon: London Em	0171-727 0771
UK Em, Yaounde	00-237 220545
Canada: London HCom	0171-258 6600
UK HCom, Ottawa	00-1613 2371530
UK Con, Toronto	00-1416 5931290
UK Con, Vancouver	00-1604 6834421
Chad: UK Em, Ndjamena	00-235 513064
Chile: London Em	0171-580 6392
UK Em, Santiago	00-562 2239166

China: London Em	0171-636 9375
UK Em, Beijing	00-861 5321961
UK Con, Shanghai	00-8621 4330508
Colombia: London Em	0171-589 9177
UK Em, Bogota	00-571 2185111
UK Con, Medellin	00-574 2463114
Costa Rica: London Em	0171-706 8844
UK Em, San Jose	00-506 2215566
Croatia: London Em	0171-434 2946
UK Em, Zagreb	00-3841 334245
Cuba: London Em	0171-240 2488
UK Em, Havana	00-537 331771
Cyprus: London HCom	0171-499 8272
UK HCom, Nicosia	00-3572 473131
Czech/Slovak FR London Em	0171-243 1115
UK Em, Prague	00-422 24510439
Denmark: London Em	0171-333 0200
UK Em, Copenhagen	00-45 35264600
Dominican Republic:UK Em,	00-1809 5015
Ecuador: London Em	0171-584 1367
UK Em, Quito	00-5932 560669
Egypt: London Em	0171-499 2401
UK Em, Cairo	00-202 3540850
El Salvador: London Em	0171-436 8282
UK Em, San Salvador	00-503 981763
Estonia: London Em	0171-589 3428
UK Em, Tallinn	00-70142 313353
Ethiopia: London Em	0171-589 7212
UK Em, Addis Ababa	00-2511 612354
Fiji: London Em	0171-584 3661
UK Em, Suva	00-679 311033
Finland: London Em	0171-235 9531
UK Em, Helsinki	00-3580 661293
France: London Em 0	171-201 1000
UK Em, Paris	00-331 42669142
UK Con, Bordeaux	00-33 56423413
UK Con, Marseille	00-33 91534332
Gambia: London HCom	0171-937 6316
UK HCom, Banjul	00-220 495135
Germany: London Em	0171-235 5033
UK Em, Bonn	00-49228 9167
UK Em, Berlin	00-4930 201840
UK Con, Frankfurt	00-4969 1700020
UK Con, Munich	00-4989 211090
Ghana: London HCom	0181-342 8686
UK Em, Accra	00-23321 221665
Greece: London Em	0171-229 3850
UK Em, Athens	00-301 7236211
Grenada: London HCom	0171-373 7809
UK HCom, St Georges	00-1809 4403222
Guatemala: London Em	0171-351 3042
UK Em, Guatemala City	00-5022 321601
Guinea: UK Em, Conakry	00-224 461734
Guyana: London HCom	0171-229 7684
UK Em, Georgetown	00-5922 65881
Haiti: UK Em, Port au Prince	00-509 573969
Honduras: London Em	0171-486 4880
UK Em, Tegucigalpa	00-504 325429
Hong Kong: London	0171-499 9821
Hong Kong government	00-852-5230176
Hungary : London Em	0171-235 4048
UK Em, Budapest	00-361 2662888

Iceland: London Em	0171-730 5131
UK Em, Reykjavik	00-3541 15883
India: London HCom	0171-836 8484
UK HCom, New Delhi	00-9111 601371
UK HCom, Bombay	00-9122 2830517
UK HCom, Calcutta	00-9133 2425171
UK HCom, Madras	00-9144 8273136
Indonesia: London Em	0171-499 7661
UK Em, Jakarta	00-6221 330904
Iran: London Em	0171-584 8101
UK Em, Tehran	00-9821 675011
Iraq: London via Jordan Em	0171-584 7141
UK Em, Baghdad	00-9641 5372121
Irish Republic: London Em	0171-235 2171
UK Em, Dublin	00-3531 2695211
Israel: London Em	0171-957 9500
UK Em, Tel Aviv	00-9723 5249171
Italy: London Em	0171-312 2200
UK Em, Rome	00-396 4825441
UK Con, Milan	00-392 72300320
UK Con, Naples	00-3981 663511
Ivory Coast: London Em	0171-235 6991
UK Em, Abidjan	00-225 226850
Jamaica: London HCom	0171-823 9911
UK HCom, Kingston	00-1809 9269050
Japan: London Em	0171-465 6500
UK Em, Tokyo	00-813 32655511
Jerusalem: UK Con	00-9722 828281
Jordan: London Em	0171-937 3685
UK Em, Amman	00-9626 823100
Kenya: London HCom	0171-636 2371
UK HCom, Nairobi	00-2542 335944
Korea: London Em	0171-581 0247
UK Em, Seoul	00-850 7357341
Kuwait: London Em	0171-589 4533
UK Em, Kuwait	00-965 24320461
Latvia: London Em	0171-312 0040
UK Em, Riga	00-70132 320737
Lebanon: London Em	0171-229 7265
UK Em, Beirut	00-9611 416112
Lesotho: London HCom	0171-235 5686
UK HCom	00-266 313961
Liberia: London Em	0171-221 1036
Libya: London via Saudia Arabian Em,	
Libyan Interests Section	0171-486 8387
Lithuania: London Em	0171-938 2481
UK Em, Vilnius	00-70122 222070
Luxembourg: London Em	0171-235 6961
UK Em, Luxembourg	00-352 229864
Malawi: London HCom	0171-491 4172
UK HCom, Lilongwe	00-265 782400
Malaysia: London HCom	0171-235 8033
UK HCom, Kuala Lumpur	00-603 2482122
Malta: London HCom	0171-292 4800
UK HCom, Valletta	00-356 2331347
Mauritius: London HCom	0171-581 0294
UK HCom, Port Louis	00-230 2111361
Mexico: London Em	0171-499 8586
UK Em, Mexico City	00-525 2072089
Mongolia: London Em	0171-937 0150
UK Em, Ulaan Bataar	00-976 358133
Morocco: London Em	0171-581 5001

UK Em, Rabat	00-2127 720905	UK Em, Cape Town	00-2721 4617220
Mozambique: London Em	0171-383 3800	UK Em, Pretoria	00-2712 433121
UK Em, Maputo	00-2581 420111	UK Con, Jo'burg	00-2711 3378940
Namibia: London HCom	0171-636 6244	Spain: London Em	0171-235 5555
UK HCom, Windhoek	00-26461 223022	UK Em, Madrid	00-341 3190200
Nepal: London Em	0171-229 1594	UK Con, Barcelona	00-343 4199044
UK Em, Kathmandu	00-9771 410583	UK Con, Malaga	00-3452 217571
Netherlands: London Em	0171-584 5040	Sri Lanka: London HCom	0171-262 1841
UK Em, The Hague	00-3170 3645800	UK HCom, Colombo	00-941 437336
UK Con, Amsterdam	00-3120 6764343	Sudan: London Em	0171-839 8080
New Zealand: London HCom	0171-930 8422	UK Em, Khartoum	00-249 70760
UK HCom, Wellington	00-644 4726049	Swaziland: London HCom	0171-581 4976
Nicaragua: London Em	0171-584 4365	UK HCom, Mbabane	00-268 42581
UK Em, Managua	00-5052 780014	Sweden: London Em	0171-917 6400
Niger: UK Em, Niamey	00-227 732015	UK Em, Stockholm	00-468 6719000
Nigeria: London HCom	0171-839 1244	Switzerland: London Em	0171-723 0701
UK HCom, Lagos	00-2341 2619531	UK Em, Berne	00-4131 3525021
Norway: London Em	0171-235 7151	UK Con, Geneva	00-4122 7343800
UK Em, Oslo	00-472 552400	UK Con, Zurich	00-411 2611520
UK Con, Bergen	00-4755 348505	Syria: London Em	0171-245 9012
Oman: London Em	0171-225 0001	UK Em, Damascus	00-96311 712561
UK Em, Muscat	00-968 738501	**Tanzania:** London HCom	0171-499 9321
Pakistan: London HCom	0171-235 2044	UK HCom, Dar es Salaam	00-25551 29601
UK HCom, Islamabad	00-9251 822131	Thailand: London Em	0171-589 2944
UK HCom, Karachi	00-9221 532041	UK Em, Bangkok	00-662 2530191
Panama: London Em	0171-487 5633	Trinidad: London HCom	0171-245 9351
UK Em, Panama City	00-675 690866	UK HCom, Port of Spain	00-1809 6252861
Papua New Guinea:		Tunisia: London Em	0171-584 8117
London HCom	0171-930 0922	UK Em, Tunis	00-2161 341444
UK HCom, Port Moresby	00-675 251677	Turkey: London Em	0171-235 5252
Paraguay: London Em	0171-937 1253	**Uganda:** London HCom	0171-839 5783
UK Em, Asuncion	00-59521 444472	UK HCom, Kampala	00-25641 2570541
Peru: London Em	0171-235 1917	Ukraine: London Em	0171-727 6312
UK Em, Lima	00-5114 334735	UK Em, Kiev	00-7044 2280504
Philippines: London Em	0171-937 1600	UAE London Em	0171-581 1281
UK Em, Manila	00-632 8167116	UK Em, Abu Dhabi	00-9712 326600
Poland: London Em	0171-580 4324	United States: London Em	0171-499 9000
UK Em, Warsaw	00-482 6281001	UK Em, Washington	00-1202 4621340
Portugal: London Em	0171-235 5331	UK Con, Chicago	00-1312 3461810
UK Em, Lisbon	00-3511 3961191	UK Con, Dallas	00-1214 6373600
Qatar: London Em	0171-493 2200	UK Con, Los Angeles	00-1310 4773322
UK Em, Doha	00-974 421991	UK Con, Miami	00-1305 3741522
Romania: London Em	0171-937 9666	UK Con, New York	00-1212 7450200
UK Em, Bucharest	00-400 120303	Uruguay: London Em	0171-584 8192
Russian Fed. London Em	0171-229 3628	UK Em, Montevideo	00-5982 623630
UK Em, Moscow	00-7095 2306333	**Vanuatu:** UK HCom, Vila	00-678 23100
St Lucia: London HCom	0171-937 9522	Venezuela: London Em	0171-584 4206
UK HCom, Castries	00-1809 452248	UK Em, Caracas	00-582 9934111
Saudi Arabia: London Em	0171-917 3000	Vietnam: London Em	0171-937 1912
UK Em, Riyadh	00-9661 4880077	UK Em, Hanoi	00-84 252349
Senegal: London Em	0171-937 0925	**Yemen:** London Em	0171-584 6607
UK Em, Dakar	00-221 237392	UK Em, Sanaa	00-9671 215630
Serbia: UK Em, Belgrade	00-3811 645055	Yugoslavia: London Em	0171-370 6105
Seychelles: London HCom	0171-224 1660	UK Em, Belgrade	00-3811 645055
UK HCom, Victoria	00-248 225225	**Zaire:** London Em	0171-235 6137
Sierra Leone: London HCom	0171-636 6483	UK Em, Kinshasa	00-24312 34775
UK HCom, Freetown	00-23222 223961	Zambia: London HCom	0171-589 6655
Singapore: London HCom	0171-235 8315	UK HCom	00-2601 228955
UK HCom, Singapore	00-65 4739333	Zimbabwe: London HCom	0171-836 7755
Somalia: UK Em, Mogadishu	00-2521 20288	UK HCom, Harare	00-2634 793781
South Africa: London Em	0171-930 4488		

DISASTERS/EMERGENCIES

The Home Office's definition of a disaster is "any event (happening with or without warning) causing or threatening death or injury, damage to property or the environment or disruption to the community, which because of the scale of its effects cannot be dealt with by the emergency services and local authorities as part of their day-to-day activities".

The emergency services refer to disasters as major incidents. The term disaster is applied to events such as floods, serious accidents, building collapses, storms and other calamities. Official plans for handling disasters are relatively public, and are collectively known as emergency planning. More behind-the-scenes are central government contingency plans for dealing with strikes and riots. In these events selected parts of the emergency planning system may be asked to help the contingency planners, discretely.

Journalists covering a "major incident" often find it difficult to obtain information. But central government departments, local authorities, the emergency services and most big industrial plants have plans to cope with any emergency, and knowledge of these should help reporters with their work.

At national level, there is an emergency government administrative structure kept in readiness for the most serious catastrophe. It can be activated either as a whole or in part, and is most likely to be used during a foreign attack, general strike or mass civil unrest. The top layer consists of the prime minister, key ministers, some senior civil servants and chief military and police officers. In the most extreme emergency this would be the national decision-making body, operating from a hardened and anonymous communications centre.

The next level consists of the Regional Emergency Committees (RECs), with one in each of the ten Home Defence Regions. The RECs are normally chaired by the regional director of the Department of the Environment, but on activation a government minister would take charge. Each REC has a command centre, where emergency service officers, the military and some local politicians would together act as a regional government.

This emergency government structure is normally not visible to the public. Enquiries about it are seldom answered in detail. The Cabinet Office has the main responsibility, with some help from the Home Office. The Cabinet Office is the home of the Civil Contingencies Unit (CCU), the government body with the prime responsibility for co-ordinating the state's response to emergencies. The CCU is a committee of civil servants and some ministers, chaired by the Home Secretary, and backed by a secretariat. It decides the state's approach to serious threats, appointing a government department (the "lead" department) to work out details and put plans into effect when necessary.

Local authorities also have some emergency planning duties. Each county-type authority has its own emergency planning officer (EPO), responsible for taking an overview of possible local problems, and drawing up plans to handle them. The EPO is the best starting point for inquiring about proposals for dealing with local disasters. contact via the county councils, listed under local government plus:

London Fire & Civil Defence Authority: Emergency Planning Division 0171-587 6350
Home Office: Emergency Planning Division 0171-273 3439

The Home Office co-ordinates the EPOs and other emergency planning work via its Fire and Emergency Planning Department.

In the front line of handling any disaster are the four main emergency services: the police, fire brigades, ambulance services and Coastguard. All four operate emergency procedures day-to-day, and have press offices for handling queries. They also have their own individual plans for handling major incidents.

The police usually take initial charge at a disaster. The Home Office says the police should, as soon as possible during a disaster, set up a media contact point run by an experienced press officer. The police also set up a central control point where liaison officers from all the emergency services, local authorities, the military, Whitehall and volunteer bodies meet and keep in contact with their respective HQs.

Many volunteer agencies help the official services, including the WRVS, Red Cross, St John Ambulance, Raynet (a network of radio amateurs) and mountain rescue teams. The government's Joint Emergency Executive Committee manages groups giving medical aid.

Guides

There are no adequate published guides to all contingency planning and the military. Following are what is available on specific aspects.

Dealing with Disaster
HMSO   Tel 0171-873 9090
A Home office booklet which outlines procedures for all emergency services to ensure proper control and co-ordination at disaster scenes.

Guide to Help in a Major Emergency
Paramount Publishing   Tel 0181-207 5599
Published 1993 for the Society of Emergency Services Officers; it covers much of the same ground as Dealing with Disaster, but in more detail, and with contact numbers.

Who's Who in the Emergency and Rescue Services Directory
Lincoln Publications   0171-240 5562
An annual listing of relevant bodies and commercial suppliers.

Lead departments

In the event of a disaster listed below, the Whitehall department named alongside provides a government response.

Flooding - MAFF and equivalents in Scottish, Welsh and Northern Ireland Offices.

Marine pollution - Department of Transport.

Military - Ministry of Defence.

Miscellaneous (building collapses, dam failures, earthquakes) - Environment Department or Scottish/Welsh/Northern Ireland Offices.

Off-shore installation blow-outs - Department of Employment (Health & Safety Executive).

Overseas disasters - Foreign Office.

Radiation inside UK - Civil: DTI and Scottish Office, or Department of Transport if civil nuclear material in transit.

Radiation from outside UK - Environment Dept.

Rivers - National Rivers Authority

Search and rescue - Civil shipping: Department of Transport (Coastguard).
Military shipping and aircraft, and civil aircraft at sea: Ministry of Defence.

Civil aircraft on land: Department of Transport.

Sports grounds accidents - Home Office, with National Heritage Department.

Transport accidents - Department of Transport.

Weather - Severe storms: Home Office or Welsh Scottish/Northern Ireland Offices initially; Environment Department later.
Other weather emergencies: Transport.

Other bodies

Air Accidents Investigation Branch,
   Department of Transport   01252-510300
BASICS (British Association for Immediate
   Care)   01473-218407
British Airways Crisis Management Team,
   Gatwick   0181-513 0917
British Divers Marine Life Rescue
   Charity   01634-281680
British Safety Council   0181-741 1231
Casualties Union   0171-235 5366
Emergency Planning College,
   Easingwold   01347-821406
Emergency Planning Society   01352-703019
Institute of Civil Defence and Disaster
   Studies   0171-588 3700
International Rescue Corps   01324-665011
Marine Accident Investigation Branch,
   Department of Transport   01703-395500
Mines Rescue Service   01623-23263
National Chemical Emergency
   Centre   01235-432919
National Voluntary Civil Aid
   Society   0181-977 2806
Royal Life Saving Society   01527-853943
Search & Rescue Dog Assoc:
   England   01579-363090
   Lake District   01768-772463
   Wales   01690-750552
   Southern Scotland   0141-944 1091
   Highlands   01847-611256
Society of Industrial Emergency Services
   Officers   0171-416 0146
Underwater Search Unit   0171-275 4421
WRVS   0171-416 0146

Mountain rescue

Military - via RAF Rescue Coordination Centres:
   Northern (in Fife)   01383-412161
   Southern (in Devon)   01752-563777
Civilian - via police force HQs
   Mountain Rescue Council   01457-853095

THE MILITARY

The strength of the armed forces in mid-1995 was: Army 120,000, RAF 70,000, Royal Navy 51,000. The budget for 1995/6 was over £22,000 million, about 40 per cent of it going on military equipment. The peace dividend means 19,000 jobs will go by the year 2000.

Britain remains committed to NATO, but has also increased its military involvement with the European Union. Two Polaris nuclear subs are being replaced by four Trident missile versions. Garrisons are maintained in Hong Kong, Gibraltar, Cyprus, Brunei, Belize and the Falkland Islands. Troops remain in Northern Ireland, although in a backstage role since the IRA ceasefire began in September 1994.

Military operations inside the UK are largely controlled by the UK Commanders-in-Chief Committee (UK-CICC), based near Salisbury. The troops have three internal British roles:

1) Military Aid to the Civil Power (Mac-P) involves providing armed forces to help the police during violent civil challenges to state authority, as in Northern Ireland 1969-74.

2) Military Assistance to Civil Ministries (Mac-M) is the use of troops to carry out specialised services for government departments, especially during strikes.

3) Military Aid to the Civil Community (Mac-C) arranges for troops to help the public during emergencies like floods.

The Emergency Planning Division of the Home Office liaises between the military, police and central government on crisis management and wartime emergency planning matters.

Ministry of Defence

Whitehall HQ main number	0171-218 9000
Chief of Information	0171-218 7900
Press office: Armed Forces	0171-218 2629
Army	0171-218 3255
Navy	0171-218 3257
RAF	0171-218 3253
Policy and procurement	0171-218 2906
Out of hours	0171-218 7907
Secretary of State's office	0171-218 2111
Permanent Under-Sec's office	0171-218 2839
Chief of Defence Staff's office	0171-218 2116
UK-CICC	01722-336222
Navy Department: First Sea Lord's office	0171-218 2214
Army Department: Chief of the General Staff's office	0171-218 7114

Air Force Department: Chief of the Air Staff's office	0171-218 6313
Commandant General Royal Marines	017705-547500
Chemical & Biological Defence Establishment (Porton Down)	01980-612000
D-Notice (or Defence Press & Broadcasting) Committee	0171-218 3820
Defence Export Services Organisation	0171-218 3042
Defence Intelligence Staff	0171-218 2407
Doctrine & Training (Upavon)	01980-615000
Hydrographic Office	01823-337900
Meteorological Office	01344-420242
Royal College of Defence Studies	0171-915 4800
Navy News	01705-722351
RAF News	0171-305 8057
Soldier Magazine	01252-349356

Army

Army HQs - UK Land Forces:	
London District	0171-414 2339
Eastern District (York)	01904-659811
12 Engineer Brg	01223-860681
15 (North East) Brg	01904-659811
19 Infantry Brg	01206-575121
24 Airmobile Brg	01748-832521
49 (East Midlands) Brg	0115-925 4811
54 (East Anglia) Brg	01206-575121
Southern District (Aldershot)	01252-24431
2 Brg/Dover Area	01303-249541
43 (Wessex) Brg/Exeter Area	01392-216980
Aldershot Area	01252-24431
Bulford Area	01980-672050
Wales & Western District (Shrewsbury)	01743-236060
11 Signal Brg	0151-228 2463
30 Engineer Brg	01785-45840
42 (North West) Brg	01772-716543
143 (West Midlands) Brg	01743-236060
160 (Wales) Brg	01874-623111
Prince of Wales Division	01543-433333
Scotland (Edinburgh)	0131-336 1761
51 Highland Brg	01738-21281
52 Lowland Brg	0131-336 1761
Northern Ireland (Lisburn)	01846-665111
Army Department HQs:	
Army Air Corps (Stockbridge)	01980-672050
Household Cavalry (Chelsea)	0171-930 4466
Infantry (Warminster)	01985-214000
Intelligence Corps (Ashford)	01233-625251
Royal Armoured Corps	01929-403550
Royal Artillery (Woolwich)	0181-855 7755
Territorial Army	01722-433960

Royal Navy

Naval Home Command	
(Portsmouth)	01705-722351
Allied Command: Channel & Eastern	
Atlantic (Northwood)	01923-826161
Naval Bases: Devonport	01752-553740
Portsmouth	01705-722351
Portland	01305-820311
Rosyth	01383-412121
Royal Marines (Portsmouth)	01705-731978

RAF

Strike Command (High	
Wycombe)	01494-461461
Logistics Command (Huntingdon)	01480-52151
No 1 Group (Benson)	01491-37766

No 11 Group (Bentley Priory)	0181-950 4000
No 18 Group (Northwood)	01923-837201
No 38 Group (High Wycombe)	01494-461461
Military Air Traffic Operations	
(Uxbridge)	01895-276009
London Air Traffic Control Centre ·	
Military (West Drayton)	01895-445566
Air Warfare Centre	
(High Wycombe)	01494-497140

Military police

MOD Police	0171-824 4444
RAF Police	0171-218 9000
RN Regulating Branch (police)	01705-722351
Royal Marines Police	0171-824 4444
Royal Military Police	0171-824 4444

INTELLIGENCE

MI5

The internal counter-subversion organisation is MI5, aka the Security Service. Its key role is defending the state against "actions intended to overthrow or undermine parliamentary democracy by political, industrial or violent means" (1989 Security Service Act). Since the IRA ceasefire MI5 has tried to justify its existence by seeking a role fighting organised crime. MI5 has been trying to become a British FBI, taking over functions from the police, but a tradition of hostility has made this difficult. A compromise should be agreed by the time director-general Stella Rimington retires at the end of 1996.
Home Office press contacts   0171-273 4610

MI6

The Secret Intelligence Service has traditionally been Britain's overseas spying agency, gathering and processing information discovered by covert means in foreign countries. The 1994 Intelligence Services Act widened MI6's role. It can now do anything "in the interests of national security or of the economic well-being of the UK, or in support of the prevention or detection of serious crime", where "persons outside the British Islands" are the suspects. The MI6 "chief" is David Spedding. Both MI5 and MI6 in 1994 took over expensive new London headquarters buildings almost facing each other across the Thames between the Vauxhall and Lambeth bridges. MI5 and MI6 have about 2,000 staff each.
Foreign Office press contacts   0171-270 3100

GCHQ

The Government Communications Headquarters is based in Cheltenham and has 6,000 civilian staff, assisted by 3,000 members of the Armed Forces in their overseas bases. The 1994 Intelligence Services Act said GCHQ's functions should be eavesdropping and providing wide-ranging technical advice (especially on languages). The primary work is electronic eavesdropping carried out in the interests of national security and of the economic well-being of the UK in relation to people overseas, and "in support of the prevention or detection of serious crime". GCHQ is dominated by the United States. The two countries run UKUSA, a worldwide intelligence listening operation. GCHQ, like MI6, is responsible to the Foreign Office. Its Director is Sir John Adye.
Foreign Office press contacts   0171-270 3100

Special Branch

Police services are supplied to the intelligence bodies by the Special Branch, the anti-subversive police, traditionally seen as MI5's foot soldiers. Special Branch must carry out arrests because legislation has never vested MI5 with official police powers. Each of Britain's forces has its own theoretically independent Special Branch squad, but in practice that of the Metropolitan Police is by far the largest and so it has the de facto national co-ordinating role.
Met press contacts   0171-230 2171

THE POLICE

British policing is carried out by 52 police forces: 39 in England, four in Wales, eight in Scotland and one in Northern Ireland (the Royal Ulster Constabulary - RUC). London has two separate forces: the Metropolitan (the "Met") and the City of London, the latter covering just the area of the Corporation. There are about 150,000 officers.

In England and Wales all forces except the Met are supervised by local police authorities. These used to have local councillors as two-thirds of the members. Following new legislation, there are now 17 (or more) members: nine councillors, three magistrates and five "independent" members chosen by the other authority members from a list supplied by the Home Office. The Met is run by a commissioner who is directly responsible to the Home Secretary. In Scotland, the police authorities are the island and regional councils. The RUC is controlled by an authority appointed by the government.

Each police force is run by a chief constable, who is nominally responsible to the police authority. In practice, the authorities have little power, leaving the chiefs largely outside authority influence. The Home Office provides just over half the finance for the forces, giving it more command than the authorities. This means Britain has a national police force in many respects, but one that is not acknowledged as such. Also largely unrecognised are the British police officers and organisations taking part in the behind-the-scenes construction of a European state system capable of cross-national action during major internal conflicts.

The Association of Chief Police Officers (ACPO), the professional body for chief constables, plays a major role in both shaping all British policy on the police and in co-ordinating the strategies of the various police forces.

Several police national services are provided centrally by the government. The National Criminal Intelligence Service (NCIS, known as Ensis) provides forces with information about serious crime and major criminals. It has a Drugs Unit, helping co-ordinate the drug trafficking intelligence material of the police and Customs. NCIS also liaises with the International Criminal Police Organisation. It has a London headquarters and five regional offices. The Police National Computer (PNC) provides all forces with a 24-hour service supplying vital information.

The National Criminal Records System (NCRS), recording all arrests and convictions, has recently been installed on the PNC, under the title Phoenix. The Police National Network of integrated voice and data communications has also just been created. Regional crime squads are co-ordinated at a national level to handle serious cases crossing force boundaries.

In June 1995 the first major review since the 1960s of police roles recommended that 26 tasks currently carried out by the police could be hived off to local authorities. But the Home Office study found there was no scope for the police to withdraw from any major area of work. This was a success for senior police officers, who had feared much greater involvement by the private sector.

In England and Wales the Home Office oversees policing through its Police Department, which has an Intelligence Services division. In Scotland the Scottish Office Home and Health Department and in Northern Ireland the Northern Ireland Office supervise the devolved functions of the Home Office.

Government services

Home Office:

Main number & Police Dept	0171-273 3000
Press offices: Police	0171-273 4610
Criminal justice	0171-273 4600
Crime prevention	0171-273 4620
Crime Prevention Centre	01785-58217
Crown Prosecution Service	0171-273 8000
Forensic Science Service	0171-273 4610
Immigration Service Intelligence & Investigation Unit	0181-897 0771
International Criminal Policy	0171-273 3000
Missing Persons Helpline	0181-392 2000
National Criminal Intelligence Service:	
Main number	0171-238 8000
Press	0171-238 8431
National Identification Bureau	0171-230 2780
Police Scientific Development Branch (equipment)	01727-865051
Police National Computer	0181-205 1855
Police Staff College, Bramshill	01252-842931
Scottish Office Home & Health Dept:	
Main number	0131-556 8400
Press	0131-244 5106
Police division	0131-244 2155

Northern Ireland Office:
Main number 01232-520700
NI Police Authority 01232-230111
Cabinet Office: Main number 0171-270 1234
Press 0171-270 0393
Foreign Office: Main number 0171-270 3000
Press 0171-270 3100
GCHQ 01242 221491
HM Inspectors of Constabulary:
England and Wales 0171-273 2116
Scotland 0131-244 5614

Specialist police forces

British Transport Police 0171-388 7541
Military: MOD Police HQ 0171-824 4444
RAF Police 0171-218 2842
Royal Marines Police 01705 836338
Royal Military Police 0171-824 4444
Royal Naval Regulating Branch
(RN police, HMS Nelson) 01705-822351
Ports: Belfast 01232-232235
Dover 01304-216084
Falmouth 01326-212100
Liverpool 0151-949 1212
London (Tilbury) 01375-846781
Tees 01642-468129
Royal Botanic Gardens Constabulary
(Kew) 0181-332 5000
Royal Parks Constabulary 0171-298 2000
UK Atomic Energy Authority
Constabulary 01235-463560

Other policing organisations

Counterfeiting Intelligence 0181-591 3000
HM Customs & Excise Investigation
Division 0171- 620 1313
Dept of Social Security Organised
Fraud Units 0181-951 1311
Dept of Trade & Industry Companies
Investigations Division 0171-215 5917
Federation Against Copyright
Theft (FACT) 0181-568 6646
Federation Against Software
Theft (FAST) 01628-660377
Gaming Board 0171-306 6200
Immigration Service Intelligence and
Investigation Unit 0181-745 2400
Inland Revenue Investigation
Office 0171-438 6622
Interpol (via NCIS) 0171-238 8431
Post Office Investigation Dept 0181-681 9259
Radio Investigations Service (Dept of
Trade & Industry) 0171-215 2086
Sea Fisheries Inspectorate
(part of MAFF) 0171-238 5798/9
Serious Fraud Office 0171-239 7272

Staff bodies

ACPO (Association of Chief Police Officers):
England, Wales, N Ireland 0171-230 7184
Scotland 0131-311 3051
Association of Chief Officers of
Probation 01924-361156
Association of Police Surgeons 01423-509727
British Assoc of Women Police 0121-626 5000
International Police Association 0115-981 3638
Police Federation:
England and Wales 0181-399 2224
N Ireland 01232-760831
Scotland 0141-332 5234
Police Superintendents Association
(England & Wales) 01734-844005
Charities:
Police Dependants Trust 0171-273 2921
Police Foundation 0171-582 3744
Police Memorial Trust 0171-603 7272

Privatised policing

Assoc of British Investigators 0181-546 3368
British Security Industry Assoc 01905-21464
Certificated Bailiffs Assoc 0121-632 5472
Institute of Professional
Investigators 01254-680072
International Professional Security
Association 01803-554849
Security Industry Inspectorate 01905-617499
Vehicle Industry Security
Association via 01203-404400

Pressure groups

There are few independent information sources
on the police. Statewatch has the largest UK
library on policing and security outside official
institutions, with material going back two
decades. It also publishes a bi-monthly journal
and runs a public computer database. Liberty
(the National Council for Civil Liberties) is a
long-established campaigning organisation, also
with a library and regular journal. Other
magazines on the police are Police Review,
Police and Policing. See also War and Peace
in the final section on Press and Advice
Groups.

Justice 0171-329 5100
Liberty (NCCL) 0171-403 3888
Missing Persons Bureau 0181-392 2000
Police Complaints Authority 0171-273 6450
Police Review (magazine) 0171-537 2575
Statewatch 0181-802 1882

Police forces

Most police forces have voice bank recorded tape message with details of incidents.

Avon & Somerset	01275-818181
Voice banks: Bristol	01426-957011
Taunton	01426-950441
Bristol	0117-927 7777
Bristol - North	0117-970 2070
Taunton	01823-337911
Weston-super-Mare	01934-635252
Yeovil	01935-415291
Bedfordshire	01234-841212
Voice bank	01426-925682
Bedford	01234-271212
Dunstable	01582-471212
Luton	01582-401212
Cambridgeshire	01480-456111
Voice bank	01426-950160
Ely	01353-662392
Hinching Brook	01480 456111
Cheshire	01244-350000
Voice bank	01426-955487
Chester	01244-350222
Crewe	01270-500222
Ellesmere Port	0151-355 4066
Macclesfield	01625-610000
Northwich	01606-48000
Runcorn	01928-713456
Warrington	01925-652222
Widnes	0151-424 7431
Wilmslow	01625-536222
Cleveland	01642-326326
Guisborough/Hartlepool/	
Middlesbrough	01642-326326
Cumbria	01768-64411
Voice bank	01426-972830
Carlisle	01228-28191
Cockermouth	01900-823212
Ulverston	01229-583311
Derbyshire	01773-570100
Voice bank	01426-955020
Alfreton	01773-830000
Buxton	01298-72100
Chesterfield	01246-220100
Derby	01332-290100
Ilkeston	0115-944 0100
Matlock	01629-580100
Devon & Cornwall	01392-52101
Voice bank	01392-452198
Barnstaple	01271-73101
Camborne	01209-714881
Exeter	01392-52101
Launceston	01566-774211
Paignton	01803-555201
Plymouth	01752-701188
Scilly Isles	01720-422444
Dorset	01929-462727
Voice bank	01426-932345
Bournemouth/Poole	01202-552099
Dorchester	01305-251212
Durham	0191-386 4929

Voice bank	01426-984458
Chester-le-Street	0191-388 4311
Newton Aycliffe	01325-314401
Essex	01245-491491
Voice bank	01426-925680
Basildon	01268-532212
Chelmsford	01245-491212
Colchester	01206-762212
Grays	01375-391212
Harlow	01279-641212
Southend	01702-431212
Gloucestershire	01242-521321
Voice bank	01242-276154
Cheltenham	01242-521321
Gloucester	01452-521201
Guernsey	01481-725111
Hampshire & Isle of Wight	01962-868133
Voice bank	01426-932024
Isle of Wight	01983-528000
Portsmouth	01705-321111
Southampton	01703-581111
Whitchurch	01256-892999
Hertfordshire	01707-331177
Voice bank	01426-934068
Hemel Hempstead	01442-277000
Hertford	01992-533000
St Albans	01707-354000
Stevenage	01438-757000
Watford	01923-472000
Humberside	01482-26111
Voice bank	01426-978223
Hull (Priory)	01482-649231
Scunthorpe	01724-282888
Isle of Man	01624-631212
Jersey	01534-612612
Kent	01622-690690
Voice bank	01622-683932
Ashford	01233-611055
Canterbury	01227-762055
Dartford	01322-280055
Dover	01304-240055
Folkestone	01303-850055
Gillingham	01634-260055
Gravesend	01474-331055
Maidstone	01622-690055
Margate	01843-231055
Medway	01634-827055
Sevenoaks	01732-740055
Sittingbourne	01795-477055
Tunbridge Wells	01892-511055
Lancashire	01772-614444
Voice bank	01772-618194
Blackburn	01254-51212
Blackpool	01253-293933
Chorley	01257-269021
Colne	01282-863161
Lancaster	01524-63333
Preston	01772-203203
Leicestershire	0116-253 0066
Coalville	01530-836300
Hinckley	01455-637881
Leicester	0116-253 0066
Loughborough	01509-231111
Melton Mowbray	01664-63676

Lincolnshire	01522-532222	Stafford	01785-58151
Voice bank	01426-957180	Stoke-on-Trent	01782-744644
Boston	01205-366222	Tamworth	01827-61001
Gainsborough	01427-810910	**Suffolk**	01473-613500
Grantham	01476-62501	Voice bank	01426-932403
Lincoln	01522-529911	Felixstowe	01473-383300
Skegness	01754-762222	Ipswich	01473-383100
City of London	0171-601-2222	Lowestoft	01986-835100
London - Metropolitan Police	0171-230 1212	Newmarket	01284-774400
24-hour press bureau	0171-230 2171	**Surrey**	01483-571212
Voice bank	0891-900099	Voice bank	01426-953808
Facility requests	0171-230 3301	Guildford	01483-31111
Area HQ press officers:		Reigate	01737-765040
1 North (at Edmonton)	0181-345 4075	Woking	01483-761991
2 East (at Wanstead)	0171-275 4125	**Sussex (East & West)**	01273-475432
3 South East (at Eltham)	0181-853 8071	Voice bank	01273-479221
4 South (at Norbury)	0181-649 1705	Brighton	01273-606744
5 South West (at Kingston)	0181-546 1212	Chichester	01243-536733
6 West (at Notting Dale)	0171-246 0052	Crawley	01293-524242
7 North West (at Harrow)	0181-733 4072	Eastbourne	01323-412299
8 Westminster (Cannon Row)	0171-321 7237	East Grinstead	01342-321155
Aliens Registration Office	0171-230 1208	Gatwick Airport	01293-531122
Firearms Unit	0171-488 5212	Hastings	01424-425000
Public Carriage Office	0171-230 1632	Worthing	01903-231821
Greater Manchester	0161-872 5050	**Thames Valley**	01865-846000
Voice bank	0891-335559	Voice bank	01426-932012
Bolton	01204-522466	High Wycombe	01296-396000
Bury/Manchester/Salford/		Milton Keynes	01908-686000
Stockport/Trafford	0161-872 5050	Newbury	01635-31000
Oldham	0161-624 0444	Oxford	01865-266000
Rochdale	01706-47401	Reading	01734-536000
Tameside	0161-330 8321	Slough/Windsor	01753-506000
Wigan	01942-244981	**Warwickshire**	01926-415000
Merseyside	0151-709 6010	Voice bank	01426-952404
Voice bank	0891-557725	Bedworth	01203-643111
All stations (including Birkenhead,		Leamington Spa	01926-451111
Southport & Wallasey)	0151-709 6010	Nuneaton	01203-641111
Norfolk	01603-768769	Rugby	01788-541111
Voice bank	01426-952342	Stratford-on-Avon	01789-414111
Gt Yarmouth	01493-336200	**West Mercia**	01905-723000
Kings Lynn	01553-691211	Voice bank	01426-913005
Norwich	01603-768769	Bridgnorth	01952-290888
Northamptonshire	01604-700700	Bromsgrove	01527-579888
Voice bank	01426-952401	Droitwich	01905-794888
Corby	01536-400400	Hereford	01432-276422
Daventry	01327-300300	Malvern	01905-723888
Kettering	01536-411411	Redditch	01527-584888
Northampton	01604-700700	Shrewsbury	01743-232888
Wellingborough	01933-440333	Stourport-on-Severn	01562-820888
Northumbria	01661-872555	Worcester	01905-723888
Voice bank	01426-979793	**West Midlands**	0121-626 5000
Alnwick/Berwick/Hexham/		Voice bank	01426-952009
Ponteland	01661-872555	Aston	0121-322 6000
Newcastle/N Shields/Gateshead	0191-232 3451	Bournville	0121-626 4000
Sunderland/South Shields	0191-510 2020	Brierley Hill	0121-626 8020
Nottinghamshire	0115-967 0999	Coventry	01203-539000
Voice bank	01426-957125	Dudley	0121-626 8000
Hucknall	0115-968 0999	Rose Road	0121-428 6000
Mansfield	01623-420999	Sheldon	0121-626 7000
Nottingham	0115-948 2999	Solihull	0121-712 6000
Staffordshire	01785-57717	Steelhouse Lane	0121-626 6000
Voice bank	01785-232525	Walsall	01922-439000
Cannock	01543-574545	Wednesfield	01902-649020
Newcastle-under-Lyme	01782-717071	West Bromwich	0121-626 9000

Wiltshire	01380-722341	Glasgow: Central (Stuart St)	0141-332 1113
Voice bank	01426-961045	Aikenhead Rd	0141-422 1113
Chippenham	01249-654455	Bridgeton	0141-554 1113
Salisbury	01722-411444	Clydebank	0141-941 1113
Swindon	01793-528111	Govan	0141-445 1113
Yorkshire - North	01609-783131	Maryhill	0141-946 1113
Voice bank	01426-979568	Northern	0141-552 6333
Harrogate	01423-505541	Paisley	0141-889 1113
Malton	01653-692424	Greenock	01475-724444
Richmond	01748-823055	Hamilton	01698-286303
Scarborough	01723-500300	Kilmarnock	01563-21188
Selby	01757-702596	Motherwell	01698-266144
Skipton	01756-793377	**Tayside**	01382-23200
York	01904-631321	Dundee	01382-23200
Yorkshire - South	0114-276 8522	Forfar	01307-462551
Voice bank	01426-952018	Perth	01738-21141
Barnsley	01226-206161		
Doncaster	01302-366744		
Rotherham	01709-828182	**Wales**	
Sheffield	0114-276 8522	**Dyfed/Powys**	01267-236444
Yorkshire - West	01924-375222	Aberystwyth	01970-612791
Voice bank	01426-979656	Ammanford	01269-592222
Bradford	01274-723422	Brecon	01874-622331
Halifax	01422-337033	Carmarthen	01267-232000
Huddersfield	01484-422122	Haverfordwest	01437-763355
Keighley	01535-604261	Llanelli	01554-772222
Leeds	0113-243 5353	Newtown	01686-625704
Wakefield	01924-375222	Pembroke Dock	01646-682121
		Gwent	01633-838111
		Voice bank	01426-950026
Scotland		Blackwood	01495-223673
Central		Newport	01633-244999
Falkirk	01324-634212	Pontypool	01495-764711
Stirling	01786-456000	**North Wales**	01492-517171
Dumfries & Galloway	01387-52112	Voice bank	01426-950443
Wigtown	01776-2112	Caernarfon	01286-673333
Fife	01592-652611	Llandudno	01492-860260
Cupar	01334-52226	Prestatyn	01745-852341
Dunfermline	01383-726711	Wrexham	01978-290222
Kirkcaldy	01592-204444	**South Wales**	01656-655555
Grampian	01224-639111	Voice bank	01656-869291
Voice bank	01224-639333	Cardiff	01222-222111
Aberdeen	01224-639111	Pontypridd	01443-485351
Bucksburn	01224-712811	Port Talbot	01639-883101
Elgin	01343-543101	Swansea	01792-456999
Lothian & Borders	0131-311 3131		
Dalkeith	0131-663 2855		
Edinburgh: central	0131-662-5000	**Northern Ireland**	
Leith	0131-554 9350	**Royal Ulster Constabulary**	01232-650222
West End	0131-229 2323	Voice bank	01232-700085
Hawick	01450-75051	Antrim	01849-463555
Livingston	01506-31200	Armagh	01861-523311
Northern	01463-715555	Ballymena, Antrim	01266-653355
Dingwall	01349-62444	Belfast	01232-650222
Fort William	01397-702361	Coleraine, Londonderry	01265-44122
Inverness	01463-715555	Cookstown, Tyrone	01648-766000
Kirkwall, Orkney	01856-872241	Derry	01504-367337
Lerwick, Shetland	01595-2110	Dungannon, Tyrone	018687-52525
Stornoway, Western Isles	01851-702222	Enniskillen, Fermanagh	01365-322823
Wick	01955-3551	Larne, Antrim	01574-272266
Strathclyde	0141-204 2626	Lurgan, Armagh	01762-325144
Ayr	01292-266966	Newtownards, Down	01247-818080
Coatbridge	01236-420155	Newry, Down	01693-65500
Dumbarton	01389-63311	Portadown, Armagh	01762-332424

FIRE BRIGADES

Fire brigades are run by county councils and the larger metropolitan authorities. In England and Wales, standards are set by the Fire and Emergency Planning Department at the Home Office. Fire service standards are supervised by the Fire Service Inspectorate, also at the Home Office. It inspects each fire brigade annually. In Scotland, these functions are overseen by the Scottish Office Home Department, and in Northern Ireland by the local Department of the Environment. See The Fire Directory, published by FMJ International (01737-768611).

England

Avon	0117-926 2061
Bedfordshire	01234-351081
Berkshire	01734-452888
Buckinghamshire	01296-24666
Cambridgeshire	01480-454651
Channel Islands · Guernsey	01481-724491
Jersey	01534-37444
Cheshire	01244-322633
Cleveland	01429-872311
Cornwall	01872-73117
Cumbria	01900-822503
Derbyshire	01332-771221
Devon	01392-873711
Dorset	01305-251133
Durham	0191-384 3381
Essex	01277-222531
Gloucestershire	01242-512041
Hampshire	01703-620000
Hereford & Worcester	01905-24454
Hertfordshire	01992-584900
Humberside	01482-565333
Isle of Man	01624-673333
Isle of Wight	01983-525121
Isles of Scilly	01872-73117
Kent	01622-692121
Lancashire	01772-862545
Leicestershire	0116-287 2241
Lincolnshire	01522-533361
London · HQ	0171-582 3811
Press	0171-587 4063
HQ Central Operations	0171-587 4803
Greater Manchester	0161-736 5866
Merseyside	0151-227-4466
Norfolk	01603-810351
Northamptonshire	01604-797000
Northumberland	01670-513161
Nottinghamshire	0115-967 0880
Oxfordshire	01865-842999
Shropshire	01743-260200
Somerset	01823-337222
Staffordshire	01785-813234
Suffolk	01473-725363
Surrey	01737-242444
Sussex · East	01273-406000
Sussex · West	01243-786211
Tyne and Wear	0191-232 1224
Warwickshire	01926-423231
West Midlands	0121-380 6906
Wiltshire	01722-334288
Yorkshire · North	01609-780150
Yorkshire · South	0114-272 7202
Yorkshire · West	01274-682311

Wales

Clwyd	01745-343431
Dyfed	01267-221444
Glamorgan · Mid	01443-237777
Glamorgan · South	01222-498602
Glamorgan · West	01792-310919
Gwent	01495-757921
Gwynedd	01286-673811
Powys	01982-553576

Scotland

Central	01324-716996
Dumfries & Galloway	01387-52222
Fife	01592-774451
Grampian	01224-696666
Highlands & Islands	01463-222722
Lothian & Borders	0131-228 2401
Strathclyde	01698-284200
Tayside	01382-322222

Northern Ireland

NI Fire Brigade HQ (Lisburn)	01846-664221
A Division (Belfast)	01232-310360
B Division (Bangor)	01247-271906
C Division (Portadown)	01762-332222
D Division (Derry)	01504-311162
E Division (Ballymena)	01266-43370
F Division (Omagh)	01662-241190

Support organisations

Home Office	0171-273 3000
Fire/Emergency Planning Dept	0171-273 2845
Chief Fire Officers Association	01827-61516
Fire Brigades Union	0181-541 1765
Fire Research Station	0181-953 6177
Fire Service College	01608-50831
Fire Service Inspectorate	0171-217 8728
Institution of Fire Engineers	0116-255 3654
NI Environment Dept	01232-540540
Scottish Office Home Dept	0131-556 8400

AMBULANCE SERVICES

Ambulance services are part of the NHS and administered in England by the Department of Health, in Wales by the Welsh Office, in Scotland by the Scottish Office Home and Health Department and in Northern Ireland by the Department of Health and Social Services. In England and Wales ambulances are the responsibility of the local health authority or NHS trusts. Scottish ambulances are run by the Scottish Ambulance Service and in N Ireland by four Health and Social Services Boards.

England

Avon	0117-927 7046
Bedfordshire (+ Herts)	01234-270099
Berkshire	01734-771200
Bucks (Two Shire Trust)	01908-262422
Cambridgeshire	01223-411444
Channel Islands · Guernsey	01481-725211
Jersey	01534-80999
Cheshire (Mersey Trust)	01244-364567
Cleveland	01642-850888
Cornwall (Westcountry Trust)	01872-78181
Cumbria	01228-596909
Derbyshire	01332-372441
Devon (Westcountry Trust)	01392-434222
Dorset	01202-896111
Durham	0191-386 4488
Essex	01245-443344
Gloucestershire	01452-395050
Hampshire	01962-860421
Hereford & Worcester	01886-834200
Hertfordshire (+ Beds)	01234-270099
Humberside	01482-561191
Isle of Man	01624-663322
Isle of Wight	01983-821655
Kent	01622-747010
Lancashire	01772-862666
Leicestershire	0116-275 0700
Lincolnshire	01522-545171
London	0171-928 0333
Greater Manchester	0161-231 7921
Merseyside	0151-260 5220
Norfolk	01603-424255
Northants (Two Shires Trust)	01908-262422
Northumbria	0191-273 1212
Nottinghamshire	0115-929 6151
Oxfordshire	01865-225577
Scilly Isles	01720-22392
Shropshire	01743-364061
Somerset (Westcountry Trust)	01823-278114
Staffordshire	01785-53521
Suffolk	01473-749333
Surrey	01737-353333
Sussex · East	01323-410434
Sussex · West	01243-532866
Warwickshire	01926-881331
West Midlands	01384-455644
Wiltshire	01249-443939
Yorkshire · North	01904-628085
Yorkshire · South	01709-820520

Wales

Clwyd	01352-700227
East Dyfed	01267-233232
Glamorgan · Mid	01443-217005
Glamorgan · South	01222-552011
Glamorgan · West	01792-651501
Gwent	01633-421521
Gwynedd	01286-674811
Pembrokeshire	01437-774281
Powys	01686-627788

Scotland

Headquarters (Edinburgh)	0131-447 7711
Control centres:	
Aberdeen	01224-662244
Ayr	01292-265061
Dundee	01382-817171
Edinburgh	0131-452 8686
Glasgow	0141-353 6111
Inverness	01463-236611
Motherwell	01698-276441
Paisley	0141-887 2168

Northern Ireland

Eastern (Belfast)	01232-795404
Northern (Antrim)	01849-428911
Southern (Portadown)	01762-335121
Western (Derry)	01504-48063

Support organisations

Ambulance Service Institute	01962-860421
Assoc of Ambulance Personnel	01749-344044
BASICS	01473-218407
British Red Cross	0171-235 5454
Cruse · Bereavement Care	0181-940 4818
Royal Life Saving Society	01527-853943
St Andrews Ambulance Assoc	0141-332 4031
St John Ambulance	0171-235 5231
Unison	01737-353322

HOSPITALS

The National Health Service employs over a million staff, occupies 46,000 acres of land and runs 1,600 hospitals. Until 1991 the hospitals were run by 160 district health authorities and overseen by regional health authorities The 1990 NHS and Community Care Act permitted the creation of quango style trusts to provide services to the NHS on a contractural basis. Nearly all hospitals are now run by trusts which are super-vised at arms-length by the NHS Management Executive. The number of RHAs has been reduced from fourteen to eight and their role will eventually be taken over by eight regional offices of the Management Executive.

Below are the hospitals with an accident and emergency department and some acute hospitals in larger towns without an emergency hospital.

Department of Health	0171-210 3000
Press officers	0171-210 5222-9

England

Avon

Bath (Royal United)	01225-428331
Bristol (Frenchay)	0117-970 1212
Bristol (Royal Infirmary)	0117-923 0000
Bristol (Southmead)	0117-950 5050
Weston-super-Mare	01934-636363

Bedfordshire

Bedford	01234-355122
Luton & Dunstable	01582-491122

Berkshire

Ascot (Heatherwood)	01344-23333
Slough (Wexham Park)	01753-633000

Buckinghamshire

Aylesbury (Stoke Mandeville)	01296-315000
High Wycombe (Wycombe)	01494-526161

Cambridgeshire

Cambridge (Addenbrooke's)	01223-245151
Huntingdon (Hinchingbrooke)	01480-416416
Peterborough	01733-874000

Channel Islands

Guernsey (Princess Elizabeth)	01481-725241
Jersey General	01534-59000

Cheshire

Chester (Countess)	01244-365000
Crewe (Leighton)	01270-255141
Macclesfield	01625-421000
Northwich (Victoria)	01606-74331
Warrington	01925-635911

Cleveland

Hartlepool	01429-266654
Middlesborough	01642-850222
North Tees	01642-617617

Cornwall

Penzance (West Cornwall)	01736-62382
Truro (Treviske)	01872-74242

Cumbria

Carlisle (Cumberland)	01228-23444
Furness, Cumbria	01229-870870

Derbyshire

Chesterfield	01246-277271
Derby (Derbyshire Royal)	01332-347141

Devon

Barnstaple (North Devon)	01271-22577
Exeter (Royal Devon)	01392-411611
Plymouth (Derriford)	01752-777111
Torbay	01803-614567

Dorset

Poole	01202-665511
Weymouth	01305-60022

Durham

Bishop Auckland, Co Durham	01388-604040
Darlington, Co Durham	01325-380100
Durham (Dryburn)	0191-333 2333
Shotley Bridge	01207-583583

Essex

Basildon, Essex	01268-533911
Chelmsford (Broomfield)	01245-440761
Epping (St Margarets)	01992-561666
Essex County	01206-853535
Harlow (Princess Alexandra)	01279-444455
Harold Wood, Essex	01708-345533
Rochford/Southend	01702-435555

Gloucestershire

Cheltenham	01242-222222
Gloucester (Glos Royal)	01452-528555

Hampshire

Basingstoke	01256-473202
Portsmouth (Queen Alexandra)	01705-379451
Southampton	01703-777222

Winchester (Royal Hampshire)	01962-863535

Hereford & Worcester

Hereford	01432-355444
Kidderminster	01562-823424
Redditch (Alexandra)	01527-503030
Worcester Royal Infirmary	01905-763333

Hertfordshire

Hemel Hempstead	01442-213141
Stevenage (Lister)	01438-314333
Welwyn Garden City (Queen Elizabeth II)	01707-328111
Watford	01923-244366

Humberside

Bridlington	01262-606666
Grimsby	01472-874111
Hull (Royal Infirmary)	01482-328541
Scunthorpe	01724-282282

Isle of Man

Douglas (Noble's)	01624-642642

Isle of Wight

Newport (St Mary's)	01983-524081

Kent

Ashford (William Harvey)	01233-633331
Canterbury (Kent & Canterbury)	01227-766877
Dartford (West Hill)	01322-223223
Gillingham (Medway)	01634-830000
Maidstone	01622-729000
Margate (Thanet)	01843-225544
Tunbridge Wells (Kent/Sussex)	01892-526111

Lancashire

Blackburn (Royal)	01254-263555
Blackpool (Victoria)	01253-300000
Burnley	01282-425071
Lancaster	01524-65944
Leigh	01942-672333
Ormskirk	01695-577111
Preston (Royal)	01772-716565
Southport	01704-547471

Leicestershire

Leicester	0116-254 1414

Lincolnshire

Boston (Pilgrim)	01205-364801
Grantham	01476-65232
Lincoln (County)	01522-512512
Louth (County)	01507-600100
Stamford	01780-64151

London - Emergency

Acton (Central Middlesex)	0181-965 5733
Ashford	01784-884488
Barnet	0181-440 5111
Bromley	0181-289 7000
Camberwell (Kings College)	0171-737 4000
Carshalton (St Helier)	0181-644 4343
City (St Bartholomew's)	0171-601 8888
Ealing	0181-574 2444
Edgware	0181-952 2381
Edmonton (North Middlesex)	0181-887 2000
Enfield (Chase Farm)	0181-366 6600
Euston (University College)	0171-387 9300
Fulham (Charing Cross)	0181-846 1234
Greenwich	0181-858 8141
Hammersmith	0181-743 2030
Hampstead (Royal Free)	0171-794 0500
Harrow (Northwick)	0181-864 3232
Highgate (Whittington)	0171-272 3070
Hillingdon	01895-238282
Homerton	0181-919 5555
Ilford (King George)	0181-554 8811
Isleworth (West Middlesex)	0181-560 2121
Kingston	0181-546 7711
Lambeth (St Thomas's)	0171-928 9292
Lewisham	0181-333 3000
Leytonstone (Whipps Cross)	0181-539 5522
Newham	0171-476 4000
North Kensington (St Charles)	0181-969 2488
Paddington (St Mary's)	0171-725 6666
Roehampton (Queen Mary's)	0181-789 6611
Romford (Oldchurch)	01708-746090
Sidcup (Queen Mary's)	0181-302 2678
Southwark (Guy's)	0171-955 5000
Thornton Heath (Mayday)	0181-401 3000
Tooting (St George's)	0181-672 1255
Wembley	0181-903 1323
Westminster, SW1	0181-746 8000
Whitechapel (Royal London)	0171-377 7000
Woolwich (Brook)	0181-856 5555

London - Non-emergency

Brompton Heart, SW3	0171-352 8121
Eastman Dental, WC1	0171-915 1000
Eliz. Garrett Anderson, NW1	0171-387 2501
Gt Ormond St Children's, WC1	0171-405 9200
London Homeopathic, WC1	0171-837 8833
Maudsley, SE5	0171-703 6333
Middlesex, W1	0171-636 8333
Moorfield's Eye, EC1	0171-253 3411
National Orthopaedic	0181-954 2300
Neurology, WC1	0171-837 3611
Royal Marsden, SW3	0171-352 8171
Throat, Nose & Ear, WC1	0171-837 8855
Tropical Diseases, NW1	0171-387 4411

Greater Manchester

Ashton-under-Lyme (Tameside)	0161-331 6000
Bolton	01204-522444
Bury	0161-764 6081
Manchester Royal Infirmary	0161-276 1234
North Manchester	01161-795 4567
Royal Oldham	0161-624 0420
Rochdale Infirmary	01706-377777

Salford (Hope)	0161-789 7373
South Manchester (Withington)	01161-445 8111
Stockport	0161-483 1010
Wigan (Royal Albert Edward)	01942-244000
Wythenshawe	0161-998 7070

Merseyside
Liverpool (Alder Hay Children's)	0151-228 4811
Liverpool (Broadgreen)	0151-228 4878
Liverpool (Royal)	0151-709 0141
Liverpool (Walton)	0151-525 3611
Whiston	0151-426 1600
Wirral	0151-678 5111

Norfolk
Gt Yarmouth (James Paget)	01493-452452
Kings Lynn (Queen Elizabeth)	01553-766266
Norfolk & Norwich	01603-286286

Northamptonshire
Kettering	01536-492000
Northampton	01604-34700

Northumberland
Ashington, Northumberland	01670-812541
Hexham, Northumberland	01434-606161

Nottinghamshire
Mansfield	01623-22515
Newark	01636-73841
Nottingham (City)	0115-969 1169
Nottingham (University)	0115-249924
Worksop	01909-500990

Oxfordshire
Banbury (Horton)	01295-275500
Headington (John Radcliffe)	01865-741166

Shropshire
Shrewsbury	01743-261000

Somerset
Bridgwater	01278-451501
Minehead	01643-707251
Taunton (Musgrove)	01823-333444
Yeovil	01935-75122

Staffordshire
Burton-upon-Trent	01283-66333
Stafford	01785-57731
Stoke-on-Trent(North Staffs)	01782-715444

Suffolk
Ipswich	01473-712233
West Suffolk	01284-713000

Surrey
Ashford	01784-884488
Chertsey (St Petr's)	.01932-872000
Camberley (Frimley Park)	01276-692777

Epsom	01372-735735
Guildford (Royal Surrey)	01483-571122
Redhill (East Surrey)	01737-768511

Sussex - East
Brighton (Royal Sussex)	01273-696955
Eastbourne	01323-417400
Hastings (Conquest)	01424-755255

Sussex - West
Chichester (St Richard's)	01243-788122
Haywards Heath (Princess Royal)	01444-441881
Worthing	01903-205111

Tyne & Wear
Gateshead (Queen Elizabeth)	0191-487 8989
Newcastle	0191-273 8811
Newcastle (Royal Victoria)	0191-232 5131
North Tyneside	0191-259 6660
South Tyneside (South Shields)	0191-454 8888
Sunderland	0191-565 6256

Warwickshire
Nuneaton (George Eliot)	01203-351351
Rugby (St Cross)	01788-572831
Warwick(South Warwickshire)	01926-495321

West `Midlands
B'ham Accident (Selly Oak)	0121-627 1627
Birmingham (Dudley Road)	0121-554 3801
Birmingham (Hartland)	0121-766 6611
Coventry & Warwick	01203-224055
Dudley (Russells Hall)	01384-456111
Solihul	0121-711 4455
Sutton Coldfield (Good Hope)	0121-378 2211
West Bromwich (Sandwell)	0121-553 1831
Wolverhampton (Royal)	01902-307999

Wiltshire
Salisbury	01722-336262
Swindon (Princess Margaret)	01793-536231

Yorkshire -North
Harrogate	01423-885959
Northallerton (Friarage)	01609-779911
Scarborough	01723-368111
York	01904-631313

Yorkshire -South
Barnsley	01226-730000
Doncaster (Royal Infirmary)	01302-366666
Rotherham Hospital	01709-820000
Sheffield (Children's)	0114-276 1111
Sheffield (Northern General)	0114-243 4343
Sheffield (Royal Hallamshire)	0114-276 6222

Yorkshire - West
Bradford (Royal)	01274-542200
Dewsbury	01924-465105
Halifax	01422-357222

Huddersfield (Royal Informary)	01484-422191
Keighley (Airedale)	01535-652511
Leeds (General Infirmary)	0113-243 2799
Leeds (St James's University)	0113-243 3144
Pontefract	01977-600600
Wakefield(Pinderfields)	01924-201688

Scottish hospitals

Borders
Melrose (Borders General) — 01896-754333

Central
Falkirk (Royal) — 01324-624000
Stirling (Royal) — 01786-434000

Dumfries & Galloway
Dumfries (Royal Infirmary) — 01387-246246

Fife
Dunfermline (Queen Margarets) — 01383-623623

Grampian
Aberdeen (Royal) — 01224-681818

Highland
Inverness (Raigmore) — 01463-704000

Lothian
Edinburgh (Eastern General) — 0131-536 7000
Edinburgh (Royal Infirmary) — 0131-536 1000
Edinburgh (Western General) — 0131-537 1000
Livingston (St John's) — 01506-419666

Orkney
Kirkwall (Balfour) — 01856-872763

Shetland
Lerwick (Gilbert Bain) — 01595-695678

Strathclyde
Airdrie (Monklands) — 01236-748748
Ayr — 01292-610555
Carluke (Law) — 01698-351100
East Kilbride (Hairmyres) — 01355-220292
Glasgow (Royal Infirmary) — 0141-211 4000
Glasgow (Sick Children) — 0141-201 0000
Glasgow (Southern) — 0141-201 1100
Glasgow (Stobhill) — 0141-201 3000
Glasgow (Victoria Infirmary) — 0141-201 6000
Glasgow (Western Infirmary) — 0141-211 2000
Greenock (Inverclyde) — 01475-633777
Kilmarnock (Crosshouse) — 01563-521133
Paisley (Royal Alexandra) — 0141-887 9111

Tayside
Brechin (Stracathro) — 01356-647291
Dundee (Royal Infirmary) — 01382-223125
Perth (Royal) — 01738-623311

Western Isles
Stornoway (Western Isles) — 01851-704704

Welsh hospitals

Clwyd
Rhyl (Clwyd) — 01745-583910

Dyfed
Aberystwyth (Bronglais) — 01970-623131
Carmarthen (West Wales) — 01267-235151
Haverfordwest (Withybush) — 01437-764545
Llanelli (Prince Phillip) — 01554-756567

Glamorgan - Mid
Bridgend (Princess of Wales) — 01656-752752
Merthyr Tydfil (Prince Charles) — 01685-721721
Pontypridd (East Glamorgan) — 01443-218218

Glamorgan - West
Swansea (Singleton) — 01792-205666

Gwent
Abergavenny (Neill Hall) — 01873-852091
Newport (Royal Gwent) — 01633-234234

Gwynedd
Bangor (Gwynedd) — 01248-384384
Llandudno — 01492-860066

Northern Ireland

Antrim
Ballymena (Wavney) — 01266-653377
Belfast City — 01232-329241
Belfast (Musgrave Park) — 01232-669501
Belfast (Royal Victoria) — 01232-240503
Belfast (Ulster) — 01232-484511
Larne (Moyle) — 01574-275431
Lisburn (Lagan Valley) — 01846-665141
Newtownabbey (Whiteabbey) — 01232-865181
Newtownards (Ards) — 01247-812661

Armagh
Craigavon — 01762-334444
Down
Newry (Daisy Hill) — 01693-65511
Fermanagh
Enniskillen (Erne) — 01365-324711
Londonderry
Coleraine — 01265-44177
Derry (Altnagelvin) — 01504-45171
Magheragelt (Mid-Ulster) — 01648-31031
Tyrone
Dungannon (South Tyrone) — 01868-722821
Omagh (Tyrone County) — 01662-245211

Military hospitals

Army

Cambridge (Aldershot)	01252-22521
Duchess of Kent, Catterick	01748-832521
Queen Elizabeth, Woolwich	0181-856 5533

Navy

Haslar, Gosport	01705-584255
Plymouth (Royal Naval)	01752-229363

RAF

PrincessAlexandra, Swindon	01793-812291
Princess Mary's, Wendover	01296-623535

Special hospitals

Ashworth, Merseyside	0151-473 0303
Carstairs, Lanark	01555-840293
Broadmoor, Berkshire	01344-773111
Rampton, Nottinghamshire	01777-248321

COASTGUARD & LIFEBOATS

HM Coastguard is responsible for initiating and co-ordinating search and rescue operations in the seas around the UK, and on the cliffs and shoreline. It is the first point of contact for any kind of maritime emergency. When an accident occurs, the Coastguard can call on RNLI lifeboats (see below), and military and civilian aircraft, helicopters and ships to provide assistance. The Coastguard has some aircraft and boats of its own as well. There are also 370 teams of 3,500 volunteer Auxiliary Coastguards who carry out rescues on cliffs and beaches. Seafarers in distress normally make radio calls on Channel 16, the distress and safety channel, which is monitored constantly by the Coastguard. In 1993 the Coastguard handled 9,611 incidents involving 17,106 people and assisting 3,754 vessels.

Day-to-day HM Coastguard operations are run from six regional Maritime Rescue Co-ordination Centres (MRCCs) and their subsidiary Maritime Rescue Sub-Centres (MRSCs). There are 21 of these MRCCs and MRSCs (listed below) around the UK coast, all staffed 24-hours a day, and each with a Publicity Liaison Officer who can talk to the press.

Each district has its coastline divided into sectors, run by a full-time sector officer, one of whose main tasks is to co-ordinate the work of the Auxiliaries in the area.

The work of Coastguards is administered by the Coastguard Agency on behalf of the Department of Transport. The Agency's aim is to: "minimise loss of life at sea and on the coasts of the UK; and minimise pollution from ships to the seas and coastline of the UK." The first of these roles is carried out by HM Coastguard, the second by the Marine Pollution Control Unit.The MPCU has equipment stockpiles at Stirling, Ipswich, Milford Haven and Buttonwood (Lancs). It has aircraft for aerial spraying and remote sensing at Inverness and Coventry.

The Coastguard Agency operates from new offices in Southampton which it shares with the Marine Safety Agency. Much of Britain's official control over marine emergencies and contingency building have thus been centralised. The Safety Agency is responsible for: implementing the government's strategy for marine safety and prevention of pollution from ships; developing and enforcing high standards of marine safety; inspecting ships in UK ports to ensure they comply with safety, pollution and operational standards; and managing the official Register of Shipping and Seamen.

Coastguard Agency
Marine Safety Agency
Spring Place, 105 Commercial Road, Southampton SO15 1EG.

Agency	01703-329100
Press	01703-329401
Press · Dept of Transport	0171-276 0888
Eves	0171-276 5999

HM Coastguard centres

North and East Scotland
Covers northern North Sea, from Scottish border north and then west to Cape Wrath, including oil and gas installations.

MRCC, Aberdeen: Ops	01224-592334
Press	01224-581206
MRSCs:	
Shetland: Ops	01595-692976
Admin	01595-693611
Pentland: Ops	01856-873268
Admin	01856-873632
Forth: Ops	01333-450666
Admin	01333-450822

Eastern

Covers southern North Sea, from Scottish border to Aldeburgh, including oil and gas installations.

MRCC, Yarmouth: Ops	01493-851338
Admin	01493-852309

MRSCs:

Tyne Tees: Ops	0191-257 2691
Admin	0191-257 2681
Humber: Ops	01262-672317
Admin	01262-606905

South Eastern

Covers south east coast from Aldeburgh to the Hampshire/Dorset border. Runs the Channel Navigation Information Service (the traffic separation scheme operating in the eastern English Channel, the busiest shipping lane in the world).

MRCC, Dover: Ops	01304-210008
Admin	01304-852515

MRSCs:

Thames (Walton): Ops	01255-675518
Admin	01255-675518
Solent	01705-551308

South Western

Covers western Channel round to near Hartland Point, plus the south west Atlantic approaches.

MRCC, Falmouth: Ops	01326-317575
Admin	01326-318103

MRSCs:

Portland: Ops	01305-760439
Admin	01305-760695
Brixham: Ops	01803-882704
Admin	01803-882702

Western

Covers Bristol Channel north from Hartland, plus Irish Sea (excluding Northern Ireland coastal waters) and western Atlantic approaches.

MRCC, Swansea: Ops	01792-366534
Admin	01792-361130

MRSCs:

Milford Haven: Ops	01646-690909
Admin	01646-692174
Holyhead: Ops	01407-762051
Admin	01407-764349
Liverpool:Ops	0151-931 3343
Admin	0151-931 3351

West Scotland and Northern Ireland

Covers Northern Ireland and west of Scotland coasts, plus north western Atlantic approaches.

MRCC, Clyde: Ops	01475-729988
Admin	01475-888588

MRSCs:

Belfast: Ops	01247-463933
Admin	01247-452997
Oban: Ops	01631-564444
Admin	01631-564444
Stornoway: Ops	01851-702013
Admin	01851-706961

Lifeboats

The Royal National Lifeboat Institution (RNLI) is supported entirely by public donations. It has saved over 123,000 lives since it was set up in 1824. The RNLI operates 210 lifeboat stations around the British Isles. It has a total of 278 operational boats, plus about 100 relief vessels. Each lifeboat station is run by a voluntary committee, whose honorary secretary authorises the launch of the boat, usually on the request of the local Coastguard. Larger lifeboats may have a paid mechanic or coxswain/mechanic; otherwise nearly all the crews are volunteers. During rescue operations the lifeboat is controlled by the coxswain, in liaison with the local Coastguard MRCC. The RNLI likes all press enquiries to go to its press office at its head-quarters in Poole, Dorset. Out of hours, contact the central operations room.

RNLI headquarters, Poole	01202-671133
Central operations room	01202-670707

Boathouses

Below are all UK and Irish Republic stations with a large lifeboat (over 10 metres, capable of off-shore work). The numbers are mainly for the boathouses themselves, rather than officers:

Aberdeen	01224-591658
Aith, Shetland	01595-810276
Aldeburgh, Suffolk	01728-452552
Alderney, Channel Islands	01481-823456
Amble, Northumberland	01665-712460
Angle, Dyfed	01646-641204
Anstruther, Fife	01333-310526
Appledore, Devon	01237-473969
Arbroath, Tayside	01241-873235
Arklow, Wicklow	00-353402 32850
Arranmore, Donegal	00-35375 21580
Ballycotton, Cork	00-35321 646903
Ballyglass, Mayo	00-35397 82072
Baltimore, Cork	00-35328 20174
Barmouth, Gwynedd	01341-280274
Barra Island, Western Isles	01871-810307
Barrow, Cumberland	01229-820941
Barry Dock, South Glamorgan	01446-735678
Beaumaris, Gwynedd	01248-810260
Bembridge, IoW	01983-872201
Berwick-upon-Tweed	01289-306217
Blyth, Northumberland	01670-352201
Bridlington, Humberside	01262-672450
Broughty Ferry, Tayside	01382-79956
Buckie, Grampian	01542-831289
Calshot, Hants	01703-893509

Campbletown, Strathclyde	01586-552414	Poole, Dorset	01202-665607
Clogher Head, Louth	00-35341 22600	Port Erin, IoM	01624-832154
Courtmacsherry, Cork	00-35323 46111	Port St Mary, IoM	01624-835015
Cromer, Norfolk	01263-512237	Porthdinllaen, Gwynedd	01758-720241
Donaghadee, Down	01247-888556	Portpatrick, Dumfries	01776-810251
Douglas, IoM	01624-621367	Portree, Highland	01478-613610
Dover, Kent	01304-852515	Portrush, Antrim	00-353265 823201
Dun Laoghaire, Dublin	00-3531 280 2667	Pwllheli, Gwynedd	01758-612200
Dunbar, Lothian	01368-863966	Ramsey, IoM	01624-812169
Dungeness, Kent	01679-20317	Ramsgate, Kent	01843-583594
Dunmore East, Waterford	00-35351 83268	Rhyl, Clwyd	01745-344040
Eastbourne, East Sussex	01323-470206	Rosslare, Wexford	00-35353 33249
Exmouth, Devon	01395-263579	St Davids, Dyfed	01437-720215
Eyemouth, Borders	01890-750293	St Helier, Jersey	01534-24173
Falmouth, Cornwall	01326-374177	St Ives, Cornwall	01736-796422
Filey, North Yorkshire	01723-513197	St Marys, Scilly Isles	01720-22347
Fishguard, Dyfed	01348-873231	St Peter Port, Guernsey	01481-721091
Flamborough, Humberside	01262-850947	Salcombe, Devon	01548-842158
Fleetwood, Lancs	01253-874000	Scarborough, North Yorks	01723-360520
Fowey, Cornwall	01726-832156	Selsey, West Sussex	01243-602833
Fraserburgh, Grampian	01346-515162	Sennen Cove, Cornwall	01736-871222
Galway Bay, Galway	00-35399 61166	Sheerness, Kent	01795-664866
Girvan, Strathclyde	01465-4454	Sheringham, Norfolk	01263-823212
Gt Yarmouth, Norfolk	01493-662508	Shoreham, West Sussex	01273-593403
Hartlepool, Cleveland	01429-266103	Skegness, Lincs	01754-763011
Harwich, Essex	01255-502258	Stornoway, Western Isles	01851-703339
Hastings, East Sussex	01424-425502	Stromness, Orkney	01856-850279
Holyhead, Gwynedd	01407-762583	Sunderland, Tyne & Wear	0191-567 3536
Howth, Dublin	00-3531 8393311	Swanage, Dorset	01929-423237
Hoylake, Merseyside	0151-632 2103	Teesmouth, Cleveland	01642-486636
Humber	01964-650228	Tenby, Dyfed	01834-842197
Ilfracombe, Devon	01271-863771	Thurso, Highland	01847-63433
Invergordon, Highland	01349-853915	Tobermory, Strathclyde	01688-2143
Islay, Strathclyde	01496-840242	Torbay, Devon	01803-853136
Kilmore Quay, Wexford	00-35353 29690	Troon, Strathclyde	01292-314414
Kirkwall, Orkney	01856-875201	Tynemouth, Tyne & Wear	0191-259 6673
Lerwick, Shetland	01595-3827	Valentia, Kerry	00-323667 76100
Lizard, Cornwall	01326-290451	Walton, Essex	01255-675650
Llandudno, Gwynedd	01492-875777	Wells, Norfolk	01328-710230
Lochinver, Highland	01571-844513	Weymouth, Dorset	01305-785817
Longhope, Orkney	01856-70333	Whitby, North Yorkshire	01947-602216
Lowestoft, Suffolk	01502-573757	Wick, Highland	01955-3723
Lytham St Annes, Lancs	01253-736316	Wicklow	00-353404 67163
Mallaig, Highland	01687-2579	Workington, Cumberland	01900-604124
Margate, Kent	01843-221613	Yarmouth, IoW	01983-872201
Moelfre, Clwyd	01248-410367		
Montrose, Tayside	01674-674341		
Mumbles, West Glamorgan	01792-366246		
New Quay, Dyfed	01545-560311		
Newcastle, Down	01396-725138		
Newhaven, East Sussex	01273-514143		
North Sunderland, Northmblnd	01665-720370		
Oban, Strathclyde	01631-63733		
Padstow, Cornwall	01841-520667		
Penlee, Cornwall	01736-731300		
Peterhead, Grampian	01779-473331		
Plymouth, Devon	01752-662623		

Disaster struck on 6 June 1995 when Southend pier burned down

TRADE UNIONS

About twenty five million of the forty four million adults in the UK are in employment. Just under 7.3 million of them are in the sixty eight trade unions affiliated to the Trades Union Congress (TUC), with another 1.5 million belonging to just over two hundred non-TUC unions. Of those classed as "not in employment", the number who are actually unemployed is unknown. The government keeps the official figure well below three million, but other experts believe the genuine total is much higher, possibly even around five million.

With trade union membership now at its lowest level since World War Two, the TUC in March 1994 relaunched itself as a slimmed down "high profile campaigning body". The number of unions has declined, with many merging in order to cope with the effects of fewer members. The largest union, with 1.46 million members, is Unison, which was created in 1993 by combining NALGO, NUPE and COHSE. The next biggest is the TGWU (950,000), followed by the AEEU and GMB (both with 835,000) and then MSF (516,000).

One of the reasons for the rapid decline in trade unionism in the 1980s and 90s has been the reshaping of their legal environment. The Certification Office for Trade Unions and Employers Associations is the statutory body overseeing many of the legal criteria and rules applying to unions. The Comissioner for the Rights of Trade Union Members helps trade unionsts take legal action against their own union.

Main contacts

Trades Union Congress (TUC)	0171-636 4030
Scottish TUC	0141-332 4946
Wales TUC	01222-372345
Centre for Alternative Industrial and Technological Systems	0114-266 5063
Certification Office for Trade Unions & Employers Assocs	0171-210 3734
Commissioners for the Rights of Trade Union Members / Protection Against Unlawful Industrial Action	01925-415771
Industrial Society	0171-262 2401
Institute of Employment Rights	0181-677 9644
International Centre for Trade Union Rights	0171-498 4700
International Confederation of Free	
Trade Unions	00-322 224 0211
International Labour Organisation	0171-828 6401
Labour Research Dept	0171-928 3649
Public Concern at Work	0171-404 6609
Tolpuddle Martyrs Museum	01305-848237
Trade Unionists for Labour	0171-828 7788
Irish Congress of Trade Unions	01232-681726

Unions and associations

Asterisked unions belong to the TUC.

Amalgamated Engineering & Electrical Union (AEEU)*	0181-462 7755
Associated Metalworkers Union	01204-793245
Associated Society of Locomotive Engineers & Firemen (ASLEF)*	0171-431 0275
Assoc of British Professional Divers	01224-595454
Assoc of First Division Civil Servants*	0171-222 6242
Assoc of Teachers & Lecturers	0171-930 6441
Assoc of University Teachers (AUT)*	0171-221 4370
Bakers, Food & Allied Workers Union*	01707-260150
Banking, Insurance & Finance Union (BIFU)*	0181-946 9151
British Airline Pilots Assoc (BALPA)*	0181-759 9331
British Assoc of Journalists	0171-353 3003
British Assoc of Social Workers (BASW)	0121-622 3911
British Medical Assoc (BMA)	0171-387 4499
British Telecommunications Union Committee	0171-628 4914
Broadcasting, Entertainment, Cinematograph & Theatre Union (BECTU)*	0171-437 8506
Civil & Public Services Assoc (CPSA)*	0171-924 2727
Equity (British Actors Equity Assoc)*	0171-637 9311
Film Artistes Assoc*	0171-937 4567
Fire Brigades Union*	0181-541 1765
GMB*	0181-947 3131
Graphical, Paper & Media Union (GPMU; ex-NGA+SOGAT)*	01234-351521
Hospital Consultants and Specialists Assoc*	01256-771777
Inland Revenue Staff Federation*	0171-834 8254
Institute of Journalists (IOJ)	0171-252 1187

Institution of Professionals, Managers
& Specialists (ex-IPCS)* 0171-928 9951
International Transport Workers
Federation 0171-403 2733
Iron & Steel Trades Confed.* 0171-837 6691
Manufacturing Science Finance*
(MSF) 0181-871 2100
Musicians Union* 0171-582 5566
National Assoc of Colliery Overmen,
Deputies & Shotfirers* 01302-368015
National Assoc of Licensed
House Managers* 0181-947 3080
National Assoc of Probation
Officers* 0171-223 4887
National Assoc of Schoolmasters &
Union of Women Teachers* 0171-379 9499
National Assoc of Teachers in Further
& Higher Education* 0171-837 3636
National Communications Union*0181-998 2981
National Union of Civil & Public
Servants* 0171-928 9671
National Union of Insurance
Workers* 0171-405 6798
National Union of Journalists* 0171-278 7916
National Union of Marine, Aviation &
Shipping Transport Officers* 0181-989 6677
National Union of Mineworkers* 0114-276 6900
Derbyshire 01246-211091
Midland 01782-837093
North East 0191-384 3515
Scotland 0131-556 2323
South Wales 01443-404092
National Union of Rail, Maritime &
Transport Workers* 0171-387 4771
National Union of Students 0171-272 8900
National Union of Teachers* 0171-388 6191
Police Federation 0181-399 2224
Printing Trades Alliance 0171-701 1950
Prison Officers Assoc* 0181-803 0255
Professional Footballers Assoc 0161-236 0575
Royal College of Nursing 0171-409 3333
Royal College of Midwives 0171-580 6523
Scottish Prison Officers Assoc* 0131-443 8105
Society of Authors 0171-373 6642
Society of Telecom Execs* 0181-943 5181
Stable Lads Assoc 01283-211522
Transport & General Workers
Union (TGWU)* 0171-828 7788
Transport Salaried Staff Assoc* 0171-387 2101
Union of Communications Workers
(UCW)* 0171-622 9977
Union of Construction, Allied Trades
& Technicians (UCATT)* 0171-622 2442
Union of Democratic Mineworkers
(UDM) 0115-976 3468
Union of Shop, Distributive & Allied
Workers (USDAW)* 0161-224 2804
Unison (ex-NALGO+NUPE+
COHSE)* 0171-404 1884
Writers Guild* 0171-723 8074

CORPORATE

Libraries

All public reference libraries should have a business sectiion, usually holding the essential reference books listed below. Here are the three main libraries in central London.

British Library Business Information Service
25 Southampton Buildings, London WC2 1XX
Tel: 0171-323 7454

City Business Library
Corporation of London, 1 Brewers Hall Garden, London EC2V 5BX
Tel: 0171-638 8215
Recorded details 0171-480 7638
Business Information Focus 0171-600 1461
The most comprehensive of the public business libraries.

Westminster Reference Library
St Martin's Street, London WC2H 7HP
Tel: 0171-976 1285
Also runs the commercial Information for Business service.

Essential reading

Directory of Directors
A listing of the 54,000 directors controlling major companies, plus 15,000 companies and 75,000 board members.

Hambro Company Guide
Hemmington Scott Publishing
Quarterly update of all 2,300 stockmarket companies.

Key British Enterprises
Dun & Bradstreet
A directory covering the top 50,000 companies.

Macmillan's Unquoted Companies
Macmillan
20,000 companies with turnovers more than £3 million.

Stock Exchange Official Yearbook
A profile of all listed companies.

UK Kompass Register
The CBI-backed six volume directory on British industry,

Who Owns Whom
A listing of the parent and subsidiary companies of major companies.

Key contacts

ACAS (Advisory, Conciliation & Arbitration	
Service)	0171-210 3000
Press	0171-210 3642
Association of British Chambers of	
Commerce	0171-222 1555
Association of British Insurers	0171-600 3333
Banking Information Service	0171-398 0044
Bank of England	0171-601 4444
Press	0171-601 4411(-5)
Bankruptcy Association	01482-658701
British Bankers Association	0171-626 8486
British Institute of Management	01536-204222
British Insurance & Investment Brokers	
Association	0171-623 9043
London Investment	
Association	0171-796 3606
British Standards Institution	01908-220022
Building Societies Assoc	0171-437 0655
Business in the Community	0171-629 1600
CBI (Confederation of British	
Industry)	0171-379 7400
Certification Office for Trade Unions &	
Employers' Associations	0171-210 3734
Chamber of Shipping	0171-417 8400
Co-operative Union	0161-832 4300
Corporation of London	0171-606 3030
Ethical Investors Group	01242-604550
Export Credits Guarantee Dept	0171-512 7000
Federation of Small	
Businesses	0171-928 9272
ICOF (Industrial Common Ownership	
Fund)	01604-37563
ICOM (Industrial Common Ownership	
Movement)	0113-246 1737
IMRO (Investment Management	
Regulatory Organisation)	0171-628 6022
Industrial Society	0171-262 2401
Inland Revenue - main number	0171-438 6622
Press office	0171-438 7356
Out of hours press	01860-359544
Revenue Adjudicators Office	0171-930 2292
Institute of Chartered Accountants:	
England & Wales	0171-920 8100
Scotland	0131-225 5673
Institute of Taxation	0171-235 9381
Institutional Fund Managers	
Association	0171-588 0588
LAUTRO (Life Assurance & Unit Trust	
Regulatory Organisation)	0171-379 0444
Lloyds of London	0171-623 7100
London Chamber of Commerce	0171-248 4444
London International Financial	
Futures Exchange	0171-623 0444
London Metal Exchange	0171-264 5555

Low Pay Unit	0171-713 7616
Monopolies and Mergers	
Commission	0171-324 1467
National Association of Pension	
Funds	0171-730 0585
Office of Fair Trading	0171-242 2858
Patent Office	01633-814000
Personal Investment	
Authority	0171-538 8860
Rural Development Commission	0171-276 6969
Securities & Investments Board	0171-638 1240
Serious Fraud Office	0171-239 7272
Eves	0171-239 7050
Stock Exchange	0171-588 2355
Takeovers & Mergers Panel	0171-382 9026
HM Treasury - press	0171-270 5238
TUC (Trades Union Congress)	0171-636 4030
UK Co-operative Council	0161-829 5290
Unit Trust Association	0171-831 0898

Companies House

Companies House is the name given to the Department of Trade and Industry's company registry. Its three main statutory functions are: incorporating and dissolving companies; examining and holding documents required under legislation; and making this information available to the public. All the 980,000 registered companies have to submit annual returns and certain other documents to the Companies House headquarters in Cardiff. Copies of this information are available by post or fax, or directly from the Companies House public offices in Cardiff, London, Birmingham, Manchester, Leeds, Edinburgh and Glasgow. Research can be carried out by the public at these offices. The information comes in the form of the "standard company search", a microfiche of the last three years data received from a company, costing £3. Viewers can be used free of charge at the offices. The information can also be supplied as paper prints, at extra cost.

England & Wales Registry -

Cardiff HQ	01222-388588
Cardiff search room	01222-380507
Press	01222-380062
General enquiries	01222-380801

Other Companies House offices:

London (55 City Road, EC1)	0171-253 9393
Birmingham	0121-233 9047
Edinburgh	0131-535 5800
Glasgow	0141-248 3315
Leeds	0113-233 8338

Manchester	0161-236 7500

Other company registries:

Alderney	01481-822817
Guernsey/Sark	01481-725277
Isle of Man	01624-685233
Jersey	01534-603000
Northern Ireland	01232-234488

Official receivers

London	0171-323 3090
Birmingham	0121-236 8831
Bournemouth	01202-558208
Brighton	01273-820577
Bristol	0117-927 9515
Cambridge	01223-324480
Canterbury	01227-462070
Cardiff	01222-230575
Chester	01244-321471
Croydon	0181-681 5166
Exeter	01392-436886
Gloucester	01452-521658
Hull	01482-323720
Ipswich	01473-217565
Leeds	0113-245 5776
Leicester	01533-2622251
Liverpool	0151-236 9131
Manchester	0161-834 4919
Newcastle	0191-232 1104
Northampton	01604-37288
Norwich	01603-628983
Nottingham	01602-9501596
Plymouth	01752-668554
Reading	01734-581931
Rochester	01634-815367
St Albans	01727-832233
St Annes-on-Sea	01253-784200
Sheffield	0114-2726691
Southampton	01703-223348
Southend	01702-602570
Stockton	01642-617720
Stoke	01782-45256
Swansea	01792-642861

Top companies

Abbey National (banking)	0171-612 4000
Alfred McAlpine (construction)	0151-328 5000
Allders (furnishings)	0181-681 5232
Alliance & Leicester	0171-629 6661
Allied Colloids (chemicals)	01274-671267
Allied-Lyons (food/alcohol)	0171-323 9000
AMEC (construction)	01606-883885
Amersham International	

(household)	01494-544000
Amstrad (electronics)	01277-228888
Argos (retailing)	01908-690333
Argyll (retailing)	0181-848 8744
Arjo Wiggins Appleton (paper)	01256-723000
Asda (supermarkets)	0113-243 5435
Associated British Foods	0171-589 6363
Associated British Ports (port operators)	0171-430 1177
Attwoods (waste disposal)	01753-662700
B&Q (DIY)	01703-256256
BAA (airports)	0171-834 9449
Balfour Beatty (construction)	0181-684 6922
Bank of Scotland	0131-442 7777
Barclays Bank	0171-626 1567
Barratt Development (building)	0191-286 6811
Bass (alcohol)	0171-409 1919
BAT Industries (tobacco)	0171-222 7979
Benetton UK (clothing)	0171-731 4564
Bernard Matthews (food)	01603-872611
BET (industrial services)	0171-629 8886
BICC (electrical)	0171-629 6622
Blue Circle (building)	0171-828 3456
BOC (chemicals)	01276-477222
Body Shop (retailing)	01903-731500
Boots (retailing)	0115-950611
BPB Industries (building)	01753-573273
Bradford & Bingley BS	01274-555555
Brent Walker (leisure)	0171-465 0111
Britannic Assurance (insurance)	0121-449 4444
British Aerospace	0171-930 1020
British Airways	0181-759 5511
British Coal	0171-201 4141
British Gas	0171-207 4141
British Land (property)	0171-486 4466
British Petroleum (oil/gas)	0171-496 4000
British Rail	0171-928 5151
British Shoe Corporation	0116-280 6000
British Steel	0171-735 7654
British Telecommunications	0171-356 5000
BTR (industrial materials)	0171-834 3848
Budgens (supermarkets)	0181-422 9511
Burmah Castrol (oil/gas)	01793-511521
Burton (retailing)	0171-636 8040
Cable & Wireless (telecomms)	0171-315 4000
Cadbury Schweppes (confectionery/ soft drinks)	0171-409 1313
Calor (oil/gas)	01753-540000
Carlton Communications (TV)	0171-499 8050
Chase Manhatten Bank	0171-962 5000
Cheltenham & Gloucester BS	01452-372372
Chemical Bank	0171-777 2000
Christian Salvesen (food)	0131-552 7101
Christie's (auctioneers)	0171-839 9060
Ciba-Geigy (chemicals)	01625-421933
Coats Viyella (textiles)	0161-728 5100

Comet (retailing)	01482-320681
Commercial Union (insurance)	0171-283 7500
Co-operative Retail Services	0161-832 8152
Co-operative Wholesale Soc	0161-834 1212
Costain (construction)	0171-928 4977
Courtaulds (chemicals)	0171-612 1000
Dalgety (food)	0171-486 0200
De La Rue (printing)	0171-836 8383
Debenhams (retailing)	0171-408 4444
Dixons (retailing)	0171-499 3494
Do-It-All (DIY)	01384-456456
Dow Chemical (oil)	0181-848 8688
Dowty (engineering)	01242-221155
Dunhill Holdings (consumer)	0171-499 9566
Engelhard (metals)	0171-588 4080
English China Clays (building)	01734-304010
Enterprise Oil	0171-925 4000
Esso (oil/gas)	0171-834 6677
Eurotunnel	0171-747 6747
Ferranti (electronics)	0161-499 9900
Fisons (horticultural/ pharmaceutical)	01473-232525
Ford (vehicles)	01277-253000
Forte (leisure)	0171-836 7744
Gallaher (retailing/tobacco)	01932-859777
Gateway (supermarkets)	0117-935 9359
General Accident (insurance)	01738-621202
General Electric (electronics)	0171-493 8484
George Weston (food)	0171-589 6363
George Wimpey (building)	0181-748 2000
Girobank	0171-600 6020
GKN (engineering)	01527-517715
Glaxo (household/health)	0171-493 4060
Granada (media/leisure)	0171-734 8080
Grand Metropolitan (food)	0171-321 6000
Greycoat (property)	0171-379 1000
Gt Universal Stores (retailing)	0161-273 8282
Guardian Royal Exchange (insurance)	0171-283 7101
Guinness (alcohol)	0171-486 0288
Halfords (retailing)	01527-517601
Halifax BS	01422-333333
Hambros (banking)	0171-480 5000
Hanson (conglomerate)	0171-245 1245
Harrisons & Crosfield (conglomerate)	0171-711 1400
Hillsdown (food)	0171-794 0677
House of Fraser (retailing)	0171-834 1515
HSBC Holdings (banking)	0171-260 8000
IBM (business machines)	01705-321212
ICI (chemicals)	0171-834 4444
Imperial Tobacco	0117-963 6636
Inchcape (trading)	0171-321 0110
John Laing (construction)	0181-959 3636
John Lewis (retailing)	0171-828 1000
John Menzies (retailing)	0131-225 8555
John Mowlem (construction)	0181-568 9111

Kingfisher (retailing)	0171-724 7749
Kleinwort Benson (banking)	0174-588711
Kwik Save (supermarkets)	0151-236 7551
Ladbroke (leisure)	0181-459 8031
Land Securities (property)	0171-413 9000
Lasmo (oil & gas)	0171-945 4545
Leeds Permanent BS	0113-243 8181
Legal & General (insurance)	0171-528 6200
Littlewoods (retailing)	0151-235 2222
Lloyds Abbey Life (assurance)	01932-850888
Lloyds Bank	0171-626 1500
Lo-Cost Stores (retailing)	01244-520900
London Regional Transport	0171-222 5600
Lonrho (conglomerate)	0171-606 9898
Lucas Industries (engineering)	0121-627 6000
Marks & Spencer (retailing)	0171-935 4422
Marley (building materials)	01732-455255
McCarthy & Stone (building)	01202-292480
McDonalds (fast food)	0181-700 7000
MEPC (property)	0171-911 5300
MFI (furnishings)	0181-200 8000
Midland Bank	0171-260 8000
Milk Marketing Board	0181-398 4101
Mobil (oil)	0171-412 4000
Morgan Crucible (industrial)	01753-837000
Mothercare (parenting)	01923-241000
National & Provincial BS	01274-733444
National Power (electricity)	01793-877777
National Westminster Bank	0171-726 1000
Nationwide Anglia	01793-513513
Nestle (food)	0181-686 3333
News International (media)	0171-782 6000
Next (retailing)	0116-286 6411
NFC (transport)	01234-272222
Northern Foods	01482-325432
Northern Telecom	0171-291 3000
P&O (shipping etc)	0171-930 4343
Pearson (media)	0171-411 2000
Pentos (retailing)	0171-499 3484
Peugeot Talbot (vehicles)	01203-884000
Pilkington (glass)	01744-28882
Post Office	0171-490 2888
Powell Duffryn (transport)	01344-53101
Powergen (electricity)	01203-424000
Prudential (insurance)	0171-405 9222
Racal Electronics	01344-481222
Rank Organisation (leisure)	0171-706 1111
Rank Xerox (machines)	01895-251133
Ranks Hovis McDougall (food)	01753-857123
Rechem (waste treatment)	01628-810011
Reckitt & Colman (household)	0181-994 6464
Redland (building materials)	01737-242488
Reed Elsevier (media)	0171-499 4020
Rentokil (chemicals)	01342-833022
Reuters (media)	0171-250 1122
RMC (building materials)	01932-568833
Rolls-Royce (engineering)	0171-222 9020

Rosehaugh (property)	0171-486 7100	Tate & Lyle (food)	0171-626 6525
Rothmans (tobacco)	0171-491 4366	Taylor Woodrow (building)	0171-629 1201
Rover (vehicles)	0121-782 8000	Tesco (supermarkets)	01992-632222
Royal Bank of Scotland	0131-556 8555	Texaco (oil/gas)	0171-719 3000
Royal Insurance	0151-283 4300	Texas Homecare (DIY)	01933-679679
RTZ Corporation (mining)	0171-930 2399	Thames Water	01734-593333
Rugby Group (building)	01788-542666	Thorn EMI (leisure)	0171-355 4848
Saatchi & Saatchi (advertise)	0171-436 4000	TI Group (engineering)	01235-555570
Safeway (supermarkets)	0181-848 8744	Tootal	0161-728 5100
J Sainsbury (supermarkets)	0171-921 6000	Total (oil)	0171-937 7777
Samuels	0121-554 3871	Trafalgar House (mixture)	0171-499 9020
Schroders (banking)	0171-382 6000	TSB (banking)	0121-600 6000
Scottish & Newcastle (beer)	0131-556 2591	**Unigate** (food)	01892-534424
Scottish Power (electricity)	0141-637 7177	Unilever (food/household)	0171-822 5252
Sears (retailing)	0171-200 5999	United Biscuits (food)	01895-432100
Securicor (miscellaneous)	0181-770 7000	United Newspapers	0171-921 5000
SG Warburg (banking)	0171-606 1066	**Vauxhall** (vehicles)	01582-21122
Shell (oil/gas)	0171-257 3000	Vickers (engineering)	0171-828 7777
Sketchley (miscellaneous)	01455-238133	Vodafone (telecomms)	01635-33251
Slough Estates	01753-537171	**Waitrose** (supermarkets)	01344-424680
Smithkline Beecham (health)	0181-975 2000	Wellcome (health/household)	0171-387 4477
Smiths Industries (engineers)	0181-458 3232	WH Smith (retailing)	0171-730 1200
St Ivel (food)	01793-848444	Whitbread (alcohol)	0171-606 4455
Standard Chartered (banking)	0171-280 7500	Wittington Investments (food)	0171-589 6363
Storehouse (retailing)	0171-262 3456	Wolseley (building materials)	01905-794444
Sun Alliance (insurance)	0171-588 2345	Woolwich (building society)	0181-298 5000
Sunblest Bakeries (food)	01784-451366	Woolworths (retailing)	0171-262 1222
Superdrug (household/health)	0181-684 7000	WPP Group (advertising)	0171-408 2204
Tarmac (construction)	01902-307407	**Zeneca** (drugs)	0171-304 5000

CONSUMER WATCHDOGS

Consumer watchdogs fall into four broad types:
1) **regulatory organisations** `
2) **ombudsmen**
3) **advisory committees**
4) **pressure groups.**

Regulatory agencies

The Office of Fair Trading (OFT) was set up to protect consumers by ensuring fair trading and encouraging competition. It administers consumer laws and monitors competition.
Individual problems are taken up by Trading Standards Departments in county councils. The Institute of Trading Standards Administration publishes an annual directory. Also listed here are the two government auditing departments, the National Audit Office (NAO) and the Audit Commission. The NAO audits accounts of government departments and public bodies. The Audit Commission examines the accounts of local authorities and the NHS.

Audit Commission	0171-828 1212
Press	0171-930 6077
British Standards Institution	0171-629 9000
Data Protection Registrar	01625-535711
National Audit Office	0171-798 7000
Offer (Office of Electricity Regulation)	0121-456 2100
Scotland	0141-331 2678
Northern Ireland	01232-311575
Office of Fair Trading	0171-242 2858
Press	0171-269 8898
Office of Rail Regulator	0171-282 2000
Ofgas (Office of Gas Supply)	0171-828 0898
Oflot (Office of National Lottery)	0171-240 4624
Ofsted (Office for Standards in Education)	0171-925 6800
Oftel (Office of Telecomms)	0171-634 8700
Ofwat (Office of Water Services)	0121-625 1300

Ombudsmen

Not all ombudsmen are government appointed; some are a form of PR exercise by industry sectors. The Department of Trade and Industry (DTI), Department of the Environment, Ministry of Agriculture and Home Office are the government departments responsible for administering government's relation with consumerism. The DTI, through its Consumer Affairs Division, has one of the most prominent general roles, particularly in consumer protection. MAFF has the main responsibility for food.

Banking Ombudsman	0171-404 9944
Broadcasting Standards Council	0171-233 0544
Building Societies Ombudsman	0171-931 0044
Data Protection Registrar	01625-535711
Department of Trade & Industry:	
Main number	0171-215 5000
Consumer Affairs Division: Press office	0171-215 5969
Estate Agents Ombudsman	01722-333306
Health Services Ombudsmen:	
England	0171-276 2035
Wales	01222-394621
Scotland	0131-225 7465
Insurance Ombudsman	0171-928 7600
Legal Services Ombudsman	0161-236 9532
Scotland	0131-556 5574
Local Government Ombudsmen:	
SE England	0171-915 3210
North of England	01904-663200
Rest of England	01203-695999
Wales	01656-661325
Scotland	0131-225 5300
Northern Ireland	01232-233821
Ministry of Agriculture, Fisheries & Food:	
Main number	0171-270 3000
Food safety press	0171-270 8435/46
Parliamentary Ombudsman	0171-276 2130
Press	0171-261 8765/75
Pensions Ombudsman	0171-834 9144
Police Complaints Authority	0171-273 6450
Press Complaints Commission	0171-353 1248
Solicitors Complaints Bureau	01926-820082
Press	01926-822043

Advisory committees

These are the officially sponsored bodies giving consumers' views of industries and services.

Advisory Committees on Telecommunications	0171-634 8700

Air Transport Users Council	0171-242 3882
Association of Community Health Councils	0171-609 8405
Central Rail Users Consultative Committee	0171-839 7338
Electricity Regional Consumers Committees	0121-456 2100
Gas Consumers Council	0171-931 0977
London Regional Passengers Committee	0171-839 1898
Post Office Users National Council	0171-928 9458

Pressure groups

The largest of the independent pressure groups is the Consumers Association, publisher of Which? magazine. The government-funded National Consumer Council (NCC) conducts research, lobbies policy makers and publishes reports. The NCC helps run the Consumer Congress, the forum for consumer bodies. Each spring it publishes the Consumer Congress Directory with details of over 150 organisations.

Buswatch	01705-814493
CAMRA (Campaign for Real Ale)	01727-867201
CASE (Campaign for State Education)	0181-944 8206
Child Poverty Action Group	0171-253 3406
Consumer Credit Trade Assoc	0171-636 7564
Consumers Association	0171-486 5544
Ethical Consumer (magazine)	0161-237 1630
Federation of Independent Advice Centres	0171-274 1839
Institution of Environmental Health Officers	0171-928 6006
Institute of Safety & Public Protection	01709-823102
Institute of Trading Standards Administration	01702-559922
Local Authorities Co-ordinating Body on Trading Standards	0181-688 1996
Money Advice Association	01752-794631
National Association of Citizens Advice Bureaux	0171-833 2181
National Consumer Council	0171-730 3469
Wales	01222-396056
Scotland	0141-226 5261
Northern Ireland	01232-672488
National Debtline	0121-359 8501
National Federation of Consumer Groups	0191-261 8259
New Consumer	0191-272 1148
Society of County Trading Standards Officers	01992-556799

RETAILING

Trade associations etc

Association of Convenience Stores	01252-515001
Assoc of Independent Retailers & Businesses	01905-612733
Bakers, Food & Allied Workers Union	01707-260150
Bookmakers Association	0121-327 3031
Booksellers Association	0171-834 5477
British Antique Dealers Association	0171-589 4128
British Association of Toy Retailers	0181-993 2894
British Clothing Industry Association	0171-636 7788
British Council of Shopping Centres	01734-885505
British Franchise Assoc	01491-578049
British Frozen Food Federation	01476-590194
British Hardware Federation	0121-446 6688
British Retail Consortium	0171-371 5185
British Shops & Stores Association	01295-712277
Consumers Association	0171-486 5544
Credit Card Research Group	0171-436 9937
Food & Drink Federation	0171-836 2460
Keep Sunday Special Campaign	01223-321812
Mail Order Traders Association	0151-227 4181
Music Retailers Assoc	0181-994 7592
National Assoc of Licensed House Managers	0181-947 3080
National Assoc of Shopkeepers	0115-947 5046
National Federation of Fishmongers	01376-571391
National Federation of Meat Traders	01892-541412
National Federation of Retail Newsagents	0171-253 4225
National Pharmaceutical Association	01727-832161
Office of Fair Trading	0171-242 2858
Radio, Electrical & TV Retailers Assoc	01234-269110
Retail Fruit Trade Federation	0181-569 3090
Retail Motor Industry Federation	0171-580 9122
USDAW (Union of Shop, Distributive & Allied Workers)	0161-224 2804

Large retailers

Allders	0181-681 5232
Allied Bakeries	01784-451366
Argos	01908-690333
Argyll	0181-848 8744
Asda	0113-243 5435
Associated British Foods	0171-589 6363
B & Q	01703-256256
BhS	0171-262 3288
Boots	0115-950 6111
Budgens	0181-422 9511
Burton Group	0171-636 8040
Co-op (CRS · retail)	0161-832 8152
Co-op (CWS · wholesale)	0161-834 1212
Comet	01482-320681
Debenhams	0171-408 4444
Dixons	0181-419 3000
Forte	0171-836 7744
Freemans	0171-735 7644
Gateway	0117-935 9359
Grand Metropolitan	0171-321 6000
Great Universal Stores	0161-273 8282
Halfords	01527-517601
Harrods	0171-730 1234
House of Fraser (Harrods, Dickins & Jones, Army & Navy, Rackhams)	0171-834 1515
Iceland	01244-830100
Inchcape	0171-321 0110
John Lewis	0171-828 1000
John Menzies	0131-225 8555
Kingfisher (Comet, Woolworth, Superdrug)	0171-724 7749
Kwik Save	01745-887111
Littlewoods	0151-235 2222
Lo-Cost Stores	01244-520900
Lonrho	0171-606 9898
Marks & Spencer	0171-935 4422
McDonalds Restaurants	0181-700 7000
MFI	0181-200 8000
Next	0116-286 6411
Owen Owen	0151-707 4000
Ratners	0121-554 3871
Sainsbury	0171-921 6000
Sears (Freemans, Selfridges, Olympus Sports)	0171-200 5999
WH Smith	0171-730 1200
Storehouse (Bhs, Habitat, Mothercare)	0171-262 3288
Superdrug	0181-684 7000

Tesco	01992-632222	Gateshead (Metro)	0191-493 2040
Texas Homecare	01933-679679	Glasgow (Princes Square)	0141-221 0324
Thorn EMI (DER, HMV, Rumbelows,		Glasgow (St Enoch)	0141-204 3900
Radio Rentals)	0171-355 4848	Glasgow (Sauchiehall)	0141-332 0726
Waitrose	0171-828 1000	Harlow (Harvey)	01279-442981
Woolworth	0171-262 1222	Hull (Princes Quay)	01482-586622
		Inverness (Eastgate)	01463-226457
		Ipswich (Buttermarket)	01473-281580
		Kingston (Eden Walk)	0181-549 9672

Large shopping centres

		Leeds (Crossgates)	0113-264 9589
		Leeds (Merrion)	0113-245 9172
Aberdeen (St Nicholas)	01224-645420	Leicester (Shires)	0116-251 2461
Bangor (Wellfield)	01248-354799	Lincoln (Waterside)	01522-529566
Bath (Podium)	01225-444678	Manchester (Arndale)	0161-833 9851
Belfast (In Shop)	01232-329719	Newcastle (Eldon Square)	0191-261 1891
Birmingham (Bull Ring)	0121-643 6261	Newport (Kingsway)	01633-258151
Brent Cross	0181-202 8095	Nottingham (Victoria)	0115-941 8722
Bromley (Glades)	0181-313 9292	Oxford (Clarendon)	01865-251493
Cambridge (Grafton)	01223-316201	Paisley	0141-848 5666
Cardiff (Capitol)	01222-223683	Plymouth (Armada)	01752-269471
Cardiff (St Davids)	01222-396041	Portsmouth (Cascades)	01705-851255
Coventry (Cathederal Lanes)	01203-632532	Redhill (Belfry)	01737-779930
Croydon (Whitgift)	0181-688 8522	Romford (Liberty II)	01708-733620
Cumbernauld	01236-736963	Rugby (Clocktower)	01788-572630
Cwmbran	01633-872121	Sheffield (Meadowhall)	0114-256 8800
Derby (Eagle)	01332-366383	St Albans (Maltings)	01727-844226
Doncaster (Frenchgate)	01302-368335	Stafford (Guildhall)	01785-223107
Dundee (Nethergate)	01382-227265	Swansea (Quadrant)	01792-460312
Dundee (Wellgate)	01382-225454	Taunton (Old Market)	01823-326556
Durham (Milburngate)	0191-386 9363	Telford	01952-291370
Ealing Broadway	0181-567 3453	Thurrock (Lakeside)	01708-869933
Edinburgh (St James)	0131-557 0050	Wandsworth (Arndale)	0181-870 2141
Elephant & Castle	0171-703 5678	Wolverhampton (Mander)	01902-711084
Falkirk (Howgate)	01324-631985	Worcester (Crown Gate)	01905-610065

TRANSPORT

Trains	**318**
Boats	**319**
Planes	**320**
Roads	**321**

Support organisations

Airport Operators Assoc	0171-222 2249
Air Transport Users Council	0171-242 3882
Alliance of Independent Travel	
Agents	01733-390900
Assoc of British Travel Agents	0171-637 2444
British Air Line Pilots Assoc	0181-476 4000

British Air Transport Assoc	0171-930 5746
British Motorcyclists Federation	0181-942 7914
British Ports Association	0171-242 1200
British Roads Federation	0171-703 9769
British Tourist Authority	0181-846 9000
British Transport Police	0171-388 7541
British Waterways	01923-226422
Civil Aviation Authority	0171-379 7311
Confederation of Passenger	
Transport	0171-831 7546
Department of Transport	0171-276 0888
Driver & Vehicle Licensing	01792-782318
Register of Shipping, Seamen & Fishing	
Boats	01222-747333
Vehicle Inspectorate	0117-954 3200
Inland Waterways Assoc	0171-586 2510

International Air Transport Assoc		Liverpool	0151-237 3010
(Geneva)	00-4122 7992525	Newport	01633-244292
London Traffic Director	0171-222 4545	Peterborough	01733-895555
London Transport	0171-222 5600	Retail Motor Industry	0171-580 9122
Press	0171-918 3271	Road Haulage Assoc	01932-841515
Passport Offices:		Society of Motor Manufacturers &	
London HQ Passport Agency	0171-279 3434	Traders	0171-235 7000
Belfast	01232-232371	Thames Passenger Services	
Glasgow	0141-332 0271	Federation	0171-231 7122

TRAINS

Ownership of railway track, signalling and stations was transferred to a new government-owned company: Railtrack, prior to privatisation. It also has overall responsibility for timetabling and safety. The operating of all passenger and freight train services remains the responsibility of the British Railways Board (BRB) until they are sold to the private sector. The BR businesses InterCity, Network SouthEast and Regional Railways have been replaced by 25 separate train operating units (TOUs). The government intends privatising 51 per cent of these by 1 April 1996. But by mid-1995 only the sale of the train operating units was well advanced: South West; Great Western and London; Tilbury and Suthend. All trains and rolling stock are currently the property of three state-owned companies: Eversholt, Porterbrook and Angel Train Contracts.

Rail contacts

British Railways Board HQ	0171-928 5151
Press	0171-957 1979
Train operating units (TOUs):	
Anglia (London)	0171-465 9000
Cardiff Valleys	01222-499811
Central (Birmingham)	0121-643 4444
Chiltern (Aylesbury)	01296-332100
Cross-Country (Birmingham)	0121-654 7400
East Coast (York)	01904-653022
Gatwick Express (London)	0171-973 5005
Great Eastern (London)	0171-928 5151
Great Western (Swindon)	01793-526100
Isle of Wight (London)	0171-928 5151
London, Tilbury & Southend	0171-928 5151
Merseyrail (Liverpool)	0151-709 8292
Midland (Derby)	01332-262045
Network South Central	0181-6672952
North East (York)	01904-522354

Northampton & N London	0171-928 5151
North West (Manchester)	0161-228 2141
ScotRail (Glasgow)	0141-332 9811
South Central (Croydon)	0171-928 5151
South East (London)	0171-928 5151
S Wales & West (Swindon)	01793-526100
South West (London)	0171-928 5151
Thameslink (London)	0171-928 5151
West Coast (Birmingham)	0121-643 4444
West Anglia & Great Northern	
(London)	0171-928 5151
Docklands Light Railway	0171-918 4000
European Passenger Services	0171-922 4494
London Underground	0171-222 1234
Press	0171-918 3274
Rail Express Systems	0171-922 6334
Rail Regulator	0171-282 2000
Railfreight Distribution	0171-922 6730
Railtrack: HQ	0171-344 7100
Press	0171-344 7293
Trainload Freight: West	01270-255123
South East	0171-713 2420
Union Railways (Channel Tunnel	
Rail Link)	0181-666 6497

Travel enquiries

BR to Europe	0171-834 2345
BR London to and from:	
London area (except below)	0171-928 5100
SE London/Kent	01732-770111
W London/South Wales/West	0171-262 6767
NW London/Midlands/West Coast/North	
Wales/Scotland	0171-387 7070
N London/East Coast/	
Scotland	0171-278 2477
BR Edinburgh	0131-556 2451
BR Glasgow	0141-204 2844
BR Northern Ireland	01232-230671

BOATS

Seaports and harbour authorities

Aberdeen, Grampian	01224-592571
Ardrossan, Strathclyde	01294-463972
Belfast	01232-554422
Bristol, Avon	0117-982 0000
Brixham, Devon	01803-853321
Cardiff	01222-471311
Clyde Ports	0141-221 8733
Cowes, Isle of Wight	01983-293952
Dover, Kent	01304-240400
Dundee, Tayside	01382-224121
Falmouth, Cornwall	01326-211376
Felixstowe, Suffolk	01394-604500
Fishguard, Dyfed	01348-872881
Fleetwood, Lancs	01253-872323
Folkestone, Kent	01303-220544
Forth Ports	0131-554 4343
Gt Yarmouth, Norfolk	01493-855151
Harwich, Essex	01255-243030
Heysham, Lancs	01524-852373
Holyhead, Anglesey	01407-762304
Grimsby, Humberside	01472-359181
Hull, Humberside	01482-327171
Immingham, Humberside	01469-571555
Ipswich, Suffolk	01473-231010
Isle of Man	01624-686628
Larne, Antrim	01574-279221
Lerwick, Shetland	01595-692991
Liverpool	0151-949 6000
London:	
PLA	01474-562200
Tilbury	01375-852200
Thames Navigation Centre	01474-562200
Londonderry	01504-860555
Lowestoft, Suffolk	01502-572286
Manchester	0161-872 2411
Medway Ports, Kent	01795-561234
Milford Haven, Dyfed	01646-693091
Newhaven, East Sussex	01273-514131
Peterhead, Grampian	01779-474281
Poole, Dorset	01202-440200
Portsmouth, Hants	01705-297395
Ramsgate, Kent	01843-592277
Rye, East Sussex	01797-225225
Scarborough, North Yorks	01723-373530
Shoreham, West Sussex	01273-592613
Southampton, Hants	01703-330022
Stornoway, Western Isles	01851-702688
Sunderland, Tyne & Wear	0191-514 0411
Swansea, West Glamorgan	01792-650855
Tees & Hartlepool	01642-241121
Tyne	0191-232 5541
Weymouth, Dorset	01305-206421
Whitby, North Yorks	01947-602354
Workington, Cumbria	01900-602301

Ferry companies

Irish Ferries	0151-227 3131
Brittany Ferries:	
Portsmouth	01705-827701
Plymouth	01752-221321
Caledonian MacBrayne Ferries	01475-650000
Condor Ferries	01305-761551
Hoverspeed: Dover	01304-240241
Irish Ferries (Dublin)	0151-227 3131
Isle of Man Steam Packet Co	01624-661661
Isles of Scilly Steamship Co	01736-62009
North Sea Ferries: Hull	01482-77177
Olau Line: Sheerness	01795-666666
P&O:	
Aberdeen	01224-572615
Cairnryan	01581-200276
Dover	01304-203388
Felixstowe	01394-604040
Larne	01574-274321
Portsmouth	01705-827677
Scrabster	01847-894180
Red Funnel Ferries	01703-330333
Sally Line: Ramsgate	01843-595522
Scandanavian Seaways	01255-240240
Seacat:	
Belfast/Stranraer	0345-523523
Dover	01304-240241
Folkestone	01303-221281
Sealink-Stena:	
All reservations	01233-647047
Info: Dover	01304-868686
Fishguard	01348-873523
Harwich	01255-240965
Holyhead	01407-606666
Southampton	01703-532099
Stranraer	01776-702262
Swansea Cork Ferries	00-35321 271166
Wightlink	01705-827744

PLANES

Airports

Aberdeen (Dyce)	01224-722331
Barra, Hebrides	01871-890212
Belfast (Aldergrove)	01849-422888
Belfast (City)	01232-457745
Benbecula, Outer Hebrides	01870-602051
Biggin Hill, Kent	01959-571111
Birmingham International	0121-767 5511
Blackpool, Lancs	01253-343434
Bournemouth (Hurn), Dorset	01202-593939
Brawdy, Dyfed (RAF)	01437-764571
Bristol (Lulsgate), Avon	01275-474444
Brize Norton, Oxon (RAF)	01993-842551
Cambridge	01223-61133
Campbeltown (Strathclyde)	01586-552577
Cardiff	01446-711111
Carlisle	01228-573641
Channel Islands: Alderney	01481-822851
Guernsey	01481-37766
Jersey	01534-46111
Coventry, West Midlands	01203-301717
Culdrose, Cornwall (RAF)	01326-574121
Dundee, Tayside	01382-643242
East Midlands	01332-852852
Edinburgh (Turnhouse)	0131-333 1000
Exeter, Devon	01392-367433
Glasgow	0141-887 1111
Gloucester-Cheltenham	01452-857700
Humberside (Kirmington)	01652-688456
Inverness (Dalcross), Highland	01463-232471
Ipswich	01473-720111
Isle of Man (Ronaldsway)	01624-823311
Leeds/Bradford (Yeadon)	0113-250 9696
Liverpool (Speke)	0151-486 8877
London: Battersea Heliport	0171-228 0181
City, Docklands E16	0171-474 5555
Gatwick, West Sussex	01293-535353
Heathrow, Middx	0181-759 4321
Stansted, Essex	01279-680500
Luton, Beds	01582-405100
Lydd, Kent	01797-320401
Lyneham, Wilts (RAF)	01249-890381
Manchester (Ringway)	0161-489 3000
Manston, Kent	01843-823333
Newcastle (Woolsington)	0191-286 0966
Northolt, Middx (RAF)	0181-845 2300
Norwich, Norfolk	01603-411923
Orkney: Kirkwall	01856-872421
North Ronaldsay	01857-633240
Papa Westray	01857-644252
Westray	01857-677271
Penzance Heliport, Cornwall	01736-63871
Plymouth, Devon	01752-705151
Prestwick, Strathclyde	01292-79822
St Mawgan, Cornwall	01637-860551
Scilly Isles: St Marys	01720-422677
Tresco Heliport	01720-422970
Shetland: Lerwick	01595-840246
Sumburgh	01950-460661
Shoreham, West Sussex	01273-452304
Southampton (Eastleigh)	01703-629600
Southend, Essex	01702-340201
Stornoway, Western Isles	01851-702256
Teeside	01325-332811
Tiree, Argyll	01879-220304
Valley, Anglesey (RAF)	01407-762241
Wick, Caithness	01955-602215

Airline bookings

Aer Lingus	0181-899 4747
Aeroflot	0171-355 2233
Air Canada	0181-759 2636
Air France	0181-759 2311
Air India	0175-368 4828
Air New Zealand	0181-846 9595
Air UK	0345-666777
Alitalia	0171-602 7111
All Nippon Airways	0171-355 1155
American Airlines	0181-572 5555
British Airways	0181-897 4000
British Midland	0345-554554
Brymon Airways	0345-222111
Cathay Pacific	0171-747 8888
Delta Airlines	01800-414767
El-Al Israel Airlines	0171-437 9255
Gulf Air	0171-408 1717
Iberia	0171-830 0011
Icelandair	0171-388 5599
Japan Airlines	0171-408 1000
KLM	0181-750 9000
Lufthansa	01345-737747
Middle East Airlines	0171-493 5681
Northwest Airlines	01293-561000
Olympic Airways	0171-493 3965
Pakistan International (PIA)	0171-734 5544
Philippine Airlines	0171-499 9446
Qantas	01345-747767
Sabena	0181-780 1444
SAS	0171-734 4020
Saudia	0181-995 7777
Singapore Airlines	0181-747 0007
Swissair	0171-439 4144
TAP Air Portugal	0171-828 0262
Thai Airways	0171-499 9113
TWA	0171-439 0707
United	0181-990 9900
Virgin Atlantic	01293-747747

ROADS

Coach/bus companies

Eastern National (Chelmsford)	01245-256151
Eastern Scottish (Edinburgh)	0131-313 1515
Greater Manchester Buses	0161-267 2828
Green Line (London)	01737-242411
Grey Green (London)	0181-800 8010
Highland Scottish (Inverness)	01463-233371
London Buses	0171-222 1234
Press	0171-918 3272
Mainline Group	0114-256 7000
Merseyside Transport	0151-254 1254
National Express (London)	0990-808080
North Western (Liverpool)	0151-525 1733
Red & White (Cardiff)	01633-485118
Ribble Motor Services (Preston)	01772-254754
Scottish Citylink (Glasgow)	0990-505050
Stage-Coach Holdings (Perth)	01738-630008
Strathclyde Buses	0141-423 6600
Yorkshire Traction	01226-202555
Western National (Truro)	01872-73954
West Midlands Travel	0121-333 3377

Motoring organisations

AA: Headquarters	01256-20123
Breakdown service	0800-887766
AA Roadwatch	01345-500600
National Breakdown: HQ	0113-239 3666
Breakdown service	0800-400600
RAC: Headquarters	0181-452 8000
Breakdown service	01800-828282

EDUCATION

Education is run by the Department for Education in England, the Welsh Office Education Department, the Northern Ireland Department of Education and the Scottish Office Education Department.

About 93 per cent of pupils attend maintained state run schools. These are usually split into primary schools for 5-11 year olds and secondary schools for 11-16. Most are controlled by Local Education Authorities (LEAs) which are part of the county councils. The exceptions are grant-maintained schools which have opted out of LEA control and are overseen by the DfE; and schools which receive public funds but are run by voluntary bodies like the Church of England.

Non-maintained schools come in many forms and names: independent, private, preparatory and public (in Scotland and most of the rest of the world "public" schools are actually maintained schools). The Independent Schools Information Service provides information.

Directories

The Education Year Book
Longman   Tel 0171-896 2424
It contains details of schools, colleges and educational bodies.

University College and Entrance
Sheed and Ward, 14 Coopers Row, London EC3N 2BH
The official guide to univeristy and college entrance.

Central bodies

Dept of Education	0171-925 5000
Press	0171-925 5096
N Ireland Dept of Education	01247-279000
Scottish Office Education Dept	0131-556 8400
Welsh Office Education Dept	01222-825111
Assoc of County Councils	0171-235 1200
Assoc of Local Authorities of Northern Ireland	01232-249286
Assoc of London Authorities	0171-222 7799
Assoc of Metropolitan Authorities	0171-222 8100
Convention of Scottish Local Authorities	0131-346 1222
Council of Local Education Authorities	0171-235 9554
Curriculum Council for Wales	01222-344946
Education Consultants Society	0181-459 5419
Independent Schools Information Service	0171-630 8793
National Council for Vocational Qualifications	0171-387 9898
National Curriculum Council	0171-229 1234
N Ireland Curriculum Council	01232-381414
Office for Standards in Education (OFSTED)	0171-421 6800
School Examinations & Assessment Council	0171-229 1234
Welsh Joint Education Committee	01222-265000

Teaching unions

Assoc of Teachers & Lecturers	0171-930 6441
Assoc of University Teachers	0171-221 4370
Girls School Assoc	0116-254 1619
Headmasters Conference	0116-285 4810
National Assoc of Head Teachers	01444-458133
National Assoc of Schoolmasters/ Union of Women Teachers	0121-453 6150
National Assoc of Teachers in Further & Higher Education	0171-837 3636
National Union of Teachers	0171-388 6191
Prof Assoc of Teachers	01332-372337
Secondary Heads Assoc	0116-247 1797
Society of Education	0171-580 5705
Society of Headmasters & Mistresses of Independent Schools	01962-862579

Universities

(Ex-polytechnics have old names in brackets.)

Aberdeen	01224-272000
Aston (Birmingham)	0121-359 3611
Anglia (Anglia Poly)	01245-493131
Bath	01225-826826
Birmingham	0121-414 3344
Bournemouth (Bourne Poly)	01202-524111
Bradford	01274-733466
Brighton (Brighton Poly)	01273-600900
Bristol	0117-928 9000
Brunel (Uxbridge)	01895-274000
Buckingham	01280-814080
Cambridge	01223-332200
Central England in Birmingham (Birmingham Poly)	0121-331 5000
Central Lancashire (Lancs Poly)	01772-201201
Coventry (Coventry Poly)	01203-631313
City (London EC1)	0171-477 8000
Cranfield Institute of Technology	01234-750111
De Montfort (Leicester Poly)	0116-255 1551
Derby (Derbyshire College)	01332-47181
Dundee	01382-23181
Durham	0191-374 2000
East Anglia (Norwich)	01603-45161
East London (East London Poly)	0181-590 7722
Edinburgh	0131-650 1000
Essex (Colchester)	01206-873333
Exeter	01392-263263
Glamorgan (Wales Poly)	01443-480480
Glasgow Caledonian (Glasgow Poly)	0141-331 3000
Glasgow	0141-339 8855
Greenwich (Thames Poly)	0181-316 8000
Heriot-Watt (Edinburgh)	0131-449 5111

Hertfordshire (Hatfield Poly)	01707-284000
Huddersfield (Huddersfield Poly)	01484-422288
Hull	01482-46311
Humberside (Humberside Poly)	01482-440550
Keele (Stoke-on-Trent)	01782-621111
Kent (Canterbury)	01227-764000
Lancaster	01524-65201
Leeds	0113-243 1751
Leicester	0116-252 2522
Liverpool	0151-794 2000
London	0171-636 8000
Birkbeck College	0171-580 6622
Courtauld Institute	0171-872 0220
Goldsmiths College	0181-919 7171
Imperial College	0171-589 5111
Institute of Education	0171-580 1122
Kings College	0171-836 5454
London Business School	0171-262 5050
London School of Economics	0171-405 7686
London School of Hygiene	0171-636 8636
Queen Mary College	0171-975 5555
Royal Academy of Music	0171-935 5461
Royal College of Music	0171-589 3643
Royal Holloway & Bedford	01784-434455
School of Oriental Studies	0171-637 2388
Senate House	071-636 8000
University College	0171-387 7050
Wye	01233-812401
Loughborough	01509-263171
Kingston	0181-549 1366
Leeds Metropolitan (Leeds Poly)	0113-283 2600
Liverpool John Moores (Liverpool Poly)	0151-231 2121
London Guildhall (City Poly)	0171-320 1000
Manchester	0161-275 2000
UMIST	0161-236 3311
Manchester Metropolitan (Manchester Poly)	0161-247 2000
Middlesex (Middlesex Poly)	0181-362 5000
Napier (Napier Poly, Edinburgh)	0131-444 2266
Newcastle	0191-222 6000
North London (N London Poly)	0171-607 2789
Northumbria at Newcastle (Newcastle Poly)	0191-232 6002
Nottingham	0115-951 5151
Nottingham Trent (Nottham Poly)	0115-941 8418
Open University (Milton Keynes)	01908-274066
Oxford	01865-270000
Oxford Brookes (Oxford Poly)	01865-741111
Paisley (Paisley College of Tech)	0141-848 3000
Plymouth (South West Poly)	01752-600600
Portsmouth (Portsmouth Poly)	01705-876543
Queens (Belfast)	01232-245133
Reading	01734-875123
Robert Gordon (Aberdeen Inst)	01224-262000
St Andrews	01334-476161
Salford	0161-745 5000

University College Salford (Salford College of Technology)	0161-736 6541	Teesside	01642-218121
Sheffield	0114-276 8555	Thames Valley (W London)	0181-579 5000
Sheffield Hallam (Sheffield City	0114-272 0911	Ulster (Coleraine)	01265-44141
South Bank (South Bank , London SE1)	0171-928 8989	Wales	01222-382656
		Aberystwyth	01970-623111
		Bangor	01248-351151
Southampton	01703-595000	Cardiff	01222-874000
Staffordshire (Staffs)	01782-294000	St Davids, Lampeter	01570-422351
Stirling	01786-473171	Swansea	01792-205678
Strathclyde (Glasgow)	0141-552 4400	Warwick	01203-523523
Sunderland	0191-515 2000	West of England (Bristol)	0117-965 6261
Surrey (Guildford)	01483-300800	Westminster (Central Lond)	0171-911 5000
Sussex (Brighton)	01273-606755	Wolverhampton	01902-321000
		York	01904-430000

RELIGION

The largest religious bodies in the UK are the the Anglican Communion group, the Roman Catholic Church and the Presbyterians including the Church of Scotland. The largest non-Christian religion is Muslism.

In the Anglican Communion group, the Church of England is the leading body. It has been the state church in England since the mid-16th century. The country is divided into the two provinces of Canterbury and York, each run by an archbishop: George Carey (Canterbury) and John Habgood (York). There are 44 dioceses within the provinces. The Church of England is governed by its General Synod, with 574 members, meeting twice a year under the presidency of the archbishops. There are about 11,000 staff and 16,000 churches. The other main Anglican churches in the UK are the Church in Wales, the Episcopal Church in Scotland and the Church of Ireland. They are independent, but have strong links with the Church of England, along with the other Anglican churches around the world. Every ten years all Anglican bishops meet for the international Lambeth Conference to discuss common issues, although without any policy-making formal power. In Scotland, the leading religious body is the non-Anglican Church of Scotland, the state church also set up in the 16th century. It has a Presbyterian structure, with 47 districts and about 750,000 members. It is governed by its General Assembly.

The Roman Catholic Church is the world-wide organisation run from the autonomous Vatican City State in Rome. The leading figure is the Pope, currently John Paul II. In England and Wales the governing body is the Bishops' Conference, headed by the President, Cardinal Basil Hume, Archbishop of Westminster. In Scotland there is a similar Bishops' Conference. The British Isles have about 12,800 staff and 8,600 churches.

Muslims are followers of the religion Islam, whose god is called Allah. Islam was conceived in Arabia by the prophet Muhammad, who was born in Mecca in 570 AD. Many Muslims have come to Britain since the late 19th century. There is no central organisation, although there are many prominent mosques and bodies around the country. The most influential of these are the Islamic Cultural Centre (the London Central Mosque) and the Imams and Mosque Council. The religion Sikhims grew up in the Punjab four centuries ago, coming to Britain in the 1950s. It has no central body, but the Sikh Missionary Society has an information service.

Religious statistics

The main religious bodies are listed here along with the membership figures.

Anglican	1,808,000
Baptist	231,000
Hindus	140,000
Jewish	108,000
Methodist	459,000
Muslim/Islam	520,000
Orthodox	276,000
Pentecostal	170,000
Presbyterian	1,242,000
Roman Catholic	2,045,000
Sikh	270,000

Anglican

Church of England
General Synod (main CoE contacts
office) 0171-222 9011
Archbishop of Canterbury (Lambeth
Palace) 0171-928 8282
Archbishop of York 01904-707021
Church Commissioners 0171-222 7010
Record Centre 0171-222 7010
Church in Wales 01222-231638
Episcopal Church in Scotland 0131-225 6357
Church of Ireland 00-3531 978422

Roman Catholic

Administration 0171-828 9808
Bishops Conferences:
England and Wales 0171-630 8220
Scotland 01236-764061
Archbishops: Westminster 0171-798 9055
Liverpool 0151-722 2379
Glasgow 0141-226 5898
Media offices: London 0171-828 8709
Glasgow 0141-221 1168
Dublin 00-35312 885043
Catholic Enquiry Centre 0181-455 9871

Other religions

African Carribean Evangelical
Alliance 0171-735 7373
Associated Presbyterian Churches of
Scotland 01862-87541
Baptist Union 01235-512077
Wales 01792-655468
Scotland 0141-423 6169
Ireland 01232-663108
Buddhists:
Buddhist Society 0171-834 5858
Friends of the Western Buddhist
Order 0181-677 9564
Church of Jesus Christ of Latter-day
Saints (Mormons) 0121-711 2244
Church of Christ, Scientist 0171-371 0600
Church of Scientology 0171-580 3601
Church of Scotland 0131-225 5722
Congregational Federation 0115-941 3801
Eastern Orthodox Churches:
Greek 0171-723 4787
Russian 0181-742 3493
Serbian 0171-727 8367
Other nationalitiies 0181-741 9624
Free Church of England 0151-638 2564
Free Church of Scotland 0131-226 5286

Free Presbyterian Church of
Scotland 0131-229 0649
Hindu Centre 0181-534 8879
Independent Methodist
Churches 01942-223526
Jehovah's Witnesses 0181-906 2211
Jewish Communities in UK/Board
of Deputies 0171-387 3952
Chief Rabbi 0171-387 1066
Enquiry Desk 0171-387 4044
Jewish Care 0181-458 3282
Krishna Consciousness 01923-857244
Lutheran Church 0171-373 1141
Methodist Church 0171-222 8010
Ireland 01232-324554
Muslim: Islam Cultural Centre 0171-724 3363
Imams & Mosque Council 0181-992 6636
Pentecostal Church bodies:
Apostolic 01792-473992
Assemblies of God 0115-947 4525
Elim 01242-519904
New Testament 01604-643311
Presbyterian Church in Ireland 01232-322284
Presbyterian Church of Wales 01222-494913
Religious Society of Friends
(Quakers) 0171-387 3601
Salvation Army 0171-236 7020
Scotland 0141-779 4661
Seventh Day Adventist Church 01923-672251
Sikh Missionary Society 0181-574 1902
Sikh Cultural Society 0181-952 1215
Union of Welsh Independents 01792-467040
Unitarian Churches 0171-240 2384
United Reformed Church 0171-916 2020

Other bodies

Church Army 0181-318 1226
Church Commissioners 0171-222 7010
Church House Bookshop 0171-340 0280
Church Missionary Society 0171-928 8681
Council of Christians & Jews 0171-794 8178
Mothers' Union 0171-222 5533
Spiritualists National Union 01279-816363
Lesbian and Gay Christian Movement
0171-739 1249
Inform (Information Network Focus
on Religious Movements) 0171-955 7654
Christian Rescue 01536-741250
Evangelical Alliance UK 0171-582 0228
Cult Information Centre 0181-651 3322
Christian Research Association 0181-294 1989

SPORT

The Department of National Heritage is the government department responsible for over-seeing sport and recreation in England. In Wales, Scotland and Northern Ireland the Secretaries of State for those countries have that role. Most of their work is devolved to the four national Sports Councils. They are policy-making, co-ordinating and grant-giving bodies, funded by the government. The council known simply as the "Sports Council" is both the English Sports Council and the one covering general issues affecting all the UK.

Working alongside the Sports Councils are many advisory, consultative and co-ordinating bodies. The Central Council of Physical Recreation represents the views of English sporting organisations to the Sports Commission, its main funder. Equivalent bodies are the Scottish and Welsh Sports Associations and the Northern Ireland Council of Physical Recreation. The CCPR set up the Institute of Sports Sponsorship,and the Institute of Professional Sport, to protect the welfare of professional sportspeople. The British Olympic Association organises British participation in the four-yearly Olympics (next Games in 1996). The association, the CCPR and the national sports associations have recently formed the British Sports Forum to represent non-governmental sports bodies.

The National Coaching Foundation provides education and advice services to coaches in all sports, via 16 national coaching centres. The National Playing Fields Association promotes the provision of recreation and play facilities, especially playing fields. The Sports Aid Foundation raises funds to help train talented sportspeople. The government's Business Sponsorship Scheme for Sport aims to secure funding for local sport from businesses.

Individual sports are overseen by independent governing bodies, which usually draw up rules, control membership and set standards. The Football Licensing Authority is responsible for ensuring football grounds comply with legal safety requirements, including the all-seating policy for top clubs. The Football Trust, set up in 1990 by pools companies, provides funds to improve safety and comfort at football grounds.

Most local authorities have an officer with responsibility for sport, usually in the recreation or tourism department.

National bodies

Dept of National Heritage	0171-211 6000
Press Office	0171-211 6266
Sports Council	071-388 1277
Sports Council for Wales	01222-397571
Scottish Sports Council	0131-317 7200
Sports Council for N Ireland	01232-381222
British Assoc of Leisure Parks, Piers & Attractions	0171-383 7942
British Assoc of Sport & Medicine	0171-253 3244
British Assoc of Sport & Exercise Sciences	0113-274 4802
British Blind Sport	01788-536142
British Deaf Sports Council	01943-850214
British Institute of Sports Coaches	0113-275 3365
British Olympic Assoc	0181-871 2677
British Paralympic Assoc	0181-666 4556
British Society of Sports History	0181-295 0188
British Sports & Allied Industries Federation	01203-414999
British Sports Assoc for the Disabled	0171-490 4919
British Universities Sports Fed	0121-766 8855
British Wheelchair Sports Foundation	01296-84848
Central Council of Physical Recreation	0171-828 3163
Commonwealth Games Fed	0171-383 5596
Foundation for Sport & Arts	0151-259 5505
Institute of Leisure & Amenity Management	01491-874222
Institute of Sports Sponsorship	0171-233 7747
National Coaching Foundation	0113-274 4802
National Council for Schools Sports	0181-656 8857
National Play Information Centre	0171-383 5455
National Playing Fields Assoc	0171-584 6445
Physical Education Assoc	0171-828 9229
Pool Promoters Assoc	0151-227 4181
Sports Aid Foundation	0171-387 9380
Sports Nutrition Foundation	0171-250 0493
UK Sports Assoc for People with Learning Difficulties	0171-250 1100
Ulster Sports & Recreation Trust	01232-381222
Womens Sports Foundation	0171-831 7863
Youth Clubs UK	0171-353 2366

National sports centres

Bisham Abbey, Bucks	01628-476911
Crystal Palace, South London	0181-778 0131
Cumbrae & Inverclyde, Ayrshire	01475-674666
Glenmore Lodge, Aviemore	01479-861256
Holme Pierrepont, Notts	0115-982 1212
Lilleshall, Shropshire	01952-603003
Plas Menai. Gwynedd	01248-670964
Plas y Brenin, Gwynedd	01690-720214
Welsh Institute, Cardiff	01222-397571
Tollymore, County Down	01396-722158

Sports bodies

Royal **Aero** Club	0116-253 1051
Aircraft Owners & Pilots Assoc	0171-834 5631
British American Football Assoc	0161-864 1250
National Federation of Anglers	01283-734735
Scottish Anglers National Assoc	0131-339 8808
National Federation of Sea Anglers	01626-331330
Wales	01222-621795
Scotland	0131-317 7192
Grand National Archery Society	01203-696631
Scottish Archery Assoc	0141-339 9188
Welsh Archery Federation	01633-874240
Amateur Athletic Assoc	0121-440 5000
Scotland	0131-317 7320
Northern Ireland Sports Council	01232-381222
Athletics Assoc of Wales	01792-456237
British Athletic Federation	0121-440 5000
Badminton Assoc	01908-568822
Scottish Badminton Union	0141-445 1218
British Balloon & Airship Club	01604-870025
British Baseball Federation	01482-643551
English Basketball Assoc	0113-236 1166
Scotland	0131-317 7260
English Civil War Society (battle re-enactment)	01430-430695
Sealed Knot (battle re-staging)	01384-295939
World Professional Billiards & Snooker Assoc	0117-974 4491
English BMX Assoc	0181-813 2838
British Bobsleigh Assoc	01985-850064
British Crown Green Bowling Assoc	0151-526 8367
English Bowling Assoc	01903-820222
Wales	01495-723836
Scotland	0141-221 8999
Northern Ireland	01232-614658
English Bowling Federation	01205-366201
English Indoor Bowling Assoc	0181-470 1237
Wales	01656-841361
Scotland	01294-468372
Ireland	01232-794869
English Womens Bowling Assoc	01297-21317
English Womens Bowling Fed	0191-413 3160
English Womens Indoor Bowling	01794-514922
Wales	01443-771618
English Bowls Council	01603-427551
Amateur Boxing Assoc	0181-778 0251

Wales	01222-623566
Scotland	01382-508261
Northern Ireland	003531-4543525
British Boxing Board of Control	0171-403 5879
Camping & Caravanning Club	01203-694995
British Canoe Union	0115-982 1100
Veteran Car Club	01462-742818
Vintage Sports Car Club	01635-44411
Caravan Club	01342-326944
National Caving Assoc	01639-849519
British Chess Federation	01424-442500
Clay Pigeon Shooting Assoc	0181-505 6221
Crafts Council	0171-278 7700
Cricket Council/Test & County Cricket Board	0171-286 4405
Marylebone Cricket Club(MCC)	0171-289 1611
National Cricket Assoc	0171-289 6098
Wales	01222-708475
Northern Ireland	0001-893943
Scottish Cricket Union	0131-317 7247
Womens Cricket Assoc	0121-440 0520
Croquet Assoc	0171-736 3148
English Curling Assoc	01923-825004
Royal Caledonian Curling Club	0131-333 3003
British Cycle Speedway Council	01508-493880
British Cycling Federation	0161-223 2244
Northern Ireland	01266-48774
Cyclists Touring Club	01483-417217
Scottish Cyclists Union	0131-652 0187
Welsh Cycling Union	01597-851550
Scottish **Darts** Assoc	01224-692535
British **Equestrian** Federation	01203-696697
Amateur **Fencing** Assoc	0181-742 3032
Football Assoc	0171-262 4542
Wales	01222-372325
Scotland	0141-332 6372
Northern Ireland	01232-777732
Football League	01253-729421
Scotland	0141-248 3844
Football Trust	0171-388 4504
Womens Football Assoc	01707-651840
Scotland	0141-353 1162
Scottish **Games** Assoc	01738-627782
Royal Horticultural Society	0171-834 4333
National Gardens Scheme	01483-211535
British Gliding Assoc	0116-253 1051
English Golf Union	0116-255 3042
Wales	01633-870261
Scotland	0131-339 7546
Ladies Golf Union	01334-475811
Professional Golfers Assoc	01675-470333
Royal & Ancient Golf Club	01334-472112
Scottish Ladies Golfing Assoc	0192-479582
National Greyhound Racing	0171-267 9256
British Amateur Gymnastics Assoc	01952-820330
Wales	01222-522012
Scotland	01324-612308
Irish	01232-381222
British **Hang-Gliding & Para-Gliding** Assoc	0116-261 1322

British Harness Racing Club	01745-854746
Scottish Official Board of Highland Dancing	0131-668 3965
Hockey Assoc	01908-241100
Scottish Hockey Union	0131-650 8170
All England Womens Hockey Assoc	01743-233572
British Horse Society	01203-696697
Jockey Club (horse racing)	0171-486 4921
Racecourse Assoc (horse racing)	01344-25912
British Field Sports Society (hunting)	0171-928 4742
Scotland	01828-27015
British **Ice Hockey** Assoc	01202-303946
Scotland	01292-266203
National Ice Skating Assoc	0171-253 3824
Jousting Assoc	01271-861200
British Judo Assoc	0116-255 9669
British Ju-Jitsu Assoc	01254-237216
English **Karate**	0181-5990711
Welsh Karate Federation	01834-813776
Keep Fit Assoc	0171-233 8898
Northern Ireland	0184-9433560
All England Womens **Lacrosse** Assoc	0121-773 4422
English Lacrosse Union	0161-928 9600
GB Luge Assoc	01432-353539
British **Microlight Aircraft** Assoc	01869-38888
The Morris Ring	01926-330771
Motor Caravanners Club	0181-893 3883
British Automobile Racing Club (motor racing)	01264-772607
British Racing & Sports Car Club (motor racing)	01474-874445
RAC Motor Sports Assoc	01753-681736
Auto-Cycle Union (motorcycling)	01788-540519
British Motorcyclists Federation	0181-942 7914
British Mountain Bike Federation	0161-223 2244
British Mountaineering Council	0161-445 4747
Scotland	01764-654962
Council for **National Parks**	0171-924 4077
Central Council for British Naturism	01604-20361
All England Netball Assoc	01462-442344
Wales	01222-237048
Scotland	0141-334 3650
Assoc of British **Orchestras**	0171-828 6913
British Orienteering Federation	01629-734042
Outward Bound	01753-731005
British **Parachute** Assoc	0116-278 5271
British Petanque Assoc	01203-421408
Modern Pentathlon Assoc	01734-817181
National Playing Fields Assoc	0171-584 6445
Assoc of Pleasure Craft Operators	01952-813572
Hurlingham Polo Assoc	01869-350044
English Pool Assoc	01922-35587
Assoc of **Railway Preservation** Socs	01233-712130
Ramblers Assoc	0171-582 6878
British Federation of Roller Skating	01952-825253
Amateur Rowing Assoc	0181-741 5314
Wales	01222-777398
Scotland	01475-722996
Henley Royal Regatta (rowing)	01491-572153
British Amateur Rugby League	01484-544131
Rugby Football League	0113-262 4637
Rugby Football Union	0181-892 8161
Wales	01222- 390111
Scotland	0131-346 5000
Salmon & Trout Assoc	0171-283 5838
British Federation of Sand & Land Yacht Clubs	01509-842292
Camanachd Assoc (shinty)	01397-772461
British Assoc for Shooting & Conservation	01244-570881
Scotland	01350-723226
Wales	01686-688861
National Rifle Assoc (shooting)	01483-797777
British Show Jumping Assoc	01203-696516
Showmen's Guild	01784-461805
British Ski Federation	01506-884343
English Ski Council	0121-501 2314
Wales	01222-619637
Scotland	0131-317 7280
World Professional Billiards & Snooker Assoc	0117-974 4491
British Softball Federation	0117-951 4475
Squash Rackets Assoc	0181-746 1616
Scotland	0131-317 7343
British Sub-Aqua Club	0151-357 1951
British Surfing Assoc	01736-60250
Amateur Swimming Assoc	01509-230431
Wales	01222-342201
Scotland	0141-641 8818
English **Table Tennis** Assoc	01424-722525
Wales	01495-756112
Scotland	0131-317 8077
Tennis & Rackets Assoc	0171-386 3448
Lawn Tennis Assoc	0171-385 2366
All England Club	0181-944 1066
Wales	01222-371838
Scotland	0131-225 1284
British Ten-Pin Bowling Assoc	0181-478 1745
Scotland	0141-334 9989
British Trampoline Federation	0181-863 7278
Tug-of-War Assoc	01494-783057
English **Volleyball** Assoc	0115-981 6324
Northern Ireland	01232-667011
British **Water Ski** Federation	0171-833 2855
Inland Waterways Assoc	0171-586 2556
British Amateur Weightlifters Assoc	01865-200339
Scotland	01475-674666
English Olympic Wrestling Assoc	0161-832 9209
Royal Ocean Racing Club (**yachting**)	0171-493 2248
Royal Yachting Assoc	01703-629962
Wales	01248-670738
Scotland	0131-317 7388
Northern Ireland	01232-661711
British Wheel of Yoga	01529-306851
Youth Hostels Association	01727-855215

PRESSURE/ADVICE GROUPS

Index to advice groups

There are thousands of pressure groups, campaigning societies, advice organisations, voluntary bodies and special interest groups. For fuller lists see:

Charities Digest
Family Welfare Association
Tel 0171-254 6251

Everywoman Directory
Tel 0171-359 5496

Directory of British Associations
CBD Research
Tel 0181-650 7745

Journalists' Source Directory
City University
Tel 0171-477 8221

Peace Diary and World Peace Directory
Housmans
Tel 0171-837 4473

Voluntary Agencies Directory
National Council for Voluntary Organisations
Tel 0171-713 6161

Who's Who in the Environment
Environment Council
Tel 0171-278 4736

Community action

Advice Services Alliance	0171-247 2441
Assoc of British Credit Unions	0171-582 2626
Charities Aid Foundation	01732-771333
Child Poverty Action Group	0171-253 3406
Childline	0800-1111
Community Development Foundation	0171-226 5375
Community Service Volunteers	0171-278 6601
Directory of Social Change	0171-209 4949
Drinkline	0171-332 0202
Everyman Centre	0171-793 0155
Festival Welfare Services	0171-700 5754
Gamblers Anonymous	0171-384 3040
Inter-Action Trust	0171-583 2652
Local Govt Information Unit	0171-608 1051
London Advice Services Alliance	0171-377 2538
Missing Persons Helpline	0181-392 2000
National Assoc of Citizens Advice Bureaux	0171-833 2181
National Council for Voluntary Organisations	0171-713 6161
National Federation of Community Organisations	0171-226 0189
Rotary International	01789-765411
Samaritans	0171-734 2800
Saneline	0171-724 8000
Scottish Council for Voluntary Organisations	0131-556 3882
Small World	0171-272 5255
Student Community Action	0171-739 4565
Victim Support	0171-735 9166

Ethnic groups

Anti-Racist Alliance	0171-278 6869
Black Environment Network	0171-713 6161
Campaign Against Racism & Facism (CARF)	0171-837 1450
Campaign Against Racist Laws	0181-571 1437
Civic Trust (Community Action)	0117-926 8893
Commission for Racial Equality	0171-828 7022
Confederation of Indian Organisations (UK)	0181-863 9089
Freedom Network	0171-738 6721
India Assoc (UK)	0181-556 5119
Indian Workers Assoc	0181-574 6019
Institute of Race Relations	0171-837 0041
Joint Council for the Welfare of Immigrants	0171-251 8708
Kurdish Cultural Centre	0171-735 0918
Legal Advice Service for	

Travellers	01222-874580
Migrant Resource Centre	0171-834 6650
National Group on Homeworking	0113-245 4273
National Gypsy Council	0161-620 3964
Newham Monitoring Project	0181-555 8151
Pakistan Welfare Assoc	0181-544 1644
Refugee Council	0171-582 6922
Runnymede Trust	0171-375 1496
Scottish Asian Action Committee	0141-331 1069
Scottish Crofters Union	01471-822529
Standing Conference of West Indian Organisations	0171-928 7861
Union of Turks in England	0171-729 1422
Youth Against Racism in Europe	0181-533 4533

Claimants

Bootstrap Enterprises	0171-254 0775
Industrial Common Ownership Movement (ICOM)	0113-246 1737
Low Pay Unit	0171-713 7616
New Ways to Work	0171-226 4026
Public Concern at Work	0171-404 6609
Rural Development Commission	0171-340 2900
Unemployed Workers Charter	0181-459 7146
Unemployment Unit	0171-833 1222
Women & Manual Trades	0171-251 9192
Working Mothers Assoc	0171-700 5771

Drugs and addiction

Alcohol Concern	0171-928 7377
Alcoholics Anonymous	01904-644026
ASH (Action on Smoking and Health)	0171-935 3519
Assoc for Nonsmokers Rights	0131-557 3139
Assoc for Prevention of Addiction	0171-251 5860
Gamblers Anonymous	0171-384 3040
Institute for the Study of Drug Dependence	0171-928 1211
Libra Trust	01273-480012
Mainliners	0171-737 3141
Medical Council on Alcoholism	0171-487 4445
Narcotics Anonymous	0171-498 9005
Release	0171-729 9904
Standing Conference on Drug Abuse	0171-928 9500

Health

Age Concern	0181-679 8000
Alzheimer's Disease Society	0171-306 0606
Arthritis/Rheumatism Council	01246-558033
ASH (Action on Smoking and Health)	0171-935 3519

Body Positive	0171-835 1045
Breast Cancer Campaign	0171-439 1013
British Deaf Assoc	0171-839 5566
British Dental Health	01788-546365
British Heart Foundation	0171-935 0185
British Holistic Medicine Assoc	01743-261155
British Homeopathic Assoc	0171-935 2163
British Kidney Patient Assoc	01420-472021
British Lung Foundation	0171-371 7704
British Medical Assoc	0171-387 4499
British Migraine Assoc	01932-352468
British Organ Donor Society	01223-893636
British Paediatric Assoc	0171-486 6151
British Psychological Society	0116-254 9568
British Wheel of Yoga	01529-306851
Cancer Relief Macmillan Fund	0171-351 7811
Cancer Research Campaign	0171-224 1333
Casualties Union	0171-235 5366
Clic (Cancer and Leukaemia in Childhood)	0117 924 4333
Crusaid	0171-976 8100
Dial UK (Disability Information and Advice Lines)	01302-310123
Disability Alliance	0171-247 8776
Disability Wales	01222-887325
Downs Syndrome Assoc	0181-682 4001
Festival for Mind, Body, Spirit	0171-938 3788
Food Commission	0171-628 7774
Foundation for the Study of Infant Death	0171-235 0965
GLAD (Greater London associatiion of Disabled People)	0171-274 0107
Haemophilia Society	0171-928 2020
Health Rights	0171-274 4000 ext 326
Health Unlimited	0171-928 8105
Hearing Dogs for the Deaf	01844-353898
Help the Aged	0171-253 0253
Herpes Assoc	0171-607 9661
Hospice Information Service	0181-778 9252
Imperial Cancer Research Fund	0171-242 0200
Incapacity Action	0171-732 1095
Inquest	0181-802 7430
Institute for Complementary Medicine	0171-237 5165
Leonard Cheshire Foundation	0171-828 1822
Leukaemia Research Fund	0171-405 0101
London Lighthouse	0171-792 1200
ME Assoc	01375-642466
MENCAP	0171-454 0454
Mental Health Foundation	0171-580 0145
Migraine Trust	0171-278 2676
MIND (National Assoc for Mental Health)	0181-519 2122
Multiple Sclerosis Society	0171-736 6267
National Aids Trust	0171-972 2845
National Asthma Campaign	0171-226 2260
National Autistic Society	0181-451 1114
Natural Medicines Society	01773-710002
Outset	0181-692 7141
Overeaters Anonymous	0171-498 5505

Parkinsons Disease Society	0171-383 3513
Patients Assoc	0181-981 5676
Pregnancy Advisory Service	0171-637 8962
RADAR (Royal Assoc for Disability & Rehabilitation)	0171-250 3222
Royal National Institute for the Blind	0171-388 1266
Royal National Institute for the Deaf	0171-387 8033
Royal Society for the Prevention of Accidents	0121-200 2461
Samaritans	01753-532713
SCODA (Standing Conference on Drug Abuse)	0171-928 9500
Socialist Health Assoc	0171-490 0057
Spastics Society	0171-636 5020
St John Ambulance Assoc	0171-235 5231
Tenovus Cancer Helpline	0800-526527
Terence Higgins Trust	0171-831 0330
Voluntary Euthanasia Society	0171-937 7770

National Childbirth Trust	0181-992 8637
National Childcare Campaign	0171-405 5617
National Childrens Bureau	0171-843 6000
National Children's Home	0171-226 2033
National Council for One Parent Families	0171-267 1361
National Society for the Prevention of Cruelty to Children (NSPCC)	0171-825 2500
National Youth Agency	0116-285 6789
PAIN (Parents Against Injustice)	01279-647171
Parent Network	0171-485 8535
Pensioners Voice	01254-52606
Pensions at 60 Alliance	0171-924 2727
Pre-School Playgroups Assoc	0171-833 0991
Rapport	01225-448343
Relate (Marriage Guidance)	01788-573241
Save the Children Fund	0171-703 5400
Third Age	0171-737 2541
Woodcraft Folk	0181-672 6031
Workers Educational Assoc	0181-983 1515

Education and family

Abortion Law Reform Assoc	0171-637 7264
Active Birth Centre	0171-561 9006
Advisory Centre for Education	0171-354 8321
Assoc of Radical Midwives	01695-572776
Baby Life Support Systems	0171-831 9393
Baby Milk Action	01223-464420
Barnardos	0181-550 8822
Birth Control Campaign	0171-580 9360
British Pregnancy Advisory Service	01564-793225
Brook Advisory Centres	0171-833 8488
Campaign for State Education	0181-944 8206
Carers National Assoc	0171-490 8818
Child Rescue	01273-692947
Childline	0171-239 1000
Childrens Legal Centre	0171-359 9392
Children's Society	0171-837 4299
Divorce Conciliation Service	0171-730 2422
Exploring Parenthood	0181-960 1678
FACE (Fight Against Cuts in Education)	01203-313375
Families Need Fathers	0171-613 5060
Family Caring Trust	01693-64174
Family Planning Assoc	0171-636 7866
Family Rights Group	0171-923 2628
Family and Social Action	0181-458 7485
Family Welfare Assoc	0171-254 6251
Gingerbread	0171-240 0953
Girl Guides Assoc	0171 834 6242
Inter-Action	0171-583 2652
Mary Ward Centre	0171-831 7711
Message Home	0171-799 7662
Mothers Union	0171-222 5533
National Abortion Campaign	0171-923 4976
National Campaign for Nursery Education	01206-799344

Sex

Albany Trust	0181-675 6669
Campaign Against Pornography	0171-263 1833
Campaign for Homosexual Equality	0171-833 3912
English Collective of Prostitutes	0171-837 7509
Gay & Lesbian Legal Advice	0171-976 0840
Gay London Policing	0171-233 0854
Lesbian & Gay Christian Movement	0171-739 1249
Lesbian & Gay Employment Rights (LAGER)	0171-704 8066
Lesbian Information Service	01706-817235
London Bisexual Group	0181-569 7500
London Lesbian & Gay Switchboard	0171-837 7324
London Lesbian Line	0171-251 6911
London Rape Crisis Centre	0171-916 5466
OutRage (against homophobia)	0171-439 2381
Sexual Compulsives Anon	0181-914 7599
Stonewall	0171-222 9007
Terence Higgins Trust	0171-831 0330

Women

Assoc of Greater London Older Women	0171-281 3485
Change	0171-277 6187
Co-operative Womens Guild	0181-520 4902
Fawcett Library	0171-320 1189
Fawcett Society	0171-587 1287
Feminists Against Censorship	0181-552 4405
Feminist Library & Information Centre	0171-928 7789
Justice for Women	0181-340 3699

Movement for the Ordination of Women	01763-848822
National Abortion Campaign	0171-923 4976
National Alliance of Womens Organisations	0171-381 3916
National Association of Widows	0121-643 8348
National Council of Women	0171-354 2395
National Federation of Women's Institutes	0171-371 9300
National Group on Homeworking	0113-246 4273
Positively Women	0171-490 5515
Rape Crisis Centre	0171-837 1600
Rights of Women	0171-251 6577
Soroptimist International	0161-480 7686
The 300 Group	01895-812229
Townswomen's Guilds	0121-456 3435
West Indian Womens Assoc	0181-521 4456
Women Against Fundamentalism	0171-272 5476
Women Against Sexual Harassment	0171-721 7592
Women in Theology	0181-533 3913
Womens Aid Federation	0117-963 3494
Womens Enterprise Development Agency	0121-525 2558
Womens Environmental Network	0171-354 8823
Womens Farm & Garden Assoc	01285-658339
Womens Health Concern	0171-938 3932
Womens Resource Centre	0171-405 4045
Women's Voice	0181-236 0050
WRVS (Womens Royal Voluntary Service)	0171-416 0146

Housing

Advisory Service for Squatters	0171-359 8814
Alone in London Service	0171-387 6184
Centrepoint (Nightshelter)	0171-629 2229
CHAR: Housing Campaign for Single People	0171-833 2071
Crisis (ex Crisis at Christmas)	0171-377 0489
Girls Alone Project	0171-383 4103
Homes for Homeless People	01582-481426
Housing Centre Trust	0171-700 0100
Institute of Housing	01203-694433
Leaving Home Project	0171-629 2229
London Connection	0171-321 0633
London Housing Unit	0171-267 9396
National Assoc for Voluntary Hostels	0171-731 4205
National Federation of Housing Assocs	0171-278 6571
National Housing & Town Planning Council	0171-251 2363
National Missing Persons Helpline	0500-700 700
New Horizon	0171-388 5560
Piccadilly Advice Centre	0171-437 1579
Residential Boat Owner Assoc	0181-892 5086
Rural Housing Trust	0171-235 6563
Scottish Crofters Union	01471-822529
SHAC (Housing Aid Centre)	0171-404 7447
Shelter	0171-253 0202
Shelter Nightline	0800-446441
Simon Community	0171-485 6639
SQUASH (Squatters Action for Secure Homes)	0171-226 8938

Animals, farming and food

Animal Aid Society	01732-364546
Animal Concern	0141-334 6014
Animal Health Trust	01638-661111
Animal Welfare Trust	0181-950 8215
Arboricultural Assoc	01794-368717
Bat Conservation Trust	0171-240 0933
Beauty Without Cruelty	0171-254 2929
Blue Cross	0171-834 5556
Breach-Whale Wars	01405-769375
British Assoc for Shooting & Conservation	01244-570881
British Beekeepers Assoc	01203-696679
British Dietic Association	0121-643 5483
British Trust for Ornithology	01842-750050
British Union for the Abolition of Vivisection	0171-700 4888
Butterfly Conservation	01206-322342
Campaign Against Angling	01179-441175
Campaign to Stop Animal Experiments	0114-253 0020
Cats Protection League	01403-261947
Compassion in World Farming	01730-268070
Country Landowners Assoc	0171-235 0511
Donkey Sanctuary	01395-578222
Earthkind	0181-889 1595
Farm Animal Welfare Council	0181-330 8022
Farm Animal Welfare Network	01484-688650
Farmers' Union of Wales	01970-612755
Farming & Wildlife Advisory Group	01203-696699
Food & Drink Federation	0171-836 2460
Game Conservancy	01425-652381
Glutamate Information Service	0171-631 3434
Henry Doubleday Research Assoc	01203-303517
Hunt Saboteurs Assoc	0115-959 0357
International Dolphin Watch	01482-643403
International Whaling Commission	01223-233971
Kennel Club	0171-493 6651
League Against Cruel Sports	0171-403 6155
London Wildlife Trust	0171-278 6612
Mammal Society	0171-498 4358
National Anti-Vivisection Society	0181-846 9777
National Canine Defence League	0171-837 0006
National Farmers' Union	0171-235 5077

NFU Scotland	0131-335 3111
National Federation of Badger Groups	0171-498 3220
National Society of Allotment & Leisure Gardeners	01536-266576
Organic Growers Assoc	0117-929 9800
Orkney Seal Rescue	01856-831463
Otter Trust	01986-893470
Peoples Dispensary for Sick Animals	01952-290999
Pesticides Trust	0171-274 8895
PETA (People for the Ethical Teatment of Animals)	0171-388 4922
Rare Breeds Survival Trust	01203-696551
Royal Agricultural Society	01203-696969
Royal Horticultural Society	0171-834 4333
Royal Society for the Protection of Birds	01767-680551
Royal Zoological Society of Scotland	0131-334 9171
RSPCA	01403-264181
Scottish Landowners Fed'tion	0131-555 1031
Scottish Wildlife & Countryside Link	01738-630804
Scottish Wildlife Trust	0131-312 7765
Soil Assoc	0117-929 0661
Ulster Farmers' Union	01232-370222
Ulster Wildlife Trust	01396-830282
Urban Wildlife Trust	0121-666 7474
Vegetarian Society	0161-928 0793
Whale & Dolphin Conservation Society	01225-334511
Wildfowl & Wetlands Trust	01453-890333
Wildlife Trusts (ex RSNC)	01522-544400
Women's Farming Union	01892-722803
Wood Green Animal Shelters	01763-838329
World Society for the Protection of Animals	0171-793 0540
World Wide Fund for Nature	01483-426444
Zoo Federation	0171-586 0230
Zoological Society of London	0171-722 3333

Countryside and environment

Action with Communities in Rural England	01285-653477
Advisory Committee on Protection of the Sea	0171-799 3033
Agenda 21 Network (London)	0171-379 4324
Alarm UK (National Alliance Against Road-building)	0171-737 6641
Ancient Monuments Society	0171-236 3934
Architectural Heritage Fund	0171-925 0199
Assoc for the Conservation of Energy	0171-935 1495
Association for the Protection of Rural Scotland	0131-225 7012
Assoc of Railway Preservation Societies	01233-712130
Black Environment Network	0171-713 6161
British Assoc of Nature Conservationists	01604-405285
British Earth Sheltering Assoc.	01600-860359
British Ecological Society	0181-871 9797
British Mountaineering Council	0161-445 4747
British Society of Dowsers	01233-750253
British Trust for Conservation Volunteers England	01491-839766
Wales	01686-628600
British Unidentified Flying Object Research Assoc	01924-444049
Campaign for Environmentally Responsible Tourism	0181-291 0692
Campaign for the Protection of Rural Wales	01938-552525
Capital Transport Campaign	0171-388 2489
Centre for Alternative Technology	01654-702400
Civic Trust	0171-930 0914
Wales	01222-484606
Scotland	0141-221 1466
Clean Rivers Trust	01636-892627
Common Ground	0171-379 3109
Communities Against Toxics	0151-339 5473
Community Recycling Network	0117-942 0142
Conservation Foundation	0171-823 8842
Council for Environmental Education	01734-756061
Council for the Protection of Rural England	0171-976 6433
Cycle Campaign Network	01908-674812
Cyclists Public Affairs Group	01483-414320
Docklands Forum (London)	0171-377 1822
Dragon	0181-691 7685
Earth First!	0171-738 6721
Earth Foundation	0181-675 7774
Earthwatch Europe	01865-311600
Environment Centre	0131-557 2135
Environment Council	0171-824 8411
Environmental Investigation Agency	0171-490 7040
Environmental Law Assoc	0171-628 2020
Environmental Transport Assoc	01932-828882
Fauna & Flora Preservation Society	01223-461471
Freedom Network	0171-738 6721
Freedom Trail	01935-863349
Freewheelers	0191-222 0094
Friends of the Earth	0171-490 1555
FoE Scotland	0131-554 9977
Georgian Group	0171-377 1722
Global Witness	0171-262 2308
Green Alliance	0171-836 0341
Green Party	0171-272 4474
Wales Green Party	01970-625143
GreenNet	0171-713 1941
Greenpeace (London)	0171-837 7557
Greenpeace Ltd	0171-354 5100
Groundwork Foundation	0121-236 8565

Historic Churches Preservation
Trust 0171-736 3054
League Against Cruel Sports 0171-403 6155
Local Agenda 21 Steering Group 01582-451166
London Cycling Campaign 0171-928 7220
London Ecology Centre 0171-379 4324
London Ecology Unit 0171-267 7944
London Greenpeace 0171-837 7557
London Lorry Control Scheme 0171-582 0852
Marine Conservation Society 01989-566017
Marine Society 0171-261 9535
Media Natura 0171-240 4936
Motorcycle Action Group 0121-459 5860
Mountaineering Council of
Scotland 0141-334 8336
National Federation of
City Farms 0117-971 9109
National Pure Water Assoc. 01924-830097
National Recycling Forum 0113-243 1562
National Society for Clean Air 01273-326313
National Trust 0171-222 9251
National Trust for Scotland 0131-226 5922
Neighbourhood Energy Action 0191-261 5677
Noise Abatement Society 0181-460 3146
N Ireland Environment Link 01232-314944
Open Spaces Society 01491-573535
Oxleas Wood Hotline 01426-921900
PACTS (Parliamentary Advisory Committee
for Transport Safety) 0171-922 8112
Pedestrians Assoc. 0171-490 0750
Pesticides Trust 0171-274 8895
Planning Exchange 0141-248 8541
Plantlife 0171-938 9111
Public Transport Campaign
Group 0161-236 1970
Rail Not Roads 0171-737 6641
Rainforest Foundation 0171-620 1556
Ramblers Assoc 0171-582 6878
Reclaim the Streets 0171-737 0100
Reforest the Earth 01603-631007
Reforesting Scotland 01971-502406
Right to Peace & Quiet
Campaign 0181-312 9997
Road Alert 01635-521770
Royal Entomological Society 0171-584 8361
Royal Scottish Forestry Society 01383-873014
Royal Society for Nature
Conservation:The Wildlife
Trusts Partnership 01522-544400
Royal Town Planning Institute 0171-636 9107
Save Britain's Heritage 0171-228 3336
Save Our Railways 0171-730 7851
Scottish Conservation Projects
Trust 01786-479697
Scottish Native Woods 01887-820392
Scottish Wildlife & Countryside
Link 01738-630804
SCRAM (Scottish Campaign to
Resist the Atomic Menace) 0131-5549977
SERA (Socialist Environment &

Resources Assoc) 0171-263 7424
Small World 0171-272 5255
Society for the Protection of
Ancient Buildings 0171-377 1644
Surfers Against Sewage 01872-553001
Town & Country Planning
Assoc 0171-930 8903
Trainwatch 0171-582 6505
Transport 2000 0171-388 8386
Tree Council 0171-828 9928
Trees for London 0171-713 5464
Trust for Urban Ecology 0171-237 9165
Urban Pollution Research
Centre 0181-368 1299
Victorian Society 0181-994 1019
Waste Watch 0171-245 9998
Waterway Recovery Group 0171-722 7217
Wild Flower Society 01509-215598
Wildfowl & Wetlands Trust 01453-890333
Woodland Trust 01476-74297
World Conservation Monitoring
Centre 01223-277314

History

British Assoc of Friends of
Museums 0161-881 8640
British Records Assoc 0171-729 1415
British Society for the History
of Science 01367-718963
Council for British Archaeology 01904-671417
English Civil War Society 01430-430695
Folklore Society 0171-387 5894
Historical Assoc 0171-735 3901
Rescue (British Archaeological
Trust) 01992-553377
Society for Folk Life Studies 0113-275 6537
Subterranea Britannica 01737-823456
Victorian Society 0181-994 1019

Science

Assoc for Science Education 01707-267411
British Assoc for the Advancement
of Science 0171-973 3500
British Astrological and Psychic
Society 01442-244360
British Society for Science History 01367-718963
Centre for Alternative Industrial
and Technological Systems 01142-665063
Centre for Alternative Technology 01654-702400
Centre for Exploitation of
Science and Technology 0171-354 9942
Royal Institution 0171-409 2992
Royal Society 0171-839 5561
Science Policy Research Unit 01273-686758
Scientists for Global
Responsibility 0181-871 5175

War and peace

At Ease	0171-247 5164
Bertrand Russell Peace Foundation	0115-978 4504
Campaign Against Arms Trade	0171-281 0297
Campaign Against Militarism	0171-278 9908
Campaign for Nuclear Disarmament	0171-700 2350
Council for Arms Control	0171-873 2065
Faslane Peace Camp	01436-820901
Housmans Peace Resource Project	0171-278 4474
Institute for Law and Peace	0181-348 6918
Irish Peace Initiative	0171-609 1743
Landmines Working Group	01296-632056
Medical Action for Global Security	0171-272 2020
National Peace Council	0171-354 5200
Non-Violent Resistance Network	0171-607 2302
Nukewatch UK	01768-898641
Pax Christi	0181-800 4612
Peace Brigades International	0171-713 0392
Peace Pledge Union	0171-424 9444
Peace Resource Project	0171-837 4473
Royal British Legion	0171-973 0633
Scientists for Global Responsibility (ex-SANA)	0181-871 5175
Troops Out Movement (out of Northern Ireland)	0171-609 1743
War Resisters International	0171-278 4040
Working Party on Chemical & Biological Weapons	01579-384492
World Court Project	01323-844269
World Disarmament Campaign	0171-729 2523

Human rights/International

Action for Southern Africa	0171-833 3133
Amnesty International	0171-814 6200
Anti-Slavery International	0171-924 9555
Article 19	0171-278 9292
British Red Cross Society	0171-235 5454
Campaign Against Asylum Bill	0171-582 6922
Canon Colins Educational Trust for Southern Africa	0171-354 1462
Central America Human Rights	0171-631 4200
Cuba Solidarity Campaign	0171-263 6452
Cymdeithas yr Iaith Gymraeg	01970-624501
Defend the Kurds Campaign	0171-586 5892
Freedom Network	0171-738 6721
Howard League for Penal Reform	0171-281 7722
Intermediate Technology Development Group	01788-560631
Interights	0171-278 3230
Kashmir Freedom Movement	0171-354 5308
Law Centres Federation	0171-387 8570
Legal Action Group	0171-833 2931
Liberty/(NCCL)	0171-403 3888
Scottish CCL	0141-332 5960
Minority Rights Group	0171-978 9498
Nicaragua Solidarity Campaign	0171-272 9619
Oxfam	01865-311311
Release	0171-729 9904
Survival International	0171-242 1441
Third World First	01865-245678
Tools for Self Reliance	01703-869697
Travellers Support Group	01258-454563
War on Want	0171-620 1111
WaterAid	0171-233 4800
World Development Movement	0171-737 6215

Update for the 1997 Media Guide

AMENDMENTS

If your organisation has an entry in the 1996 Guide which needs changing, please photocopy it, show amendments and paste into the space on the right.

ADDITIONS

If your organisation has not been mentioned in this Guide, please use the space above for details you would like to see included next time around.

Photocopy this page and send it to:

Paul Fisher, Guardian Media Guide, 119 Farringdon Road, London EC1R 3ER

THE INDEX